Cory Booker, Proof Through the Night

Cory Booker, Proof Through the Night

Disclaimer: This work is not commissioned or endorsed by Senator Booker or any related entity and no relationship is claimed or implied.

Copyright © 2025 by V. September McCrady, Kenneth Stuczynski, Amorphous Publishing Guild
All rights reserved. Apart from quoted and reproduced public domain content, no part of this book may be reproduced in any manner whatsoever without written permission except in the case of brief quotations embodied in critical articles and reviews.

Cover Flag photo by September McCrady; Photo of Senator Booker from his government website.

First Printing, 2025

Amorphous Publishing Guild
Buffalo, NY, USA
www.Amorphous.Press

CONTENTS

FOREWORD vii

Introduction 1
7:00 PM - Necessary Good Trouble 3
7:22 PM - Letters 8
7:33 PM - Healthcare 12
12:15 AM - Social Security 89
3:08 AM - Education & Reseach 146
4:43 AM - Borders and Liberties 174
7:13 AM - The President 212
7:24 AM - Cuts, Chaos, and Crisis 215
8:02 AM - Deportation Injustices 226
8:26 AM - Security and Foreign Policy 232
8:31 AM - Spiritual Values 234
8:53 AM - Challenges and Solutions 241
9:42 AM - The World Stage 255
10:13 AM - National Security 265
10:32 AM - Medicaid (and Sports) 270
10:43 AM - Tariffs 274
10:49 AM - Social Security and USAID 277
11:25 AM - Housing 287
11:29 AM - Empty Promises 288
11:51 AM - Tax Cuts and Housing 294
11:59 AM - Energy and Environment 297
12:01 PM - Prayer 298

12:03 PM - Agriculture and Frozen Obligations 299
12:17 PM - Questions and Praise for a Colleague 304
12:44 PM - Food Concerns 312
12:44 PM - Looters and Polluters 315
1:06 PM - Impact on Veterans 319
1:30 PM - Child Tax Credits 327
1:46 PM - Health and Human Services 332
1:55 PM - Setting the Record Straight 335
2:06 PM - Fear, Anger, and Courage 339
3:11 PM - Personal Comments 356
3:32 PM - Betrayal of Veterans 363
3:56 PM - The Economy 372
4:25 PM - Canada 379
4:31 PM - Democracy and Tyranny 381
5:02 PM - Paying the Price 390
5:19 PM - Our Children 395
5:24 PM - Tax Policy Failures 398
6:00 PM - Chaos and Abuse of Power 412
6:38 PM - Historical Moment 422
7:15 PM - Final Words 432

BIOGRAPHIES 443
THE CONSTITUTION OF THE UNITED STATES 456
THE BILL OF RIGHTS 465
THE FEDERALIST PAPERS, NO.51 467
DECLARATION OF CONSCIENCE 471
LIFT EVERY VOICE AND SING 475
ABBREVIATION GUIDE 477
ACKNOWLEDGEMENTS 481
PUBLISHER'S NOTE 482
ABOUT AMORPHOUS PUBLISHING GUILD 485

FOREWORD

I guess this starts with who I am. My website sums it up as "a mother and a maker, a pagan and a politician, an ally and an advocate". This also demonstrates my penchant for alliteration, lol. I've been podcasting for years now and keep naming them after that convention. Geek Grills, Heresy and Hearsay, Tipple Theory...

I'm a Gen X-er through and through, born in 1968. I didn't get involved in politics until the 2000s. I had small children and felt I needed to do something to make the world a better place. I figured using a system in place was an efficient path. I had also moved to North Carolina, far from friends and family, and wished to find like-minded folks in this Red/Purple state. I hadn't affiliated with a political party when I lived in New York (Western New York, not NYC — you learn when you move away you always have to explain that). So, I read the party platforms. I chose the Democratic Party as most closely aligned with my ethics and morals. Then, I dove in.

First, I found that I had to go to a newspaper to find a listing for a meeting. It was listed as a meeting of the Democratic Men's Club or something like that. This was around 2004. I found the party chair's number through the Board of Elections. His name was Gene Mahaffey. I called and he said everyone was welcome — they just called it that. I said I wanted to get involved and he referred me to our local Board of Elections because they needed Poll Workers. Great! I trained and became the "Chief Judge" at my polling place. Someone had just quit; they needed a replacement. I'm glad I did that. I learned A LOT. I firmly believe that everyone who is able should do hands on election work so they have a real understanding of the process. It should be drawn like jury duty or something.

It wasn't what I had in mind though, so I called Gene again and asked when the meetings were because I wanted to come. They met usually once a month at a restaurant called the Captain's Galley. I started attending. I offered to make them a website. I got smiles and nods, pretty much. Younger folks had come through a few times with such ideas, but always moved away or wandered off. Now, I was in my mid-thirties. Here's the thing about the standing organization of Democrats in Iredell County at the time — they had been holding down the fort since the great Reagan exodus. It was a handful of older folks having the meetings and filing the paperwork. They were organizing the precincts they could, recommending folks to work the polls to try and keep things balanced, and working the polls themselves in many cases. I revere them for those efforts. I made a Yahoo Group to try and find more people and tell them about the meetings. The party treasurer moved to Florida, and I guess I seemed smart enough and so they made me treasurer. This was probably four months in to showing up for the meetings. Not long after, Robert Stidd found the party through the Yahoo group only to find out the party was taking a couple months off from meeting for the holidays. I went to meet him myself. He handed me a check and told me to put the website up — a go ahead and get forgiveness rather than permission sort of thing. I did, and got the party to vote to make it the "official" website sometime later. Rob Stidd was elected Chair of the Iredell County Democratic Party not too long after that.

So, there's a lot of long boring details to follow. The takeaway though, my elevator pitch for getting involved in politics, is that We The People do still have power in this system. The dark, smoky rooms full of rich people are not really where it happens, I promise. Within a year of my showing up for meetings and the county convention, I was on a committee of like four or five people who got to choose who filled a vacancy in the State Legislature! They don't teach you in school that this is how things actually work! I attended State Executive Committee meetings, as a proxy at first, and was able to affect the national party platform! I was elected to be an Obama delegate to the Democratic National Convention from my district in 2008, and again at the state level in 2012. I was appointed to serve on the DNC Delegate Selection committee (ensuring diversity) for the 2012 convention in Charlotte, NC. We The People have the power to get things done. No small part of that is constantly changing and refining the party platform of our choice. You just have to show up. This is where I finally get to explaining how and why I ended up helping to make this book — it's all about making our country A More Perfect Union.

My friend Ken wrote a book called "40 Days In...The Beginning of the Second Trump Presidency". He acknowledged me in that work, as we've engaged in civil discussions on subjects like politics for a long time. We used to be ideologically further apart than we seem to be these days. His acknowledgement was very flattering (I mean, a man even saying he might have been wrong about some things? Progress! lol). He kindly sent me an autographed copy. I thanked him, and pretty much immediately questioned him about using editors. I'm just a nerd like that. Typos will yank me right out of a read. It's a really good book, and was done in an amazingly short timeframe to capture the moment in history. I admire Ken for doing it. He accepted my unsolicited criticism with good grace, and understood I meant it to be constructive.

He told me about this book, this Keepsake Edition of the record-breaking Booker speech. I was excited to hear about it. I intentionally resisted the urge to offer to edit. These days, I recognize the value of my time. He did eventually ask me if I'd do it for the credit. This isn't something I normally espouse, for instance my husband is a musician so I'm averse to the "exposure" bullshit. However, this credit had value. I could use it to launch into previously unavailable prospects in editing, which I felt I would be very good at, so I accepted.

I started editing the transcript of the speech, and Senator Booker early on used the phrase "A More Perfect Union'. This really struck a chord with me, and I called Ken to tell him. I'd previously mentioned to him that I have a keepsake copy (a big fold out one) of President Obama's A More Perfect Union speech from March 18, 2008. It captures a moment in time in my political history for several reasons. I cherish it. Senator Booker's use of the phrase really impacted me, and I wanted to explain that whole thing to Ken. If you've read this far, you can tell that I'm passionate about people having ownership of the process of making our union more perfect. That conversation and the work I'd done so far in editing led to being offered co-authorship. I gratefully accepted.

I've been diligent. I had been reading the transcript Ken compiled (as I understand it) from a combination of AI and the Congressional Record. I'd correct obvious typos, and go check the video for clarification if something was just weird or said "inaudible". This process ended up not being good enough — for me. I queued up the video of the entire speech on Mr. Booker's YouTube channel. I went back to the beginning. I watched the whole thing while editing the chapters. I corrected mistakes in the official record, and was shocked to learn some speakers were misattributed. I did some research and suggested footnotes in places. Other than the video footage, I believe this book is the only documentation of the thanks he offered after conceding the floor. I appreciate Ken for letting me take ownership of this work the way I have. This has been a great collaboration.

I am eternally grateful to Senator Cory Booker for giving this speech. I'm so glad I took the time to experience it in its glorious entirety. Sharing it with folks, making a clean and true written record of it, has been an honor. It's been giving me hope during this troubled time in America. Even compiling the short biographies of the other speakers, I've been seeing the speeches they are giving since, the committee work they are doing, the hearings they are having, and the bills they are presenting. I see the successful blocking that the judiciary and We The People are enacting against the unlawful actions of the current administration. I see its momentum.

Sure, I go to protests sometimes, and write to my representatives. This book, though — this is a way I hope to pick up the torch that Mr. Booker lit and pass it on. It's a historical record, sure, but the important thing I hope it does is to inspire even more of John Lewis's "Good Trouble".

September McCrady, co-Editor
23 September 2025

Introduction

If we're going to give context to Senator Cory Booker's record-breaking speech, we ought to start with the record that was broken.

The year was 1957. The date was August 29th. It was a Wednesday, 8:54 in the evening to be exact. Strom Thurmond, representing the state of South Carolina in the United States Senate, rose to speak. The purpose was simple: to delay the passing of the Civil Rights Act of 1957.

He had an axe to grind. To understand it, we must go back to the Fifteenth Amendment to the United States Constitution. It was the last of the three Reconstruction Amendments, ratified on 3 February 1870. It reads {omitting section designations}: **The right of citizens of the United States to vote shall not be denied or abridged by the United States or by any State on account of race, color, or previous condition of servitude. The Congress shall have power to enforce this article by appropriate legislation.** However, Jim Crow laws ruled the roost in many states since the Civil War, supported by the Supreme Court's 1896 Plessy v. Ferguson ruling in favor of the "separate but equal" doctrine. He wanted that status quo to be maintained.

The next day, at 9:12 in the evening, he retired from the podium.

His speech lasted 24 hours and 18 minutes.

On Monday, the 31st of March, 2025, Senator Cory Booker took the Senate floor. It was 7:00 in the evening. In addition to C-SPAN, there were live feeds by the Associated Press, PBS, CBS News, MSNBC, and The Guardian, and was livestreamed on Booker's TikTok, YouTube, Twitter, and Instagram accounts.

He had an axe to grind. He once said that it "just really irked me, that [Thurmond] would be the longest speech — that the longest speech, on our great Senate floor, was someone who was trying to stop people like me from being in the Senate."

During his speech, he stated, "To hate him is wrong, and maybe my ego got too caught up in if I stood here maybe, maybe—just maybe—I could break this record of the man who tried to stop the rights upon which I stand. [...] I'm not here, though, because of his speech. I'm here despite his speech. I'm here because as powerful as he was, the people were more powerful."

But Senator Booker's stand must be seen in a much greater context. Since Trump's inauguration on 20 January 2025, a flurry of Executive Orders – many blatantly unconstitutional – sent the federal government into chaos. The keys to most agencies were turned over to Elon Musk, the richest man in the world, as head of the Department of Government Efficiency (DOGE), who stopped funding and mass-fired workforces and contractors. All this was before Congress even met, after which the federal budget was proposed under a Republican majority, codifying huge budget cuts while lowering taxes for higher brackets and increasing the deficit. And as unimaginable as it may seem, the rights that were recognized in 1959 are now under threat in 2025.

Senator Booker had not drunk water since the day before the speech and had fasted for days. Over the hours, his staff delivered ten black binders of notes, letters, and documents, totalling over 1,164 pages of material. As per custom, he was granted permission to speak, and continue to speak, so long as he could 'remain standing' and 'speak more or less continuously'.

The next day, at 8:05 in the evening, he retired from the podium.

His speech lasted 25 hours and five minutes.

7:00 PM - Necessary Good Trouble

I am really grateful, Mr. President — grateful you're in the chair and I'm grateful to be able to rise right now and speak. I want to say at the top that I have a tremendous love for this institution and a lot of that's born from the people that are here, from the pages I get to know in every class to the folks that work the doors, the clerks, the parliamentarians. This is a special place and a lot of the people who are known here are not the ones who really keep this place functioning.

I come in here days and I have good moods or bad moods, but always find myself lifted when I walk onto this floor. It's a sacred civic space. It is extraordinary and I'm always aware of the weight of history when I walk in here, no matter good day, bad day, whether I'm in a rush or not. When I touch the Senate floor, I feel something really magnificent. I don't think that our founders would've ever imagined a body like this with Black people on both sides of the aisle, with women serving here, with folks from many different backgrounds. We are in many ways doing what this Senate, what the founders had envisioned, which was this idea of every generation making this a more perfect union.

But there have been times in this journey where our union was in crisis and was in peril. There have been times in this great American journey over our 250 years where so many heroes had to emerge — people that I've come to revere, like Joshua Chamberlain from Maine, who played such a pivotal role in the Battle of Gettysburg. What a noble soul he was. He would later go on to be the governor of his state and go on to great things, but his heroism lay that in a time of crisis, he stood up. I know there are veterans in this body, and I admire them so much who have answered that call to serve our country and put their lives at sacrifice. There are people that I admire that are heroes of mine that were suffragists, who were people who fought as abolitionists. There are people more recently that I've come to lionize and admire because they did so much for this country, not with titles, not with high rank or positions, but folks when this country was facing crossroads, was facing crises, they stood up, they spoke up.

One of my greatest heroes of life was a man I got to serve with, named John Lewis, and I served with him in this body and every opportunity I had. I would ask him about the times when he was just a 20-something. He was the youngest person who was a feature speaker on the march on Washington. He was called the bravest man in the Civil Rights Movement because he kept putting himself in harm's way to dramatize, to let folks know, to bring attention to the injustices in this world and to say very strongly that what is going on in our country is not normal. What is going on in our country is wrong.

I stand on this floor as a United States Senator, but I revere people who never stood on this floor. People who before they even got to their 30s and 40s and 50s in life were out there as great patriots fighting for this nation. I rise today in an unusual manner, and I want to be clear and explain that, but I just want to tell you what John Lewis said. It's a quote so many people know, and he really spoke not to members of the Senate or the Congress. He was really speaking to Americans. He said, "Get in good trouble, necessary trouble. Help redeem the soul of America."

John Lewis died in 2020, in July, at a time that it was Donald Trump's first term in office, and he did what Congresspeople did, but he also did some really extraordinary things to fight for healthcare. My friend Chris Murphy knows about that. He was there when John Lewis did open Facebook chats, not in this chamber or in the house chamber. He sat on the steps and people were there. I remember when he did a sit-in, they had to shut the cameras off on him. He got in good trouble on the House side too, and so I start tonight thinking about him. I've been thinking about him a lot during these last 71 days — get in good trouble, necessary trouble, help redeem the soul of America and had to ask myself if he's my hero, how am I living up to his words? I think Democrats and Republicans have made a lot of mistakes.

No side has a monopoly on the truth. No side has been perfect servants of this country, but what's happened in the last 71 days is a patent demonstration of a time where John Lewis's call to everyone has I think become more urgent and more pressing and if I think it's a call for our country, I have to ask myself how I'm living these words.

So tonight I rise with the intention of getting in some good trouble. I rise with the intention of disrupting the normal business of the United States Senate for as long as I am physically able. I rise tonight because I believe sincerely that our country is in crisis, and I believe that – not in a partisan sense – because so many of the people that have been reaching out to my office in pain, in fear, having their lives upended. So many of them identify themselves as Republicans.

Indeed, conversations from in this body, to in this building, to across my state and recently in a travel across the country, Republicans as well as Democrats are talking to me about what they feel is a sense of dread about a growing crisis or what they point to about what is going wrong. That bedrock commitments in our country that both sides rely on, that people from all backgrounds rely on, those bedrock commitments are being broken. Unnecessary hardships are being borne by Americans of all backgrounds and institutions which are special in America, which are precious, which are unique in our country are being recklessly – and I would say even unconstitutionally – affected, attacked, even shattered. In just 71 days, the President of the United States has inflicted so much harm on American's safety, financial stability, the core foundations of our democracy, and even our aspirations as a people, from our highest offices, a sense of common decency.

These are not normal times in America and they should not be treated as such. John Lewis, so many heroes before us, would say that this is the time to stand up, to speak up. This is the time to get in some good trouble, to get into necessary trouble. I can't allow this body to continue without doing something different, speaking out. The threats to American people and American democracy are grave and urgent and we all must do more. We all must do more against them, but those ten words – "If it is to be, it is up to me." – all of us have to think of those ten two-letter words, "If it is to be, it is up to me." Because I believe generations from now will look back at this moment and have a single question, "Where were you when our country was in crisis and when American people were asking for help?"

"Help me." Did we speak up?

Did we speak up when 73 million American seniors who rely on social security to have that promise mocked, attacked, and then to have the services undermined, to be told that be no one there to answer if you call for help. When our seniors became afraid and worried and panicked because of the menacing words of their president, of the most wealthy person in the world of cabinet secretaries. Did we speak up? When the American economy in 71 days has been upended when prices at the grocery store were skyrocketing, and the stock market was plunging when pension funds 401K's were going down, when Americans were hurting and looking up. Where the resounding answer to this question was no, are you better off economically than you were 71 days ago?

Where were you? Did you speak up at a time when the President of the United States was launching trade wars against our most close allies, when he was firing regulators who investigate America's biggest banks and biggest corporations and stop them from taking advantage of the little guy, or the little gal, or my grandmother, or your grandfather, dismantling the agency that protects consumers from fraud that the only one whose sole purpose is to look out for them? Did you speak up when the President of the United States, in a way that is so crass and craven, peddled his own memecoin and made millions, upon millions, upon millions of dollars for his own bank account at a time so many are struggling economically.

Did you speak up when the President of the United States did what amounts to a car commercial for the richest man in the world right in front of America's house, the White House when the President tried to take healthcare away, where were you? Did you speak up? Threatening a program called Medicaid [that] helps people with disabilities, helps expectant mothers, helps millions upon millions of Americans, and why? As a part of a larger plan to pay for tax cuts for the wealthiest amongst us who've done the best over the last 20 years. For billionaires, it seems so close to the President that they sat right on the dais at his inauguration and sit in his cabinet meetings at the White House.

Did you speak up when he gutted public education, slashed funds for pediatric cancer research, fired thousands of veterans who risked their lives for their country, when he abandoned our allies and our international commitments at a time when floods, fires, and hurricanes, and droughts, are devastating communities across this country, when countries all around the world are banding together to do something and he turned his back? Did you speak up when outbreaks of dangerous infectious diseases are still a global threat, but yet we have stopped engaging in the efforts necessary to meet those threats? Where were you when the American press was being censored, when international students were being disappeared from American streets without due process, when American universities were being intimidated into silence, challenging that fundamental idea of freedom of thought, freedom of expression, when the law firms that represent clients that may not be favored were attacked, and attacked, and attacked, where were you?

Did you speak up when they came for those firms or what about when the people who attacked the police officers who defended this building, and American democracy, on January 6th, who just outside those doors put their lives on the line for us and many of them would later die? Where were you when the President pardoned them, celebrated them and even talked of giving them money — the people who savagely beat American police officers? Did you speak up when Americans from across the country were all speaking up, more, and more, and more voices in this country speaking up saying, "This is not right. This is un-American. This is not who we are, this is not America." Did you speak up?

And so I rise tonight because I believe to be about what is normal right now, when so much abnormal is happening, is unacceptable. I rise tonight because silence at this moment of national crisis would be a betrayal of some of the greatest heroes of our nation, because at stake in this moment is nothing less than everything that we brag about, that we talk about that makes us special. At stake right now are some of our most basic American principles that so many Americans understand are worth fighting for, worth standing for, worth speaking up for. Like if you work hard your entire life and pay into Social Security, it should be there for you when you retire and you should not have to question if those paychecks will arrive, and the government should strive to improve service to you, not brag about cutting it.

Basic American principles like if you serve your nation in the military, if you put your life in danger abroad, you will be respected and taken care of. You'll be cherished and honored and not forced to worry that the federal employees who provide you with care, many of whom who are veterans themselves will be fired or the benefits that you rely on will be denied or that your healthcare needs won't be met. Basic American principles like your child will have access to a high quality public education that every child has a unique genius, even our children, beautiful children with special needs, they have genius and then our children can go to school and parents and teachers know that they will be safe there. At stake now are those basic American principles that the people you elect to serve you in government will represent you and not try to make themselves richer, not run some scam and call you a sucker.

These basic ideals of our nation that everyone's rights will be equally protected and everyone will be held accountable under the law. Right now, all of this, things that make our country different are under attack. Our constituents are asking us to acknowledge this. Everywhere I travel now, I hear from Republicans and independents and Democrats who are afraid, who are worried, who are angry, and I think about John Lewis who taught me that fear is not something to be shunned. It's almost a signpost that you're headed in the right direction. It is something that is a necessary precondition. You cannot have great fear without great courage. John Lewis would tell us that this is a time for great courage. He would tell us that anger is a fuel. It can consume you, debilitate you, or it could fuel you to put yourself in service of others.

I feel if my friend was here, if my hero was here, he would tell us and try to teach us that this is a moment to know that despair is only possible if you don't meet it. As an agent of hope, if John Lewis was here, he would look at me and say, "What are you doing?" What are we doing? So tonight I rise in an unusual way. I rise with the intention to stand here until I can stand no longer, until I'm physically unable to stand anymore. I'm going to speak up. I'm going to try to cause some good trouble in this body I respect so much. I'm going to try to cause what I believe is necessary trouble.

I'm going to try to honor the legacy that I know I've inherited as an American. The legacy I think about when I come to this floor and feel sometimes overwhelmed with all the sacrifice and struggle that had to get me here. Good people who caused good trouble in the face of slavery. Good people who caused good trouble in the face of the denial of the right to vote. Good people who caused good trouble in the cause of equal rights. Good people who caused good trouble in the fight against hate.

Good people who caused good trouble in the fight against demagogues, from McCarthy to Father Coughlin, to big people who showed such small character when they tried to suppress others. I want to cause good trouble and prove worthy of those who came before.

This is not normal. Listen to America. Listen to Americans, they seem to always be ahead of this body. They're rising up in state after state, not along partisan lines, but as an American line. Not because they hate other Americans, but because they love America, and know that. What does love look like in public? It looks like justice, and there is so much injustice going on. I don't know how long I can stand, but I will stand and speak up.

7:22 PM - Letters

I want to start by reading some of these letters to try to give folk a flavor of what's happened in my office for 71 days.

The calls we've gotten have gotten more and more numerous. I know I'm not the only one because the calls became so numerous to the Senate as a whole, it locked up the lines. The letters I'm getting, the emails I'm getting, people taking scraps of paper and just writing their hearts out and sending it in to say this is not ordinary times, these are painful times, frightening times. Times where people question what's happening to America and worry that there are powerful people trying to fundamentally change our nation in a way that will hurt people to the benefit of the powerful and the wealthy.

I look at these letters like this one, I won't read the name, but they say:

> Hi, Senator Booker. Medicaid has saved my life many times. Without it, many people in America will die. Please help us. {Underlined multiple times.}

Here's another scrap of paper where somebody writes their heart out:

> Dear Senator Booker, when I got out of the Navy, I had mental illness. I needed psychiatric medicine to stop going in and out of the hospital. Because of Medicare, I have medicine that has kept me out of the hospital for 18 years. Without Medicaid and my medicine, I will wind up in the hospital.

Americans telling me their most vulnerable pains, their most terrified realities, are now confronting them, rendering their pride and telling their truth. Here's another one:

> Dear Senator Booker, I'm writing you today as a constituent. In addition to being a concerned citizen, I'm a 25-year employee of the local Board of Education and a parent of a permanently disabled daughter who has just started receiving Medicaid. Even with her Master's Degree, my daughter is only able to work 19 hours a week. Therefore, insurance is not provided. Medicaid is a necessity to maintain her physical and emotional health and provide services to assist with her independence so she can continue to be a contributing member of society.
>
> By withdrawing funding for Medicaid, the policy would disrupt programs serving disabled and elderly people in New Jersey and throughout the country, and Medicaid is only one area which will potentially be affected by Donald Trump's funding freeze. Please protect Social Security and Medicare for the hardworking Americans who have earned it.
>
> Social Security isn't quote, "a handout". We've paid into it with every paycheck throughout our entire working lives and the 66 million seniors relying on Medicare could have their healthcare put on hold or canceled. We deserve to know these programs will be there for us. If federal grants are limited, medical and science research limited, including vaccines and disease prevention, they'll all be severely impacted. The United States should be a world leader in healthcare, in education and scientific advancement.
>
> This is an embarrassment to us as a country. It should not be possible in America for one single man, even an elected president, to stop funds which Congress has already allocated. I implore you to use your power as my Senator and a key member of our government to stand up for what is important to the people of your district. We want to go to work, take care of our families, and ensure all citizens have health services they deserve. These latest orders are inappropriate, untenable, and illegal. As a senator, please take action. Please take action to defend and protect these programs. Thank you for your time.

> Cory Booker, recently it's come to my attention that my students' rights in New Jersey are under threat from new legislation. This has caused distress and uncertainty in my classroom from my students who depend on funds for Medicaid. My students depend on consistency and a lapse in their education and care would result in regression, trauma, and worse. I teach students in New Jersey who are supported by your legislature. I teach all abilities meaning many of the students live with ADHD, autism, and other disorders that require extra care and attention. It's my life's mission to bring what I know to those who want to learn it.
>
> I love the job I do. I love that I get to spend time with those who need it most and deliver care and education. The job that I do helps my students live more independently and achieve richer and more fulfilling lives. I live out of state, but most of my students are from the state you help legislate. My students' rights are in trouble and need you to advocate for them. I urge you to continue to fight for Medicaid. Please work to oppose any and all cuts or caps to the Medicaid program.

> Dear Senator Booker, I'm a registered voter in New Jersey. I'm writing today to strongly urge you and your fellow policymakers to oppose all cuts to the Medicaid program as it is a lifeline for individuals with disabilities. Oppose all cuts or caps.
>
> I was a special education teacher for 30 years, and after I retired, I volunteered as a special education advocate for ten years. I had the privilege of advocating for many disabled children and young adults who were receiving Medicaid services.
>
> Medicaid gave many of my clients the opportunity to participate in society by providing daily life skills for independence. Skills reinforced through Medicare programs include shopping, safety, job search, speech and language — just to point out a few of the services provided by Medicaid.
>
> My clients require repetition of these skills to function in their daily lives. Without these programs provided by Medicaid, regression will occur and learned skills will not be retained. Without Medicaid, this community will struggle, isolate, and lose any quality of life they've enjoyed since receiving Medicaid services. Medicaid has made a critical difference in the lives of my clients. Cutting and capping Medicaid will have devastating consequences for them and their family.
>
> Senator, there are 1.6 million New Jersey residents with disabilities who rely on Medicaid for access to vital care, resources, and essential medications needed to survive. Please support and fight for these vulnerable New Jersey citizens. Please take action to protect these vital programs provided by Medicaid. Thank you in advance for your anticipated efforts in my request of your support for our most vulnerable residents.

I'm going to rise tonight as I said and stay for as long as I physically can, and I'm going to go through issue area after issue area, after issue area, and talk specifically to the concerns, the fears, the actions taken to the hurts that are already being felt throughout America, elevating others' voices who don't have the privilege of standing in this body, honoring those Americans who even though they don't have such a position, they are raising their voice. I will rise for as long as I can to honor them and raise mine.

7:33 PM - Healthcare

The first area I want to talk about is Medicaid, Medicare, and healthcare, as my constituents spoke to. I don't need to tell anyone the importance of healthcare to humanity. Without our health, we would not be able to do anything else. We would not be able to provide for our families, spend time with our loved ones, do all of the things that make life worth living, and that's why I'm going to stand here and explain to people what's going on and how our healthcare programs are at risk and being undermined.

The Trump administration and Republicans in Congress are right now discussing how to cut these programs in a way of putting those savings either into tax cuts for the rich. I say either because they're going to be putting in the taxes for the rich, but those tax cuts as we know are still going to blow massive trillion-dollar holes in our deficits. They're trying to gut Medicaid and Medicare programs on which nearly a third of our country rely, all to pay for those tax cuts to billionaires and corporations. They're also dismantling the very institutions meant to safeguard our nation's health and well-being. And this is not the first time. They tried this before during Trump's first administration, when he unsuccessfully tried to repeal the Affordable Care Act, and cut Medicaid despite its popularity across the nation, across the political aisle. He was going after something that wasn't Left or Right, that Americans were saying in a chorus of conviction that this is about right or wrong, it is wrong to take away healthcare from millions of people.

Let me explain, if I can, or speak to a few points from a recent report by Protect Our Care to explain what the administration is trying to do to our healthcare system. They want to slash almost a trillion dollars, about $850 billion, from Medicaid, forcing people to choose between healthcare and putting food on the table. In every state, hundreds of thousands of seniors, children, and working families could lose their health insurance thanks to Republican plans to cut those hundreds and hundreds of billions of dollars from Medicaid. It would impose ... they seek burdensome work requirements for people on Medicaid. The last proposal coming from Republicans of that work requirement has one goal, to make it harder for people to qualify for Medicaid, to slash benefits and deny up to 36 million people access to healthcare so they could fund, again, those tax breaks for the wealthiest and for corporations.

Work requirements only increase the red tape that hard-working families already burdened by working multiple jobs, caring for children and more. They're simply increasing the red tape working families have to go through to obtain affordable care. Their intention is also to hike premium costs. Millions of families who use private health insurance saved an average of $2,400 per year on their premiums thanks to the Inflation Reduction Act advanced premium tax cuts, but now the proposals Republicans are putting forth want to end these savings and raise costs for over 24 million Americans.

The proposal wants to take away protections from people with pre-existing conditions. The GOP plans to repeal and undermine the ACA, meaning, if they're successful, 135 million people with pre-existing conditions like asthma, cancer, and diabetes, would lose critical protections — that private insurance companies can charge them higher premiums. The efforts that they're discussing – Republicans are discussing – would raise prescription drug prices. It would stop medical research and stop medical debt relief. Over the first three months of his administration, Donald Trump and Republican allies have increased the prices of prescription drugs, including cancer and heart medications, as well as vital antibiotics, delayed the implementation of a Biden administration rule that barred medical debt from showing up on credit reports, cut NIH grants, halted all studies and activities within the NIH relating in any capacity to the health of LGBTQ Americans, including active research programs, and President Trump violated court orders to halt funding freezes to organizations like the NIH.

Republicans rejected legislation to cap insulin costs for millions of people with diabetes nationwide. Now, they want to raise costs for seniors by repealing the cap for people who rely on Medicare. As many as one in four of the 7.5 million Americans dependent on insulin are skipping or skimping on doses – I want to say that again – As many as one in four of the 7.5 million Americans dependent on insulin are skipping or skimping on doses. This is a life-threatening practice. No one in this country should have to bear that. This week we know Republicans in the Senate will make us vote on a budget that will inevitably intended to harm the strength of programs like Medicaid and vital health programs in general. Here's what a few organizations are saying about the impact of the budget that will soon be put on this floor, what impact it'll have on our health systems.

According to this nonpartisan Center on Budget and Policy Priorities, a nonpartisan policy and research institute, this is what they write:

> The House Republican budget would require deep cuts to Medicaid, and recent statements from House Energy and Commerce Chair, Brett Guthrie, suggests the Affordable Care Act's Medicaid expansion to adults with low incomes, which cover more than 20 million Americans, will be a prime target. Cutting Medicaid by hundreds of billions of dollars and focusing many of those cuts on the Medicaid expansion would lead millions of people to become uninsured.
>
> Eliminating Medicaid expansion was a key goal of Republicans' failed effort to repeal the ACA eight years ago and Congress should once again reject efforts to undermine it. Recent Republican proposals such as reducing the federal matching rate for Medicaid expansion, repealing the 2021 Rescue Plan incentive for new states to expand, or taking away Medicaid coverage from certain adult enrollees by imposing work requirements would leave expansion enrollees at risk.
>
> They could lose their coverage due to the work requirements, or their state might drop their coverage due to a drastic increase in state costs. Twelve states, 12 American states have poison pill laws that would automatically end expansion coverage or review of the coverage if the federal matching rate drops below 90%. In those states, expansion enrollees are even in graver risk. Representative Guthrie's recent statement confirms that House Republicans are eyeing proposals such as work requirements, a reduction in the federal matching rate, or a per capita cap on funding for the expansion group. This last option could shift 72 billion and 190 billion in costs from states from 2026 to 2034, putting that burden from 72 billion to 190 billion on states, increasing the state costs expansion by 41 to 108%, and that's jeopardizing medical coverage for millions.
>
> Forty states plus Washington DC have adopted the Medicaid expansion, helping adults with low incomes become healthier and more financially secure. Health coverage through expansion improves people's access to something that makes so much economic sense, it improves people's access to preventative care, to primary care. It also provides care for people with chronic illnesses, prevents premature deaths, and protects people from catastrophic out-of-pocket medical costs.

Let me pull away from the nonpartisan group's remarks for a second, because I saw this as a mayor. When you scrimp on regular treatment for people with chronic care, when you scrimp on preventative disease, it costs more to taxpayers. I saw that because folks would end up in my emergency rooms in Newark, and the care there is so much more expensive for a taxpayer, you get a much better deal in helping someone treat their chronic disease. You get a much better deal in giving them regular access to doctors, but to cut that makes no sense.

Not only are you cutting it to give, again, those larger tax cuts, to billionaires and corporations, but you're cutting it and you're just going to add even more and more to the overall healthcare costs of our country to the size of the debt. Let me go back to the text.

> Having health coverage also makes it easier for adults to work or look for a job. Consider that Medicaid supports work, and that nine out of ten Medicaid adults are already working, caring for family, attending school, or are ill or disabled, work requirements are unnecessary, they're burdensome, they're more red tape and hassles, proposals to use work requirements as a way to take away Medicaid coverage from certain adults are just another way to undermine Medicaid expansion. Attacks on the Medicaid expansion are often based on false claims that covering adults with low incomes takes away care from groups traditionally eligible for Medicaid.
>
> In reality, Medicaid expansion supports better outcomes for all groups, including children, older adults, and people with disabilities. Medicaid expansion has driven coverage gains for parents, which improve their access to care as well as their overall well-being, the overall well-being for their children."

Stepping away from the text, there's not a parent in America that knows when you're sick, when you are being hurt by your chronic disease, it's harder to take care of children and their well-being suffers. Back to the text.

> Expansion has also driven coverage gains among people with disabilities. People with disabilities who receive supplemental security insurance income generally also qualify for Medicaid. About two out of three people with disabilities who participate in Medicaid qualify on another basis, meaning Medicaid expansion is an important path to coverage for those with low incomes.
>
> Medicaid expansion also supports hospitals and other healthcare providers by reducing their uncompensated care costs and improving their operating margins especially, especially, especially for rural and safety net hospitals. If all states in America were to drop the Medicaid expansion in response to a decline in federal support, a recent analysis found that the provider revenues would fall by $80 billion and uncompensated care costs would increase by $19 billion in 2026 alone.

That's the end of the article.

This is not a hyperbole or scare tactic. These are real possibilities. Even the nonpartisan Congressional Budget Office has said there is no way to meet the Republican budget resolution dedicated cuts without cutting Medicaid or Medicare. Tonight and into tomorrow morning, I'm going to do everything I can to elevate the voices of Republicans, because this is not intended to be a partisan speech. From the Cato Institute to The Wall Street Journal to nonpartisan groups to [our] own Congressional Budget Office, everyone is pointing to what is happening as not normal, not what the president says it is, as something that's going to hurt Americans, something that's going to cost us more money in the long run. Someone's going to take people with disabilities and put them even more in the shadows and margins when they should be centralized and empowered. What they're proposing is not just morally wrong, it actually adds to the fiscal crisis of our country. It will drive up healthcare costs in America. It will drive up chronic disease in America.

An issue so important to me, I've been fighting for it since I got here because America, this great nation, this great land is one of the leading countries on the planet earth in the Western world and leading democracies, I should say, that has maternal mortality rates that are extraordinarily high. Well, 40-plus percent of our babies are born on Medicaid. Here's an article from NBC.

> Republicans can't meet their own budget targets without cutting Medicare or Medicaid. House Republicans can't meet their own budget target that is necessary to pass President Donald Trump's legislative agenda without making significant cuts to Medicare or Medicaid, the official budget scorekeeper confirmed on Wednesday, House Republicans adopted a budget blueprint last week that opens the door to pass Donald Trump's policy priorities on immigration, energy, and taxes. It instructs the House Energy and Commerce committee to cut spending under its jurisdiction by $880 billion.
>
> The Congressional Budget Office, a nonpartisan in-house think tank that referees the process, said that when Medicare is set aside, the total funding under the committee's jurisdiction is 8.8 trillion over the next 10 years. Medicaid accounts for 8.2 trillion of that, or 93%. When Medicare and Medicaid are excluded, the committees oversee a total of 581 billion in spending, much less than the $880 billion target, the CBO said.
>
> The letter outlining the figures was in response to a query by... {I take away from the article for a second by my friend and longtime New Jerseyan representative...} Frank Pallone. He's the ranking member of the Energy and Commerce Committee, and Brendan Doyle, a Democrat of Pennsylvania, the ranking member of the budget committee, they asked the question that leaves Republicans in a deep predicament.
>
> The budget resolution adopted by the slimmest of margins is in a narrowly divided house was the delicate product of negotiations amongst conservative hardliners who demand steep budget cuts and swing district GOP lawmakers who say they don't want to slash funding for health programs their constituents rely on.

Off the article for a second — God bless you for caring about your constituents.

> Reversing the target would mean upsetting one of those factions and potentially risking the support of key votes to pass the eventual budget reconciliation bill that advances Trump's agenda.

Democrats have made protecting Medicaid a centerpiece of their attack on the party-line GOP agenda, accusing Trump of trying to cut healthcare for the working class to pay for tax cuts for the wealthy.

> "The letter from the CBO confirms what we've been saying all along, the math doesn't work without devastating Medicaid cuts," Pallone said Wednesday in a statement. "Republicans know their spin is a lie, and the truth is they have no problem taking healthcare away from millions of Americans so that the rich can get richer and pay less in taxes than they already do."

You see, stepping away from this, they are saying, "We're going to make these cuts to balance the budget," but their budget blows a bigger hole in our deficit.

If this is what Trump said, then why are they proposing to cut 880 billion from critical healthcare programs like Medicaid, Medicare, and Children's Health Insurance Program? You can't have it both ways. Donald Trump promised to make America healthy again, but gutting healthcare for millions of Americans, rolling back healthcare for millions of Americans, rolling back support for new mothers, slashing innovative cancer treatments, this doesn't help families. I love what Dr. King said. Martin Luther King famously stated, "Of all the forms of inequality, injustice in health is the most shocking and inhumane." *Of all the forms of inequality, injustice in health is the most shocking and inhumane.*

Paul Farmer, extraordinary leader, physician, anthropologist, renowned humanitarian, pioneer of global health — I read his book, "Mountains Beyond Mountains".

In another one of his books, "Pathologies of Power: Health, Human Rights, and the New War on the Poor", he wrote, and I quote, "If access to healthcare is considered a human right, who is considered human enough to have that right?" I think in a country this wealthy, where we are seeing stratospheric wealth created here in individuals, we're seeing some of the richest people in the world, and yet we still are targeting for tax bucks breaks for them, we're targeting millions and millions of Americans who rely on things like Medicare.

I started my speech with John Lewis — let me quote him now. In 2012 he said, "Healthcare is a right and it is not a privilege, not just for some people but for all people." John Lewis was a visionary. So let me tell you a bit more about Medicaid. If you're watching, let me break it down and show just how critical it is for millions of Americans.

Medicaid right now is in the crosshairs of many, many Republicans in Congress. It's on this precipice. It's not abstract policy. It's not just numbers in a line item in a budget. At stake, when you talk about Medicare, is millions and millions of Americans' health. It goes to this question is how deeply do we care for one another? I love what our founders said in the Declaration of Independence. At the very end of that they say, "**We must mutually pledge, pledging to each other, our lives, our fortunes and our sacred honor.**" Are we living up to that when we are saying we're going to take away healthcare for millions of Americans in order to have greater tax cuts? You see, people want to just say, "Oh, it's a government program," as if that's a slur, when really it's something that We the People, in order to create a more perfect union, created as a lifeline to tens of millions of Americans that, but for programs like this, would be succumbing to diseases, succumbing to ill health, and we as an entire country would suffer.

Think about this not as that slur where they try to call this in ways to try to shift public opinion away from human beings, fellow Americans, our patriots, think of it instead as a lifeline. It is the reason a child with asthma can breathe easier. It is the reason a senior can receive the care they need in a nursing home, our elders. It is the reason a low-income mother can take her child in for vaccinations or a person with a disability can live with dignity and independence. Congress is entertaining proposals now, conversations are being had in this building and in Senate and House office buildings about how we can gut programs.

God, I wish somebody said in a bipartisan way, "Let's come together and find healthcare savings." I offered that. I literally said to the now Secretary of Health, I told stories about private sector folks who saved money by expanding access to food, to healthy fresh food. Let's save that because I know private sector companies that have bent their cost curves, saved money, not by cutting healthcare, but by giving people better access to nutritious healthy foods. You are what you eat. We're not coming up with bipartisan proposals to save money, to create efficiencies, to do things that can make programs run better. Heck, when I was mayor, we were able to lower expenditures, create more efficiency, have more happier customer service. There are ways to do that, but no, this is folks coming with an ax to cut your healthcare or your neighbor's healthcare or your elder's healthcare.

It's not a government program. It's a commitment we make to each other in the greatest nation on the planet Earth, we say we'll take care of our children, we say we'll take care of expectant mothers, we say we'll take care of our own, but they pass that House budget resolution. Republicans who called themselves moderates on budget... They all voted for it except for one who had the crazy thing to do in Washington to tell the truth. Massey said that by their own numbers, this don't add up — what they're pushing on the American people is going to steal from the future generations by racking up trillions of debt. He stood on principle.

They're not even doing what they're telling us they're going to do. $880 Billion in Medicaid funding cuts — it's not trimming the fat, it's not finding efficiencies, it's not a plan to cut out any possible corruption. It is to make children and expectant mothers and seniors and people with disabilities have a harder time accessing healthcare, which we already said that Martin Luther King, of all the forms of inequality, injustice in healthcare is the most shocking and inhumane. Not bigotry, not poverty, two things he fought so nobly against. He said the most inhumane, the most unjust are what we're talking about here, take away access to healthcare from children, take away access to healthcare from our elders, take away access to healthcare to people with chronic diseases.

Why? Why? To cut the deficit? Well, there's some Republicans willing to tell the truth, it's not going to cut the deficit. To take from the poor and give it to the rich and powerful? Well, we know the rich and powerful will get bigger tax cuts. They're not shrinking the government, folks. They're creating bigger and bigger governmental obligations. And what do they mean? When you look at ten years out and have trillions and trillions and trillions or more, it means that future generations, or maybe ten years from now, that their debt payments are going to grow more and more and more, taking away more money that we have as a collective body as Americans to invest in scientific research, to invest in cutting edge medical technology.

So let's be clear. Let's be clear. Children from low-income families would lose access to routine checkups, vaccinations, and emergency care.

Seniors who depend on Medicaid for long-term care, many of whom are already exhausting their life savings, would be left without options. People with disabilities who require constant medical attention, specialized equipment, and home-based services would face uncertainty and loss of those services. And let us not forget the low-income adults who gained coverage through Medicaid expansion, who work hard every day, they got access to Medicaid through expansion under the Affordable Care Act. For them, this is not ideology. For them this is not political philosophy. For them this is life or death. It's about survival.

These proposed cuts would also devastate the very infrastructure of our healthcare system. I've heard this from hospitals. Again, Republicans and Democratic leaders in my state who know our hospitals are speaking to this injustice. Medicare provides nearly 19% of all hospital revenue. It allows rural hospitals already on the brink to keep their doors open. Rural hospitals, it would take safety net hospitals that serve uninsured and underinsured populations. Without Medicaid, with these cuts, these institutions would crumble. That's not rhetoric. I've talked to my safety net hospital. I did an event and I remember the fear in this hospital administrator's eyes, who lives every day to help the poor, to help the uninsured, in many ways we share a faith and I know he believes he's answering the highest calling of his country and his faith to help those who come with nothing.

Because when hospitals close, when Medicaid staff lose their jobs, entire communities lose access to care, ambulances end up having to drive farther and farther, wait times increase, lives are at risk. The ripple effects are vast. Schools will suffer. When children with disabilities lose access to Medicaid-supported services like physical therapy, transportation and mental health support, children's ability to learn and thrive is compromised. Schools in rural areas where Medicaid often funds on-site nurses and telehealth programs, they would be stripped of essential support. What we are witnessing is, again... Don't get caught in this Washington parlance — this is not a normal time. This is a threat to millions of Americans. It's not a budgetary proposal.

It is like the metaphorical Sword of Damacles; it is people all over this country who are beginning to see what this really means. It's an economic crisis that would be rolled upon states and rural areas and communities and cities. It is a moral crisis that speaks to the soul of our nation. Calculated and being calculated right now, it is a deliberate and calculated attack on healthcare for Americans in order, again, to give tax cuts to the wealthy.

If the enhanced Federal Match for Medicaid is limited, one of the things on the chopping block, states would be forced to absorb the difference, an estimated $88 billion every year. That is a 29% increase in state-funded Medicare spending per resident. To fill those holes, states would be left with impossible choices: either raise taxes or slash services, education infrastructure, public safety. For them, they would have to figure out where to get the money from, or else they'd be slashing services. It's an unholy choice.

Cutting Medicare doesn't make us stronger. It will weaken our economy. It will raise healthcare costs for everyone and push millions of Americans into crises that will ripple and radiate through their lives, their families lives, their work lives. Hospitals will pass unpaid bills onto insured patients.

Healthcare premiums will rise. People will delay care, omit medications, and then show up in emergency rooms later, more sick, and therefore more expensive to treat. And in the end, who pays for it? Who pays for this moral failure, this financial failure? Who pays for it? We do. The American people.

And who gets rich on this? Well, I know the last tax cut that they want to extend the people who make the most money off of this system and this cuts because of the tax cuts they will get will be billionaires. And working families in America, people who paying insurance rates, hurt ... is hard, is difficult — people who have high premiums and copays. It's the rest of us that pay.

So, I want to talk about the people at risk. There's nearly 12 million people who qualify for both Medicare and Medicaid — our nation's most vulnerable. They'd lose critical wraparound services. Services like long-term care, dental care, vision and non-emergency transportation services that are not luxuries for these folks but their lifelines.

A higher share of those with both Medicaid and Medicare have cognitive impairments and conditions like Alzheimer's. And God ... my father, who had dementia. We're a well-off family. I saw the challenges, the resources, the drains, the physical challenges for his primary caregiver, my mother.

Millions of Americans though, would rely on Medicaid. And they would face devastating choices, quit their jobs to provide full care, full-time care, or leave their loved ones while they go off to work on a job without the support they need. When it comes to Alzheimer's and dementia, I know personally you cannot leave someone without the care.

Nursing homes may be forced to shut their doors or cut staffing levels to dangerous lows. In fact, people who can't take care of their elders, they might be going to nursing homes, which again increases costs for taxpayers. Home healthcare services, often the only thing keeping people in their communities out of institutions, that would disappear. This would be a crisis for elder care. This would be a crisis for disability services.

What it is when a nation isn't taking care of its elders? It's a crisis of our national character.

Medicaid also plays a profound role in the success of children and their well-being. Nearly half of all children in the US are covered by Medicare – excuse me – are covered by Medicaid and CHIP. Research shows that when children have access to care, they are more likely to stay in school, graduate, and earn more as adults. That's not surprising to people, just to think it through. It's true. If kids have access to healthcare, they succeed more in life. Medicaid helps diagnose learning disorders, treat chronic conditions, and ensure children don't fall behind simply because they're born into poverty.

It's essential to the American dream that just because you're poor, it shouldn't affect your destiny. And for us to be the America of which we speak, a child born in poverty shouldn't have their future cut off because they can't get the healthcare to empower them to thrive. Talk to any school district in any state, in any county — those resources are necessary to help children. Medicaid pays for nearly half of the births in the United States.

The United States, as I said earlier, has a shameful distinction of a massive maternal health crisis. We have the highest rate of maternal deaths of any high-income nation. I'm going to say that again. America has the highest rates of maternal deaths, women dying in childbirth or in the days after, of any nation. A majority of these maternal deaths take place during that postpartum period, the days after birth. For years, I have fought for Medicaid to provide coverage for women for up to one year postpartum, instead of just 60 days. In 2022's Congress, I was so happy that states had the option to expand Medicaid coverage for up to one year postpartum. It is one of the solutions to this maternal healthcare crisis that expert after expert after expert says, "Just make sure those women who gave birth are not knocked off of healthcare after two months." As of this January, 49 states plus the District of Columbia have expanded postpartum Medicaid coverage past those 60 days.

Hey, we're stepping in the right direction to show that we love our moms. We value those life-givers that are mothers. We value them. But cutting Medicare means potentially eliminating the progress we made towards ending that maternal mortality crisis. It's just no justifying that. In a nation this great and this wealthy, we talk so much about children and motherhood. All of us should be coming together about this maternal health crisis. But what's happening now, again, is the very program that's helped us to begin to address this is under attack.

When we invest in Medicaid, we are investing in the future, in children who grew up to be healthier, in seniors who age with dignity, in rural communities with limited access to healthcare and services, and families who don't have to choose between a prescription and rent.

This is about health, but I want to tell you that, for all those doing the math at home, you cannot have a thriving economic engine without good healthcare. The two are incompatible, widespread sickness, illness and disease, and people who can't get their health issues covered. It takes away from our economic strength.

In fact, just cutting Medicaid would cost jobs. Nurses aides, support staff, medical technicians, entire communities depend on funding that Medicaid provides. Cutting it would destabilize state budgets, force those impossible trade-offs, and widen the gap. Widen the gap between the richest in our country and the rest. A gap that's already widening at stunning rates.

These cuts are not about efficiency. Don't let anybody tell you these cuts are about efficiency. I know a lot about making government more efficient. This is not about innovation. There's so many things that we as a country should be doing to deal with medical innovation. And I'll be the first to say, Republicans and Democrats have failed to step up to the 21st century and do things that really can create more efficiencies in our healthcare system. I really hope to see more bold thinkers about creating real efficiency. But what they're doing now is not about efficiency. It's not about innovation. It's not about the heart priorities of Americans who know everything that I'm saying.

The letters I've gotten, Republicans and Democrats and independents in my states, scared people, they know what this is about. Republicans in New Jersey who run hospitals know what this is about. This should be a bipartisan strategy [on] how do we make our society more healthy and less dependent on healthcare. And when it comes to healthcare, heck, let's not do the stupid things like cutting scientific and biosciences, and the research that often leads to medical breakthroughs. Let's come together and figure out how to deliver services more efficiently.

Making Americans healthier? I don't believe them. They're cutting access to kids, to fresh and healthy foods, or cutting school lunch resources. There's a way to do this that should be bringing the best ideas from both sides of the aisle to deal with these issues. But that's not what they're doing.

Every data point, every story, hospitals from rural areas to urban areas — everyone is saying the same thing and illustrating the same point: Medicaid is critical to the health of some of the most vulnerable Americans. It's critical to our elders, to our children, to our mothers. It is a lifeline for more than 72 million people.

With control of the Senate, the House, and the Presidency, Republicans have the opportunity to dream big. They have an opportunity to lead with a vision for better health in America, to come before the people, and Congress, and hearings, and say, "This is our vision for American health and well-being. We're going to show what some private companies did. They cut their healthcare costs and improve the health of their employees by providing better access to food."

There are so many good ideas that I've learned when I was mayor from Republicans, from private sector people. But those aren't the ideas that are coming forward. The ideas that are coming forward is, "Hey, let's just send to the Energy and Commerce Committee the mandate to cut $880 billion. Let's rush now. Let's rush now. Let's get it done before our narrow majority somehow gets undermined. Let's just cut, cut, cut, cut, cut." And in the end, what's the result? Americans get sicker, driving up overall healthcare costs, all to get billionaires more of a tax cut. I know the character of so many of my friends in this body on both sides of the aisle. This is not who we are. It is not who we are. But God, there's no big vision. There's no big dream for healthcare.

Instead of improving Medicaid and increasing funding, as 42% of Americans support, they want to make extraordinary cuts that will demolish a program. They are proposing that $880 billion cut from Medicaid and taking healthcare away from millions of Americans. They want to impose work requirements, even though 90% of Medicaid beneficiaries are already working or cannot work for legitimate reasons.

Arkansas actually tried this. (I love case studies.) They tried this in 2017, and the results were disastrous. People lost coverage that they shouldn't have, and employment didn't increase. Nationally, such requirements could put 36 million people at risk of losing their healthcare.

They're proposing failed policies, not breakthrough ideas, not a bold vision that I know is in America's heart. This repeal that some folks are saying that they want to do to save money. A hatred for previous presidents, they want to repeal Biden-era rules that made Medicaid and CHIP enrollment easier, less red tape, easier for seniors and children. "Let's repeal that," they say. They want to end a rule requiring minimum staffing standards in nursing homes, including 24/7 access to registered nurses, one of the hardest, most underappreciated jobs in America. Let's get less access to these noble, noble professionals. They propose per capita caps that would upend Medicaid's financing model in every state, leaving states with less money to meet their residents needs.

And in states that expanded Medicaid under the ACA, these cuts could jeopardize coverage for 20 million people who gained access. The budget that they're proposing would require deeper cuts. Speaker Johnson claims these changes are about rooting out fraud, waste, and abuse. But that's not what's happening, folks. What's happening is an assault on a program that provides dignity, health and stability, economic growth, improved outcomes for kids, more respect for our elders, care for the disabled.

Nearly 2 million New Jerseyans – 2 million people in my state – rely on Medicaid. And yet, our state is slated to see cuts of up to 5.2 billion. Medicaid accounts for a quarter, more than a quarter of New Jersey's state budget. Think about that. It accounts for more than a quarter of our state's budget.

And my state, one of the hardest working states that's out there, just their work requirement would put about 700,000 of my neighbors, my fellow statespeople, at risk of losing their healthcare.

Medicaid covers about one-fifth of hospital spending. At University Hospital in Newark, New Jersey's only level one trauma center, more than 149 million in the potential cuts loom.

I know this hospital, I have been there when my officers have been injured. I've been there when my firefighters in Newark were injured. I've been there when heroic citizens are injured and brought there. It is our level one trauma center. People from all around our region are sent there. These emergency room workers are incredible. Heck, they've treated me coming out of an emergency, and they're facing $149 million in cuts. And their leadership, knowing how vital that hospital it is, how that hospital stands in the breach between life and death, health and illness, they know what it would mean.

We should be strengthening this program through innovations that come from people on both sides of the aisle. We should be coming together as a body and saying, "Okay, let's spitball this. Let's put up the best ideas in America to make things more efficient. Oh, wait a minute. You mean if we treat chronic diseases with access to healthy food, we might actually be able to lower diabetes rates, lower hypertension rates, lower obesity rates?" Well, that's one great way to make this investment happen.

"You mean there is technology and innovation that's happening right now with our best scientists that could create better access to telehealth? It could create more efficiency in medical records?" It could cut down on mistakes that are still made in medical care, like combining the wrong drugs or other challenges that up costs.

There's systems that we could create that could create more transparency, and eliminate more real fraud, and go after the fraudsters themselves in a more efficient manner. There are so many things that we could do if we came together as a body. But what are we doing instead? Following our President that wants his tax cuts renewed.

What did those tax cuts do? The first time around, most of the benefits went to the wealthiest people and corporations. And it drove trillions of dollars, the largest deficit growth that we have seen in a generation. Rapacious, rapacious, misguided budgeting, creating bigger and bigger debt payments.

I remind you, Clinton? Balanced budget. Bush? The first president in American history that didn't call for the common sacrifice to go to war. We spent trillions of dollars in those foreign wars and guess what he said? No common sacrifice. Only about 1% of our people will fight in those wars. I'm going to give you a tax cut.

Well, that makes no sense. You're going to drive up deficits that my children will have to pay for. Obama comes along, and at least he lowers his deficit spending. But then Trump comes in and increases it by trillions of dollars on the backs of working Americans, to give those benefits to the wealthiest.

And now Biden, who shrunk the deficit a bit – didn't eliminate it – still spent. What any fiscally prudent person might say is really problematic. Let's not make this blindly partisan. But for anybody who would criticize Biden and follow Trump into what he's doing with this budget proposal that's going to slash healthcare for millions of Americans, increase the deficit by trillions and trillions of dollars, and make Elon Musk richer and richer — is that your solution? It violates our values. It violates our national character. It violates the highest principles put forth by the most noble people in American history.

And I stand today, and I will not sit down for hours and hours, if God gives me the ability to stand here, because I want to read the voices of Americans. I want to share their voices in this body. I want it to echo in history. I want it to be recorded by these extraordinary people who stand here every day and record my words and my colleagues' words. I want it to be in the Congressional record.

Anecdotes

I want Deanna to tell her story. Deanna's daughter is disabled and Medicaid provides her with life-saving medications, medical equipment, orthotics, and multiple specialists for her rare disease diagnosis. She has life- threatening seizures and requires rescue seizure medications, oxygen and CPR, and has nurses that accompany her to school and meet her medical needs during the day so that she can go to work.

Deanna is terrified. She uses this word. She is terrified of her daughter losing her Medicaid. She's so afraid, she's literally talking openly about going to Canada and asking for asylum there so that her daughter has the healthcare needs met. That is outrageous to me, that an American who's fearful for their child would think about fleeing to Canada for better healthcare.

Wendy and Cassie. Wendy is the mother, and she wrote about the threats that Medicaid cuts would pose to her daughter, Cassie. Cassie is 32 years old. She has Rett syndrome, RTT, a rare neurological disorder that significantly impairs even basic motor functions, requiring the individual to have life-long care and supervision. Without Medicaid funding, Cassie and Wendy would not be able to afford housing, the day program, the prescriptions that she needs on a daily basis.

Tanya and Cameron. God, Tanya uses Medicare and Medicaid to care for her son, her beloved child, Cameron. Cameron is battling stage four cancer and is confined to a wheelchair. Due to the severity of his illness, he cannot be without his cancer treatment and prescription medication. Medicare and Medicaid coverage is for them, they say, a matter of life and death for Cameron.

Here's this amazing group in New Jersey, in Cherry Hill, amazing group. The Cherry Hill Free Clinic. Volunteers sustain the Cherry Hill Free Clinic. Doctors give up their own time, because they are driven by the conviction that in America we take care of each other. We love each other. And when you say love your neighbor, love requires sacrifice and service. These doctors and professionals that volunteer their time at the Cherry Hill Clinic, I just want to tell you, God bless you. Thank you for living our American values and the values of your faith traditions.

The Cherry Hill Free Clinic provides free healthcare treatment and medication to low-income individuals, not in Cherry Hill, but throughout New Jersey. Without the support of Medicare and Medicaid coverage for their parents, a free clinic would not be able to provide the extent of services and care that their patients desperately need. They would not be able to be the source of light to so many people that are facing scary darkness.

Think that it's not going to happen to me, that cancer diagnosis. It's not going to happen to me, that rare diseases that affects the child. It's not going to happen to me. But when it does and they can't imagine how they will make ends meet, they find in the Cherry Hill clinic doctors and medical professionals willing to step up. And they've been doing extraordinary things that would make every American proud. And now they see what's coming from this Republican, from this Donald Trump proposal.

Jean is an awesome soul. She's a disabled citizen. She relies on Medicaid coverage for her frequent hospitalizations. Without Medicaid, she would be unable to receive the critical care that she needs. God bless you, Jean.

Susan writes to us. She's a disabled person who's confined to a wheelchair. Susan relies on Medicaid for her healthcare. Medicaid provides her wheelchair transportation to get her to her medical appointments. Without Medicaid, she would not have medical coverage or the transportation means to receive the essential healthcare.

Edna. Edna. Edna's 98, God bless her. Ninety-Eight, what a life. And now, as a 98-year-old, she now has dementia. Her daughter is 78 years old. And I can't imagine this moment, when you realize at 78 that you can't any longer care for your 98-year-old mom due to her worsening dementia, Edna received Medicaid coverage and is now able to have full-time care at a rehabilitation center for senior citizens. Her daughter at 78 years old is so grateful, so grateful to live in a country that her 98-year-old mom can be in a rehabilitation care center. But they know what savage cuts in Medicaid would do.

Randy and Dylan. Randy enrolled her son, Dylan, in Medicaid. Dylan is ten. He is wheelchair-bound due to Duchenne muscular dystrophy. Dylan requires frequent medical care and daily heart medications to prevent illness with his heart functioning. To prevent the issues with his heart functioning, forgive me. Randy relies on Medicaid to provide medical care for Dylan, who Randy loves so much. Medicaid covers the costs, and his critical prescription medications.

And then there's Teresa, who recently lost her job and required urgent medical assessments due to a medical issue that was discovered by her doctor. During what was a difficult time, when you go to the doctor and a doctor discovers something that is so urgent that you need immediate support, Teresa was without insurance and needed to receive care as instructed by her doctor. Due to her enrollment in Medicaid, she was able to receive the diagnosis, the diagnostic testing that she needed. It's a good story, but stories like that will become more difficult.

Pamela writes that Medicaid is essential to her 22-year-old son's life. He has epilepsy, cerebral palsy, vision impairment, and too many other complex medical issues for Pam to list to us. Medicaid provides his health benefits and his funding source to attend his day program and receive therapies. Private-duty nursing comes to his home, and it pays for vital medications. She writes to me that

> Our private insurance is not enough to cover our son's complex medical needs. We would need to be able to pay for his monthly prescription costs. We would not be able to pay for his monthly prescription costs, nor the lengthy hospital stays when he's sick. We would not have the nursing hours to support his care for him to be able to continue to live at home, nor would we be able to leave home on weekdays and have a day program to attend. {Pamela writes...}
>
> As his parent, I need to take an early retirement from public school teaching to care for our son because the medical coverage he has just isn't enough. It doesn't provide for his transportation and his day program.

So she's leaving her job early. She writes and she bolds this, "Our disabled community members and their families deserve better. Medicaid provides for a bare minimum existence." And she has a message for the lies being told by too many. She says, "There are no excesses here in my house."

Sally and Mike:

> We rely on Medicaid for our two adult children with disabilities for long-term care, especially for my daughter, who just finished her two-and-half-year chemo treatment regime. We will need it for monthly checkups and prevention of a relapse. We use the funding to provide the much-needed care she needs at home. We also have 90-plus-year-old parents who need Medicaid in order to survive. We are the real sandwich generation, caring for two adult children with special needs, and two very elderly parents who couldn't survive on their own. Please do everything in your power to help fund and not cut Medicaid in any way. Thank you for your time and your commitment helping the more vulnerable population.

I mean, Sally and Mike, you're not alone. That sandwich generation taking care of children and parents. You're taking care of adult children and 90-plus-year-old parents. I hear you. I hear you.

Carol:

> My son Jason is 41 and autistic. He has severe behavioral issues. Medicaid has enabled my son to attend a day program three days a week. The program bills Medicaid for his participation. We would not have the financial resources to pay for my son's day program. Medicaid helps us to use our son's living at home with his loved ones, not in a group home. We save the state money by taking care of him. Do not cut. Do not cut this vital program.

Now, Rosemary says that she has an adult son and that son has CP, a seizure disorder. This is where maybe I should have gone to medical school and not law school ... cystic encephalomalacia.

My cousin the doctor is here, she would be able to help me if she was down here. But her adult son is on the autism spectrum, yet he earned a BA.

> Yet he earned a BA on the autism spectrum and lives 'independently', but with our support and works a part-time job." She put independently in quotes. If he loses his Medicaid coverage, he will not be able to afford to live where he lives, or most importantly, he will not be able to afford his meds. He has medications that would run $500 a month.
>
> We live with that anxiety that millions of Americans live with, that erodes them, that burns at their spirit, that anxiety that has put millions of Americans into bankruptcy, that anxiety that I can't afford my medications, that anxiety that I can't care for my children, that anxiety that I won't have that resources, that anxiety. We live with the anxiety of Medicaid cuts with every report about what House Republicans are doing. We support anything that can be done to maintain Medicaid. Please, Senator.

Danielle, she writes that,

> I'm the oldest sibling to my two younger brothers, Matt and Christian, who have been living with a rare neuromuscular disease since they were diagnosed as babies. Throughout their lives, Matt and Chris, along with my parents and family, have fought to ensure that they have the best care possible despite how unknown and under-researched their condition is. Taking Medicaid away from them would strip Matt and Christian of basic access to specialized care that they rely on and therefore strip them of their dignity and their independence. As someone who has had a front row seat watching two people I love suffer from a neuromuscular condition and as a human being who believes in the right to access medical care, I implore, I implore, I implore our representatives and the Trump administration to consider the devastating impact that these cuts would have on people like my brothers.
>
> Slashing funds for an already underfunded program is not only the wrong target in the name of 'efficiency', but also a decision that would cement our nation's treacherous path toward becoming a nation that does not seek justice for all. Instead, a nation that only serves those in power, only serves the powerful, only serves the wealthy. As your constituent affected by neuromuscular disease, I'm concerned about the potential unintended consequences of the efforts to so-called reform Medicaid. 72 million Americans rely on Medicaid for affordable, accessible and state health coverage, including children, pregnant women, parents, seniors, and individuals with disabilities. Any effort to reform Medicaid should not inadvertently prevent patients from having access to the healthcare that they deserve.

Danielle, I hear you.

Judith, she goes right to the point.

> Please stop Trump. Please stop Trump now. He's going after Medicaid. I have an adult severely autistic granddaughter who relies on Medicaid for her special needs program. A country is judged by how it meets the needs of the weakest people {she writes} Please stop him.

I want to read your words again, Judith. "A country is judged by how it meets the needs of the weakest people. A country is judged by how it meets the needs of the weakest people."

Elizabeth writes,

> Medicaid helps me access healthcare and direct supports in my home, in my community. Cuts to Medicaid would mean I wouldn't have the services I need to live on my own with supports and would be forced to live in a more restrictive setting.

Sandra writes,

> Medicaid has allowed my son's needs to be met at home and not in a group home. It has allowed my husband to participate in his caregiving, not a stranger. It has allowed him to be employed with the aid of a job coach. These are just a few things, in addition to healthcare. If the cuts to Medicaid happen, it goes away.

Alicia:

> Medicaid provides healthcare and services to my developmentally disabled adult child. If Medicare funding is cut, my son will not have the healthcare they need and the programs to attend.

Maggie:

> My 28-year-old son Will has down syndrome. He currently lives a full and active inclusive life. His life is full, his life is active. He's in the community where he's cherished. He lives in the community, he's cherished. He has wonderful support staff and lots of activities that keep him healthy and happy. His days include volunteering at a senior citizen center, working at the local gym, shopping, leisure activities, speech therapy. He does music therapy. We follow the self-direction model, which is work on my end, but I would not have it any other way. But if Medicare funding is cut, these cuts would impact his livelihood.

Nibble:

> Without my Medicaid, I would not be able to be as mobile nor independent. Without Medicaid evaluating my physical disability, cerebral palsy and related limitations, and prescribing me an electric-powered wheelchair for daily independence and assistance with mobility and even pain management due to not being able to walk well. I am actually up for a new wheelchair this year, as it was allowable every five years for a new wheelchair prescription.
>
> Without my Medicaid, I would not have been properly diagnosed with things like sleep apnea in 2017. I now use CPAP machine to force air into my body so I can sleep peacefully instead of gasping for air at night. Without my Medicaid, I would not be able to be fitted for a leg brace for my physical support and mobility, enabling me to actually stand up straight and walk without my wheelchair. Without my Medicaid, I would not be able to be a full-time employee, a full-time worker.

Laura:

> Medicaid has provided my sister with benefits to help support her medical and mental health issues since she graduated high school. She's now 33 and living with me and my husband after being separated from our parents that are now in assisted living and nursing home arrangements. {Wow.} Susan has never worked or been married because of her mental disability and she is dependent on her Medicaid benefits. Please keep these benefits in place for people like my sister who don't have much in their lives they can depend on.

Laura, your sister's now living with you after being separated from your parents who are now in a nursing home. I see you.

Michael:

> I need Medicaid because it provides me the ability to get my anxiety medication and to afford my therapist. I use Medicaid for medical, dental, and visual visits. I wear glasses. Without Medicaid I am unable to live or function in this world.

Robin:

> Courtney is my 35-year-old daughter with severe disabilities. From 2009 to present she has needed crucial surgeries as well as medications and hospital stays. Medicaid has made the financial support for these procedures possible. It has saved her life.

And I know, I can tell from her letter that Robin loves her 35-year-old daughter Courtney.
Mary:

> Medicaid is helping to improve my daughter's life through the services of the division of developmental disabilities. Without it, she would be left to whittle away at home seven days a week with no community interaction. She is learning prevocational skills in a manner that she is validated and viewed as a person with strengths.

Thank you, Mary.
Allison:

> I'm my daughter's caregiver in New Jersey. Medicaid funded programs allow her to remain an active part of our community at home with her family. If Medicaid is cut, we would lose our healthcare. It would be devastating.

Gi-Han:

> My daughter has a disability. Through Medicaid she receives a lot of services to help her improve and progress, also to help her stay active and social. She gets speech therapy, occupational and physical therapy. People come to our home to help her as well. If Medicaid cuts happen, she will stop all the services she receives and her life will be threatened. Please, she must keep her Medicaid, because as a parent, I don't know what I can do with my daughter if that is happening. It will be so hard for her and us.

Roseanne:

> Medicaid has supplied the nurses that take care of my disabled granddaughter I'm raising at home instead of being sent to an institution. She will put her life at risk for a medical emergency or fatal injury without nurses here.

Ash:

> My daughter takes speech therapy, occupational and physical therapy and tutoring. So if that is all gone, she will stop progress and she'll be more disabled and will be unable to do anything by herself or live inadvertently. She needs a lot of help, and if these Medicaid cuts happen, I don't know what I will do with her and it'll make life so hard.

These Americans are facing challenges that I can't imagine, and what's amazing about so many of them is they find the goodness and the decency of their neighbors, of people who are helping and supporting them, of people who do the jobs, the occupations that many Americans would find incredibly challenging; the occupational therapist, the physical therapist, the person who does the transportation, the nurses that take care of folks. It is a community of people out there that are trying to make our nation stand for what we say we do. They are trying to show that we are a loving and caring and compassionate community.

Other Voices

And what I love is that this is not partisan. I keep saying this over and over again. For this whole time I could stand, I hope it's as many hours as possible, I'm going to be bringing in the voices of Republicans and Democrats because this is not a partisan issue. Maybe it is in Congress, but the Republicans and Democrats of America don't want Medicaid cuts. They especially don't want them to benefit the richest amongst us who don't need more help, God bless them. They're doing all right. And it's not going to solve our budget problems. Their budget proposal, as was said by the one lone Republican who voted against it because he's such a fiscal hawk, he said, "If you just read their own numbers, this is a lie, a sham. It increases the deficit by trillions."

But let me go to some Republicans. Joe Lombardo, the governor of Nevada:

> An abrupt reduction in federal funding would not only disrupt care for those who rely on Medicaid, but would also destabilize public and private healthcare providers leading to workforce reductions, service limitations and financial strain on already overburdened healthcare facilities.

The Governor of Nevada knows it. My mom, my aunt, my uncle, my other aunt, they live in Nevada. My mom lives in a retirement community there. This governor knows that that state would be hit so hard by a reduction of these services, it would be like an impact that ripples out throughout the state, raising costs, lowering care, hurting Americans, hurting Nevadans.

My colleague, Mike Rounds of South Dakota said,

> That's not a cost-cutting measure. That's a cost transfer. And when you've got partnerships with states, you shouldn't be doing that without having them involved in the discussion.

I tell you, I have conversations with lots of my Republican colleagues and I appreciate this quote from one of them.

Coalition of State Medical Associations writes,

> On behalf of 50 state medical associations and the District of Columbia, the hundreds of thousands of physicians we represent, {I'm adding this, I am sure of both political parties and independents, back to what they write} and the 80 million Medicaid patients we serve, we are united in urging the United States Senate to protect Medicaid from the devastating $880 billion cuts in spending-out targets in the House Budget resolution. If these cuts are enacted, millions of Medicaid patients will lose their coverage, and we expect all Medicaid patients to lose some of their existing benefits. {All Medicaid patients.} All Medicaid patients to lose some of their existing benefits and access to essential healthcare services.

The American Academy of Pediatrics, Children's Defense Fund, Children's Hospital Association, Family Voices National, First Focus Campaign for Children, the March of Dimes and National Association of Pediatric Nurse Partnerships, they all came together to jointly write,

> By reducing vital support for Medicaid and CHIP, you would not just be cutting a budget line, you would be eliminating the health prospects of our children, leaving them without the care they need to grow into healthy adults.

AARP:

> More than half of all the funds for longterm care in America come from Medicaid. As our country gets older and as millions of baby boomers continue to age, our country is on the brink of a serious longterm care crisis. AARP would welcome the long overdue debate about how to address the challenge, which should involve reforms to remove Medicaid's bias towards institutional care and increase support for families who take care of their loved ones at home. Large scale cuts, however, threaten millions of seniors with disruption to the care they need.

Listen to AARP. We would welcome the long overdue debate. We would welcome the long overdue debate on how to address this challenge. But we're not having a long overdue debate. We're not bringing together the world's most deliberative body to focus on how to solve these problems.

Michael Tuffin, the president and CEO of AHIP, America's Health Insurance Plans:

> Medicaid is indispensable to low income people and working families. If their Medicaid coverage is disrupted, these Americans will lose access to primary care and be unable to fill prescriptions for drugs to treat chronic illnesses. Many will end up in the emergency room, the costliest site of care. Loss of Medicaid coverage means people will be less healthy and the care will ultimately cost more.

Rick Pollack, who's the president and CEO of American Hospital Association:

> On behalf of the hospitals, nurses, doctors, and those who care for and serve the needs of 72 million patients that rely on Medicaid, we urge you to consider the implications hinging on the budget reconciliation bill's fate on removing healthcare for millions of our nation's patients. These are hardworking families, children, seniors, veterans, disabled individuals who rely on essential care services. We ask the House to construct a path forward that protects Medicaid from these harmful cuts that would impact the care for millions of Americans.

We did Republican governors, here's a Democrat, Colorado Governor Jared Polis who joined with Oklahoma Governor Kevin Stitt. They're the chair and vice-chair of the National Governor's Association, Democrat and Republican, and they write,

> Without consultation and proper planning, congressionally proposed reductions to Medicaid would impact state budgets, rural hospitals and healthcare service providers. It is necessary for governors to have a seat at the table when discussing any reforms and cuts to Medicaid funding. States and territories should be afforded more flexibility when it comes to administrating these programs in a manner that best suits the needs of their states.

What a radical thing, that a Republican and a Democratic governor are simply asking for a seat at the table in the conversation. What's the table? Is there a hearing? Are there discussions? Did we form a national commission? None of that. None of that. And they warn about what it'll mean to their states.

The American Academy of Family Physicians, American Academy of Pediatrics, the American College of Gynecology, the American College of Physicians, the American Psychiatric Association all together write,

> Our organizations, representing more than 400,000 physicians who serve millions of patients, are alarmed by the proposals to implement cuts or other structural changes to Medicaid during the budget reconciliation process. Cuts to Medicaid will have grave consequences for patients, communities and the entire healthcare system.

Lisa Lacasse, president of the American Cancer Society Cancer Action Network:

> ACSCAN opposes cuts that will increase the number of uninsured nationwide by severing the lifeline that Medicaid provides for cancer patients and those at risk for cancer. It is imperative for cancer patients and millions more at risk that this valuable health insurance program be protected for decades. ACSCAN has advocated in support of Medicaid and we will continue to advocate at the federal and state levels in support of expansion of access to the program and against policies that jeopardize individuals' access to lifesaving health insurance coverage.

Bruce Siegel, president and CEO of America's Essential Hospitals:

> The budget resolution will open the door to devastating Medicaid cuts that will impact millions of Americans, especially those middle to low income working Americans in both rural and urban communities who rely on Medicaid for access to critical healthcare services. This budget resolution and its directive to the House Energy and Commerce Committee to cut $880 billion of federal spending will slash the Medicaid program and threaten to discontinue lifesaving safety net services in many communities.

Thirty-eight national parent organizations – I didn't know there were 38 national parent organizations – but they wrote in a chorus of conviction:

> Cuts on this magnitude would require enormous changes, such as instituting per capita caps, reducing the federal match rate for Medicaid expansion, adding barriers to coverage, including work requirements, and repealing rules that strengthen enrollment processes and access to care and Medicaid that would severely harm many individuals fighting serious and chronic health conditions. Our organizations, all 38 national parent organizations, oppose any cuts to either traditional or Medicaid expansion that take away coverage, jeopardize access to services and providers, shift costs to states and reduce parents' access to care.

Now, here is a huge group that includes the National Alliance on Mental Illness, the March of Dimes, Muscular Dystrophy Association, the National Cancer Coalition, the National Health Council, National Kidney Foundation, National Multiple Sclerosis Society, National Organization for Rare Disorders. It is about, I will estimate and give it for the congressional record, about 25 to 30 organizations. [

> On behalf of the undersigned chapters of the American Academy of Family Physicians, representing over 130,000 family physicians and medical students across the country, we write to convey our deep concerns regarding proposals to reduce Medicaid funding or implement further eligibility restrictions. We strongly urge you and your colleagues to reject any reforms that have the potential to impede access to essential care for millions of Americans who rely on Medicaid, including our nation's most vulnerable populations.

SENATOR CHUCK SCHUMER (NEW YORK): Would my colleague yield for a question?

SENATOR BOOKER: I will yield specifically for the question, yes.

SENATOR SCHUMER: Thank you. I first want to thank my colleague for taking the floor, for showing the American people how horribly this administration is treating average families, working families in so many ways. And I know he intends to hold the floor for a long time to make sure that's the case, letting America know how bad this is. Healthcare has been the focus right now, and it's amazing. I would say to my colleague, "Isn't it incredible? All these cuts they're proposing in healthcare are done with a purpose in mind, and that is to reduce the taxes on billionaires." And doesn't it bother my colleague that these people who he's been documenting who so desperately need healthcare are going to lose that, if our Republican colleagues have their way, simply to cut taxes for the very wealthy? That's my question.

SENATOR BOOKER: Leader Schumer, that's the pain in these stories. The families that I read, the fear that they have, that they're relying on these lifelines that are going to be cut, services that are going to be cut, that are going to affect their beloved parents or their children with disabilities. When they ask the question, "Why? Is it for a noble purpose? Is it for a collective sacrifice?" No. The answer that they have to stare at is that you're going to cut services for my vulnerable child or my parents in order to give tax cuts to the wealthiest Americans, in order to give tax cuts to billionaires.

And here's the insult added to that injury, also this lie that we're going to be focused on the fiscal strength of our nation. They're going to give all those tax cuts away and take away healthcare benefits and the result's going to be even bigger deficits. So people like Elon Musk and Donald Trump, billionaires, where most of these tax cut will accrue to their benefit, will get more, more, more money than if you were spending a hundred thousand dollars a week for the rest of your life, you wouldn't get near the net worth of Elon Musk.

SENATOR SCHUMER: Will my colleague continue to yield for another question?

SENATOR BOOKER: Yes, yes.

SENATOR SCHUMER: From what I understand, and tell me if this is correct, that if they did this tricky thing that even our Republican colleagues are calling fakery and hocus pocus, our conservative Republican colleagues, that it might increase the deficit by $30 trillion. Is that accurate?

SENATOR BOOKER: That is accurate. And that's stunning, that they know that they can't do this, so they're going to use some budget trickery to mask the truth. Math doesn't lie. Numbers don't lie. You may be able to mask it so you could use rules of reconciliation to try to force it through, but the result for the American people is going to be the same. Chuck, people will lose healthcare, healthcare benefits, and watch the deficit of this nation not increase, but explode. Which means the cost of our debt payments alone are going to be more than the very programs that they're going to be slashing for families. That is outrageous, cruel, unacceptable, and we have to do everything we can as a people to stop it.

SENATOR SCHUMER: Will my colleague yield for another question?

SENATOR BOOKER: Yes sir.

SENATOR SCHUMER: Despite this fiscal hocus pocus, this fakery, this trickery which my colleague has alluded to, when they cut Medicaid, when they cut social security, when they cut Medicare, those cuts remain just as devastating no matter what kind, is that accurate, no matter what kind of bunk they put on their balance sheets to say it doesn't matter?

SENATOR BOOKER: I was reading stories and many of them will live with me. There's a family that's taking care of their two parents in their 90s and their disabled adult children, desperately relying on these programs. No matter what you do or say or call it or label you slap on it, those are the kind of Americans who are stepping up to take care of their loved ones who will get hurt.

SENATOR SCHUMER: Will my colleague yield for another question?

SENATOR BOOKER: Yes.

SENATOR SCHUMER: So just today I visited a nursing home on Staten Island and a nursing home in Long Island, both in Republican congressional districts, and I spoke to people there. The nursing home I visited, if Medicaid were cut significantly, the nursing home would close according to the head of this nursing home. He was there. 300 people would lose their jobs, and these people, hundreds of people in this nursing home, would have nowhere to go. They say, "Oh, they can move in with their kids." First, isn't it accurate that many of them are in a condition where their kids can't take care of them? And second, given the housing shortages we face, and the tariffs will make that worse with the wood — isn't it true that many families just don't have room to take an elderly person, particularly one who needs care into their homes and that this would cause chaos to all sorts of people who are not on Medicaid themselves, but have loved ones who need it in assisted living, in nursing homes, in care facilities?

SENATOR BOOKER: Yes, Senator Schumer, to tell a family to just double up or triple up drives up their costs. Often that elder that's living with them that might have dementia demands care. So the family member that's caring for them has to decide, "Oh my God, am I going to give up my job, which I need to pay the rent to stay home and take care of them, or go to the job and let really difficult things happen?" And this is the thing that the Leader is pointing out that I think is really important.

SENATOR SCHUMER: One final question.

SENATOR BOOKER: Yes, please. Please...

SENATOR SCHUMER: Would you share something personal with us? You're taking the floor tonight to bring up all these inequities that will hurt people, that will so hurt the middle class, that will so hurt poor people, that will hurt America, hurt our fiscal conditions, as you've documented. Just give us a little inkling, give us a little feeling for the strength and conviction that drive you to do this unusual taking of the floor for a long time to let the people know how bad these things are going to be.

SENATOR BOOKER: I appreciate the Democratic Leader's question. I think that all hundred of us in this body are getting what I've gotten. I can't go to the grocery store. I can't walk my neighborhood. I just did a travel around the country to do what a lot of us elected officials do and getting stopped in the airport by people who want to tell me stories about a parent with dementia or a disabled child, or a child with a rare disease that has seizures. Story after story after story, the people who've been writing in to me, some of them on scraps of paper just to try to tell us, "Please." And they're not saying don't do 880 billions of cuts. They say they live on such a precipice that any diminution of resources would drive their families into crisis and despair.

Many of the professionals that I'm quoting are saying we don't need to be cutting, we need to be finding ways to extend services to do more. How can we do more? I talked earlier about the fact that you helped with this, Senator Schumer, when we were battling many of us. And I know my friend Lisa Blunt Rochester, she was a leader on the House when we said, "Why are so many women dying in childbirth in the postpartum period in America?" Shameful that we're the worst nation of all the wealthy nations, and that's for us as a whole, but for Black women, it's almost four times as much. And so what do we do here, Chuck? You remember this. Excuse me, Senator Schumer, what do we do here?

SENATOR SCHUMER: Chuck is okay.

SENATOR BOOKER: Chuck is okay.

We came together and we said this is a time for Medicaid expansion. To say to a woman, "You don't just get 60 days postpartum, but we're going to expand that beyond 60 days state after state." Red and Blue states said, "You're right, this is a crisis. That which should be the happiest period of a woman's life is the most devastating with women hemorrhaging and dying." We began to treat that, and now what's the threat? The threat is that they're going to cut these things that we did to help more people, to stop more folks from dying. And here's the trick: you know this battle well. I wasn't here, Chuck. You were here, and I know my chief of staff was on your staff writing this in, and this is why you all said, "We are going to try to incentivize states to expand Medicare. We're going to cover 90% of the costs."

I still don't understand why some states, just to talk about cutting off your nose to spite your face, said no. My state, Republican governor, said, "Heck yeah, sign New Jersey up." But many of those states have this automatic trigger that if the funding is cut, even if they say we're not going to cut 880 billion, just 250 billion. Well, that's going to trigger many states to give up that Medicare expansion, go back to the days where millions upon millions of Americans don't have coverage at all. So, again, this whole speech is because Chuck, because Senator Schumer, business as usual in this place when that kind of threat is happening, when the stories that I read I had to struggle through, we should be doing hearings, we should be bringing in people. I know the values that we share on both sides of the aisle. How could we be so abjectly cruel and why to push through a tax break plan that families in the neighborhood I live in won't see benefits?

SENATOR SCHUMER: I thank my colleague for his strength, his courage, his effectiveness in letting the American people know how badly this upcoming bill will affect them if our Republican colleagues insist on passing it, and thank him, and yield the floor back to him.

SENATOR BOOKER: Thank you.

SENATOR SCHUMER: I thank him for his courage and strength.

SENATOR BOOKER: Thank you for-

SENATOR SCHUMER: And effectiveness.

SENATOR BOOKER: Thank you for allowing me to yield the floor for you to ask a question.

I see my colleague here from Delaware. I'm going to read a few more stories, but I suspect that she too has a question because she and I did not just meet when she was sworn in here in January. God bless her. She is my colleague, but she's my sister. She has inspired me for years, and when she heard I was doing this, I'm not sure how much this has done on the Senate floor, but my sister came over and prayed with me that I could stand for a long time because she knew what we were trying to do, which was to try to create with who we served with John Lewis-type good trouble in this institution to not do things normal. To begin to say that the voices I'm reading are Democrats and Republicans, the voices I'm reading are Democrat and Republican governors, Democratic and Republican heads of hospitals, Democratic and Republican heads of medical associations, Democratic and Republican constituencies. This is not Right or Left — this is right or wrong.

And my colleague, my colleague, I'm going to put her on blast, but God bless your friends that remind you of who you are when you forget. She didn't know that I really wanted to give a speech that was speaking to all of America, but she came up here and when we were praying, she said, "I pray that you speak words of love." Because she and I know love is ferocious. It's the strongest force on the earth. It's not soft, it's not saccharine. She asked God to give me words of love today. And so I know that this friend of mine, my sister here, my colleague who I've worked with for years and years and years, asked me if she could come to the floor and ask a question. So, as I've been instructed to do, if you were asking me to yield for a question, then I'm going to say go ahead if you want to ask me.

SENATOR BLUNT ROCHESTER (DELAWARE): I would ask my colleague, the great gentleman from the state of New Jersey, if he would yield the floor.

SENATOR BOOKER: I will yield for a question. I yield for a question while retaining the floor.

SENATOR ROCHESTER: I want to begin by thanking you so much, Senator Booker, for your leadership, and thank you for the opportunity to ask you a question. As I stood and listened to you, I was reminded of why we are in this place in the first place. I see my colleague, Mr. President, a member of my class, and I think one of the key things that you talked about was ensuring that we recognize that we are all in this together. I think it might have been Martin Luther King who said, "We may have come over on different ships now, but we're all in the same boat now." *We may have come over on different ships.* I feel like in this very present moment, we have to recognize we're all in this together.

And to your point, when we think about the importance of Medicaid to this country, a lot of people don't even realize that they're on Medicaid. They might think of a health program that they're on, but they don't even make the connection to the fact that they're on Medicaid. That almost half of the babies in this country are born because of Medicaid. That it's not just from birth, but it goes all the way to seniors who are aging with dignity because they have access to Medicaid and allowing their family members to go to work because they don't have to worry about that family member. And so I wanted to, number one, in addition to asking my question, say thank you to you for not only shining a light on these potential dangerous cuts, but also ringing the alarm.

It is alarming that we are faced with this kind of question of do we take money from those who are in need and are connected, because we're all connected, and give it to a few. And so as I think about our work on maternal mortality and how we are trying to make sure that our country is not of one of the richest in the world, but the lowest in our maternal mortality numbers. As we look at issues of families who might have a family member who has a special needs child, or when I went home in our recess break, I was able to meet with folks from our developmental disability council and I heard a gentleman named Emmanuel. He is a wheelchair user. He said to me something that just stuck. He said, "If you pull the thread of Medicaid out of my life, it will unravel."

He had been sleeping in his car before Medicaid. He wasn't sure if he was going to have employment before Medicaid. And even he and his wife thought about what impact it might have, whether they were able to stay married or whether he would have to go into a facility. And so I want to thank you for shining the light and ringing the alarm, and I want to ask you, what do you think will be the impact on children in this country without Medicaid?

SENATOR BOOKER: I am so grateful for that question and it sobers me when you ask it because just a reduction in Medicaid – I love that metaphor you used – is pulling a string out for families who are barely holding it together right now. Families with children with disabilities, or developmentally disabled who have been struggling so much to get their children into programs that could help move them, some of them to independence, some of them into adulthood where they can get a job. So many of these things that help to propel these children would be undermined. Just transportation services going away would create hardship and devastation on families.

So, here we are in America where costs are going up, housing is going up. We're about to have these awful tariffs where the price of vehicles will go up, the price of transportation will go up, and so the ripple effect of an impact on children just by a fraction of the cuts that they're proposing, not to mention the grandeur of the $880 billion, would have a devastating impact on millions and millions of children. But it doesn't stop there. You quoted King. King said that in the Letters from Birmingham Jail, "We're all caught in an inescapable network of mutuality tied in the same garment of destiny." To think that there could be an injury to a family and their child and have it not affect you is not only a self-defeating ignorance, it's callous and uncaring and it demands us to step up for those children that you so rightfully ask me in your question.

SENATOR ROCHESTER: Gentleman, yield for another question.

SENATOR BOOKER: I will definitely yield for a question.

SENATOR BLUNT ROCHESTER: As the former executive of a major city in this country, can you talk a little bit about the impact that these cuts will have on cities, municipalities, and states? Because some might think, oh, this is just a nice issue. No, this is an economic issue as well. If you could talk a little bit about the impact that this is going to have and why mayors across this country should care, why governors across this country should care and city councils, why should they care?

SENATOR BOOKER: The thing that is so significant already, governors and mayors are writing letters and speaking up. When I go to different cities in New Jersey, I'm often called by local leaders because they know, number one, the stories of the people who rely on Medicaid, the seniors, the children, the disabled families. But more importantly than that, they know there are hospitals who already have very fragile budgets to carve out millions and millions of dollars. As I told, over tens of millions of dollars for our level one trauma hospital in New Jersey, that would devastate the entire economic model for our hospital. It would affect jobs, it would affect the economy, it would affect small businesses. It would be devastating.

SENATOR ROCHESTER: I will end my questions at the moment by saying again, thank you so much, Senator Booker, for your leadership. We've had an opportunity to work on food as medicine, maternal mortality. There are so many more important things to work on, but the fact that you are spending your time, your energy, your intellect to stand up for millions of Americans, I commend you for that. I'm grateful to serve with you. I had the opportunity to serve with John Lewis in the house and get in good trouble, and I'm glad to be here with you in the Senate. I yield back my time.

SENATOR BOOKER: Thank you very much.
I'm going to continue elevating here, throughout the hours and hours of the speech, the voices of Americans from all backgrounds, all geographies. Elevating the stories of leaders, Democrat, Republican, independent, and I want to start with Matthew Cook, who's the president and CEO of Children's Hospital Association. And Matthew Cook writes,

> The House budget resolution directive to the Energy and Commerce Committee to cut 880 billion in spending will almost certainly lead to deep reductions in Medicaid funding for children who rely on the program and destabilize the financial viability of the providers caring for them.
>
> {To the point that my colleague from Delaware asked:} Slashing funding would mean fewer healthcare providers, fewer services, and longer wait times for patients who already face significant barriers to care. These cuts will impact the 37 million children on Medicaid program, including the nearly 50% of children with special healthcare needs. Three million children in military-connected families. {I'm going to repeat that...} Three million children of military-connected families, more than 40% of the children living in rural areas and small towns, patients in rural communities would be hit especially hard as hospitals and clinics in these areas rely heavily on Medicare funding to stay open. Here's from the Mental Health Liaison Group. In the midst of our nation's ongoing mental health crisis.

I'm going to pause there.
When I ran for president, and moved around the country in town hall meeting, after town hall meeting, after town hall meeting, I was even surprised on how many Americans ... I don't think we had a town hall where someone didn't want to stand up and tell me about the mental health crisis in America and how poorly we were doing. When the Mental Health Liaison Group starts off with that, it hits me very hard. I still remember meeting with a guy in a New Jersey diner who had mental health issues, was a teacher at a high school, and stabilized his mental health because of his prescription drugs, but then stopping unable to afford them, started skimping on the drugs, had a mental health crisis, lost his job, and his whole life destabilized. Just because of not access to a costly prescription drug, a valued teacher had his life upended.
So I start this letter again:

> In the midst of our nation's ongoing mental health crisis, including its devastating impact on youth and our ongoing overdose epidemic, it is paramount that access to life savings MHSUD services is not reduced and the integrity of the Medicaid program to serve as a vital federal and state-partnered safety net is preserved. Limiting access to Medicaid threatens to undermine gains in reducing overdose mortality rates and could lead to increasing rates of incarceration and hospitalization.

And my colleague from Delaware knows this. The biggest mental health institutions in America, the biggest ones — pick your state. From Illinois to Los Angeles, the biggest mental health institutions are LA prisons, are Chicago's prisons, and jails wasting taxpayer dollars. Where folks got their mental health care treatment, their lives could stabilize. They could be workers; they could be helpers; they could not be sick.

Here's Chip Khan, the CEO of Federation of American Hospitals, in quotes,

> Key Republican lawmakers recognizing that so many constituents rely on Medicaid for critical care made it clear that their vote today was based on an understanding that the final reconciliation bill would not include devastating cuts or changes. I believe that's gratifying {Chip Khan writes} It is important that these members came to the same conclusion: Medicaid cuts should be off the table. Medicaid cuts should be off the table. It is up to these lawmakers to follow through and ensure spending cuts don't come at the expense of care for over 70 million Americans, including kids, seniors, and hardworking families.

I love the appeal in that letter because it was an appeal that I'm reminded of that my colleagues, Lisa Murkowski and the great John McCain and an extraordinary friend, Susan Collins, when they voted to save the Affordable Care Act. They listened to the appeal of people like this gentleman and my colleague sitting there and it's like often we resort to words of vicious cruelty. John Lewis didn't do that when he advocated against the most horrific racist, he didn't take on words of hate. We've got to appeal to colleagues of good conscience not to let, as this person says, no Medicaid cuts. No Medicaid cuts.

I know President Trump has said that Medicaid cuts are off the table, said that over and over and over again. We'll see. We'll see.

Modern Medicaid Alliance:

> With over 70 million children, seniors and hardworking families relying on Medicaid for their health and wellbeing, it is critical Congress listens to state and local government officials, faith leaders, healthcare providers, and hardworking Americans, and blocks proposed cuts to the program. As organizations representing and caring for the millions of Americans who receive coverage and benefits through Medicaid, we know firsthand how the current level of cuts being considered by Congress would impact their care. They will cause Americans to lose coverage, reduce health access, and increase costs. We oppose any cuts, we oppose any cuts, we oppose any cuts or harmful policy changes to Americans' Medicaid benefits as part of the budget reconciliation process and call on congressional leaders to reverse course and protect the program moving forward.

Here's the Modern Medicaid Alliance:

> The latest House vote breaks a vital promise to more than 70 million Americans who depend on the Medicaid program and now face the potential for unprecedented destabilizing cuts to their coverage and access to care. The full extent of cuts being considered go far beyond addressing waste, fraud and abuse and would undermine Medicaid coverage for those who depend on it. Already, senators are issuing stark warnings about the impact of Medicaid cuts on the stability of their communities, state budgets, hospitals and providers. We urge members of the House and Senate to block any Medicaid cuts or harmful policy proposals as part of the ongoing budget process.

Sister Mary Haddad, President and CEO of Catholic Health Association:

> We are deeply concerned that the budget resolution would force the House Energy and Commerce Committee to slash $880 billion from the Medicaid program, an essential health care program for nearly 80 million low-income Americans. Medicaid provides coverage for one in five individuals, funds 41% of all national births, and is the largest payer for long-term care and behavioral health services. These cuts would have devastating consequences, particularly for those in small towns and rural communities where Medicaid is often the primary source of health coverage. Medicaid is not just a health program. It is a lifeline. It provides access to care for those who need it most: poor and vulnerable children, pregnant women, elderly adults, and disabled individuals in our nation while ensuring their dignity. {*Their dignity.*}

Here's The Partnership for Medicaid again.

> The Partnership for Medicaid, a nonpartisan nationwide organization representing clinicians, healthcare providers, safety net health plans and counties calls on Congress to reject cuts to Medicaid during the budget reconciliation process. The Partnership for Medicaid stands ready to work with policymakers to identify more sustainable strategies to strengthen Medicaid and improve upon its promise of providing high-quality coverage and access to care populations.

Another organization saying, "Hey, put me in. Let us help you improve this program and maybe we could achieve some of our mutual goals."

Here is Dr. Susan Kressly, President of the American Association of Pediatrics, the great AAP:

> The American Academy of Pediatrics urges lawmakers to reject the budget resolution before the US House of Representatives and to protect programs that are vital to the health and wellbeing of children. We oppose the proposed funding cuts to programs like Medicaid and the Children's Health Insurance Program, which cover nearly half of all US children as well as the Supplemental Nutrition Assistance Program. These cuts would have devastating consequences for children and families.

We're going to talk about cuts to SNAP later, but I love how the Dr. Susan Kressly, President of the American Association of Pediatrics, can't help but mention them together. Why is a doctor concerned about healthcare also mentioning SNAP?

Well, fundamental to our children's health and wellbeing is having access to fresh and healthy foods. This is me being a little critical of people saying their MAHA, Make America Healthy Again, and then immediately cutting kids' access to fresh, healthy fruits and vegetables. I love this doctor. It's almost like you're doubling down on the injury to our children. We are cheapening highly processed and sugar-filled, empty-nutritious foods, denying access to fresh, healthy fruits and vegetables, and then not letting people with chronic diseases get healthcare. I love this doctor for pointing out those connections.

But now I'm going to go to Brian O'Connell, who is a vice President of The Leukemia and Lymphoma Society.

> The fiscal year '25 budget resolution would create not just the opportunity by the obligation for the House Committee on Energy and Commerce to make dangerous cuts, dangerous cuts to Medicaid program in the budget reconciliation process expected in the coming week, the hundreds of billions of dollars cuts demanded by the budget resolution cannot be achieved without slashing benefits for enrollees or altogether taking away Medicaid coverage for millions of Americans. To be clear, The Leukemia and Lymphoma Society and the patients we represent are clamoring for Congress to lower healthcare costs. But the framework before the house today would pave the way for policies that do just the opposite, putting affordable access to healthcare out of reach of millions of Americans.

Feeding America (I love this organization):

> Cuts to vital federal nutrition programs like SNAP necessitated by this resolution and the Senate version passed last week will make families grappling with high food costs, hurt rural economies and strain food banks already overwhelmed by the rising demand. We urge the house to reject spending cuts to nutrition programs in the budget reconciliation process and support the work the House and Senate agricultural Committees are doing to create a strong bipartisan Farm Bill.

The Federal AIDS Policy Partnership:

> We are writing on behalf of 95 national, regional, and local organizations advocating for federal funding legislation and policy to end the HIV epidemic in the United States. We urge Congress to reject all proposals to enact cuts to Medicaid, whether through per capita caps or block grants restrictions to the Federal Medical Assistance Percentage or FMAP or mandatory work requirements during reconciliation for the 2025-2026 fiscal year budgets. Medicaid is the most important source of health coverage and lifesaving care for people living with HIV. The most important source of health coverage and lifesaving care for people living with HIV, providing coverage for more than 40% of the people living with HIV and contributing 45% of all federal funding for domestic HIV care and treatment.

The next letter starts:

> To be clear, the cuts outlined above are being proposed for one simple reason to pay for 4.5 trillion in tax breaks that disproportionately benefit the wealthy. Congress can and must take a different path. Congress must take a different path, one that lifts more families out of poverty and provides more Americans with the opportunity to reach their full potential. A people-first agenda should include expanding the child tax credit for the 17 million children who don't receive the full credit due to low family incomes, expanding rental assistance, increasing SNAP benefits to reflect rising grocery prices and closing the Medicaid coverage gap. If Congress focused on ensuring that wealthy Americans pay their fair share rather than providing additional tax breaks, we can fund these initiatives and so much more.

This is a group of groups that you'll recognize or many people will recognize. American Association of Nurse Practitioners, Gerontological Advanced Practice Nurses, the Association of National Nurse Practitioners in Women's Health, National Association of Pediatric Nurse Practitioners, the National Organization of Nurse Practitioners Faculties. They write:

> We are deeply concerned with the impact of these cuts on the healthcare system and their potential to harm our most vulnerable patients. Further, these cuts will threaten the viability of practices that treat Medicaid patients, financially destabilizing and having a disproportionate impact on those who provide care to underserved and rural communities.

Association of American Medical Colleges, AAMC:

> We remain extremely concerned that the budget resolutions reconciliation instructions would result in unsustainable cuts to federal healthcare programs, specifically Medicaid by requiring at least 880 billion in savings from the House Energy and Commerce Committee. Cuts of this magnitude would jeopardize both access to care for millions of Medicaid enrollees and the financial stability of the providers who care for them.

Here's one from CHIMES International or Chimes International:

> Cuts in Medicaid will have a dramatic negative impact on our healthcare system and the first responder community. Millions of Americans will be at risk of losing access to housing, thereby increasing homelessness for some of the most vulnerable members of society, especially in areas that already lack affordable housing. Provider organizations like ours will be forced to close the doors of residential facilities and reduce support staff, which is already in short supply.

Katie Smith Sloan, who is the President and CEO of LeadingAge:

> States would have to fill in massive budget holes if federal funding to Medicaid programs were cut. Even if a cut such as the change to the expansion ... FMAP proposal does not seem to directly impact aging services. It would, because the cost of the cut would have to somehow be absorbed by state budgets. That type of hole cannot be filled in via more efficiency. Balancing the 10-year program budget cycle on the back of Medicaid program is not a good trade-off for the American people.

Alan Morgan, who is the CEO of the National Rural Health Association — this letter is powerful. He represents the National Rural Health Association:

> Any cuts to the Medicaid program will disproportionately affect rural communities. Rural Americans rely on Medicaid coverage with about 20% of non-elderly adults and 40% of children living in rural areas enrolled in Medicaid and CHIP. In almost all states, rural areas have higher rates of Medicaid enrollment than metropolitan areas. Cuts to Medicaid would shift healthcare costs onto rural families, many of whom already struggle with financial instability. Medicaid cuts would force families to face higher out-of-pocket expenses, leading many to delay or forego necessary treatments. The burden would worsen health outcomes, especially for those managing chronic conditions like diabetes, heart disease, and cancer.

To the extraordinary prescience of my colleague from Delaware who knew this letter was coming, I imagine, this is a letter from the US Conference of Mayors, the National League of Cities, the National Association of Counties, the National Conference of State Legislators, the Council of State Governments, the International City County Management Association...

I'm going to pause for a second just to remind folks – because I've been involved in the US Conference of Mayors, National League of Cities – I've dealt with the National Association of Counties on things that were important here in the Senate. All of these groups are bipartisan. All of these groups represent Democrat and Republican mayors, Democrat and Republican city councilpeople. I was an actually non-partisan mayor. Newark does not have partisan elections, so they have non-partisan folks. This is a group of people who have those jobs where the rubber meets the road.

A change in state policy, a change in federal policy. We had to eat it when I was mayor, if it cost us more money. I was a mayor that talked like lots of mayors do, not in partisan lingo. They just talk about, "Hey, that's an unfunded mandate. Hey, that's adding more bureaucracy. Hey, that's going to cause more people in my community to be homeless. It's going to cause more children in my community to use an emergency room as their primary care physician." When I meet a mayor, I look at them and I thank them because it's one of the hardest jobs in America.

So, this organization that represents Democrats and Republicans, they write:

> As a coalition of bipartisan membership organizations representing state legislators, mayors, cities, and counties, we are committed to working collaboratively to strengthen the Medicaid program so that the states and localities can continue to meet the needs of their residents effectively. We write to express concern over proposed changes to Medicaid financing and requirements that could significantly impact state and local budgets, healthcare infrastructure, and millions and millions of Americans who rely on the program.

I would say, so far, there's at least half a dozen to a dozen of these letters where bipartisan groups are saying, "Let us help you. Don't rush this through in a way that is going to cause havoc to state and local governments. Cause havoc to children and seniors and the disabled. Cause havoc to hospitals and businesses. Cause havoc to rural communities. Cause havoc to the idea of what it means to be an American." That we take care of our own. That we stand up for each other. That we lend a hand. That we lift folks up. And here it is, this voice of bipartisan sensibility that says, "Hey, hold a hearing. We'll come. Put some of us on a commission."

This group that is called Advocates for Community Health:

> Medicaid Successes as a national program, derives from its variations across different states {different states doing things in different ways}. Medicaid looks different in every state and territory because the program is able to reflect and accommodate the specific needs of the state's patients, providers, and communities. These state-based programs are vital to the patients by community health centers, patient directed primary care providers that serve rural and underserved communities nationwide. As the House and Senate work towards a budget reconciliation package, Advocates for Community Health encourages a cautious approach to changes to Medicaid policy, as broad changes have the potential to destabilize state Medicaid programs and community health centers, impact local economies and job creation, and further exacerbate rural healthcare access challenges.

Families USA, their executive director, whose name is Anthony Wright:

> Americans are storming town halls calling their representatives in Congress and demanding that House Republicans stop their plan to massively cut the healthcare that Americans want and need. President Trump and some Republicans have said they won't touch Medicaid. But their vote today is when we see who walks the walk. The vote is the walk-the-plank moment for moderates who say they don't want Medicaid cuts but are being asked to cut over $880 billion to the care and coverage of their constituents. Policymakers and public alike understand that there is no version of this budget resolution that does not include deep cuts to vital program services and benefits the American people use every day to help them see a doctor, pay rent, or feed their families.

Justice in Aging — It's an organization that's led by its executive director, Kevin Prindiville. He writes:

> With this vote, lawmakers endorsed taking away Medicaid from millions of Americans, including older adults, all to bankroll tax cuts for the wealthy. Thanks to our collective advocacy, the vote to pass this dangerous budget blueprint did not come easily. And we will make sure lawmakers know that voting to enact these cuts would be voting to abandon older Americans.

The National Alliance for Caregiving:

> The House Budget Blueprint to eliminate at least $800 billion in federal funding, near funding unfairly targets criminal health care and supportive services that older adults, people with diabetes and their family caregivers depend upon to maintain health and economic security for families and themselves. Home and community-based services funded via Medicaid are cost-effective. They save millions of taxpayer dollars on unnecessary and often unwanted institutional care. Most of all, Medicaid funded HCBS {Home and Community-Based Services} offers consumers a choice in how they receive care in the dignity of their own homes.

In the dignity of their own homes — dignity.
The Coalition for Whole Health Legal Action Center:

> Among the options being discussed, are work requirements for enrollees. Despite the fact that most people receiving Medicaid do work and other cuts to federal funding that would disproportionately harm people with substance abuse and mental health conditions. And those with arrest and conviction records by making it harder to access critical health coverage and service medications and supports.
>
> Such individuals already face pervasive stigma and discrimination, including significant barriers to employment, that threaten their stability and wellbeing. At a time when overdose and suicide are claiming more than 400 lives a day, we cannot afford to reduce access to comprehensive healthcare services that people with substance abuse use, mental health conditions, and those rebuilding their lives after incarceration, desperately need to recover and thrive.

So, let me tell you something about that that really strikes me. I was blessed to go to colleges. And there, people would use drugs. And now I live in a community where the consequences for drug use often means jail time. In fact, if you look at low income people, their chances of being incarcerated are far greater than college kids who have drug usage rates at about the same. And so, now you say to somebody who's got an arrest record, served some time, that when they come out they can't get help? Or people with mental illness are over incarcerated and you're going to say to them, "You've got this mental illness, now you've got a record and you also can't get healthcare services?" That's again, self defeatist when it comes to our nation trying to give people ways of elevating themselves above their past mistakes or the diseases that challenge them.

Here's another group, Community Catalyst: "These cuts will hit hardest where healthcare access is already fragile."

Here's the Alliance for Aging Research:

> We, the undersigned organizations, urge you to oppose any cuts to Medicaid and the Supplemental Nutrition Assistance Program, SNAP, including those called for in the proposed budget resolution. We are concerned about the negative impact these deep cuts will have on the Americans living with chronic disease and other disabilities.
>
> But we are willing to draw your attention now to how devastating they will be on those with Alzheimer's and related diseases. Including frontotemporal degeneration and Lewy body dementia and their family caregivers.

April Barrett, president of SEIU:

> Let's be clear, Americans have flooded Congressional phone lines, rallied the town halls and lifted their voices to make it clear that they do not want massive cuts to the healthcare and public services they depend on. Despite that, today, Speaker Johnson, pressed a budget resolution forward that puts our nation on a disastrous path to ripping away healthcare from 80 million children, pregnant women, veterans, seniors, people with disabilities by gutting Medicaid.

Lee Sounder, the president of AFSCME:

> This budget proves that extremists are more concerned with giving wealthy trillions in tax cuts, than helping working people. Voters across the country are packing town halls to demand no cuts to Medicaid and SNAP. They're calling representatives asking them, 'Please save these services.' They want their elected leaders who will lower rising costs, who make it easier to afford rent and food. But instead of listening to workers, the House moved forward on a budget plan that will cause millions to lose their healthcare, increasing food insecurity for families, and jeopardize Medicare and social security in the long term.

He calls this shameful.

The Diabetes Leadership Council and Diabetes Patient Advocacy Coalition:

> We are deeply concerned about the budget resolution passed in the House of Representatives this week. This budget resolution will likely lead to cuts to the safety net Medicaid programs, which provides health insurance to almost 80 million Americans, including children, pregnant women, elderly adults, people with diabetes and low income adults and families.
>
> This action would disproportionately impact Americans who most need us, including those with diabetes or other chronic conditions who rely on Medicaid to access medications and technology that they need to manage their conditions.
>
> Members of Congress should instead work to ensure access to health insurance through the Medicare program, work to ensure access to healthcare without barriers for the most vulnerable Americans.

Here's the Alliance for Childhood Cancer:

> Work Requirements may also impact [care]givers of children with cancer who are unable to work due to the demands of cancer treatment for young adults with cancer who may not be eligible for insurance via their employer or may not be able to work due to their diagnosis. Many young adults rely on Medicaid, especially the Medicaid expansion for coverage. And research shows a clear increase in survival for young adults with cancer in Medicaid expansion states.

Unidos US:

> The proposed resolution would slash at least 880 billion from programs that have long provided lifesaving affordable coverage to millions of Americans. Medicaid alone serves 80 million people, covering nearly 40 million children. Half of those with special healthcare needs and more than 40% of all births.
>
> In Latino communities, Medicaid reaches 20 million individuals, protecting nearly one third of community members, more than half of Latino children and roughly 30% of Hispanic elders. Without these vital programs, there'll be higher hospitalization rates, delayed diagnoses, and increased mortality. This would become the norm. Placing an unsustainable strain on public health and national financial security.

As UnidosUS recently pointed out, these proposed cuts would represent the largest cuts to Medicaid in US history.

The Coalition of Survivors of Domestic Violence and Sexual Assault:

> On behalf of the adult and child survivors of domestic violence and sexual assault, we serve and advocate for them. We, on behalf of them, write to ask you to reject cuts to federal Medicaid funding.
>
> Survivors rely on Medicaid every day to escape abuse, to rebuild their lives after violence, to care for their children and families.

Catholic Health Association of the United States and the United States Conference of Catholic Bishops and Catholic Charities USA:

> Weakening Medicaid through structural challenges such as per capita caps or block grants, would undermine these values and risk leaving millions without access to essential health services.
>
> Furthermore, policies like work reporting requirements have shown clear evidence of creating artificial barriers to care generating paperwork and bureaucracy, while doing little to support people looking for work. These requirements also fail to recognize that most people on Medicaid already work and ignore the realities of low wage workers. Caregiving responsibilities, health limitations and studies have shown they frequently result in loss of coverage for eligible individuals and children.

The Disability and Aging Collaborative and the Consortium for Constituents with Disabilities on behalf of 107 national organizations and more than 230 state and local organizations:

> The undersigned members of the Disability and Aging Collaborative, the health and long-term service and support task forces of the consortium for constituents with disabilities, and allied organization's right to urge you to exclude Medicaid cuts work requirements or any changes that limit funding or eligibility from budget reconciliation or other legislation.
>
> People with disabilities, older adults, family caregivers and their children, direct care workers and other low-income individuals and families depend on Medicaid every day for their health, safety and independence. Medicaid enables our communities to go to work and to care for loved ones. It is our community's lifeline and we cannot afford for any part of it to be cut.

The Jesuit Conference:

> Programs that meet basic needs such as SNAP, Medicare, and Medicaid health insurance, premium tax credits and social security should be protected and remain as robust as possible. We oppose modifications that would have the effect of reducing important benefits of excluding vulnerable people from participating.

Thank you, The Jesuit Conference.

Why? I mean, we have just read dozens and dozens of letters from real people who are relying on these programs to take care of their elderly parents, take care of their loved one with the dementia, to take care of their children, to take care of their adult children with disabilities, to take care of their children with special needs, to take care of their families, to take care of their communities, to take care of rural towns, to take care of the hospitals, to take care of people. Why? Why? Why are all of these people lifting their voices now pointing to the crisis that can't be normalized? Pointing to the challenges? Because we've seen this reconciliation process call for $880 billion of cuts.

When as I read earlier, there's only one place that the majority of those cuts can come from, and that would be hundreds of millions of dollars of cuts to Medicaid. Which organization after organization told you, it is already a delicate balance that cuts to these programs could ultimately tear down people's access to lifesaving benefits. People use the word dignity over and over again. Dignity. It is a value in our country that we treat our elders with dignity. That we give people struggling with chronic disease dignity. That we give parents who are slammed with the unimaginable diagnoses for their children. We help them to access dignity.

People that we talked about that read their letters, they all said, "We can help you find efficiencies. We can help you make the programs work better. We can help you." But why are you doing this if it is all a part of a larger package to give tax cuts to the wealthiest Americans, to give tax cuts to billionaires? How does that work? That Elon Musk should get richer, and richer and richer, and families, the love in these letters, who love their children, who love their aging parent, who love that person with dementia, even though they don't recognize them anymore, but that doesn't stop their heroic love. And they piece together their finances in a nation where housing costs are going up, food costs is going up, transportation's going up. They piece together the fragile finances of their lives. The Medicaid funding is one part of it that gets yanked away and everything unravels. Why? They ask. Why? They plead for help. They ask us to do something.

I want to read some articles coming from a variety of backgrounds, but perhaps this one from PBS, A closer look at who relies on Medicaid.

So, what PBS wrote:

> As Congressional Republicans seek about $4.5 trillion, $4.5 trillion to extend expiring tax cuts, the federal government will need to find savings elsewhere. If you're going to give those $5.5 trillion that disproportionately go to the wealthy, you're going to have to find savings elsewhere.

You are going to give that $4.5 trillion that disproportionately go to the wealthy, and you are going to have to find savings elsewhere.

> Experts say budget cuts could affect Medicaid coverage for as many as millions of Americans at a time when the program may need more funding, not less. The proposed House bill requires the Committee on Energy and Commerce to find $880 billion in spending cuts. Which means some aspects of Medicaid, which the committee oversee may be on the chopping block.
> Medicaid is a massive program that provides free and reduced cost healthcare for eligible enrollees. It offers critical coverage to a wide variety of Americans, including children, adults with disabilities and older people in nursing homes.
> Even for Americans who have private insurance, Medicaid can play a part of their healthcare. That's because Medicaid is such a large ending of funding, that so many aspects of the countries, so many benefit from the aspects of this country's health coverage.

So many benefit from these aspects of this country's health coverage.

> The public health insurance option is funded in part by the federal government and in part by states covering around 72 million Americans. The government spends about $880 billion on Medicaid in fiscal year 2023, the most recent year for which there's data, according to an analysis by the nonprofit Health Policy Research Organization, KFF.
> Medicaid is an extremely popular entitlement program, said Robin Rudowitz, director of the program on Medicaid and the uninsured at KFF.
> More than nine in 10 adults say Medicaid is very or somewhat important to their local community, according to recent KFF polling. 40% of respondents said they wanted Medicaid funding to remain the same, while 42% wanted to increase funding for the program. Just 17% wanted to decrease funding a little or a lot.
> Some studies have found that expanding Medicaid can save money for states, including in spending reductions in corrections, healthcare, as well as mental health and substance abuse.

Pulling away from the article for a second, that is so logical. "Expanding health coverage for people with mental health challenges or substance abuse means an investment now and saves a lot of money for society later and saves them from being rearrested because of their disease."

Back to the article.

> President Donald Trump has said his administration will not cut Medicaid benefits and will instead reduce spending by eliminating waste and fraud. Well, according to health policy experts, there may not be a way to fund the tax cuts without gutting Medicaid. Doing that will have real implications, said Allison Orris, senior fellow and director of Medicaid policy at the Center on Budget and Policy Priorities. Another non-partisan group. It's fair to say that if Medicaid is cut by hundreds of billions of dollars, people will lose coverage. But some of the ways in which they will lose coverage and healthcare access are a little bit tricky, she said. So, who and what relies on Medicaid?
>
> Medicaid covers low income Americans in all 50 states, as well as DC and the American territories. But the program's benefits are farther reaching. Medicaid pays for around two in every five births in the country. The program accounts for about 20% of both hospital funding, and long and total healthcare spending nationwide, according to KFF. That organization's analysis of hundreds of studies concluded since 2014 largely found that Medicaid expansion helped cut hospital costs associated with uninsured patients. Many studies also found that Medicaid expansion helped with overall hospital funding and resulted in fewer hospital closures. And Medicaid, not Medicare, is the single largest payer of long-term coverage, including nursing home care.
>
> Here are some of the ways Medicaid is crucial for so many Americans' healthcare. Long-term care for people with disabilities according to KFF analyses. 35% of Americans with disabilities have Medicaid. It's about 15 million people. That compares with 19% of people without disabilities and the majority of whom have employer provided health insurance. Currently, Medicaid covers about 60% of long-term care coverage, much of which provides care for younger adults with disabilities.
>
> Nursing homes: Medicaid is the primary payer of nursing care in the United States. It covers 63% of nursing home residents. For many older adults, Medicaid is the safety net.
>
> David Grabowski, professor of healthcare policy at Harvard Medical School says "an individual can be middle income their entire life, and then reach the older long-term care years and have to enter a nursing home. Because nursing homes can be so expensive, families can quickly deplete all of their assets, then rely on Medicaid to cover long-term care."
>
> {Another group, children...} 37% of people enrolled in Medicaid are children. But they account for only about 15% of the programs spending. And 2023 KFF found that of the 72 million people enrolled in Medicaid, about 30 million were children. Millions more children are enrolled in the children's health insurance program, which some states run with Medicaid expansion funds.

They're tied. Forgive me, that's off this article. Back to the article.

> So far, political conversations have not yet focused on cutting CHIP.
> Rural maternal health: Medicaid covered around 40% of births nationwide in 2023, KFF found. And nearly half {nearly 50%} of all rural births.
> Studies also show that being enrolled in Medicaid leads to improved health outcomes for children, including declines in infant and child mortality, preventative care visits on par with privately insured children and even potentially positive outcomes into adulthood, such as improvements in education.

That's what studies show being enrolled in Medicaid leads to. How about Native Americans and Alaskan Indians?

> Four in ten American Indian, Alaskan native people are enrolled in Medicaid. The highest enrollment rate among any race and ethnicity category. This includes about 23% of non-elderly A-I-A-N adults and 44% of American Indian Alaska Native Children.
> How the federal government funds states Medicaid plans: Medicaid began as an optional program in 1966, alongside Medicare, with around eight million people eligible for enrollment. By the 1980s, all states had opted into providing health insurance through Medicaid.
> Though eligibility requirements have changed over the last 60 years and vary by state, the most significant change to Medicaid was the enactment of the Patient Protection In An Affordable Care Act in 2010. It requires states to cover adults with incomes up to 138% of the poverty line. After the Supreme Court ruled in 2012 that expansion for states should be optional, 40 states and Washington DC have expanded Medicaid.

Forty of our 50 states accepted federal funds at a much higher rate than the match rate for non-expansion. That is a good summary by PBS of how far-reaching this program is. How many Americans in every single state, from all backgrounds, both sides of the political aisle, independents, old, young, hospitals, businesses, care professionals, and more...

This is who we are. We've expanded the program. We've made it better. We've brought improvements. And yet we're doing a process; it's not going through a committee. We are not soliciting the best ideas from both sides of the aisle about how to make it more efficient, more effective. We're not bringing in private sector professionals to give advice and input or hospital providers or people that are seeing things that we could learn from and craft legislation to make the program better, and the letters are even showing. We're not even doing any of those things, and then we're cutting the very programs that allow people access to fresh, healthy food that then cause us to need more healthcare for chronic diseases. This alone would be bad enough, if we were gutting a program with no input from professionals. If we were taking away healthcare from seniors, children, expectant mothers, the disabled, that would be bad enough. But why? Again, why? Because it's part of a larger budget package to give trillions of dollars of tax cuts disproportionately to the wealthiest Americans and still add trillions to the national deficit. I talked about American Indian and Alaska Natives. I mentioned that I've recently visited some proud Native Americans and heard their stories and was inspired by their conviction and their grit and how, under incredible odds, they were able to create better lives. After extraordinary oppression and vicious policies and more, they found a way forward. There's a disproportionate number of Native Americans in Alaska — Natives that rely on these programs, people who have maintained extraordinary dignity despite promises made and promises broken.

So many people are talking about that idea of a sacred trust, that the richest nation in the world, to honor its ideals of freedom, has to focus on keeping people free from fear that one medical bill will throw their family in crisis, or fear that one diagnosis for their child will unravel their lives, or fear that if their parent gets dementia, there will be no care for them. So much of this conversation is within this larger understanding of who we are and what do we stand for.

I want to take a look at some of the things the Trump administration is doing that is going to undermine not just Medicaid, but health insurance coverage for Americans, for all Americans, and raise the cost of healthcare and negatively impact our health. At a time when basic prices of everyday goods are going up, the President is making healthcare harder to access and drug prices even higher. I want to explain this.

On his first day back in office, Trump rescinded a policy that extended the enrollment period for ACA plans. This policy gave Americans sufficient time to enroll in healthcare for the year, and enrollment in the ACA continues to go up as people see how affordable this program is and how they can get quality healthcare. But the first thing, one of the first things he does, is rescind the policy that extended the enrollment period. In addition to this, Republicans in Congress want to take away the tax credits that make healthcare more affordable for so many people. Millions of working-class Americans rely on Affordable Care Act tax credits to access affordable quality healthcare and coverage.

I could go on with the things. For example, currently, these tax credits, they're set to expire at the end of this year. If these tax credits are taken away, families will pay up to 90% more for their healthcare, and five million Americans could lose their healthcare altogether. Again, if this goes through in 2025, billionaires and CEOs will get a huge tax break while working Americans relying on this tax credit will lose it. Think about that. This would allow billionaires and CEOs to get more of a tax break while these tax credits that help more Americans access healthcare would expire. For New Jerseyans, ending the ACA tax credit would make health insurance less affordable for 352,000 hard-working people and their families and would force 75,000 people to go uninsured — 75,000 people in my state alone. Last year, 24 million people chose Affordable Care Act plans during the most recent open enrollment period, due to these expanded tax credits that made plans available to people for little or no monthly premiums and extended the enrollment period, which I just said the President has rolled back.

President Trump also overturned an effort for Medicare to lower drug costs, like implementing a two-dollar monthly out-of-pocket cap on certain generic drugs, as well as a measure that would reduce Medicare payments for rare disease drugs and drugs that treat life-threatening conditions. I just don't understand that one. I really see that as cruel. Americans struggling to afford their drugs had a cap of out-of-pocket expenses on certain generic drugs, and that was overturned. Costs are going up. Costs are going up, and now this president is expanding costs for out-of-pocket generic drugs, as well as Medicaid payments being eligible for rare diseases.

I had the privilege of becoming close to John McCain. I came here within the Senate and got this admonition, almost, from Bill Bradley, somebody who held my seat beforehand, and he challenged me to go and have lunch with or meetings with all my Republican colleagues at the time. That was way back in 2013, and I was told by John McCain's staff that I had like 10, 15 minutes, but I was going to take it. This is John McCain — he's a legend. And I go in, and I meet with him, and I didn't come out of that office for about 90 minutes. And we both got emotional as he showed me pictures and documentation from his time as a prisoner of war. In 2017, he was under extraordinary pressure in this healthcare crisis, and there were thousands of Americans descending on our capitol.

I'll never forget the Little Lobbyists, they call themselves, kids in wheelchairs that would roll up to Congresspeople and raise their little voice respectfully and ask them not to take away their health coverage. I remember people coming in here with preexisting conditions and saying, "Don't repeal my healthcare and not even have a plan to replace it." President Trump was asked about healthcare when he was Candidate Trump for this office, and he said he had, I think, it was 'conceptions of a plan'. And since he's been in office, I haven't heard a vision for healthcare, besides budget proposals that would cut people's healthcare.

But John McCain, I will never, ever forget that moment. I was actually standing on the Republican side, if I remember correctly, having conversations, and he came to the floor, after listening to Arizonans tell stories like the ones I've been reading, and put his thumb down. He wrote a speech about his decision, and I want to read a part of that now.

> I have been a member of The United States Senate for 30 years. I had another long, if not as long, career before I arrived here, another profession that was profoundly rewarding and in which I had experiences and friendships that I revere. But make no mistake: My service here is the most important job I have had in my life, and I'm so grateful to the people of Arizona for the privilege, for the honor of serving here, and the opportunities it gives me to play a small role in the history of the country I love.

I've known and admired men and women in the Senate who played much more than a small role in history. True statesmen, giants of American politics. They came from both parties and various backgrounds. Their ambitions were frequently in conflict. They had different views on the issues of the day, and they often had very serious disagreements about how to best serve the national interest, but they knew that however sharp and heartfelt their disputes, however keen their ambitions, they had an obligation to work collaboratively to ensure the Senate discharged its Constitutional responsibilities effectively. Our responsibilities are important, vitally important to the continued success of our Republic, and our arcane rules and customs are deliberately intended to require broad cooperation to function well at all. The most revered members of this institution accepted the necessity of compromise in order to make incremental progress on solving America's problems and to defend her from her adversaries.

That principled mindset and the service of our predecessors who possessed it come to mind when I hear the Senate referred to as the world's most deliberative body. I'm not sure we can claim that distinction with a straight face today. I'm sure it wasn't always deserved in the previous eras either, but I'm sure there have been times when it was, and I was privileged to witness some of those occasions.

Our deliberations today, not just our debates, but the exercise of all of our responsibilities, authorizing government policies, appropriating the funds to implement them, exercising our advice and consent role, are often lively and interesting. They can be sincere and principled, but they are more partisan, more tribal, more of the time, than any other time I remember. Our deliberations can still be important and useful, but I think we all agree they haven't been overburdened by greatness lately, and right now, they aren't producing much for the American people.

Both sides have let it happen. Let's leave the history of who shot first to historians. I suspect they'll find we all conspired in our decline. Either by deliberate actions or neglect, we've all played some role in it. Certainly, I have. Sometimes I've let my passion rule my reason. Sometimes I made it harder to find common ground because of something harsh I said to a colleague. Sometimes I wanted to win, more for the sake of winning than to achieve a contested policy.

Incremental progress compromises that each side criticize but also accept just plain muddling through, to chip away at problems, and keep our enemies from doing their worst isn't glamorous or exciting. It doesn't feel like a political triumph, but it's usually the most we can accept from our system of government, operating in a country as diverse and quarrelsome and free as ours.

Considering the injustice and cruelties inflicted by autocratic governments and how contemptible human nature can be, the problem-solving our system does make possible, the fitful progress it produces, and the liberty and justice it preserves, is a magnificent achievement.

Our system doesn't depend on our nobility. It accounts for our imperfections and gives an order to our individual strivings that has helped make ours the most powerful and prosperous society on earth. It is our responsibility to preserve that, even when it requires us to do something less satisfying than winning, even when we must give a little to get a little, even when our efforts manage just three yards in a cloud of dust. While critics on both sides denounce us for timidity, for our failure to triumph, I hope we can again rely on humility, on our need to cooperate, on our dependence on each other — to learn how to treat each other again, and by so doing, better serve the people. Learn how to trust each other again, and by so doing, better serve the people who elected us.

Stop listening to the bombastic loudmouths on the radio and television and the Internet. To hell with them. They don't want anything done for the public good. Our incapacity is their livelihood. Let's trust each other again. Let's return to regular order. We've been spinning our wheels on too many important issues because we keep trying to find a way to win without help from across the aisle. That's an approach that's been employed by both sides, mandating legislation from the top down, without any support from the other side, with all the parliamentary maneuvers that requires.

We're getting nothing done. All we've really done this year is confirm Neil Gorsuch to the Supreme Court. Our healthcare insurance system is a mess. We all know it, those who support Obamacare and those who oppose it. Something has to be done. We Republicans have looked for a way to end it and replace it with something else, without paying a terrible political price. We haven't found it yet, and I'm not sure we will.

All we've managed, all we've managed to do, is make more popular a policy that wasn't very popular when we started to try to get rid of it. I voted for the motion to proceed, to allow debate to continue and amendments to be offered. I will not vote for the bill as it is today. It's a shell of a bill right now. We all know that. I have changes urged by my state's governor that will have to be included to earn my support for final passage of any bill. I know many of you will have to see the bill change substantially for you to support it.

We've tried to do this by coming up with a proposal behind closed doors and consultation with the administration, then signing it on, then springing it on skeptical members, trying to convince them it's better than nothing. Asking us to swallow our doubts and force it past a unified opposition. I don't think that is going to work in the end, and it probably shouldn't.

I mean, that is prescient. As a great New Jerseyan, Yogi Berra, said, "That feels like deja vu all over again." Do you hear what John McCain was criticizing? One party, behind closed doors, without consultation of experts, against the wishes of Republican governors, is trying to force something through, past a united opposition. He literally is describing what's happening right now and condemning both sides of this institution for playing this record over and over and over again.

Yes, I'm a Democrat, and I admit that our healthcare system needs so much help and so much reform. One out of every three of our tax dollars is being spent on healthcare. That's ridiculous, and what are we getting from it? A society that's getting more and more sick. And what of our solutions as a body? Did we come together as a team? Did we set up a special conference, set up a special committee to study the issues, to bring in the experts, to involve the best technology, to learn the lessons from private sector and public sector, from universities, from scientists? Are we doing that, or are we doing exactly what John McCain said we shouldn't do? Exactly what he described, why he voted no.

It is maddening in this country to create greater and greater healthcare crisis and for us not to solve it, but to battle back and forth between trying to make incremental changes or to tear it all down with no plan to make it better. Leaving more Americans suffering what is still one of the most significant ways people go bankrupt, which is not being able to afford their healthcare. And what are we doing it for this time, John? Senator McCain? I know you wouldn't sanction this. I know you would be screaming. I've seen how angry you can get, John McCain, I've seen you tear people apart on this floor, Democrat and Republican, for doing the same stupid thing over and over again.

Listen to John McCain explain why he voted no the last time the Republican party tried to unite and tear down healthcare with no idea how to fix it and threatening to put millions of Americans in financial crisis and healthcare crisis.

I can't believe we are here again, with thousands upon thousands upon thousands of Americans writing letters, storming into town halls. Hospital leaders, private sector leaders, Republican governors, Republican mayors, Democratic governors, Democratic mayors, all saying, "What are you doing in Congress, and why?" I think what's even more outrageous this time is the why. To redo the tax cuts that independent budget analysis know that the overwhelming benefit went to the billionaires that sat on stage with Donald Trump during his inauguration.

We're not saving any money in our budgets. Their plan is to expand our budget crisis. Their plan will add trillions of dollars to our budget and give tax cuts to the wealthiest and not help the people that John McCain is talking about. His echoes haunt me, that he said, "We are mistaken when we don't come together across the aisles, across our differences, to try to make things better."

There is a healthcare crisis in this country. One out of three dollars in our government is going to healthcare, and we have more chronic disease in this nation than we have ever had before, and there's no solution being offered in this reconciliation to deal with that. In fact, we're making it worse because we're denying children access to healthy foods. This is ridiculous.

If they're successful, what kind of country will we be? With more stratifications of wealth, with people who have done so good.

I'm not one of these Democrats that hates successful or wealthy people. Heck, people in my neighborhood, as the only senator that probably lives in a low income neighborhood, strive to be wealthy. They are doing great. The top quartile of our country for the last 20 years has made extraordinary wealth. God bless them.

But when you see that 70, 80% of Americans don't want Medicaid cuts, it's because most Americans know neighbors, family members, church members who rely on Medicaid. They know that their grandmother in a nursing home relies on Medicaid. They know that the disabled child next door relies on Medicaid. And now we want to gut it? $880 Billion?

John McCain — most people remember the thumb down, they don't remember his words, they don't remember the warnings. This man is in heaven now and his words, they speak to us in this moment. Again, why won't we listen to them?

> Our deliberations today, not just our debates, but the exercise of our responsibilities, authorizing government policies, appropriating the funds to implement them. They can be sincere in principle, but they are more partisan, more tribal, more of the time than any I remember.
>
> Our deliberations can still be important and useful, but I think we'd all agree that they have overburdened, they've been overburdened, and right now they aren't producing much for the American people.
>
> Both sides have let this happen. Let's leave the history of who shot first to the historians, I suspect they will find we all conspired in our decline either by deliberate actions or by neglect.
>
> {Listen to John McCain...} Our system doesn't depend on our nobility. It accounts for our imperfections and gives an order to our individual strivings that has helped make ours the most powerful process of society on earth.
>
> {Listen to us...} Let's trust each other. Let's return to regular order. We've been spinning our wheels on too many important issues because we keep trying to find a way to win without the help from the other side. That's an approach that's been employed by both sides, mandating legislation from the top down without support from the other side. We're getting nothing done. All we've done this year is to confirm Neil Gorsuch.
>
> I voted for the motion to proceed to allow debate to continue and amendments for office. I will not vote for the bill as it stands today. {I will not vote for the bill.}
>
> We've tried doing this by coming up with a proposal behind closed doors in consultation with the administration {Donald Trump} then springing it on skeptical members, trying to convince them it's better than nothing, asking us to swallow our doubts and force it past a unified opposition. I don't think that is going to work in the end, and it probably shouldn't.

Well, this shouldn't work either. This shouldn't work either. This is wrong. This is wrong. I see the Leader here. I'm sorry, sir. I should be conserving my energy.

SENATOR SCHUMER: Would the gentleman yield for a question?

SENATOR BOOKER: Yes, I would yield for a question while retaining the floor.

SENATOR SCHUMER: First, your impassioned remarks are so meaningful. I hope all of America is watching. And if some people are not up at this hour, watch it tomorrow. It's inspiring. And I would just ask my colleague a question. I was there, I spent four hours with John McCain before he voted. And we talked and talked, and talked and went over the courage of his father and his grandfather in the Navy, and the courage that he hoped to show as they did. And I'd ask my colleague this question, isn't it eerily reminiscent that after John McCain did his courageous act, that here we are years later, almost a decade later, a few years less, and they're doing the same thing again, cutting people's healthcare to give tax breaks to the wealthiest people? And isn't it true that John McCain saw the suffering of people who wouldn't get healthcare and urged people to come together on a bipartisan solution?

And wouldn't it be much better if our colleagues from across the aisle – they may not agree with us on everything – but instead of trying to jam another bill down our throats like they did back in 2017, came and worked with us for the betterment of the country, for the betterment of the 80% of the people who need healthcare, who will struggle without that healthcare? Some will be ill, some will die — will die. So does it strike the gentleman that how could the people on the other side of the aisle try to do this again after John McCain made such a courageous stance? It's not echoing. It doesn't seem to be echoing in their ears, is it? I'd ask my colleague to just answer that general line of questions.

SENATOR BOOKER: So Collins, Murkowski and McCain — it took a lot of courage, they were getting a lot of pressure from the White House. John McCain was viciously attacked afterwards. But his private conversations with members and you, Senator Schumer, know at the last lap around his track of life, he didn't want to be remembered as someone doing something – to use John McCain kind of language – boneheaded to hurt a lot of innocent, fragile people and leave them without a plan. When his own governor, Republican governor – I read Republican governors earlier – were saying don't do this.

I want to say something else to the Senator in response to his question. I watched you that night and I just loved something you did, and I've never said this to you. People over here tried to start applauding and you stood up angrily and told them not to because what John showed was something bigger than partisanship. He talks about it, one side trying to win the other side, trying to... It's more ego sometimes than it is ideals. And you stood up and said, "No, this is not that moment. We're watching a man take a position that was not easy, that didn't serve his politics, but served his spirit." I don't know if my staff has that envelope of the articles that I wanted specifically, because there's a story in there and I don't have it now, I'm going to read it later about John McCain in the prison camps.

I wasn't here when we had this moment. But when I got here weeks after this moment, Mr. Leader, all my colleagues on both sides, I want to talk about it was a special conference in the old Senate chamber. I was not there but the Democrats and Republicans — it actually changed our behavior in here. It didn't last, but I came here and people said, because of that, we're all going to partner up and for State of the Union addresses, you have a Republican partner and a Democrat. We go as couples, basically. It was something about this man where the dignity that he had, that we all treasured in a moment like that, that he began to elevate... I had my partner senator here say to me when I got here, "You are not a full senator until you get ripped by John McCain's anger."

SENATOR SCHUMER: Will the Senator yield? I am well aware.

SENATOR BOOKER: Okay. And I never got ripped by him. After my meeting I mentioned earlier, in his office, he started inviting me with him. My first CODEL was with him and telling me... He told me all the time, "Booker, there are two types of senators here." (I don't mean that he was casting aspersions on others.) "There are people that represent their states and there are statesmen." And he kept challenging me, "Be a statesman. Not a great Democratic senator, but be a great American senator." He would challenge me over and over, and over again. I would go to his national security conferences out at his ranch. And one of my favorite moments as a senator, if I had top ten favorite moments as a US senator, this is one of them. The Leader knows that I am a vegan. And when you go to one of his open barbecues, there is nothing vegan. I mean, they even saturated every vegetable in butter and mayonnaise was everywhere. But I'm not going to complain, I'm just going to sit and enjoy the conference conversations.

And so now I'm in a golf cart going home at the end of the night and the young man who was shuttling me home goes to me, "How was the food? Did you enjoy the dinner?" And I go, "Well actually, if I'm going to be honest, I didn't eat." And they go, "You haven't had dinner?" And I go, "No." I said, "I'm a vegan." And they go, "Well, we're about to pass John McCain's home, where he lives. And it's late, I'm sure he's asleep, but maybe we can break in and see what's in his fridge." And I'm like, "Dude, I'm from Jersey. I love this. Breaking into John McCain's house and I won't have to worry about getting arrested?" I said, "I'm all in." And so we went in and as soon as we rounded the kitchen, I looked through the kitchen and John McCain was sitting there with another elderly tough-looking man on the couch, engaged in conversation, so I didn't get my joy of breaking into John McCain's house. But I walk in and he's sitting there with a former secretary, if I remember correctly, of the Navy.

And they're like, "Booker, sit down." I go, "I haven't eaten." He goes, "Ah." So I'm sitting there eating peanut butter and celery or whatever, and these two men are talking about government inefficiency. And they say the place that we could be saving the most money, former secretary, if I remember correctly, of the Navy and one of the great men on national security, they started detailing the waste in the military. They both claim that we could have much more capacity, greater military effectiveness for billions and billions and billions of dollars less. I'll never forget. Again, this is me new to the senate, I don't know foreign policy like I do 12 years later or the military like I do 12 years later. But I was listening to these two experienced men complaining about the gross waste that was undermining our overall effectiveness and efficiency.

And that's why to this day, I'm infuriated that when people come in and say they want to cut budgets, the first thing they want to go for is not to take a real – because the military hasn't passed an audit in years – to have a real conversation about a lot of the baked-in corruption and misspending in the military. But they're going after programs that hospital after hospital, healthcare provider after healthcare provider, leader after leader, governor after governor says, are you crazy? And so this is one of the more preposterous moments that you and I both know if John McCain was here right now, he would reject this whole thing because we were literally repeating the same thing we did in 2017, eight years ago.

SENATOR SCHUMER: Would the Senator yield for a question?

SENATOR BOOKER: I will yield for a question while retaining the floor.

SENATOR SCHUMER: Isn't it true when McCain talked about waste in the military, he studied it, he documented it, he said, 'this is a good thing', 'this is a bad thing'? He helped guide me on many of these things. I voted for some weapon system, getting some people upset because he showed me they worked, and I voted against a lot of them because he showed me they didn't. But isn't it so that our colleagues on the other side, when they talk about waste in the healthcare system, they don't document a thing. They use just a meat axe or a chainsaw as Elon Musk perversely, but proudly said he's going to carry one. And they don't document waste that they say exists and then they just slash things that people need that's not waste at all, that's life support for people. Isn't that a huge difference between the way McCain looked at waste, whether it's in the military or anything else, and what we're hearing here today?

SENATOR BOOKER: Resoundingly, yes. I'm just laughing that every time DOGE puts up their supposed savings, they then try to take them down because as soon as they're fact-checked, so many of them are not done. And I'm not saying all of them — I don't want to paint with a broad brush. I know having Microsoft licenses (too many), yeah, this waste, I wish we were doing this in a bipartisan way. Those cuts would be bigger and probably have a lot more staying power than what they're doing, which is ready, fire, aim, and then having to beg people to come back to work because they fired FAA people or nuclear regulators or what have you. But this is the bigger point that you're making, that really is getting me. So you know this, I used to be an executive. There's nobody in this body...

Here's a bold and braggadocios thing to say, but fact check me, anybody — there's nobody in this body that was a governor, a county executive like Coons, or a mayor that cut government as much as I did. I had to cut my government by 25%. Imagine that here on the federal level. And I had to do it because I can't print money. It was a national recession, I was left with a mess, had to do it. But we found ways to do it cooperatively with a legislator, bringing in experts. But this is the point I want to make to you, one thing I couldn't cut was my healthcare costs. And so I started asking people what can I do? And you know who I found? I found a big business owner who had tens of thousands of employees, who said I have the same problem. And you know what I did?

I went into my cafeteria where thousands of people eat, (big, big place,) and I saw deep fryers and Cinnabon-like products and all this unhealthy stuff. And I ripped it all out, had the union ready to go crazy on me. But then I brought in the best chef. I paid extra money to get the best kind of all healthy, nutritious whole foods. And then they loved it. And then they started asking me, can we get food to take home for our kids? Because we stopped through McDonald's or Burger King on the way home. Long story short, he said, "It began to bend their cost curve." What do we do in the United States of America? What is Donald Trump ... I just read all the things he is doing. He's cutting access to healthy lunch programs. They're threatening to cut SNAP program. They're threatening to cut the things that would give our residents in America not the cheap hyper-processed, empty nutrition foods, but the stuff that is healthy for our kids.

So there's so much hypocrisy based in this that even the private sector folks are saying, you are going to drive up costs for your country when you make people get their healthcare in emergency rooms. You're going to drive up costs for your country when you're going to force people to have to quit their jobs so they can come home and take care of their loved one with dementia. This will drive up costs ultimately for our country, put more hardship on people, all while giving the most wealthy people who don't need it, bigger tax cuts. It makes no sense, and that is the spirit of why John McCain voted against this effort in 2017.

SENATOR SCHUMER: I thank the gentleman. It's a hope, maybe forlorn, that maybe one of John McCain's words will influence a few folks over there before we proceed disastrously. I wish the gentleman strength and yield the floor to him.

SENATOR BOOKER: I appreciate you allowing me to yield to you to answer a question while retaining the floor.

I'm going to continue with a little bit more here before we change topics for the night. I want to point out how grateful I am for my friend, Chris Murphy. The last time I stood on this floor for many hours was just in support doing like my colleague is doing for me right now. After the Pulse shooting*, we wanted to vote on common-sense gun safety, bipartisan-supported, common-sense gun safety. We didn't get it. Chris Murphy right down there held the floor for 15 hours and I paced around, walked the floor, helped to support things, stayed up with him all night. And it is profound to me that when I told my brother that I wanted to cause some good trouble, that I was going to rise, that he said, "I'm in. I'm in." And so there he is helping me out, especially as we approach 11 o'clock at night and the fourth hour. I'm just grateful for him. I'm grateful for him.

I want to go now to cuts that are being made to local and state health department funding and again, Republican and Democratic governors. We have letters from people on both sides of the aisle who are saying that this is just wrong and it makes no sense, but here we go. It is actually really what I would call a dangerous reversal, that Trump's HHS recently announced the cancellation of almost 12 billion in federal grants that state and local health departments have been using to track infectious diseases, health disparities, vaccinations, mental health, substance use and services. Because of that reversal, my state, for example, is going to lose $350 million in federal funding for health programs due to these cuts. My Governor, Phil Murphy said that these cuts would create an unfillable void in funding that will have disastrous ramifications for our most vulnerable neighbors.

Last week we learned that HHS planned to cut an additional 10,000 jobs. In total since January, HHS has cut 20,000 of its employees. That's over a quarter of its workforce. These are people who inspect nursing homes to ensure that they're safe. They improve diagnostic and treatment services for children, regulate health insurance to make sure that they are not discriminating against you based on your health conditions and health status, to protect you from infectious diseases, conduct inspections to make sure that infant formula is safe. And I want to tell you that Secretary Kennedy has committed to bringing radical transparency to the HHS, I would love radical transparency. But at the end of February, Secretary Kennedy announced that HHS is no longer required to undergo the public comment period, a practice that's taken place at the agency since 1971.

Another critical resource of health information for the American public is the CDC's morbidity and mortality weekly report that has been published since 1952 and is often called the Voice of the CDC. But unfortunately, on January 23rd, the first time since its inception, the report was not published in a direct response to the Trump administration's freeze on public communications. In addition to pausing the critical publication, it also reported that the pregnancy risk assessment monitoring system had halted operation. This PRAMS, which was developed in 1987, is designed to identify groups of women and infants at high risk for health problems, to monitor changes in health status and to measure progress towards goals and improving the health of mothers and infants. Over the last 38 years, the program has collected essential data on maternal behaviors and experiences before, during, and shortly after pregnancy. Maternal care providers rely on that data collected by PRAMS, the sole source of this type of information to enhance prenatal and postnatal care.

The US is in the midst of a mortality crisis, which we mentioned before. We have the highest rate of maternal deaths of any high income nation. As I learned when I was a mayor, data is power. You can't manage a problem unless you have measures on the problem. To pull back things like that, again, you're reducing transparency, you're cutting back on vital reports that people who are trying to meet this crisis rely on to inform their strategies. And again, here's the frustration, is that we are the worst in maternal health outcomes for developed nations, but even in our country, African-American women are three times more likely to die from pregnancy related causes than the majority. This is one of the countries where it's profoundly dangerous to have kids. And again, this is yet another thing that HHS is doing, that's leaving us more vulnerable, less informed, less empowered to deal with the health challenges that we still deal with.

Since the Trump administration made the disastrous decision for agencies to pause external communications, we've been seeing significant delays in critical information from other key agencies. There have been avoidable delays in critical data from the CDC, that states are starting to speak out, saying that they need to protect the health of their communities. As of March 20th, when it comes to vaccines, what we're seeing in America, talk about getting less safe, there are 378 confirmed cases of measles throughout the United States. As one of my doctor friends said, "There are more children with measles right now than there are trans athletes in the NCAA." This is a real crisis. For the first time in a decade, a child who was not vaccinated for measles tragically died in that outbreak. And while measles is spreading across our nation and we are having one of the worst flu seasons in the last decades, HHS has delayed the convening of critical advisory councils at the CDC and FDA. These advisory councils are responsible for determining the vaccine schedule, what vaccines must be covered by insurance and the safety, effectiveness and appropriate use of vaccines. They do essential and timely work to keep people safe and disruptions to their work can be harmful to the health of the American people.

Let me go to the National Institute of Health. It's the largest public funder of biomedical research in the world. It's facing devastating cuts. The NIH is one of the greatest successes in publicly funded scientific research in all of human history. The US is one of the best places to do scientific research because it has had more capacity than any other country to fund and conduct research at the highest levels. Pauses, lapses and elimination of NIH funding will drive researchers to do their research in other countries and undermine the efforts to cure diseases, to find solutions to conditions from obesity, to Alzheimer's, to cancers. One of the best taxpayer dollars we can invest is in NIH because it returns more than five taxpayers dollars back in the breakthroughs that they make.

We have put the future of scientific research in the United States at grave threat with what the Trump administration is now doing. They've imposed cuts and a number of harmful orders on the NIH, that have both stalled its research and confused its partners. 99.4% of the FDA-approved drugs come from the NIH-funded research. Let me just say that again. NIH-funded research has led to 99.4% of all the FDA drugs that are out there. The NIH funding cuts will directly affect your access to future novel treatments that can improve your quality of life or your children, or if you love your neighbor, like so many religions call us to do, with your neighbor's children as well.

Here's an example of that. Hepatitis C is a liver disease caused by the virus HCV, and it is one of the most common types of viral hepatitis in the United States. It is estimated that three to four million Americans have hepatitis. In 2014, the first complete treatment for hepatitis C was approved by the FDA. The development of this revolutionary new treatment that has since been used to cure millions of people around the world was funded by NIH research. This is a type of life-saving innovation we will lose out on if we defund the NIH as the Trump administration is currently doing. American enterprise and knowledge will be drained, we will fall behind.

We already know there's fierce competition for the researchers by countries like China. They are aiming, in fact, they are upping their investments in scientific research, doing everything they can to keep scientific researchers in their country. I was just talking to an innovator out in the West Coast, was telling me that they're starting to take passports away from their researchers. There's a fierce competition going on to keep the best minds here in this country or be drawn away to other places from Europe to China. And we're stopping our funding? I've heard from academic institutions that are telling me that they're not even offering as many PhD programs in some of these key areas of science because of the attacks that are happening on our universities, all while China is upping their investments in the universities. I can't believe that they're trying to out-America us and we're trying to turn our back on our most successful traditions.

One of his first actions, President Trump imposed a communications freeze on all US health agencies, effectively silencing some of our nation's top researchers, scientists, and public health experts. This action stalled 16,000 grant applications for around $1.5 billion in NIH funding. The NIH has since begun to incrementally send notices to the Office of the Federal Register to resume reviews. The combination of these actions irresponsibly have stalled our nation's primary source of life-saving biomedical research. It is our understanding that full communications have not been resumed and that it continues to impede critical research at the NIH. As I've been told time and time again by experts in this area, just to pause funding could set research back years because when you're conducting research, whether it's in a test tube and biomedical research, you can't pause. Whether it's in a human body, and biomedical research, you can't pause.

Across the nation, brilliant researchers have been finding out daily that the Trump administration has canceled their research. Research on critical issues like maternal health, long COVID, diabetes, new pharmaceutical drugs, cancer, and so, so much more. The NIH has decided to cancel its 2025 summer internship program. On average 1,100 interns participate in this program each year, helping develop the next generation of scientists and researchers. A small number of summer interns had already accepted their offer to join the NIH in 2025. The decision follows the Trump administration's federal hiring freeze. Again, in my faith there's a saying, "Train a child in the way he shall go, and he will not depart from it." These are our young people, these are the future scientists, now aren't getting the experience of the lifetime. I've met people in this institution who first came here as college summer interns.

The NIH has decided not only to cancel those internships, but to shut the door to many kids who had already made their summer plans. Many people here know what it's like to have a summer plan, have a summer internship, not apply for other ones. It's another act of just meanness and cruelty. Let this class come in and then say, "Okay, I'm going to cut the program next year." But the way they're doing things is mean and cruel, and having an impact on people's lives. Congressionally-directed medical research programs. I've worked across the aisle with my colleagues. I have friends in here that have worked with me on specific diseases in a bipartisan way. I'm so proud of some of that work.

Well, we've long appropriated about $1.5 billion a year in federal funds for medical research, nearly half of which typically goes to cancer. It's something that we have found common ground on in my 12 years here in significant stretches. The medical research program was created and sustained by Congress, competitively awards funds to hundreds of projects each year at both the defense department labs and outside research institutions, including at many American universities to study everything again, from cancer to battlefield wounds, to suicide prevention. In 2024, $130 million was specifically appropriated in a bipartisan way in this body, incredibly good senators of good conscience coming together and saying we should do more in these areas.

They approved $130 million for research in breast, kidney, lung, melanoma, ovarian, pancreatic, prostate, and a handful of very rare cancers. Why? Because there are people of good conscience here. We meet folks who come to this... They're not lobbyists, they come and they tell us about their stories of rare cancers. There are people on both sides of the aisle that have marched for prostate awareness, for breast cancer awareness. There's a goodness and decency here, but in 2024, this funding... It's a bill that passed in March. It was now slashed, slashed by 57%. And I told you earlier that data, one of the best taxpayer dollars we can spend, is in medical research. We've all heard this in this body, when the NIH has come through and shown, $1 invested could get more than $5 back. Any Wall Street executive that would get five times their money back from an investment, who is this helping? And do we think about the people? I thank God, I don't have many family members that are going about your day, go to the doctor, come back with a cancer. I know lots of people though. I know their stories, when they're diagnosed with a cancer and they're told there's no cure.

I've seen people go through what you go through in that. And so, how could the country that has led humanity for more than a generation or two suddenly have a president come along and say, "I'm going to slash all of these things. And oh, by the way, I'm going to give billionaires a big tax cut." So what do we say when these folks come to our office? Some of the people with rare diseases came to my office a couple weeks ago. And the amount of their funding is so small. And maybe if it was to solve our budget deficit, if we're going to do this as a country, we got to come together in a bipartisan way. The debt is... I'm one of these Democrats that believes it's a real crisis. But we are not solving the deficit in what they're proposing here. They're cutting and cutting and cutting things that make no sense to cut, and they're doing it for a tax breaks which disproportionately go to the wealthiest and to rack up even more debt.

I want to read this article, and my staff told me that we have lots of sections to go through and it's been four hours and 11 minutes. But this is one that hurts me, because I've met so many people who fall into this category. I want to read an article that deals with an issue called medical debt, and the ongoing impact it has on people as part of their lives. The Affordable Care Act, when we did that, we lowered the costs, and implemented protections for Americans requiring insurers to cover pre-existing conditions, expanding Medicaid, which we've talked about a lot tonight, implementing caps on out-of-pocket costs for Americans. All of these helped in alleviating medical bankruptcy for some. Medical bankruptcies in America have gone down, but not all. We still live in a country where one of the top reasons for bankruptcy is medical debt.

One of my staffers kind of shook me with the reality she was dealing with which is, she's got stratospheric medical debt. So here's an article from Healthcare Insights. It's not a partisan rag — it's a scientific journal. *How medical debt is crushing 100 million Americans*. It's from October of last year. This author – I just want to give a little more understanding of what kind of article this is – it's John August. He is the Scheinman Institute's Director of Healthcare.

> George Curley is one of 52 million people, or one-third of Americans in the workforce, who earn $15 an hour or less. I had the opportunity to interview George recently about his experience with medical debt, and how it has impacted his life.

Having suffered an industrial accident, and even though his employer was responsible for his injuries, and he carried health insurance, he still accumulated $20,000 in medical debt.

George grew up in Dallas and spent his life working hard as a full-time warehouse and retail worker. At one point in his life, he found a job and he enjoyed working as a forklift driver in a factory that produced ceramic tile. In time, he switched jobs working on the production line. One fateful day, a piece of metal struck him in the foot. He had to have surgery and underwent the amputation of one of his toes.

He had to take a month off from work. And when he returned, he went back to driving the forklift. He found that due to his accident and surgery, he couldn't operate the forklift to his satisfaction. He became frustrated in not being able to operate the forklift. He grew depressed, and left the job.

> "It took me three months to get back on my feet after the toe amputation. There were nursing care for two months to help me work again. This life-saving medical procedure left me with over $20,000 in debt. Even with insurance, exclamation point, I avoided doing necessary follow up with doctors due to not being able to afford additional care. There were hard times on top of this. I suffered a great deal of depression due to losing my job during my leave of absence. This medical debt is currently following me. There was a point of time that I was rebuilding my credit. Before the surgery I built it up by over 120 points. With a medical debt on my credit report, my credit score dropped 60 points. The big drop in score has not allowed me to get my own place. I'm not able to continue to pursue my dream of being a voice actor due to not having proper financial footing to get back to school. I can't travel and do things I would like to do. I'm working, but things are very financially tight. The medicine I need is being paid out of pocket. After paying my bills, I'm in the negative. There is no money left over to pay my medical debt. I can't save money right now, not even towards retirement. To have this medical debt on my credit score means not being able to pursue a better life."

He went on short-term disability for a while, but then found the part-time job he holds now at Walgreens. He had to return to work to pay for the house he and his brothers had purchased. Through this period, George had to take payday loans. And between those loans and his weekly wages, he attempted to pay back the money he owed the hospitals. He learned that because of his medical debt, his credit rating was destroyed by credit agencies, who learned that he had fallen behind on his payments to the hospitals. According to the Consumer Finance Protection Bureau {which I guess barely exists now} 100 million Americans owe 220 billion in medical debt.

So 100 million Americans owe $220 billion in medical debt ...

> George told me that the medical debt has had several devastating impacts on his life — inability to borrow money for a mortgage or a car. Employers ask for credit reports, and reports that show an applicant for a position are often rejected to a poor credit report. This has impacted his ability to find a better job than his part-time job at $15 an hour, with no benefits, working at Walgreens where he lives in Garland, Texas. Incredible stress that further impacts his health conditions including diabetes.

An additional note, Garland, Texas, where George lives, is near Dallas, which includes Garland and Dallas, is a locality with high medical debt, and high profit for healthcare systems in the region.

> Though George makes very low wages, medical debt is a broadly shared experience by Americans across income groups. Clearly, low wage workers suffer the worst burden, but the problem is pervasive, and a broad feature of American life.
> Some background: In the off-sided study, as many as 65.5% of people who file for bankruptcy blame medical bills as a primary cause.

I'm going to repeat that in the article. 66.5% of Americans who file for bankruptcy blame medical bills as their primary cause. Two-thirds of Americans who are filing bankruptcy point to medical bills as the cause.

> As many as 550,000 people file for bankruptcy every year for this reason.

More than half of 1 million Americans, year, after year, after year, after year, after year, after year, for no fault of their, own because of a metal bar shoved up through his toe, because of a diagnosis of cancer, because of diabetes, because of things outside of their control, they rack up medical debt, that as this man can enrode their well-being.

> This data has been known about how many Americans affected, and has continued even with the passage of the Affordable Care Act. Lesser known is the amount of medical debt that Americans carry.
>
> What are the causes of this burden on so many? Well, more Americans have health insurance today than ever before. Coverage has many gaps. High deductibles and narrow networks, which prevent patients from seeking health providers of their choice and common cause of accumulation of high-cost bills. When patients understandably seek care from a preferred provider, too often that care is not covered.
>
> Most healthcare plans only provide 80% of payment for covered costs; 20% {twenty percent!} patient responsibility of high medical bills can leave people unable to pay their bills. Approximately 14 million people in America, 6% of adults in the US owe over $1000 in medical debt. And about 3 million people, 1% of Americans owe medical debt of more than 10 grand.
>
> Additionally, this government report identifies many of the components of medical debt which are completely out of control of the patient. In most cases these practices are unlawful but, hospitals use these tactics frequently to press patients to pay, including ...
>
> **Double billing**: Companies cannot attempt to collect on medical bills that have already been paid by the consumer insurance, or a government program such as Medicaid or Medicaid. This practice can coerce consumers into paying twice for the same service.
>
> **Expanding legal limits**: Companies must not attempt to collect amounts that surpass Federal or state caps, such as those set by the Federal No Surpass Act, or state laws on 'reasonable' rates. These violations can saddle consumers with unjustly high medical debts, burdening their finances.
>
> **Falsified or fake charges**: Debt collectors must not collect on bills that include upcoded or exaggerated services or charges at service the consumer did not receive.
>
> **Collecting unsubstantiated medical debts**: Debt collectors must not attempt to collect medical debts.

These are all awful practices that go on. Here's Paul Sugar's story, compelling and tragic:

> Paul spent much of his life starting as a child as learning about jewelry, living in a small town near Albuquerque, New Mexico. At an early age, he earned enough money selling silver and turquoise necklaces to be able to buy a motorcycle. As he became an adult, he developed a successful business in the mining and selling of silver and turquoise used in making jewelry.
>
> He also worked at GE, the GE Engine plant, but was laid off during the time of industrial downsizing. He went to work for Qwest, installing communications infrastructure, but was laid off from that job when Qwest was acquired by US West, so he returned to his business.
>
> On January 9th, 2019, he was terribly injured in a fire at his home. He's still recovering physically and economically, after losing 66% of his skin, and getting care at a specialty trauma unit in another part of the country. He ended up owing over $82,000 in medical bills. The medical debt on his credit report means, he has not been able to get loans to expand his business and earn more after the fire. His medical bills totaled $550, 000.
>
> Insurance covered most of it, but it was still more than he could pay. He made payment plans with all of his various bills. But when his credit card number changed, some of the automatic payments he had arranged for did not go through, and the bills ended up in collection before he even knew he was behind.
>
> Prior to the fire, he always had stellar credit rating. But since this medical debt, it has gone down. In his business it's important to be able to take out short-term loans to supply the company, but now he can't do that at reasonable terms and rates. He spent his retirement savings account trying to pay back all of his medical bills, his retirement savings, but it wasn't enough. Now he worries about his future. How will he retire? Will he have enough for his daughter's college education? Can he move homes if he needs to?
>
> At one point, he needed to replace his car, because he and his wife had to travel 18 hours round trips every couple of weeks to receive prescriptions for pain medication. He was denied the credit to do so. All our healthcare professionals are on the front lines of the impact of medical debt. Doctors and other healthcare professionals experience first-hand when patients are denied care due to medical debt.

This article describes how healthcare systems deny patients with medical debt. Dr. Matt Hoffman, who is a leader in the successful effort to form a union with Doctor's Council in 2023, talked about this problem. They instructed staff to stop providing care to patients with more than $4,500 in overdue bills. Going beyond the more common practice of turning such debts over to collection agencies, he and his fellow doctors protested their health care system's decision to deny patients access to care due to medical debt.

Minnesota Attorney General Keith Ellison banned the denial of care for patients with medical debt. I mean, these practices sound like they're Byzantine. They don't sound like America, or at least who we should be.

There's a lot of New Jerseyans who are dealing with medical debt. There are a lot of New Jerseyans who are impacted by these programs that the president has already rolled back. I'm standing today because of this crisis in our country. And one of the strategies that Donald Trump and his team have talked about is to flood the zone, flood the zone, flood the zone. And so, sometimes the press doesn't even cover the cutting of some of these programs, some of these benefits that help people who are struggling with medical debt, or are struggling making ends meet, help them access healthcare. It's a level of distraction and cruelty. And again, why? Why are they cutting this? They're saying they're trying to make government more efficient or more effective. Well, it's not effective for these folks, and what are the savings going to go to?

Is it going to go to expanding medical research, expanding those things, that when taxpayers invest money on they get returned? No. They're cutting medical research. They're cutting the things that empower children to grow up and have healthy productive lives. And again, what they're aiming to do with it is to provide massive, massive tax cuts. I'm coming to the end of this section, but there are more voices that I want to include.

I'm going to read a few, and then, I think I'm going to get a question from my colleague. So a few more pages if I may, before we begin to dialogue. Or at least I'll receive a question I imagine. But I just want to elevate some of these voices. This is a person writing to me on February 28th.

> Dear Senator Booker, I'm writing to you as a concerned citizen, and most importantly as a proud aunt of a PhD in neuroscience, dedicating her life to research that could lead to life-saving treatments. As a minority in science, she has worked incredibly hard to break barriers in the field that is not always welcomed to people like her.
>
> Watching the current political attacks on research funding is not just heartbreaking, it's dangerous for our country's future. Science is not political. It serves all people regardless of race, background or party affiliation.
>
> Yes, funding cuts to agencies like NIH and the National Science Foundation threaten to halt critical research slowing the development of treatment for diseases that impact millions. These cuts will push out brilliant young scientists, many of whom have already had to fight to get where they are to do the research they're doing.
>
> This is not just about my niece, or scientists in general, it's about every American. Disease does not choose a political party. Cancer, Alzheimer's, Parkinson's and countless others, affect Republicans and Democrats alike. Without strong investment in research, we are all at risk of losing the chance for better treatments, new cures, and improved healthcare.
>
> Beyond health, defunding science will hurt our economy. Scientific research drives innovation, creates jobs, and ensures that the US remains a global leader. A country that does not invest in science is a country that falls behind.
>
> I urge you to continue standing with the scientific community, supporting young researchers from all backgrounds in fighting to protect and expand research funding. This is one of the most critical investments we can make for health, for economic growth, and for the future of every American. Thank you for your time, leadership and dedication to building a stronger, smarter, and healthier nation.

A couple New Jersey sources. This is a letter from someone in Somerset, New Jersey:

> At my university, I am extremely concerned that we are not as large an institution as some of the others, and do not get as much state aid. We rely on these funds far more than running facilities. If this goes into effect, it will ultimately lead to the loss of jobs, research, opportunities for students, and will stunt our growth as we embark on our journey to become an R1 institution. I'm not sure we could recover from this anytime soon.

Another person on these cuts to the NIH:

> I'm a postdoctoral researcher performing basic science research on bacterial communication. In short, I'm seeking to understand bacterial chemical communication to find new pathways for therapeutic development. Antibiotic research resistance is already killing thousands of Americans each year. We need new treatments provided by indirect costs to find these cures.
>
> Indirect costs actually directly funded my day-to-day work, providing funds for building maintenance staff, university-shared resources such as electron microscopes, and common laboratory supplies such as liquid nitrogen. Without any of these resources, my job and those of other researchers seeking new cures would be impossible. Thus, eliminating or reducing these funds will have a negative repercussions on the health and well-being of the American people for generations to come.

That's my constituent from Plainsboro, New Jersey.
Related to Federal grant funding freezes, another New Jerseyan writes:

> I'm a researcher at the University of New Jersey, where I study ways to combat cancer, and promote infant health, critical research that ensures generations grow into healthy adults. My aspirations aline with yours, fostering a strong, healthy and educated population.For this region, I urge you, Cory Booker, to take immediate action to restore normal Federal grant operations, so that my colleagues and I can continue making paradigm-shifting state-of-the-art discoveries with the potential to save millions of lives.
>
> This university is dependent upon Federal grants, a testament to the world-class quality of our research and its leadership in the biomedical field. These grants enable groundbreaking advancements that position the United States at the forefront of scientific information. I had planned to apply for a Federal grant in 2025 to further my research, but with the current uncertainty I'm deeply concerned about my application's future.

Here's another scientist:

> My five-year NIH grant is in its second year, and although my first-year budget ended and I submitted all the required documents, my second-year funding was cut. We need the funding to be able to continue our critical research.

Here's another patient story:

> At age 17, a large black spot blocking his vision suddenly appeared in my patient's right eye. Over the next couple of months, multiple trips to increasingly specialized doctors led to a clinical diagnosis of Von Hippel-Lindau disease, the diagnosis received by phone on his 18th birthday. This is a genetic disease in which the damaged VHL tumor suppressor gene fails to stop tumors from growing. Patients experience randomly occurring tumors in up to ten organs. And the only available treatment was surgery to try to remove the tumors.
>
> The patient is one of about 10% of patients who are de novo, the result of random genetic mutation. In this patient's case, scans had revealed not only a large tumor on the optic nerve of his right eye, but also a huge tumor encompassing one of his adrenal glands, that in retrospect had been causing him headaches, inability to concentrate, and anxiety due to consistently elevated adrenal levels. While MRI scans also related tumors in his spine, kidney, and pancreas, that this tumor and entire adrenal gland needed to be removed.
>
> After months of injections, his eye interspersed with laser treatment, he lost the vision in his right eye. The time needed for medical care required for him to give up his team sport, losing both his support group and the chance to compete at the Division One level. But he continued with his final exams, graduation, and plans to study engineering at the university. With continued regular monitoring, he was able to attend the university, but the trauma of his diagnosis and the processing of the impact of what it might mean for his life, coupled with the stress of engineering studies, brought on significant mental health challenges. He did go on to graduate, traveling to the NIH for his regular surveillance supported by various specialists.
>
> In 2022, a kidney tumor had grown large enough that he needed surgery again. The kidney is a sensitive organ, and will normally have full nephrectomy of the affected kidney. Doctors were treating him. And now at age 24, his tumor was removed in a successful kidney sparing robotic operation. Yet tumors on his spine continue to grow.
>
> This experience of my patient and many others encapsulates the miracle of medical research funding, that has such a powerful impact on people's lives. We were able to get seriously miraculous things done. But without funding for these diseases, we may never have a chance to test the ideas and develop them in a way that led to a drug that ultimately helped this patient with these tumors.
>
> This is a success story, but will we have more? Will we have others? The drug we developed is expensive. Current recommendations are to take it daily. Nothing is known about its long-term side effects, more research is done. It's not known whether patients can take breaks from the drug. Stopping at some point might mean tumors would resume.
>
> One of the Congressionally-directed medical research program grants recommended for FY25 funding is going to look precisely at many of these questions. Two others will examine other aspects of critical treatment. These are life or death issues

for the patients. And yet, this funding now is threatened. Yet this research now is threatened. Please continue to fully fund the Congressionally-directed medical program.

I'm going to read a few more and then pause, just in case my colleague wants to ask a question. But this is Kerry Muller from Texas:

> My family has benefited from Congressionally-directed medical research programs, because my thirteen-year-old daughters have neurofibromatosis, a rare genetic disease which causes uncontrolled tumor growth. My daughter, Caitlin, was diagnosed with a brain tumor two years ago. And thanks to a drug whose research was seeded with Congressionally-directed medical research program, her brain tumor has decreased to the point that is now undetectable on an MRI.
> Without this drug, she would have had to try other chemotherapy treatments that would've been more invasive, in addition to brain surgery to bypass a blockage the tumor would've caused.

This is Samantha Pearson from Las Vegas:

> For just over four years, I've been on a clinical trial at UCLA. The meds were just recently FDA approved. While the side effects sometimes made me question agreeing to the trial, being told my tumors have drastically shrunk, made it all worthwhile. My pain is decreased. My plexiform neurofibroma is 90% smaller, and I am so happy that I get to be a part of this clinical trial made possibly by NFRP, because of my participation in the drug trial.

There is story after story here of people — Camille Ollenberg, Jan Dmyutsky, Lola Newdecker, Professor Alexander Robachevsky, Kyle Retz, Carissa Heberkamp from Illinois, Samuel Curtin, Dr. Stephanie Buchs-Hoveden, Katharina Hopp, Jared Tehr, Dr. Terry Watnick, Scott Howe (Marine Corps retired), Van Stewart (United States Navy), Reid Novotny (Colonel Maryland Air National Guard), Alex and Leslie, Chip and Kristen. Greg and Molly from Denver.
William Tuttle, United States Navy:

> After my son's birth and diagnosis, I was diagnosed with tuberculosis sclerosis Complex at the age of 43, just three months after I retired from the 23 year Naval career. The complexity of this disease means that it remains to be seen whether my young son will be able to live the typical life that I have been fortunate to live. Because of research conducted through the TSCRP, my son has effective treatment options available to him, that were not even just a decade ago, but there's still so much to learn.

Again, another person benefiting from our research, benefiting from the funding that's now being threatened and cut. Beth Inland from Nevada, Shelly Mitzner, Reed Hoffman, David Brooks Carpenter, Military family, Major David Long, United States Air Force, Deborah Moritz, Fran Hyler.

I just want to say that the Declaration of Independence clearly states, "**We hold these truths to be self-evident, that all men are created equal. That they are endowed by their creator with certain unalienable rights. That among these are life, liberty, and the pursuit of happiness.**" How can you have life, liberty, and the pursuit of happiness without health? Health is at the core of life. Health is at the core of true liberty. Health is at the core of the pursuit of happiness. The right to health is fundamental for over well-being, and for the realization of other human rights.

In his annual State of the Union address to Congress on January 6th, 1941, President Franklin Delano Roosevelt underscored the importance and shared commitment to four freedoms. Many of you know them. The first freedom is freedom of speech and expression. The second is the freedom of every person to worship their own way. The third is the freedom from want, which means every person deserves peace and health, among other things he said. The fourth freedom is freedom from fear, which in our country of great wealth, no one should fear their healthcare going away.

We have known from our country's beginnings and throughout, that we must do all we can to provide for our people, and we have tried to do that over the years from Social Security Act of '65, which created Medicaid and Medicare, the Health Insurance Portability and Accountability Act of 1996, HIPAA, to the Patient Protection and Affordable Care Act of 2010, the ACA.

We should be adding to these protections and benefits trying to get more people health coverage. We should be caring for each other. We should be loving each other. We should be fighting for the justice of each other. We should be hearing the cries of parents worried for their children. We should be hearing the agony of a partner whose spouse has Alzheimer's.

We should be standing up for these folks. This is why we fight. This is why I stand.

SENATOR CHRIS MURPHY (CONNECTICUT): Senator, yield?

SENATOR BOOKER: Yes. I'll yield for a question while retaining the floor.

SENATOR CHRIS MURPHY: Senator Booker, first of all, I want to express my gratitude to you for recognizing the gravity of this moment. Your ability to see that we are facing a series of threats that are not normal, a series of threats to families, to children, to individuals, threats to our democracy, threats to our rule of law. I think it's really important and you have endeavored to do something extraordinary here, to stand on your feet for as long as you can to convey both to our colleagues and to the public that because these are not normal times, what is required of us is something different than a normal response.

And I know maybe we have extended the amount of time that you had planned to talk on this particular topic of the threat to Americans healthcare, but I don't know that there's anything more important than we're talking about today in the United States Senate, because the scope of what Republicans are talking about here is absolutely extraordinary, and I want to lay out for you a few additional facts and numbers and ask you to respond to them as you wrap up your time talking about this particular topic.

But let me just underscore what you have laid out very well. We are talking about nearly $900 billion worth of cuts to Medicaid in order to pay for about a trillion dollars worth of tax cuts for the wealthiest 1% of Americans. There will be table scraps in the Republican bill for middle-class consumers and families, but the bulk of the tax cuts are going to the very, very wealthy millionaires and billionaires, frankly, people who have done tremendously well in this country over the past several decades who are not in need of more. And so you were very right to point out the immorality of the 2017 attempt to cut the Affordable Care Act, which insured 20 million Americans, but Medicaid covers 70 to 80 million Americans. And the new wrinkle is that this proposal doesn't just cut healthcare for tens of millions of Americans. Estimates are that it could be 30 million Americans that lose healthcare under the Republican proposal.

No, this is even more difficult to swallow for the American public than the 2017 attempt to cut and eliminate the Affordable Care Act because this measure is a direct transfer of money from the poor and the middle class, the people who are on Medicaid to the very, very wealthy. Frankly, it could turn out to be the biggest transfer of wealth in the history of the country from the poor and the middle class to the wealthy, which is why I think you are taking this extraordinary step to make sure that our colleagues and the American people know the gravity of this moment. A lot of Republicans all across the country are not doing town halls any longer. They are not meeting in person with their constituents.

And so there's a lot of Americans that are going to be in the dark that have a lot of questions, have a lot of questions about what's happening here, about why it is necessary to cut a program like Medicaid that ensures 24% of Americans to the bone in order to finance the tax cut for the very, very wealthy. One of the things I just wanted to set up for you here is just to note that Americans may be surprised to know that 24% of Americans are actually on Medicaid today. Because some Americans may say, "Well, my insurance isn't Medicaid, my insurance is through MississippiCAN", or "my insurance is through ACCESSNebraska", or "my insurance is through Centennial Care" or in Connecticut, "my insurance is through HUSKY Health". In New Jersey, it's New Jersey Family Care, right? So Medicaid normally isn't called Medicaid. It's called something different in every state.

And so it's important for you to understand that so many of your neighbors are on Medicaid even though it may not be called Medicaid in your state. That's how we get to 24% of American families on this particular program. And the Joint Economic Committee, which is a Committee of

Congress, did a study, issued a report talking about how many people would lose their healthcare insurance on a state-by-state basis if this $880 billion cut to Medicaid went through, and I won't go through the whole list, Senator Booker, but I just pulled out some states that are represented by our Republican colleagues. In Alabama, 20% of Alabamans are on their Medicaid program and in total 330,000 people in one state, in Alabama would lose their healthcare if this cut went through. In Arkansas, 25% of families are on the Arkansas Medicaid program. A quarter million people would lose their health insurance. In Florida, 17% of the state is on Medicaid, 1.3 million Floridians could lose their healthcare because of these Medicaid cuts.

We can just go on and on. 20% of Iowans are on the Medicaid program. 20% of Indiana residents, 25% of Kentucky residents, 30% of Louisianans are on their state's Medicaid program. Five-hundred-thousand residents of Louisiana could lose their healthcare. Some of that would happen in a sort of slow-moving catastrophe. But as you pointed out, Senator Booker, a lot of that would happen immediately because many of the states that have taken advantage of the Affordable Care Act Medicaid expansion have a built-in clause to their state's law that says the minute the reimbursement rate declines, even if it declines by only a few percentage points, the entirety of the Medicaid expansion program is eliminated. So overnight you will have millions of people who will lose their healthcare insurance. But as you have rightly pointed out, that's just the beginning of the disaster because there are hundreds of rural hospitals in this country that are right now living on the brink of disaster.

If Medicaid reimbursements drop just by 5 or 10%, those rural hospitals are out of business. Same can be said of thousands of drug treatment centers in this country, addiction treatment centers. And so you're ultimately talking about hundreds if not thousands of hospitals and health centers closing, millions of Americans losing their healthcare insurance and for what, and for what? To be able to hoard a bunch of money so that the richest Americans can buy a third vacation home so that millionaires can double their landscaping budget. Who's asking for this in America today?

Of course there's a conversation to be had about efficiency in our healthcare programs, but none of that conversation is happening here. If it was, you wouldn't be reading the letters of all of these associations representing healthcare groups predicting disaster. They would actually be in the room at the table because if you really wanted to save money, you'd actually put the doctors in the hospitals and the medical providers who know something about the system in a room.

But instead, this is a political decision that's been made to cut a certain amount of money that does not coincidentally line up to the amount of money that the Republican budget bill wants to give in tax cuts to the very, very wealthy. And so you, I think rightly put emphasis and drew attention to John McCain's decision. And of course, we should always give credit to Lisa Murkowski and Susan Collins who also voted no in 2017 on the repeal of the Affordable Care Act bill because it's just a reminder that you are under no obligation as a United States Senator to do the wrong thing if you know what the right thing is. You work so hard to get this job, spend your entire life working to become somebody who can make important decisions like we can in the United States Senate, and you are under no obligation to outsource your decision making to the President of the United States or your party leadership.

Everybody here gets to make an independent decision on what's right or wrong, and this just feels plain wrong. A thoughtless, unplanned, massive cut in Medicaid that's going to throw millions of people off their healthcare in order to finance a tax cut, the majority of which is going to go to people who don't need it. Every senator here can make up their own mind as to whether that is the right thing or the wrong thing to do for this country. And the exercise that you are engaged in, Senator Booker, is a simple one. Just trying to make sure that all the facts are on the table. That last segment you did on the impact on medical research should be reason alone for folks to reconsider the path this administration is taking, but the Medicaid cuts as a mechanism to further enrich those that are already plenty rich. Man, I just don't imagine that is anything that the American public are clamoring for.

And so, Senator Booker, I just wanted to really thank you for standing up and making this moment possible and I want to leave you with just two stories on this topic that have come into my office and then ask you a question. This is all a lead up to a question. So I have a constituent who was paralyzed about a decade ago and he now exists in a wheelchair and the only insurance program that can provide him with what he needs from a mechanical and technological standpoint, plus the drugs he needs to survive is Medicaid. It's his only option. It's his only option. He can't work, he's paralyzed. Medicaid is his only option and for him and for millions of others, Medicaid is life or death. It's just life or death.

If you're talking about cutting Medicaid by as much as 20%, that's what we're talking about here today, an $880 billion cut to Medicaid represents about 10% of the overall program. But you have to assume that states are not going to continue to match if the federal government isn't putting in their share. So that 10% cut could very quickly become something closer to a 20% cut. There is no way that you can cut the Medicaid program by 20% without it impacting people like my constituent in a wheelchair who comes to many of my events when we protest these Medicaid cuts. This is life or death for many Americans, but that's not the full extent of the horror that will happen.

I was just reading a letter the other day from an 80-year-old constituent of mine who lives at home with his wife, but his wife is very frail and it is Medicaid and Connecticut's Medicaid waiver that allows for her to receive in-home healthcare services. And he is panicked. He wants to spend the final years of his life with his wife and he knows that if Medicaid gets cut even on the margins, that Medicaid waiver likely is gone and either his wife will pass or she will have to be in an institution. Query whether that institution will be able to even give her a place because two-thirds of nursing home beds in this country are paid for by Medicaid. And so one way or the other, he is staring separation from his wife in the eye. She either doesn't make it without the Medicaid reimbursement that gives her the services at home or she is forced to go to an institution and they live separately for their final days.

This is the reality facing people who rely on Medicaid whether you are disabled or elderly, this is the reality that will be imposed on millions of Americans in order to finance a tax cut for the wealthy. The scope of this is just enormous, Senator Booker. And so I guess this is the question I wanted to ask you. You and I have been in government for a long time. We've served in a variety of different capacities. I don't think this country is really ready for the scope of the healthcare cataclysm that could come with a trillion dollar cut to the health insurance program that is responsible for the care of one-quarter of Americans, two-thirds of nursing home beds, and the budgets of literally tens of thousands of vital healthcare institutions in this country.

And so nobody is better than you at conveying the moral consequences of the decisions we make here. Just share with us for a minute as you sort of wrap up a conversation on this topic of the healthcare priorities of the Trump administration and the Republican Congress, what America may look like in a world where we have decided to gut the program, the health insurance program of last resort for the most vulnerable Americans and the health insurance program that ensures 24% of Americans, two-thirds of which are working for a living. Just give us a little bit of a sense of the enormity of the consequence that this ultimately would bring to this country.

SENATOR BOOKER: So first of all, thank you for the question, but I just want to reiterate the friendship I have with Chris Murphy and his willingness to spend the night with me here on the floor as we go hour after hour after hour. And I just want to say this again and I'm going to say it a few times in this long speech that will go on for as long as I'm physically able.

Chris, the last time we spent 15 hours on this floor together was a health issue. It was yet another stunning mass shooting, this time at the Pulse Nightclub. And you and I talked a lot before we got on this floor, and I think the agony that you and I were feeling was, how can this be the strongest nation in the world ... organized government? If you read our founding documents, if you read our Founding Fathers, one of the first things they organized this government for — it's good to carry around the Constitution.

It is so important to understand what the preamble to the Constitution says we are about: "**We the People of the United States, in order to form a more perfect union, establish justice, ensure domestic tranquility, provide for the common defense, promote the general welfare and secure the blessings of liberty to ourselves and our prosperity, do ordain and establish the constitution of United States, which each one of us, each one of us in this body went down there and swore an oath to uphold.**" Those are the first words of this, Chris, and God, I remember your agony.

Folks, I want you to know when I came to this body, my staff was talking about the maiden speech, the maiden speech. Please don't go look back and look at my maiden speech. It was not great. But the maiden speech my staff wanted me to watch was yours and it was gut-wrenching about Newtown, gut-wrenching that the strongest nation on the planet earth should now be this nation where we tell our children in this implicit lesson, not explicit, but implicit lesson, we are going to teach you how to hide. We're going to run actor shooter drills because we can't protect you.

And my mom lives in Vegas, in that Vegas shooting, shooting at a synagogue in Pittsburgh. And so here we were in yet another of these maddening realities in our country that the leading cause of death for our children is shooting. And in our conversations leading up to it, I still remember you and I saying, "We need to come to this floor." And you said, "I'm going to stand and do something different." And we again, just like tonight, we had no end to that. We were nine years younger, my friend, and we said we were going to stand down here and try to get this body to do something different, to try to get this body to recognize the gravity of what was going on in the strongest nation on the earth that was having child after child after child, American after American dying to gun violence.

And the response we were getting from this body, the world's most deliberative body was, "Nothing's going to change. We can't do anything." I mean, I'm going to give you respect. Years later, you were part of the first gun legislation to pass out of this body in 30-something years. And now I just found out that the community violence intervention money that you allowed me to fight so hard to get in that bill is being clawed back by Donald Trump, our bipartisan bill, our bipartisan-approved finances, money. And I think of taking away of our power in this body from the bill that you were one of the main architects of with Republican colleagues, God bless them, people like Cornyn and others. And so I just want to take people back to what the insider conversations and you were generous. I want to remind you just teasingly on the floor, you never asked me if you could publish my text messages, but you put them in your book.

SENATOR MURPHY: I did.

SENATOR BOOKER: It's a great book. I actually learned, I read lots of my colleagues' books. I learned a lot of data about gun violence from your book. And we were talking about this belief that these words, this belief in our country, that these words, why this government was formed, is so important. Just America, this is who we are, these imperfect geniuses. We form this, "**We the People, in order to form a more perfect union, establish justice, ensure domestic tranquility, provide for the common defense, promote the general welfare and secure the blessings of liberty.**" And so you stood right down there for 15 hours. I paced this room pledging to you that I wouldn't go to the bathroom, I wouldn't sit down and I was hurting after 15 hours. But you were steadfast until we finally got Mitch McConnell to give us something. It was one or two votes. It was two votes. And both of them failed.

We didn't get 60, but at least what we forced this institution to duke to confront the horrendous horrors of that nightclub shooting. And so you ask me now as you and I and my dear brother who I've known since he was coming out of college, three of us on this floor at a new day. It's past midnight, a new month, it's past midnight as we sit here. Why? Because of your question. I can't stand anymore to live in a country where it seems that these convulsions come, that threaten our most vulnerable over and over again. I can't stand it. I have to stand up. I have to speak up.

We have to do something different yet again, you and I talked about this last week. America, we are not doing a good job right now. We read the section about medical debt. Tens of millions of Americans are saddled with medical debt — 66% of the people that declare bankruptcies because they can't afford their medical bills because something that happened to them could happen to us and our families. My mother, my brother, and I have a lot of challenges, a lot of problems, but we weren't saddled with a rare disease. We didn't have tumors springing up all over our bodies. I don't know what that would've done to my family.

SENATOR MURPHY: Will the Gentleman yield?

SENATOR BOOKER: Yes.

SENATOR MURPHY: There is so much similarity between the debate that you are forcing this Senate to have tonight and the debate that we were having back in 2016 on this epidemic of gun violence. I always describe it this way, the only thing that matters, the thing that matters more than anything else in your life is protecting your loved ones from physical harm. You would give anything, anything, you would give your life-saving, your house. You would perhaps give your own life in order to protect your child or your brother or sister or mother or father from physical harm. And so when you and I have sat across from the victims of gun violence, many of which live in your neighborhood, in my neighborhood, in Newark and Hartford, we are looking at a kind of desperation and sorrow that is unique. That is unique that comes with not just losing a loved one to gun violence, but feeling powerless in that exercise, feeling like there was nothing you could do.

And watching your elected leaders stand by and allow for this reality to continue to occur in your neighborhood, where kids are being shot down in cold blood, and your elected leaders, the adults in charge of your community are standing idly by. That is not fundamentally different than the reality that will be visited upon millions of families if this size of a cut in Medicaid funding goes into effect because families out there who rely on Medicaid to keep alive their son or daughter who has a complicated medical disease have no other quarter, have no other last resort besides Medicaid.

And so Medicaid stands between life and death for their son or daughter. There is no other place for them to go. And so that same empty hollow look that we have seen so many times in the eyes of a mother or father who lost a son or daughter to gun violence, that is the look that we are choosing to visit upon millions of families in this country who when faced with the loss of their only health insurance option for their disabled child will watch their child potentially face the same fate as those young men in your neighborhood and my neighborhood. And so that's the reason why I pose this question to you that you're answering about the moral gravity of this moment because it is not fundamentally different than the one that brought us here in 2016.

SENATOR BOOKER: In answering this question, and again, I'm going to continue to yield the question to you while retaining the floor. I want to just compound this for people because I know these numbers, 880 billion, 100 million Americans that would be affected directly by Medicaid cuts or the people that work in the hospitals that would be affected by Medicaid cuts or the nursing homes that are affected by Medicaid cuts. These are big, big numbers, but people, these are human beings. I live in a community that had a horrible lead poisoning problem for their kids that had horrible toxic sites and children born around toxic Superfund sites, as you know they're called, have higher rates of autism, higher rates of birth defects. And so even coming up as a city council person, I saw that the environmental injustices surrounding my community were causing parents to have to deal with medical complications amongst their children at alarming rates and needed help. And Medicaid was the program, no fault of their own — environmental injustice. Now here's the double insult of the Trump administration. One is they gutted the environmental justice section at the DOJ.

They're not investigating corporate polluters. They're not investigating the injustices environmentally that big, powerful, wealthy people do that often cause people – we all saw Erin Brockovich – that cause people to get seriously hurt. And then the second part of that insult is we're not only not going to hold people accountable and let them get away with that, the polluters or the folks causing often the source of the disease. We're now not going to help get healthcare to the families who often live in fragile communities that have these resources. These are the people when you sit with them in your office, as you and I have, as me and the other senator from New Jersey on the floor tonight have, as you sit with them and they tell you their stories and you see that this is a lifeline, that this Medicaid program and you are so good by telling people because I saw this during the Affordable Care Act. Just the name alone, people [were] like, "I don't have Obamacare."

Yes, you have the ACA. And let me explain it to you. It's under many different names, including in my state that people don't know that this is a Medicaid-funded program. So they don't know that this is a sort of damocles at their family's well-being.

But this is the larger issue, Senator Murphy, is that these are real people in every county, in every state. It's why they're representatives. It's why I read statements demanding there not to be cuts by the organizations bipartisanly read the League of Cities, the largest mayor association, Republican governors and others are all saying, "Do not cut this program." They're not even saying, "Don't do 880 million, maybe just do 400 million." They're saying, "Do not cut this program."

And many of them are saying, "In fact, we need to find ways to expand the program because there's still gaps that people are falling into." And it doesn't make economic sense because if you get regular care, if your chronic disease is treated, it ultimately could be cheaper to the taxpayer as opposed to people ending up in hospitals. But those hospitals now, because of what's being threatened in this bill, rural hospitals, and tier one trauma hospitals are all being threatened in their care. And so tonight it's not normal.

At a mass shooting on 12 June 2016 at Pulse Nightclub in Orlando, 49 people were killed by a lone gunman. Deemed a terrorist attack by the FBI, it was the deadliest mass shooting in the United States since 1949 until the 2017 Las Vegas shooting.

12:15 AM - Social Security

I ask everybody to understand this is not a normal moment in America. This is a crossroads moment in America. It's one of those times where the values that we talk about in the Constitution are at stake. What is going to define us, our commitments to ideals of justice, fairness, of being there for each other.

And one of those other programs that is now in crisis is what I want to switch to. And I think that my colleague was joking with me because we have – for anybody who's watching – we have a whole list of things we wanted to get to. And my staff now seemingly, very ambitiously, Medicaid, Medicare, healthcare, Social Security's coming up now, tariffs and economic policy, education, national security, public safety, immigration, housing — chapter by chapter, each one about an hour or so. This would be enough to make it until tomorrow evening if I can stand that long.

And who knows? But we're behind schedule, so I'm going to jump into talk about Social Security. And I want to start because as I said earlier, I get to stand here. I get to come on this floor, but so many millions of people don't. And I want to elevate their voices tonight because as I go across New Jersey, as I go across my nation, I see Republicans, Democrats, independents, veterans, so many people stopping me in airports, stopping me in the community, stopping me in the grocery store, wanting to tell me that they're afraid, that they're angry, that they're worried, that they believe we are in crisis. That our nation is at a crossroads. Who are we going to be as a nation? And this topic ... I don't know. If maybe I will just let you all know that this topic; my mom chewed into me about this topic.

She lives in a senior citizen retirement community, mostly Republican. I visit her many times. It's a great community. I hate how we go to this idea of Right or Left. These are great seniors that live in a great community and they're talking about Social Security. So I want to read... start before this section by just reading. This is how people are sending it to me. This is a small postcard, handwritten from somebody from Hamilton Square, New Jersey:

> Dear, Senator Booker, I'm writing to ask you if my Social Security is now in danger, please let me know. It is very important to me, thank you.

I'm going to try to answer that tonight, fairly and candidly.

Here's another person who writes. My staff is protecting their identity. I just want to say where they're from — South Plains New Jersey.

> I am one of your constituents in a proud New Jersian, and I'm writing to let you know how upset, distraught, and worried I am about the current state of our country. I hope you'll take time and read my letter as this is the first time I have felt compelled to write a government official.

I want to tell you, I'm reading your letter again, and I'm now reading it on national TV, if C-SPAN can be. (Presiding Officer might challenge me with a factual error, but C-SPAN is national TV, I think.)

> I want to start by telling you a little about myself. I am 64 years old and I am currently working full time. I am a breast cancer survivor. My plan was to retire in the next three years, but with the current state of chaos and turmoil, I honestly don't see how I can retire. I'm concerned about Medicare, which I will definitely need when I retire. I will also need a supplemental plan for whatever Medicare does not cover. I do not qualify for retirement benefits through my job. With the cuts being made to federal programs, Medicare will not be enough. I would need a more expensive supplemental plan to cover these cuts.
>
> I am also concerned about Social Security. I have worked since I was 16 except for nine years when I was home with my three children. I have worked hard and paid into Social Security and believed that the money was for my retirement. Now I hear that Social Security is a Ponzi scheme and it may be privatized. This is so unfair for people like me that worked hard all their life and counted on this money to retire. I was planning on working past 65 to get my full Social Security benefits, but now I begin to wonder if it's worth it. {Now I begin to wonder if it's worth it.}
>
> So at this point I'm in a holding pattern due to the unstable climate in which we are all living. As I said, I have three children who are all adults now. My son has been diagnosed as being bipolar. He's been hospitalized a few times due to this. He's currently on medication that he needs to function and sees a therapist. He is in grad school and is on Medicaid. He works part-time since he is a full-time grad student, so he does not qualify for benefits.
>
> I worry about what these cuts will do to my son and others like him. No one seems concerned with the people who rely on these programs to live their best life. Someone needs to look out and take an interest in helping people in these circumstances.
>
> My daughter is a teacher in a district that receives Title I funds. She works very hard as a teacher and is devoted to her students. With the supposed dismantling of the Department of Education, I'm concerned about what this means to the education field. Teachers, administration and students. My daughter's school is making a difference in the lives of these students and they need the funding that is received from both the state and federal government. Programs like the Title I and other federally funded programs need to stay in place.
>
> On another topic...

This constituent is getting a lot into her first letter to a government official and I appreciate it.

> On another topic, inflation increasing prices and the overpriced housing market is a huge problem. Placing tariffs on our biggest trade partners is beyond unfair. This drives the cost of goods up and the consumer is the one who ends up paying the increase. A lot of families are food insecure wondering where their next meal is coming from. A lot of parents go without so their children can eat. Food pantries and banks are scrambling to meet demand. Something needs to be done so families can survive.
>
> The housing market is also an issue. Owning your own home is now unreachable for most young people starting out. Interest rates are high and housing prices in New Jersey are unaffordable. Thank you for reading my letter. I'm asking you as our senator, please stand up for what is in the best interest of families, seniors, adults, and children in your district.
>
> Tariffs, dismantling departments like Social Security, Medicare, Medicaid, education and other services that are important to the everyday person is not the answer. You are our voice in the Senate. Please do the right thing and speak up and continue to fight for everyday Americans.

This is why I'm standing up. This is why I will stand here as long as I'm physically able. This is why I will continue to tell story after story, but first a little important history. [For] 90 years our country has made a promise to people that if you pay into the Social Security program your whole life, that money will be there for you when you retire. Franklin Roosevelt signed the Social Security Act into law 84 years ago, and this is his quote. He called it a "cornerstone and a structure which is being built, but it is by no means complete". Social Security is still a cornerstone. It's still the bedrock, according to FDR, it's the bedrock of an edifice being built in a nation where we belong to each other. We the People building this, that's our cornerstone. He called it the Social Security.

Today, 73 million Americans count on Social Security. Millions more than that are planning on those benefits they earned being there for them. You heard from the first letters I read that people are really worried. [The] President of the United States stood up in a State of the Union Address and talked about rampant fraud because payments are going out. All that from conservative papers to ones on the other side have showed that what he was saying was not true, but they're sowing chaos. They're attacking, delegitimizing it, calling it a Ponzi scheme — DOGE leader Musk and the President. But 73 million Americans are counting on sociality benefits and 1.6 million in my state. 40% of people rely on Social Security. Forty percent have no other source of income. They live paycheck to paycheck. Social Security checks, excuse me, Social Security checks.

And despite mocking Social Security, calling it a Ponzi scheme, that had communities like my parents, my mom's, people beginning to worry, they actually took real actions to lay off thousands of Social Security employees, making it harder to process Social Security applications and troubleshoot questions from beneficiaries. They didn't roll out a plan to say, "Hey, this is how we are going to show that we can do the best customer service ever. We're going to bring some of the best private sector people in to advise on how we can use technology and innovation to give the best customer service. Hell, roll in AI, do all these things. We're going to make a model of responsiveness to our seniors because we're a society that respects our elders, values them, wants them to retire in dignity and security and peace of mind. That's the big ambition." No, that's not what was said.

Social Security employees, like many employees, got letters that they didn't expect, saying they were laid off. Didn't matter how well they performed, it didn't matter what function they performed, and it put in jeopardy just trying to contact Social Security if you're retiring. Just trying to contact Social Security, if you need to apply for benefits. They tried to eliminate service by phone, saying that they wanted to require in-person visits, which is absurd for many seniors that don't have access to transportation or live in rural areas, because you know what they're doing also is that they're trying to close down many Social Security offices. I'm going to get to the specifics of that later. These actions are harmful enough, but they're just the beginning of what our President and Elon Musk are saying they want to do to a program that for millions of Americans, it's their only check a week. It's essential for them and others, it's how they make their retirement secure.

You don't protect the future by punishing the people who built this country. You don't fix America by throwing seniors or veterans or Americans with disabilities under the bus. That's not how we do things. That's not how we should do things. There's so many hardworking families that believed in this idea, if I work hard all my life in America, I can make ends meet, I can raise my kids and I can retire with dignity. Congress does have a responsibility to be good stewards of taxpayer dollars. We should do more of that. I want to do more of that. I want to help lead in that fight, but none of us were invited to a table when it came to this. This congressionally established program – FDR, I read – but it was Congress that established it is now not being included in the planning or procedures to try to improve Social Security or make it more efficient or more effective. We haven't convened hearings or task forces in a bipartisan way to find out what we can do to better serve our seniors.

Instead, lies are being proffered about Social Security making wrongful payments. Lies are being proffered by the highest office in the land. The most richest person in the land, who does not need Social Security, is calling it a Ponzi scheme, telling people who are relying on it, they're part of a Ponzi scheme. But remember this, Social Security is not the government's money to spend. It's the hard-earned savings of working Americans and it belongs to Americans. The President and Elon Musk need to keep their hands off of it. It's not theirs to take, and it's not theirs to break. Their scheme ... they're the ones that have a scheme. And it's not about efficiency, it's not visionary. What we need in America now is visionary leaders that have bold, exciting visions for what things like Social Security can be and what they're doing is not only wrong, it hurts people. It scares people.

And not just people — our elders. The people who raised us, the people who built roads and highways, the people who served food, made food, who started small businesses, raised generations. That's who we're disrespecting. And so what happens in this context, why am I standing here? Is because the people of New Jersey are saying, "Why aren't you doing more? This is unacceptable Senator Booker, it's unacceptable." Here are voices — and my phones have exploded with people that the President and Elon Musk have made terrified about what's happening to the Social Security Service and what's happening to their checks.

My staff said that we were overwhelmed with phone calls and emails from people who are worried about the direction that the President is taking Social Security. They use words to be that people who called were angry and terrified. I want to share some of these calls from constituents. Here's someone from the great Cherry Hill, New Jersey:

> I'm very concerned that the President along with his cruel and inept administration and DOGE are working to privatize and ruin the Social Security program. I am a constituent, Senator Booker. I live in Cherry Hill, New Jersey and I'm a senior who relies on Social Security income for my basic needs, food and housing. The mere idea of not having those funds has caused me sleepless nights and wondering if I will become homeless.

I'm going to stop there for a second. I remember this President FDR growing up, hearing that what he did was get on the radio not to stir up fear, not to stir up chaos, but to comfort people, to remind them that we are Americans. You have no need to fear, but this President, just with his rhetoric alone about Social Security, is driving my constituents to write me notes like this. I continue with the letter from my constituent from Cherry Hill.

> I hope you'll convince both Democrats and Republican colleagues to prevent this from happening. Trump lied when he promised during his campaign he would not touch the Social Security Administration, but now we see threats and already some actions towards making severe cuts and making the program less accessible. I urge you to continue to fight for us.

Pennington, New Jersey:

> My sister and I are older Americans who are each disabled. One from a severe accident because of a drunk driver and the other from a life-changing illness. We are alone and take care of each other. For me, SSDI is my one and only income. I have a few years before I am at full retirement age. Even with my check and splitting rent costs between us, it is taking right under 50% of my monthly check for rent alone.
>
> {Fifty percent. *Fifty percent.*}
>
> This does not leave much to cover even the bare necessities of health, vehicle insurance, utilities, foods, medicine, even a tight budget, especially with costs on everything continuing to rise. Senator, as seniors, we are petrified about what's happening to SSA. I must ask you, Senator, what do we do if our monthly SSA benefits are interrupted? How do we keep a roof over our heads as disabled seniors. With very limited savings, it would only take a few months before the roof over our heads would be in jeopardy. We just spent a small fortune for us to move into a smaller lower cost apartment because we could not afford significant ongoing rent increases. I realize we are far from alone in our fears, but that is of very little comfort as we spend our nights unable to sleep, fearful we do not lose our only income along with the roof over our heads.

This is our elders. Here's a constituent from Egg Harbor Township:

> My husband and I live Social Security check to Social Security check. Without those checks we earned... Without those checks we earned, we are dead. Please don't let this outrageous administration take our benefits away.

This is a constituent from Runnemede, New Jersey:

> I am a 75-year-old New Jersey resident. I received my working papers in 1964. At the age of 14. I worked continuously until I reached the age of 70 in 2020. I enlisted in the United States Navy in '67 and retired in '99. I was on active duty from 1970 to '77. I finished my career in the Naval Reserve for 56 years. I paid my taxes and contributed to Social Security. I have collected my Social Security for four years and as you are no doubt aware, the amount of money paid me monthly by Social Security Act was calculated by them based on my contribution.
>
> I'm currently a full-time, 24/7 caretaker for my invalid wife and do not have the luxury of earning a supplemental income. My sole income is from Social Security and a small Naval reserve pension. My total healthcare comes from Medicare and TRICARE for Life. The contract I made with the United States government was that they could use my money during my working life with the understanding that they would take care of me when I could no longer earn for myself. I have kept my part of this bargain for 56 years.
>
> Now after only four years, the government is threatening to renege on our agreement. Please sir, do not let this happen, Senator Booker. That is my money. I earned it. I earned my Social Security by my contributions and I earned my pension by my service.

Another constituent named Sarah:

> I have been a teacher in Atlantic County for 26 years. My husband is a 100% disabled veteran who receives VA disability payments as well as SSDI. We depend on the VA and SSDI for approximately half of our income for our family of five. We are currently preparing our oldest for his first year at college and awaiting financial aid packages from several schools.
>
> We are petrified that Trump and Musk's agenda is dangerous and will have life altering consequences for families like ours. We are counting on you Senator Booker, to do the hard work to protect the essential benefits. The destruction of the Department of Education is another completely horrifying situation. We need to protect our special needs students and federal financial aid for college bound students. We need to protect the idea of education is for all. {Education is for all.} Education is for all instead of a few elites who could just afford it.

Rosie is another constituent. She starts off proudly:

> I am a senior, 84 years old. {God bless you, Rosie. My mom is 85.} My only income is Social Security. {She generously gives me confidential information.} My only income is Social Security. $1,179 per month and I am terrified that the current gang of thieves in the White House will tamper with it under the guise of "saving money". If Social Security is cut off, I am on the streets.

I again can't keep harping enough on the traditions of our country where Presidents, whether you agreed with them or not, whether they're from your party or not, Ronald Reagan didn't whip up fear on bedrock commitments like Social Security or health. Barack Obama didn't shake people so that Republicans and Democrats in my state would write me letters using words like fear and terror — wouldn't use worries about losing sleep when you have enough things to stress over.

Here's Deborah:

> I am a retired widow. I depend on Social Security to pay bills each month. I'm concerned about the reports that Elon Musk is to revamp and in my opinion, ruin the Social Security Administration. I'm worried that payments will be disrupted. There are many other things going on in the government today that I'm also concerned about. I hope that the seniors and congresspeople, along with the judicial system, can stand up to him and take back control of government. Look, it's going to revamp and ruin Social Security.

This is just somebody simply saying it like, "Be plain. Don't make up lies about false payments. Don't call it a Ponzi scheme. Give us a bold vision of how it's going to help more seniors. How are you going to serve more seniors? How are you going to improve the system? How are you going to make it better? How are you going to serve the dignity of our seniors?"

This is Holly — Holly is a constituent too.

> I am one of your constituents who's retired and relies 100% in order to live on my earned Social Security benefit in which I paid throughout my entire working career. I call on you to maintain Social Security program as it stood before the ascension of Trump and Musk. You must ensure that there are no missed earned benefit payments or late payments made to recipients, especially accessible Social Security offices must remain open and fully staffed, staffed with trained, experienced Social Security employees in order to provide the kind of regular necessary customer service by phone, online and in person. And the Trump Musk administration's endless terrorist threats of dismantling the Social Security Administration insidiously calling it a Ponzi scheme, working in order to privatize it must cease and desist immediately.
>
> Moreover, you, Cory Booker, must reverse and or stop whatever draconian changes are being made to destroy the Social Security Administration with thousands of cuts to needed employees with almost no notice and no public imput. Social Security is being dismantled by an unelected billionaire, at least for now, Musk and his band of DOGE boys, not a real government department who have illegally and callously rifled through our most private personal information and done God knows what with it, with their ultimate goal to risk and or steal the retirement funds of older Americans by placing the Social Security Trust fund in the hand of private corporate equity firms.
>
> Seniors do not agree to this. Seniors do not agree to this and such action is a legal and completely unacceptable! {This constituent continues...} Furthermore, I'm deeply concerned that the ceaseless chaos will invite criminals to exploit confusion around identity verification. Ironically, while the administration claims these changes are meant to combat fraud, they may very well do the opposite. Hastily introducing new, unfamiliar technology and verification steps without any real public education campaign will create the perfect environment for criminals to deceive and defraud.
>
> This latest ill-conceived change also comes at a time when the Social Security Administration is already struggling with a customer service crisis. Long hold times, low staffing, delayed callback systems, confusing announcements about possible office closures. This chaos has to be stopped now Senator Booker. I urgently ask you to please use your congressional power to reverse these changes which are creating more confusion for older Americans.
>
> Senior Americans earn Social Security through a lifetime of hard, honest work. I know I did. The money is ours and we deserve a properly run Social Security Administration, which continues to be administrated honestly through the federal government as established in 1935.
>
> In fact, the narrative of the Social Security Act running out of money could be easily fixed if Congress wrote laws that slightly increased the amount that high net worth individuals, the wealthiest of the wealthy paid into the program.

Holly, God bless you. My mother, in her senior community, is seeing this rise in scammers trying to steal people's money, and she's amazed at the technology they're using. Scams that involve the voices of their relatives asking them for help. They're in a crisis. All that technology and the wisdom of my mom. She's like, "Why aren't we using the technology and innovations to make Social Security easier to use, easier to engage with?" Common sense questions.

Carly, a constituent from New Jersey:

> Please include disabled people when you talk about Social Security and Medicare, Senator Booker, if you don't mention us, every time. I paid into Social Security for 16 years, I worked full time. I was sick almost every day. I finally had to leave my job in 2015. I was granted SSDI and I'm on Medicare and until I was injured last year, I had a part-time job where I continued paying into the system.
>
> I fear that the first people they will go after are the disabled. We are not as capable of fighting. People see us as lazy or fakers and we're almost never included in the conversations about marginalized communities. Please don't let me be erased.

Carly, you are not. I see you and I'm standing here for as long as I possibly physically can so that I can elevate your voice and others.

Patricia, a constituent from New Jersey:

> I am 65 years old, a senior. I have worked my whole life and paid into Social Security. Will you please work hard and push back to preserve these benefits. Without Social Security monies and Medicare as well, I will not survive. I am outraged {Patricia writes...} to see what is happening recently. Help. If there's anything you, quest of me, if there's anything you... {My constituent says...} If there's anything you need of me, please let me know.

It's one of the most beautiful sentiments in America is that people in crisis, who are wrapped with fear and worry, they still are standing up to volunteer. Retired seniors. I'm always moved when a constituent just not only tells me what's on their mind, how they're angry, how they're worried, what their concerns are, but they also say, "Let me help you. Let me help you." Patricia, it's late at night. You're probably sleeping, but you help me tonight at 12:41 AM.

The goodness and the decency of our seniors, the kindness and generosity of our communities and what does our President do to these people? He spends time of his State of the Union Address not calling us together, not calling us to common cause, not reminding us that we share common values and common virtues. He spreads lies about Social Security and unleashes the wealthiest man in the world to cut before he even understands the agencies he's cutting. A guy who with the same kind of cynical nature, who I can't even fathom being as wealthy as he is. It's not what I've sought in my life. He tells a Ponzi scheme when constituent after constituent tell me that is their only source of income that they paid into all of their lives and now the most powerful person on the planet and the richest person on the planet are striking fear and worry into seniors.

And yet all of that power, all of that money, a constituent from New Jersey tells me about what she's concerned with and then says, if there's anything you request of me, "Please let me know. I am here to help. I'm here to help." That's the country I know and love. Not the fearmongers and the demagogues and the spreaders of lies, but the good decency of Americans who even in their time of crisis ask the question, "How can I help? How can I help?"

Helen from New Jersey:

> Senator Booker, please stand up to Musk and Trump to save, protect Social Security and Medicare. My life and my husband's life depend on it. We are senior citizens who worked and paid our share of taxes for over 50 years. We now need those benefits to survive.

And here is Janet, one of the hundreds – I'm sorry to my staff – thousands of people who've written, emailed, and called.

One more, Janet:

> I oppose the closing of Social Security field offices. If anything, more field offices should be opened if phone support is cut back. In 2022, while living in Wyoming, I started on Social Security. There were issues. Thank and thank God for the local field office in Cheyenne because they were the only people who could physically look at my documentation, realize what was happening to me, submit corrections and enter notes in the system that the Social Security phone support could see. It took four or five trips to my local field office to resolve it. I had previously gotten nowhere with Social Security phone support.
>
> Today I read the list of field offices that are slated to be closed and they appear to be in rural areas. The people who live there might have to drive a full day's drive several times to apply for and follow up on their benefits. It is not fair.

It is not fair. It is not fair. It is not fair...

Across the country my office hears from... it's not just New Jersey. Across the country, people who are frustrated, who feel like nobody will listen to them, we get calls from across the country. My staff doesn't say, "You're not from New Jersey so we're not going to talk to you." My staff, just incredible people I have surrounding me in the office who remind me of the values I treasure, and so they wanted me to include tonight people not from New Jersey, because again, we hear from thousands of people in my state and so many around the country.

Here's Maria Karachi from Springfield, Delaware County, Pennsylvania:

" My name is Maria Karachi. {Forgive me, Maria, if I'm pronouncing your name wrong.} I am 78 years old and live in Springfield, Delaware County, Pennsylvania. When I was 16, I received my first paycheck, and so money was taken from my earnings. I learned then about FICA, the special government savings account that I would put part of my earnings into until I retired. This was how I could pay my bills in my old age, it was something I could always count on. My earnings history shows the good and bad times, including the gaps when I received unemployment. My chosen career was in mortgage banking, bank mergers, dramatic changes to interest rates and even bank lending regulations meant times of unemployment with few options or jobs or accepting temp employment. I had to make the choice. Every paycheck withheld FICA.

I was almost 65 when I began my career at the bank offering decent pay with overtime. It was 2010 and I had two goals to meet for my retirement, a mortgage-free home and working until I was 70 earning the maximum benefit. Underwriters that I worked with had shown me what they felt added security to my personal finances, so I was diligent with setting up my emergency savings account. It would be there for any time my Social Security check didn't cover my expenses on my home or me getting older, so I often worked until 10:00 PM at night, delayed taking days off, making my goals possible.

The Social Security Administration sent information about my future benefit payments, so I made a budget and determined my escrow for taxes, insurance and home maintenance to be taken from my benefit. I knew how much I would have per week for my living expenses once my mortgage was paid. I used the overtime income for my emergency savings account. Everything relies on my receipt of my monthly check from Social Security.

The recent assault on Social Security has me terrified. People who were not elected, vetted, or made to swear an oath to protect our US Constitution have taken our personal data saying that they are searching for fraud. Errors are being made with this new regime and no clear resolution in sight.

Why do they need my personal information, that includes my Social Security number, work history and bank information? In February, my identity was stolen. When thieves moved my mail using a postcard sent to USPS, my bank statement, and a copy of my paycheck were forwarded to the thieves before I got the USPS notice of the change. I froze my credit then, and have done so later, since TransUnion has the BOSE address listed as a fraudulent one on part of their report, but also has it on another address for mail that has been returned to the sender.

I have quit fighting the data entry mistake, but I remain diligent and alert if mail is due and doesn't arrive. What can I do about this new group of identity thieves known as DOGE?

Until recently, I had confidence in my ability to provide for myself because I lived in the United States of America, a republic governed by the people, for the people. My parents were children of the Great Depression, so they instilled in me how to be financially solid and survive. Now, at 78, I'm learning everything that I hold dear is to be attacked by the 47th president using a contributor to his reelection as his advisor and the leader of a group named DOGE.

I do not feel safe due to cuts in so many who have kept us safe, cuts in the CDC, cuts in the FBI, cuts in the EPA, cuts in the FAA and Social Security. I worry about losing our foreign allies and the release of convicted domestic terrorists pardoned by the President, while suspected immigrants might be whisked away before anyone even knows they are.

Everyone I know receiving Social Security benefits relies on those payments for their daily life. As prices increase under President Trump's leadership, many are not as fortunate as me who had a solid plan for increased expenses. We worked putting into FICA with every paycheck that we received. The thought of delaying payments or making errors so that anyone must prove their right to receive their benefit is stealing from people.

Are we still the land of the free and the home of the brave? I'm counting on our elected officials like you and the courts to preserve it.

Lisa Bobaki, Fleetwood, Pennsylvania:

Hello, my name is Lisa, and I live in Fleetwood, Pennsylvania. Fifteen years ago, my healthy 42-year-old husband was found deceased on our couch by our then 13-year-old son. Our 10-year-old and 3-year-old stood quietly crying on the stairs. Sudden cardiac death was the cause. The same day, my daughter asked if we would need to move to another house. I promised her, I promised to keep them in the only home they'd ever known. Those early days remain blurred in my mind.

I remember my father taking me to the Social Security office, and shortly thereafter, survivor's benefits for my children began showing up in the bank account to assist with their care. If not for these benefits, I would not have been able to keep my promise to my children. It's not much money, amounting to roughly the salary of a minimum wage job, yet it was a lifeline to some piece of normalcy for my family — not a Ponzi scheme.

My kids have now aged out of the system. I'm about to begin widow's benefits, as my body cannot continue to work multiple jobs as a physician therapist, which I've needed to do to make ends meet for myself and my family. Social Security benefits were essential to the care and being of raising my children. It was a promise from their father who had paid into the system his entire working life. We must work on continuing to expand these essential benefits and never consider dismantling or privatizing them. Thank you, Senator Booker.

Here's Kayana Spooner from Chippewa Falls, Wisconsin, who writes me,

> My name is Kayana Spooner, and I live in Chippewa Falls, Wisconsin. I'm 63 years old. My husband, Joe, and I have five children and three grandchildren and live a wonderful life as our family is growing. {God bless you and your family.} We owned businesses and worked to contribute Social Security for ourselves and our employees. We did all the things we could do to secure our future and contribute to the larger community of those in need.
>
> We felt that we were living the American dream, until one day in 2012, {I know this personally with my dad and I feel for you, Ms. Spooner.} Until one day in 2012, I was diagnosed with Parkinson's disease. Parkinson's disease is a degenerative brain disease that progresses over time. {Sorry, I'm thinking about my dad.}
>
> It is unrelenting and affects motor and nerve processes. Loss of benefits will have a direct and daily effect on me and my family as we navigate the medical needs we will be facing. I will need progressive and comprehensive care as I age, I will need medication every single day of my life, and I will need the security of a generous society to care for me. Millions of others join me there. Please, Senator Booker, please protect my Social Security.

I just thank God that my mom had the resources to take care of my dad, and I watched that degenerative disease take from his life for 20 years and how much it cost, the thousands of dollars it cost my mom to take care of him. I know my friend, Andy Kim, who's in the Senate right now, is facing health challenges with his father. I know so many people personally whose parents have Alzheimer's.

I know so many Americans who are not powerful, they're not rich. I know so many Americans who live in fear every day that one little thing will happen to them that will destabilize their financial wellbeing, and now those millions of Americans, because of a president and a man named Musk, are striving fear into them, are whacking away the people that answer phones or firing the people in an agency that already was struggling with wait times and already was struggling with slow response times.

These people, who are hanging on by a thread in their lives or are facing the people they love the most, who are struggling with the diseases that so many of us in this body have been affected by, they are now worried. They're writing me letters with words like fear and terror. They're talking about staying up at night and not being able to sleep because they don't have a president that comforts them. They have a president that talks down to them, that lies about the services that they rely on. What is this? It is not normal. It is not normal. This is America. How can the most powerful people in our land not comfort others, not tell them they have nothing to fear but fear itself, not tell them to have malice towards none but have charity towards all?

What kind of man is in our White House that makes fun of the disabled, who lies so much that the fact-checkers lose count, that minimizes the pain and the suffering? Where you have cabinet secretaries, that are billionaires themselves, that say, "If my mom misses a Social Security check, ah, but if somebody else complains about it, they're probably a fraudster." These people are not fraudsters, they're hurting, they're afraid, they're worried.

For God's sake, this is America. Every one of our founders' documents is riddled with words that speak of our commitment to each other. Yeah, they weren't perfect geniuses, but they were people that aspire to virtue. They read the greatest philosophers of their times. They said, "What does it mean to be good to one another? What does it mean to create a society that is not run by despots and dictators who are so disconnected, who talk down, 'let them eat cake?'"

They dreamed of a different country than this folks. They dreamed of a different country than this. They dreamed of a country that stood for not just get all I can for me, the biggest tax cuts possible to the wealthiest people. They dreamed of a nation where any child born in any circumstance from any place could grow up and have their American dream, and God, it gut wrenches me when I hear people not as privileged as me, and I'm not Musk and DOGE, but my mom had the resources and the family to support her as she watched my dad die of Parkinson's disease.

But this person's writing in, she herself has Parkinson's, she underlines and bolds the part of her letter, she says, and I'll read it again, because Spooner, I want you, from Chippewa Falls, Wisconsin, to know you are seen, to know you are heard, know that maybe the President will talk down and cut and malign your only paycheck, your only hope, but I won't, I won't. I see you, I feel you.

You can't lead the people if you can't love the people, and I'm sorry, our President is not showing that. He may be saying those words. She writes with Parkinson's, I still remember my dad telling me he had it. She writes that,

> It is unrelenting, Parkinson's, and affects my motor and nerve processes. Loss of benefits will have a direct and daily effect on me and my family as we navigate the medical needs we are going to be facing. I will need progressive and comprehensive care as I age, I will need medication every single day of my life. {I know this. I know you will. I know you will.} I will need the security of a generous society to care for me. {...a generous society to do the basic for families in this kind of struggle.} Millions of others join me there. Protect my Social Security, Senator Booker.

I tell you, I'm going to fight for your Social Security, I'm going to fight to protect the agency, I'm going to fight against unnecessary cuts that hurt the service it gives. And today into tomorrow, I'm going to stand as long as I can, as long as I can, I'm going to stand and read stories like this, because you are seen, you are heard. Your voices are more important than any of the hundred of us. More of your stories should be told on this floor, of people that are scared right now, terrified right now, people living in rural areas that see their local Social Security agency on a list that Elon Musk put of places he's going to sell away to the private sector and you're going to lose your agencies. Well, I will fight. I'm sorry.

Margaret Hebbring* from Chippewa Falls, Wisconsin... Chippewa Falls, two letters, my staff is keeping me on my toes. This is another person from Chippewa Falls, Wisconsin:

> My name is Margaret Hebbring, and I live in Chippewa Falls, Wisconsin. I'm 77 years old, and I am a member of the Lac Courte Oreilles Band of Lake Superior Ojibwe. My husband is a veteran, who currently {...I'm so sorry, I'm so sorry} My husband is a veteran who currently has cancer and he's receiving chemotherapy at the VA hospital, which we have to travel to, which is over 100 miles away, and without our Social Security, I'm not sure what would happen to us.
>
> We would for sure have to sell our home. I have savings that will last me one month. I have savings that would last me one month right now. We live paycheck to paycheck, so please, please, protect our Social Security.

This is Judith Brown ... We're moving away from the great State of Wisconsin, we're going to the great State of North Carolina, where my dad is from, up in Hendersonville, Asheville. But this person, Judith Brown, is from Charlotte, North Carolina, one of my top five favorite non-New Jersey states. I don't know if my friend Andy Kim has his top five favorite non-New Jersey states. New Jersey obviously is the best. Don't look at this, Senator from Connecticut, and I hate to tell him that Connecticut is not on my top five non-New Jersey states, even though I got educated there. I'm sorry about that, I'm sorry about that. The presiding officer is such a good man. His state is not on my top five non-New Jersey states, but North Carolina is, and I'm going to read a letter from Judith Brown.

> My name is Judith Brown, and I live in Charlotte, North Carolina. I was 17 when I started working, and worked for another 20 years as an administrator until I had to be declared disabled. Without Disability, I would not have been able to see my specialist, get an eyecare or any of the other needs that I had. I was also the mother of two young sons who were on the autism spectrum. Without Disability, I wouldn't have been able to take care of them and get the care they needed to be independent young men. {God bless them.}
>
> I hear that they want to close the field offices and change the customer service line. As a person with mobility and vision impairments, this is outrageous. I need to be able to access it the best way I can on the times that I can access it. Please, Senator, fight to protect Social Security for a senior like me and for young people with disabilities like my sons. Thank you.

No, thank *you*, Judith Brown. Thank you for writing a letter. Thank you for speaking up. Thank you for not being silent. Thank you for advocating not just for your family, but for the millions and millions of other Americans who lean heavily not just on their Social Security checks, but on the incredible public servants that keep that agency working and who wish to have a president that said, "I'm going to bring the best of business experience to my customer service. I'm going to bring the best of caring and technology and innovation. I'm going to call the best computer technologists, scientists, in the country. We're going to make this the best Social Security in the history of our country.

And you know what? My friends, the billionaires I had on stage with me when I was inaugurated, I'm just going to ask them to pay a little bit more, 0.00001% more of their net worth, to make sure that Social Security is safe forever." I'm sorry, it's crazy.

I'm going back to Pennsylvania... It's almost like you can't make this up, honestly. I just know my country. I know our character. I know how good of a people we are. I know how much we love one another. I know our faith in Red states and Blue states and Right and Left. I've sat next to people on planes who introduced themselves to me as Republicans from a red state, and by the end, we're laughing and talking and sharing stories. We are a good nation together. We can be so great, we've shown that. But how can we have a president that in 71 days drives this much fear into our country? It's absurd, everybody, it's absurd. This is why I can't let this be normal anymore.

Michelle, from Lancaster, Pennsylvania:

> My name is Michelle Groover {I love your last name, Michelle} from Lancaster, Pennsylvania, and I would definitely be impacted if something would happen to my Social Security. {Michelle also has Parkinson's} And I'm on disability, and the money that I have goes pretty much to the most of my medications and foods that I need to eat to keep myself going and strong. That's how it would impact my family. I wouldn't be able to afford also my insulin for my diabetes. {Parkinson's and diabetes.} So it's a challenge every month as it is, even with the amount that we have, because the cost of pharmaceuticals and things keep us going. {Yes.} So that's why Social Security is really important to us as a family, it helps us get by every day. Thank you.

This is Patricia Harvey-Porter from Johnstown, Pennsylvania:

> Hello, my name is Patricia Haney, {excuse me, Ms. Porter} Patricia Haney-Porter. I reside in Johnstown, Pennsylvania. My work is varied. I've been employed as a secretary in the private sector, as a statistician for the government agency, as a real estate agent, and most recently, as a legal secretary. This is my story as to how Social Security has affected my life. My mother passed away in 1956, my sisters and I, {God bless you...} were eight, ten, and eleven. My maternal grandparents stepped in and they raised us with the help of Social Security survivor benefits, resulting in good educations and allowing other needs to be met. We had almost normal lives due to these benefits.
>
> While raising two children, I worked as a real estate agent. My income was based on commissions rather than salary, so I made the entire Social Security payments based on my income. We had a roof over our heads, healthy food on the table. One of my children had serious medical issues, and I paid for her bills out of pocket, never asking for a penny from any government agency. These expenses were paid for from my income and I paid taxes every year.
>
> I waited until I was 70 to collect my Social Security benefits, as I realized the later you collect, the better the benefits. I have no pension and I live almost entirely on Social Security benefits. I am always looking for part-time work, but few people want to hire me as I will be 80 in June. {God bless you, God bless you.}
>
> Based on the benefits I receive, I'm able to pay my mortgage and all monthly expenses. I receive Medicare, which help pay the medical bills. Should Social Security and Medicare be taken from me, I will likely lose my home. I could no longer afford medical costs, groceries. I have a medical condition which requires regular visits with a specialist who is 70 miles away. Without Social Security and Medicare, I would no longer be able to see him, and my condition would result in death sooner rather than later.
>
> Thank you for all you are doing to see that the benefits received through Social Security, Medicare and Medicaid will continue.

As Senator Murphy and I was talking, it's all interrelated. This is somebody on Social Security, but they have to drive just for medical attention. We are in a hospital crisis in America. There's so many rural areas where rural residents of our country have to drive so far just to get to a hospital, and cuts in Medicaid, we've heard it from the letters I read in the last section, will endanger those hospitals' survival.

Charlotte, North Carolina, again — Kevin Woodson. I get a lot of letters, my staff, from Wisconsin and Charlotte, North Carolina. Okay...

> My name is Kevin Woodson. I'm a 69-year-old retiree living in Charlotte, North Carolina. I worked 38 years for two Fortune 500 companies. Two Fortune 50 companies, {I'm sorry, Kevin} and I thought that I would have a fully funded pension plan to live off in my retirement. However, I never got to the 25 years in, so only got partial pensions. This is why I need Social Security. It covers the holes that the pensions don't cover in terms of medical benefits. It allows me the freedom to enjoy my life, take care of activities that I need in order to keep myself healthy.
> Social Security is dependable, something I rely on, not a Ponzi scheme, and I hope that we don't touch Social Security and that we don't have any issues trying to keep that money flowing. It's money I paid into.

Margarita Silver from Surprise, Arizona. (I love that name, Surprise, Arizona.)

> Hello, my name is Margarita Silva. I live in Surprise, Arizona with my husband. I started working at the age of 15 doing volunteer work as a candy striper at the hospital where my mother worked. I did not get paid. After that, I started working as a waitress, earning 50 cents an hour. After graduating from high school, I took various jobs, earning a little more. And then, I started working at Mountain Bell, and I retired after 30 years from Qwest. So if they do Social Security cuts, I don't know what I'm going to do. I'll be forced, at the age of 74, to look for a job. So those are my hard-earned benefits. I worked for that, more than 30 years, I worked for that. Thank you.

Wayne Bank from Chippewa Falls, Wisconsin... I need to go to Chippewa Falls, Wisconsin — this is the third letter that are included that are people reaching out to me from Chippewa Falls. God bless you, I need to visit your community.

> Hello, I'm Wayne from Chippewa Falls, soon to be 69 years old. I've been on Social Security for a couple of years, my wife and I. I spent years in the service, Navy, and again, like I said, my wife and I are going to have been on Social Security. Saying that, we would, if we lost our Social Security tomorrow, we would lose our house, our cars, and pretty much our livelihood, because this is what we've worked for and we don't need to lose it. Why do you work for 55 years and pay into Social Security and then lose it?
>
> Recently, I tried get back online, get on *my Social Security* account, I wasn't able to. Because of that, I went down to the Social Security office in Eau Claire, Wisconsin, and they said they couldn't do anything for me, that I had to set up an appointment. So I come home later, called, set up an appointment, and it's still three days out before I can get my appointment, and they don't know if they can help me.
>
> So at this point in time, I really need to know what's going on with Social Security, Senator Booker, because if we lose it, everybody else that's on it loses it, we're going to be in a really sorry state.

Those folks who answer phones and set appointments, they're sure important when somebody is in a crisis. They have to wait a few days, their check is missed, it's real consequences for real people.

> Hello, my name is Manuel. My wife and I live, {surprise, surprise} in Surprise, Arizona. We're both on Social Security, and that's what we depend on to live our lives in our retirement years. We have to pay our bills, we have to buy food, we basically have to live off that, so if you take our Social Security, what are we going to live off? Are you going to take good care of us? You know, we're American citizens and we deserve and we paid into it and we've earned it, and it's not just something given to us. So leave our Social Security alone, let us live our lives. Let us live our lives out the way they should be.
>
> And we're supposed to be in our golden years, so it's important to us, it's important to all Americans out there that are seniors. Let us live our lives. Thank you very much, Senator Booker.

Patricia Naughton from Pittsburgh, Pennsylvania, I lift your voice:

> My name is Patricia Naughton, and I'm from Pittsburgh, Pennsylvania. I've been paying into Social Security since I was 16 years old. I am currently 70, and have been collecting Social Security for the last five years. Without Social Security, I wouldn't be able to pay my mortgage, utilities, food, medicine, copays, and many other things. I would not be able to survive without Social Security. There's no reason that seniors should be held hostage over Social Security. This is our money, our money that we put into the Social Security system for many years. We deserve not to be threatened by the loss. Thank you.

Kathleen Wilverding* from Hanover, Pennsylvania:

> Hello, my name is Kathleen Wilverding, and I currently live in Hanover, Pennsylvania. I'm originally from New Jersey and taught in the public school system for 29 years as a school librarian. When I retired, I decided to move to Hanover, Pennsylvania {Kathleen, you're missed in Jersey} and at the age of 62, I started collecting Social Security because of COVID. I needed the extra stability that Social Security provides. I no longer have to work a full-time job because of Social Security, although I do work a part-time job and still pay into the system.
>
> Social Security provides me with stability, financial stability. It helps pay the bills, and I really don't have to worry about my finances because it's Social Security. If Social Security is taken away, I'll lose everything I've worked for over the past 60 years. I feel that Social Security is a godsend. Protect it, Senator Booker, thank you.

Cynthia Marino from Pennsylvania:

> My name is Cynthia Marino. I'm a retired registered nurse from Lancaster, Pennsylvania. My husband... {I'm sorry, Cynthia} My husband died in 1990, and two of my children received survivor's benefits for eight years, during which time I was able to get my bachelor's degree in nursing and work part-time. All three of my children went on to get college degrees. When I was 61 years old, I went on Social Security Disability, having a hip replacement. I was switched to regular Social Security when I turned 65.
>
> I now deeply depend mostly on Social Security for my husband and myself, with small pensions from both of our jobs supplementing the Social Security. I'm now able to live independently in a handicapped mobile home thanks to the money from Social Security in the past and present, much cheaper than Medicaid funds to keep me in a nursing home. Thank you, Senator Booker, protect it.

Thank you, Cynthia, for your story.

These are just some. These are just some. I read their voices, I lift their voices with mine. I want to go to the Detroit Free Press, but before I read this article, I know my senator from New Jersey is here. I'm going to read this article, and if he is interested in our sixth hour, if he has a question, I will yield a question while retaining the floor, but I'm going to read this article and then we'll go. This is from the Detroit Free Press.

(My mom was born in Detroit, I love the city, my family owes it a lot. My grandfather went to find a job on the assembly lines in Detroit, building bombers during World War II.)

It says Kathleen Sherrill's been retired for 10 years now and typically didn't think twice about whether she'd received Social Security payments on time. For the first time ever, the 74-year-old Troy retiree went online in March on the very day that $2,800 was to hit her bank account through direct deposit. She suddenly felt compelled to make absolutely certain that her Social Security money was there when it was supposed to be. Sherrill and other retirees are on edge, big time. Call it Social Security insecurity.

"I have never really worried about it much as I have this year," Sherrill said. The money thankfully was sitting in her account in March and she knew her checks and payments for her ongoing bills would not start bouncing. "I think anybody, future or current people on Social Security, are definitely targeted," she said. "It's a worry that I'm sure everybody is having right now."

I know it because I heard from my mom and her whole senior community. Seniors uncertain what to do next for Social Security.

> Since early February, AARP has seen nearly double the calls to its customer service care line as more people began being troubled about Social Security and it has shown no signs of abating, according to the AARP spokesperson. Since February 1st, AARP said it has been receiving more than 2,000 calls into its call center per week on concerns relating to Social Security. "Social Security has never missed a payment and AARP and our tens of millions of members are not going to stand by and let that happen now," said John Hishta, AARP Senior Vice President of Campaigns, in a statement last week.[1]

While those words sound reassuring, it's frankly not comforting to realize that seniors need to hear that their monthly Social Security payments will arrive as usual. I don't imagine anyone had this one on their bingo cards for March 2025, this kind of worry and stress.

On social media, I spotted one comment that said,

> Folks, the federal workers began advertising last month that all Americans remove all funds from the account where they normally receive any federal payments, Social Security, federal tax funds, and the like. Keep the account but only use it as a place for feds to transfer money. Immediately move all transferred cash to a separate account.

The concern, according to the post, "DOGE can declare you dead and force your bank to send back any funds paid to you." Whoa, a lot of retirement angst there and, yes, some wild notions and really bad advice. Moving Social Security money around to hide it in another account, different from where it's directly deposited, actually could put more of your money at risk when it comes to some debt collection.

Anyone who's tracked retirement policy, as I have, knows that the potential unraveling of Social Security system has been discussed for decades, many retirees just never imagined a convoluted scenario when someone would think Social Security possibly could implode.

The health of Social Security, which marks its 90th anniversary this year, isn't all that makes many retirees and those about to retire nervous. Their anxiety can go into overdrive watching the stock market slide on Trump's tariffs news and seeing all the political ping-pong with Social Security money that belongs in their pockets. The Trump administration has maintained that it wants to cut costs and fraud when it comes to the Social Security program, not benefits. But people remain skeptical and some commentary isn't helping.

Acting Social Security Commissioner Leland Dudek in interviews last week, including one with Bloomberg News last Thursday, actually threatened to temporarily shut down Social Security after a federal judge temporarily stopped members of Elon Musk's Department of Government Efficiency from digging through personal data at the Social Security Administration. The DOGE operatives, according to the court, will first need to receive proper training on handling sensitive information, which some might say is the least they can do.

The American Federation of State County and Municipal Employees, or AFSCME, Alliance for Retired Americans, and the American Federation of Teachers filed a motion for emergency relief on March 7th to halt DOGE's unprecedented, unlawful seizure of sensitive data regarding millions of Americans. No surprise, Dudek soon found it politically prudent to back off from his threat.

"I'm not shutting down the agency," Dudek said in a statement, indicating he had received clarifying guidance from the court about the temporary restraining order. "President Trump supports keeping Social Security offices open and getting the right check to the right person on time," Dudek said.

Financial tech CEO Frank Bisignano, who was nominated by the President Donald Trump to lead the Social Security Administration, ended up being grilled by Democrats about the bedlam during confirmation hearings before the Senate Committee on Finance on Tuesday.

The angst isn't about to go away, particularly if people continue to face even longer waits on the phones or see Social Security offices closing in their community, thanks to some key changes being made now by Trump's administration.

Customer service is on the chopping block, as the Social Security Administration reduces the number of employees, restricts what services can be handled by phone, and shutters some local offices where people could talk to someone face-to-face.

On Wednesday, the Social Security Administration announced that it would initiate a two-week delay for implementing a highly criticized move to end phone services and require in-person visits for some services. "In-person identity proofing for people unable to use their personal, *my Social Security* account for certain services will be effective April 14th," according to the announcement. But individuals applying for Medicare, disability and Supplemental Security Income who cannot use a personal *my Social Security* account can complete their claim entirely over the telephone without the need to come to the office, according to the March 26th announcement. That's good news for many.

Even so, merely delaying the change doesn't help others and, frankly, customer service could still suffer in the long term. And it will get very ugly if current Social Security recipients miss out on even one dime of their benefits.

At one point last week, U.S. Commerce Secretary Howard Lutnick suggested that his 94-year-old mother-in-law wouldn't complain about missing a Social Security check for a month or so. "Only fraudsters would call," he said during an All-In podcast.

My thought: Have you ever watched an exchange where someone on the Social Security is being denied a coupon or a senior discount at a store or restaurant? It's not pretty. Worse yet, has Lutnick ever talked with a friend or relative in his or her 70s or 80s who depends on Social Security to cover basic bills? Social Security provides retirement, survivor and disability payments to 73 million people each month. The number includes about 56 million people who are aged 65 or older.

Some people, and even Sherrill includes herself in that group, are better off than others. They won't miss paying an electric bill or the rent because they can turn to retirement savings or money from a traditional pension. Even so, Social Security remains an integral source of income each month for all retirees and others who receive benefits. "I'm concerned about my financial future," Sherrill told me. Social Security now represents about half her monthly income. She never imagined that any Social Security fix would involve cutting benefits for existing retirees. Some GOP proposals have suggested increasing the age for full retirements from 67 to 69 over an eight-year period beginning in '26. But now she fears it's possible her benefits could get cut at some point down the road.

Overall, Sherrill has had fun in retirement. She has nine grandchildren, 12 great-grandchildren and wants to spend more time with them, not less. Sherrill and her friends who are retired are cutting back on eating out and entertainment just in case something happens to Social Security. High prices for many things put pressures on fixed incomes as well. She wants to take less money out of her retirement savings now so she has more money on the sidelines in case her Social Security benefits get cut. Even so, she's staring at an unexpected $600 new monthly car payment ahead because she needs to replace a car that was in an accident a few weeks ago. "If Social Security payments are cut or stopped, I may be selling it."

The wild swings for the stock market, 401(k) plans, going down in America has created more jitters for more people. The economy seems uncertain. Consumer confidence is in worse of a place. Leaders are threatening Social Security services, offices are being cut, people are being laid off, so people are worrying.

Taking a rough guess on just her 401(k) plan, she believes she's lost about $30,000 on her retirement savings as the stock market has tumbled. Over the years, she said cuts to Social Security we're always a part of the political realm, but she felt that Congress provided a stopgap to any dramatic moves. She doesn't believe it's true anymore. "I'm hoping Congress wakes up, looks in the mirror and decides they don't like what they see," she told me.

One big problem with fueling an atmosphere of chaos is that many people do start worrying about everything. One big problem with fueling an atmosphere of chaos means people stop believing that Social Security is a system they can depend on. Sherrill said she took a call from her college roommate who mentioned that she was going to look at her bank account online to see whether her monthly Social Security payment was stopped or it arrived as usual. "I said, 'You're going to be okay. I got mine this month.'"

So many people afraid right now.

SENATOR ANDY KIM (NEW JERSEY): Will the Senator yield for a question?

SENATOR BOOKER: Yes, I will yield for a question while retaining the floor.

SENATOR KIM: Thank you, Senator Booker, and thank you for coming to the floor tonight and speaking up. I have a few questions for you, so why don't you catch your breath. I wanted to start by saying how proud I am of you to represent our great state of New Jersey alongside each other. And it's not just me. I want to tell you because I know you've been here in this chamber nonstop for hours, but I want to tell you that the people are paying attention and they join me in thanking you in this moment. In fact, I saw a few posts I thought I'd share.

Stacey from Bayonne said on Facebook, "I couldn't be prouder to be a lifelong New Jerseyan that I am tonight. Keep it up, get in that good trouble, lead the way and hopefully others will follow."

Janie in Princeton said, "Thank you. Proud that you are my senator and that you are bringing Big Jersey energy to DC tonight.

Vicki in Ewing said, "We are sending our strength to you. Medicare and Medicaid should not be touched.

And someone on Reddit even said, "I hope he wore the most comfortable and supportive shoes he could find."

In your opening, you said something that resonated with me. You said, "Our constituents are asking us to acknowledge that this is not normal, that this is a crisis."

I can't tell you how important it is to internalize it, and that's why we're here at this late hour in the US Senate. That's why you are leading here to make the case to the American people that this is a crisis. That resonated with me because I hear this over and over again. I hear it from people all over our home state, whether at town halls or other rooms that are packed, people saying this moment is not normal. This moment constitutes a crisis.

And I'm glad you're speaking on the floor and said that because what you've said isn't just Cory Booker saying that, it's that millions of New Jerseyans that we represent are saying it. And you are lifting up their voice. It's not just you're saying that, it's that millions of Americans who see something fundamentally wrong and they're angry about it.

Now, I have some questions for my colleagues, but I want to add some context for this because I want to dig in a bit on why people are so angry in this moment and why what we're seeing from Donald Trump and Elon Musk isn't in response to that anger, it is the cause of it. A common refrain in the town halls that I've held is that people just feel like nothing is working for them. There is a promise, a uniquely American promise, that is simply going unfulfilled for too many. Now, that promise is simple. Your government will work for you. Your economy will allow you to advance if you work hard and give your kids a better future. And your country will keep you safe by ensuring the world is stable and secure.

And Senator, you and I are here because we know that this promise is going unfulfilled. To say that the American promise is going unfulfilled would be a tragedy in its own right. It would be something that we as a Congress should put our entire focus into restoring. But the sad fact is that this isn't just about a promise unfulfilled. It's about a promise that has been hijacked. It's about a promise that has been distorted to work for those who have been paid to play, to be denied for everyone else.

Now, let's start with the promise that your government will work for you. This is the basis of our democratic republic. We are public servants in that we serve the people. It's the people's priorities that we put first. It is their lives that we work to make better every day. It is their futures that we are endeavoring to brighten.

But when the people look at Donald Trump and his administration, they don't see that. They see Elon Musk who donated nearly $300 million to buy his way to a seat of power. And the world's richest man has been handed the keys to our government. And the same person who has been handed nearly $40 billion in your taxpayer dollars to prop up his own corporations is now working to fire veterans from their jobs, make the Social Security Administration less responsive to seniors, and make it harder for your government to work for you.

Now, that's what we've seen in the collection of billionaires that buy their way into fulfilling their own American promise, a government that works for them and only them, a government that keeps them rich at any cost from your Medicaid to your Social Security, to the food you put on the table, a government where they pay and they benefit. And if you can't, you're left behind.

That's not the government our parents were promised. That's not the government we were promised. That's not the government we want to pass down to our kids. As Senator Booker mentioned, our nation is in crisis. Bedrock commitments are being broken. That starts with the first American promise. We can rebuild and restore that promise by actually working to make our government work for the people. Where we see corruption, we must call it out and combat it. And the corrupting power of money in our politics is one example. And the extreme wealth of billionaires like Elon Musk are drowning out working Americans, and that must be addressed.

And as we approach the 250th anniversary of our independence of our country, we have an opportunity to remind people that the promise of America is something bigger than ourselves. And that public service, not private enrichment for those at the very top, but that public service is core to what makes this country special.

So let's talk about that second American promise. This is the promise of the American dream. That Rockwellian notion of the house, and the white picket fence, and the kids in the yard, only works if you can pay for that house. It only works if you can afford child care and healthcare for those kids. It only works if you can work hard and deliver something bigger and better than you were handed. And right now, that is not happening. While we are fighting to bring change to our economy to make life more affordable and the middle class more accessible, what we're seeing from Donald Trump and Elon Musk is another promise hijacked for those at the very top.

Senator Booker, I want to just take a step back as I get into these questions here because you're talking about Social Security, talking about Medicaid, talking about so many of these other issues here. But in that broader context, well, let's situate it here, which is this recognition that we live in the time of the greatest amount of inequality in our nation's history. So it isn't just about these programs and how we rely on them, it's that we are seeing the wealth gap widening and it's happening faster and faster. And in many ways, I consider this to be the great fragility of America right now — that we are the greatest, richest, most powerful country in the world, but not for everybody.

And what we see right now is it's not just about the Social Security, it's not just about the checks, but as you mentioned, Social Security offices are closing, worry about customer service if people call on the phone lines, and it feels like efforts are underway to try to sabotage our Social Security, our Medicare, our Medicaid, and then have people say, "Hey, look, it's not working, and that's why we need to get rid of these things." And that sabotage is something people see right before their very eyes.

I mean, you've heard the Commerce Secretary talk about how seniors won't mind if there are late payments. And he said that those that complain are fraudsters, as you mentioned. That's directly trying to undermine people who are working hard over the course of their lives. And I have to say, it's a great irony in many ways, this idea that the richest man in the world is criticizing the hard-earned savings of seniors that are just getting a little bit every single month for them to just try to get by, and then he calls it a Ponzi scheme.

And my father, as you mentioned, is one of those that depends on Social Security for his entire livelihood right now. And I heard another person at a town hall, I did, she described the feeling that she has right now, and I think you can connect with it. She said, it feels hard to breathe right now because there's so much anxiety in the American people. So I'm glad that you're shining a light on this because people are scared and they're worried and they want to know what comes next.

So my question to you here is something that was actually shared by a constituent of both of ours talking about all the concerns of Social Security of this time, but I thought it was very poignant in pointing out that what we also need to put forward to the American people right now is a vision going forward of how to not just restore and protect this promise, but how we take it to the next step. If we live in the time of the greatest amount of inequality, not just to think about how we on to a receding tide, but how to try to put forward some vision that can try to inspire in the same way that Social Security did and put forward generational change, so I wanted to ask you that sense.

Do you believe in that sense that right now, more than ever, as people are faced with this anxiety that's hard to breathe, that, yes, we'll stand here on the floor of the Senate and do everything we humanly can to be able to protect what they have, but do you agree that we also have to put forward that positive vision of where we take Social Security? Where do we take Medicaid, Medicare? Where do we take our economy, the Better Work for Everybody, so we're not just trying to figure out how to better divide and hold onto the pennies that the billionaires are willing to share with the rest of us while they don't give us anything else to be able to move forward on?

And how do we come up with a vision that tries to shrink that inequality and live in a society that's willing to share that wealth and recognize there's more than enough to go around? And that it's not zero-sum? And that we can be stronger together in that way? And I love to hear how you can paint that vision for the American people.

SENATOR BOOKER: So I will answer your question, but knowing that my mom's watching right now, before I answer the question, I just want to tell folks who may not know about my relationship with my other senator from New Jersey. It is probably one of the more interesting relationships in here. I always tell New Jerseyans I voted for Andy Kim before anybody else did because I was on an interview committee for the Rhodes Scholarship in New Jersey, and I was a former Rhodes, and I really wanted the experience of what it was like to be on the other side because my experience was quite interesting. And these incredible folks came in. Young people from New Jersey were amazing, applying for this extremely competitive scholarship. And Andy Kim was one among that number and he blew the committee away.

So way back, I'm going to retain the floor, but ask you a question. What year was that?

SENATOR KIM: That would've been 2004.

SENATOR BOOKER: 2004.

SENATOR KIM: Twenty-one years ago.

SENATOR BOOKER: How many years?

SENATOR KIM: Twenty-one years.

SENATOR BOOKER: Twenty-one years ago. In 2002, I had lost a run for mayor. In 2006, I would run again. So I was sort of in between trying to do my work in Newark. And Andy blew me away. And I knew then that he was this extraordinary man of character and brilliance, this great mix of hearts and head, this great mix of honor and a fierce ambition to make a contribution to the world.

And if you follow Andy's career, he has been a public servant in some of the highest levels in the administration. But then he ran for Congress and I remember that race, and you electrified not just the district you represented, but really the whole state of New Jersey, and then he came here.

But the moment that I remember most was during the January 6th attack. I was here on the Senate floor in this very seat and will never forget how back here, Mark Kelly, an unbelievable senator, who... He and I were two of the last people off the floor along with one of our Republican colleagues, just trying to make sure if anybody broke through, we would be there. I couldn't believe that I was a senator. I was thinking about having to fight my way off the Senate floor.

But I remember that we got to an undisclosed location, and then a lot of senators were in safe spots and a lot of House members were safe spots, debating about what to do. I'm so happy we came back late and continued the business of the government, the transfer of power. But while all these senators were dealing with the big issues and whatever, Andy Kim took a broom, plastic bags, and just began cleaning up under the Capitol dome. Remarkable humility shown in a humble gesture about his love of country.

And now here we stand on the Senate floor, at the earliest hours of the morning, closing in on 2:00 AM, and you asked me this question that I didn't expect, which is, "Hey Cory, this now seems to be a time where Democrats are defining themselves about what they're against. Shouldn't we be talking about a vision of what we're for?"

I'm very upset watching what's happening to Social Security, watching what's happening to insinuate fear amongst seniors who should be retiring with security and peace, cuts and undermining, thousands of people being laid off. All of that is worthy of us standing, and the things we're reading, but what I think Senator Kim is really pointing to the fact is that there is bold visions for who we are going to be as a country. He is one of these big believers that we can be a nation that boasts about [that] we are a country where somebody doesn't retire and lives on such a meager check that they're technically at the poverty line. Like Senator Booker, we have more wealth than nations all around the globe, stratospheric wealth in this country, GDP growth, and can't we design a system that doesn't have seniors stressed out and living... those that live off of their paychecks living there?

And the other thing I know you know about, and I just recently did a talk with a Republican friend of mine, Senator Young, we worked on a bill together because we both recognized with seniors that generation, baby boomers, a generation ahead of me, I was about to say ahead of us, but you're technically a millennial.

SENATOR KIM: That's right.

SENATOR BOOKER: You're a millennial. I'm an Xer. But the generation ahead of me is so big that we're seeing this massive group of Americans soon to be retiring. And lots of people recognize it and calling it the great retirement crisis — not because Social Security checks won't be there.

You were asking me, "Cory, what's the great vision for they're going to be there?" But because just the reality of that the Social Security checks themselves are so meager and many other people don't have jobs where they have 401(k)s and the like.

And so, Senator Young, again, this is not a partisan speech. Later, I'll be quoting from the Cato Institute, the Wall Street Journal editorial, lots of conservatives who point to this not being a normal time in America, this being a crisis moment in America, not just people on my side of the aisle, but Republican governors, Republican thought leaders. A lot of folks are saying that there's a real crisis in our country being caused by the current president, who in 71 days, most people can't say yes, most people say no to the question, are you better off than you were 71 days ago?

And so, I want to answer your question by saying this. Everyone should retire with a secure Social Security. I believe there's ways to secure the programs by asking the wealthiest people who pay the smallest percentage of their income into Social Security, while people like the names I'm reading are often paying the most, but the wealthiest people paying a little bit more in Social Security taxes on their income, which is minuscule.

As you said, with the gravity of the wealth that's being created in this country – which is again something that I'm not against in terms of just people being successful – but this idea that we have a system that creates a fair, secure retirement. That's one thing that we can do. I think also one of these things that we should be talking about right now is how do we make the Social Security system not frustrating for people who complain before Donald Trump laid off tens of thousands of people with Musk, who complained about wait times and other things? There's ways we can improve Social Security services as well.

So I think we can do things to secure Social Security in the long term with a simple fix. Not by raising the retirement age for people who are struggling, but by doing things, by simply saying, you know what? Social Security taxes already are regressive because they cap out at a certain amount. Maybe skip some of the people in the middle, under $400,000 or $500,000 a year, make people who are the wealthiest in our country pay a little bit more. That would be my vision. A very small amount would create a secure system. I think we can also do a lot to improve the Social Security services. And then what I did with Senator Young, this is what's special about this place when it happens, is for people to reimagine what economic security could be about.

I'm now very quietly – I think I've told you about this – have this great idea that I've been talking about for years, called Baby Bonds, or that every child born in America. And this is not a new idea. We actually scraped it from people years and years ago on both sides of the aisle in here had this idea that why not in a capitalist society that every child be born with a savings account? Excuse me... a growth account. That government seeds it with some money and their entire lives, people can contribute into that tax-free and it can grow. And so that by the time – not retirement – by the time they're 20, 25, 30, they have thousands, if not tens of thousands of dollars to invest in things that create wealth.

Because right now, lots of people are working paycheck to paycheck and don't have stock accounts, don't have the kind of things that could actually produce a lot more wealth. I'm just throwing that out as one idea, Andy. And I'm going to pause because I know you have another question and I'm going to yield to the question while retaining the floor, but I just want to say there are so many bipartisan ideas to deal with wealth inequality. The child tax credit, that was unfortunately not made permanent, cut child poverty America in half. It worked for an entire year. And I remember some of my colleagues from Marco Rubio to Mitt Romney talking about, "Hey, we should be expanding the child tax credit." We should be having a bolder vision for American retirement security, for wealth creation, for economic security. But we're not talking about those bold ideas.

We have a president who's come in and one of the first things he's done in 71 days is insinuate fear and insecurity about Social Security by threatening it, by telling lies about it and by having somebody like Elon Musk calling it a Ponzi scheme, and that's why we get fear. And then they take a hatchet to the actual agency that undermines its ability to deliver service in a good way.

SENATOR KIM: Will the Senator yield?

SENATOR BOOKER: I will yield for a question while retaining the floor.

SENATOR KIM: Yeah. What you raised is absolutely right and it's front and center in everyone's minds. When my parents immigrated here 50 years ago, they didn't know anybody in the entire western hemisphere of planet Earth. But America — it called them. It inspired them. And I asked them once, "What was it that drew you here?" And they said that they felt that here in America they could guarantee that the family that they raised, that their kids, me and my sister, would have a better life and more opportunities than they did. And that was that sense, that generational progress that is made. But now, I'm standing here with a seven-year-old and nine-year-old, I'm hoping fast asleep right now, and I don't know if I can make that same promise to them right now, that I could guarantee them that they will have a better life and more opportunities.

So there is that growing cynicism and pessimism about that American promise I talk to you about and I just feel like there's an unraveling happening here where we see this sense of concern and it's being weaponized by some to create that sense of zero-sum, to push us away from this idea that we're part of something bigger than all of us and that we can all lift each other up in that great American project. And it's sad because as we're getting to that 250th anniversary. It should be a time when we rededicate ourselves to the American project, right? Like recommit ourselves to what the next 250 years would be. But we're entering it now with this sense of pessimism on that front.

So I guess my question to you here is how do we break out of that tailspin on that front?

SENATOR BOOKER: Andy, you got me really excited. You've seen me pacing back here, because I love that you're a millennial. I'm an X generation. I love the baby boomers, but they're quickly leaving Congress. This is the last baby boomer president we will ever have. I'm confident of that. And the new generations are coming forward to lead in America. And it is time that we dream America anew. It really is. It is time that we revive and redeem the dream. I just am one of these people that thinks, okay guys, we have some of the brightest minds on the planet earth. Some of our founding fathers said we need a little revolution every once in a while. We need new thoughts and new ideas and new visions that excite and energize people, that take a lot of the old divisions in our country and erase them and remind people we have common cause and common purpose. And I want to get people excited again about the American dream.

I want to renew the dream, redeem the dream. We can do that. I'm so excited about it. And financial security, it is absurd that we don't have the greatest plan to create wealth, not for the favored few simply. Again, the top quartile in America has crushed it the last 25 years. Heck, under Obama alone, the stock market doubled. But most Americans don't own stocks. So people who are sitting on passive wealth were able to grow and grow and grow and grow, while working Americans saw their prices going up, housing becoming unaffordable, and the idea of the American dream under assault. And it ticks me off that other countries are trying to out-America us. They're trying to take our secret sauce that we seem to be turning our back on. Affordable higher education, apprenticeship programs. Some of our European competitors, job disappears at 40, you can go right into a apprenticeship program where you can earn and learn and end up in a career that gives you not just success but you thrive in.

There is no idea that we can't conceive as a country. This is an idea and a time that I just think that we need to start being bold again in our visions for collective prosperity, for everyone to thrive.

Not just the favored few, but the many. And I'm telling you, those ideas are out there, whether it's baby bonds, a child tax credit, investing in science and research. There's so many things. But you are, can I say this to you affectionately. You are a nerd. As am I. We're two guys that love to read, that love American history. We're two guys that this body, go back a century, they never imagined that we'd be here. Okay?

And one of my favorite speeches of all time was when Daniel Webster got on Bunker Hill and he delivered the speech. I'm going to read the introduction to it.

To commemorate the 50th anniversary of the Revolutionary War battle at Bunker Hill in which the outnumbered colonists inflicted such heavy losses on the mighty British forces attempting to invade. I love one of the quotes – I can't remember it exactly – but the general, the person that was leading the British attack wrote in their diary or wrote back to the king, "We won the battle, but a few more victories like this, we're going to lose the continent." That's how great these people were. And this is what I want you to know. It's a new generation, right? Those leaders are no longer around. I read this and I get excited about the possibilities for our generation, the new leaders that are emerging in America that have to. It is their obligation not to let the dream die, to redeem the dream.

And so here it is. I'm just dying to read this to you. Here it is, Andy. I don't want to read too much of it to you. Okay, here we go:

> If in our case, the representative system is ultimately a fail, this idea of a democratic government, popular governments must be pronounced impossible. {He's saying that we have the obligation to make a more perfect union.} No combination of circumstance is more favorable to this experiment can ever be expected. The last hopes of mankind, therefore, rest with us. Can we make this democratic experiment work? And it should be proclaimed that our example had become an argument for the experiment. The principle of free government adheres to this American soil. It is bedded in this soil. It's as immovable as this nation's mountains. And let the sacred obligations... {This is the part Andy, Senator Kim:}
>
> And let the sacred obligations which have devolved on us, this generation and on us sink into our hearts, the sacred obligations. Those are daily dropping from among us who established our liberty and our government. The generation that established this nation are now dying.
>
> The great trust now descends to our hands. Let us apply ourselves to which is presented to us as appropriate object. We can win no laurels in our generation in a war for independence. Earlier and worthier hands gathered all of those laurels. Nor are there places for us by the side of Salon and Alfred and other founders of our state. Our fathers have filled them, but there remains to us a great duty of defense and preservation. And there is open to us also that noble pursuit to which the spirit of the times strongly invites us. Our proper business is improvement. Let ours be the age of improvement. In a day of peace, let us advance the arts of peace and the works of peace. Let us develop the resources of our lands, call forth its powers, build up its institutions, promote all its greatness, and see whether we also in our day and generation may not perform something worthy to be remembered.
>
> Let us cultivate a true spirit of union and harmony in pursuing the great objects which our condition points out to us. Let us act under a settled conviction, and an habitual feeling that these 24 states are one country. Let our conceptions be enlarged to the circle of our duties. Let us extend our ideas over the whole and vast field in which we are called to act. Let our object be our country, our whole country, and by the blessings of God, may that country itself become a vast and splendid monument, not of oppression and terror, but of wisdom, peace and liberty upon which the world may gaze with admiration forever.

That's a bold vision. This bold vision that doesn't give up on America, doesn't surrender to cynicism about America. That's who you are, Andy Kim. And that's what gets me excited.

Right now, we're fighting against what I think are tyrannical forces. I'm sorry that when a leader stands up, not with humility like George Washington's farewell address or some of the great founders in their inaugural addresses, but stands up and says, "Only I can solve these problems," who doesn't use his speeches to heal and to comfort, but to talk about the enemies he's going to pursue, and those enemies are not the adversaries who seek to destroy us. Those enemies are other Americans.

And to create an environment where our seniors who should be retiring in security are fearful that their Social Security or their Medicaid or their Medicare is going to be under threat, that's insidious to me. This is a un-normal time. This is why I'm standing here. But you, my friend, my partner in the Senate, God, this partnership, I'm so excited about the future. I'm so excited about the promise. Let us fend off all attempts to cut Social Security and Social Security services.

Let us fend off all attempts to cut Medicaid and Medicare and CHIP and all the other things that we rely on. But let us also not forget that our obligation is not to defend what it is, but to have a vision for what can become. We now, when so many people are giving up on the American dream, on the idea of America, on what you said so wonderfully, that my children will do better than me, that basic bedrock that our children generation after generation will do better and better and better, it's time to redeem the dream and dream America anew with bold visions. Not how we will just help people survive in retirement, but visions of how we all can thrive in this great nation that has enough resource and enough abundance, abundance to provide for everyone's hopes and dreams.

SENATOR KIM: Thank you so much. Keep up your energy. I yield back.

SENATOR BOOKER: Thank you. You're giving me energy. I'm sourcing myself from you. Now, I don't want to just cast aspersions on... And we are saying things that I just want to back up in fact. All those letters from seniors. I see my dear friend from Pennsylvania is now the presiding officer. You missed all the letters I read from Pennsylvania. All those letters where people were using the word Ponzi scheme. Where did that come from? I just want to read The Joe Rogan Experience. I actually like and enjoy listening to Joe Rogan.

Elon: "Social Security is the biggest Ponzi scheme of all time."

Now that's a big statement. "The biggest Ponzi scheme of all time," Elon says.

And Joe Rogan says, " Why? Explain that."

> Oh, {Elon says} So well, people play into Social Security, um, and and the money goes out of Social Security immediately, but the obligation for Social Security is, uh, your entire retirement career, so you're paying, uh, with your... {And I'm reading this verbatim...} You're paying, uh, with, you're the kind of people you're paying, like, uh, if you look at the future obligations of Social Security, it far exceeds the tax revenue, far... If you've looked at the debt clock... {Rogan says, "Yes?"} Okay, there's, there's, there's... {Three there's. I'm reading it verbatim.} Our present-day debt, but then there's our future obligations. So when you look at the future obligations of Social Security, the actual national debt is double what people think it is because of the future obligations. {Rogan, "Uh..."; Elon...} So basically people are living way longer than expected.

That was the evidence of a Ponzi scheme.

Now, let's correct something. The reason why we have a massive debt in America – lots of people should take ownership over it – but the biggest debt creator in the last, say, 25, 30 years is the President of the United States. Current one. In his first term, by blowing massive holes in our deficits to give tax cuts that went way disproportionately to the wealthiest Americans and corporations, and he wants to renew those tax cuts that independent budget folks are saying could add trillions of dollars to our national deficit.

So if he's talking about the debt clock or whatever he was talking about, he's a part of administration, even though he's unelected and not approved by Congress and whatever, he and his president, the richest man in the world and the most powerful man in the world together, they're driving an agenda that's going to drive this deficit much bigger and they're going to try to pay for some of it. Not all of it, because it's trillions of dollars of projected debt. They're going to try to pay for some of it by cutting NIH grants, by cutting Medicaid, by cutting staff at Social Security. So no, Social Security is not a Ponzi scheme. People paid into it, and as Andy Kim and I just talked, there are ways to preserve it, strengthen it, make it better.

It's a program that pays benefits after a lifetime of work. It's never missed a payment. It's never run out of money. It's an insurance program, but don't take my word for it. Here is Current Affairs magazine editor Nathan Robinson writing on March 7th, *Why Social Security is Not a Ponzi Scheme*. That's a great title.

> Old age insurance is not a scam and it's not destined to collapse. Proponents of privatizing or eliminating Social Security are constantly telling lies about it. {So here's the article...}

Elon Musk has called Social Security a Ponzi scheme, comparing it to a scam in which a con man must keep finding new suckers in order to disguise the financial unsustainability of the enterprise. The term has also been used by libertarian commentators as reasons in the Hoover Institute, who try to convince people that the program is fundamentally broken and unsustainable because both Social Security and Ponzi schemes take money in the form of new contributions which they pay to old ones.

It is easy to craft a superficial resemblance between the two, but Social Security is not a Ponzi scheme, and it's important to understand why. Because the comparison is used to generate the illusion of Social Security crisis that can be used to justify major benefit cuts or even the elimination of the program altogether. Under the Ponzi scheme, differences between old age insurance and Ponzi schemes, we can train ourselves mentally to resist the propaganda that is used to try to convince the public to support undermining one of our most important social welfare programs. Let's think about a few different cases in which money is pulled and paid out. First, let's imagine a company has a pension scheme. I realize this may be difficult to imagine it these days, but stick with me for a minute. Workers pay 5% of their income. The employer pays in an equivalent amount to 50% of the worker's income.

When the worker is retired, they get a fixed benefit every year for the rest of their life equivalent to some percentage of what their salary was. Let's call that scenario A. Now let's imagine a different scenario. Five uncommonly astute middle schoolers create a rudimentary insurance scheme to guard against being punished by their parents. The children all go to the mall every week and play arcade games together. They each get an allowance of $10 a week, which they spend at the arcade. What they decide to do is to spend $9 each week instead and put $1 a week into a fund. If one of them has their allowance taken away by their parents, the fund will pay the arcade money for the week. That way nobody in the friend group is ever deprived of this ability to go to the arcade. We're going to call that scenario B.

Finally, let us imagine a scenario in which a fraudster tricks a group of old people into giving them their money. He says that if they invest their retirement money with him, he can guarantee them a 20% year return risk-free. They invest. He provides them with statements showing that their money indeed is growing at 20% a year. When they ask him to pull a portion of their money out so they can spend it, he disperses it. But what he actually is doing is spending all their money and providing fake statements. He's able to keep paying withdrawals because he's constantly recruiting new suckers just enough to cover what people are withdrawing. Eventually people get suspicious. Too many try to withdraw their money at once and he flees the country. This is a Ponzi scheme named after the Italian con man, Charles Ponzi, who fleeced people in this way.

We will call this Ponzi scheme scenario C. Notice that there are similarities and differences between the three scenarios. The similarity is that there is a fund that some people are paying into while others are being paid. Another similarity is that all three are potentially unstable. In scenario A, company pension, employee starts living a very long time. In retirement, the amount of money in the pension fund might not be able to cover the promised benefits necessitating an adjustment of the contributions from the next generation of workers. Or if in scenario B, middle school arcade insurance, one of the kids might be so unruly that his parents are suspending his allowance every other week requiring adjustments of the rules of the payouts or contributions to keep the funds stable. Scenario C, the Ponzi scheme is the most unstable of all because it depends on elaborate fraud, on fake accounting that disguises the fact that nobody has the amount of money that they are being told they have.

It only lasts until people try to actually use the money. But scenarios A and B could also collapse if they're not managed well. We can see that despite the commonalities, there are fundamental differences between scenarios, A, B, and scenario C. The first two are legitimate ways for people to pool and distribute money, and they can work just fine accomplishing their intended purpose. The third is a fraud in which people's money is being stolen. The difference is more important than the similarities. I have laboriously laid out these examples in hopes that we can better understand why Social Security can be made to look like a Ponzi scheme, but it isn't one at all. 'Social Security is the biggest Ponzi scheme of all times,' said Musk. 'People pay into Social Security and the money goes out of Social Security immediately, but the obligation for Social Security is your entire retirement career.'

Now, it's true that in an insurance system, the incoming payments from new people might be used to fund outgoing payments to people who are already part of a Ponzi scheme, but that's not what makes a Ponzi scheme a Ponzi scheme. Musk, not for the first time, doesn't know what he's talking about. One of the reasons Social Security can be made to seem like a Ponzi scheme is because people may misunderstand how it works. People might think that Social Security saves their money over time and then when they retire, it pays their money back. Not quite how it works. It's not like a savings account. The money I pay in is not saved up for me. It's paid out to today's beneficiaries. When I retire, my benefits will be paid by the incoming next generation of workers. Discovering this fact can make people think that Social Security is Ponzi scheme, but it's not.

A Ponzi scheme is a fraud in which returns are fake. There is nothing fake about Social Security as long as enough money is in the pool to pay out beneficiaries. The operation is sustainable and perfectly honest. The only reason it matters that retirees do not pay for their own benefits but depend on the payments of the next generation of workers is that if there isn't a next generation of workers, we got a problem. But unfortunately, there is every reason to believe that human beings will continue to exist, work and pay Social Security taxes.

Now, what Musk and others who claim Social Security is a scam or in crisis say is that in the future there will be not enough workers to pay retirees the promised benefits. Musk says, and I quote, 'If you look at the future obligations of Social Security as far extends the tax revenue, there's our present-day debt, but then there's our future obligations. So when you look at the future obligations of Social Security, the actual national debt is double what people think it is because the future obligations. Basically, people are living way longer than expected and there are fewer babies being born. So you have many people who are retired that live for a long time and get retirement payments. However bad the financial situation is right now for the federal government, it'll be much worse in the future.'

But what he's trying to get you to think, this is a major problem or some deep fundamental flaw with Social Security, it isn't. Every insurance plan has to make adjustments over time. If there are a lot of wildfires burning down houses, a company selling fire insurance might have to raise premiums. The increased premiums might be small, but without them, the program would go bankrupt. This doesn't mean, however, that we'd be justified in saying fire insurance plans are a Ponzi scheme destined to go bankrupt. The adjustments needed to be made to Social Security in the long-term are minor. Yes, people are living longer and having fewer babies. That means that there ultimately has to be some kind of adjustment to either how much is being paid in, how much is being paid out, or both. Republicans want to cut benefits. Defenders of Social Security instead want to raise the money going into it by increasing taxes paid by the wealthy.

So interesting that we just saw that in the dialogue with my ideas with Andy Kim.

> The amount of taxes that would need to be raised in order to make Social Security solvent is negligible. The Social Security Administration has estimated that increased in the combined payroll tax from 12.4% to 14.4% to make the program would make the program sustainable for the next 75 years. As Dean Baker and Mark Westbrot put it in the introduction to 1999's Social Security book entitled The Phony Crisis, the only real threat to Social Security comes not from any fiscal or demographic constraints, but from the political assaults on the program by would-be reformers. If not for these attacks, the probability that Social Security will not be there when anyone who is alive today retires would be about the same as the odds that the US government will not be there.

Of course, in the next 25 years since that was written, the chances that the US government itself may someday not be there conceivably have gone up." This is a funny author. "Musk is certainly trying to make sure that little of it remains as possible. But the point remains, the theory behind Social Security is sound. It is not like an unsustainable con, although it's also not like a savings account. It can easily be sustained indefinitely with some minor adjustments to ensure that enough money is coming in to keep it going. It is also the case that even the need to keep enough money flowing in is artificial. As Stephanie Kelton explained, the restrictions on Social Security's ability to pay out are created by a legal choice, not an actual financial constraint facing the US government, which could keep paying benefits even when Social Security's funding 'runs out' if it was authorized by Congress to do so.

Beware the rhetoric of those who describe it as in 'crisis or being a scam.' They either do not understand the fundamentals of how it works or they have deliberately tried to deceive you. I cannot say for certain whether Musk is knowledgeable enough to understand the basics and is lying or simply cannot wrap his head around the basic way an old age insurance program works." The author continues. "As Alex Larson of Social Security Works explained to me, the Right has been trying to destroy Social Security since its inception. This is for a few reasons. First, a lot of vultures stand to benefit from privatization, just as the privatized Medicare Advantage program has enriched insurers like UnitedHealth. Second, the Right believes that individuals should be responsible for their own fates. Has an ideological opposition to government social welfare programs, even if this results in a bunch of old people being poor.

They see Social Security as an offensive, big government intrusion into the free market, something that compels people to put money into a retirement program whether they want to or not. The problem is that most of the public doesn't share this hatred for the concept behind Social Security, and the program is overwhelmingly popular on both sides of the political aisle because they have failed to win the ideological argument. The Right must therefore convince the public of a different argument. That the program is collapsing and doomed and can only be saved through major benefit cuts, which will be stated as a euphemism of raising the retirement age. Hence, the propaganda about unsustainability and Ponzi schemes. This can be effective if you don't know much about how Social Security works. It's easy to be convinced that there's something fishy about its payment structure or that it's heading for some dire financial apocalypse, but this is not the case.

Baker and Westbrot are right that the threats to Social Security come from those who say they're trying to save it from a crisis. We need to have a clear understanding of what's going on so we can fight to save the program that works just fine and can easily be made to continue providing retirement benefits to every subsequent generation of Americans, ideally ensuring that nobody has to endure old age poverty.

And so why are they cutting Social Security staff, thousands of people? Again, I've said this time and time again. I'm standing here because this is not a usual time. I think our country is facing a growing crisis. But I am quoting so many Republicans because a lot of us who've run stuff know that you don't just fire people and then realize the mistakes you've made and beg them to come back to work. They know that you don't just fire people that do essential functions in a program before you've even done assessments of what your goals and ambitions are for social security. It's clear that their goals and ambition isn't the best customer service to improve the complaints that I've heard over the years about waits, unreturned calls, challenges at Social Security offices. That's not their ambition.

We've missed a big opportunity to come together in this nation and start to really reimagine our government that works for people, that can do big things, that can serve folks, and instead, we are trying to demonize people. We're trying to lie about critical programs, call it a Ponzi scheme, make up out of thin air that somehow we're paying thousands of people that are over 150 years old, fraudulently. We're better than that. To that point, I just want to again, make my facts clear.

Here's an Associated Press fact check from the President's speech:

> Tens of millions of dead people aren't getting social security checks, despite Trump and Musk's claims. The Trump administration is falsely claiming that tens of millions of dead people over 100 years old are receiving social security payments. Over the past few days, President Donald Trump and billionaire advisor Elon Musk have said on social media and in press briefings that people who are 100, 200, or even 300 years old are improperly getting benefits.

"A HUGE problem," Musk wrote, as his Department of Government of Efficiency digs into the federal agencies to root out waste fraud, to allegedly root out waste, fraud, and abuse. It is true that improper payments have been made, including to some dead people, but the numbers thrown out by Musk and the White House are way overstated and misrepresent Social Security data.

Here are the facts.

What has the Trump administration said about payments to centenarians? On Tuesday, Trump said in a press briefing in Florida that we have millions and millions of people over 100 years old receiving social security benefits. "They're obviously fraudulent or incompetent," Trump said. "If you take all those millions of people off Social Security, all of a sudden we have a very powerful social security with people that are 80, 70, 90, but not 200 years old,"President Trump said. He also said that there's one person in the system listed as 360 years old. Last Monday, Musk posted a slew of posts on social media, including, "Maybe Twilight is real, and there are a lot of vampires collecting Social security," and, quote, "Having tens of millions of people marked in Social Security as alive when they're definitely dead is a huge problem. Obviously, some of these people would have been alive before America existed as a country. Think about that for a second..." {End quote.}

On Wednesday, Social Security's new acting Commissioner Lee Dudek acknowledged recent reporting about the number of people older than 100 who may be receiving benefits from Social Security. He said, quote, "The reported data are people in our records with a Social Security number who do not have a date of death associated with their record. These individuals are not necessarily receiving benefits." Quote, "I am confident that with DOGE's help and our commitment of our executive team and workforce that Social Security will continue to deliver for the American people," Dudek said.

How big of a problem is Social Security fraud?

A July 2024 report from the Social Securities Inspector General states that, "From fiscal years 2015 through 2022, the agency paid out almost 8.6 trillion in benefits, including 71.8 billion or less than 1% in improper payments. Most of those erroneous payments were overpayments to living people.

In addition, in January, the US Treasury clawed back more than 31 million in a variety of federal payments, not just social security payments, that improperly went to dead people. A recovery that former Treasury official David Lebryk said was just the tip of the iceberg.

> The money was reclaimed as part of a five month pilot program after Congress gave the Department of Treasury temporary access to the Social Security Administration's full death master filed for three years as part of the omnibus appropriation bill in 2021. The SSA maintains the most complete database of individuals who have died, and the file contains more than 142 million records, which go back to 1989...
>
> [The] Treasury estimated in January that it would recover more than 215 million during his three-year access period, which runs from December, 2023 through 2026.

So are tens of millions of people over a hundred years old receiving benefits? No. No, no. But the letters I read from scared people across the country show what happens when a president lies. When his unelected, biggest campaign contributor, richest man in the world just continue to make public statements to insinuate fear and doubt and chaos, and then make announcements that they have to take back, that they're going to end the call in service, which so many seniors rely on.

Then they create more fear when people see that posted government buildings that are to be sold at auction to the private sector are actually the addresses of their Social Security offices. Why, everywhere I'm going around my state, everywhere I have gone around the country in the last few weeks, and my mom and her mostly Republican senior community are all up in arms and feel this fear. Or the people that we read about who write letters about losing sleep. It's because of the chaos, the crass cruelty, the unjustified cuts and attacks on a program that is the bedrock between security and financial ruin for so many Americans.

Here's a Wall Street Journal writing about this, how Trump and Musk are undermining Social Security.

> Dealing with Social Security {Wall Street Journal writes} is heading from bad to worse. The agency administers benefits is cutting staff and restricting services as part of the Department of Government Efficiency's review." {The Wall Street Journal writes...} The federal agency that administer Social Security benefits is facing a customer service mess. The Social Security Administration is cutting staff, restricting what recipients can do over the phone and closing some local field offices that help people in person. The number of retirees claiming benefits has risen in recent eight years as Boomers age.
>
> Few federal agencies reach as far into American's lives as Social Security, which delivers a monthly check to some 70 million people. Many of those people now fear that the changes, part of President Trump's powerful overhaul of the federal government through the Department of Government Efficiencies, are eroding confidence in the nearly 90-year-old program. {The Wall Street Journal continues...} Agency officials have acknowledged that because of planned reduction in services over the phone, there will be longer wait and processing times. An estimated 75,000 to 85,000 additional visitors a week could show up at local field offices, according to an internal memo sent by Doris Diaz, the acting deputy commissioner for operations.
>
> (Details of the memo, which were reviewed by the Wall Street Journal, were reported earlier by the Washington Post.)
>
> This is likely to tax the agency's 800 number, where people typically make appointments for office visits. Already, Social Security recipients have complained about customer service.
>
> Holly Lawrence made several unsuccessful attempts to reach a human before she filed her Social Security claim. Holly Lawrence, 64-year-old, made several unsuccessful attempts to reach a human before she filed her Social Security claim online. The Washington DC based freelance journalist said she called the agency's 800 number several times starting in February. Each time, she got an automated voice that warned of a two-hour wait on the phone. Her calls were disconnected before she could leave a message or request a callback.
>
> She gave up trying to reach a customer service agent and created an online account on the agency's website on March 3rd. She had to wait two weeks for an account activation code to arrive in the mail before she could submit her claim. She's still waiting for that claim to be reviewed and processed.
>
> Lawrence said she has virtually no retirement savings. 'I'm financially strapped and cannot afford to get a financial advisor. It was important for me to be able to talk to someone at Social Security,' she said.' adding that she's concerned that the customer service delays she encountered could negatively affect others 'who don't have the strength to persist'.
>
> {Wall Street Journal continues...} Social Security has a reputation as the third rail of American politics, a benefit to which elected officials make cuts at their own risk, make cuts risking their reelection. Donald Trump has vowed not to cut benefits, but

> he and DOGE's leader, Elon Musk, have made unfounded claims of widespread fraud in the program.

I'm going to repeat that sentence from the Wall Street Journal. "He and DOGE's leader, Elon Musk, have made unfounded claims of widespread fraud in the program."

> Commerce Secretary Howard Lutnick said in a recent podcast interview that if social security checks were hypothetically delayed, it might catch those guilty of fraud because they would make the loudest noise, screaming, yelling and complaining.
>
> Critics say turmoil at the agency is undermining trust in the safety net programs. "The killing those programs from the inside," said Illinois Governor Pritzker, "the result of which is we don't know what they are doing to tear down the scaffolding that holds Social Security together."
>
> DOGE has gained access to systems containing personal information, but a federal judge has temporarily blocked those efforts. On Friday, Leland Dudek, acting Social Security Commissioner threatened to shut down the agency because of the judge's order, but later reversed course. Dudek, the acting Commissioner said, "The changes are designed to make sure the right payment is to the right person at the right time. It's a common sense measure.
>
> Even before DOGE's plans went into motion, the agency's customer service operation had shown signs of strain.
>
> Roughly 47% of the quarter million people who call Social Security's 800 number on an average day have gotten through to a representative this year. Only 47% got through to a rep. This is down from nearly 60% in 2024. The average time to wait for a callback is over two hours. There has been a steady decline in the agency staff and DOGE plans to cut employment by another 12%. That would bring the total number of employees to about 50,000 from about 57,000 today and nearly 68,000 in 2010. "Customer service has been going downhill for years," said Bill Sweeney, senior vice president at AARP.

It's going to get worse. Some Social Security Administration changes amounts to cuts in services. Wall Street Journal continues:

> "Starting March 31st, people who want to file for retirement, survivor or disability benefits, or change their direct deposit information can no longer complete the process by phone," the agency said Tuesday. "Instead, they must do so online or at a field office."
>
> The agency said it's stopping phone calls as part of an effort to reduce fraud and strengthen identity proofing procedures. So Social Security Agency has estimated that improper payments represent 0.3% of total benefits. Dudek too, acknowledged that recent changes including the shift away from claiming on the phone are likely to drive up the numbers, making appointments at field offices over the next 60 days.
>
> He said field employees would be trained over the next two weeks to respond to the changes. "We're going to adjust our policy and procedures to adapt to the volume," he said. 'These changes are not intended to hurt our customers." Dudek said in the call Monday with advocates that the phone service policy change and quick timeline were directed by the White House, according to people familiar with the call. {Directed by the White House.}
>
> Kathleen Romig, director of Social Security and Disability policy at the Center on Budget and Policies Priorities says, "It isn't clear why the agency chose to discontinue identity verification over the phone while allowing it online and in person." She says, "Other advocates say that by discontinuing the phone option, the agency is creating hurdles for those who lack internet service or live far away from the field office."
>
> "The agency has also largely stopped serving walk-in customers in field offices," said Maria Freese, senior legislative representative at the nonprofit National Committee to Preserve Social Security and Medicare. "Most waiting in person must book appointments on the 800 number."
>
> In February, 45% of people who schedule a phone or in-person appointment to file a claim got one within 28 days. DOGE plans to close nearly 50 of the agency's approximately 1200 field offices, according to Social Security works. Although spokesman for the nonprofit said some of the offices on the list 'don't seem to exist'. The chairman and CEO of Fiserv, Inc. [Frank Bisgnano] has been picked by Trump to serve as Social Securities Commissioner and will appear before the Senate Finance Committee on Tuesday."

I mean, this is the Wall Street Journal pointing out utter incompetence. Utter incompetence. And they're rolling back trying to catch up, but they don't seem to care and the way they're going about this, they're hurting seniors. They're undermining the security of the program. The title of the Wall Street Journal's article is the best, it's *Social Security Services Are Now Going From Bad to Worse*, under this leadership who promised they were going to serve people. I see the senator standing and I'll yield for a question while retaining the floor if he has one.

SENATOR MURPHY: Senator Booker, I'm going to pose to you a pretty simple question here, but first let me lay down a little bit of a predicate. We've heard already some talk tonight about this extraordinary statement, but not terribly surprising from the Secretary of Commerce. This is a close friend of the president, somebody who's very close to all the decisions being made in the White House where he said that if a Social Security recipient misses their check for a month, then they should not complain.

"My mother-in-law wouldn't complain." ... that's easy for him to say.

Maybe you wouldn't complain if your son-in-law was a billionaire. You probably are not going to be harmed by missing a Social Security check if you've got a billionaire in the family. But 99.99% of Americans do not have a billionaire that they can get on the phone if they miss a month, and one month's Social Security check disappearing is a cataclysm for a lot of families. As I was listening to you, I just did a little bit of easy back-of-the-napkin math. So the average Social Security check on a monthly basis in this country, it's somewhere around $2,000. Obviously, it varies based upon how much money you put in and what your income was, but on average it's about $2,000.

Now, some Americans have supplemental retirement income, but fewer and fewer do today because it's just not the case any longer that employers are going to provide for you a defined benefit plan. So if you were working minimum wage your entire life, or if you were working a low wage job, you're not going to have money to put away in Social Security. I remember during one of my walks across the state of Connecticut, spending about a half an hour walking with an elderly gentleman in Willimantic, Connecticut, and he told me a story that is not atypical. He worked his entire life, most of his adult life. He worked for Walmart. He was really proud of working for Walmart. He helped a whole bunch of people in his community.

He was working for a great American company, a company he was proud of. He was helping people every single day that lived in his neighborhood get what they needed when they came into the store. But you know the wage he was making at Walmart, he was making very little and they didn't have any defined benefit plan. They would let him save a little bit of money if he could find the means, but he couldn't because every single dime that he made from Walmart had to go to rent and groceries and medicine and cell phone bill and transportation. And so he worked for 20 years at Walmart and when he retired. You know how much he had in savings? Zero. Zero.

And he felt like he had done everything people had asked him for. He worked for a great American company. He helped people. He worked full time. He didn't miss time, he didn't goof around. And when he retired, he had nothing, nothing saved. So the Social Security check, which to him was probably about $2,000 a month, was everything he had. And he's walking with me explaining to me what his life is like today. He was coming out of the liquor store and that was one of the things he did every day was go down to the liquor store and buy a nip or two and just pass a couple hours.

He didn't like to spend a lot of time in his house because he has roommates. He lives in a small apartment with two other guys, strangers. He doesn't know them. And he says to me as we're walking, "This is not how I expected my life to go. I thought if I worked my entire life and I played by the rules and I worked hard, that'd have a little bit more dignified retirement than this. I share a room with two other guys that I don't know." And that's the reality for a lot of Americans. That's the reality for a lot of retirees. Two thousand dollars is the average social security check.

I don't know why I picked Tallahassee, but I just picked Tallahassee. I said, what's the average one bedroom rent in Tallahassee? It's $1,200. Utilities, probably another couple hundred dollars. The average senior citizen spends about $500 a month on food. Rent, utilities, food — that's it. That's your $2,000. You got nothing left. If you are one of the seven million Americans who rely only on Social Security like my friend from Willimantic, you got nothing left for medicine, for transportation. You have nothing left for a cell phone. You have nothing left to go to the movies once a month. You have nothing left for presents for your grandkids for Christmas or for their birthday. If you're relying on Social Security, and many people who work their entire life are, you go without that check for one month, your whole life falls apart.

And so this just cavalierness that Musk and Trump have about Social Security, that the billionaires that advise them have about social security, "Don't worry about it," if you miss a check for a month or two months. You're a fraudster. You're trying to defraud the government if you complain about missing a Social Security check. It is so disconnected from reality. I know we're going to talk later today about the plans to shut down the Department of Education. It shows this similar disdain for public education, the way that they are showing a disdain for working Americans who are relying on social Security as their primary means of retirement income — the disdain for the 40 million working Americans who rely on Medicaid.

And it's not hard to understand why. Because if you're a billionaire, if you're Elon Musk, if you're Donald Trump, you don't have to rely on the public school system. Your kids go to fancy private schools. You will never need to rely on Medicaid. You have lived fortunate lives. In Donald Trump's case, because he was born into wealth. You'll get a Social Security check, but that's not going to be your primary retirement.

And so you can understand, if you put a bunch of billionaires in charge of the government who don't lead lives that are remotely connected to how average people live, they will say things like, "Social Security is just some big Ponzi scheme, and that's the big one to eliminate", or, "You know what? America will be all right if we impose $880 billion of cuts to the insurance program for 24% of Americans", or, "Let's shut down the Department of Education because, I don't know, public education doesn't matter to me." So I think it's just the reality that we're living in today in which we have people who are making these decisions who just don't understand how normal people's lives work.

And in particular, how a person's life falls apart if they have any diminution in their Social Security income when the average check is $2,000 a month, and the average expenses in most cities for a senior citizen who relies on social security is going to be far higher than $2,000 a month.

Here's my question for you. You laid out what's going on in Social Security today. It's like the opposite of efficiency, right? It's called the Department of Government Efficiency. And what we know for certain in the Social Security system is that everything they're doing has the intent of making the system less efficient, right? You don't just close dozens of offices and shut down the phone system to make the system more efficient. You do that to make the system less efficient. And so I'm trying to figure out why. I'm trying to figure out why. And I'll give you two theories and then let you tell me if you think I'm right or I'm wrong.

It could be a pretext to eradicate the whole system. What did they say about USAID? They said that USAID was a corrupt enterprise. It was corrupt. No evidence of corruption in USAID. No evidence of corruption, no allegations of specific corruptions, but they just made these accusations that USAID was criminal. Musk and Trump said this, "It's a criminal enterprise; it's a corrupt enterprise," and that became their justification to eliminate it. Within weeks, USAID, one of the most important vehicles of US national security was gone, was gone. They didn't run on that. Nobody saw that coming. It was two weeks of allegations about criminality and corruption, and then USAID vanished and people were looking around, "What happened? They didn't tell us they were going to do that," and now it's gone.

They certainly didn't run on eliminating Social Security or cutting people's benefits. But boy, the playbook seems a little familiar here that all of a sudden there are these lies being told, lies being told. Let's say what it is about the corruption inside Social Security. As you said, the improper benefit payments are minuscule, right? 0.3% of overall payments. And so is this a pretext to ultimately make big cuts in Social Security? Or alternatively, is it just part of a plan to just sort of put the entire country on edge? To just make everybody wake up in the morning wondering whether they're next, right? "Is it my Medicaid benefit that's going to be cut? Is social security going to be there for me if I'm a federal employee? Is my job here next week?"

And is that a means of distracting you from the corruption and the thievery that's happening at the highest levels of government? Is that in service of an agenda to try to convert this country from democracy to something else? If everybody is just so focused on the next hit, Medicare, Medicaid, Social Security, my son losing his federal job... Is that a means to ultimately try to drive an agenda through the back door while people are looking at the threats coming at them through the front door? It's clearly not about efficiency. I mean, that's what we know. The changes they're making to Social Security are not about efficiency. The question is, what's the agenda here if it's not efficiency?

SENATOR BOOKER: Again, you and I, Presiding Officer, there's a lot of people here I know that operate from just a place of just decency. There are problems with government, we need to fix them. We need to make government more efficient. We need to deal with the national debt. There's so many things that people on the Right and the Left in this country can agree on. You and I could agree that – God bless America – government can be a lot more efficient. But the question is they're not playing on the level. There are lies about USAID, like, I don't know, 5 million condoms going to Gaza or something outrageous, and easily proven false, time and time again.

A President of the United States, again, this doesn't shock people anymore, he's a president more than any other modern president, by independent fact-checkers has proven to lie over and over again. But as I sat there listening to his speech, and he just goes on and on about transgender mice, when that was proven to be utterly a lie. Or else somebody just misreading the kind of mice that are used in medical experiments, which have a similar word. So are they lying in order to attack these programs? DOGE is insidious in the fact that they keep posting things and then having to pull them down because just independent folks.

And I have article after article, we're so far behind in this agenda of things to get through, I'm not going to read them all. Some of them I'll submit to the record, but not people on the Left calling them out for what they're doing and saying being a lie about Social Security. So you're pointing out a pattern. First, they tell terrible lies to try to whip up public sentiment against entities created in a bipartisan way – by the way, using congressional powers – approving spending, approving programs, approving agencies. Let's create incredible lies, magnify them on social media, try to spread them with our influencers and everybody.

So now people believe that somehow, "Oh, the president talked about all this money going to transgender mice." That's a lie, but we're going to use that as an excuse to attack scientific funding. We're going to use that as an excuse to attack Medicaid. We're going to use that excuse to pull the people fighting Ebola out of East Africa. And so I was told by a colleague, a Republican colleague of mine, "When you come here, don't try to get into the head of your colleague and understand what their motivations are." But this to me is a pattern in which they're trying to undermine public confidence. And the result of this pattern has seniors, letter after letter wrote using things like 'I'm losing sleep', 'I'm terrified', 'I'm scared', 'help me please', telling the most painful stories about retirement insecurity, about health challenges.

And so again, I have this expectation, whether you're a Republican or a Democratic president, you don't insinuate fear amongst vulnerable communities. You don't insinuate fear amongst our elders who deserve our respect and deserve to retire with dignity. You don't do that. You stand boldly in front of them and say, you know what? There are some things we're going to improve. We're going to try to bring the best minds in America to make the best customer service because every independent group has been saying that customer service is failing.

And yeah, we want to go after fraud and abuse, but we're not going to do it. First thing we're going to do is fire the Inspector Generals who have a better record than Elon Musk has over this last decade in rooting out fraud and abuse under Democrat and Republican presidents. So it just doesn't add up. It's not on the level. And so before I allow you to ask the next question, what does this amount to, Senator Murphy? Ultimately, what this amounts to is an attack on the programs, the healthcare, the services, the retirement security that millions of Americans rely on. And often for them what they're relying on is the difference between safety and security and chaos and destitution. I'm not exaggerating that. When somebody's Social Security check is the only income they have and they've already downsized, as you said, brought in roommates doing everything they can to cut costs because under this president, costs are going up.

This is why we have to stand and not let this happen.

SENATOR MURPHY: The gentleman yields?

SENATOR BOOKER: Yes, I will yield for a question while retaining the floor.

SENATOR MURPHY: So there's also a third agenda here. We were not necessarily both here at this time, but a few Republican administrations ago, there was an attempt to privatize Social Security, to take the corpus and move that money into the hands of the private sector for them to manage the money and, of course, charge a fee or a commission for the management of the money. The Social Security Trust Fund, if sort of fully handed over to investors on Wall Street, could make a lot of money for that industry. The American people rose up against that. It was stopped in its tracks, but that is still a priority for a lot of allies of the president, to get their hands on that money inside Social Security. And, again, I'm previewing a future conversation, but I keep on making the analogy to what is happening inside of the education space because those same industries, whether it be investment banks or private equity firms, get wide-eyed at our public education dollars as well, because they would love to get their hands on those public education dollars and have private equity companies running our elementary schools, and middle schools, and high schools, and skimming a little bit of money off the top to pay back their investors.

And so the other potential agenda here is to attack the public administration of Social Security, attack the public administration of our public schools in order to shift that administration and the oversight of the investments, in the case of Social Security, to the private sector so that the president can hand those functions and that oversight to friends in the private sector. And once again, it just becomes a moneymaking vehicle for folks who already are doing very well instead of an exercise in just trying to promote good governance. Instead of the agenda simply being the education of our kids or the administration of a benefit program, it just becomes about making somebody else money.

I pose that as a question to my friend because we saw this attempt to try to privatize Social Security, and you can certainly see at the end of this assault, this false assault, on the inefficiency of the public administration, the solution being to turn the program over to the private sector, the privatization of Social Security that many Republicans have wanted for a long time finally coming to fruition.

SENATOR BOOKER: So that's the problem, right, is that if you have an idea, bring it. Let's have a national debate. Let's bring in experts. Let's have a debate. The person you're talking about, Bush, who had that idea, he had the good sense to say, you know what? I'm not going to try to kill the agency. I'm not going to lay off thousands of their employees. I'm not going to drive the services it provides, make them worse to be called out by right-leaning newspapers and right-leaning writers. I'm actually going to bring my idea forward and let's have the debate in Congress. Let's bring people together. Let's hold the hearings. Let's have the conversation.

I can deal with that because – this is going to surprise you, Senator Murphy – is I've had conclusions about policy positions that I've changed over the years. When I've had a debate, I had a contest of ideas, people have persuaded me. But that's not the way Trump operates. He tried to kill healthcare without a plan. The powerful letter I read by John McCain about why he voted no is because it was 'first, kill this thing that people rely on, don't worry, trust me, we'll figure it out later'. That's what's happening with Medicaid right now. There's no conversation about how to better provide healthcare to the tens of millions of people that rely on Medicaid, from our seniors to expectant mothers to people with disabilities. No conversation. They're just sending people into dark rooms and saying, here's $880 billion I need. Find a way to cut it. Let's kill it, and then see what happens.

SENATOR MURPHY: Ready, fire, aim.

SENATOR BOOKER: Ready, fire, aim.

Look, Senator Murphy, I prepared for so many days on this and we are talking about the point, so I'm going to submit... There's lots of articles here that I'm going to submit to the record. Without objection from the presiding officer, I'd like to submit a Washington Post article about long waits, waves of calls, website crashes, Social Security is breaking down[2]. May I submit this for the record?

PRESIDING OFFICER: Without objection.

SENATOR BOOKER: Thank you to the presiding officer and my friend who I'm keeping up at 3:00 AM. He's a kind, generous man to be here. Here's a closure of Social Security offices, 47 closures across the country in red states and blue states, everywhere in between, closures of Social Security offices. I know everybody's talking about cutting Social Security, but what they're doing right now, right now, is grinding the services of Social Security, grinding them down. So with the permission of the... I'd like to submit an article for the record from the Associated Press, a list of Social Security offices across the US expected to close this year.

Thank you very much. I want to read some of the places. Without the rest of the language I just put in the record, but just for folks out there that are watching, these are the places Social Security offices provide really important services to your community that this administration, Elon Musk, are closing: Alabama, 634 Broad Street; Arkansas, 965 Holiday Drive, Forrest City, 483 Jefferson Avenue in Texarkana.

In the great state of Colorado, they're closing 825 North Crest Drive, Grand Junction. In Florida, they're closing 4740 Derry Road in Melbourne. In Georgia they're closing 1338 Broadway, Columbus. In Kentucky they're closing 825 High Street in Hazard. In Louisiana, they're closing 178 Civic Center Drive, Houma.

In Mississippi, there's three places they're closing: 4717 26th Street, Meridan ... Meridian (excuse me to the great people that live there); 604 Yalobusha Street in Greenwood; 2383 Sunset Drive in Grenada, Mississippi.

In Montana, they're closing 3701 American Way. They're closing Social Security offices in North Carolina, 730 Roanoke Avenue, Roanoke Rapids. They're closing 2123 Lakeside Drive in Franklin, North Carolina.They're closing 2805 Charles Boulevard in Greenville, North Carolina. (I know that town.) They're closing 1865 West City Drive in Elizabeth City, North Carolina.

In North Dakota, they're closing 1414 20th Avenue, Southwest... forgive me, the great people that live in this community, but 'Minot' I'm pronouncing it and I'm sure I'm butchering it.

In Nevada where my mom lives, in the city my mom lives, they're closing 701 Bridger Avenue, Las Vegas. In New York, 75 South Broadway, White Plains, my mom worked there and 332 Main Street in Poughkeepsie, New York. In Ohio, 30 North Diamond Street, Mansfield; in Oklahoma, 1610 Southwest Lee Boulevard.

In Texas, they're closing two offices: 1122 North University Drive ... I know that people are going to write me letters that I'm mispronouncing their town's names, Nacogdoches. Anybody from Texas here? No? I'm sorry. 8208 Northeast Zac Lentz Parkway.

In West Virginia, they're closing 1103 George Kostas Drive. In Wyoming, they're closing 79 Winston Drive, Rock Springs, Wyoming.

There're cuts to Social Security staff. How deeply are they cutting? They're cutting thousands.

We've already talked about it, but, if I can, from the Associated Press, can I enter this article, *Social Security Administration Could Cut Up to 50% of Its Workforce*?[3]

PRESIDING OFFICER: Without objection.

SENATOR BOOKER: Thank you. The article that I won't read, out of generosity to my dear friend who's presiding, but it details in painful ways what these cuts could mean to people in our country. Just trying to move a little quicker through my documents because I'm way behind. The impact of these cuts, one of the big places they're going to impact is in rural America, is already suffering so much. There's a lot of sources that are talking about the rural areas of our nation they're going to cut.

And I'd like to enter the record another Associated Press article entitled *New Social Security Rules Present Barriers to Rural Communities Without Internet and Transportation*, A new requirement that the Social Security recipients go online or in person to a field office to access key benefits instead of just making a phone call will be difficult for many people to meet in those rural areas. This is an article from March 22nd. Can I enter that into the record?

PRESIDING OFFICER: Without objection. [SEE APPENDIX]

SENATOR BOOKER: Thank you. Thank very much to the kind friend who's up with me late or early, I should say. One more article I want to read, I want to ask for the record. I feel like I can take liberties with the presiding office because I've known him for 20-plus years. I consider him a real friend. He married up and he's going to teach me how to do that. I guess I'm not allowed to insult a colleague on this. That's a violation of Rule 19, I think. But it was a joke. But you did marry up. You know that.

Okay, so this is a former Social Security officers who are speaking out about what's happening, people that have worked in the agency, see what's happening. Two former senior officials at the Social Security Administration, one under a Democratic president, one under a Republican president, wrote this column published in The Hill. The title of the column is *Social Security Faces A Crisis With Staff Cuts, Closures*[4]. Again, these are folks from both sides of the aisle yelling into the wilderness, hoping that more people will understand what is happening to Social Security, what these cuts and staff are actually going to do to the quality of life of millions of Americans who rely on Social Security, disproportionately impacting people that are living in rural areas, red states, blue states, Republicans, Democrats. This is not a normal time, America, that a bedrock commitment made is being undermined by the most powerful man in our country and the richest man in the world. And the title the article, *Social Security Faces a Crisis With Staff Cuts and Closures* written by, again, somebody who worked under a Republican, somebody who worked on a president.

May I enter this into the record?

PRESIDING OFFICER: No objection.

SENATOR BOOKER: And I want to end with what I've been trying to do since I started some, I think, about eight hours ago. Yeah, eight hours ago I began. I want to begin by doing what I said I was going to do is not just lift my voice but lift the voice of New Jerseyans and Americans. And so here's some words.

This is one employee from New Jersey who contacted me to say that,

> The teleservice center has received many calls from the public, from New Jersey to Georgia and other states. They all have in common is the fear of losing their livelihood as a result of identification verification in-person visits. Seniors, disabled, and others that are economically disadvantaged need a voice, Senator Booker, and the voice I hear all throughout the day from seniors are voices of fear. Please review any policy of in-person identification for the public.

— [A] person from my state begging because they're hearing the fear of the seniors that they've pledged themselves to serve.

Another Social Security employee from New Jersey who contacted me said, I quote,

> I worked at Social Security for almost 19 years. I was approaching my 19 years in July. However, I took the early-out retirement because there's a lot of uncertainty within the agency. The resignation of others also brings additional phone calls and workloads into the office. This adds additional stress and no additional bodies to handle the workloads. It also provides poor unfair service to the public.

Here's another story from a Social Security employee in New Jersey.

> I am a claims representative for our Social Security field office. The most dramatic changes I've noticed from our recent change in operations is that our appointment calendar seems to be filling up more quickly for simple post-entitlement changes that were formerly handled over the phone. This occupies appointment space for most urgent and critical issues that would warrant an office visit. We have identity verification protocols already in place to keep identities thieves in check. To the extent that some fraudsters are still getting through, requiring people to come into our office to verify their identity is an obviously less efficient solution to the problem.
>
> A better solution to enhance security question protocols is to use two-step verification systems and document fraud attempts in our technician experience dashboard so scammers can't just shop around for field offices to fool. Regarding the in-person identifying policy, I believe that it is causing more harm than good. I've had claimants appearing in person frantic that they will lose their benefits because of this. My office has lost four staff members, two who are members of management. This is nothing but chaos here and I can foresee more loss and a further decline in employee morale.

That's from a Social Security employee in my state describing what's going on in their office. Another New Jersey Social Security worker:

> I work in one of the smaller offices in New Jersey, and we are currently combined with another office that is undergoing renovations, which has caused the number of claimants coming into the office to double over the last few months. And although we do have extra staff because the staff have been deployed to our location, it doesn't change the infrastructure of the building, such as the number of desks available to do in-person interviews and provide adequate waiting space for double the amount of claimants.
>
> In our office we only have nine desks where we can interview the public due to safety and safety protocols. Three of these are front windows where we can do quick changes and six of them are where we could do short interviews or benefit applications. Right now, being that most interviews are being done over the phone, we have over 20 people interviewing at a time now. Imagine having to do these interviews in person. We can only have six to nine interviews at a time instead of 20-plus because there's only six by nine desks available. This doesn't seem very efficient.

Maybe they should... Too bad they can't call the Department of Government Efficiency who caused the problem.

Here's another Social Security worker, their story:

> The foot traffic in the field office on a daily basis is already overwhelming. The public coming in randomly to show their identity would be a disadvantage for the elderly, people with vision issues, disabled, and someone with no car. This really hits home with me. My older brother lost his right leg to diabetes, is legally blind, and unable to drive. He called me concerned about this, knowing there is no way he can get to his field office and cannot afford to lose his retirement. I'm hoping this is reconsidered.

Social Security is not a program, it's a promise. We owe it to seniors and working people who've paid into the Social Security their whole lives to make good on the promise of a secure retirement, not to attack Social Security, to drive them into fear and worry, and, when they call for help, to put them on hold for hours or drive them into offices that may be closing or are overcrowded or are unable to help our elders. Does this sound like America at its best? Does this sound like America being made great again? This is outrageous. These are our elders. They deserve dignity, respect, and they deserve their Social Security.

I'm going to move on to the next item, but I want to reiterate again, I'm determined to stand here as long as I physically can. We're eight hours into it.

Dozens and dozens of people, I've read their stories. As I've gone around the country, I've gone around my state, there's this growing anger and rage and fear. There's chaos, there's confusion, and they read the newspapers and see that programs are helping them when an unexpected disease or cancer or a crisis hits them. And they see that a bunch of folks are trying to figure out how to cut $880 billion from things like Medicaid. The stories got me a little emotional just because hearing about so many people who, not to their fault, not to their problem, were hit by a crisis, a challenge, an accident at work, are now sitting back and are going to see what we do. People who have told us that their whole delicate, fragile world works because they have a transportation program that could be on the blocks of cuts in Medicaid or that their home healthcare worker or that their medications...

And even while these big issues are being discussed, we're seeing, as we've been documenting here again from Republicans and Democrats, how the administration's already taking steps to roll back programs, to seize funding that people have been used to access the ACA or to lower their prescription drug costs, or that are funding their research that we're competing with China through the NIH. Republicans and Democrats we've read already who have been saying, "Hey, wait a minute, you shouldn't cut the things that actually produce money for your country in the long term."

Incorrectly spelled as "Hebring" and "Woverding", respectively, in the Congressional Record.

(1) *Seniors now worrying if one day they won't get their Social Security money on time*, Susan Tompor, Detroit Free Press, 27 March 2025

https://www.freep.com/story/money/personal-finance/susan-tompor/2025/03/27/social-security-turmoil-makes-retirees-insecure-about-their-finances/82591386007/

(2) *Long Waits, Waves of Calls, Website Crashes: Social Security is Breaking Down*, Lisa Rein and Hannah Natanson, Washington Post, 25 March 2025
https://www.washingtonpost.com/politics/2025/03/25/social-security-phones-doge-cuts/
https://www.congress.gov/119/crec/2025/03/31/171/57/modified/CREC-2025-03-31-pt2-PgS1961.htm

(3) *Social Security Administration Could Cut up to 50% of its Workforce*, Associated Press, 27 February 2025
https://apnews.com/article/social-security-layoffs-doge-musk-trump-93efbed33957af5ec8ac37744d0592d
https://www.congress.gov/119/crec/2025/03/31/171/57/modified/CREC-2025-03-31-pt2-PgS1961.htm

(4) Social Security Faces a Crisis With Staff Cuts, Closures, Jason Fichtner and Kathleen Romig, 29 March 2025
https://thehill.com/opinion/5220147-social-security-crisis/
https://www.congress.gov/119/crec/2025/03/31/171/57/modified/CREC-2025-03-31-pt2-PgS1961.htm

3:08 AM - Education & Reseach

But now here's something that I want to get into, which is education in our nation.

I believe that genius is equally distributed in the United States. There's as many geniuses being born in the wealthiest parts of New Jersey and Pennsylvania as are being born in the lowest incomes. And in the global knowledge-based economy, the most valuable natural resource any nation has is the genius of its children. One genius, one Einstein, one Madam Curie, one genius could change humanity forever. And I hear these stories about China graduating more people in STEM than we have total graduates in our entire country. It's a global competition.

And if we are to be this nation that Andy Kim talked about, where every generation has the right as an American to expect that the next generation will do better, not worse, so much of this revolves around what we all know: how important education is to a democracy, especially the best ideas, the best innovations, the best artists, innovators, entrepreneurs, scientists, doctors, teachers. We need to invest in the best pipeline possible, but now – not with Congress who established the Department of Education but by executive fiat, undermining the separation of powers – the administration wants to dismantle, defund, destroy the Department of Education and scatter its responsibilities across agencies that themselves are going through massive personnel cuts and are not equipped to handle them.

This is ultimately about whether or not we as a nation believe that every child deserves an education and we should organize ourselves to meet that calling. Our nation's children are that precious resource. One of the most noble professions are those people that teach our children. And so let's go right into it. At the signing ceremony to commemorate the establishment of the Department of Education, President Jimmy Carter said, "Today's signing fulfills a longstanding personal commitment on my part. My first public office was as a county school board member. As a state senator and governor, I devoted much of my time to education issues. I remain convinced that education is one of the most noble enterprises a person or society can undertake." Pastor Carter also said, "The Department of Education was created because education is so important to our nation's future that it must have a robust level of national support."

Now, here's a letter that I really wanted to read. I'm a member of a Baptist church with the great Pastor Jefferson, but I actually study Torah. And in my Torah study with Rabbi Davidson, when I heard about all these cuts to the Department of Education, he wanted me to hear from the great rebbe, Rebbe Menachem Schneerson, the Lubavitcher Rebbe, who in 1979 wrote a letter, not in support of religious schools, but wrote a letter in support of public education, in support of the creation of a special Department of Education. He wrote this letter in 1979. I was so moved by it, thank you, Rabbi Davidson, I want to read it here. This is the Rebbe:

> I am certain that you will agree that the state of education in this country, as in many others, leaves much to be desired. {He was not happy.} And the status quo as reflected in juvenile delinquency, et cetera, is far from satisfactory and, what's worse, has been steadily eroding and that some determined nationwide effort is called for us to upgrade the quality of public education in this resourceful country. I trust you will agree that such an enormous effort, which is surely in the highest national interest, can come only from the federal government with the fullest cooperation of state, county, and city.
>
> In my view, a separate, adequately funded, cabinet-level Department of Education subject to legislative safeguards to ensure that the traditional primacy of the states and localities in education affairs would not be jeopardized could well meet the challenge. The main reason why I support said proposal are as follows: one, the creation of a distinct cabinet-level Department of Education would have a salutary impact on all who are involved in education, particularly parents, teachers, and students. The very innovation of upgrading the status of education from that of an adjunct to or division of another national agency would pointedly underscore its proper place among the nation's priorities.

Look how prescient the Rebbe was and what he might say if he was alive today.

> Number two, the workshops of education are the school and the home. For various reasons which need not be discussed, I'm worried about the home. {He basically says...} Too much of school is left to the streets. In so far as the street is concerned, there is very little that we can do. As things stand more can be done and needs to be done, but in the final analysis, it's the public school where the greatest improvement can and must be achieved.
>
> Among the factors that lie in the roots of the shortcomings of public education too, in my opinion, command primary attention. One has to do with the general curriculum, which should place much greater emphasis on character building and moral and ethical values. The other has to do with the quality of teaching by qualified, dedicated, motivating teachers. The latter point requires the upgrading of teachers' salaries on par with comparable professions in other fields of science and relieving them as far as possible of other frustrations and stresses.

I just want to do a side note here. I'm a big believer that we should slash public school professionals' tax rates. We need the best minds coming into the profession. Why not as a country to say, if you're going to take a job as a teacher, which unfortunately pays too low in our country, let's do that instead of, again, giving these massive tax cuts disproportionately to the wealthiest in our country?

> The upgrading of our nation's educational system will of course require considerable federal investment. But this is one area where spending has built-in returns, not only in the longterm but also in the immediate gains in terms of diminishing expenditures in the penal system, crime prevention, reduction of vandalism, drug abuse. In the longer term, it would also bring savings in expenditure on health and welfare and, one may venture to say, even in the defense budget, since a morally healthy, strong, and united nation is in itself a strong deterrent against any enemy.

And finally, five, he says,

> The creation of a separate cabinet-level Department of Education, as I understand it, has been conceived not for the purpose of merely improving administrative efficiency nor merely as a coordinator of existing programs or for technical reasons. The main purpose is to breathe new life into the whole educational system of this nation and to involve the whole nation through its federal government in this massive concerted effort, and as such, I am convinced a national Department of Education cabinet level deserves everybody's support.

Thank you, Lubavitcher Rebbe. Unfortunately, this administration has not listened to the Rebbes. What does the Department of Education do, and how is this administration attacking it?

Let me read you an excerpt from The New York Times. *Can Trump Abolish the Department of Education?* It's from March 20th.[1]

> President Trump signed an executive order on Thursday to the director of the Federal Department of Education to come up with a plan for its own demise. Only Congress can abolish a cabinet-level agency, and it is not clear whether Mr. Trump has the votes in Congress to do so. I will tell you, in the Senate if you need 60 votes, he doesn't. But he's already begun to dismantle the Department, firing about half of its staff, gutting its respected education research arm and vastly narrowing the focus of its civil rights division, which works to protect students from discrimination.
>
> Mr. Trump's long history of attacking the Department of Education represents a revival of a Reagan-era Republican talking point. It has unified Democrats in fiery opposition. {Yeah.} But is shuttering the Department possible? And if not, how has Trump begun to use the agency to achieve his policy goals?

> What does the Department do?
> It's founded in 1979. Its main job is distributing money to college students through grants and loans. It also sends federal money to K-12 schools targeted towards low income and disabled students and enforces anti-discrimination laws. The money for schools has been set aside by Congress and is unlikely to be affected by Mr. Trump's executive order.

I don't agree with the New York Times, because time and time again, the money set aside by Congress is being clawed back by the President against the people that the Constitution of the United States of America says has spending power.

> The federal dollars account for only about 10% of K-12 school funding nationwide. While Mr. Trump has said he wants to return power over education to the states, states and school districts already control K through 12 education, which is mostly paid for with state and local tax dollars. The federal department does not control learning standards or reading lists in countries. The agency plays a big role in funding and disseminating research on education, but those efforts have been significantly scaled back by the Trump administration. It also administers tests that track whether American students are learning and how they compare with their peers in other states and countries.

God forbid we measure people's performance. It's unclear whether those tests will continue to be delivered given the drastic reductions in the staff and funding necessary to management. Still, closing the Department would not likely have much of an immediate effect on how schools and colleges operate. The Trump administration has discussed tapping the Treasury Department to disperse student loans and grants, for instance, and the Health and Human Services to administer funding with students with disabilities.

> Any effort to fully eliminate the Department would have to go through Congress. Republican members would most likely hear opposition from superintendents, college presidents and other education leaders in school districts. Schools and Republican regions rely on federal aid from the agency just as schools in Democratic regions do. "They're going to run into opposition," said Joe Valant, an education expert at the Brookings Institution. "They have a laser-thin majority and a filibuster to confront in the Senate."
> Even if congressional Republicans stuck together, Dr. Valent predicts their constituents would protest given the Department's role in distributing money from programs like Pell Grants, which pay for college tuition, and IDEA, which provides support to students with disabilities. "It's a very hard sell. I'm skeptical."

Efforts to eliminate the Department threaten the enforcement of critical laws. There's the Elementary and Secondary Education Act, which has supported school districts since 1965 in low-income areas, Individuals with Disabilities Act, which ensures 7.5 million students with disabilities receive an education. The Higher Education Act, which helps more students afford college Title IX protections to guard against sex discrimination. This doesn't just hurt our country, but undermining those resources for our students hurts generations to come.

I want to submit for the record New York Times article entitled *Trump Firings Gut Education Department's Civil Rights Division*[2]. Thank you, my friend. Thank you, Presiding Officer, sir.

How Education Department Cuts Could Hurt Low-Income and Rural Schools in Particular, an article on March 21st, 2025[3]. May I submit that too, sir? Again, rural communities are really taking a hit.

And if I can give disability rights testimonials.

Gutting the Department of Education will be devastating for students with disabilities. Right now, the Department of Education, the Individuals with Disabilities Act, which guarantees more than seven million students in America the right to a free, appropriate public education, it ensures that provides services like speech therapies, counseling, personalized learning plans. Without federal oversight, these protections could disappear, schools could delay evaluations, cut corners or deny support altogether for parents.

Consider Catherine a resident of Westwood, New Jersey. Right by Harrington Park where I grew up. Catherine has seven-year-old twin boys who receive special services. They currently attend an out-of-school district specialized program, but are very much a part of Westwood Regional School District, and may even one day transition back into the school.

In her words,

> The Department of Education plays a critical role in enforcing the IDEA and ensuring that students with disabilities receive the accommodations and support they need to succeed. Without this oversight, many students risk losing essential services, widening existing gaps and disparities and they will face greater barriers to academic success and reaching their highest potential. This is not a partisan issue. It's a matter of ensuring that all students, regardless of ability, have equal access to education.

Her story is one of thousands of parents, educators, and advocates across the country who are standing up for children's rights to an equitable education, for Catherine's family, for her boys, and for every child who deserves a fair shot at success. Their fight for an inclusive education is essential.

Here's Ashley from Wayne, New Jersey who knows firsthand how important the Department of Education's funding is. Her daughter who is legally blind relies on Bookshare, an online learning tool that provides accessible materials to students with print disabilities at no cost to schools or families. Without it, her daughter would be left behind. As Ashley put it,

> This is a service she absolutely needs in order to access information that regularly-sighted people do not even have to think about. Cutting programs like this isn't just irresponsible, it would be cruel.

Kimberly from Dumont, New Jersey, the mother of twin boys with nonverbal level three autism. They attend an amazing school in Nutley because of IDEA. Without it, their future would be uncertain. In her own words, she says,

> It was not long ago that kids like them would've had to have been institutionalized. Now they're able to have a beautiful life and go to school. I am terrified of the future if IDEA is eliminated. I am begging you, please consider families like mine.

Kimberly, I see you.

Michelle from New Jersey shares this fear. Her daughter who has neurofibromatosis, who's one, and has apraxia, depends on in-class support to succeed. She knows firsthand how essential the Department of Education is in protecting students with disabilities. This is her words now, "Gutting, weakening, and ultimately closing the Department of Education is disastrous and dangerous for the disabled students who depend upon it." She reminds us that education is a civil right and laws like IDEA and Section 504 ensure that students with disabilities receive the support they need to succeed. Alana from my state is deeply concerned about her 20-year-old son who depends on the protections of Section 504 to have a fair shot at the future. Her 10-year-old child with autism relies on these protections every single day. She's asking for help because as she put it, "Section 504 and its rules are very important to the disability community. We need your help to save it."

Roger, who's a grandfather from New Jersey, is also pleading for action. His granddaughter has relied on a 504 plan since seventh grade and will continue to need it as she applies to college. He raises the essential question, "Which programs are directly helping students?" The answer is clear laws like IDEA, IEPs and Section 504, they're not luxuries, they're lifelines. Again, this is not about politics, and as we see from various writings, people from both sides of the aisle are worried and concerned.

I'd like to submit for the record this article from one of the publications in my state, *What Happens to Special Education Programs in New Jersey if Trump Shuts Down the Department of Education?*[4] It's by Gene Myers.

PRESIDING OFFICER: Without objection. [SEE APPENDIX]

SENATOR BOOKER: Thank you very much. I want to say something about student loans, too. The Department of Education is also responsible for operating the $1.6 trillion student federal loan program, which benefits 42.7 million borrowers in America and allow students to access higher education, something that is shown unequivocally to strengthen our economy. This administration plans to move student loan funding to the Small Business Administration, a plan that even some of my Republican colleagues in Congress have expressed serious concerns about.

Here's an article that Republicans are hesitant to stand behind Trump's plan for student loans:

> Although SBA managed a wealth of COVID relief programs, it normally runs a much smaller operation than the student debt program. President Trump has yet to win over his own party to push "immediately" in transfer of the Department of Education's massive student loan operation to another agency that's slated for deep staff cuts. Trump was expected to propose moving the agency's $1.6 trillion portfolio to the Treasury Department, a concept long discussed on Capitol Hill and suggested in Project 2025, the Heritage Foundation's conservative policy blueprint. Instead, the President announced this month that the SBA would get it, surprising many lawmakers and conservatives who track the issue. Although the SBA, which provides financial support to companies for disaster relief, training, and other needs, managed a wealth of COVID relief programs, it normally runs a much smaller operation then student debt. It's also slated to lose 43% of its staff.

Now Republicans are worried about the size of the debt and the staffing needed to manage the complex system of servicers, borrowers and loan applications, and with about 43 million borrowers and a record number of them starting to fall behind on their payments since the pandemic era hiatus ended in 2023, transferring this work may be one of the most challenging hurdles for unwinding the agency President Trump has pledged to close. "A lot of us were thinking it would go to Treasury. We're talking about the huge nature of student loans," House Education and Workforce Chair Tim Walberg said in an interview. "They have much larger staffing capabilities right now than SBA, but the President may have something specific in mind that I'm not aware of."

Early legislation from Senator Mike Rounds aimed at dismantling the Education Department also recommended the Treasury Department for the job. At a recent House Rules Committee meeting, Walberg suggested that moving the portfolio to the SBA, which likely requires an act of Congress to complete, might not be permanent. Some Republican lawmakers have been hesitant to say the move is official. Neither the Education Department's Federal Aid office, which manages the loan program, nor the SBA have provided a timeline or detailed plans to move the portfolio, but Education Department officials skeptical of Trump's SBA plan met the week after his announcement to discuss if the Treasury Department should manage this massive portfolio instead of the SBA, according to a person with granted anonymity to discuss the manner.

Some conservatives are concerned about the SBA's lack of experience with colleges and universities and the time crunch and staff will be under to learn the complex student loan system. "The plan to move the portfolio sounds rushed. It sounds like no one has been briefed on it and it's not clear what the purpose is," said Jason Delisle, who served on the Education Department's Review group on Trump's presidential transition team. FSA largely works with direct loans, meaning that instead of a bank lending the money, the Education Department disperses the funds directly to institutions in the students' names. Colleges and universities, however, aren't on the hook. If the loan isn't repaid, the borrower is. The SBA only started working with the REC loans at a massive scale in the aftermath of the pandemic.

"They're laying off 43% of the SBA staff at the same time SBA is being handed $1.6 trillion portfolio. That's three times the size of what they have and they're laying off 43% of the staff," said Michael Negron, who worked on the small business and student loans for the National Economic Council during the Biden administration. The administration has not clearly stated whether the FSA workers who have expertise on the student debt system would be transferred to the SBA, which is a concern for Negron. "That doesn't mean it's impossible. The SBA could be a fit," he said, "But the conditions need to be right. "There is a world where this can work," he said optimistically, who is now a fellow at Groundwork Collaborative, a left-leaning think tank. The White House did not acknowledge questions about how it would transfer.

"President Trump is doing everything he can within his executive authority to dismantle the Department of Education and return education back to the states while safeguarding critical functions for students and families," said press secretary Karoline Leavitt in a statement. "The President has always said Congress has a role to play in this effort and we expect them to help the President deliver."

You know, that sounds like a president who doesn't care about Congress, cares about what he's trying to do, hasn't approached this in a intelligent way, making grand statements and opinions without not considering that the department you're transferring loans to might actually be incapable with a severely diminished staff of doing the job.

Here's an incredible article by Fareed Zakaria about what this is really going on and how it affects the United States, especially relative to other nations.

" There is no area in which the United States' global dominance is more total than higher education. With about 4% of the world's population and 25% of its gross domestic product, America has 72% of the world's top 25 universities by one ranking and 64% by another, but this crucial US competitive advantage is being undermined by the Trump administration's war on colleges. Hat tip to the New York Times' Michelle Goldberg for raising this issue as well. "We have to honestly and aggressively attack the universities in this country. The professors are the enemy," said JD Vance during a speech to the National Conservatism Conference in 2021.

The administration has put those words into action. The most dramatic assaults have been financial. A freezing or massive reduction in research grants and loans from the federal government. Some of these efforts are under court review, but the cumulative impact could be that billions of dollars in cuts to basic research, much of its disrupting ongoing projects and programs.

High quality research in the United States has emerged in a unique ecosystem. The federal government provides much of the funding through prominent institutions such as the National Institute of Health and the National Science Foundation. Private foundations and companies account for the most of the rest. Professors at universities both public and private use these funds to conduct research. No other country has a system that works as well.

What is risked now is what Holden Thorp, the Editor-in-Chief of the Science of journalists calls the social contract that the federal government institutions have had to enable the scientific research enterprise in America in the last 80 years. {That is what is at risk.}

Take Duke University, which ranked number 11 in total grants received from the NIH last year. Of its 1.33 billion research budget, 863 million came from Washington according to the AP. That includes funds for critical research projects on cancer and other diseases, but also supports more than 630 PhD students at the medical school. If the cuts go through, these projects and students will have to be pared back substantially. Just on Thursday, John Hopkins announced huge layoffs, saying it would let go of more than 2000 employees after losing $800 million in federal grants.

One crucial mechanism to cut funding is through a massive reduction in the overhead or indirect costs that universities get reimbursed for by the federal government. Overhead makes up 40 or 50% of a grant, but last month the NIH ordered that it be capped at 15%. That sounds more rational than it is. Universities divide their costs on science grants into research costs, the salaries of the professors and graduate students, and overhead, the costs of the buildings, labs, energy and utilities and administrative staffs. When you are building a complex lab to conduct experiments, the structure and equipment is often far more costly than the salaries and stipends of the researchers. Michigan State University has declared that these cuts could make its stop construction of a 330 million research building for cancer research, for cardiovascular disease and neuroscience studies.

Government funding plays a unique role in America. It often supports basic research, the kind that companies have less incentive to do and its results cannot be hoarded by any one company, but rather are provided free to the entire scientific community, to the entire technological community so that all can use it to experiment and innovate. It's an incredible American system that has reaped billions and billions of dollars of rewards to our economy.

Take the mapping of the human genome. It costs less than $3 billion and took 13 years because it was government funded. One of its key requirements was that the research should be made publicly available for all within 24 hours of being generated.

"The other assault on the universities is a strange new attack on free speech... {Fareed writes}. It began from a principled critique that bureaucracies, universities, and elites all became too woke, but the government response to this problem has been Orwellian. Searching through these institutions for any mentions of the words diversity or identity or inclusion, and then shutting down those programs without any review. Worse, it now punishes universities on their campuses people who might espouse certain views on topics like Israel and Palestine and now is punishing the protestors themselves.

I have long argued that universities have a huge problem. They have far too little intellectual and ideological diversity, which is the most important kind of diversity on a campus, but the way you fix that is not to restrict radical left-wing speech, but to add voices and views from other parts of the spectrum. The answer to censorship by the left is not censorship by the right.

The fury with which of the Trump administration has turned on academia resembles nothing so much as the early days of the Cultural Revolution when an increasingly paranoid Mao Zedong smashed China's universities, their established universities, and a madness that took generations in China to remedy. Meanwhile, in Beijing last week, the Chinese government announced its intention to massively increase funding for research and technology so that it could lead the world in science in the 21st century.

So as America appears to be copying the worst aspects of Chinese history, China is copying the best aspect of America's, striving to take the edge away from the United States as though we are going through our own Cultural Revolution.

Learn from the fascist in China. (Fareed's article's over. This is me now...) Learn from the fascist in China and don't do what the Chinese did. Do what America has done to lead humanity in the sciences, in innovation, in research, in breakthroughs, in science. We are the global model and one administration in 71 days has our best universities cutting the number of PhD students they bring in, cutting the research that they're doing, cutting the planned development of research buildings.

This is insanity. Insanity. We are America. Why is the President of the United States attacking the science and research at the top universities on the planet Earth? Bullying them, undermining them. I've had universities from my state. I've had universities from my neighboring state — not Connecticut, New York. I've had my college Stanford come to see me. Top researchers. The academic community, not the political community, not the history majors, not the political scientists, not the literature students, not the AFAM [African American Studies] departments, the scientists of America have been coming to the Senate to say, "What the heck? What is going on? How could you take America's edge, America's advantage, America's strength, America's brilliance and undercut it in 71 days of your administration?"

We are killing the golden goose. Why? Because we have a president who is taking money that we already approved – the Article I branch of government – and claiming that he could claw it back all on some trumped-up charge that these institutions are too woke. The solution to that is not to cut science funding. This should make people mad, but more importantly, it should make people stand up and not be bystanders and wait until we lose our edge because our adversaries globally are smiling as we destroy our institutions from Duke to Rutgers, to University of Michigan, to Berkeley to Stanford. This is madness. This is insanity and one of a dozen reasons we're going through, a dozen reasons I'm standing here that we should not be doing things normal. If we are complicit in what Donald Trump is doing...

I'm hearing it not from political people but from scientists that show up in my office from Cornell, medical researchers that show up in my office from our research hospitals in New Jersey and are saying they're not political, they're just saying, "What the heck? You are undermining the research of today that will affect the breakthroughs five years from now, 10 years from now." What's China doing while we're doing this? They're investing record numbers, record levels. The country of Tiananmen Square cracking down on college students is now trying to out-America America, while America is acting more like them because our president is violating the separation of powers, taking away the money we approved and we're letting it happen by doing things normally here and not holding one hearing.

Here's another example of what Fareed was talking about. It's an article entitled Graduate Student Admissions Paused. *Graduate Student Admissions Paused and Cut Back as Universities React to the Trump Orders on Research*. And again, this is not from a political magazine, it's not from the New York Times or the Washington Post or the Wall Street Journal. This is from STAT News*. When did science become political?

> Acceptances for biomedical graduate students and professional scholars are being cut back at some universities and medical centers across the country as many grapple with the potential impact of the Trump administration's order to cut National Institute of Health research funding.

That paragraph alone should have people all in this chamber upset.

Let's just give European universities, Australian universities, Canadian universities, Chinese universities a leg up because we're going to cut the number of graduate students and postdoctoral students. The geniuses in our country will have less opportunity. Here goes the article, it continues...

> The cuts come even as the proposed reductions to funding for overhead expenses set to start on February 10th were temporarily halted last week by federal judges at least until a court hearing. Universities appear to be exercising caution with some freezing positions and not taking new applications or accepting fewer students than normal, according to interviews, public announcements, and internal emails obtained by STAT. The abrupt narrowing of training opportunities is leaving many future researchers at the start of their scientific journey in limbo.
> The academic calendar runs to the rhythm of its own sessions right now. It's typically this time of year when offer letters for PhD programs and postdoc positions in labs start hitting inboxes. Universities and academic medical centers were in the thick of that process when the NIH {under President Donald Trump} put out a policy about overhead costs known as indirect costs.
> "This couldn't be worse timing for doing this." — Waverly Ding, an Associate Professor at the University of Maryland who studies the biomedical sciences workforce. "It's creating a jolt in the market that is going to be disabling for labs, especially the smaller labs because they won't have the human capital to do their science. It's also going to create chaos for PhDs. It's going to be a cascading chain effect through the entire ecosystem."

I know we don't read science... Actually, we have a few doctors in here that do. But look at the alarm that they're sounding that this is not normal.

> The slowdown is happening at some universities and not at others. Some students may be unaware of the issue as they anxiously await acceptance letters without fully understanding the role national politics is playing in those decisions. Some faculty are grappling with admissions that are paused and then unpaused, while others say they're receiving little information or guidance from leadership. At the University of Southern California...

And as a former Stanford football player, it's hard for me to talk about USC. I had to jab them, Senator Murphy.

> ... At the University of Southern California, faculty in some departments were told last week to pause admissions and not formalize offers to students, even those who had visited and been given verbal acceptances. The awkward part is that we already told these applicants that they were provisionally accepted and invited them to an in-person recruitment day. Many have already purchased a flight and made hotel reservations. {I mean, that is just cruel.} One professor said in a faculty discussion, listserv observed by STAT. {I know Senator Murphy hangs out in faculty discussion listserv...}

The pause on admissions in psychology was lifted this week" {STAT was told}.

Jennifer Unger, a professor who runs a doctoral program in health behavioral research in the Department of Population and Public Health Sciences at the University of Southern California, keck School of Medicine said Wednesday she was still not able to admit the six graduate students for her department that had been accepted after a visit day on February 3rd. We had flown them out. We told them, "We love you, we want to admit you. And then, everything just stopped," Unger said.

On the day Donald Trump announced they were cutting indirect costs, USC paused all PhD admissions. "I just don't know what to tell them," Unger said of the students. "Some of them have their offers and will likely go somewhere else. We've probably lost them." Despite USC's unpausing of all admissions in many departments, Unger said Wednesday she was still not able to admit students. She hoped her portal of admit students would open soon, but said, "This disruption was coming at a time when her field," public health, "was already reeling from the actions of the Trump administration, something affecting potential graduate students as well. It's very stressful for them. This is a major life decision," she said, adding, "They were already worried about their futures. They were asking, 'Do you think we'll be able to get jobs in this environment? Do you think we'll get grants?'"

The dean of the graduate school at USC told STAT late Friday that the university's briefly paused PhD admissions to assess the uncertainties around federal funding, but that the admissions process was now open. Some schools though were continuing to accept students who had accepted graduate students before the recent turmoil and said that offers were there intact. "We have no knowledge of any disruptions to graduate student admissions in the science fields," Rachel Zentz, Senior Director of Communications, said.

In some cases, the pauses in hirings and admissions were implemented ahead of the NIH policy change, evidence of how quickly the Trump administration's threats to withhold federal research dollars over diversity, equity, and inclusion efforts are shifting the financial footings of universities. On February 6th, faculty at Vanderbilt University were instructed to reduce graduate admissions by half across the board according to an email obtained by STAT. {Reduce graduate admissions by half.} On the same day, the faculty at the University of Washington School of Public Health received an email to pause offers to doctoral students as well as offers of financial support to graduate students. "Faculty hiring was also frozen," the email said.

This Tuesday, the public health school sent out another email informing the community that some faculty hiring and PhD students would continue, some, but at a greatly diminished level. The school is also planning to take more cost containment measures, including a hiring freeze, a reimportment freeze through the end of the academic year due to the volatility caused by the Trump administration.

"Existing offers will be honored" {wrote Hillary Goodwin, Dean of the University of Washington School of Public Health}.

Marian Pepper, Chair of UW's Immunology Department said she was instructed by the university leadership to keep her program's next generation cohort smaller than the usual five to nine students admitted each year. That's easier said than done because the proportion of students who accept offers of admissions varies year to year. Pepper told STAT that while she expects the incoming class to be slightly smaller than usual, she has spoken with program heads at UW and elsewhere who are reducing class sizes by half or more. "I know for other programs they're feeling bleak about how they're going to keep labs running without funding or students," Pepper said. "It's pretty overwhelming."

Medical schools are hit hard. Medical research, hit hard.

> It's unclear how many other universities are taking similar preemptive belt-tightening measures, but schools of public health and medical schools are particularly vulnerable because they tend to have many faculty postdocs and graduate students supported by grants. Boston University School of Public Health has also ordered an across-the-board hiring freeze on all new faculty and staff positions including student workers and postdocs. In a campus-wide announcement, Dean Ad-Interim, Michael Stein said, "The move was being made due to the uncertainty of the moment."
>
> A spokesperson for the school told STAT that the graduate admissions are unaffected by the freeze. Unger said, "USC had cut funding for some teaching assistants in their department early in the year before the executive orders," which reduced the number of graduate students in her program from 10 to 6.
>
> On February 11th, Columbia's University Medical School faculty were told that the school was putting a temporary pause on hiring as well as other activities like travel and procuring equipment according to an email obtained by the Columbia student newspaper, the Columbia Spectator. A Spokesperson for Columbia declined to comment on the pause.
>
> In other cases, schools may accept fewer graduate students than they had planned, not because of an overt directive from university leaders, but because faculty feel unsure about the future, given the Trump administration's intent to cut billions of dollars in overhead funding.
>
> At the University of North Carolina, Chapel Hill, "25% fewer graduate students will be admitted this year" {twenty-five percent fewer}, "based on a survey of faculty members taking new students said, Mark Pilfer, a professor in cell biology there. "That means the school will admit about 75 students across the biomedical sciences". {He noted:} "The number of graduate students vary each year, so the decline was not unprecedented...

And the numbers continue to go down.

> In an interview with STAT, Robert Farms, Director of UNC's Lineberger Comprehensive Cancer Center said, "The hiring freezes, fewer PhD students, and other similar cost containment measures are being considered as the Center is eyeing the same financially turbulent waters of other research institutions. Every one of these things is on the table, unfortunately," Ferris said. "There's so much uncertainty. Can we hire this faculty member? Can we purchase this equipment? They just don't know exactly what or how many measures the Center has to take," he said, "as there are simply still too many unknowns. For instance, the outcome of the NIH indirect rate cut policy is still up in the air. Not knowing how it's going to shake out, it just freezes everybody into inaction."

Adding to the uncertainty is disruptions to key parts of the National Institute of Health approval process for proposed grants. Although some meetings of study sections in which grant applications are reviewed resumed at the start of the month, meetings of advisory councils have not. Each of the 27 institutes of the National Institute of Health have its own advisory council, which meets three times a year to issue final recommendations on new research projects. None of these councils, none, have met since January 22nd. Communications freezes were ordered across all health agencies.

A law called the Federal Advisory Committee Act requires that advisory councils post meeting details in the Federal Register 15 days prior to their scheduled date. But because submissions to the Federal Register have been put on hold indefinitely, these meetings can't take place. And without these meetings, no new grants can be funded.

According to one NIH employee, "At least one NIH meeting scheduled for this Friday to allow an institute director to provide updates that could proceed because it has been posted to the Federal Register was nonetheless canceled Wednesday." This was because the meeting was specified it would include a session open to the public. But because a ban remains in place on any public communications, meetings with open sessions cannot be held, and they can't update the Federal Registry with a revised agenda stating no open session because the Federal Registry is closed.

Principal investigators who had been counting on awards to pay the salaries of new graduate students and postdocs are now left wondering if their labs will be able to make it through the summer, let alone take on new members. Referencing the hold on submissions to the Federal Register, MIT Neuroscientist, Nancy Canwisher proposed on social media Wednesday, "So much for the grant I submitted last September, which was supposed to be reviewed last week. Hardly the biggest tragedy on the current scale of things, but it will force me to severely downsize my already small lab."

Fears were similar for one computational genomics researcher at a prominent East Coast institution who asked for anonymity for fear of being targeted by the Trump administration. "We have people coming to visit the lab next week and these are students we haven't made offers to yet because we can't. I don't know what I'm going to tell them."

Beyond the immediate harm to young scientists, he worries about the long-term damage to fields like computer science and biomedical engineering, areas where the US has long been the world leader. "If we stop training students, we're going to lose the lead very quickly," he said. "It's not clear anyone else is going to pick up the ball. We're just going to be worse off and people won't even be aware of it. It's hard to notice when it takes 20 years instead of 10 to get a cure."

Cuts within the NIH are also adding to the rapidly constricting pool of places prospective scientists can go and train. Since the 1960s, the NIH has provided opportunities for recent college graduates to spend one or two years in a full-time research position within one of the institute's labs, which many scientists see as a key tool for recruiting young people into biomedical fields. On February 1st, a notice appeared on the NIH website announcing that all training programs had paused recruitment pending guidance from Health and Human Services. "The NIH post-bac program, which provides recent college graduates with research positions in career advising, and last year admitted roughly 1,600 people, will not be accepting any new applicants for 2025" according to an NIH employee who asked for anonymity {for fear, of course — that's my add...} of repercussions.

It's a vital link in the training of doctors and biomedical scientists in the country. The NIH employee said, "You can't find a medical school or a biomedical program that doesn't have students from the post-bac program." {And it's ended.}

While the Trump administration may be hoping that the headwinds in creating for academic hiring may push recent graduates or newly minted PhDs into the private industry, it's unlikely to play out that way because of the speed and scale of the disruption. "Pharmaceutical firms are not going to suddenly open up more jobs for graduates to adapt to this situation," said Ding. "More likely is that people will start looking for opportunities outside the United States or wind up without jobs altogether.

At this point, it's still too early to say if these are the first signs of losing a generation of scientists." But even people like Ding who track the data that could provide clues about how extensive the damage will be are facing uncertainty about their ability to continue their own work. Her plan to hire a postdoc are currently on hold as she waits to find out if a grant she has through the National Science Foundation, which is facing its own dramatic cuts, will come through.

I mean, honestly, I'm here because I said at the beginning, some nine hours ago, that I was going to stand here because what is going on in America is not normal. We've gone through healthcare cuts, we've gone through Social Security being attacked and undermined and slashed the Department of Education, but if those things don't worry you, statements like this should. "It's still a little too early to say that these things are the first signs of losing a generation of American scientists."

I know this. I've been privileged. I've studied at Oxford University overseas, have studied at Stanford University in Silicon Valley, and I've studied at Yale, and watched friends get degrees in the sciences in things I couldn't spell, and they had options not just in America, but the brightest minds on the planet Earth. There's a global competition going on for them from Canada to Oxford to countries in Asia. If you are telling me thousands of people right now, 71 days into the Trump administration, are losing opportunities in the sciences to do research in the most important areas of human endeavor, can't get hired, they will go elsewhere.

For over a generation, America has led the planet Earth because of this combination between research universities, private sector industry, and government. How do I know this? Because I'm here because of it. The whole computer revolution in America was because incredible computer science researchers at academic institutions were partnering with industry and being funded in many ways by the government, and it helped companies like IBM with their mainframes dominate. My dad was one of IBM's first Black people hired as a salesman in the Washington DC, Maryland area. My parents were IBMers, because when scientific endeavor explodes into new industry, new ideas, new biomedical breakthroughs, it creates a ripple effect through our economy lifting so many people up, and in 71 days, Donald Trump's actions have led scientific articles like this to talk about a postdoc program which provides bright recent college graduates, brilliant people, 1600 of them, to usually get jobs, has been canceled. And this article laments from scientists, not political people, not politicians, that this is a crisis.

It's a crisis in America and we haven't held one hearing on this in Congress. Yet, university after university. I can't be the only senator having this happen, not just from my state, the universities are coming from New York to California, sounding the alarm that we are going to lose our competitive edge against one of our greatest competitors, China, who is doubling down as the article said in research on the sciences.

But let me just give you some examples and then I'll yield for a question. I just want to talk about some New Jersey institutions that have written me out.

> Rutgers has been a partner in the Air Force Research Laboratories, Minority Leaders Research Collaborative Program. That grant, which has been led by the Ohio State University, is on pause. {God forbid they use the word, minority.} And the annual program review and summer internship programs are not expected to happen this year.
> Rutgers School of Nursing has been with the Institute of Human Virology in Nigeria on an action to sustain precision and integrated HIV response towards epidemic control, and they were funded through a CDC and PEPFAR grant, a stop work order came in.
> Multiple Rutgers entities have received communications from federal agencies related to DEIA cancellation of apprenticeship programs.

Many conferences have been canceled that are trying to find the best minds wherever they might be, because there's many geniuses at Howard and Fisk and Morehouse that are often overlooked.

Anika Barber faculty of the Rutgers Department of a Molecular Biology and Biochemistry writes me this:

> Rutgers holds an NIH initiative for maximizing student development training grant that supports an additional five doctoral students. This grant expires in January 2026, and we put in for a renewal this fall for which I wrote a letter of support. However, it seems likely that this grant proposal will not even be reviewed.
>
> I just completed the first year of funding on my NIH Maximizing Investigations Research Award and put in my progress report for the next years of funding. These are non-competing renewals, which means they don't go through peer review. In the past, they were reviewed by the NIH program officials to ensure that the funds are being managed in accordance with the approval grant and the research findings.
>
> However, NIH has been extremely slow to process even these non-competitive renewals. This type of grant requires a plan for enhancing the work.

I want to read this last letter. It's handwritten.

> I am writing you not only as a concerned parent who believes in progress, education and the power of science improves lives. My daughter is a PhD in neuroscience, dedicating her life to research that has the potential to save countless lives. As a minority in science, she has worked tirelessly to overcome barriers in a field that is already competitive and demanding. Watching the current political attacks on research funding is devastating not just for her future, but for the future of the American country. Science is not political. It serves all people. Yet funding cuts to agencies like NIH and the National Science Foundation threaten to halt critical research that leads to medical breakthroughs.
>
> These cuts will not only slow progress in fighting diseases like cancer, Alzheimer's and Parkinson's, but they will also discourage young, diverse scientists, many of whom have already fought hard to be in these spaces, from staying in the field. This is not just about scientists. It's about every American. Diseases do not know political parties. Without adequate research funding, we are all at risk of losing the chance for better treatments, new cures, and improved healthcare. If we truly want a stronger and more innovative America, we must invest in science, not abandon it. Defunding research will also harm our economy. Scientific innovation drives job creation, medical advancements, and global progress. A country that does not invest in science is a country that falls behind.

SENATOR MURPHY: Does the Senator yield?

SENATOR BOOKER: I will yield for a question while retaining the floor.

SENATOR MURPHY: I thank the senator. What the senator's outlining is an extraordinary assault, not just on education but on the knowledge economy. I want to bring manufacturing jobs back to this country, but I understand, I think everybody understands, that we are not going to be a nation filled with low-skill manufacturing jobs. We are going to be a nation that does high- skill manufacturing. We are going to be a nation that invents things. We are going to be a nation that is dependent on engineering and on invention. We're going to be a knowledge economy. We are today, but we're going to be even more reliant on maintaining and expanding our knowledge edge on the rest of the world given the fact that the pace of change and the oncoming transformation that will come from robotics and AI will make it even more important for a nation to have the most highly skilled, most highly educated workforce possible in order to stay ahead of the curve and not have employment be buried by automation and artificial intelligence.

So this is a moment in which we should be doubling down on our support for the knowledge economy on that integration of public sector research and private sector research, which has always been the genius of the American economy. We did that integration better than anybody, and it is not coincidental that we leapfrog the rest of the world when it came to that innovation economy. But what the senator is explaining is that the Trump administration is waging a war on the knowledge economy, is literally signing our economic death warrant by coming after the foundational strength of our nation, which is that public-private sector integration.

I just checked in with the University of Connecticut, which is going to lose $165 million dollars because of this illegal change that the Trump administration has implemented, dramatically cutting the amount of research dollars that go to institutions with NIH grants. I'll just read half their list. They gave me the list of all the research projects that are going to either be eliminated or slowed or diminished: [a] project for improving physical and cognitive function in aging; a project on improving outcomes for people with autism; a project on understanding neural mechanisms for language and reading, including for people with dyslexia, funding for prevention and care for HIV patients; projects for studying the leading causes of death and disability in the United States, including cancer, obesity, Alzheimer's disease and substance abuse; a project studying treatments for rare diseases and genetic disorders with specific impacts on health including sickle cell, mitochondrial disorders, Rett syndrome and Prader-Willi syndrome, muscle and bone regeneration research, tick-borne diseases.

The University of Connecticut faces the same crisis as all the other institutions listed in that incredibly long and comprehensive STAT news article.

And as you mentioned, researchers are not going to wait around for this crisis to pass. They are going to accept offers from research institutions in other countries, from our European allies to our Asian competitors. We are going to lose our competitive edge when it comes to research.

It is worth noting that this change in research funding is illegal. Article I vests the spending power of the federal government in Congress. That's plain and simple and there's lots of good reasons why our Founding Fathers did that, Senator Booker. They were determined to keep the spending power out of the hands of the executive branch because they had seen how the British King had used the Treasury in order to compel loyalty and to punish opposition. You get money if you're loyal to me. I withhold money from you if you are disloyal to me. And so Congress got the spending power.

We decided the exact rate of reimbursement for medical research. We were very specific about it in the statute that we passed, Republicans and Democrats. This cut in funding for institutes of higher education's research that has been implemented by the administration is illegal on its face. Congress said exactly how research funding should be allocated. The president is ignoring that statute and implementing a unilateral cut. It has been enjoined by the federal court. Hopefully if the courts follow the law, it will be permanently stopped.

But it is important to note that it stands in a larger context of the federal government using its spending power... Excuse me, the Trump administration trying to seize control of federal spending in order to do that work that our Founding Fathers were so worried about. We have seen over the past several weeks the administration march through school after school, trying to cut individual deals with institutions of higher education. We will release your funding only after you sign a bilateral agreement with the administration lining your Institute of Higher Education's priorities up with the political interests of the administration. This is exactly what our Founding Fathers were trying to avoid. The executive using the spending power to compel loyalty from individuals and institutions.

What they are doing is illegal, and it is beyond me why my Republican colleagues, our Republican colleagues, stand idly by while the spending power vested in Congress by the Constitution is ripped from us.

But Senator Booker, I guess I'm going to ask you the same question I did when it came to this assault on Social Security, and it's a simple question and I'll lay out a little bit of a predicate. The question is why. What the administration has done is extraordinary, proposing to close the Department of Education. Wildly unpopular. Nobody's asking for that. Waging this illegal and unconstitutional assault on our knowledge economy, suspending funding for institutions of higher education. Research budgets, when plainly the statute says they cannot do that. So why engage in this extraordinary action to essentially destroy America's knowledge economy from elementary school all the way up to graduate education?

Well, as we've talked about, as you laid out, it can't be because you're trying to help the economy. This destroys the economy. I mean, this is the worst thing that you could probably do for the economy is to wage this open, transparent, proudful assault on research because we will not survive as an economy unless we are the place where cutting edge research and invention happens. We just won't. And so researchers now who are having all of their offers suspended by major colleges and universities, they're looking elsewhere. Maybe they're hoping that the offer still comes through, but they're dialing up other competitors, many of them outside of the United States. There was a story out of the University of Cambridge in England a couple of weeks ago in which their administrators were talking about the bounty that they are receiving as some of the highest class researchers in the world are coming to them because they don't believe that they'll have any source of stable funding from the United States.

So it can't be about helping us create jobs or supporting our economy. This is no doubt an assault on the economy. One of the complaints that I hear often about elementary and secondary education is that the Department of Education was engaged in micromanagement, right? That it was a federal school board and we want to get the federal government out of the business of dictating what local schools will do. Well, that's not a credible explanation for what's happening because in fact, the Trump administration is telegraphing that they are going to actually jump into the micromanagement of our local schools. Nobody has any idea what DEI means. Like let's just be honest. It means something different to every single official in the Trump administration. It's just a proxy to impose a set of reactionary right-wing values on our schools or on our federal agencies.

I asked a question of the nominee to be the alleged last Secretary of Education as to whether or not African-American history could be taught in our high schools any longer. And her answer was essentially, maybe not, I don't know. But DEI might mean that you can't teach African-American history. It might mean that the federal government is going to comb through every syllabus in every high school in the entire country and tell you what courses you can teach and what courses you can't. And if there's any words in there that our AI algorithm doesn't like, like 'African', can't teach it. That's a level of micromanagement never seen before in the federal government. And so the reason that they are cracking down on the Department of Education or eliminating funding for research is not because they're trying to get the federal government out of the management of our schools, because they're doing exactly the opposite.

They're telling you that your school is not going to be able to make decisions on what classes it offers its students. It's going to be Linda McMahon, the former CEO of the World Wrestling Federation, that is going to be in charge of whether your school can teach African-American history. So then what's the reason, Senator Booker, and I'll just give you a couple suggestions.

Well, maybe it's just to compel loyalty, right? Maybe it's just to use that money to compel loyalty so that boards of education or colleges are only teaching conservative or right leaning curriculum. Maybe it's to try to quell protest on campuses so that there isn't an ability for students to robustly protest the policies of the regime. Maybe it's just to destroy the idea of objective truth. I mean, this whole scandal over Signal [Pete Hegseth's use of the messaging phone app] has lots of elements to it, but I think one of the most worrying things for the American public, why it's still a story a week later is because the Secretary of Defense looked the American public in the eye and said, two plus two equals nine, right?

He said, those Signal texts you saw did not involve war plans, did not involve classified information. And the American public was like, wait a second. We read them. I'm not dumb. I know those were war plans. I know that that was classified information. But if you are in the business of trying to unwind a democracy, you have to destroy objective truth. You have to make everything political. You have to make everything subjective. Where is objective truth midwifed? In our education system, that's where we learn that two plus two equals four every time. But if you want to undermine the foundation of a democracy, then you undermine the place where truth happens. Okay. Maybe it's the same agenda with Social Security. Just come up with an excuse to privatize it all. Just take all the money that's going to good public sector research and just move it all into the private sector so it can be a source to reward the friends of President Trump. That could be a rationale as well. Or maybe it's even simpler. Maybe it's just to own the libs. Maybe it's just that historically, Democrats in the left have maybe talked about education more than Republicans have. Even though to me it was always something we both cared about. Whether or not I agreed with George Bush's No Child Left Behind plan, at least he was walking into the capitol with a plan to try to improve education.

But maybe it's just that Democrats on the left have historically talked more about education, and if you believe as Donald Trump does, that all politics is zero-sum, anything that Democrats are for must be by definition bad for America.

And Democrats seem to like college and they seem to really support our schools. So we have to destroy our colleges and we have to destroy public education because if the left is for it, it must be evil. Maybe that's the reason they're doing it, but that's the question I pose to you because it has nothing to do with our economy. It has nothing to do with getting the federal government out of the management of schools and colleges. There's another agenda here, and it doesn't seem to be an agenda that squares with anything the American people have been asking, Senator Booker.

SENATOR BOOKER: Well, I just want to answer you. Again, I would drive myself mad trying to understand what the ambitions of Trump was or the ambitions behind some of the crazy stuff in Project 2025 that he said wasn't there. They tried to run away from it because it was so unpopular, and now so much of it is being done. It almost sounds like too partisan, too insane. What I do want to do Senator Murphy, in answer to your question, all I can do is try to be as fair and factual and describing what's happening in our country and appeal to people who are moderates in this country. The people who are fair arbiters of what's happening to try to appeal to them that this is a crisis.

So when university, after university, after university is cutting scientific research, stopping bringing in the best minds, PhD candidates, post-docs, when they're telling you that they're stopping investment in state-of-the-art research buildings, when they're telling you that they're shutting down programs to bring the youngest brightest minds in, and our competitor China is doing the exact opposite, flowing money through, because China understands if we get two steps ahead of America on quantum computing, we can break all kinds of encryptions. We could locate every submarine they have. China understands if we can get two steps ahead of America on artificial intelligence, it's an end game for them.

This is a global competition and a president in 71 days, if you are a moderate in America and just want America to win in human endeavor, look at what the president is doing. And here's to the point you were driving Senator Murphy. It is Orwellian, the bastions of freedom that are our universities. As an article from Fareed Zakaria has said, "Even if universities got too woke and had two excesses, the antidote to that isn't to try to shut down the thought of the left. It's to try to make a fair more competitive marketplace for ideas from all around the political spectrum." But this isn't about politics, it's about science, it's about research. It's about cutting NIH funding, science funding. But I want to stick with that because that's the controversial nub, right? We need to go after DEI programs. I'm hearing it all the time.

It was like the confusion I had five years ago when people were asking me, oh, the Republicans are talking about critical race theory. As my father says, I got more degrees in the month of July, but I'm not hot. But I had to go back and research what is critical race theory. Oxford, Stanford, Yale grad here... I wasn't sure what they were talking about. And this is the rub on that because I don't want to just talk about what's obvious, which should enrage people on both sides of the aisle. Not just enrage people on both sides of the aisle because of China outcompeting us, but because we allocated this money in a bipartisan way that he's now trying to pull back. That should — it raises a violation of Article I of the Constitution. But I want to stick in this more controversial era that you talked about that has — all across the country people banning books.

When I heard Tony Morrison's "The Bluest Eye" was being taken out of libraries, when I heard my favorite author James Baldwin was being taken out of libraries, what kind of world do we live in? Where somehow studying what they call black history is something that Trump feels like is a rally people to stop where a person going for the Department of Education can't look you in the eye and says, yes, we need to study black history. Well, I get upset with that because black history is American history. I had a brilliant friend of mine, brilliant, look with me in deadpanned embarrassment and tell me he just found out that year about the bombing in Tulsa, Oklahoma, something I worked with Senator Lankford to do more to memorialize, but just never knew about it. That this thriving African-American financial community was the first recorded aerial bombing, not Pearl Harbor, in the United States of America. And he was never taught it.

Is that Black history or is that American history? Why do these people who attack our history think they have to sanitize, homogenize, Disney-ify American history to make us proud? I am more proud of our country when we tell the truth about what happened, when we learn from the wretchedness and the difficulties and the bigotries and the hates and the demagogues who pit us against each other and how we all overcame that. That's our greatness. How the genius of inventors that were women or blacks in the most oppressive of times still manifested their genius to transform humanity. These are stories that should make every American more proud.

So yeah, when you have a president now that is making people scrape through programs that they don't even know what they're doing, but if they've word diversity in it, that's bad? That's insanity. My mom worked for IBM before they used words like DEI, and one of her jobs was to find a bigger pool of highly qualified applicants. And so you know what she did is what is being stopped by the Trump administration. She just made sure that they were going to HBCUs to find the brightest students, so that their applicant pool would be better. This isn't about preferential treatment for one group over another. It's about trying to create a more competitive pool where we get the best of the best. It's about merit based. And this president talks about merit, and I watched Senator Whitehouse ask one of the top lawyers in the EPA if he'd ever brought a case, if he had had a hearing, if you ever did a deposition.

"No, no, no, no, no." And he's like, wait a minute. How are you qualified for this job? And that's the conflict in the logic that I'm observing. In one sense, they're exalting the wealthy elites. I have never imagined that I would see a presidential inauguration where billionaires, leaders of tech companies would sit in front of cabinet members, many of whom were billionaires themselves, but that kind of elitism, but yet they call academic excellence, brilliance and achievement in the sciences at these universities, the elites that we need to go after. If we start going after our educational institutions and weakening their ability to advance excellence in human endeavor, we are injuring ourselves and we have models for that. As Fareed Zakaria says, "The best model is Mao Zedong and the Cultural revolutions where one of the first groups they went after were their universities." But now they're reversing that and they watched what we did so well that they're doubling down on their funding of universities.

They're taking their best scientists and taking away their passports because they don't want them to come here and study. Because they're trying to get ahead of us with DeepSeek and AI. They're trying to get ahead of us in quantum computing. They're trying to get ahead of us in robotics. They're trying to get ahead of us in biomedical engineering. They're trying to get ahead of us in all of these things. And they know the way they do it is to do what America did in the 60s, the 70s, 80s, the 90s, the aughts, the 2010s to do what they did in all those times and look at them now. Look at them now.

SENATOR MURPHY: Will the gentleman yield?

SENATOR BOOKER: I will yield while still retaining the floor.

SENATOR MURPHY: I take the gentleman's point, my friend's point, right? I am probing tonight for the why, right? Because it's the obvious question. It doesn't make sense. On its face, this intentional chaos, this intentional chaos in Social Security, in Medicare, in higher education, it doesn't make sense. It's not about efficiency. It's not about jobs. So what is it about? But your point is a good one. That may not actually be the conversation that a lot of apolitical Americans are asking. They may just be looking at this on the face and say, how does it impact me? It doesn't matter to me why it's happening. It just matters to me how it's going to impact me. And there's just no doubt that this assault on higher education has an impact. It does. Because we are – as you've said it better than I have – we are just in a race. We are just in a race, and we just decided to slow down to a walk, which is a shame because we're fast.

We're fast. This country is quick, and our coach just told us start walking while the other guys speed up. And this is why we have urgency because the rac is ... this one's not a... Maybe it's a marathon, but it is one of those races where if the other team gets too big a lead, it's going to be hard to catch up. And so in the next three and a half years, if we just stand down in terms of supporting the knowledge economy, we are going to shed millions of jobs, millions of jobs. And once those centers of excellence, research excellence are outside of the United States, it's not like the next president can just come back in and fix it.

That becomes a permanent liability for us. So the reason that I'm here on the floor with you, Senator Booker, is because I agree with you that this is not normal, but I also agree with you that we now wake our colleagues up fast because a second ago, I thought we all agreed on the fact that we need to support the knowledge economy. Two seconds ago, we were all raising hands together, Republicans and Democrats, that we finally started putting big new dollars into NIH. We did a $2 billion increase I think a few years ago, and it was a big bipartisan achievement. And all of a sudden, just because Donald Trump is in the White House, we've lost the bipartisan consensus around supporting the knowledge economy.

SENATOR BOOKER: Then you go back to your question. I know you want to get your last question out before I jump into the next area. So related to this, immigration. I mean the brightest minds on the planet earth that are coming here now are terrified to come here, but we'll talk about that.

SENATOR MURPHY: I made my point.

SENATOR BOOKER: You made your point.

I just wanted to say something to you because you just got me triggered when you said we had some consensus over the last four years that we were here. I love how you said just yesterday, I remember the Chips and Science Act. That was a bipartisan bill. I was sitting in a skiff with all of us, and I watched our whole national security apparatus talk about why science endeavors and chip making and the breakthroughs that are happening on chips are so essential for our national security and how we had to stay ahead of the competition and we marched out of that meeting in a bipartisan fashion. We saw this in the bipartisan work we've been doing on AI here, talking about how America has to lead in this area. And with all of that bipartisan vigor, we let a president come in, in 71 days and halt scientific research, pausing, literally experiments in their tracks, halting researchers in their tracks, shaking universities to the core that are afraid of free expression for getting on the wrong side of dear leader that it might cost them their science funding.

So you are putting your finger on it, but can I just say something on a personal level? Because I just want to remind folks as we close it in the 10th hour that you and I were here for 15, and you are here. You are here because you agree with me, you agree with me, that from science and research to higher education, to the Department of Education, Social Security, to healthcare in America, we are at a crisis. Any one of those alone should have Americans. But the case we're making going through all these, pulling from people on the left and the right, we've quoted Republican governors, we've quoted Republican mayor organizations represented by organizations. We've quoted public and business people. We've quoted from the Wall Street Journal and Cato Institute's coming up. This is not a partisan crisis that people across the spectrum are pointing to.

But I do want to point out that you've been such a good friend to me to spend 10 hours almost on the floor, and it means a lot to me tonight. So thank you for that as I switch to healthcare. And I appreciate the sentiment that you have and that you had after the Pulse shooting that you were so worried about when I listened to your maiden speech when you first got here to the Senate, that we would normalize gun violence in this country. And what I'm worried about, I share your worry there. I grew up in a time where fire drills were the big thing, and that space between people ducking and covering because of nuclear fears and left school before... We were a country that had more active shooter drills than fire drills. And we just sort of are normalizing this terror in our country and haven't stepped up to the challenge of really doing something about it.

But this is one of these crises where if we act like business as usual, 71 days so far of the Trump administration, when we get to a hundred days catastrophic things could have happened to Medicaid and healthcare. The crashing of research for science, the attacks on the programs our senior citizens rely on. We as a country have to, as I said at the very beginning, 10 hours ago almost, we have to do what John Lewis challenged us to do, to stand up, to speak up, to get into good trouble, necessary trouble. And tonight, my friend, in the wee hours, so many songs about 4:00 in the morning, it's like the hour that nobody should be awake, and I want to thank the presiding officer for being here. I want to thank the clerks and the parliamentary staff and the impositions, but the cries of American citizens for their leaders to do something different, to stand up, to speak up.

I felt like this has to be done, and so let's keep going.

*STAT is a news outlet that reports on health and medicine - https://www.statnews.com/

(1) Can Trump Really Abolish the Department of Education? New York Times, 20 March 2025 https://www.nytimes.com/2025/03/20/us/can-trump-dismantle-education-department.html; Text of section "What does the Department do?" can be found in *What a Smaller Education Department Is Doing Under Trump*, Dana Goldstein and Michael C. Bender, The New York Times, 14 July

(2) *Trump Firings Gut Education Department's Civil Rights Division*, New York Times, 13 March 2025
https://www.nytimes.com/2025/03/13/us/politics/trump-education-department-civil-rights.html

(3) *How Education Department Cuts Could Hurt Low-Income and Rural Schools in Particular*, Jonaki Mehta, NPR, 21 March 2025
https://www.npr.org/2025/03/21/nx-s1-5330917/trump-schools-education-department-cuts-low-income

(4) *What Happens to Special Education Programs in New Jersey if Trump Shuts Down the Department of Education?* Gene Myers
{Unable to reference}

4:43 AM - Borders and Liberties

I felt like this has to be done, and so let's keep going. Almost 10 hours in. I'm thankful, but we're going to start the next section, and I'm trying to do in all of these is I'm trying to elevate the voices that don't get to come to this place. The voices that I'm hearing from. Voices that identify themselves sometimes as I'm a Republican veteran and I'm a Democrat, but most of them are just people that are just saying, "this is not normal." Many of them are saying, "do something." Some of them who get me very emotional saying, "what can I do?" I get that question a lot. "What can I do? Tell me what I can do to try to stop this."

We're going to take this issue of immigration, and here is... I'm not sure where this person is from. My staff has covered it up probably to protect a person's identity, but I'm going to read this handwritten note. Oh, it's from New Jersey. Thank you.

> Senator Booker, please continue to fight the good fight against the injustices being done by the current administration. I am the pastor of Emmanuel Lutheran Church in New Brunswick. As a faith leader and your constituent, I'm deeply concerned about the treatment of LGBTQ people and immigrants by this administration. The demonization and marginalization of these groups is unchristian and deeply offensive to the values of my faith. I ask that you continue to oppose all executive orders and legislation that targets these groups. You have been a consistent ally. Please continue to be a champion for justice for all people, but especially the most vulnerable.

Another person, late yesterday, in fact, court filings from the Trump administration revealed that they mistakenly deported a Maryland father with protected legal status to this horrific prison in El Salvador. Abrego Garcia is married to a United States citizen and has a five-year-old disabled child who is a US citizen. He has no criminal record in the United States, but despite receiving a legal status called Withholding Of Removal, where a United States immigration judge found that it is more likely than not to face persecution if deported to El Salvador, the Trump administration deported him, where? To the very country from which he fled gang violence.

Here's the story that was written about him in the Atlantic.

> The Trump administration acknowledged in a court filing Monday that it had grabbed a Maryland father with protected legal status and mistakenly deported him to El Salvador, but said that the US courts lack jurisdiction to order his return from the mega prison where he is now locked up. The case appears to be the first time the Trump administration has admitted to errors. When it sent three planeloads of Salvadorans and Venezuelan deportees to El Salvador's grim Terrorism Confinement Center on March 15th, attorneys for several Venezuelan deportees have said that the Trump administration falsely labeled their clients as gang members because of their tattoos. But in Monday's court filing, attorneys for the government admitted that the Salvadoran man, Kilmar Abrego Garcia, was deported accidentally.
>
> Although ICE was aware of his protection from removal to El Salvador, Abrego Garcia was removed to El Salvador, because of an administrative error the government told the court. Trump lawyers said the court has no ability to bring him back now that Abrego Garcia is in Salvadoran custody.
>
> Simon Sandoval-Moshenberg, Abrego Garcia's attorney, said he's never seen a case in which the government knowingly deported someone who had already received protected legal status from an immigration judge. He is asking the court to order the Trump administration to ask for Abrego Garcia's return, and if necessary, to withhold payment to the Salvadoran government, which says it's charging the United States $6 million a year to jail US Deportees.
>
> The Trump administration told the court to dismiss the request on multiple grounds, including Trump's primacy in foreign affairs.

Primacy in foreign affairs? I'm not going to stop now, but I ask anybody who's read the Constitution to understand that the President of the United States is not king. He does not have primacy in foreign affairs. I continue with the article ...

> The claim that the court is powerless to order any relief, Sandoval-Moshenberg told me, 'If that's true, the immigration laws are meaningless, all of them, because the government can do whatever they want, whenever they want, wherever they want, and no court can do anything about it once it's done.'

Court filings show Abrego Garcia came to the United States at the age of 16 in 2011, fleeing gang threats in his native El Salvador. In 2019, he received a form of protected legal status, known as Withholding Of Removal, from a US immigration judge who found he would likely be targeted by gangs if he was deported back. Abrego Garcia, who is married to a US citizen and has a five-year-old disabled child, who is also a US citizen, has no criminal record in the United States, according to his attorney. The Trump administration does not claim he has a criminal record, but called him a danger to the community. They called him an active member of MS13, the Salvadorian gang that Trump has declared a foreign terrorist organization.

Sandoval-Moshenberg said those charges are false, and the gang label stems from a 2019 incident when Abrego Garcia and three other men were detained in a Home Depot parking lot by a police detective in Prince George's County, Maryland. During questioning, one of the men told Officers Abrego was a gang member, but the man offered no proof, and police say they didn't believe him, filings show.

Police did not identify him as a gang member, Abrego Garcia was not charged with a crime, but he was handed over to US Immigration and Customs Enforcement after the arrest to face deportation. In those proceedings, the government claimed that a reliable informant had identified him as a ranking member of MS13. Abrego Garcia and his family hired an attorney and fought the government's attempt to deport him. He received Withholding Of Removal six months later, that protective status, it's not a path to permanent US residency, but it means the government won't deport him back to his home country, because it's more likely than not that he'll face harm there.

Abrego Garcia has no contact with any law enforcement agency since his release, according to his attorney. He works full-time as a union sheet metal apprentice, has complied with requirements to check in annually with ICE, and cares for his five-year-old son who has autism and a hearing defect, and is unable to communicate verbally.

On March 12th, Abrego Garcia had picked up his son after work from the boy's grandmother's house, when ICE officers stopped the car, saying his protective status had changed. Officers waited for Abrego's wife to come to the scene and take care of the boy, then drove away with him in handcuffs.

Within two days, he had been transferred to an ICE staging facility in Texas, along with other detainees the government was preparing to send to El Salvador. Trump had invoked the Alien Enemies Act of 1798 and the government planned to deport two plane loads of Venezuelans, along with a separate group of Salvadorians. Abrego's family has no contact with him since he was sent to the mega prison in El Salvador, known as the CECOT {C-E-C-O-T}.

His wife spotted her husband in the news photographs released by Salvadorian President Bukele on the morning of March 16th, after a US district judge had told the Trump administration to halt the flights. 'Oopsie,' Bukele wrote on social media, taunting the Judge. Abrego Garcia's wife recognized her husband's decorative arm tattoo and scars. According to the court filing, the image showed Salvadorian guards in black ski masks frog-marching him into the prison with his head shoved down toward the floor. The CECOT is the same prison Department of Homeland Security, Kristi Noem, visited last week recording videos for social media, while standing in front of a cell packed with silent detainees.

If the government wants to deport someone with protective status, the standard course would be to reopen the case and introduce new evidence arguing for deportation. The deportation of a protective status holder has even stunned some government attorneys I've been in touch with who are tracking the case, who declined to be named, because they weren't authorized to speak to the press. One of those people texted me, 'What. The. (expletive).'

Sandoval-Moshenberg told the court he believes Trump officials deported his client through extrajudicial means, because they believed that going through the immigration judge process took too long, and they feared that they might not win after all their cases. Officials at ICE and the Department of Homeland Security did not respond to a request for comment.

The Monday court filing by the government indicates officials knew Abrego Garcia had legal protections shielding him from deportation to El Salvador. ICE was aware of this grant withholding the removal at a time of Abrego Garcia's removal from the United States. Reference was made to a status on internal forms. Abrego Garcia was not on the initial manifest of the deportation flight, but was listed as an 'alternate'. The government attorneys explained as other detainees were removed from the flight for various reasons, Abrego Garcia moved up the list.

The flight manifest did not indicate that Abrego Garcia should not be removed. The attorneys said through administrative error, Abrego Garcia was removed from the United States to El Salvador. 'This was an oversight,' the government admitted, but despite this, they told the court that Abrego Garcia's deportation was carried out in good faith.

I'm going to go into this section now, and I'm going to read things by Conservative justices, and Liberal justices, to some of the most conservative Supreme Court justices, that say, "This is outrageous in this nation."

No one – there are parts of this Constitution – and I'm going to talk about them, that talk about due process, about fundamental American ideals, but this story, and the few others I've heard, where Americans that have the status to stay here, that have an American spouse, American children who will be traumatized by this. This case, a disabled child whose working father who is struggling to take care of one of our children, an American child with an American mother. We were told that the President said he was going to be focusing on criminals, and these trumped-up charges, where they admit in court, and made a mistake, but write such mocking things to judges like, "Whoopsie" on social media ... This cruelty, this is not who we are.

So let's talk about the Constitution first. — the Fifth and the 14th Amendment. The Fifth and the 14th Amendment.

The Fifth and the 14th Amendments say that, "**No one shall be deprived of life, liberty, or property without the due process of law.**" The central promise of those words is an assurance at all levels of the American government must operate within the law and the bonds of this Constitution that everybody in this chamber swears an oath to uphold the Constitution. But every single day it just seems our President is challenging constitutional principles, pushing past constitutional boundaries. Every day we're hearing new stories of immigrants, some here legally, some awaiting trial, most charged with no crimes, being rounded up, detained, arrested, deported, often just disappeared. This is happening without charges, evidence, trials, hearings, without what the Constitution says, "Due process." This is what other governments done, we've talked about it. In the Foreign Relations Committee, we complain about it. To nations across the earth when they do not show due process, where they disappear people.

Maybe you're an immigrant that's never broken the law. Maybe you're a citizen. Even if you think the administration's immigration agenda doesn't apply to you, please know that the reckless behavior we're seeing erodes all of our rights. And the American mother and the American child, right now, whose husband was unjustly and illegally deported and is right now in an El Salvadorian prison. Think about them.

Denying due process is a slippery slope. We've seen it in other countries with democratic backsliding — it is a slippery slope. If people can be detained and deported without a hearing, detained and deported without due process, without seeing a judge, nothing will stop from slipping towards deporting others, making mistakes with an American.

I am one of these people, in this body, that thinks our immigration system is in desperate need of reform. It was last updated 40 years ago. 40 years ago was the last time we acted to update our immigration laws. The failure to update our laws has resulted in our country's inability to manage unprecedented levels of global migration, that are not just affecting our country, but are affecting others. It's an unprecedented influx of applications to enter the United States. It's put pressure and strain on our immigration system. It's slowed down processing times for millions of people trying to immigrate or naturalize legally, and made it more difficult to incentivize the world's brightest minds to come here to contribute to our country's long-term success.

For millions of Americans, immigration is not a political issue, it's a personal one. There are immigrants around my state, and in every state, who have waited year after year for Congress to find bipartisan agreement to improve our system in ways that most Americans agree on, whether you're right or left. They've been waiting for Congress to fix our outdated immigration laws, to secure our borders, to dedicate the resources necessary for USCIS to fix the outrageously long processing times for immigrations, and provide a pathway to legal status for long-term American residents who have followed our laws, contributed to our societies, and some of them know no other country because they came here when they were just months old.

Our immigration laws are so outdated, even the conservative Cato Institute published a comprehensive policy analysis in 2023 titled *Why Legal Immigration is Nearly Impossible*. In it, the Cato Institute explains, I quote,

> Today, fewer than 1% of the people who want to move permanently to the United States can do so legally. Legal immigration is less like waiting in line and more like winning the lottery. It happens, but it's so rare that it's irrational to expect it in any individual case. {The Cato Institute continues... } For some immigrants, this restrictive system sends them back into the black market of illegal immigration. For others, it sends them to other countries, where they contribute to the quality of life in their homes. And for still others, it requires them to remain in their homeland, often underemployed, sometimes in danger. Whatever the outcome, the system punishes both prospective immigrants and Americans who would associate, contract and trade with them. Congress and the administration can do better.

I've met with conservatives, I've met with business groups, I've met with agricultural leaders, who all talk to common sense things we should be doing to improve our immigration system, to protect our borders, yes, but to improve our economy, to improve our scientific research, to improve our quality of life.

The only way to fix our broken immigration system is for Congress to fix it — to pass comprehensive immigration reform. But instead of a leader, strong leaders, who go before Congress taking on the most complex issues, but yet have the courage to stand before Congress and pull them together to do hard things, instead of doing that, the last time we made progress in this body, President Trump actively blocked bipartisan legislation. Now he's imposed policies that aren't just going after criminals, they're dragging in so many others.

When President Trump stopped Republicans from voting on the bipartisan bill that was negotiated in the Senate last year, he stopped us from making strides towards the larger fixes we need. The administration's immigration plans are not helping American citizens who are submitting applications so that their spouse, or fiance, who is waiting in another country can finally join them in the United States. The administration right now is not helping American citizens who have been waiting for years for a visa for their brother, or their sister, or their mother, or their father, uniting families is an American value. Americans aren't getting any relief from these extraordinary long wait times.

On the USCIS website, you can check the average processing times for these cases, and most Americans would be shocked, maybe even horrified, to learn just how long it will take for you, as an American citizen, to bring a husband, or a wife, or even a child, back to the United States with you.

We checked this past weekend and here are the numbers. For the I-129 Fiance Visa, the processing time for 80% of the cases is eight months to three years. For an I-130 visa, if you're a US citizen petitioning for your spouse, parent, or minor child, then the waiting time is any time from 17 months to 64 months. That's an average from anywhere from a year and a half to over five years. For an I-90, if your green card is destroyed in a flood or a fire, 80% of people will be waiting for almost a year and a half – 17 months – to just get a new copy.

These numbers are shocking, and they don't even take into account long wait times for visa appointments at the US consulate or embassies. In India, for example, the average wait time for an appointment is well over 400 days. American citizens, including thousands of my constituents in New Jersey, are so angry, they're waiting far too long for the cases to be prioritized and adjudicated.

But when Trump relocates all the resources within our immigration system to conducting the largest mass deportation of people in history, American citizens are paying the price, not just from USCIS processing times, we pay the price, because to do this, he is diverting actual law enforcement resources away from solving crimes and stopping terrorisms, his actions are actually making us less safe. We pay the price, because these policies are eroding constitutional principles, as well as making us less safe, by taking law enforcement away from their efforts. This plan is about conditioning Americans to the suspension of due process. First for immigrants, if we let due process erode for immigrants, it erodes for Americans.

Let me outline a little bit about how this is happening and why this is a crisis. Two weeks ago, Trump invoked the Alien Enemies Act. The Alien Enemies Act of 1798 allows the President to detain or deport the natives and citizens of an enemy nation that we are at war with. 1798 Act, the President can detain or deport these immigrants without a hearing, with no due process, even ones who are lawfully present in the United States.

The Alien Enemies Act was last used during one of our country's darkest moments, the internment of Japanese, German, and Italian nationals during World War II. But even then, we still ensured that due process was followed prior to detention. People subjected to the Alien Enemies Act in the 1940s appeared before the Alien Enemy Hearing Board, where they could at least present evidence that they had no ties to Axis Powers.

As one circuit court judge recently said of Trump's use of the Alien Enemies Act,

> There's no regulations and nothing was adopted by agency officials that were administrating this. The people weren't even given notice. They weren't told where they were going. They were getting those people on the planes on Saturday, and had no opportunity to file habeas, or any type of action to challenge their removal.

The standards of 1940, during World War II, were higher than the standards of this President? The following are people that Trump has targeted and removed without criminal charges, without a hearing, without evidence to a prison rife with human rights abuses in El Salvador. These are the people that he has sent there: a tattoo artist seeking asylum who entered the country legally; an aspiring pop musician with a tattoo of a hummingbird; a 24-year-old who used to teach swim classes for children with developmental disabilities and has a tattoo of an Autism Awareness ribbon in honor of his brother; a Venezuelan who had fled violence in Venezuela last year and came to the United States to seek asylum. His lawyer wrote on social media, "ICE alleged that his tattoos are gang related. They are absolutely not. Our client worked in the arts in Venezuela. He is gay. LGBTQ. His tattoos are benign. He has no criminal record." Another Venezuelan removed to this El Salvadorian prison is a barber with no criminal history. Another professional, is a professional soccer player, has a tattoo with a soccer ball and a rosary closely resembling the logo of his favorite soccer team.

This is stunning, what we're doing. These people were swept up and sent to another prison known for its human rights abuses, because they were Venezuelan and had tattoos. Benign tattoos. An article was published in one periodical about the anguish from families. Here are a few excerpts from the article *You are here because of your tattoos*:

> The Trump administration sent Venezuelans to El Salvador's most infamous prison. Their families are looking for answers. On Friday, March 14th, Arturo Suarez Trejo called his wife, Natalie Sanchez, from an immigration detention center in Texas. Suarez, a 33-year-old male native of Caracas, Venezuela, explained that his deportation flight had been delayed. He told his wife he still would be home soon. Suarez did not go back to Venezuela. Still, there was at least a silver lining.
>
> In December, Sanchez had given birth to their daughter Naira. Suarez would finally have a chance to meet their three-month-old baby girl he had never ever seen. But Sanchez told the outlet she had not heard from Suarez since. Instead, last weekend, she found herself zooming in on a photo the government of El Salvador published of Venezuelan men the Trump administration had sent to President Nayib Bukele's infamous Terrorism Confinement Center, or CECOT. 'I realized that one of them was my husband,' she said. 'I recognized him by his tattoo, by his ear, and a scar on his chin. Even though I couldn't see his face, I knew it was him.' The photo of Sanchez examined a highly-produced propaganda video promoted by the Secretary of State and the White House, showed Venezuelans shackled in prison uniforms as they were pushed around by guards and had their heads shaved.
>
> The tattoo on Suarez's neck is of Colibri, a hummingbird. His wife said it was meant to symbolize harmony and good energy. She said his other tattoos, like a palm tree on his hand and an homage to Suarez's late mother's, use of Venezuelan expression about God being greater than a coconut tree, were similarly innocuous. Needless to say, they may be why Suarez has been effectively disappeared by the US government into an El Salvadoran mega prison.

We must keep our country safe. Violent criminals, people with long criminal records who are not citizens, I think every American would agree, they should be deported. Immigrants to this country, surprisingly, have a much lower rate of breaking laws, but if they break laws, I agree. But maybe you're an immigrant that's never broken a law. Maybe you're a naturalized citizen. Maybe you were born here. The problem with this idea of disappearing people with no due process, is once that foundation is laid, if they're able to defend that lack of due process to use that law from the 1700s, we begin a process in this country, that even conservative justices of the Supreme Court, said is unjustifiable.

Denying people due process pushes us down a road where more exceptions can be made. You cannot deny fundamental rights to another and not endanger them for yourself. We have created a system, now, if Trump is successful, where you can just say, you can just claim, you can just point to someone and say they're from X country, or claim that they're part of a gang, and without any due process, without any vetting, without going before any independent arbiter, you are disappeared, because there's just no way to challenge them. No due process for non-citizens means that we are a country in violation of those ideals I talked about from here [HOLDS UP POCKET COPY OF CONSTITUTION], that says at the beginning of this country, that says very simply, "**No one shall be deprived of life, liberty, or property. No one without due process of law.**" As soon as we break that, as soon as we violate that, we're going down a road.

Anton Scalia, I confess I've disagreed with him on so many things, but this conservative justice once sat in an interview with Ruth Bader Ginsburg. They had a relationship that I think was special, and shows that even people that have distinctly different views can still make real human connection in our country. They were asked by an interviewer whether undocumented people have the five freedoms, freedom of religion, freedom of speech, freedom of the press, freedom of assembly, and freedom to petition the government. Here is what the conservative Justice Scalia said, "Oh, I think so. I think anybody who is present in the United States has protections under the United States Constitution. Americans abroad have that protection. Other people abroad, do not. They don't have the protections of our constitution, but anyone who is present in the United States has the protections of the United States Constitution. Antonin Scalia, one of the most conservative members of the highest court in our land. And of course, Ginsburg, his ideological opposite, she concurred when she said, "When we get to the 14th Amendment, it doesn't speak of citizens as some constitutions grant rights to citizens, but our constitution says persons, and that the person is every person who is here in our country, documented or undocumented." Our Constitution is clear on the face.

If you are an originalist like Antonin Scalia and you read the Constitution's words, you have to stand for the idea that no one should be denied due process, that the government can't walk up to a human being and grab them off the street and put them on a plane and send them to one of the most notorious prisons in the world and just say, as one of our authority did, "Oopsie." Think about that. And that happened to a father of an American child. Think about that. That happened to a husband of an American woman. Think about that. That happened to a man who a judge already said he had the right to stay. When the rights of some are violated, they are a threat to the rights of all of us.

In January, ICE agents in New Jersey raided a small business without a warrant and detained a Puerto Rican military veteran of Boricua, an American citizen, detained him, even after he presented his valid ID to those ICE agents. This is one example of so many.

Some Americans Have Already Been Caught in Trump's Immigration Dragnet. More Will Be — an article by Nicole Foy ...

> About a week after President Trump took office, Jonathan Guerrero was sitting at a Philadelphia car wash where he works when immigration agents burst in. The agents didn't say why they were there and didn't show their badges, Guerrero recalled. So the 21-year-old didn't get a chance to explain that although his parents were from Mexico, he was born right there in the City of Brotherly Love. An agent pointed his gun at Guerrero and handcuffed him. Then they brought in other car wash workers, including Guerrero's father, who's undocumented. When agents began checking IDs, they finally noticed that Guerrero was a citizen and quickly let him go. "I said, 'Look, man, I don't know who these guys are and what they're doing. With anything law-related, I just stay quiet.'" Less than two months into the Trump administration, there has been a small, but steady beat of more and more reported cases like Guerrero's.
>
> In Utah, agents pulled over and detained a 20-year-old American after he honked at them. In New Mexico, a member of the Mescalero Apache nation more than two hours from the border was stopped and questioned by agents who demanded to see their passports. Earlier this month, a Trump voter in Virginia was pulled over and handcuffed by a gun-wielding immigration agent. It's unclear exactly how many citizens have faced the Trump administration's dragnet so far, and while previous administrations have mistakenly held Americans, too, there's no firm count on these incidents either. Government doesn't release figures on citizens who have been held by immigration authorities, neither Customs and Border Protection, neither Immigration and Customs Enforcement, which handles interior immigration enforcement.
>
> Experts and advocates say what is clear to them, though, is that Trump's aggressive immigration policy, such as arrest quotas for enforcement agents, make it more and more likely that citizens will be caught up in immigration sweeps. {In quotes} It's really everyone, not just non-citizens or undocumented people who are in danger of having their liberty violated in this kind of mass deportation machinery.
>
> Asked about reports of Americans getting caught up in administration's enforcement policies, an ICE spokesman told the outlet in a written statement that agents are allowed to ask for citizens' identification. Any US immigration officer has authority to question without warrant any alien or person believed to be an alien concerning his or her right to be or to remain in the United States. The agency didn't respond to questions about specific cases.
>
> The US has gone through spasms of detaining and even deporting large numbers of citizens. In the 1930s and 1940s, federal and local authorities forcibly exiled an estimated one million Mexican-Americans, including hundreds of thousands of American-born children.

That's our past. An estimated one million Mexican-Americans, including hundreds of thousands of American-born children, swept up and deported.

> The US Government Accountability Office report found that immigration authorities had asked to hold roughly 600 likely citizens during Trump's first term. The GAO also, the Government Accountability Office, also found that Trump actually deported about 70 likely American citizens. The GAO report did not get into any individual cases, but lawsuits brought against federal immigration agencies detailed dozens of cases where plaintiffs received a settlement.

This will accelerate if there's no due process. In his first administration, there was some process. But this will accelerate if there's no due process. I live in Newark, New Jersey, and there are dozens of languages spoken in my city, and some of the elders from some of these many different ethnic groups, from European folks who don't speak English to folks from Asia that don't speak English, and imagine one of these Americans gets stopped and doesn't have papers on them, and they see a tattoo, and next thing you know they're sent to Louisiana or Texas, and next thing you know they're on a flight. That's not hyperbole. That's not some impossible thing. We know once due process is eliminated in this country for some, all are in danger. It is a constitutional slippage that Scalia and conservatives who believe in the Constitution nobly object to.

Canadian citizen Jasmine Mooney was detained by ICE for two weeks. I saw an interview of her, this white woman stunned. Here's what she wrote. It's Canadian...

> There was no explanation, no warning. One minute I was in an immigration office talking to an officer about my work visa, which has been approved months before and allowed me, a Canadian, to work in the United States. The next, I was told to put my hands against the wall and patted down like a criminal before being sent to an ICE detention center without the chance to talk to a lawyer.

I grew up in Whitehorse, Yukon, a small town in the northernmost part of Canada. I always knew I wanted to do something bigger with my life. I left home early and moved to Vancouver, British Columbia, where I built a career spanning multiple industries, acting in film and television, owning bars and restaurants, flipping condos, and managing Airbnbs. In my 30s, I found my true passion working in health and the wellness industry. I was given an opportunity to help launch an American brand of health tonics called Holy Water, a job that would involve moving to the United States. I was granted my trade work visa, which allows Canadian and Mexican citizens to work in the United States in specified professional occupations. I got it on my second attempt. It goes without saying, then, that I have no criminal record. I also love the United States and consider myself to be a kind, hardworking person.

I started working in California and traveled back and forth between Canada and the US multiple times without any complications until one day, upon returning to the United States, a border officer questioned me about my initial visa denial and subsequent visa approval. He asked why I had gone to San Diego border the second time to apply. I explained that that was where my lawyer's offices were and that he had wanted to accompany me to ensure there were no issues. After a long interrogation, the officer told me that it seemed, quote, shady and that my visa hadn't been properly processed. He claimed I couldn't work for a company in the US that made use of hemp, one of the beverage ingredients. He revoked my visa and told me I could still work for the company from Canada, but if I wanted to return to the US, I would need to reapply. I was devastated. I had just started building a life in California.

I stayed in California for the next few months and was eventually offered a similar position, but with a different health and wellness brand. I started the visa processes and returned to the same immigration office in San Diego at the border, since they had processed my visa before and I was familiar with it. Hours passed with many confused opinions about my case. The officer I spoke to was kind, but told me that due to my previous issues, I needed to apply for my visa through the consulate. I told her I hadn't been aware I needed to apply that way, but I had no problem doing it. Then she said something strange, "You didn't do anything wrong. You are not in trouble. You are not a criminal." I remember thinking, why would she say that? Of course I'm not a criminal.

Then she told me they had to send me back to Canada. That didn't concern me. I assumed I would simply book a flight home. But as I sat searching for flights, a man approached me and said, "Come with me." There was no explanation, no nothing. He took me to a room, took my belongings from my hands, and ordered me to put my hands against the wall. A woman immediately began patting me down. The commands came rapid-fire, one after another, too fast to process. They took my shoes and pulled out my shoelaces. "What are you doing? What's happening?" I asked. "You are being detained." "I don't understand. What does that mean? For how long?" "I don't know." That would be the response to nearly every question I would ask over the next two weeks, 'I don't know.' They brought me downstairs for a series of interviews and medical questions. They searched my bags and told me I had to get rid of half my belongings because I couldn't take everything with me. "Take everything with me where?" I asked.

A woman asked me for the name of someone they could contact on my behalf. In moments like this, you realize you don't actually know anyone's phone number anymore. By some miracle, I had recently memorized my best friend Britt's number because I had been putting my grocery points on her account. I gave them her phone number. They handed me a mat and a folded-up sheet of aluminum foil. 'What's this?' 'Your blanket.' 'I don't understand.' I was taken to a tiny, freezing cement cell with bright fluorescent lights and a toilet. There were five other women lying on their mats with aluminum sheets wrapped around them looking like dead bodies. The guard locked the door behind me. For two days we remained in the cell, only leaving briefly for food. The lights never turned off. We never knew what time it was, and no one answered our questions. No one in the cell spoke English, so I either tried to sleep or meditate to keep from having a breakdown. I didn't trust the food, so I fasted, assuming I wouldn't be there long.

On the third day, I was finally allowed to make a phone call. I called Britt and told her that I didn't understand what was happening. No one would tell me when I was going home and that she was my only contact. They gave me a stack of paperwork to sign and told me I was being given a five-year ban unless I applied for reentry through the consulate. The officer also said it didn't matter whether I signed the papers or not. It was happening regardless. I was so delirious, I just signed. I told them I would pay for my flight home and asked when I could leave. No answer.

They then moved me to another cell, this time with no mats or blanket. I sat freezing on the cement floor for hours. That's when I realized they were processing me into real jail, the Otay Mesa Detention Center. I was told to shower, given a jail uniform, fingerprinted, and interviewed. I begged for information. "How long will I be here?" "I don't know your case," the man said. "Could be days, could be weeks, but I'm telling you right now, you need to mentally prepare yourself for months." Months? I felt like I was going to throw up.

I was taken to the nurse's office for a medical check. She asked what happened to me. She had never seen a Canadian there before. When I told her my story, she grabbed my hand and said, "Do you believe in God?" I told her I only recently found God, but now I believed in God more than anything. And she said, "I believe God brought you here for a reason. I know it feels like your life is in a million pieces, but you will be okay through this. I think you're going to find a way to help others." At the time, I didn't know what that meant. She asked if she could pray for me. I held her hands and wept. I felt like I had been sent a guardian angel.

I was then placed in a real jail unit, two levels of cells surrounding a common area, just like in the movies. I was put in a tiny cell alone with a bunk bed and a toilet. The best part, there were blankets. After three days without one, I wrapped myself in mine and finally felt some comfort. For the first day, I didn't leave my cell. I continued fasting, terrified that the food might make me sick. The only available water came from the tap attached to the toilet in our cells or a sink in the common area, neither of which felt safe to drink. Eventually, I forced myself to step out, meet the guards, and learn the rules. One of them told me, "No fighting." I joked, "I'm a lover, not a fighter." He laughed. I asked if there had ever been a fight in there. "In this unit? No," he said. "No one in this unit has a criminal record."

That's when I started meeting other women. That's when I started hearing their stories. And that's when I made a decision. I would never allow myself to feel sorry for my situation again. No matter how hard this was, I had to be grateful because every woman I met was in an even more difficult position than mine. There were around 140 of us in our unit. Many women had lived and worked in the US legally for years, but had overstayed their visas, often after reapplying and being denied. They had all been detained without warning.

If someone is a criminal, I agree they should be taken off the streets, but not one of these women had a criminal record. These women acknowledged that they shouldn't have overstayed and took responsibility for their actions, but their frustration wasn't about being held accountable. It was about the endless bureaucratic limbo they had been trapped in. The real issue was how long it took to get out of the system with no clear answers, no timeline, and no way to move forward. Once deported, many have no choice but to abandon everything they own because the cost of shipping their belongings back is too high.

I met a woman who had been on a road trip with her husband. She said they had 10-year work visas. While driving near the San Diego border, they mistakenly got into a lane leading to Mexico. They stopped and told the agent they didn't have their passports on them, expecting to be redirected. Instead, they were detained. They were both pastors.

I met a family of three who had been living in the US for 11 years with work authorizations. They paid taxes and were waiting for green cards. Every year, the mother had to undergo a background check, but this time she was told to bring her whole family. When they arrived, they were taken into custody and told their status would now be processed from within the detention center.

Another woman from Canada had been living in the US with her husband who was detained after a traffic stop. She admitted she had overstayed her visa and accepted that she would be deported, but she had been stuck in the system for almost six weeks because she hadn't had her passport. Who runs casual errands without their passport?

One woman had a ten-year visa. When it expired, she moved back to her home country, Venezuela. She admitted she had overstayed by one month before leaving. Later, she returned from a vacation and entered the US without issue. But when she took a domestic flight from Miami to Los Angeles, she was picked up by ICE and detained. She couldn't be deported because Venezuela wasn't accepting deportees. She didn't know when she was getting out.

There was a girl from India who had overstayed her student visa for three days before heading back home. She then came back to the US on a new visa to finish her master's degree and was handed over to ICE due to the three days she had overstayed on her previous visa.

There were women who had been picked up off the streets from outside their workplaces, from their homes. All of these women told me that they had been detained from time spans ranging from a few weeks to ten months. One woman's daughter was outside the detention center protesting for her release. That night, the pastor invited me into a service she was holding. A girl who spoke English translated for me as the women took turns sharing their prayers, prayers for their sick parents, for their children they hadn't seen in weeks, for the loved ones that they had been torn away from. Then unexpectedly, they asked if they could pray for me. I was new here, and they wanted to welcome me. They formed a prayer circle around me, took my hands and prayed. I had never felt so much love, energy, and compassion from a group of strangers in my life. Everyone was crying.

At 3:00 AM the next day, I was woken up in my cell. "Pack your bag. You're leaving." I jolted upright. "I get to go home?" The officer shrugged. "I don't know where you're going." Of course, no one knew anything. I grabbed my things and went downstairs, where ten other women stood in silence, tears streaming down their faces. But these weren't happy tears. That was the moment I learned the term transferred. For many of these women, detention centers had become a twisted version of home. They had formed bonds, established routines, and found slivers of comfort and friendships they had built. Now, without warning, they were being torn apart and sent somewhere new. Watching them say goodbye, clinging to each other was gut-wrenching. I had no idea what was waiting for me next. In hindsight, that was probably for the best.

Our next stop was Arizona, the San Luis Regional Detention Center. The transfer process had lasted for 24 hours, a sleepless, grueling ordeal. This time, men were transported with us. Roughly 50 of us crammed into a prison bus for the next five hours, packed together, women in the front, men in the back. We were bound in chains that wrapped tightly around our waists, with our cuffed hands secured to our bodies and shackles restraining our feet, forcing every moment into a slow, clinking struggle.

When we arrived at our next destination, we were forced to go through the entire intake process all over again, with medical exams, fingerprinting, and pregnancy tests.

They linked us up in a filthy cell, squatting over a communal toilet, holding Dixie cups of urine while the nurses dropped pregnancy tests in each of our cups. It was disgusting. We sat in freezing cold jail cells for hours waiting for everyone to be processed. Across the room, one of the women suddenly spotted her husband. They had both been detained and were now seeing each other for the first time in weeks. The look in their faces, pure love, relief, and longing, was something I'll never forget.

We were beyond exhausted. I felt like I was hallucinating. The guard tossed us each a blanket and said, "Find a bed." There were no pillows. The room was cold as ice, and one blanket wasn't enough. Around me, women lay curled into themselves, heads covered, looking like a room full of corpses. This place made the last jail feel like the Four Seasons. I kept telling myself, "Do not let this break you."

Thirty of us shared one room. We were given one styrofoam cup for water and one plastic spoon that we had to reuse for every meal. I eventually had to start trying to eat. Sure enough, I got sick. None of the uniforms fit, and everyone had men's shoes on. The towels they gave us to shower with were hand towels. They wouldn't give us more blankets. The fluorescent lights shined on us 24/7. Everything felt like it was meant to break you. Nothing was explained to us. I wasn't given a phone call. We were locked in a room, no daylight, with no idea when we would get out. I tried to stay calm as every fiber of my being raged toward panic mode. I didn't know how I would tell Britt where I was.

Then, as if sent from God, one of the women showed me a tablet attached to the wall where I could send emails. I only remembered my CEO's email from memory. I tapped out a message, praying he would see it. He responded. Through him, I was able to connect with Britt. She told me that they were working around the clock trying to get me out, but no one had any answers. The system made it next to impossible. I told her about the conditions in this new place, and that was when we decided to go to the media. She started working with a reporter and asked whether I would be able to call her so she could loop him in. The international phone account that Britt had previously tried to set up for me wasn't working, so one of the other women offered to let me use her phone account to make a call. In that cell, we were all in this together.

With nothing to do in my cell but talk, I made new friends. Women had risked everything for their chance at a better life for themselves and their families. Through them, I learned the harsh reality of seeking asylum. Showing me their physical scars, they explained how they had paid smugglers anywhere from $20,000 to $60,000 to reach the US border, enduring brutal jungles and horrendous conditions. One woman had been offered asylum in Mexico within two weeks, but had been encouraged to keep going to the US. Now, she was stuck living in a nightmare, separated from her young children for months. She sobbed telling me how she felt like the worst mother in the world. Many of these women were highly educated and spoke multiple languages, yet they had been advised to pretend they didn't speak English because it would supposedly increase their chances of asylum. Some believed they were being used as examples as warnings to others not to come.

Women were starting to panic in this new facility, and knowing I was most likely the first person to get out, they wrote letters and messages for me to send to their families. I felt like we all had been kidnapped, thrown in some sort of sick psychological experiment meant to strip us of every ounce of our strength and dignity. We were from different countries, spoke different languages, and practiced different religions, yet in this place, none of that mattered. Everyone took care of each other. Everyone shared food. Everyone had held each other when someone broke down. Everyone fought to keep each other's hope alive.

I got a message from Britt. My story had started to blow up in the media. Almost immediately after I was told I was being released, my ICE agent, who had never spoken before, told my lawyer I could have left sooner if I had signed a withdrawal form and that they hadn't known I would pay for my own flight home. From the moment I arrived, I begged every officer I saw to let me pay for my own ticket home. Not a single one of them ever spoke to me about my case.

To put things into perspective, I had a Canadian passport, lawyers, resources, media attention, friends, family, and even politicians advocating for me, yet I was still detained for nearly two weeks. Imagine what the system is like for every other person in there.

A small group of us were transferred back to San Diego at 2:00 AM. One last road trip once again shackled in chains. I was then taken to the airport where two officers were waiting for me. The media was there, so the officers snuck me through a side door trying to avoid anyone seeing me in my restraints. I was beyond grateful that at the very least, I didn't have to walk through the airport in chains. To my surprise, the officers escorting me were incredibly kind, and even funny. It was the first time I had laughed in weeks. I asked if I could put my shoelaces back on. "Yes," one of them said with a grin, "but you better not run." "Yeah," the other one added, "or we'll have to tackle you in the airport. That'll really make headlines." I laughed and then told them I spent a lot of time observing the guards during my detention, and I couldn't believe how often I saw humans treating other humans with such disregard. "But don't worry," I joked, "you two get five stars."

When I finally landed in Canada, my mom and two best friends were waiting for me. So was the media. I spoke to them briefly, numb and delusional from exhaustion. It was surreal listening to my friends recount everything they had done to get me out, working with lawyers, reaching out to the media, making endless calls to detention centers, desperately trying to get through to ICE or anyone who could help. They said the entire system felt rigged, designed to make it nearly impossible for anyone to get out.

The reality became clear. ICE detention isn't just a bureaucratic nightmare. It's a business. These facilities are privately owned and run for profit. Companies like Core-

Civic and GEO Group receive government funding based on the number of people they detain, which is why they lobby for stricter immigration policies. It's a lucrative business. CoreCivic made over $560 million from ICE contracts in a single year. In 2024, GEO Group, more than 763 million from ICE contracts. The more detainees, the more money they make. It stands to reason that these companies have no incentive to release people quickly.

What I had experienced was finally starting to make sense. This is not just my story. It is a story of thousands and thousands of people still strapped in a system that profits from their suffering.

I am writing in hopes that someone out there, someone with power to change any of this, can help do something. The strength I witnessed in those women, the love they gave despite their suffering, is what gives me faith, faith that no matter how flawed the system is, how cruel the circumstances, humanity will always shine through. Even in the darkest places, within the most broken systems, humanity persists. Sometimes it reveals itself in the smallest, unexpected acts of kindness, a shared meal, a whispered prayer, a hand reaching out in the dark. We are defined by the love we extend. {We are defined by the love we extend. *We are defined by the love we extend.*} We are defined by the love we extend, by the courage we summon, and the truths we are willing to tell.

That's the end of the article. And the stories continue. A ten-year-old citizen in Texas recovering from brain cancer was detained at a border patrol checkpoint, and eventually the American citizen was deported to Mexico with her undocumented parents, even though they were in need of medical attention for their brain cancer.

Here's the article from NBC — *US citizen child recovering from brain cancer removed to Mexico with undocumented parents*:

> A family that was deported to Mexico hopes they can find a way to return to the US and ensure their ten-year-old daughter, my fellow American, who is a US citizen, can continue her brain cancer treatment. Immigration authorities removed the girl and four of her American siblings from Texas on May 4th, five Americans in total.
>
> When they deported their undocumented parents, the family's ordeal last month when they were rushing from the Rio Grande City where they live to Houston, where their daughter's specialist doctors are based for emergency medical checkup. The parents had done the trip at least five other times in the past, passing through an immigration checkpoint every time without any issues according to attorney Danny Woodward from Texas Civil Rights Project, a legal advocacy and litigation organization representing the family. In previous occasions, the parents showed letters from their doctors and lawyers to the officers at the checkpoint to get through, but in early February, the letters weren't enough. They were stopped at the checkpoint. They were arrested after the parents weren't able to show legal immigration documentation. The mother who spoke exclusively to NBC News said she tried to explain her daughter's circumstances to the officers, but they weren't interested in hearing that.
>
> "Other than lacking valid immigration status in the US, the parents have no criminal history," Woodward said. Protection which detained and deported the family according to the lawyer, said in an email Wednesday, "For privacy reasons, we do not comment on individual cases." On Thursday, a CBP spokesperson said via email that the reports of the family situation are inaccurate because when someone is given expelled removal orders and chooses to disregard them, they will face the consequences of the process.
>
> They reiterated that they couldn't speak about the specifics of the case for privacy reasons. The ten-year-old girl was diagnosed with brain cancer last year and underwent surgery to remove a tumor. "The doctors practically gave me no hope for life for her, but thank God she's a miracle," the mother said. An American citizen is a miracle. The swelling on the girl's brain is still not fully gone, the mother said, causing difficulties with speech and mobility of the right side of her body.
>
> Before the family was removed from the US, the girl was routinely checked in with doctors monitoring her recovery, attending rehabilitation therapies, and taking medication to prevent convulsions.
>
> "It's a very difficult thing," the mother said. "I don't wish anyone to go through this situation."
>
> What is happening to this family is an absolute tragedy and is something that is not isolated to just them," said. Rochelle Garza, president of the Texas Civil Rights Project.

"This is part of a pattern in practice that we've seen in the Trump administration," Garza said, adding that she has heard of multiple other cases concerning mixed-status families, but for now, this is the only case of this nature the organization has taken on. The Trump administration's border czar, Tom Homan, has said families can be deported together regardless of status. Homan said it would be up to the parents to decide whether to depart the US together or leave their children behind.

But undocumented parents of US-born children, if picked up by immigration authorities face the risk of losing custody of their children without the power of attorney document or a guardianship outlining who will take care of their children left behind, the children go into the US foster care system, making it harder for the parents to regain custody of their children in the future.

According to the girl's mother, she recalled feeling like she could not do anything, she said in Spanish, "You're between a rock and a hard place." NBC News is withholding the name of the mother and the rest of the family members since they were deported to an area in Mexico that is known for kidnapping US citizens. In addition to the parents and their ten-year-old sick American daughter, four of their other American childrens, ages 15, 13, 8 and six were also in the car when they were detained. Four of the five children born in the US.

According to the mother, the family was taken to a detention center following their arrest where their mom and daughters were separated from her husband and sons and she realized she wouldn't be taking her daughter to the doctors. "The fear is horrible. I can't explain it, but it's something frustrating, very tough, something you wouldn't wish on anyone," she said, adding that her sick daughter was laying on a cold floor beneath incandescent lights. Hours later, the family was placed in a van and dropped on the Mexico side of the Texas Bridge. From there, they sought refuge in a nearby shelter for a week.

... [T]he mom said the safety concerns keep coming up at night and the children haven't been able to go to school.

The ten-year-old daughter and 15-year-old son who lives with a heart disorder known as Long QT syndrome, which causes irregular heartbeats and can be life-threatening if not treated well, have not received the healthcare they need in Mexico. The teen wears a monitor that tracks his heart rate. "The authorities have my children's lives in their hands," she said in tears.

{"The authorities have my children's lives in their hands."}

Both parents arrived to the US from Mexico in 2013 and settled in Texas hoping for a better life for their family, the mother said. She and her husband both worked for a string of different jobs to support their six children. The couple also has a 17-year-old son they left behind in Texas following their deportation.

Just two weeks ago, another undocumented mother in California caring for her 20-year-old daughter, a US citizen undergoing treatment for bone cancer, was detained by immigration authorities and later released under humanitarian parole. "We are calling on the government," Garza said, "to parole the family, to correct the harm and to not do this to anyone else."

SENATOR MURPHY: Gentleman yield?

SENATOR BOOKER: I think I need to. I'll yield to a question while retaining the floor and I thank my brother — I thank my friend who's now stood with me for almost 11 hours.

SENATOR MURPHY: Those are hard stories to read, Senator Booker, but I appreciate you showing the coldness of this current administration's immigration policy. The tragedy to me is that there's an opportunity to fix what is undoubtedly a broken immigration system, and yet we're into day 71 and Donald Trump has not proposed to us any proposals to fix the broken system. Instead, what he is doing is spending like a drunken sailor on an enforcement system that wastes tens of millions of taxpayer dollars.

You described this harrowing experience that this Canadian woman had and as I was listening to this two-week ordeal that she went through, being transported from site to site, being processed and reprocessed, as the top Democrat on the Homeland Security Subcommittee of Appropriations, I'm just cataloging in my brain how much money that cost us.

Ultimately, this was somebody working in the United States. This was somebody that posed no threat to United States citizens, but we probably spent several million dollars on that two-week ordeal. Overall, the Trump administration is going to blow through all of the money allocated to border patrol. They're going to have to come back to Congress for a massive additional appropriation, all at the same time that they are shuttering medical research in this country. They are closing down social security offices. There are measles outbreaks all across the country. Planes seem to be falling out of the sky as the FAA is enduring layoffs. There are consequences to these spending decisions. The amount of money that's being spent at the border, much of it wasted in a showy ineffective response, the consequence of that is that the services that average everyday Americans need, like help on their social security claims are being impacted.

But we need to fix the broken immigration system, and we had an opportunity to do that last year when Republicans and Democrats came together and wrote a bipartisan border security bill that frankly would've allocated tens of billions of additional dollars that would've fixed our broken asylum system, would've given the president new authorities and Donald Trump instructed all the Republicans in this chamber to oppose it. In the end, I think four senators, including the author, Senator Lankford, supported it, but every other Republican here opposed it. And the reason Donald Trump told them to oppose it was that he would fix it when he became president. But we are now in day 72 and there has not been a single proposal from Donald Trump to fix the broken immigration system, just a whole bunch of spending essentially money down the drain because the system itself needs to be reformed.

And so it speaks to my confident belief that Donald Trump does not want to fix our immigration system. He wants to keep this issue open as a sore in our politics. If I was wrong, he would've proposed legislation here to deal with the underlying inefficiency of the system instead of just throwing money at the problem. And so we will see what the result of this campaign is. We were told that immigrants to this country represented a very specific national security threat, that we needed to crack down on immigration including expelling from this country legitimate asylum seekers because that was what was necessary to protect the nation. Well, we'll see what the crime data tells us for the first few months of this administration. I have a feeling I already know what the story is, crime is not going to have gone down. Why? Because in fact, whether people want to acknowledge this or not, natural-born American citizens commit crimes at rates higher than first-generation immigrants or people born outside of the United States of America.

But Senator Booker, I guess the question I want to ask you is this, I think you and I agree that Americans, right, left, and center, acknowledge that the immigration system is broken. They didn't love it when they saw thousands of people crossing on an average day, and they know that when it takes ten years to process an asylum claim, something's wrong and that it then just provides an incentive for people to come here without documentation.

But my impression is that that cross-section of Americans that believes that the existing immigration system is broken also believes three other things. One, that the way to fix it is to change the laws and that they believe that we have not done our job until we have changed the laws. For instance, building a better asylum system. And once again, not a single proposal from the Trump administration on how to fix our broken immigration system, not a single proposal. Second, I believe that they understand that immigration is a core strength of this nation, not a liability. And that if we want to thrive as an economy, we are going to have to bring people to this country legally. But to turn our backs on immigration as a mechanism to grow economically, that's not in line with what Americans believe, even those that think the existing system is broken.

And then lastly, I just don't believe this country is as mean as Donald Trump thinks it is. I get it that everybody wants this nation to be a nation of laws, but when an American citizen looks at a child with a medical condition, when American citizen looks at an individual who will face certain death from a drug gang if they stay in their home country, when they look at individuals in war-torn nations overseas, they believe that America is strong enough, is big enough, is generous enough to be able to protect those people from harm. Why? Because that's what America always has been.

And so this idea that President Trump has that Americans are mean and spiteful and don't want to help people just because they were born outside of the United States or their parents were born outside of the United States, I just don't think that's right. It obviously betrays the best traditions of this nation. But I think it also fundamentally misreads the American people.

So I think people want our immigration to be fixed, the system to be fixed, but I think they want us to do it. They understand the laws are broken. They do not want to abandon America's tradition of bringing people here from all around the world. They understand that our economy and our economic prosperity is linked to our ability to bring hard-working immigrants to this country, and they're just not as mean as Donald Trump thinks they are.

SENATOR BOOKER: Senator, I appreciate your question, but I just have to say this to you. You worked so hard with Senator Lankford and one of the things I have to say, and I hope I don't hurt his politics by telling people how much I love Senator Lankford, we disagree fundamentally on a lot of issues maybe that will help him, we both are people though of faith. We just recently were together at a massive, I think there must've been like a thousand people there, maybe 500 at least at a national prayer breakfast event. He's such a man of character and what I like about him is I know his values because he every day tries to be a good Christian.

And this idea of "love thy neighbor" or "you were a stranger in a strange land," I just kind of took a lot of pleasure watching you, my friend, who I know for the last 12 years and him sit down in this honest, sincere negotiation. And let's be real, everybody on your side of the aisle didn't agree with you and everybody before Trump's involvement on his side of the aisle didn't agree, but you guys had the makings of a comprehensive bill that would've passed.

Now, I'll tell you also that I came here in 2013, right after a Gang of Eight* had done the same thing. They actually got the bill out and it died in the house. There are people in America despite Lankford and you, who many people would put on opposite sides of a political spectrum, that on these issues they agree. And why do they agree, Senator Murphy? Why? Because our economy is dependent upon immigration.

You want to talk about a conservative leaning group, Senator? Republicans, the Chamber of Commerce will tell you, the National Chamber of Commerce will tell you, our economy will be crippled if we don't find a way to bring more people in legally to work on work visas. When I go to the tech community or the biotech community or the AI community or the community who's trying to go forward in quantum computing, all of them are saying this is crazy that we are not allowing the brightest minds on the planet when they get here and get PhDs and have things half of Congress can't spell, that we drop-kick them out of the country. There are so many points of agreement. Take dreamers, who people on both sides of the aisle have held up as a group of people that are Americans in every way except for the piece of paper. They have no memory of another country. I could keep going through all the things in the immigration world we agree on, including the need to secure our southern border.

And so I listen to you on this section and I look at you and I remember your frustrations. You're standing up in front of our caucus, saying we're so close.

SENATOR MURPHY: Will the Senator yield.

SENATOR BOOKER: I will yield for a question while retaining the floor.

SENATOR MURPHY: I just want to drill down on this for a moment because it gets back to a theme that you've been hitting on throughout the evening and early morning. And that is not everything has to be zero-sum politics. I mean, this is part of what is so exhausting about the last 71 days for many, many Americans. I think it's part of why Donald Trump's approval ratings are sinking by the day. Because listen, you and I are pugilists when we need to be. We fight when we think that there's a worthy fight. That's what this is today — it's a fight. We understand it's a fight for our values, but we don't think everything has to be a fight. We see our jobs as standing up for our convictions, but then finding that common ground. I did not expect to be in that room with Senator Lankford.

I was surprised, pleasantly, when we came to an agreement. You spent months and months hammering out really difficult criminal justice reform with a colleague of yours that you have equal numbers of disagreements with because we feel like we have a call from our constituents to fight, but then find the common ground. But this administration has zero interest in common ground. Every single day they wake up thinking only about conflict, thinking only about defeat of their opposition. And they have been frustrated because they've been trying to do a lot of illegal things and the courts have been telling them no.

They're now talking about extraordinary measures like impeaching judges or defunding the courts. Instead, they could reach out to Democrats, they could decide to do what every previous president has tried to do, which is instead of ramming through a one-side only policy on immigration, for instance, come to people of goodwill on the opposing party and try to work out a compromise. This is what exhausts the American people is this administration's complete total unwillingness to find common ground on anything. That is not where the center of this country is.

And on the issue of immigration, we found common ground last year. It was hard. It did not satisfy everyone. But we have proven that on this issue that is hot, that is difficult for even family members to talk about sometimes, that even on this issue of immigration, we can find that common ground. And so we are here, you are here because there's a fight to be waged. But I think we both wish on a litany of these topics, we were instead sitting down with our colleagues. But that is just not in the DNA of this administration. And that is part of why this president is becoming more and more unpopular by the day is because they expect any president, any president to make at least a minimalist effort to try to reach out and find compromise. And that never happens from the Trump administration.

SENATOR BOOKER: For the question I see in there, and again, great presidents have great ideas they bring to Congress and they fight to pull together and cobble together legislation that will last. The problem we have right now is this whiplash between Trump's executive orders and Biden's executive orders and Trump's executive orders. And it's not solving the problems. And we've shown that there's enough common ground to do something on it. But I don't want to stick with common ground now actually because there's some things in here that are not common ground, like private prisons.

I'm one of these folks that doesn't want to criticize. I've flown out to a private prison Down South to get a tour, met really kind and nice people. But there is something problematic to me about a profit motive for imprisoning, shackling, detaining and holding people and this combination of that and a corporate reality where you are giving campaign contributions to people that will then turn around and give you government contracts to restrict the liberties of human beings. And the story that I read about this woman feeling like they lied to her lawyer and said if she had only said she could pay for her own flight home, but they were keeping her and every day they were keeping her they were getting more money from American taxpayers. This wasn't a system designed for justice. This isn't a system that's designed for the rights of human beings in our country. This is a system that has every day an incentive to deny the liberty, to hold people. It's wrong, it's wrong. It's broken. And with a president that doesn't care about these things, that is giving greater latitude so that more stories like the Canadian woman's story, it's stunning.

I want to keep moving though, and I just want to talk about children and the way this system is extended to children.

Last week, the government canceled the contract to provide legal services to 26,000 unaccompanied immigrant children. Remember, remember what Anton Scalia said about due process in his strict interpretations of the literal writings of our founders. But 26,000 unaccompanied migrant children no longer have legal representation. We started on that idea. We started on that idea. We started on the idea, the fifth and the 14th Amendment, "**No one shall be deprived of life, liberty, or property without due process.**" And our country has now rolled back. Trump got rid of a policy that prevented ICE from arresting kids at schools and people from their places of worship. Now, every day, families face the impossible choice of whether to send a kid to school and risk permanent separation from their families.

There's a story from New Jersey and I quote, "Recently, when I was home in Newark, New Jersey, a woman in my neighborhood came up to me to tell me a heartbreaking story. One morning she was on her way to walk to school the mom of another child's children..." I won't make this anonymous. One of my closest friends, she's like a sister to me, she lives in the Ironbound in Newark and was very emotional because her neighbors were so terrified that they came to her and asked her to walk their children to school. They're American children. There are so many teachers and school administrators who are speaking out now that they've been ordered that they must allow ICE to enter their schools. Trump has plans to revoke temporary protected status protection for hundreds of thousands of people from various countries, from Venezuela to Haiti, paving the way for those deportations, we know who they are. He's done this despite the State Department maintaining a level four do not travel warning to Haiti and Venezuela due to widespread violence, danger, sexual assaults, kidnappings and more.

He claims that he's tough on crime because he wants to go after child sexual abusers, but when you're sending children, running into schools and churches, and sending them back to environments that are known for sexual assaults on young girls.

The Department of Justice Office of Civil Rights recently dropped its case it had filed against Southwest Key, the nation's largest provider of housing for migrant children in which the DOJ alleged sexual abuse and neglect perpetrated against undocumented children in federal custody. It was a case the DOJ brought against this company who housed migrant children because of alleged sexual abuse. And what did our government do under Trump? They dropped charges. They dropped charges.

Why? Why? Children being sexually assaulted, it's not worth an investigation? Is it because the administration thinks that pursuing the lawsuit and holding perpetrators accountable will somehow interfere with their immigration agenda? They literally let alleged sex abusers go free with no explanation. The hypocrisy.

The family detentions are restarted. They fail. Failed in the past to meet basic child welfare standards and exposed children to trauma. President's own Department of Homeland Security concluded in 2018 that family detention centers posed a high risk of harm to children and families. And despite his own Department of Homeland Security back in 2018 saying that, they've restarted it.

One of the points I want to make is crime. I was a mayor. The number one issue my residents were concerned about was fighting crime, fighting crime, fighting crime. I went back to Newark recently for a horrible, tragic death of a police officer by a 14-year-old with a ghost gun. It was horrible to send off hundreds and hundreds and hundreds of police officers from all over our state, from New York. This police officer was murdered by a 14-year-old. I still pray for their family, his mom. And as I was standing there looking at this parade of police officers who were waiting for the casket, I had police officers come to me and complain that they're having harder and harder time in New Jersey solving crimes because now victims of crime, victims of sexual assault, victims of robbery who happen to be undocumented, are afraid to go and talk to local police because of all this rhetoric that's creating the fear that they'll be turned over to ICE.

Imagine in our country there are people out there that are sexually assaulting people, but are getting away with it because they're targeting immigrants. And if you don't think that hurts American safety, you're wrong. Afraid to go and talk to police officers to report crimes. They're subverting people's constitutional rights, incarcerating people in foreign prisons who have no criminal records, the harms to children. We've talked about all of this, but diverting law enforcement resources away from investigating national security threats, terrorism, drug smuggling, human trafficking, illegal arms exports, financial crimes, and sex crimes, taking law enforcement away from investigating those crimes, and forcing all federal law enforcement agencies to enforce low-level immigration crimes, or I should say undocumented people with no criminal activity beyond their being in our country.

Reuters wrote about this misguided redirection of federal resources. I read their article:

> Federal agents who usually hunt down child abusers are now cracking down on immigrants who live in the US legally. Homeland Security investigators who specialize in money laundering are raiding restaurants and other small businesses looking for immigrants who aren't authorized to work. Agents who pursue drug traffickers and tax fraud are being reassigned to enforce immigration law. As US President Donald Trump pledges to deport millions and millions of, "criminal aliens," thousands of federal law enforcement officers from multiple federal agencies are being enlisted to take on new work as immigration enforcers. Pulling crime fighting resources away from other areas, from drug trafficking and terrorism and sexual abuse and fraud.
>
> The account of Trump's push to reorganize federal law enforcement, the most significant since September 11th, 2001 terrorist attacks, is based on interviews with more than 20 current and former federal agents, attorneys and other federal officials. Most had first hand knowledge of the changes. Nearly all spoke on the condition of anonymity because they were not authorized to discuss. "I do not recall ever seeing this wide spectrum of a federal government resources all being torn turned towards immigration enforcement," said Teresa Cardinal Brown, a former Homeland Security offer who has been served in both Republican and Democratic administrations. When you're telling agencies to stop what you're doing and do this now, whatever else they were doing takes a back seat.

In response to questions from Reuters, Homeland Security assistant secretary Tricia McLaughlin said, "The US government is mobilizing federal and state law enforcement to find, arrest and deport illegal aliens." The FBI declined to respond to questions about its staffing. In a statement the FBI said, "It is protecting the US from many threats."

The Trump administration has offered no comprehensive accounting of the revamp, but it echoes the aftermath of 2001 attacks when Congress created the Department of Homeland Security, and pulled together 169,000 federal employees from other agencies and refocused the FBI on battling terrorism. Trump's hardline approach to deporting immigrants has intensified America's already stark partisan divide. The US Senate's number two Democrat, Dick Durbin describes the crackdown as wasteful, misguided diversion of resources. It's making Americans less safe by drawing agents and officials away from finding corporate fraud, terrorism, child sexual exploitation, and other crimes.

The focus of immigration is drawing significant resources from other crime fighting departments according to the more 20 sources we spoke. Until January, pursuing immigrants living in the country illegally was largely the part of two agencies — ICE (Immigration and Customs Enforcement) and Customs and Border Protection, with a combined staff of 80,000 other departments spent on crime. In Detroit where immigration prosecutions have been rare, the number of people charged with immigration offenses rose from two in February to 19 last month. Case managements from the Justice Department show that fewer than 1% of the cases brought by prosecutors by the DEA, ATF over the past decade involved allegations that someone had violated immigration law. Since January, however, DEA agents have been ordered to reopen cases involving arrests up to five years old where prosecutors have declined to bring charges.

As Trump and billionaire Elon Musk slash the size of the federal government bureaucracy, jobs that deal with immigration enforcement appear largely exempt. In January 31st, email to ICE employees, a human resource official told them they wouldn't be eligible for retirement, buyouts offered to some 2.3 million federal workers. All ICE positions are excluded, they said recently in a previously unreported email.

SENATOR PETER WELCH (VERMONT): Will it, Senator... will Madam President... will the Senator yield for a question?

SENATOR BOOKER: Yes, I will yield for a question while retaining the floor.

SENATOR WELCH: Thank you, Senator. I have been listening to many of your hours of the speech. And you're talking about immigration now. And I have another question about the immigration policy. You know... I think all of us understand that it's absolutely essential that our country secure its borders. And from time to time the country forgets that. But I think we've had this debate about immigration that's been going on for several years. And I don't know if the senator had an opportunity to address the opportunity we had in the Senate, when last year there was a realization on the part of both the Republicans and Democrats, that the only way we were going to get a secure border in a sensible, beneficial immigration policy was to work together. I know the Senator was watching that very carefully.

And we had the terrific work of Senator Langkord from Oklahoma, Senator Murphy from Connecticut, and Senator Sinema, of course, from Arizona. And despite the enormous political tension that surrounds the immigration issue, and for understandable reasons, the three of them worked very hard and came together for a tripartisan proposal in effect. Senator Sinema, of course being the independent who always played a constructive role in trying to bring the parties together. And what was included in that legislation was a major commitment embraced by Senator Murphy on behalf of the Democrats for border security. There was an acknowledgement we can't just have, we have to control our borders. It's really that simple.

But when you control your borders, you also have the opportunity to have an immigration policy that the Congress and the President, I think, will benefit the American people. And it benefits us of course if there's security at the border. But it also benefits us if we have legal immigration that is controlled by the American people. And of course I've noticed that Elon Musk who is against immigration, he's for everything that President Trump is for, he likes having very highly educated computer people. It can help him go from very rich to even richer. So he carves out an exception for people that will be beneficial and helpful to him in his various enterprises.

But we've got in Vermont, a lot of dairy farms, and we have a tourist industry, and we have a real hard time filling those jobs. So legal immigration can really be helpful and constructive and beneficial to the people of the State of Vermont. And I know talking to my colleagues on both sides of the aisle, many of us in our states have tourist industries and we have agricultural enterprises. Just to mention two, where the reality is we don't have the number of people we need to fill those jobs. And it's not just a matter of paying more because I do think we have to be very mindful that we want to do every single thing we can to help elevate the wages of American workers. Which by the way, this is a little bit of an aside. Why in the world haven't we raised the minimum wage? I know Senator, you're for that, and I certainly am. But it astonishes me that we still have, what is it, $7, 7.50? It's unbelievable what the minimum wage is. A lot of the states have raised it. Vermont certainly has.

But we on immigration had the opportunity, and the bill, and the will to make enormous progress so that we'd have an immigration policy that secured the border, had the validation of bi-partisan majorities in the house and in the Senate, would have also addressed issues about legal immigration that would help us strengthen our economy, and also would've included a pathway to citizenship for dreamers, folks who were brought here by their parents, who when they were four or five or six years old, and whose the only country they know is the United States itself.

And my understanding from talking to my colleagues on the other side of the aisle is that there's an enormous amount of respect for many of these dreamers, many of whom have been heroes for us in the military. So this is not a republic... my view, it's not a Republican-Democratic situation. It is a desire on the part of almost everyone in this body to accommodate a reality of a child being brought here by his parents, going to school, getting an education, serving their country, firefighters, Marines, teachers, doing all these things that are really helpful to our country and where they're here through absolutely no fault of their own. And if we were to require them to be deported... And that's an effort that the current administration is making, you'd literally be taking people who might be 30 or 40 years old now, have families, and send them back to the country from which their parents brought them — and they don't even speak the language.

And that obviously makes no sense. And when I talked to the Vermonters who have very, very strong views of having a strong border, and I asked them what about this situation? They think, wait a minute, well that's different. That's a person who lives here. That's like my neighbor. So I was so disappointed when we were on the cusp of being able to get this legislation passed. When then candidate Trump in his candid way said, "Kill it." And he was candid about why. It would, "Give the Democrats a win." I never saw this as a win for Democrats. I saw this as a win for America. And the reality is that when we have to do really hard things here, and we're not doing hard things these days, but when we're trying to do hard things that are really important for the American people, my experience is you really do have to get to a bipartisan place.

Because we've lost elections and we lost the last one. And that is on us. It's not on the voters. They made a decision. That's their right to do. And we have to learn and we have to listen. But when we were listening, and hearing loud and clear from the American people that we want a secure border, and then we worked with our colleagues on the other side of the aisle to get a secure border, why in the world would the leader of the party kill it? Why? We know the reason. He thought it was good politics. But this is not about what's good partisan politics. It's about what's good policy that's going to help the American people.

So I'm really, among the many things you're focusing on of course, is this question of immigration. And this is incredibly important, but I want it to be clear that I, as one member of the United States Senate, am absolutely all in for the immigration reform that we need. And that is a secure border. That is legal immigration as we determine the type of immigration will be beneficial to the American people, and sustainable. And it also includes a pathway to citizenship for these children in many cases who were brought here by their parents, who had no agency, no involvement whatsoever in the decision to come here, how they got here.

[PHONE ALARM GOES OFF]

Pardon me. For those of us who don't stay up all night, some of us use alarms to wake up. So pardon me for being here earlier than I thought I'd be here. And you're here later than maybe than you thought.

But it's such a privilege for you, and it's such a privilege for me. It's such a privilege for the other 98 citizens of this country who serve with us in the United States Senate. That any chance we get, any chance we get to do something that's helpful to the people we represent, don't we want to grab it? Don't we want to do it? And it doesn't matter if our name lives in memory that we were here. It doesn't. What matters is what we do here. And whether when we leave, we can look back and have the satisfaction of knowing we gave it our best. And I hope there's enormous pressure on folks in this job from the crosscurrents of the political world that we live in.

And all of us are fallible, and all of us have plenty of opportunity to get it wrong. And we do. But what I've seen in the people I've admired on both sides of the aisle, I think of Senator McCain who Senator Murphy worked with so much, there was a heart and soul to that man. And it was the heart and soul in his spirit that guided him. And when I think about immigration and we're talking about how tough it is, he worked together with the so-called gang of eight to come up with a reform that the Senate passed years ago. I was in the house then. And I remember being so excited. So excited when I heard that the Senate had actually come up with a proposal. It just made sense. It wasn't perfect. What is? You know, Senate to Earth: What's perfect? We do the best we can. That's about it. But you know what? When I say that's about it, that's what life is. Do your best and then move on.

And by the way, that's one of the reasons why I think, Senator, the bipartisanship, which we don't have now at all, but why it has to ultimately, we have to have enough humility to understand that either side has the answers, and where we try in earnest to come up with the best solution we can at the moment, where we listen to each other, what happens is that if we didn't get it fully right, and we never will, we understand that we have an opportunity to fix it and make it better based on that experience. And when there's just our way or the highway, there's no resolution and no progress. Number one, you don't get the bill passed as we saw with the immigration bill. And then number two, if you get it passed the other side just tries to tear it apart and repeal it, as opposed to improve it.

Now, every single one of us knows that the American people want progress. But what we're talking about with something is hard, it truly is hard, the issue of immigration. When we're talking something that's hard politically, that spirit of wanting to get to a solution, that was what animated the work of Senator Langford, Senator Murphy, and Senator Sinema. They wanted to get to a solution even though they had significantly different points of view going in, on what was the right outcome. But they wanted to get to a solution. And where they represented the points of view of the disparate views of our caucus, and they came up with a compromise that by all accounts would be such a better place for us to be now than what we're in. No progress.

We haven't been able to act on that immigration bill since the Senate acted with the leadership of Senator McCain and others. And I was mentioning how excited I was. I was in the house at the time. And I was so excited that this bill came over. And Vermonters were asking me all the time, "Peter, we've got to do something about our borders. We've got to do something to make sure our farmers don't fear having their farms raided, and them not being able to milk their cows." It's that essential. And I'm talking a lot of pretty conservative people who politically sometimes agree with me, sometimes don't. But what was so exciting to me was that on the cusp of this coming to the house, I was thinking, I'm going to have a chance to vote for secure immigration, for securing our borders, rational immigration plan, and I'm going to be able to give a fairness to the dreamers. I was so excited about that.

And then what happened is it was announced that the house would not even take up the bill. And why? It was the same reason that then candidate Trump proposed to his colleagues or to his party members in the house, or pardon me, in the Senate — kill it. And why was that? Really in all candor, it's the most cynical of all reasons. Sometimes people in politics prefer to have the issue that they can fight about rather than use the responsibility and opportunity they have to solve the problem. And that's pretty much what happened with that. And here we are and we're seeing it again.

The other, there's another thing that's happening with the immigration policies of the current administration. There's a lot of cruelty that's part of it. Yes, we have to have a secure border. Yes, criminals who came here illegally should be deported. But should the consensus that we have about a secure border, about the legitimacy of deporting criminals who are here illegally be used to justify a wholesale roundup? Where the people who are rounded up are almost randomly picked up. Some may be on the basis of good information, but it's clear in this roundup where so many people were flown to the jails in El Salvador that the minimal amount of due process, which is inquiry into who is this person. Where are they from? Does that tattoo mean they're in a gang or is that a tattoo of Mom? Are we a society where we don't provide that minimal inquiry? It's called due process. Our country was founded on it. And it appears in many cases we haven't done that.

And then what we're seeing also is that a number of people are being rounded up who are here legally. They're here on a student visa. And they published an opinion in a school newspaper, expressing their point of view about the suffering in the Middle East. And this country, of course, is founded among other things, on the First Amendment right, the free speech. And it's a pretty astonishing thing that people who express that, who are here legally by the way. Legally, legally, legally, I want to emphasize that, are suddenly confronted by people who are essentially wearing mask, put in handcuffs, taken away, and then put in a jail at some unknown place until something maybe days later you find out where they are.

How does that solve the border crisis? How does that protect the liberties that have been the hallmark of the United States of America since the Constitution? It is cruel. You have a person who essentially disappears, and that's a term I know Senator Murphy used once, and I think unfortunately accurately. So we have a challenge. And it's really not who wins this vote and who wins that vote. And it's not even who's in the majority and who's in the minority, because this country only works, and this Senate only works when, whatever your political views are, you approach the problems that

America has from the perspective of your obligation as the United States Senator to make progress, to make it better.

And I was in the State Senate for 13 years. I'm not going to say my life's been downhill since then, but what I so appreciated about the Vermont Senate and I learned working with other people there. Bipartisan doesn't have a meaning almost now because it's like you've got to be on one side or the other. But I remember when I first went to the State Senate, Senator Booker, I won an election that was an upset. So I was feeling pretty good about myself. And when I got there, it was a majority in the Republican Party. And I was ready to cause trouble. And not necessarily in the John Lewis good way. It might've been more of a Peter Welch ego way. So I had a lot to learn. And what I remember was showing up and these two Republican Senators who were just really icons for me in my life, as it turns out, they and the Lieutenant Governor made decisions about who would be on what committees, and I really wanted to be on the finance committee, but that's not a committee you get on when you just show up and you've won an election and you're acting like you're more important than you are. They put me on the finance committee and I said, "I'm doomed," and the reason is I knew I had to cooperate. They've been so good to me and so generous. They gave me a seat at the table, and it was such a thrill for me to be able to actually sit at the table with these people that I held in such high regard and who knew so much more than me, but they invited me in. They didn't push me aside just because I had different points of view and was from a different party.

A few years later, I became Senate president, so I had a lot to do with who was on what committees. I remember, I started then the process that we still do in Vermont, and I appointed a number of Republicans to chair committees. I was in the Senate a second time with the now governor of Vermont, Phil Scott, and he became the chair of the institutions committee, which was kind of, that's a big deal in Vermont. When I tell folks we did that in Vermont, where sometimes you'd appoint somebody who's on the other party, they want me to have a mental status exam around here. You just don't do that kind of thing. What I do know and what I do see is that there are a lot of people here who do have that, I'll call it the Murphy/Lankford/Sinema attitude. "Let's solve the problem. Let's make progress. Let's find a way where we can move ahead." You're talking about immigration, which, because we've been going around and around on this for so long without making progress, it's almost creating this cul-de-sac or this sinkhole where people think it's pointless. "Why even talk about it? Why try to solve it? Can't be done." Well, we know it can be done because we are the people here, 100 of us, that actually have the ability to do it, and I would say we have the responsibility to do it because it's a serious issue that faces the American people, and they're entitled to the safety of a secure border. The Dreamers are entitled to some justice and respect for the commitment they've made to being fully participating citizens here in the United States.

I just applaud the efforts of my colleagues, who, despite all of the outside noise, do want to make some progress. When we don't make progress, we descend into a bad place. Yes, deport a criminal. Our people are entitled to safety. People are not entitled to come here illegally, and people who are [here] illegally, certainly are not entitled to commit any crimes, but when we go round and round and just use the challenge of immigration reform as a political cudgel, we end up going into some pretty dark places, and that's where we're heading now, where a person gets rounded up who's legally here, because the administration doesn't like the opinion they expressed. It's not that their opinion was necessarily subversive, and it's not even wrong. It's debatable. You and I would have a free opportunity to debate. What should be our policy in the Middle East? What should be our policy on immigration? But, the administration decides, "That speech, I don't like, arrest that person, disappear that person." Then we get into debates that are really not about making progress, but mutual recrimination. I'm just very delighted that you're focusing a good part of your effort here on the vital question of immigration.

I do hope ... I haven't been watching everything, but if it's okay, I just want to direct your attention to these tariffs that are happening, a little bit. I know you're going to have an opportunity to talk about a fair number of things, you already have, but I've never seen anything so dumb and reckless as these tariffs on Canada. We have a library in Newport, Vermont. Derby Line, actually, the Haskell Free Library. Half of it is in Vermont, half of it is in Canada. Is that cool or what? Canadians come into what I call the back door, but they call the front door, and we come in the front door, which they call the back door, and we read books together. We've had this library for decades, and I was with the ... We had a roundtable up in the Canadian border – Canadian-Vermont border – and the Member of Parliament from Stansfield, which is the town next to Newport, Madame Bibeau, was with us.

When we were with some folks who ran businesses on the Vermont side and on the Canadian side, and some of whom had operations on both sides, most of these were family businesses. Some were very large, some were small, and it ranged from farmers on the Vermont side who got a lot of their fertilizer from Canada. That's true, by the way, all across the northern border, so it can be Minnesota, it can be Idaho, so many of our farmers all along the Canadian-American border have cross relationships with Canada and they get their fertilizer. It's going to cost 25% more, and we all know how hard our farmers work. Nobody works harder. The margins of what they make is tiny, and you add a 25% tariff? I mean, these people are just ... They don't know what's going to happen, and our maple syrup makers, back and forth, we get a lot of syrup from Canada and blend it and make it into products with Vermont syrup. Canada's the biggest producer of maples, the second-best maple syrup in the world. Vermont is the biggest producer of the best maple syrup in the world, in the United States, but the equipment is largely made, that our sugar makers use, is largely manufactured in Canada. 25% tariff on that. That's going to hammer the Vermont maple producers.

Again, they operate on a small margin, and a lot of these farms, as you know, and the sugar producers, or, we've got a family company up there, second generation, that makes high-quality furniture, these are family businesses and they have tight margins. They're competing, they're really working hard. The Northeast Kingdom is really a pretty low-income part of Vermont with wonderful, incredibly hard-working people who are very proud of where they live and who they are, and who their neighbors are. They're asking really tough questions about how they can make it and whether they can stay in business, and this is not the same as immigration, but there's an element here that is the same as immigration.

Shouldn't any policy that we pursue start with the premise that we'll do no harm? Madam President, it might be a policy you're advocating, and I know when you served in your previous job, you'd be wanting to make certain that what you did did no harm. In fact, you'd be insisting that it did some good. My question with the tariffs is whether the administration is starting out from the premise that I think all of us should start with. Yeah, we may have an idea, we hope it might work, but we've got to make sure it does no harm.

SENATOR BOOKER: I'm sorry, I was going to answer that question, but-

SENATOR WELCH: Yeah, go ahead.

SENATOR BOOKER: Did the Senator finish his question?

SENATOR WELCH: Yeah, well, that's a long question and I'm waiting for a long answer.

SENATOR BOOKER: Okay. I want to first start by saying that the Senator has a reputation around this place, that there's a deep penetrating goodness that's in you. I love to watch my Senate colleagues when the other people are not. It's a habit of mine, because I think what you do when no one is watching is really telling. It's a belief I have that someone who is nice to you but not nice to the waiter is not a nice person, and we have a body full of people that show some deep, decent goodness. You are one of those people, and what I love watching you is that it could be the farthest ideological person away from you, and you just have this ... You look at people like you see their divinity, whether it's a person at the highest position, a leader of the Senate on either side, or someone that holds the door.

What I love about you is when I watch you, you're one of the Senators ... Some people just keep to their side of the aisle. I always look up and I find you over there talking to somebody, and I just rely on that decency in you as a friend and I've come to love you like a brother, and I want to thank you for being here before your alarm in the morning goes off. It really touches me, and I don't know if you remember this, but about 12 hours ago and you sat right here and you embraced me in a hug, and I leaned on that hug because I wasn't sure that I would even make it 12 hours. I take strength from you, my friend, and I take strength from you to hold to my kindness, to look for it everywhere.

This is a story I don't think I've ever shared with you, but it speaks to how we get things done and how we should get things done. When I first got to the United States Senate, my mentor, Bill Bradley, gave me three real lessons for me to learn. I think I've obeyed two out of the three. One was to know the rules of procedure really well. That's the one I've probably failed. I'm still learning things 13 years into this, about the rules of procedure. The second one was, become a specialist in some areas, don't be a mile wide and an inch deep, and I feel like I've done a pretty good job on that. The one that he called me, that was most fruitful, I've already mentioned one of the benefits I had in doing this with John McCain earlier in this 12 hours, but he commanded me to go and meet with all your Republican colleagues, take them out to dinner, sit with them for lunch, whoever they are.

I went out to dinner with Ted Cruz. It was hard to find a restaurant because I'm a vegan and Ted Cruz is from Texas, but I still remember that we went out and how people were sort of shocked just to see two human beings breaking bread. The story I want to tell my friend about is when I went to see Jim Inhofe, Republican from the same state as Lankford, and I couldn't get him to meet with me. Couldn't get on his schedule, and I found out that he had Bible study in his hideaway, and so I go up to his hideaway for Bible study. Thune was there, and we all have implicit biases. We all have implicit biases. My implicit bias was that I did not expect this older conservative man, that I would walk in and see on his mantle this beautiful picture, centered, of him hugging a little Black girl.

I'm embarrassed by that, that it so surprised me, and I, especially in those days, I didn't talk to the senior giants in the Senate, I didn't call them by their first names. I still have a problem calling Senator Durbin by his first name, for example. He's a lion of the Senate in my opinion, and one of the kindest people to me since I've been here. I go to him, I go to Jim Inhofe, I go, "Mr. Chairman, sir," and I look at the picture and I go, "Who dat?" He smiles and chuckles, and then he tells me the most beautiful story of his family adopting this little Black girl out of some of the most terrible circumstances. I was so moved, and thinking about my friend Bill Bradley. I would've never known this incredibly beautiful thing about somebody who, ideologically we disagreed on so many things, but knowing this personal moment, it created this thread between us. Not a rope, not a cord, but a thread that connected me to him and created a deeper affection.

Fast forward many months in this body, and there's a big education bill, which Chris Murphy referenced earlier. A big education bill was going through the Senate because No Child Left Behind, we were going back the other way, and Senator Durbin has told me about this. Pendulum sometimes swings and swings back in this place, and it was a deal. Lamar Alexander was, in the well of the Senate, he was the manager of the bill, and there was no amendments allowed, no amendments allowed.

Of course, I'm sitting back here – this is where I sat – and you talk about egos. My ego, I think I had this great amendment and I was frustrated that they were having this rule, no amendments, but I've got a great amendment to do something about homeless and foster children that have the worst educational outcomes. I thought I had a modest amendment to try to make a difference for American children that are in foster care or that were homeless, and I'm frustrated.

I'm sitting back here, something that I dream of doing again one day, sitting, and just kind of upset. Then I see walking through those doors, Senator Jim Inhofe, and he walks to the well, kind of talking, and I remember the story he told me about this little Black girl and his family, and something tells me to get up. I walk into the well, down these steps, and I say to him, "Mr. Chairman, sir, I know how much you care for children in tough circumstances. I have an amendment." I explained my amendment to him, and he looked at me and he gave me the Senate version of no, which is, "I'll think about it." I got frustrated and I said, "Thank you, sir, for considering it," and I walked back and I sat down right here, and then when I picked my head up, he's marching into our side like you do on the other side, like his GPS coordinates were off, marches up to me and just sort of grunts at me, "I'm in," and then turns around and starts walking away from me.

I step up, I go, "Wait, excuse me. What do you mean?" He goes, "Cory, I'm going to co-sponsor your amendment," and I was so happy. Now I go over to Senator Grassley and say the same thing to him, a relationship that, thanks to Dick Durbin, I really bonded. I have this sweet relationship with him, even though, again, we disagree on so much, and he doesn't even make me wait. He looks at me and he goes, "You got Inhofe?" He signs on my …

By the time I go to Lamar Alexander, I look at him and I'm like, "I've got a full house. I'm sorry, I got no other Democrats, but I got all these Republicans," and he looks at me and he laughs and he goes, "Really?" He puts the amendment on the bill. It's the law of the land now.

SENATOR WELCH: That's great.

SENATOR BOOKER: What you said in the beginning of your long windup question, my dear friend, my dear brother, is how real change is made. That man, Dick Durbin, when I first got to the Senate, he knew how much I cared about criminal justice reform. He brought me to the table, and I started working. As I presided, I started working in conversations with Mike Lee, in conversations with Chuck Grassley. We cobbled together a bill. It wasn't done by Executive Fiat, it was done in the Senate, 87 votes. It's the law of the land. Thousands have been liberated from unjust incarceration, and so my point to the Senator is, his spirit is so right, is so true about what it takes to make real change, but the President we have right now doesn't seem to be coming to this body with any kind of bold, bipartisan legislation to solve the problems of our nation, to cobble together the common ground of this country on immigration.

No, he's not acting like that. He's using language like, "Presidential primacy." He's defending his corrupt practices in immigration by saying things like, "Presidential primacy." He's invoking the Alien Enemies Act. He's invoking the Alien Enemies Act, an act from the 1700s, to deny due process, which Anton Scalia, a textualist, says that whether you're born in this country or not, you have due process here.

The Constitution states only one thing twice. Both the 5th and the 14th Amendments say that no one – not "no citizen" – no one shall be deprived of liberty or property without due process of law, and yet this President is disappearing people, and as we documented here, disappearing the wrong people. As we documented here, detaining unjustly Americans, separating families, all while pushing his agenda and doing things that the values of people on both sides of this aisle don't believe in, like stopping the investigation of children for alleged sexual molestation.

This is wrong. I sat down with some of the advocates who were telling me and who were trying to fight to stop the law from being broken, and they scared me, Dick Durbin, because they said what I said on this floor. If someone is willing to violate the Constitution for some, it endangers the constitutional rights for us all.

Do not think this is, 'oh, those people'. If they are violating rights of some, it is a threat to the rights of all. I am standing here because of a national crisis that is growing. We talked about Social Security, we talked about Healthcare, we talked about Education. This is a crisis for *us*.

And this is what the person said. They talked about the Insurrection Act. They've been hearing people in the administration talk about the Insurrection Act. Every person in this Congress and across the country wants a safe and secure bordering, but scapegoating immigrants to erode basic constitutional freedoms does not make America safer, does not make our community safer, does not reform our immigration system like we should be doing, in a bipartisan manner like Lankford and Murphy. It does not stop our longstanding problems from our agricultural industry to our tech industry. History has shown that when due process and basic constitutional rights are eroded for some people, it does not stop. It continues to erode. The shoreline that kept you safe will shrink until it reaches you.

I am reminded of German pastor Martin Niemöller's quote about fascism in Germany.

> They first, they came for the socialists, and I did not speak up because I was not a socialist. Then they came for the trade unionists. I did not speak out because I was not a trade unionist. Then they came for the Jews. I did not speak out because I was not a Jew. Then they came for me, and no one was left to speak.

Well, everything that has happened in the last few months contradicts American values, shared values. I am most concerned about what this signals for the future and the potential invocation of this President of the Insurrection Act. Some of our country's most prominent lawyers have warned that the invocation of these two antiquated laws, the Alien Enemies Act and the Insurrection Act, may result in the true erosion of our constitutional rights. Trump's recent invocation of the Alien Enemies Act is the first step to disappearing people without due process, as Justice Scalia says is wrong.

Then, on the first day in office, Trump directed the Secretaries of Defense and Homeland Secretary – excuse me, the Secretary of Defense and the Secretaries of Homeland Security – Trump directed them to initiate a 90-day review to determine whether the President should invoke the Insurrection Act of 1807. That 90-day review, when do those 90 days come up, folks? This month, in 19 days, April 20th. The President of the United States, who's already invoked a 1780-something law, also asked his immigration folks, his Homeland Security folks, to do a 90-day review about the Insurrection Act of 1807. Now, there's people probably watching and saying, "What is the Insurrection Act?" I bet a lot of folks. I had to look up what the Alien Enemies Act was, so let me tell folks what the Insurrection Act that our President on his first day in office, of all the things a President has to do, he turned to the Secretaries of Defense and the Secretary of Homeland Security to initiate a 90-day review of the Insurrection Act.

America, what is the Insurrection Act of 1807? It's among the President's most powerful authorities that he can deploy the US Armed Forces and militia during a national emergency. He can declare a national emergency. This president has already wrongfully declared national emergencies. He called, declared a national emergency on energy. Senator Kaine talked about the outrageousness of somebody declaring a national emergency on energy when we were at the highest level of petrochemical extraction in our country's history, and until he started rolling back what we were doing on wind and solar, we had an all-of-the-above strategy. Nobody 'drilled-baby-drilled' more than Joe Biden.

The Insurrection Act gives the ability of the President to declare a national emergency to suppress insurrections, to quell civil unrest or domestic violence and enforce the law when he believes it's being obstructed. When can the President invoke the Insurrection Act? Well, nothing in the text of the law defines insurrection, rebellion, or domestic violence. Those are the prerequisites for deployment, but they don't define those things.

One of Trump's first executive orders, signed the evening he took office on January 20th, was titled Declaring a National Emergency at the Southern Border of the United States. In that order, he said American sovereignty is under attack. He has already declared a national emergency. Neither Congress nor the courts played a role in deciding what constitutes an obstruction or a rebellion. If

Trump does unlawfully invoke the Insurrection Act, he can conceivably use our military to carry out his deportation agenda within our country's borders, all while any due process or opportunity to prove that their presence in the US is lawful or even that they are a citizen. Trump himself said he wants to deport American citizens to foreign countries. Trump himself has said, "I want to deport American citizens to foreign countries." On February 4th, he said, and I quote, "I'm just saying, if we had a legal right to do it, I would do it in a heartbeat. I don't know if we do or not. We're looking at it right now." This is what he has asked his Secretary of Defense and the Secretary of Homeland Security to say. "Can I invoke the Insurrection Act?"

Don't be mistaken. This is not just about immigrants. This is not just denying immigrants the due process that Anton Scalia said that immigrants have a right to, so you don't disappear the wrong people, like the Trump administration has done, that you don't wildly disagree with what a citizen is saying and use that as a pretext to disappear them. He is creating the pretext to invoke that 1800 law, 1807 law, the Insurrection Act, and if he does that, when they came for the immigrants and denied them due process, he's trying to get us to surrender our commitment to the constitutional guarantees that Americans have. He has said he would invoke, he would deport Americans if he could. When the President denies due process to some in America, it threatens the due process of all.

Let's see what happens on April 20th, if this President who's already invoked the Alien Enemies Act follows through and invokes the Insurrection Act, but why wait until April 20th? Raise your voice now. Stand up now. Do something now. Cause some good trouble now. Let this President know that if he does ever do that, there will be a rising up of people's voices, a rising up of good trouble, as John Lewis would say, to say, "Not in my country. This is unacceptable."

The "Gang of Eight" here refers to a bipartisan group of eight United States Senators who wrote the Border Security, Economic Opportunity, and Immigration Modernization Act of 2013: Sen. Michael Bennet, D-CO; Sen. Dick Durbin, D-IL; Sen. Jeff Flake, R-AZ; Sen. Lindsey Graham, R-SC; Sen. John McCain, R-AZ; Sen. Bob Menendez, D-NJ; Sen. Marco Rubio, R-FL; and Sen. Chuck Schumer, D-NY.

7:13 AM - The President

SENATOR DICK DURBIN (ILLINOIS): Will the Senator yield for a question?

SENATOR BOOKER: To Senator Dick Durbin, somebody who's been my mentor and friend, I will yield for a question while retaining the floor.

SENATOR DURBIN: Thank you. I first want to acknowledge this extraordinary moment in the history of the Senate. I believe you've been holding the floor now for more than ten hours, and perhaps will go on even longer, and you've been joined by your colleague and friend, Senator Murphy of Connecticut. I'm sorry to take the early morning shift, but I didn't want to miss this moment in history, not just for the historic nature of it, but for the substance of it as well.

I just remind my colleague and fellow member of the Senate Judiciary Committee, it was only three, maybe four weeks ago that we had witnesses before the Judiciary Committee. I asked a question, and one of them is pending on the calendar, the executive calendar on the floor. His name is Dean Sauer of Missouri, and he's seeking the position of Solicitor General of the United States. Along with him was the lady aspiring to be the Assistant Deputy Attorney General for Civil Rights, Harmeet Dhillon, and Aaron Reitz, who has been approved by the Senate for a legal policy position. The questioning went to the basics of our Constitution, which you have noted here today, and that is, what is the check and balance on a President? What is the accountability of a President under the Constitution?

As I read it, and I don't profess to be expert, I'm still learning, as I read it, the accountability of the President is in Article Two ... in Article Three, I'm sorry ... Article Three, the Judiciary. Ultimately, the President can be held accountable by impeachment in Congress or by decision of court, that some of the orders that he is promulgating are inconsistent with law and the Constitution, and the question that was asked of the witnesses who are seeking positions in the Department of Justice, does a public official, can a public official defy a court order?

It seems so fundamental and basic. The answer is no, of course, but these three witnesses all equivocated in their own ways, which raises the question, if this President is not held accountable by a court order, what then can control a President who misuses their office to the detriment of the nation or the people who live here? That I thought was a fundamental question. It was interesting to note.

You may remember that one of our Republican colleagues on the Senate Judiciary Committee, Senator John Kennedy of Louisiana, after hearing these witnesses equivocate on whether a public official can defy a court order, came to the committee and basically said, "What are you saying? The answer is obvious. You can criticize a decision of the court within the bounds of propriety as a member of the bar, you can appeal a decision of the court, but if that doesn't satisfy you, your recourse is to quit, resign, leave. The Constitution has the last word. The courts have the last word."

I think that's the question that you're raising today. Where is the accountability of the President of the United States when he misuses the power of office? In the cases that you've mentioned, the Alien Enemies Act — it's a law that's been around since I think 1807, or somewhere that time. I think it's clear. Unless you have declared a war or unless you are invaded, you cannot invoke the Alien Enemies Act, as this President has done, and he's being challenged in that regard. Yesterday, our friend Senator Grassley, who chairs the Judiciary Committee — and I say 'friend'. Some people back home say, "Don't say that anymore, we don't talk to those people." They're wrong. This is a body where we do talk to one another, and we should, for good reason. Well, he raised the question yesterday — why is President Trump being challenged so often in court?

Well, he has issued 102 executive orders. I don't know if that's a record, but I'll bet it is. One hundred two executive orders, questioning something as basic as birthright sovereignty, birthright citizenship. The point that I'm getting to is, in obvious situations here where President Trump has gone too far, where is the accountability? It's not going to be an impeachment. We're realists. We know that the Republican House of Representatives is not likely to ever consider that. It could be in the courts, and if it goes to the courts, the question is, will this President follow a court order if it goes against his policy? If he won't follow that court order, where is the accountability? Where is the check and balance? Where is the constitutional framework, which is supposed to be at the foundation of this democracy?

I think you're raising important questions, and the Insurrection Act, the use of our military for political purposes is a frightening prospect. It's something we have avoided throughout our history and should continue to. And I just commend you for raising this point because I believe it's timely. It's as timely as the questions that we asked of these Department of Justice nominees, about the enforceability of court orders. And the question is now will the American people speak up? I'm counting on some of our Republican friends to speak up too. Throughout history, there have been moments when the party, other than the President's party, showed extreme courage, political courage, and spoke up. We need that kind of voice now, I thank you for raising that on the floor this morning. My question to you is at this moment in time, as we ask these nominees whether they would follow a court order or defy a court order, doesn't that get to the basics of our constitutional democracy?

SENATOR BOOKER: Yes. Yes. Yes, it does. I mean, you put forth this litany where what we have to ask ourselves is at what point do my colleagues in the House or the Senate and the Republican Party say, "Enough. Enough"? God bless John Kennedy for calling out the absolute absurd. I was in that hearing where you have nominees for some of the highest positions in the administration failing to say that they will abide by a court order. I mean, that is something we haven't heard people on either side of nominees just say so bluntly now, not, yes I will follow the orders of a court. They're equivocating. And God bless one of my colleagues, John Kennedy, who said, "That's absurd. You either obey the order or you resign." Because we have a constitution. And so when is it enough? When is it enough?

This is the month of Passover, and there's a wonderful song I love singing when I'm at a Pesach, Dayenu. It Would Have Been Enough, is the song, if God just delivered us from the [Land of] Egypt, it would've been enough if he parted the seas, it would've been enough. *Dayenu, dayenu, dayenu.*

This is a kind of a twisted version of that. When is it enough? When the President of the United States starts a memecoin on his first day, violating the emoluments clause immediately and enriching himself? When is it enough? When he takes an agency that is on the front lines of stopping infectious diseases like Ebola or drug resistant tuberculosis from coming here? Is that enough? When we created that in Congress and he has no right to stop that agency, would that been enough? When is it enough? For him to issue executive orders that trample on the highest ideals of this land. When he mocks members of the court so badly that even the current Chief Justice admonishes him? When is it enough? When Elon Musk is indiscriminately firing people and then realizing, oops, we need the FAA safety folks. Oops, we need the nuclear folks who are helping us keep our regulation. When is it enough that you will say, okay, I'll call them in and have a hearing to create some transparency in what he's doing? When is it enough? When he activates the alien enemies acts and starts disappearing human beings without due process? When is it enough?

Well, it's enough for me. It's enough for me.

Twelve hours now, I'm standing, and I'm still going strong because this President is wrong. And he's violating principles that we hold dear and principles in this document that are so clear and plain. The powers of the Article I branch are spelled out and he is violating them. Don't take my word for it. Republican appointed judges, Democrat-appointed judges are saying it and stopping him and then he maligns the judge that did that. When is it enough for people to speak out and not just fall in line? To put patriotism over a person that's in the White House?

So to your question, sir, to my friend, and I'm sorry to get a little animated at this early morning hour, but I am so frustrated and not just because of that, but I'm reading the stories. We're going into the next section, which is national security, and I'm reading the stories of our citizens of this country, not just New Jerseyans. There's a lot we've read in these 12 hours, but there are people from all over the country are reaching out to my office, and I know they are yours. You're the second-highest-ranking Democrat in here. I know they're reaching out to you because you're a man that stands for justice. I know they reach out to your office, too because you're one of these outposts for sanity in a Congress that is being too complicit to an executive that is overstepping his authority and violating the Constitution and hurting people who rely on healthcare and Social Security.

I'm reading these stories, sir, because the voices of the Americans that don't have the privilege that the 100 of us don't get to stand here, but I believe the power of the people is greater than the people in power. That's the ideals of our democracy in our constitution. So I'm rip-roaring and ready.

7:24 AM - Cuts, Chaos, and Crisis

I'm wide awake. I'm going to stand here for as many hours as I can – 12 hours – and I recognize that my other friend, another person I consider more than a friend, like a sister to me from the state of New York, my neighbor.

SENATOR KIRSTEN GILLIBRAND (NEW YORK): Senator Booker, would you yield for a question?

SENATOR BOOKER: My sister, for you, I will yield for a question while retaining the floor.

SENATOR GILLIBRAND: Senator Booker, I've been listening to this debate all night, and I got to say, you're on fire. And you're on fire because the American people are very, very angry about what is happening. They are not happy with what this administration has done. It's contrary to what was promised. It's contrary to what was expected. And I know we're going to talk about national security in a few minutes, but can I ask a question about one of the topics you talked about last night? Because it was exactly what my constituents were talking to me about yesterday.

So I was in New York yesterday and we talked about these cuts to Social Security. I have to say I was stopped by the gentleman who worked at Amtrak and said, "Madam Senator, Madam Senator, I just want to thank you for protecting my Social Security," that has never happened to me before, never happened at Amtrak to be stopped by someone who worked there to thank me for one thing I had done that day.

But I'm telling you, Senator Booker, when Elon Musk starts firing people at Social Security and tells the Social Security Administration, "You cannot answer the phone." What are our mothers and fathers and grandmothers and grandfathers supposed to do? Many of them are not readily available to be on a computer. Many of them can't ask their question online. And worse, Elon Musk is expecting them to show up in person at a Social Security office. How many of our older Americans are not able to drive anymore? Or are uncomfortable driving? How many of our older Americans feel uncomfortable getting in the subway to get to a Social Security Administration because there's stairs, or because the lighting's not good enough? These are the challenges that our older Americans have. And so I just want to talk about the things you told us last night about the risk to Social Security.

Social Security is our seniors' money. It's not the government's money, it's their money. So what happens when you make it hard for a senior to call and make sure their check's on the way or their check never showed up and they can't find it? For a lot of older Americans that Social Security check is the only money they have for that month. It pays for food, right? It pays for heating bills; it pays for their medicine; it pays for their rent. It pays for everything they need to survive. Elon Musk's office doesn't believe anybody should be answering the phones. Who is he to tell America how to run its Social Security Administration when our seniors need those checks?

They've crippled the phone service. Even though get this one, can't answer the phone crippled the phone service, you can only make an appointment on the phone. So how are you supposed to make an appointment if you are going to go in? I mean, that's absurd. They plan to cut 7,000 staff. That's a lot of staff, 7,000 staff, even though the Social Security Administration staffing is already at a 50-year low. So they are lying when they are saying this is about efficiency. They just want the money. And what do they want the money for? Tax cuts for billionaire buddies of Elon Musk. It is an obscenity. It is an absurdity. It is an outrage. And everyone in America should be concerned. Hands off our Social Security, Elon Musk and President Trump, hands off! They are rallying all across the country to say, hands off my Social Security, hands off my Medicare, hands off my Medicaid. It's an outrage. And I don't think people should stand for it. Because your Social Security check is your hard-earned money. It is not for Elon Musk to play with to shift around or send it to tax breaks for his billionaire friends.

Now I have to say, my office has been working closely with one senior. Now she's a New Yorker with a disability, and she was told that she had to call a specific representative's extension by the end of March. Well, that was yesterday. And if she didn't get this person, her application could be denied. She's called every day, sometimes more than once a day. She has been on hold for four to five hours just to reach this representative. As of yesterday, when we reached out to her, she had still not reached the representative. So Americans across the country are panicked. They are stressed.

They're worried that they won't get their hard-earned money back, their retirement to pay for the things that they need. Now this is the money they've spent their entire careers paying into. Every time you get a paycheck, Senator Booker, there's a line that says Social Security because that money's been taken out of your paycheck and put into Social Security. So it's there for you when you retire. It's your retirement. The page is sitting here, right here. You are paying into your Social Security. Now imagine this is your first paycheck, isn't it? I bet it is your first paycheck. Your first paycheck, you're putting in dollars that you want saved so that when you... You can't even imagine what it's going to be like to be 65, but the day you're working here, the fact that you spent all night here supporting Senator Booker, that's your retirement. Wouldn't you be pissed off if Elon Musk took your retirement money? You should be. He doesn't have any right to it. And what he's doing is he's doing it by cutting staff. So if you need help because your Social Security didn't arrive, then how are you supposed to get that check? They can't issue you a new one unless they know that it didn't show up in the mail like it's supposed to.

Ultimately, cutting individuals from Social Security doesn't just affect them, it affects the entire economy. So you can imagine if all our seniors are getting this Social Security benefit, you can't go then buy your groceries. You're not going to be able to then go buy whatever you need for your home. Those stores will get less money, and that means there'll be less resources in the economy. Social Security, if you didn't know it, it's our country's largest anti-poverty program. It keeps people out of poverty. That's what it does.

When we designed Social Security however many decades ago, it was so that our seniors don't die in poverty, because they were dying. About half of seniors at that time were dying in poverty. They didn't have enough food to live. And so we created Social Security. It's one of the most popular programs. It's one of the most effective programs.

So reducing access to this key program, Senator Booker, is an outrage. It's harmful, it's cruel, it's hurtful. So I know that this is something that you've really spent a lot of time on last night, but don't you think it's cruel to not allow phone service? Don't you think it's wrong to make it harder for people to get access to their hard-earned money? Don't you think this is something that America did not sign up for in this election?

SENATOR BOOKER: I read last night – thank you for the question my friend – I read last night some of the most painful letters of people over and over again from throughout my state and through other states who are living in fear, who use words like terrified and told stories that they couldn't sleep because of the rhetoric of this president, the rhetoric of Elon Musk calling it a Ponzi scheme telling lies during a joint address. And then I read stories from people that work in Social Security. They're telling about not having desks and the waiting lines and the inefficiencies that this has created and the horrible deteriorating customer service. And I've been trying as much as I can during this last 12 hours to read the stories of Republicans.

SENATOR GILLIBRAND: Yeah, this affects everyone.

SENATOR BOOKER: Yes, to read editorials from the Wall Street Journal to just show that this isn't a partisan thing. This isn't about left or right, it's about right or wrong. It's about will we as a country honor our commitments that we made? And then I read independent folks that are saying, this is crazy that this program is even in jeopardy.

SENATOR GILLIBRAND: I have another question for you, because I know you want to move on to some national security issues this morning.

SENATOR BOOKER: I will yield for a question while retaining the floor.

SENATOR GILLIBRAND: Thank you, Senator Booker. So the other thing that stressed out my constituents that I talked to about this weekend is air safety. They're very, very stressed out about these cuts to the FAA. There was a plane crash not too far from here — helicopter crash. Everyone on that helicopter perished. We've been reading about stories across the country about flight safety and the fact that there are near collisions all the time. We had a horrible crash in New York, in Buffalo, the Colgan air crash. I've gotten to know the families over the last several years because they've worked together for legislation to make sure we have pilot safety. But what I've been watching in terms of this administration is they don't seem to care. They just have made up this idea that cuts across the board are necessary to get rid of fraud and waste in the budget.

And I agree, we can make government more efficient, but the way you do that is at least learn what each of these agencies do, study what's happening in them and how to make them more efficient. Make sure the right number of personnel are hired. Make sure the right training is offered. Make sure there's no wasteful programs. That's good government. That is not what Elon Musk and his DOGE boys are doing. That is nothing like what they are doing.

They're just cutting everything because they want to make space for these tax cuts for their billionaire buddies. It's really disgraceful. It's something that I don't quite understand. So over the past two months, just the past two months, we've seen horrifying accidents and near misses at airports all across the country. And there was another close call just this past Friday, again at DCA. Many of these accidents have been a result of chronic understaffing and antiquated technologies at the FAA.

But instead of fixing those problems, the first thing that Trump administration did when it came to power was fire people. I think he's kind of stuck in the loop of The Apprentice. You're fired. You're fired. You're fired. I don't get it. Good government is important. I support efficiency. That's not what they're doing. It's like they're on a power trip and they just want to fire everybody across the board. Just fire them all.

So while a court forced the FAA to rehire workers, thank God for the courts. Thank God for the judges that are doing their jobs and looking at these lawsuits appropriately. Many federal workers have simply moved on and found new jobs because these are highly skilled, highly sought-after employees, people that we really want working in the federal government to keep our country safe. Now, just weeks after the horrific plane crash here with 67 people getting killed in Washington, the administration fired hundreds of Federal Aviation Administration employees, jeopardizing the public safety and threatening our national security. So that made no sense. It was right on the heels of some horrific accident that we all witnessed.

Now, over 90% of US airport terminal towers don't have enough air traffic controllers. Critical shortages remain for other aviation safety personnel as well, such as safety inspectors and mechanics because to make sure when we get on that plane, plane's ready to go. In New York, nearly 40% of positions are unfilled at two facilities on Long Island, that direct air traffic for Newark, our shared airport, JFK and LaGuardia. As a result, over these past few years, the US has experienced a substantial and alarming increase in the number of near misses. According to an analysis from The New York Times in 2023, close calls involving commercial airlines occurred on average multiple times each week. And a number of significant air traffic control lapses increased 65% over the previous year.

What did they cite as the major reason behind the increase? A shortage of air traffic controllers. While the Trump administration claims no air traffic controllers or critical safety personnel were fired, we know that many of those who were let go played an essential role in maintaining those and maintaining our air traffic control infrastructure. Others were responsible for maintaining navigational, landing, and radar systems. We also know that safety inspectors, systems specialists, maintenance mechanics, are among workers who are affected. And at least one of the employees fired worked for FAA's National Defense Program, which protects our airspace from enemy drones, missiles, aircraft used as weapons. I want to talk about those missiles and drones as well. I really want to talk to you about what your thinking is here, that we don't have a plan. You had the incursions in New Jersey, incursions in New York at the same time, and we don't have assurance that those drones aren't being operated by China or Russia or Iran or another adversary for a nefarious purpose. We have to get to the bottom of this. And that's something that Senator Booker, you and I have been at the forefront when questioning the administration about what they're doing on this issue.

So the question I have is why did the administration fire these workers and so easily part with them? Who will perform these duties going forward? What risk analysis was performed to ensure this won't make flying less safe? Now, I asked these questions of the Secretary of Transportation in a letter on February 20th, over a month ago, and what was their response? We don't know. They haven't answered my letter. They're not willing to engage the Senate in actually policy and decisions that keep our state safe. What's worse is that we don't know if this is where it ends or if more reductions are coming, and more reductions that allow for safety for our FAA. Now, DOGE's so-called Workforce Optimization Initiative — it's BS. They don't do the analysis first. They just make the cuts.

We need the secretary and the acting FAA Administrator to be responsive to Congress's questions and oversight. The American people deserve to have a federal aviation agency that is dedicated to actually doing the job of protecting us, protecting this country. The Trump administration needs to take immediate steps to address FAA staffing shortages across the entire agency, not just air traffic controllers.

So Senator Booker, the question I really want to ask you is for your state, for New Jerseyans, what are they thinking? How do they receive this information? What do they say when they read about drone incursions over one of your arsenals, over one of your sensitive military bases? What do they think about cutting staff to the FAA when they watch all this information about crashes? I know my constituents are pretty stressed out about it. They don't understand why someone's making these cuts. Again, the why is the most important question. It's not for efficiency. It's not to get rid of the fat. It's not to get rid of the fraud. Never heard an allegation, "There's fraud in the FAA." Never heard an allegation, "There's fat in the FAA." They've been understaffed forever. So they're lying about the purpose. What is the purpose? What is the purpose? What are they going to do with that money, Senator Booker? I'd like to know.

SENATOR BOOKER: I appreciate this more than you know, and there's a line threaded throughout your entire question about the way they're going about doing this from so many agencies. First, they're trying to kill certain agencies, Department of Education, which they can't legally do. The USAID, they can't legally do. We created that. It's the Article I branch of government. But on some of these other agencies like Social Security where you started, we know it's ready, fire, aim, and actually the aim part never happens. They're savagely cutting personnel and organization after organization, seniors, thousands of them are already writing in about the undermining of service. The Wall Street Journal article we read last night said that the customer service, that Social Security is going from bad to worse, and painted horrific pictures that are putting seniors in crisis, not to mention the closing of Social Security centers in rural areas where people have to now drive hours and hours and hours.

And so the FAA, it was one of the early outrages that they fired people that they then realized they needed and tried to find some way to pull some of them back. And you and I both know that the way they talk about government workers, a large percentage of them are veterans. The way they demean and degrade them, the way they accuse them of being parts of corruption, fraud, or fat, when the stories we've been reading of what some of these folks do is extraordinary. And so your question though brings up a lot of national security issues. I'm going to bridge to that because you and I both were really, really incensed that we weren't getting enough information when we had these incursions.

And I want to start, what I've been doing in other sections is just reading, elevating on this floor, the voices of people from our country trying to elevate more of the voices to let people know we see you, we hear you. Your outrage. Your hurt. Your fears. They have value.

SENATOR GILLIBRAND: I have another question before you start your letters, Senator Booker, if you'd like to entertain another question, if you'll yield.

SENATOR BOOKER: I will yield a question while retaining the floor.

SENATOR GILLIBRAND: Okay. Because you're going into the national security section, and I want to give you a couple of questions to pepper your answers. I sit on the special committee on intelligence in the Senate. I also sit on the Armed Services Committee. And so national security is an area where New Yorkers care a deep amount about. And I've been spending the last 15 years focused on how we keep this country safe and what we should be doing. And so I get a lot of questions from New Yorkers about this issue. So I want you to address the drone issue for sure because that is something you and I have been working on continuously since we've seen these incursions.

And just to give a little more context for New Yorkers who might be listening to this debate, we've had drone incursions over sensitive military sites for quite some time now, and it's something that I've been working on on a bipartisan basis on through the Intelligence Committee. And some of these incursions are every night over and over again — over sensitive military bases. There was one over Langley. We've had them over arsenals in New Jersey, over sensitive sites in New York. We've had them over military bases across the country. And I don't like it when the answer is, "Oh, we know where most of this is. This is mostly FAA traffic." And I don't like it when I hear it from this administration – or any administration – because it's not true. Some of the drone sightings are planes in the air, helicopters, maybe weather balloons, maybe enthusiasts. But they do not know if all are.

And in these specific incursions, they do not know the origin of them. They do not know whose they are. They do not know who is operating them. They do not know the purpose of these drones. These drones could easily be spying. They could be planning attacks, they could be doing anything nefarious. We have no basis to say it is all known and we are not concerned. And so this is something we are going to get to the bottom of. I am very incensed about it. It does not leave our personnel as safe and does not leave our secrets safe. So drones is one issue.

The second issue, if you could address on the national security side is cybersecurity and election security, one of the cuts that the DOGE boys made, which I literally cannot understand why they would ever do this. This is making us weaker. It is making us less safe. It is not good for America. And it shows how ill-advised this process is, and how uninformed this process is and how we can see through these cuts how insincere this process is. This is not about waste. This is not about fraud. This is not about good government. This is about making massive cuts for tax breaks for billionaires, because that is where they want to spend your tax dollars. New Yorker's tax dollars and New Jerseyans tax dollars, they want to take it and give it to tax breaks to the billionaires. Okay. So this is the question.

These cuts — they have cut all the personnel or the main personnel at an organization called CISA that were supposed to be doing election security, the people who actually were working with the states to make sure our election system can't be hacked. They fired those people. They fired the senior personnel at the Department of Defense, our most experienced generals across the board, members from the Joint Chiefs of Staff — just fired them. For what reason? I don't know. No substantive reason was ever given. But these are the senior personnel who actually keep us from wars who have the judgment and the experience to advise the president, to advise Congress, to advise us on how to keep us safe. And then the last group they cut were the lawyers. Do you remember that Shakespeare play? The first thing we do is kill all the lawyers. Well, the context in which that was given was in order to have a coup.

So Shakespeare, hundreds of years ago said, "If you want to have a coup, the first thing you do is kill all the lawyers." Well, they fired all the lawyers, the senior lawyers at the Department of Defense. They fire the generals who actually know how to keep us safe. And then they fire the personnel at CISA who are responsible for election interference. They fired the people at the FBI who are also responsible for election interference. So again, these firings make no sense. I don't think they're making us more safe. I think they're making us less safe. When you fire the people who know what they're doing and are dedicated to keeping us safe, doesn't make us safer.

What do you think Senator Booker about any of the topics that I raised, specifically the drones, the firing of the election protection personnel at CISA, the firing of the generals, the firing of the senior lawyers at the Department of Defense, firing of the FBI personnel, also expert at election interfering? These are the smartest, most capable, the most sophisticated senior personnel that are there to help us keep this country safe. I really want to hear what you're hearing for your state and what you're thinking about this reckless, reckless approach to national security.

SENATOR BOOKER: I'm so grateful for the questions from my colleague, from my friend. I want folks to know that probably the best dinner I had when I came here was with the Senator from New York who really gave me a quick rundown on how to get things done in this body. I've watched her work on both sides of the aisle relentlessly to get things over the finish line to help people in our region from 9/11 folks who were our first responders to get their healthcare, to fight, to support the military, empower the military, but to fight against sexual assault in the military. She's one of these phenomenal people. And a lot of her questions we're going to get to, including that question that was obviously painful about national security, is that like, "Hey, one of the strategies of Russia – we know this – is to attack elections of other democracies, to try to sow discord, to try to undermine the very voting process."

And the Trump administration pulled away a lot of the people in the DOJ and elsewhere that their sole purpose was to fight against foreign election interference. And so how can we have a nation where the president's in charge of national security is not doing things to address the issues that were in your questions.

And I want to start by reading a couple of constituent letters. I know we want to step back and talk a little bit about immigration because my colleague and my friend and my partner in leadership in the Senate, Tina Smith is here. But I want to get into some of these letters because I said over 12 hours ago that we were going to continue to elevate the voices of people out there. And so this is coming from someone from New Jersey.

And they're writing,

> Dear Senator Booker, I'm writing to express my deep concern regarding the current state of our nation and the lack of response to the looming constitutional crisis. It is becoming increasingly difficult to ignore the actions of a president who routinely lies and makes outrageous proposals such as annexing Greenland, Mexico, and Panama, or even renaming the Gulf of Mexico. Those proposals not only undermine our international standing, but also disrespect the foundations of our country. Furthermore, I'm alarmed by the growing threat to press freedom.
> Recently, for example, the Associated Press was barred from the White House press room simply for referring to the Gulf of Mexico rather than the Gulf of America. A clear sign that the president's disregard for free speech and free press's role in holding power to account, The President is actively trampling on the Constitution and blatantly ignoring the rule of law {as Senator Gillibrand was saying} ... he has taken steps to slash vital federal agencies and disaster relief programs undermining our nation's capacity to respond to crises. His decision to appoint unqualified individuals to high positions for the purpose of following his will is another example of how our democratic systems are being systematically weakened.
> Additionally, his reckless and irresponsible approach to foreign policy is making the world more dangerous. His insistence on blaming Ukraine for Russia's invasion and ongoing war is not only historically inaccurate, but also deeply damaging to our allies and global stability. Even worse, his administration has entertained so-called "peace settlements" that exclude Ukraine from the process entirely, effectively allowing Russia to dictate terms without any Ukrainian input. Such actions to betray our commitments to sovereignty and democracy and embolden authoritarian regimes worldwide.
> Domestically, his agenda is destructive. His administration has pursued the withdrawal from USAID, the gutting of critical global humanitarian and development efforts that have long served U.S. interest abroad. At home, he's enabling tech billionaires like Elon Musk to take a chainsaw to government agencies, arbitrarily dismantling institutions that provide essential public services. His attacks on the NIH and its funding jeopardized critical medical research and public health initiatives undermining scientific progress for purely ideological reasons. Beyond these threats, his treatment of our closest allies is both reckless and embarrassing. His taunting of Canada, whether through inflammatory rhetoric or deliberate policy snubs, weakens our diplomatic ties and disregards the importance of maintaining strong relationships with our neighbors. This petty shortsighted approach to international relations is isolating the U.S. at a time when global cooperation is more critical than ever.
> My greatest frustration, however, is the lack of action from our representatives and governors. Too many are cowering in fear of the President's authoritarian tactics. I am troubled by the absence of pushback. {I am troubled by the absence of pushback.} I'm troubled by the absence of pushback. We are witnessing the erosion of checks and balances and the consequences could be dire. I was heartened by Governor Janet

> Mills of Maine standing up to the President's orders. Unfortunately, his response was a threat to her political future, further evidence of the intimidation tactics being employed. I implore you, Senator Booker, to show some moral courage and take meaningful action to stand up to this growing threat to our democracy.
> Please let me know how you are responding to this situation and what steps you, Senator Booker are taking to defend our Constitution and the rule of law. Thank you for your time and I look forward from hearing from you soon.

I hope at this early morning hour, at almost eight o'clock, that maybe you are listening because I hear you. I see you. And I'm standing here because, in part, of letters like yours. This is not normal. These are not normal times. We must begin to do as John Lewis says, get in good trouble, get in necessary trouble. I want to read another constituent. I just want to see where this person's from. I'm not trying to violate the privacy as my staff doesn't want me to do.

SENATOR MURPHY: Chippewa Falls.

SENATOR BOOKER: What's that?

SENATOR MURPHY. Chippewa Falls.

SENATOR BOOKER: We know Wisconsin's getting a lot of love here. I know my colleague, I kept seeing folks from two towns and one in your state and one in the great state of Pennsylvania. But this person, alas, is from *Joisey* [Jersey].

> I wrote to ask you to do all you can to resolve funding for the National Institute of Health and USAID. I work in information technology at Princeton University and I've seen firsthand the destruction, the termination of funds is causing to e-research and education. We are losing the momentum of research and causing deep and lasting loss of educational resources.
> The NIH and the National Science Foundation provide funds for basic research as well as applied topics. The benefits of this research will be long-lasting and the cost of disruption will be very high. Similarly, the disruption of USAID is tragic. My daughter works for an organization working with USAID on climate mitigation and adaptation. She has lost job security as a result of the Trump administration's actions. Work she has built on in Ethiopia, Kenya, and elsewhere will be disrupted due to lack of funding.
> Thank you for your leadership as our Senator. I'm proud to be represented by you as well as our new Senator, Andy Kim. The promise of our country is great, but we must redefine our purpose and imagine a new future. Your experience and knowledge will be critical to our country's success.

Let me go with two more and then turn to my colleague. This is a short one.

> I'm writing to express my concerns about the chaos and lawlessness coming out of the White House. USAID must be restored. Please use powers to restore democracy to the United States of America. This is not what democracy looks like. Thank you.

Somebody from New Jersey ... and one more, one more. One more voice:

> As a parent of a USAID Foreign Service Officer recently in Ukraine, now in Kenya, I am outraged and horrified by the coup now being staged by Elon Musk under the authority from the President. To be called criminal after putting your life at risk in the service of America's interest is itself to be a victim of criminal-like behavior. I have seen the beautiful roads and railroads in Africa built by Chinese. In one fell swoop, Trump has given that continent to the Chinese and the Russians.
>
> He did the same thing years ago by canceling participation in the Pacific Free Trade Pact, forfeiting our power and our goodwill, making China the largest player in the region. I saw the goodwill in the eyes of passersby from the Philippines to Georgia to Tajikistan. Now I hear it turned to hostility. Think of sports fans in Canada booing our national anthem. Think also of the infants that will now die from AIDS because of USAID's treatment program was abruptly stopped along with vaccination programs and programs for stopping diseases such as Ebola, monkeypox, hemorrhagic fever. These diseases will come home. With even a 90-day pause in workers in these programs, we will lose jobs and rent and some never will return.
>
> Refrigeration of medicines will be at risk. Clinics and offices will be become unavailable. Humpty Dumpty will not be quickly put back together again. Some of what Trump wants to do will ultimately need approval of Congress. I urge you to fight every one of his proposals and appointments, slow the legislative process as much as you can, please. I hope Trump will lose his majority. Thank you for your attention. I will be of service in any way possible to right these wrongs.

I love when constituents don't only point out what's wrong, but stand up and say, "I will be in service. Let me know how I can help." Your voice is helping tonight. Speaking to these issues is helping tonight.

8:02 AM - Deportation Injustices

I know my Senate colleague is here. If she has a question, I will yield while retaining the floor.

SENATOR TINA SMITH (MINNESOTA): Mr. President.

PRESIDING OFFICER, SENATOR CASSIDY: The Senator from Minnesota.

SENATOR SMITH: Thank you, Mr. President, and thank you to my colleague from New Jersey for yielding for a question. And I want to just start by thanking my colleague, one of my dearest friends in the Senate for using his voice in such a powerful way over the many, many hours that you've been holding the Senate floor. And I know you well enough to know that you are not doing this because of your belief in the power of your voice. You are doing this because of your belief in the power of all the voices that you've been amplifying all through the night and your belief of the importance that the millions of Americans who are so frightened and concerned and horrified by what they see this administration doing and wanting to feel like there is somebody here that is fighting for them and that is listening to them.

And the way in which you are reading these letters today and all through the night, Senator Booker, I think is a tribute to your respect for all of those Americans. And so I'm so grateful for that. And I wanted to take a moment if I could, to ask you to yield for a question related to what you've been talking about. And I certainly agree with you that these are not normal times in our nation and as elected officials, it is our duty to speak up and to fight back against the abuses and the overreach of this administration and to raise up our voices, raise up the voices of our constituents who, as I said, are both frightened and furious about what's happening. So my question to you, Senator Booker, is about some of the Trump administration's recent actions regarding immigration. And my question is in three parts.

First, I think that we can all agree that our current immigration system in this country is broken. It is not working well for anyone. It's not working well for American businesses that depend on a global talent pool. It is not working well for families who want to reunite with their loved ones and it is not working well at all for those who seek refuge from persecution and believe in the promises that are carved into the Statue of Liberty. And to my colleague, I asked these questions and I think about these issues about the shortcomings of our immigration system as the Senator from Minnesota where our meat processing sector relies so much on immigrant labor, where the University of Minnesota is a beacon for international students studying science and technology and agriculture, where the resorts in Minnesota rely on folks from all over the country to come and make them work. The little mom-and-pop 12 cabin operations up on lakes in northern Minnesota and the manufacturers who rely on, as I said, the best and the brightest from all over the world coming to serve in our state and serving our economy.

And I think we know my colleague from New Jersey that there have been real and serious bipartisan attempts at comprehensive immigration reform debated in this body. And while I might not have agreed with everything in these proposals, I suspect you might not as well. I think we both, I'm sure, strongly believe that immigration is an issue that merits real debate and real policy solutions. Our colleague who is here on the floor with us this morning, Senator Murphy from Connecticut, has worked so hard to find real bipartisan solutions. And I believe that comprehensive immigration reform needs to ensure our national security. It needs to provide a fair and workable path for immigrants who want to come and contribute to the American dream, which is what truly makes this country great.

But here's the rub. The Trump administration's recent actions show that they are not interested in serious policy reforms that would make Americans safer or make our immigration system work more efficiently and fairly. Instead, what I think we can see is this President has prioritized using our immigration system as a tool to restrict First Amendment freedoms, to subvert due process, and to further weaken America's global standing with our allies and our regional partners, as he seeks to emulate the authoritarian regimes that he so openly admires.

There's just one example. In recent weeks, we've seen a number of international students targeted for arrest and deportation merely on the basis of their pro-Palestinian advocacy. Now these are young people who played by all the rules. They've entered this country with permission in order to further their educations and have not been accused of or charged of any criminal activity. Their views on the war and Gaza may differ sharply from mine or others, but I believe that the First Amendment guarantees them the right to express those views without facing punishment or reprisal from our government. Nonetheless, the Trump administration has admitted that they're doing exactly that, seeking to punish lawfully present immigrants, in some cases, even green card holders, because of the political views that they've expressed. The Secretary of State has invoked a rarely used section of statute that allows him to unilaterally designate for removal any alien who may cause, "Potentially serious adverse foreign policy consequences", and if that's not enough, many of these arrests have been carried out in a manner that seems calculated to maximize fear and intimidation in immigrant and activist communities.

Here's an example to my colleague for him to respond to. I want to take the case of the recent arrest of Rümeysa Öztürk, a Turkish graduate student at Tufts University who was studying the relationship between child development and our social media-saturated globally connected world. She is here on a valid student visa. She is not accused of any crime and by all accounts, she is a loved and valued member of the Tufts community. Her only purported offense was being one of four co-authors of an op-ed in the student newspaper that urged the administration of Tufts to engage with student calls to divest from businesses with ties to Israel and the IDF. And for that offense, her visa was revoked with no notice and she was arrested on the street and spirited more than 1500 miles away, which is likely a violation of a judge's order to await her probable deportation. And I'm sure many of my colleagues, including my colleague from New Jersey, has seen the video of her arrest, which was captured by a neighbor's security camera and it is utterly chilling.

She is surrounded by officers in plainclothes with no visible insignia, no markings at all on their clothing. She was handled roughly, her belongings are taken away from her, hands are cuffed, before being loaded into an unmarked car. It is no exaggeration that her arrest looks like a kidnapping — one that you might expect to see in Moscow rather than in the streets of Boston. And of course, the terror of what she experienced is horrible to think about. But I also think about the thousands and thousands and thousands of other students here with a student visa or other lawful means who see this and think to themselves, this could happen to me. This could be something that happens to my roommate or my student or anybody. It seems like such a breakdown in the rule of law and the way that our country should operate.

So I would like to ask my colleague, to you, does this seem normal or appropriate for federal law enforcement officers of the United States to conduct routine arrests in plain clothes with unmarked cars and with this overwhelming show of force for individuals who pose no obvious physical threat to those law enforcement? Furthermore, is this not exactly the sort of operation that you would order if your goal is to intimidate and dissuade immigrant and activist communities from exercising their constitutional rights to free speech? Does punishing people for their political speech seem consistent with American democratic values? I can't believe that we would think that it would be consistent. And I wonder if my colleague from New Jersey would like to respond in any way to this.

SENATOR BOOKER: I want to respond deeply. I first want to thank my colleague for being here in the morning. She's one of my colleagues I confided in when I told her it was 'enough was enough' for me, I needed to do something different. And she readily encouraged me to be here on the floor for what is now about 13 hours. And she's encouraged me. She has encouraged my heart and is just one of my dear friends and I'm just so grateful to see her this morning. I want to say something before I begin answering her question. In my home county, the one I grew up in, Bergen County, there's a family, the Alexanders, whose son Edan* is an American who is being held by Hamas and he is being likely tortured and in trauma and in pain. He's a U.S. citizen — he's an American.

I had a friend give me this recently – a young man who was driving me around – this ribbon that I will often use, just keep in my pocket and remind me of him and our determination to bring him home, to bring him home. I want his family to know that stays center in my thoughts. And I also feel because of so many New Jerseyans who are affected by this crisis, who have lost family members in that region that we must bring peace. And then my friend Senator Smith asked this question, which is a real test because when you disagree with someone's statements so much, but the very nature of the First Amendment, what makes this document so precious is that it says that no matter how reprehensible your speech is, this document says you have the right to say it.

I remember the controversy over a NFL player who kneeled and one of the voices – it just sticks into my head – is a man who, a White guy from the military, who just said,

> I fought battles. {I think it was Afghanistan.} And I am offended by his taking a knee. But the very reason I fought was so that he would have the freedom to do it. And so I came back, I was there on October 7th, and I have very hurt, strong feelings about what's going on over there and urgent desires to end the nightmare to bring people like Edan home to end the nightmare for so many Israelis and Palestinians. And I find some of the things people are saying so unhelpful to the crisis and to the moral truths that I believe in, but I will fight for people's rights.

And so here is a situation where you see video and it just doesn't seem like who we are. If you're revoking somebody's visa, make a phone call, tell them that you have 30 days to leave. But there should be due process and you should have to prove your claims in court if this person is somehow allying with some kind of enemy, prove it. But what I saw there doesn't reflect the highest ideals. God, if this constitution was easy, it wouldn't be worth the paper it's written on. And so I love my friend because she wades into some difficult waters, but she's guided by the oath that she took to defend the Constitution. And in these complex and difficult times, she's standing up. And I tell you, when we were in the immigration section last night, or earlier, I should say, we read the most painful stories.

My brother, over on the other side of me... I've got some of my really dear friends on the floor right now — Senator Murphy, Senator Warnock, Senator Smith. My brother, Senator Warnock knows that we are a nation that is paying hundreds of millions of dollars over the years of the Trump administration to fund private prisons that are being paid, incentivized to take away people's liberties. We read stories in the immigration section about people that got trapped in those systems that should never be there. Horrible stories, painful voices. I've read about folks who were caught up in a system and I just loved that one article from that Canadian that was for weeks put in a private prison. And suddenly when she heard the lies of the people who found ways to keep her there, the aha moment that she realized that these people every day I am there, they get profit. They're not incentivized by justice, they're incentivized by profit. I read stories, Senator Smith, of people that were sent to that horrible jail in El Salvador that the government admitted they made a mistake. They disappeared someone who has American family members.

Story after story I read that just are such a betrayal, not of democratic values, but of American values, because we all in this body know we need to do more to protect our borders, to keep us safe, to arrest criminals, be they undocumented or documented. That's an urgency we all feel. But when you sacrifice your core values, you sacrifice them to a demagogue who says this is all about your safety, when you sacrifice your core principles for your safety, you will achieve neither. You will neither be safe nor morally strong. The true leaders on both sides of the aisle that I've heard over the years talk on these issues say, we can do both. We can make our country safe and we can abide by our values. And in a complex world where country after country disappears people, when authoritarian countries disappear their political enemies, their political adversaries, disappear people who say things they politically disagree with, those countries are looking to us.

8:02 AM - DEPORTATION INJUSTICES

Did you know when Donald Trump started using that phrase, 'fake news, fake news, fake news', that in Turkey, Erdoğan started arresting people on charges of 'fake news' — because we are looked to. I believe like Reagan said, we could be that city on a hill, but we are up high and folks are going to look to us for what is the world order going to be. What is democracy globally going to look like? Are we going to defend democracy and democratic principles or will we behave like the authoritarians that we should be against? So this is a fundamental question you ask and it has been resonating all these 13 hours. We keep coming back to the Constitution because so many of the things the Trump administration are doing from the separation of powers to violating the very first words of our Constitution, the very first words, this commitment we make when we swear our oaths, all of us, we the people of the United States of America, this is our mandate. In order to form a more perfect union, establish justice. It comes really quick. It comes really quick.

Is it just to disappear a human being with no due process? I quoted Antonin Scalia, this conservative that was sitting on a stage where somebody had a lot of affection for Ruth Bader Ginsburg. And the moderator asked them, "Does somebody in our country have the rights of this document?" And he said, "Yes." Especially the 14th Amendment that doesn't say 'any citizen', that says 'no person' — nobody. And so where do we stand when our Founders, those imperfect geniuses, say we the people, in order to form a more perfect union, we the people, the United States, in order to form a more perfect union, establish justice, ensure domestic tranquility, provide for the common defense, promote the general welfare and secure the blessings of liberty to ourselves and our prosperity, what nation are we turning over to the next President? To the next Congress, when this Congress is sacrificing the powers that are given right underneath that preamble, it's Article I which spells out, "**All legislative powers herein granted shall be vested in the Congress of the United States, which shall consist of the Senate and the House of Representatives.**"

And then it goes on to talk about what we have the power to do. We set the laws. This President is invoking emergency powers like the Alien Insurrection Act, a 1780-something law that the last time was used in World War II to detain Japanese-Americans, something so shameful to put them in concentration camps here in America. He wants to take power from our Congress and the thing that is killing me, that is actually breaking my heart, brother Warnock, the thing that's actually breaking my heart is that we're letting them — that we're letting him take our power. If Elon Musk was a democrat and Joe Biden said, "Hey, go after the spending power of Congress, all the things that they approved, it's hard to do bipartisan things here." God bless Patty Murray and Susan Collins coming together and getting, spending bills – hard work – done.

Lord knows I sometimes play a little Motown in here, *Ain't Too Proud To Beg*. I go to the appropriations leader and say, "Hey, my New Jerseyans in this county, need this in this county." We work on all this. I fight for programs with Lindsey Graham and USAID, with the now Secretary of State, Marco Rubio programs that he approved. The Department of Education — I've worked with Republicans to put things in the Department of Education. There are people here that worked in a bipartisan way to try to simplify the FAFSA forms. I could go through all the work we've done that now this body, the Article I branch of [the] Constitution, right under the mandate of the United States of America, as Tina Smith is telling us right after we the people of the United States, in order to form a perfect union, established Justice as the Senator, my friend. And so that's why we're here.

That's why now the Senate is filling up. Its friends galore. We got Amy Klobuchar now on the floor. That's why we're here. No business as usual, no business as usual. We're not doing the usual order.

We're talking about these things. We're making the case. We talked about immigration, we talked about Medicaid, we talked about Medicare. We talked about healthcare. We talked about medical research. We talked about social security. We're marching through. We're marching through. 13 hours, I got more in the tank. And so I thank you for that question. It brings up very emotional things for me. I'll be honest. It brings up pain and frustration and hurt. It brings for me the pain of so many New Jerseyans that have reached out, the Palestinian doctors in my state who've worked with my office to get Palestinian babies into America for care. It brings up the hurt of being there and seeing the worst slaughter of Jews since the Holocaust. So many things are painful, but if we sacrifice our values, it reminds me of the mosque being built, 9/11. It reminds me of all these difficult points, the marchers in Skokie of the KKK, all these difficult points where the values of this constitution were tested, where we were being measured.

But I have to say what this President is doing with Alien Insurrection Act, what this President is doing with no due process, what this President is doing with flushing the Department of Education, with getting rid of the USAID, with attacking thousands of people that serve our veterans, that serve our social security, those things should be obvious to this institution, to the Senate, that that's wrong. That they have unelected... the biggest campaign donor, unelected, who's getting our personal information, and there's no transparency. Nobody in this body can say they know what confidential information Elon Musk has and knows what they did with it because they never brought him here to answer for it. So I thank my colleague for the question, and I know Reverend Warnock is going to ask me one. I just want to take a couple pages into this for a second.

Edan Alexander was abducted 7 October 2023, and was released in a Trump-brokered deal in May 2025.

8:26 AM - Security and Foreign Policy

The American people alone... our approach to foreign policy practiced by the President — what the President has done has left our allies feeling abandoned, feeling degraded and insulted that he's left our adversaries feeling emboldened and has done things that has hurt our national security that has made Americans less safe. In the short time President Trump has been in office for a second term, Americans have already been put in harm's way because of the reckless approach of the administration.

It all begins in fact with his extremely poor judgment. This administration has prioritized the obsequious point, the obsequiousness to Donald Trump over the expertise when it comes to some of the most important national security jobs. And it has sidelined dedicated professionals who've devoted their lives to keeping our country safe. This administration has also demonstrated an inability to distinguish between America's adversaries and America's allies, and a disturbing failure to understand how America's partnerships and investments abroad protect and benefit communities here.

I'm reminded of General Mattis to say, "If you're cutting things like the USAID or the State Department, buy me more bullets." But this is something that folks on the floor have talked about. I see one of my friends and somebody I really look up to — I see Tim Kaine, who sits a little bit higher up on the dais than me on the Foreign Relations Committee, somebody I've turned to many times. And he was astonished by this, and I know he, like me, has had private conversations with our Republican colleagues about this. But this body has not called for one hearing or one investigation. No accountability. What am I talking about? It's when last week we learned Vice President JD Vance, Secretary of Defense, Pete Hegseth, Secretary of State, Marco Rubio, Director of National Intelligence, Tulsi Gabbard, Director of the CIA, John Ratcliffe, Trump's National Security Advisor, Mike Waltz, special envoy for the Middle East, Steve Witkoff and several other high ranking officials in the Trump administration discussed attack plans against the Houthis in Yemen in a group chat over the commercial messaging app Signal.

We learned of this because the president's national security advisor mistakenly invited the editor and chief of the Atlantic, Jeffrey Goldberg, on the text chain. And after Jeffrey Goldberg published a story describing this jaw dropping national security failure where they could have broken at least two laws that I'm aware of just by doing that, from the preservation of public records all the way to disclosing national security highly classified information.

The president, this cabinet, the members didn't step up and say, "We made mistakes", didn't step up and say, "this is clearly abjectly wrong", didn't step up and say, "there will be accountability", didn't step up and say, "we'll take actions". No. What they decided to do when they were exposed is actually target the reporter with a barrage of insults and not acknowledging any wrongdoing.

Unsurprisingly, the Trump team's response led Jeffrey Goldberg to publish the rest of the Signal chat messages, which expose more administration lies.

We're going to go into that, but I really want to turn to my brother, and I said earlier about Senator Murphy's speech, one of my favorite I've ever heard when I was in the Senate, Brother Warnock gave a speech that's one of my favorite in the Senate too, when he talked about difference between January 5th America and then that fateful day, January 6th. He has been a friend of mine for a long time, and I think he might be the only person in this body... I started this talk 13 hours ago by talking about getting into good trouble. I think he might be the only person in this body that was arrested in this building for protesting before you came to serve in this building as the United States Senator. I'm going to stick to what I'm told to say. If you ask me that you'd like to speak, you have to say it, "I'd like to ask you a question." I think that's how this goes.

8:31 AM - Spiritual Values

SENATOR REV. RAPHAEL WARNOCK (GEORGIA): Will the senator from New Jersey yield for a question?

SENATOR BOOKER: Why yes, I will yield for a question while retaining the floor.

SENATOR WARNOCK: Well, good morning. And let me just say, Cory Booker, how very, very proud I am of you. It's a real honor to serve in this body. I know that all of my colleagues who are here agree that it's an honor for the people of your state to say that when we take stock of all the issues that we wrestle with, as we look into the eyes of our children and consider what we want for them, and in the eyes of our aging parents as they deal with the blessings and the burdens of getting older. That since all of us can't go to Washington, we're going to send you. And we're going to trust that in rooms of power where decisions are being made, that you're going to center the people and not yourself. You're going to be thinking about ordinary people. And so Cory Booker, I want to thank you for holding vigil.

As I prepare to ask you a question, I just want to thank you for holding vigil for this country all night. Rabbi Abraham Joshua Heschel said that when he marched with Dr. King, he felt like his legs were praying. And so in a very real sense, your legs have been praying as you've been standing on this floor all night. And thank you for praying not just with your lips, but with your legs for a nation in need of healing. I just got off a prayer call that I do every Tuesday morning at 7:14 AM, 2 Chronicles 7:14, *"If my people who are called by my name would humble themselves and pray, if they would seek my face turn from their wicked ways, then I will hear from heaven. I will forgive their sins and heal the land."* The nation needs healing. And we need spiritual healing. We need moral healing. But literally, there are people all across our country who need healing, who need healthcare.

And so that's why I was so proud to come to the Senate after being arrested in the Rotunda a few years before that. Proud to join you in the Senate. Proud that we were able to pass, just a couple months after I got here – the American Rescue Plan – which did so much incredible work. In that American Rescue Plan there was the expanded child tax credit, which literally cut child poverty more than 40% in our country. I wish we could get it extended. But one of the other things we did was we lowered Georgians and Americans healthcare premiums by hundreds of dollars on average. We passed a tax cut. And that's so relevant in this moment because that's what this body is prepared to do right now, I guess, in the next few days, pass a tax cut. But that tax cut is literally going to be for the richest of the rich, the wealthiest among us. But we passed a tax cut that brought healthcare into reach for tens of thousands of Georgians and millions of Americans in the American Rescue Plan. These tax credits are so critical that the nonpartisan congressional budget office said that the number of Americans without healthcare would grow by 3.8 million people in just one year if the premium subsidies were allowed to expire.

Forgive me for my phone ringing. My eight-year-old and six-year-old are calling me. They're not impressed with what I'm doing.

(SENATOR BOOKER: That's an important call.)

SENATOR WARNOCK: They're not impressed.
But we know that this impact, this would impact thousands of Georgians who've only recently been able to receive healthcare. So we pass in that American Rescue Plan these tax credits, which put healthcare in reach, and now they're set to expire if we don't do our work. And that's why what you're doing, Cory Booker, is holy work. It's within a political context, but this is holy work.

If these tax credits are allowed to expire, a 45-year-old in Georgia with $62,000 annual income would see premiums go up by $1,414 a year. A 60-year-old couple in Georgia with an $82,000 annual income would see premiums go up by a staggering $18,157 a year. Think about that. Nearly one third of Americans have less than $500 in savings in their bank account. Imagine the healthcare costs for a 60-year-old couple going up by more than $18,000. A health insurance premium hike like this would be more than an inconvenience. It wouldn't just be a nuisance. It's literally the difference between having healthcare coverage and not having healthcare coverage.

And so I'm thinking about people like that and I'm thinking about my constituent Cassie Cox from Bainbridge, Georgia. She wasn't able to afford healthcare on the Affordable Care Act marketplace until the premium tax credit brought healthcare into reach. And shortly after she became insured, she severely cut her hand, which landed her in the emergency room with 35 stitches. And with insurance, it still cost her about $300. Had it not been for the tax credits that allowed her to get healthcare, she could have been in financial ruin.

She's one of the hundreds of thousands of Georgians at risk of losing their coverage if these tax credits are allowed to expire if we don't do our work. If we're more focused on the wealthiest of the wealthy rather than the concerns of ordinary people. Senator Booker, should Democrats and Republicans come together to extend the premium tax credit for hardworking folk in New Jersey and in Georgia? What do you think?

SENATOR BOOKER: My easiest colleague question I've gotten over these 13 hours. Yes, they should. I was talking in the healthcare section about while there's these big issues that we should be concerned about, 880 billion from Medicaid, cutting all of that out to give the wealthiest, as you said... God bless them, they don't need our help. They don't need more tax cuts — to give them tax cuts and explode the deficit. This is literally taking from working Americans. The letters we read, the voices of Americans, the fear, the anguish, the hurt, the worry. People who were suffering from Parkinson's, who had children with disabilities, who had elder parents living with them. So many people telling them, not 880 billion... Their whole financial well-being was hanging on a thread in just cutting the transportation programs involved. But I said while all that was going on, the Trump administration was still doing other things to attack ACA enrollment, to attack the tax credits that people are relying on, doing other things to drive up costs. I know some of my colleagues were on the floor, like Amy Klobuchar. We've centered the lowering of prescription drug costs and he is doing things to drive out pocket costs up. There's a cruelty in that.

And I intend to still be standing at noon when we have to pause in the Senate for the pledge and the prayer. And Pastor, I want to talk to you in the way that you talked to me last night. I called my brother, I called my friend and told him I was doing this. And Warnock shifts gears a lot in my life. Sometimes he's my colleague, sometimes he's my brother. Sometimes we talk about the state of two unmarried guys in the Senate. I don't mean to put you on blast, sir, but-

SENATOR WARNOCK: Bald headed caucus.

SENATOR BOOKER: The bald headed caucus. But the one time you shift those gears into being my pastor and my friend, we prayed together last night. And most Americans identify in our faith, Christian faith. And you and I know, I would yield for you to ask a question, but I'm yielding just to have you talk about Matthew 25.

SENATOR WARNOCK: Right. I'm a Matthew 25 Christian*.

SENATOR BOOKER: You and I both. That's what we hold in common.

SENATOR WARNOCK: And it's a long chapter, but the section we're talking about-

SENATOR BOOKER: Yes.

SENATOR WARNOCK: -in Matthew 25, Jesus says, "*I was hungry and you fed me. I was thirsty and you gave me something to drink.*" I was sick.

SENATOR BOOKER: What were you?

SENATOR WARNOCK: I was in prison and you came to visit me. And someone asked, Lord, when were you sick? When were you in prison? When were you an undocumented immigrant?

SENATOR BOOKER: Yes ... yes.

SENATOR WARNOCK: And the answer comes in as much as you've done it to the least of these, you've done it also unto me. Another part of that text says, and when you don't do it for the least of these, you don't do it for me. The scripture says that the one who gives to the poor lend this to the Lord. This is holy work.

SENATOR BOOKER: Sir, my friend. I don't understand how a nation could allow a president to be so cruel that he would take away healthcare from people struggling with children that are facing the worst of health challenges. People who have a spouse like the person who wrote me, no, it wasn't the spouse. She wrote me herself. She had Parkinson's. I got upset because that's how my father died. And I watched for year after year after year how it affected my family, how it demanded from my mother, how it cost thousands of dollars for his care. And thank God we had the privilege, but this person was writing because they were afraid and they didn't. Of what the costs would be.

How can our country say that kind of cruelty, how can a nation with a majority of its people are people of faith, be they Muslims or Jain or Bahai or Hindu or Jewish, how can the central precept of our country founded on principles that are reflected in the good book, how could we say that we should cut healthcare from the sick and the needy to give bigger tax cuts to Elon Musk?

SENATOR WARNOCK: Will, the senator from New Jersey-

SENATOR BOOKER: I will yield to you, my brother, while retaining the floor.

SENATOR WARNOCK: This is the reason why every Sunday and every weekend when I leave here, I return not only to Georgia, but I return to my pulpit. And some folk ask, "Well, why do you continue to lead Ebenezer Church?" I return to my pulpit every Sunday because, notwithstanding wonderful people like you, I don't want to spend all my time talking to politicians — I'm afraid I might accidentally become one. [laughs] And so I want to connect and check in with ordinary folks. Because I was focused on this healthcare issue long before I came to the Congress. Dr. King said that of all the injustices, inequality in healthcare he said is the most shocking and the most inhumane.

SENATOR BOOKER: I read that last night, pastor. I read that last night.

SENATOR WARNOCK: The most shocking and the most inhumane. And it's the reason why as a pastor inspired by Dr. King leading the congregation that Dr. King led, way back in 2014 when the Affordable Care Act was passed, were you here? You came after?

SENATOR BOOKER: I came after.

SENATOR WARNOCK: You came right after that. I got arrested in the governor's office in Georgia fighting for healthcare.

SENATOR BOOKER: I didn't know you were a two-time arrestee, man.

SENATOR WARNOCK: I got a long record, brother. But all for good trouble — good trouble.

SENATOR BOOKER: All for good trouble.

SENATOR WARNOCK: Good trouble.

SENATOR BOOKER: Good trouble.

SENATOR WARNOCK: And we had a 1960 sit-in in the governor's office. Waves of us got arrested, they arrested one wave, and then another wave came and another wave came. And we were trying to get Georgia to expand Medicaid.

SENATOR BOOKER: Yes, I remember that.

SENATOR WARNOCK: We had passed the Affordable Care Act here, but Georgia was digging in its heels and saying, "No, we're not going to expand Medicaid." And so when I got here, Senator Klobuchar, I made it a priority of mine to get incentives for Georgia to expand Medicaid. And you remember I went to our caucus-

SENATOR BOOKER: Yes.

SENATOR WARNOCK: -and I said, look, Georgia, and about nine, then ten other states have not expanded. They should have done it a long time ago. Let's see if we can make it even easier for them. And as a freshman Senator, I was able to convince our caucus to give $14.5 billion for non-expansion states, which includes $2 billion just for Georgia to incentivize Medicaid expansion. Why? So that working people in the gap, people who literally go to work every day, can get healthcare. Georgia has left that $2 billion sitting on the table and almost 600,000 Georgians in the gap. The governor's plan has literally enrolled a whopping 6,500 people in healthcare. But we've got nearly 600,000 people in the gap.

And this is not theoretical stuff. Every time I talk about this, I have to talk about Heather Payne, because Heather Payne is a resident of Dalton, Georgia. She spent her career taking care of others. She's a traveling nurse. Heather worked throughout COVID as an ER and labor and delivery nurse. Yet often she did not have healthcare coverage herself because she fell into the healthcare coverage gap. Sometimes she had health insurance coverage, sometimes she didn't. She made too much money to qualify for Medicaid, but the only coverage options available to her were unaffordable, costing anywhere between $500 and a thousand a month.

And so about two and a half years ago, Heather Payne, a traveling nurse, noticed that something was wrong in her body. And even though she noticed that something was wrong, Senator Klobuchar, she literally had to wait for months before she could see a doctor to save up the money. And then she finally went and saw a neurologist who said, "You know what? You've actually had a series of small strokes." And even after getting that diagnosis, she had to put off serious medical procedures because she cannot work as an ER nurse anymore and is still waiting to get approved for disability so she can get Medicaid coverage.

And so this nurse who has spent her whole life healing other people can't get healthcare. I think it's wrong that in the richest country on earth, we don't want to lower the cost of healthcare for people who are working hard in our communities every day, literally keeping us healthy. I'm going to ask you another softball question, Senator Booker, should people like my friend Heather Payne have access to affordable healthcare?

SENATOR BOOKER: Yes.

SENATOR WARNOCK: In the first few months of the Trump administration, it's been clear that this administration is not working for ordinary people-

SENATOR BOOKER: I'm going to just say this – just to try to stay in the parliamentary – I yield for a question while retaining the floor. I yield for another question while retaining the floor.

SENATOR WARNOCK: The administration is working for billionaires; they're working for people like Elon Musk. Healthcare is a human right. Healthcare is basic. And while we're speaking about health, we've got to cheer on our federal workers who are keeping us healthy. And there are folks in this administration who say that they want to make them the villains. That's what Russell Vought said, that when they wake up in the morning, "We want them to not go to work" – our federal workers – "because they are increasingly viewed," he said, "as villains." I got news for Russell Vought. The people who staff our VA hospitals are not villains. The people who keep our food safe and our water clean are not villains. The people who keep our military bases operating are not villains. And so we stand with them in this moment because they are indeed keeping all of us healthy.

And so in closing, and nobody believes a Baptist preacher when he says in closing, let me say that again you're doing holy work here, brother, by holding this floor. You are literally holding vigil for our nation.

We are beset by the politics of fear. The scripture tells us that perfect love casts out all fear. We are witnessing, again, this ugly game, the politics of us and them. And there are a lot of folk who, because so much of what has been going on in our nation across Republican and Democratic administrations, let's be honest, has not been working for ordinary people. And the gap between the haves and the have-nots has gotten larger and larger. And when people are vulnerable, sometimes they give in to the politics of fear, somebody telling them that they've got all the answers. And so we saw this in this last cycle. We're seeing it in this moment in our country, the politics of us and them. And sadly, hardworking working class people are waking up this morning and they're discovering that they thought they were in the 'us' and they're discovering that they're in the 'them'. That the 'them' is larger than they thought.

And so we've got to hold vigil for each other, for workers, for women, for immigrants, for immigrant families, for our sisters and our brothers, red, yellow, brown, Black and white, for the aging who need social security, for the working poor who need Medicaid, for those who are seeking asylum and they just need a dignified path, for those who've been working here for years and they need a dignified path to citizenship. We've got to hold vigil for each other.

And so thank you for this work. This is not the end but the beginning, the struggle continues. Dr. King said that the true measure of a person is not where he stands in moments of comfort and convenience, but where he stands in moments of challenge and controversy. So thank you for praying for this nation with your lips and with your legs.

I'm going to ask you one last question. Do you intend to keep praying?

SENATOR BOOKER: Amen. Hallelujah. Yes, I do. Thank you for that question. I know there's been a question coming to me. I just want to say, pray Isaiah 40:31** for me. I think you know what that is.

SENATOR WARNOCK: Got it. I'm going to ordain this man.

A contemporary movement in American Christianity that focuses on social justice and works of mercy as preached in the 25th Chapter of the Gospel of Matthew.
*** "They will soar on wings like eagles; they will run and not grow weary, they will walk and not be faint."*

8:53 AM - Challenges and Solutions

SENATOR BOOKER: All right. The article, I was going to start reading.

SENATOR AMY KLOBUCHAR (MINNESOTA): Senator Booker?

SENATOR BOOKER: I yield for a question while retaining the floor. If the Senator has a question, I yield for a question while retaining the floor.

SENATOR KLOBUCHAR: So you'll yield for a question?

SENATOR BOOKER: Yes. While retaining the floor, yes.

SENATOR KLOBUCHAR: Very good. I want to, first of all, thank you. Thank you for waking us up this morning, literally. All night, as Reverend Warnock would tell you, I know you were in here doing your work, but it was raining, there was thunder, it was really bad. And then when we woke up this morning, you were still talking. You were still talking, and the sun was out. And you're giving people hope. When I think about what you're doing, you're like an alarm clock right now for this country. And slowly but surely we've seen people realize this isn't just a bunch of campaign rhetoric that's going on. This is actually happening. And people are stepping up. They're fighting it in the courts, they're fighting it in Congress with what you're doing today, with what, as you know, last week when we got the horrible news that the Defense Secretary of the United States was using an unauthorized line to just talk with his friends like he was spiking a football about putting the lives of our service members at risk. People stood up, Democrats stood up. They asked the tough questions.

And one of the things that bothers me is that it is so hard to see your way out of it. And a lot of people feel like we're just wallowing right now. But what you're telling us today is there is another way. Because if we just wallow, these guys are going to continue to cut kids' cancer treatment. If we just wallow, they're going to cut Medicaid when one out of two seniors in my state who are in assisted living are on Medicaid. Or they're going to continue to mess around with these tariffs, which really are national sales tax, something like $2,500 for every single family. They are going to continue to be callous. I had someone say to me last night, "Do they care when those US aid workers who devoted their lives to feeding the hungry around the world, when they have to stand outside their building and watch them literally take the name of their life's work off the brick on that building, do they care?"

And one of the things that we have done, the Democrats, have done has stood up. And what is coming upon us in these next few weeks is this tax bill that basically will give billionaires tax cuts on the backs of regular people, ransacking the government, firing veterans, messing around with Social Security. I had a guy tell me that he spent three days after his wife died in Minnesota, Reverend, three days just trying to figure out how he gets the death benefit. Why did this thing, check show up at his door? He's trying to do the right thing. He calls, he gets put on hold. He sends an email, no one writes him back. He drives into Brainerd, Minnesota, 30 mile drive. He's like 80 years old. He drives in there and then they finally help him. Then he gets back, then something else goes wrong. Then he tries to call again. He finally ends up at our door, at our office and we figure it out for him. There's 70-some million people that that's going to happen to these guys don't get their act together. So it's a real good question, do they care? But when we have this tax bill coming up in front of us in these next few weeks, I think people got to understand what's going on. They have to understand that even in the short... the thing, the house budget that came out, that'll be the subject of this, it's over 2 trillion tax cuts for people making over $400,000 a year like Elon Musk that don't need it. And so there's actually a way to stop it that's in the hands of the Republicans right now. If just two or three of them stood up on the house floor and did what you did, Senator Booker, who they said no. And if four of them in the United States Senate, four of them stood up, four Senators stood up, then we could have the discussion about, okay, let's make government work better.

We're all in, but let's not do it on the backs of regular people. Let's not do it on the backs of kids that are in cancer research or veterans who are trying to simply get their well-earned benefits because they put their lives on the line in the battlefield. Or let's not do it on the backs of farmers in Minnesota and Georgia who simply have these small farms and they're trying to get by. And then suddenly, wham, Donald Trump decides shock and awe, let's do a tariff and let's get mad at all our allies across the country like Canada. Oh, that's a good idea.

Those are the things that they're doing. So my question of you is how many people need to stand up in the US Senate to make this happen? Because I know Democrats are united. I know we're all standing up, but tell me how many people can stand up on the other side. If they stood up and joined you, what a difference it would make.

SENATOR BOOKER: So I want to thank the Senator for the question. And when I think of people who stand in adversity, I still see you standing in a snowstorm. And the strength that you've had as you've stood up to fight for affordable healthcare, stood up and fought for affordable prescription drugs, stood up and fought for farmers and for police officers and for communities. You are that kind of person that gives me strength, that I've learned so much from. And you have brought this issue up. What you just said on the floor to let you know this is not performative for her, she has brought this up in our small meetings with Chuck Schumer. She has brought this up in our caucus meetings. I've seen her talk about it in her own state. This question of what will it take?

And here's something that pains me to hear — that Elon Musk is calling Republicans up and saying, "If you take this stand, I'm going to put $100 million in a primary against you." That they are bullying people who dare to stand up and say, "Maybe this appointee is not the most qualified person you could find to lead this cabinet position," or maybe it's wrong to cut this agency that we together created in Congress."

There are people who are asking those questions, but we have seen them get dragged through X, mob attacked when it comes to their virtual presence and threatened to be primaried.

But we know, because you're somebody that works on both sides of the aisle, that there are really good people of conscience on both sides of the aisle. And as the great pastor said, there are enough sins in this body to go around for all of us. But this is not a partisan moment. It is a moral moment. This is not a Left or Right moment. It is a right or wrong moment.

We have a president that is shredding the very agencies that Americans who are struggling are relying on. Working people that, over the last 71 days, are finding higher prices, that are finding housing prices going up.

Farmers in my state, too. It's our fourth-largest industry. I've had farmers that will come to me from as far away as Texas and tell me that they're clawing back these contracts that we've already relied on to buy things already and now you're putting me in a situation where I might lose my farm. You see veterans who come to our offices. I know they come to your office, Senator Klobuchar, you're a Senator from Minnesota, but you are a national figure. So I know they're coming to your office. And they're saying things to me like, "I'm a veteran, I could go do other jobs. I wanted to work on suicide prevention and mental health issues and I'm being fired?" And you said it right. I've heard you say it in private. I've heard you say it in public. I know it irks you. Because you're one of these sort of balanced people.

Okay, we have a big deficit that is a real problem. Maybe they're trying to lower the deficit. But they're not. That's the irony — they're not. They're about to explode trillions of dollars, most of which disproportionately will go to the wealthiest people, as you've been pointing out in our private phone calls over and over again, Senator Klobuchar. And so your question to me is spot on. It's spot on. And it's why I am standing here right now at the top of another hour because of what you are saying relentlessly, persistently, and unyieldingly.

Why are we hurting Americans? From our farmers, we just talked about rural hospitals here for about 20, 30 minutes and what the threats are to them. We talked about rural Social Security centers and the threats that are to them. We talked about communities all over our country who are being hurt. And your question, why? To give tax breaks that will disproportionately go to the wealthiest Americans, who you and I are not those people that demonize wealth. We don't demonize success. I want more people to start businesses. I want more people dream of moving on up like the Jeffersons. I want more people to have that vision. I am not one of those people that are going to be mad at you because you're very successful. I'm going to be one of those people that says you don't need more tax cuts.

And we as a society have an obligation to each other, to those farmers, to those rural folks, to the cops I stood with at the funeral of one of their colleagues in Newark two weeks ago. We have an obligation to them to help them get equipment to protect themselves. This country cannot do something that is so monumentally fiscally irresponsible. Who was the one person in the House that voted, a Republican that voted against it? A guy named Massie? And I watched it. I had to smile and laugh because he said the quiet part out loud. He's sitting there looking at something, I saw him in an interview, and he says, "By their own numbers, this doesn't add up. They're adding to our deficit by the trillions." He stayed true to his principles. What happened to all those mighty deficit hawks in the House of Representatives on the Republican side that caved to the pressure of a President?

SENATOR KLOBUCHAR: Will the Senator yield?

SENATOR BOOKER: I'm so happy you asked it in the right fashion as I'm... I yield for a question while retaining the floor.

SENATOR KLOBUCHAR: Very good. That was perfect. So I think one of the things you talked about was just this deficit and what's happening and what we seeing with their proposal right now, that's going to come right before us. By some estimates it's going to add $37 trillion – 37 trillion – in 30 years as we go ahead. I mean, I literally cannot believe that when in fact we could step back now and we could say, "What things can we do? What things can we do on the Tax Code?" Because there's a whole lot of things we can do to strengthen Social Security, strengthen what we have in our government.

And what really when you step back and look at the economy... And I heard this the other day on a business channel, just about a month or two ago, man, we were coming out strong. We are a country that came out of the pandemic in a stronger way than so many other countries did around the world. We're ready. Inflation was at least steady and it was starting to come down here. And now all of a sudden we see chaos is up, corruption is up, and yes, costs are up. Ask anyone at the grocery store. And one of the problems when you look at what we could be doing to address the debt is that the proposals out there are just going to make it worse. That means more interest payments. That means... Or more interest payments on the backs of regular people. And that means less we can do to help them, as we look at what's happening right now.

And one of the things you raised, Senator Booker, which I appreciate how much you know about this, is just this prescription drug negotiation and Medicare. So what did we finally do? So decades before you or Senator Murphy or Senator Warnock got here, before I got to this place, they made a sweetheart deal with the pharmaceutical companies, and they actually baked in so that they didn't have to negotiate prices for 73 million people and anything. They could just charge whatever they wanted for these prescription drugs. What happens? Well, guess what happens. Suddenly, the drugs for our seniors are two to one what they are in places like Canada, our neighbor, our friend. Two to one what they are over there. You got people driving up to Canada from Minnesota because we can see Canada from our porch and they are going up there trying to get less expensive drugs. And then they [say], "What's going on?" So a whole bunch of people started to say, "Let's look at this."

It took years to get this done. Finally, finally, we passed a bill. It said they've got to negotiate and we took the first ten drugs. And the last administration got to pick those drugs and they picked blockbuster drugs, drugs like Eliquis, drugs like Xarelto, drugs like Januvia, Jardiance. I memorized them because I can't always find people that take them. I don't make them raise their hand, say they take them. But these are blockbuster drugs and they reduced the price by like 70% for our seniors. That's going to kick in soon. But not if this administration messes it up.

And for we have seen from everything from giving Signal lines about secret battle plans to reporters to deciding they're going to shut down people that worked on protecting our nuclear facilities and, "Oops, we made a mistake." Or how about when they said, "Okay. We want to do something about avian flu but we're going to fire all the people that work at — Oh, no! We're going to hire them back"? That's what's been going on right now.

So when I look at this really complicated prescription drug negotiation where you're taking on some of the biggest companies in the world, I look at, I say to myself, "Okay. So our Secretary of Health, Kennedy, he won't even agree when he's asked under oath if he's going to keep this up." They fired a bunch of people that would work on it. They haven't shown they're going to keep this negotiation going. Meanwhile, we've got put in place a $2,000 cap for a seniors out-of-pocket on drug costs under Medicare. That's really good. We put in place that insulin limit on 35 bucks a month. And we thank Reverend Warnock, and we thank you, Senator Booker, Senator Murphy, everyone that worked on that. We got that in place.

So now we got the big thing, which is the negotiation of all these drugs because 15 more drugs are coming their way for negotiation. Again, blockbuster drugs, Ozempic — blockbuster drugs. Those drugs are coming their way for negotiation. But they have not committed to do that. They have not committed to do that. And even if they did commit to do it, do they even have the people to negotiate to take on these major companies?

So my question of you, Senator Booker, after being up all night, after getting us through the storm of last night and into the bright sunshine of today, after holding the floor all this time – I can't even imagine how much your feet must hurt, but those feet hurting is nothing compared, which is why you're doing it, to how the rest of the people in this country right now feel and how they're hurting – my question is, how can they move forward without trying to save money for the people of this country? Because what I see happening, and there's so many signs, you see it every single day, when they are getting rid of some of these people that work on it, then you're not going to be able to get the Social Security for my friend that I met from Cross Lake, Minnesota, then you're not going to be able to get that stuff done.

But I think as we look at those cuts, it's not just the word 'cut', it's what effect does it have on real people when they can't get their services, when our veterans who also have complex ways that they've got to deal with the government, when they have no one answering the phone, when they've gotten rid of veterans who've actually done the work? So my question here is, for people that like translate this into the real world, is what is all this going to mean for people in the real world what they're doing right now?

SENATOR BOOKER: Thank you for the question, Senator Klobuchar. I love that you're bringing back to real people and what effect it's having. And what you're spelling out is something that's really important. There's a strategy that they have expressly said. They want to overwhelm you, not us. They want to overwhelm the American people. They want to flood the zone. And so I see a whole bunch of trying doing things to distract us, Gulf of Mexico, Gulf of America, Greenland, all these things to try to whip us up and not pay attention to what most Americans are concerned with, is can they make ends meet. Even the big Reconciliation Bill that they're going to try to do that we have to find a way to appeal to a small group of Republican Congress people to stop of cutting $880 million out of Medicaid, we went through in great detail at length last night, why that's bad.

But you are pointing to something even more insidious is that big things going on. They actually are cutting the support to get more people signed up with the ACA. Already happened. Make it harder to sign up for the ACA. They've already cut the tax credits that are helping people that are in the ACA get resources to help with their healthcare costs. They're going after these things. Here's one that you know really well. They're going after... As we talk about all of these parents struggling with children and family members with chronic diseases, we know one of the things that help people with chronic diseases is having access to fresh, healthy foods. But they're cutting access to that for our kids going to school. This administration has not only overseen in 71 days a rise in inflation, a rise in the cost of groceries, lowering of people's 401(k)s with the stock market going down, it's not only bringing economic chaos, but they are already hurting people on their basic delivery of their services, from taking thousands of jobs off Social Security, making harder for people who have some problem to get it solved to the VA to the ACA.

SENATOR KLOBUCHAR: Will the Senator yield for a question?

SENATOR BOOKER: I will definitely yield for a question while retaining the floor.

SENATOR KLOBUCHAR: I was thinking as you talked about the Affordable Care Act and all the work that went into it and what came out of it, I was remembering the constant attempts to repeal that bill. I was remembering when Senator John McCain, I think you were here for this, came in and did the unexpected. He went in here. He bucked his party and he said no. He didn't agree with Donald Trump about this. He didn't agree with his leaders on this. He did what he thought was right. And my issue is that we all have those moments where we have to make decisions about what we think is right.

And I think about Donald Trump and he is... Just now, just this week, he said he wanted to violate the Constitution – which he says practically every single hour – but he said that he would try to serve another term, that he would do this, he would do that. He is literally treating this presidency like he's the king. And I guess Elon Musk is thus the court jester at his side, or the White House IT guy. But the point is that he's treating this like a king.

And you serve on the Judiciary Committee. You are a student of history. You're also a scholar in terms of understanding this government and how it works. And I think one of the things that's most unsettling for people that they just don't understand is how you could have a President in place that doesn't respect that democracy. I remember when we all gathered for the inauguration and I had the four minutes, because of my job with the Rules Committee, to address those gathered in that rotunda. And I noted that our democracy can be a hot mess right now, but it's still the best form of government that we've got, that our democracy is truly our shelter in the storm. It's our shelter in the storm, to quote a great songwriter from the State of Minnesota, that the reason that we don't have... I know you may have a few songwriters from there. If the Senator could yield for one question, who is your best songwriter and singer from the State of New Jersey? Just to make clear who is-

SENATOR BOOKER: Is that your question?

SENATOR KLOBUCHAR: You yield for a question from me? Yes-

SENATOR BOOKER: I will answer that question by avoiding it because in New Jersey there are so many great patron saints from the great Bon Jovi to the great Bruce Springsteen to the incredible Queen Latifah, the chairman of the board from New Jersey, the great Frank Sinatra. So I'm not going to pick. We have so many great singers, rappers like Red Man. We are just a thriving state of... Count Basie. There's just too many. I would not force you to do that. Of course it's Prince, I think, from your state. Prince-

SENATOR KLOBUCHAR: You mean Prince and Bob Dylan, but that aside, I am very impressed, Senator Booker, that after what, 12 hours now, 13 hours? That you still are able to make sure that you mention every songwriter. But that aside, Bob Dylan once had that great line, "*Shelter in the storm*". Our democracy, shelter the storm. And then I noted that day that in some countries' presidential inaugurations, they're held in gilded palaces. Not in the United States of America. United States of America, it's held in the People's House. That's what you're doing right now, Senator Booker, because the People's House is where the action should be. That's Article I. And the Constitution specifically says here we have equal branches of government. And the final thing is that the power in that rotunda that day, and this is where we get into Donald Trump thinking he's king, the power of that rotunda didn't come from the people in there. It came from outside, came from the people. So that's why you see the people standing up right now.

Our constituents going to these town halls, standing up, breaking the phone lines in the US Senate, sending in the emails with their stories that we are able, that you've heard the Senators and you have read on the Senate floor about things that have happened to your constituents. So that's the power from the outside. So the question that I ask of you is just tell me what you think people can do when you've got a President in there that he thinks he is king and he thinks that a democracy is just something that he can just shove aside and say whatever he wants and break what every rule the people depend on, that they depend on to be able to vote, to be able to participate and have their case made. Tell me what you think.

SENATOR BOOKER: Thank you. Thank you-

SENATOR KLOBUCHAR: What's the answer to that?

SENATOR BOOKER: Thank you, Senator. I'll answer that. And I see Ron Wyden has come to the floor who's, for both Amy and I, one of the chair people of, or this point, ranking members of one of the great committees. To Amy Klobuchar's question, I read a lot of angry letters, people who were demanding of me to do something to stop them. "Do something different. Stand up. Speak up, Senator. I'm afraid. Stand up. Speak up, Senator. I'm so angry. Stand up. Speak up, Senator. The services for my disabled child are threatened. Stand up. Speak up." So it's one of the reasons why I'm doing this, why my staff and I talked about this for so many days to do something to show, to let our constituents know, to elevate their voices on the floor, to read their letters, to read their statements, not just New Jerseyans, but, like you, the hundreds and hundreds of people that are calling us from other states.

But I am most moved by the letters who tell me about their pain or their challenges or their fears, but they end that question with your question. "But I am here to help. Tell me how I can help. I am here to help. Tell me how I can help." And you said it, Senator. I read the letter of John McCain last night, his letter explaining his vote. It was so beautiful. It was tough like he was. It was hard on the whole body. But he called to principles. Senator Schumer was here when I read it. It was eerie because he was describing what went wrong then, which is the same thing here, that we do need to make our country better.

We do need to have a bolder vision for healthcare, a bolder vision for Social Security. We need to make them work for the people. But we're not doing it here in this body. And this man who's not acting like a President but is trashing our constitutional traditions, is violating our laws as he's getting tied up in court but ignoring court orders, and when he gets a decision he doesn't like, he trashes, he trashes the judges so badly that the Supreme Court itself finds that it has to go out and tell him to stop it.

What stopped healthcare from being taken away in the last time wasn't the persuasive powers of anybody in this side of the political aisle in the Senate convincing anybody over there. I would like to think it was my eloquence with Lisa Murkowski. I would like to think it was my high-minded intellect that somehow, it was damaged playing too much football, but that somehow I got a right argument to Susan Collins. That wasn't it. I'd like to think it was my ability to stand up to John McCain himself. No. None of that. It was the people. It was the people. You remember, the little lobbyists in their wheelchairs rolling up to Senators and speaking their hearts, telling them of their pain and their fear. It was people coming here and marching, people coming and flooding the calls, like they did — like they're doing now. People writing letters. People marching people in their states from all political spectrums coming in and saying, "This is wrong. This is wrong. This is wrong." And so if you're asking me what we can do, I know what we can do, but we've got to, as the great song.

Senator Klobuchar, I had my staff print a bunch of things I sent them. I sent them because I knew they were some of my favorite people from history. There's one here, Webster. There's one by Jefferson. It's the letters from the Birmingham Jail, Langston Hughes, something by Harper Lee, Emma Lazarus. But here's one. Here's the answer in a poem. And forgive me for reading this. I wanted to do it at some point today and this is perfect. And I see my Senator here, he may have a question, but I... I love this poem. It was written and put to song by a man named James Weldon Johnson. He was an educator, a poet, a diplomat, a civil rights activist, was born in the great State of Florida.

And he said that this is what we have to do.

> Lift every voice and sing. Lift every voice and sing till Earth and Heaven ring, ring with the harmonies of liberty. Let our rejoicing rise high as the listening skies. Let it resound like the rolling sea. We must sing a song full of the faith that the dark past has taught us, sing a song full of the hope that the present has brought us. Facing the rising sun of a new day begun, let us march on, let us march on, let us march on, until victory is won.

It doesn't ignore the wretchedness of our history. It speaks to the truth and the excitement and the hope about that past and the virtues that our ancestors gave us.

He goes on:

> Stony the road we trod, bitter the chastening rod felt in the days when hope unborn had died. Yet with a steady beat, have not our weary feet come to the place for which our father's sighed. We have come over away which tears have been watered. We have come treading our path through the blood of the slaughtered, out of the gloomy past till now we stand at last where the white gleam of the bright stars is cast.

The last stanza:

> God of our weary years, God of our silent tears, thou who has brought us thus far on the way, thou who has by thy might let us into the night, keep us forever in the path we pray lest our feet stray from the places, our God, where we met thee. Lest our hearts drunk with the wine of the world we forget thee. Shadow beneath thy hand, may we forever stand true to our God and true to our {to this, to this} native land.

What can we do? Do like our ancestors did. What can we do? Do like the people who never gave up, who, even when this country that they loved, didn't love them back. They kept fighting and kept pushing. And we know that, Senator Klobuchar, because we've witnessed that. In my time in the Senate with you, we've seen the most amazing shocking moments with the Obergefell case at the Supreme Court recognizing the humanity, the dignity and the equal rights of LGBTQ Americans to have love and marry. We've seen fights in this time that we've been here where we've seen victories on healthcare that made such a difference in people's lives. We've seen the fights while we've been here, some of the most painful moments where we've seen the arc of the moral universe bent not by the people here, not by the people in this body.

You think we got suffrage because a bunch of men on the Senate floor said, "Okay, guys. Come on. Put your hands in here. Ready? Give women the right to vote on three. Ready. Break."? That's not how it happened. It's not how it happened. It happened because the power of the people is greater than the people in power. You think we got civil rights because one day Strom Thurmond after filibustering for 24 hours... You think we got civil rights because he came to the floor one day and said, "I've seen the light. Let those Negro people have the right to vote."? No. We got civil rights because people marched for it, sweat for it, and John Lewis bled for it.

And so I am scared too, but fear is a necessary precondition to courage. I am angry too, but my mom told me, "Never let your anger consume you. Channel it. Fuel it so it can help your love be greater and stronger." Amy Klobuchar, that's what this moment needs. And our job in this body is to be truth tellers. Our job, just as you said so brilliantly, is to elevate the voices of the people of the country, because you're right, Amy Klobuchar.

This is the People's House. It's Article I of the Constitution and it's under assault. Article 1 is under assault. Our spending powers, our budgetary powers, the power to establish agencies like the Department of Education and USAID, it's under assault by a President that doesn't respect this document. And how do we stop them? I'm sorry to say we hold powerful positions. We are elected by great states, but we're the minority right now. And you spelled it out at the beginning of your questions to me. It will take three people of conscience on that side. It will take four here.

I'm going back to my book because there's somebody that you know. I don't know if my staff put it in at the last moment. Yes, they did. Margaret Chase Stevens, who you know. Margaret Chase Smith, excuse me. A US Senator from Maine — a Republican. When a demagogue had rose in the land exploiting people's fear, deporting Jews who were not citizens of this country because they were accusing them of being communists at a time that this body was being twisted and contorted to the will of a demagogue, where nobody had the courage to stand up. It was a woman from the Republican Party that stood, I don't know, somewhere in this body. Her feet might've been tired. Her heart might've been hurt. She might've been afraid of the consequences to stand up to people preaching the Red Scare.

But this woman in this body, rare thing in those years – this woman in this body who are our founders – those imperfect geniuses that wrote this Constitution, the woman in this body who wasn't imagined by our founders, thank God they called upon us to make a more perfect union, and generations of activists finally made it real that women could serve in this body. She had the courage, the audacity, to call her own party to task. I read her words*. She said,

> I don't believe that the Republican Party is any sense a party of fear, but I do believe that the Republican Party has made an alliance with the four horsemen of fear, the fear of communists, the fear of labor unions, the fear of the future, the fear of progress. I think it's high time that we remembered that we have sworn to uphold and defend the Constitution. {She continues...} I think it's time that we remembered that the Constitution as amended speaks not only of the freedom of speech but also the freedom of trial by jury.

This great Senator, this great Republican, said,

> Whether it is criminal prosecutions in a court or character prosecution in the Senate, there is little political distinction when the life of a person has been ruined. Those of us who shout the loudest about Americanism, in making character assassinations all too frequently, those who by our own words and acts ignore some of the basic principles of what it means to be an American, the right to criticize {without thinking the President is going to drag you from the Oval Office for criticizing him}, the right to hold unpopular beliefs. {That if you have beliefs that I find contemptible, it doesn't mean that I can disappear you from a city street. She goes on ... }The right to protest. {That just for assembling and speaking up that's not a right to cut hundreds of millions of dollars to that university's science funding.} The right to independent thought.
>
> The exercise of these rights should not cost one single American citizen his reputation or his right to a livelihood nor should he be in danger of losing his reputation or livelihood merely because he happens to know someone who holds unpopular beliefs. {Like a law firm that represents suing the President and now has their very firm, their very livelihoods, the legal secretaries and others come after them}

Margaret Chase Smith goes on to call her party, to be a woman of conscience, to stand up and say, I quote:

> The American people are sick and tired of being afraid to speak their minds lest they be politically smeared as communists or fascist by their opponent. Freedom of speech {she says} is not what it used to be in America. It has been so abused by some that it is not exercised by others.

So dear God, if I stand up in this body and say it is wrong to put Pete Hegseth in the cabinet as Secretary of Defense because he's unqualified, he's unqualified, he's unqualified. Look at a Signal chat to see how unqualified he is.

Margaret Chase Smith continues,

> As a Republican, I say to my colleagues on this side of the aisle that the Republican Party faces challenges today that is not unlike the challenge faced by Lincoln back in the day. The Republican Party so successfully met that challenge that it emerged from the Civil War as the champion of a united nation. In addition to being the party which unrelentingly fought loose spending and loose programs, I doubt if the Republican Party simply could do so simply because I do not believe the American people will uphold any political party that puts political exploitation above the national interests.
>
> Surely we Republicans are not so desperate for victory. I do not want to see the Republican Party win that way. While it might be a fleeting victory for the Republican Party, it would be a more lasting defeat for the American people {...she says} Surely it would be ultimately be suicide for the Republican Party and the two-party system itself that has protected American liberties from the dictatorship of a one-party system.

You ask me, Amy Klobuchar, what do we need to do? We need to call to the conscience of our comrades in the people's branch and say, "How could you go along with a reconciliation that will put trillions of dollars of debt on our children and our children's children? How could you go along with cutting $800 billion from Medicaid only to give tax cuts to the wealthiest, to disproportionately go to the wealthiest? How can you in good conscience, if you're a fiscal hawk, if you're a Christian Conservative, how could you hurt the weak to benefit the rich and powerful?" That is the answer to your question. The people of the United States of America — all of us have to stand up and say, "No. Not on my watch. I'm a Republican. I'm a veteran. I'm a police officer. I'm a firefighter. I'm a teacher. Not in America. We won't allow this. We won't allow this. We won't allow this."

SENATOR RON WYDEN (OREGON): Will the Senator yield – the Senator from New Jersey – yield for question?

SENATOR BOOKER: I will yield for a question while while retaining the floor.

SENATOR WYDEN: I thank my colleague and I have been listening to this and a Herculean presentation for hours and hours. And your remarks reflect the urgency of our times, Senator Booker. And I thank you for it. Let me frame the question this way. I hold open to all town hall meetings in every county in my state each year. I've had more than 1,100 of them. And since Donald Trump took office what we have seen in these town hall meetings is fear and terror and I might add record turnouts. I was in a small town in central Oregon recently, Sisters. We had almost 1,400 people here. And what people asked about, and you've touched on this morning, is of course Medicaid and Social Security because these are programs involving healthcare and retirement that are really the connective tissue between the government and our people. And these programs make it possible for people to pay for essentials. They're not going to fancy places. They're buying groceries. They're paying rent. They're buying medicine.

We had one separate town hall meeting, I say to my colleague, just with federal employees whose goal is to get out in the woods and help prevent fire in Oregon. I organized this meeting. They too are terrified. They've dedicated their lives to trying to help. Now, we serve the American people. And I'm telling you, I've seen service in action over the last few hours with your reflecting the urgency of our times. Our salaries are paid for by taxpayers and I'm particularly troubled by the fact that we're getting all these reports that many Senators are saying, "I'm not going to do town hall meetings." They're on the other side of the aisle. As I said, I've had 1,100 of them, ten of them so far this year. Seems to me that's refusing the answer to constituents. And you've been here all night and you're setting a very clear example about what it means to push back against authoritarianism.

So just like I have town hall meetings, my question to my friend from New Jersey is, what are you hearing from home? Pretty straightforward question, but it sure as heck is what the times are all about because people are saying, "What are you doing back there? What's important to you?" And I talk about town meetings. I had a tele-town hall. I say to my friend during the speech that was made on the floor of the House, I had 30,000 people participating. That's a lot for my small state. So I know what I'm doing and I think the American people would like to hear a bit about what my colleague is hearing from his state and why it's so important that he's out here mopping his brow today, trying to stay on his feet, making the case for the urgency of our time. What are you hearing?

SENATOR BOOKER: Thank you, Senator. I'm hearing a lot of fear, a lot of anger. I'm hearing head of hospitals say that this is outrageous — the threats to our hospitals in New Jersey. I'm hearing heads of critical health services tell me what the Medicaid cuts will mean to their organizations. I'm hearing from Catholic priests that are doing extraordinary things in service of their communities. I'm hearing from citizens who are veterans who got fired from their jobs. I'm hearing from people, as I read letters from people who work in the Social Security Agency, and what the chaos that's been created and the lack of... The deteriorating service to seniors. I've heard from seniors who are terrified about what's being done to Social Security and how it might affect their lives. I'm hearing demands from our constituents, people demanding, Senator, that we do something about the outrages they're seeing.

And I think that when I hear New Jerseyans, by larger and larger numbers. And I'll be back in my state. I know we were planning meetings in the town hall and a lot more this weekend. But I have to say now more than ever, we need more of it. We need more of it. And one of the reasons I'm here is because I want to elevate those voices of my constituents. I want to tell the stories that my constituents are writing in about and lift their voices and tell them that they're seen, they're heard.

I've been going through section by section, as you pointed out, Social Security section on healthcare or section on education and the Department of Education and that work that it does. I've been going point by point through. This is the agenda. I didn't know how much I can get through, but we laid it out. We have binders for each one of these issues. Immigration, we went through. We have housing, the environment, farmers and food, veterans, the corruption that's been normalized by this president, the rule of law, public safety, all of the ways that we know that there is a crisis in our country and we as a nation need to be more tuned to it and doing more to meet this crisis, to rise up and defend our country, defend our well-being.

And all while things are happening that you know. You're the chairman of the finance committee and you have these insights. We've talked about them, about what's about to happen in this reconciliation process. I mean, that's one of the most stunning things. It's almost immediate on this floor.

I think we're going to see about the tariffs tomorrow and see how far the president will go, but we do know whatever it is, it's going to affect prices that are going to continue to go up for Americans as inflations continue to go up for Americans, as the stock market has continued to go down, as people's 401Ks have lost so much money. The uncertainty I'm hearing from businesses in New Jersey, the chaos that they feel about the economy, the consumer confidence in this country has gone way down. If you ask the question, "Are you better off than you were 71 days ago?" not many Americans would say that they're better off.

Their costs are higher, their groceries are higher. They're soon to see everything from car prices to food go higher. Their retirement security is under attack, their healthcare is under attack. They're losing their department of education. They're less safe from infectious diseases abroad. There are so many things that we have to talk to and try to stop, and you're our leader on the finance committee and you know that the tax thing, they're trying to run through this now. I am trying to get my head wrapped around these wacky parliamentary things that even the podcasts I listen to in the morning to inform me. They even spoke about this years and years ago, but they said, "Oh, this is too crazy. We can't do this."

To try to tell the American people somehow that the trillions of dollars of tax cuts that we're going to give disproportionately to the wealthiest people of all, oh, there's nothing to see here. That has a zero impact on the budget so we can do it through reconciliation. That is the biggest hocus-pocus, manufactured artifice that I've ever seen to obscure the truth in America. That what the Republicans are trying to do is cut massively into healthcare for Americans in order to give tax cuts to the wealthiest – disproportionately to the wealthiest who don't need it – and to drive up the deficits, making our children and our children's children have a more dangerous economy and higher and higher debt payments to make. Debt payments that will skyrocket higher than any expense the government makes.

We are literally about to see something go through reconciliation that threatens to sacrifice our children's future so that the richest of the rich can get richer. And so I know there's a lot of people who are angry, who are worried, who are feeling overwhelmed, who are struggling to make ends meet, but I know of only one way to do this and I'm trying to do it myself, is to do things differently, to stand up, to speak up, to not act like this is just normal in our country.

Margaret Chase Smith, "Declaration of Conscience", 1 June 1950. A copy is provided at the back of the book.

9:42 AM - The World Stage

There's not a president from Eisenhower to Reagan to Bush on the Republican side that could ever imagine a day where in a UN vote, we side with Russia and China against the Western democracies that we saved in World War II. That we stormed beaches of Normandy for. That we did the Berlin Airlift for. That we did the Marshall Plan for. We designed the world order and now we're turning our back on it. We designed the rules-based world order and we're turning our back on those organizations, from trashing NATO, to getting out of the World Health Organization, to getting out of the group of countries coming together to deal with climate change. We're not leading the planet earth anymore. Our allies are saying openly they can't trust us. The quotes are unbelievable by our allies.

Generations of Americans all know one thing: Russia is our adversary. This principle was reinforced after Russia's brutal unprovoked invasion of Ukraine in February of 2022. The American public knows a lot about Putin and his cronies and what they've done to the brave people of Ukraine. Russia has abducted over 19,000 children, taking them from their families and homeland. Russia has targeted civilians, bombing hospitals and schools, including a strike on a children's hospital during the supposed ceasefire negotiations just a few weeks ago. Russian forces have raped and assaulted Ukrainian civilians, and Russia has tortured prisoners of war.

One would think given all the horrors inflicted by Russia, that the United States would continue to treat Russia as the adversary and the pariah that other Western democracies treat it. But that's not what Trump has done. He's done the opposite. On the third anniversary of Russia's unprovoked invasion of Ukraine, the Trump administration joined Russia and North Korea in voting against a UN resolution condemning the invasion that has killed over 12,000 Ukrainian civilians and injured 30,000. Imagine that. I had the foreign minister of a great ally in NATO in my office looking at me and saying, basically, "What the heck?"

My friend, Chris Murphy, on the floor — we sit close to each other. He's further up the dais than me in foreign relations and this stuff is insanity.

Here's NBC News:

> President Donald Trump has said Ukraine, not Russia, started the war. He called Ukrainian president Vladimir Zelenskyy, not Vladimir Putin. He called Zelenskyy a dictator. Meanwhile, Trump's administration is standing down on a suite of tough anti-Kremlin policies. In just over a month, Trump has executed a startling realignment of American foreign policy, effectively throwing US support behind Moscow and rejecting the title alliance with Kiev, cultivated by former president Joe Biden. The extraordinary pivot has upended decades of hawkish foreign policy towards Russia that provided a rare area of bipartisan consensus in an increasingly divided nation.
>
> Trump's recent moves have drawn international attention, unsettling US alliances and thrilling conservative populists who favor a turn away from Zelenskyy. The new posture was put in stark relief on Friday during a tense Oval Office meeting {we all remember this} between Trump and Zelenskyy. The leaders clashed in front of the press raising questions about the future of American support for Kiev.

Alliances and partners around the world are our biggest strength against any US adversary or competitor, from China to Russia to Iran to North Korea. We are the strongest nation on the planet Earth, but our strength is multiplied and magnified when we stand in alliance with those nations that share our values and are bonded to us and are committed to us. In fact, the only time Article 5 in the United Nations, that article that says that if one person in NATO is attacked, everyone is attacked, and they all join together. That one time it happened was 9/11 when our NATO allies stood up with America. And so look at NATO. It's been the bedrock of the international order for 80 years. It was created in 1949 by 12 countries including the United States to provide collective security, and in many ways to provide collective security against the Soviet Union.

Since then, 20 more countries have joined NATO through ten rounds of enlargement bringing the total number of NATO countries to 32. The most recent additions were Sweden in 2024 and Finland in 2023, who applied to join NATO in 2022 after Russia invaded Ukraine, because those countries are realizing that the authoritarian dictator that Putin is – who threatens his smaller neighbors – those other nations have realized they should be standing with NATO. That we have a principle of collective defense, as I said, enshrined in Article 5 of the North Atlantic Treaty. Collective defense means an attack on one ally is considered an attack against all allies.

A strong NATO has made America safer and stronger and more prosperous. My colleagues on both sides of the aisle have recognized this. I've been in this body for 12 years. I've been told by people who I've learned from about foreign policy. When I came here as a mayor and leaned on people like Chris Coons, and lean on people like Chris Murphy, leaned on people like John McCain, leaned on people like Lindsey Graham, leaned on people like Senator Rubio. He helped pass a law that enshrined congressional action before the president can withdraw from NATO. That law passed with overwhelming bipartisan support. Eighty seven senators voted yes. Senator Rubio, now Secretary of State, said, and I quote, "NATO serves as an essential military alliance that protects shared natural interests and enhances America's international presence. Any decision to leave the alliance should be rigorously debated and considered by the US Congress with the input of the American people."

Two weeks ago though on March 19th in 2025, in response to news that the Pentagon may give up the role of Supreme Allied Commander in Europe, a position held by an American general since the NATO alliance was formed in 1949, Republican Senator Wicker and Representative Rogers signaled their oppositions in an extraordinarily joint statement warning to Donald Trump that that change would risk undermining American deterrence around the globe. I want to read some of the comments of NATO partners about the damage that has been done in just the last 71 days of Trump's leadership in upending the world order that has helped to keep America strong and stronger and safer and more prosperous.

The EU's top diplomat said the free world needs a new leader. Think about that. Think about that. The EU's top diplomat has said in response to Donald Trump that now the free world needs a new leader. Every president of my lifetime was seen as the leader of the free world and now the rest of the free world, its top diplomat, is saying it's time for that to change. The new German Chancellor said, "My absolute priority will be to strengthen Europe as quickly as possible so that step-by-step we can really achieve independence from the USA." He went on to say, "I never thought I would have to say something like this on a television program, but after Donald Trump's statements, it is clear that the Americans, at least this part of the Americans, this administration, are largely indifferent to the fate of Europe."

Our ancestors saved Europe. Our ancestors stormed beaches in Normandy, paratrooped into Europe, liberated concentration camps. Our ancestors sacrificed blood and treasure for Europe. It turned Germany from one of history's worst despotic states into a global economic power and a democracy. We were there at the Berlin Airlift. We were there for the Marshall Plan and now Europe is saying it is clear that the Americas, at least that part of the Americas, this administration, are largely indifferent to the fate of Europe. That is not true. That is not true, and as long as I have breath in my body and blood in my veins, I will join in with the other people on both sides of the aisle.

God bless you, Roger Wicker, for standing with the understanding that America is the strongest nation in the world, but our strength is multiplied and magnified when we stand with our allies from Germany to Japan, from Australia to Iceland. That when our country stands up, we don't bully our neighbors like Canada. We don't threaten our allies like Iceland, like Greenland. We don't threaten smaller, weaker nations like Panama. We don't upend the world order. Donald Trump does not speak for me. He does not speak for the traditions of this body. He doesn't speak for the people that are buried, Americans that are buried in fields in Germany and in France and all over Europe.

Here is former Secretary of Defense, Lloyd Austin's speech to NATO and the Atlantic Council:

> On April 4th, 1949, 12 democracies came together in the wake of two world wars and the dawn of a new Cold War and they all remembere, as President Truman put it then, the "sickening blow of unprovoked aggression". {That's what Truman said.} They were coming together against the sickening blow of unprovoked aggression. {You hear that, Putin?} And so they vowed to stand together for their collective defense and to safeguard freedom and democracy across Europe and North America. They made a solemn commitment, declaring that an armed attack against one ally would be considered an attack against all.

Now, that commitment was enshrined in Article 5 of the North Atlantic Treaty. It was the foundation of NATO and it still is. And on that bedrock we have built the strongest and most successful defense alliance in all of human history — and I'll say one of the most prosperous blocs of democratic countries. Throughout the Cold War, NATO deterred Soviet aggression against Western Europe and prevented a third world war. In the 1990s, NATO used air power to stop ethnic cleansing in Bosnia and Herzegovina and in Kosovo and the day after September 11th, 2001, when Al-Qaeda terrorists attacked our country, including slamming a plane into the Pentagon not far from here, NATO invoked Article 5 for the first and only time in history.

SENATOR CHRIS COONS (DELAWARE): Will the senator yield for a question?

SENATOR BOOKER: I yield for a question while retaining the floor — I yield to one of my best friends in the Senate. I yield to one of the smartest guys I know. I yield to the guy who handed me the chairmanship of the committee that oversaw world public health in Africa and still reminds me that he knows more Swahili than I'll ever know. I yield to the guy who when he speaks up in the Senate, people on both sides of the aisle listen. I yield to my friend who has real friendships, who when I came to and said, "We are seeing the worst famines on the planet Earth, that Joe Biden didn't put enough money into the world feeding programs," he went to another appropriator over there, another friend of ours, Lindsey Graham, and together we got billions of dollars or more that saved hundreds of thousands of lives.

You are a prince of a man. You are my friend. You are somebody that is a hero who folks don't know their name in the countries that you've affected with your strength on foreign policy. Dear God, my friend, I yield the floor for a question while retaining the floor.

SENATOR COONS: I asked my friend-

SENATOR BOOKER: Excuse me, I'm going to say that correctly. I yield for a question while retaining the floor. I do not yield the floor.

SENATOR COONS: I asked my friend and colleague from New Jersey if he is familiar with Psalm 30 verse five.

SENATOR BOOKER: Not at this moment.

SENATOR COONS: I offered to repeat it because I think it speaks to this moment. *"Weeping may endure for a night, but joy comes in the morning."* This is a holy month. It is the month of Lent, it is the month of Ramadan. It is the period of reflection preceding Passover. And my question to my colleague is rooted in a scripture in the Torah, in the Psalms – forgive me, known to both of us – one widely engaged in in these days. *Weeping may endure for a night, but joy comes in the morning.* This is a reminder, both of the possibility of redemption, of the urgency of hope and of your night-long sacrifice on this floor.

Let me ask you if I might, two more questions of my friend and colleague. To my colleague from New Jersey, are you familiar with a front-page story on the Washington Post entitled *Trump's USAID Cuts Cripple American Response to Myanmar Earthquake*, an article running today in the Washington Post?

SENATOR BOOKER: I have not read the paper this day, but I-

SENATOR COONS: I had suspected that that might be the case given that my colleague from New Jersey has dedicated his night to standing tall and fighting hard to make sure that the people of the United States know what is going on. And I'll share with you just for a moment that it hurt my heart to watch the National Evening News last night and see a Chinese humanitarian emergency response team celebrated as they pulled survivors out of the earthquake rubble in Myanmar.

It did not hurt my heart that there are Chinese nationals providing emergency relief, but it hurt my heart that exactly those people who are the very best in the world at responding to humanitarian crises — exactly those people had just received termination letters and their work with USAID had just been suspended. Normally in every humanitarian crisis I've known in my lifetime, the first in are the men and women of USAID and the US Armed forces. Whether a tsunami, a tornado, wildfires or an earthquake, we had world-leading humanitarian response capabilities and I think it is a tragedy that we have not... [Fixes microphone]

I think it is a tragedy and it is reflected in both this article that I've asked my colleague about and in the response of the world that we have created an enormous opening for the PRC [People's Republic of China] to come in and do what we previously did so well. Let me ask another question, if I might, of my colleague. Are you familiar with what has just happened to food banks all over our nation in terms of an announcement about impending deliveries of badly needed surplus food? This I suspect will be the focus of your future comments on agriculture, but I mention it as something that has impacted my state and I suspect yours as well.

SENATOR BOOKER: Well, first of all, I want to say, Mr. Flynn, when you asked me to yield for a question, I want to say a yield for a question while retaining the floor, and I want to say to the colleague, I'm familiar with some of this, but as a part of a question to me and not anything resembling a colloquy, I will yield for a question while retaining the floor if you have another question.

SENATOR COONS: To my colleague, are you familiar with an article *USDA halts millions of dollars worth of deliveries to food banks*?

SENATOR BOOKER: I'm pretty sure I am. I am.

SENATOR COONS: I will simply then ask my colleague a question.

SENATOR BOOKER: Therefore, if you were going to ask me a question, I yield for a question while retaining the floor.

SENATOR COONS: To my colleague, I ask the question, are you familiar with the cuts that have been imposed to the US Department of Agriculture suspending hundreds of millions of meals to Americans in need and the justification for that being offered?

SENATOR BOOKER: I am familiar. I've mentioned it earlier in this last 15 hours, so thank you.

SENATOR COONS: Last question.

SENATOR BOOKER: I yield for a question while retaining the floor.

SENATOR COONS: To my colleague from New Jersey I ask the question, are you familiar with when, whether and why NATO has invoked Article 5? And how the service and the sacrifice that followed reinforces exactly the point I believe my colleague was beginning to speak to, which is the common cause and the common purpose shown by all of our NATO allies in America's greatest moment of need in recent decades after the attacks of 9/11?

SENATOR BOOKER: I am very familiar with that. It haunts me that when America was in crisis, I live 11 miles from Ground Zero.

SENATOR COONS: And to my colleague, are you aware which of our European NATO allies lost per capita the highest number of their soldiers in combat serving alongside American service members? A nation I visited, a nation whose service members I visited. A nation that is today aggrieved by comments made recently. Are you familiar with our trusted ally, Denmark?

SENATOR BOOKER: Yes, I am. That country that has shed more blood than any of our allies side by side fighting with America is Canada. Is Canada.

SENATOR COONS: Denmark.

SENATOR BOOKER: Oh, it's Denmark?

SENATOR COONS: Denmark lost per capita, I believe... Excuse me? Let me simply ask of my colleague one more question.

SENATOR BOOKER: Thank you very much. I yield for a question while retaining the floor.

SENATOR COONS: Is my colleague aware that broadly distributed across our NATO allies is service and sacrifice, including the loss of their troops in combat and that every single loss in combat was a loss of great service and sacrifice by our NATO allies?

SENATOR BOOKER: Yes, I am familiar and I'm grateful for you making those points as we threaten Greenland and Denmark and try to bully them in a way that, with a rhetoric that fashions more after the behavior of Vladimir Putin's threatening before the Ukrainian invasion, as opposed to what allies do who are grateful for shared sacrifice, who are grateful for shared honor, who are grateful for shared prosperity.

What is happening right now to me is shameful. How we're treating our allies is unacceptable and the tariffs that will be imposed will indeed hurt Canada and other NATO allies, but they will hurt us in the long run more, not only in the immediacy of the driving up of prices for Americans, what the president is doing as he turns his back on Republican traditions and American and democratic traditions. It's going to hurt us more as a nation in the long run as other countries look to other places for leadership of the free world.

SENATOR COONS: Will my colleague yield for another question?

SENATOR BOOKER: I yield for a question while retaining the floor.

SENATOR COONS: Is my colleague familiar with the testimony of General Jim Mattis, a decorated four-star Marine Corps general who served as Secretary of Defense in the previous Trump administration, who testified about what the consequences would be if we were to defund development and diplomacy?

SENATOR BOOKER: I hope that the colleague of mine, who again has been a mentor, a friend on all things foreign policy, my belief is that he's referring to when General Mattis sat before the United States Senate and said very pointedly if you cut the foreign aid, if you cut organizations like USAID, if you cut the programs of the State Department, then buy me more bullets.

SENATOR COONS: Will my colleague yield for a final question?

SENATOR BOOKER: I yield for a question while retaining the floor.

SENATOR COONS: Does my colleague have an opinion about whether it strengthens or harms America in our national security to have an earned reputation as a nation of compassion, a nation that comes to the aid of those suffering through humanitarian disasters, a nation of compassion that provides healthcare and access for retirement and decency, a nation that cares for the least of these on the margins of the world and that has a just and inclusive society at home? Does my colleague have an opinion about whether it strengthens or weakens our nation at home and abroad to earn a reputation for compassion and reliability, or instead to deserve a reputation for unreliability and cruelty?

SENATOR BOOKER: So this is the powerful thing about my friend who I went with on my first trip to the continent of Africa as a senator. And I remember flying in to Zimbabwe. The leader of that country had passed away. And you always correct me on my pronunciation, so I'm going to try my best. "Emengagwa".

SENATOR COONS: Mnangagwa, yes.

SENATOR BOOKER: Mnangagwa, thank you sir. The alligator was his reputation, had taken over as his leadership. And we, this bipartisan merry group of senators, were going there to sit in a unified bipartisan way and say to this new leader, "You need to honor democratic principles. You need to honor free and fair elections. That we want to be your partner. We want to be your friend, but it's time for a new, peaceful, democratic Zimbabwe." And as we landed, I don't know if you remember, he was landing too in the airport and he was coming from China. He was coming from China, who has different values than we have. In fact, you and I both see now all over the continent of Africa a competition. We come with USAID, we come with PEPFAR [President's Emergency Plan for AIDS Relief], we come with a program called AGOA [African Growth and Opportunity Act], helping with economic development. We come with scientists that stand in the breach against the worst infectious diseases.

One of the most courageous things I saw Chris Coons do in my life was when the Ebola scare was happening about eight years ago and was starting to show up on our shores, you did something that people were afraid to do. You went to Africa to visit with the people from our country that are there fighting Ebola. You had to come and quarantine when you came back to make sure you didn't have it. It was amazing because you were going there to say to the world, "I, Chris Coons, Senator for Delaware here, but America is here."

America knows that an infectious disease anywhere is a threat to public health everywhere. America knows that when it comes to the globe, Martin Luther King was right in his spiritual proclamation in the letters from the Birmingham jail, that we are all caught in an inescapable network of mutuality tied in a common garment of destiny. That injustice anywhere is a threat to justice everywhere.

I have been to where you've been, from Kenza and Tanzania to traveling with you to Ouagadougou. You used to make me smile when I used to say the capital of Burkino Faso. Ouagadougou, my friend. There's a word I learned from a language, the Bantu language. It basically roughly translates into this: I am because we are. *I am because we are.*

America has learned the power of soft power. General Mattis knew much cheaper investment, much more success. String of successes that we've had in the last 25 years have been with our soft power, not with our 20-year wars in places like Iraq and Afghanistan. General Mattis knew that. He gave wisdom. He said, "Do not cut the State Department. Do not cut USAID. They are making an invaluable contribution to fighting terrorism, to fighting instability, to spreading democracy, to fighting infectious diseases where we go and stand."

But now we're shrinking, we're retreating, we're pulling back, we're cutting aid. And when crises are happening like we're seeing in Myanmar right now, we don't even have the personnel to be there to help people.

But you know who does? China. And they show up and they leverage influence. You and I know this in the continent of Africa. "Here, take our money, take our money. Be in debt to us now, and we have control. By the way, we want a military port here." Like they have right next to us in Djibouti. The Chinese are playing a long game and Trump is playing into their hands and weakening our nation, not just against infectious diseases, not just against the global fight against climate change, not just against the economic opportunities that we're missing out on in the continent in Africa.

And guess what? If you don't know this, by 2050, one out of every four people on the planet Earth will live on the continent of Africa. One of every three working-age people on the planet Earth will be on the continent of Africa. China's playing the long game, not only critical rare earth minerals, but the economic power of the most populous continent on the planet. And what are we doing with Trump? We're doing Michael Jackson. We're moonwalking away from that continent saying, "China, go ahead."

I love you, Chris Coons. I am the ranking member of this subcommittee inspired by you, Chris Coons. And the work that you and me and Lindsey Graham and John McCain did over the last ten years is being swept away as our allies are saying frightening things that they have to look elsewhere for leadership and not to the people that save the free world. It is a shame that we're doing to my grandparents' generation. With my grandmother, with her war bonds and her victory garden and my grandfather building bombers at the Willow Run Bomber plant in Michigan. All the country came together and sacrificed for the war effort. We saved Europe, we bled and died on that European continent.

There are, and you've seen them, these fields of crosses, and you see some stars of David and you see some Muslim graves, you see it all. Our American boys died, and yet we still invested in that continent. We still invested with the Marshall Plan. We still invested with the Berlin Airlift. We still stood up to communism. And a great Republican president, a great Republican president stood up in front of a Russian autocratic leader and said, "Gorbachev, tear down this wall." And what is Trump going to be remembered for? "I really love Vladimir Putin. Zelenskyy is a dictator. You're my friend."

You and I both visit VA halls and occasionally we meet a World War II veteran. In my state, there are some incredible men that still wear their hat. And if they can, they stand with pride. They are called the greatest generation. And what are we doing to their legacy? What are we doing to their legacy, Chris Coons? I'm going to keep talking unless somebody wants to say, "Will the Senator yield for a question?"

10:13 AM - National Security

SENATOR ED MARKEY (MASSACHUSETTS): Will the Senator yield for a question?

SENATOR BOOKER: I yield for a question while retaining the floor.

SENATOR MARKEY: First of all, thank you so much for what you are doing, Senator Booker. You are drawing our nation's attention to what Donald Trump and Elon Musk and DOGE are seeking to do to our country, especially the most vulnerable in our society.

And you, Senator Booker, you have been a champion for the poor, for the sick, for the disabled, for those most in need throughout your entire life. That is who you are. You are absolutely a champion for those who need help the most.

So as we look at what Donald Trump is proposing: to destroy the Department of Education, just to level it, knowing that Title I money goes to the poorest children in Newark, in Boston, so that they can have as close to an equal footing is possible so that they too can compete, to ensure they enjoy the American dream; to gut Medicaid, knowing that there's 338,000 people just in Massachusetts alone who are on disabilities, who need Medicaid in order to deal with those afflictions which their families need a little bit of help to deal with; to begin a process of saying that social security is a Ponzi scheme.

SENATOR BOOKER: Yes.

SENATOR MARKEY: Knowing that ultimately they need the billions of dollars for the tax breaks for millionaires and billionaires. And they have to get it out of education, they have to get it out of Medicaid, they have to get it out of veterans' benefits. They have to get it out of Social Security. We know what their plot is. The plot is to get $2 trillion out of the programs that affect ordinary people in order to have tax breaks for the wealthiest people in our nation. And most of it will come out of healthcare. It'll come out of Medicaid, ultimately out of Medicare, out of the Affordable Care Act, out of veterans' benefits. Healthcare, healthcare, healthcare, healthcare for every family, for the wealthiest in our society who don't need a tax break.

That one thing they don't need right now is a tax break. Especially when Elon Musk and Jeff Bezos and Jeff Zuckerberg now control more wealth than the bottom 50% of our nation combined. Did they really need a tax break? I know the President put him right behind him at his inauguration, but oh my God, the Cabinet sits behind billionaires? The Founding Fathers are spinning in their graves thinking about how they've inverted what is supposed to be the way in which our government, our country works.

So I thank you for your incredible leadership. You are putting the spotlight on what is going wrong in this country right now, this oligarchy seeking to take over our nation. So I thank the Senator for what he's doing. It is just so consistent with his whole life, what he stands for, what he stands for on the floor of the Senate today, a conscience, a conscience for the nation. So can the Senator tell the Senate today, the nation, what this could mean if we continue down this path of Donald Trump and Elon Musk and DOGE for those families who need help the most in our society?

SENATOR BOOKER: I so appreciate the Senator, and I want to tell folks, when I wrote my book, I thought I knew this man here. But I did a lot about environmental justice in my book. I did about a lot of these toxic chemicals out there that are threatening our people. And I came to the office, to the office of the Senate one day, so humbled because I told him, "I knew you as my colleague. We both got here around the same time. But I had no idea of the kind of things you did in the United States House of Representatives, how many bills that made a difference for people's lives in Boston and Newark and Camden and Passaic." You are one of the people that after a few years here, I discovered in 2015 writing my book how amazing your career is. And now having served in the Senate about the same amount of time, I'm so grateful for you. And you have been so consistent in why you came here and not forgetting the people you've been fighting for your whole career. And so, your question is right aligned with that point.

It was said earlier about this humanity's biggest fight, humanity's biggest consistent theme, us versus them or just us. I don't like when we pit one group in this country against another group. It's not us versus the billionaires or us versus the Republicans. It's understanding what is best for We the People. How can we create a more perfect union?

And I will tell you this right now, we are a union in trouble compared to our global peers. We have higher disease rates, higher diabetes rates, higher cancer rates, higher maternal mortality rates, higher premature birth rates, higher infant mortality rates. There are so many things going on in this country that should not go on. But yet, we are a nation of utter abundance. We are a nation of incredible wealth and resources. And we've proven in our past to be a nation of incredible vision, and that's why I don't understand why we are playing so small, why we have a president that is playing so small.

It's not coming here like presidents of the past and saying, "We together." From Reagan to Clinton to Obama, there's a big challenge, America. We together are going to get into the room and do sausage-making, Republicans and Democrats, and we're going to find a way to write great legislation. Whatever you want to say about Joe Biden, he was a big president because he didn't try to do things by executive fiat or as a quote of Donald Trump's I put here, "The primacy of the executive," ignoring our Constitution.

You know how many bipartisan bills were hammered out here? I see another dear friend of mine, Mark Warner. You know how many bipartisan bills Mark Warner was at the table for, my senior Senator who is Chairman of Intelligence? We did bipartisan Infrastructure Act when Trump in his first term had infrastructure week every other week. We did a CHIPS and Science bill. He's trying to claw back with the money, but we together, I still remember that skiff, that classified skiff where the whole Senate was there and our National Security Team and Gina Raimondo put forward the crisis in our country, the vulnerabilities. And we came out of that room, we got into our rooms, and we hammered out a great CHIPS and Science bill.

Decades went by in this body with doing nothing on gun violence — decades. And courageous people on the Republican side, friends of mine that surprised me that stood up like Senator Cornyn and said, "We're going to do something. I've got my lines. You've got your lines, but let's find the space in the middle." And we did programs that if you come to New Jersey, the Community Violence Intervention money is lowering murder rates in places like Newark by over 50% helping to get it done along with our great law enforcement officers. And the incredible thing about that now is Trump is trying to claw back that money, violating the separation of powers, because we decide how we're spending money in America, not the Executive. Read the Constitution.

And so, you and I both know that a big president would come to here and say, "Let's do some legislation." And I read it in the middle of the night, but John McCain, it's really important, John McCain, I won't read it but I'll tell it, voted against the healthcare last time, the taking away of healthcare for millions of Americans, and said, "That's because of the dysfunction of this body, that we don't come together and do something bigger and bolder to provide better healthcare, to bring the ideas from both sides and expand the opportunities for Americans and replace the imperfections of the Affordable Care Act with smarter and better things."

Not Donald Trump. He's repeating the mistakes, but not with the ACA, which affects tens of millions of Americans, with Medicaid that affects 70 to 100 million Americans. Why? You ask why? Well, we know why. There's two things that this will achieve — two things. One, as you said it, it is because he wants to not just renew the Trump tax cuts, but expand them that have disproportionate benefits to the wealthiest. And I wish the wealthiest in the country, names that we know, people like Elon Musk would say, "I don't want a tax cut." I wish he would say the truth. "I don't need a tax cut." But no, that's one of the reasons he wants to renew a program that gave disproportionate money.

But that's not the only reason. There's a cruelty in what he's doing. It's so offensive. He seems to have no respect for people with disabilities. He made fun of a journalist with a disability once. He seems to have no respect for people who are working hard and struggling, but still can't make ends meet. No respect for people that are afraid of his language, of his threats. They think that what he's doing to Social Security might mean they don't have it; that what he's saying to Medicare and Medicaid are lies because he's got more registered lies than any president of my lifetime. They don't think they can trust this President not to hurt them because he already is.

And so, I was told by my parents, "What defines you as a person is not what happens to you, but how you choose to respond." What happens to us as a nation is not what happens to us. They can bomb us from Pearl Harbor to attack us at 9/11. The American character was defined by how we responded to those crises. And yes, there have been major political crises before, but we responded by bending the arc of our nation more towards justice, taking care of more and more people saying that we belong to each other in America. It is We the People. It is *We the People*.

I see the standing of my friend, Mark Warner. I don't know if he has a question, but I know what I'm told to say. If he asks me to yield for a question.

SENATOR MARK WARNER (INDIANA): Will the Senator yield for a question?

SENATOR BOOKER: I yield for a question while retaining the floor.

SENATOR WARNER: Well, Mr. President, let me join my friend and colleague from Massachusetts, one to celebrate the Senator from New Jersey's endurance, his willingness to continue to make this case in as clear terms as possible. Not having been here last night at 6:30, I do wonder when he started this speech-athon at 6:30 whether the bob and the weave and the move was quite as strong, or was he firmly attached to the podium? The fact that you are going on more than 12 hours now and look like you've got hours ahead and hours before you sleep, and knowing that there are other members that have got a question, including the Majority Leader.

I just want to be brief with mine. You've talked a lot with great passion about the damage done domestically. As Chairman of the Intelligence Committee, now vice Chairman, I have been aghast at the sloppiness of this administration time after time after time in terms of their treatment of classified information. The first two weeks of the administration, strangely, a couple hundred CIA agents' identities were revealed on a non-classified chain. These probationary employees, it means new employees, the American government had spent a couple hundred thousand dollars on each of them. You've got to get a security clearance, you've got to get them trained. Unfortunately, these folks can't deploy abroad. They can't deploy undercover because their names were carelessly put on an unsecured channel.

If you say, "Well, that went just a one-off." Well, what about a week or so later, the DOGE boys, they print a whole list of federal properties that should be for sale. They quickly take it down a few hours later realizing they once again have screwed up. But in putting up that list, they put on classified dark sites that the American government again spends millions of dollars to protect. Or more recently as well, the DOGE boys, either ignorantly or maliciously, either one just plain stupid, put out the list of a classified agency, its budget, total headcount. Again, all classified information.

And Senator, one thing I can tell you, and I know you know this as well, if this had happened to a line intelligence officer or a line military officer, there'd be no question. Your butt would be fired. Matter of fact, we got information yesterday there had been a DHS employee who had inadvertently, inadvertently put a journalist on a chat line. Guess what happened? The guy is fired.

So when it came to this incident now called Signalgate or Signalgate Fiasco, where you've got the leading members of this administration debating where and how we should bomb the Houthis, including specific information of who will be hit and when, Senator Booker, I was down in Hampton Roads this weekend, these were the communities that surround the Norfolk Naval Station. Norfolk Naval Station is where the Truman, the aircraft carrier, has been deployed from. It is the aircraft carrier that the flights that attacked the Houthis flew off of. I can tell you one thing, Senator Booker, these people were pissed off that there'd been this level of carelessness about their loved ones, that if it had gotten in the wrong hands would've cost American lives.

So Senator Booker, as you put down the litanies of all of the challenges that have been raised by this administration, I'll ask you a simple question. Do you agree that this pattern – not one-off – pattern of sloppiness, endangers our national security?

SENATOR BOOKER: Yes, absolutely, yes. I love that you gave that litany, Senator. I have benefited from your leadership on the Intel Committee. You are one of the people that when things go down on the planet Earth, you're one of the small handful of people with the highest security clearance here. You know before rank-and-file senators do. And we've had so many conversations about threat matrixes and what our enemies are doing. You've sent me to the skiff and say, "I can't talk to you about this. Go down to the skiff and ask for the information" to help me to fill out my understanding of national security threats.

I am stunned by this President, all that I've read in the skiffs about what Russia is doing to this country. I am stunned and angry by this President and what he is doing to us by cozying up to Putin and turning his back on our allies. But the sloppiness, the unqualified leaders that he's put in place, it has caused us to be more at risk.

And the Signalgate, you said it, if that had happened under any other president, Republican or Democrat, whoever controlled the Senate would have hearings. They would want know was this pattern in practice? Did these Signal conversations happen before and we only know about this one because somehow you pulled in a journalist?

Well, that's a violation of the law, because they're disappearing messages, were destroying government documents that the executive branch has a legal obligation. And the classified materials, putting it out there first saying, "Oh, there was nothing classified about that," lying. And then, they put out the actual, said, "Okay, if there's nothing classified," they release the whole thing. And to the wisdom of people like you, and again, more wisdom and experience at Intel than me, it's clearly that that was sensitive, probably classified, but we should be having hearings and accountability.

I keep going back to how this document is being undermined and attacked by this President. And one of the powers and responsibilities that we swore to uphold, every one of us swore to uphold this, was that we are to be a check on the administration.

10:32 AM - Medicaid (and Sports)

Before I yield to the next question from Senator Schumer, I want to talk about Senator Schumer. I just want to say something, get it off my chest. Senator Murphy, we've passed the 15-hour mark. I want to thank Senator Murphy in particular because he's been with me the whole night. He hasn't left my side. And in some ways the debt's repaid. We passed 15 hours. Because we called Chuck Schumer nine years ago, nine years ago. I remember exactly where I was standing when we, three of us were on the phone, and we asked Chuck to help us for you to take the floor right down there and do a filibuster. We didn't know how long it was going to last, but I committed to you that I would be your aide-de-camp. Fifteen hours you've stood, Chris Murphy, saying that this nation shouldn't do business and usual for the Pulse massacre. And the leader of the Senate nine years ago said, "I support you guys. Go ahead."

And so, one of the first people I called, Senator Schumer, and talked to about this actually was Murphy. And he did full circle for me and has been with me the whole 15 hours. His debt is paid, but I've got fuel in the tank, man. And the only reason you stopped wasn't because you couldn't go on anymore. It was because we got a concession from Mitch McConnell. We got his concession to get two votes on common sense gun safety that Republicans had put forward, like universal background checks in the past. But we lost that vote. But in both occasions, nine years apart, once where Murphy was the principal and now here we have a leader that said, "Yeah, how can I help?" And so, I want to thank Senator Schumer before I suspect he might ask me to yield for a question, for being a friend, a partner, and one of the first people I turned to with this idea and that encouraged me to go for it. To go for it, Cory. And so, thank you, Chuck Schumer.

SENATOR SCHUMER: Would the senator yield for a question?

SENATOR BOOKER: I yield for a question while retaining the floor.

SENATOR SCHUMER: And I have two questions, frankly, one on Medicaid cuts which we talked about last night and one on tariffs. But first, let me say before I get to this question, your strength, your fortitude, your clarity has just been nothing short of amazing. And all of America is paying attention to what you're saying. All of America needs to know there's so many problems, the disastrous actions of this administration in terms of how they're helping only the billionaires and hurting average families. You have brought that forth with such clarity. People from one end of America to the other admire you. Our whole caucus is behind you, and we admire your stamina, your strength, your passion, your intelligence. The list of adjectives could go on.

My question first relates to the Medicaid cuts. As we talked about last night, I visited three Republican districts, one in Staten Island, one right on the border of two Republican districts in Long Island yesterday to talk about Medicaid cuts. I went to nursing homes, and it was clear that the Medicaid cuts that are proposed in this proposal, $880 billion in the House, would be devastating. On Staten Island, the nursing home we visited – they love it – Silver Lake nursing home, would close. Three hundred people would lose their jobs, hundreds would be thrown out. And most of them said their children can't take care of them. Their needs are more advanced. And even some who said their children might be able to take care of them, didn't have room in the house, etc.

So it's affecting Staten Island's middle class, [who] voted for Trump. But we made a plea to their Congresswoman to not vote for any bill that had these Medicaid cuts and the tax breaks for billionaires. And a lot of the people there — it was bipartisan. There were both parties there. We estimated that about 18,000 people total would lose their jobs with these Medicaid cuts, creating a recession on Staten Island. We estimated the harm that would've caused. And so, this was devastating. Same thing on Long Island. Again, Republican areas with Republican congresspeople who hold the balance.

If those three congresspeople alone would say, "I'm not voting for a bill that cuts Medicaid to give tax breaks for the billionaires," the bill would fail. And I know that you in New Jersey and my colleagues in Massachusetts, Connecticut, and elsewhere are doing the same thing, Congressmen and Senators. And I've talked to Leader Jeffries, he's doing the same with his folks.

So my question to you is very simple. If these people in New Jersey, in New York, across America are kicked out of nursing homes, of assisted living facilities, of healthcare facilities, what would they do? And how does the Senator, with his passion and everything else, feel when the only reason they're doing this is to give tax breaks to the wealthiest of Americans? Would you please answer my question, sir?

SENATOR BOOKER: Yes, I will, Leader Schumer. Late last night, I read dozens and dozens and dozens of letters from terrified people. The stories were heartbreaking as people rendered their pride and gave us insights into the more painful aspects of their lives. I got emotional over one about a person talking about being diagnosed with Parkinson's and know that the disease would get more and more debilitating like I saw with my father and demand more and more help. And she was paranoid that the burden on our family, that they couldn't afford it. I had this is one amazing letter about a person that said they were the sandwich generation, two 90-something year old parents they were taking care of and two adult men, children with disabilities.

And for all of these people, like you saw in the nursing homes, Medicaid wasn't a plus or some kind of abundance heaped upon their lives. It helped them keep the fragile financial world they were living in stable. And then, not just an $880 billion cut, Senator Schumer, but even just half of that or a quarter of that would cut services that would pull apart their whole lives, their ability to care for their loved ones, their ability to still work.

One person just said, "Just the transportation we get through Medicaid for my disabled child is the link that holds it all together." And callously and cruelly, they're talking about this not in any kind of insightful way, not any kind of, "Well, here's we can make it more efficient and actually help to keep some..." None of that kind of thought or logic of bringing in experts, because we read page after page after page of rural hospital leaders, of urban hospital leaders, and more and more and more.

So your question is clearly that it is this crazy scheme right now to expand the Trump tax cuts that overwhelmingly disproportionately go to the wealthiest of us in America who need not our help; that would still yet expand the deficit by trillions of dollars, which means your children – and I know how proud a grandfather you are – your grandchildren would have to pay for that debt. They're stealing from your grandchildren so that the wealthiest amongst us could get bigger tax cuts, and at the same time taking away medical coverage from the most vulnerable.

What is that? It's not who we are. It's not who we are, America. And as much as people, thousands descended on this to save the ACA, Medicaid affects millions and millions of more people. Wake up. They're coming after a vital program for American expectant mothers, for American children, for American disabled, for the seniors like the ones you visited.

SENATOR SCHUMER: I thank my colleague.

SENATOR BOOKER: Now, I have one more thing to get off my chest, sir.

SENATOR SCHUMER: Please.

SENATOR BOOKER: This is a little lighter. You heaped so many kind things on me. I don't know if you realize that never before in the history of America has a man from Brooklyn said so many complimentary things about a man from Newark.

SENATOR SCHUMER: But I would remind my colleague that we are both New York Giants fans.

SENATOR BOOKER: Who play where? In New Jersey. This is not a colloquy. I hold the floor. I do not yield. [Laughter in the chamber]

Brooklyn stole the Nets, it's an injustice, from Newark. They stole the Nets. I do not yield the floor for a rebuttal. And the Giants and the Jets play in New Jersey. There's only one football team in New York, and that's the Bills.

I do not yield, but I do love and respect. But when I've got the floor, I don't have to yield. This is the one time in my life I get the last word with my much more senior, much wiser friend and Senator who supports me.

SENATOR SCHUMER: My colleague, I do have another question.

SENATOR BOOKER: Oh, okay.

SENATOR SCHUMER: Unrelated subjects.

SENATOR BOOKER: On a different subject.

SENATOR SCHUMER: On an unrelated subject.

SENATOR BOOKER: Okay. Unrelated.

SENATOR SCHUMER: But I will say, go Bills.

SENATOR BOOKER: As long as he gives me that commitment, I yield for a question while retaining the floor.

SENATOR SCHUMER: First, let me say before I ask my question, go Bills. Second, given the 15 hours which you've shown such amazing strength of an All-American athlete who could probably, given what you've shown tonight, be a star on our Giants. So I will not even try to rebut-

SENATOR BOOKER: Thank you, sir.

SENATOR SCHUMER: -where the Giants are. But I will ask you this question second.
And just going back, before I get to tariffs, one of the leading hospitals in New York told me if there were only a 20% cut at Medicaid, less deep than they show, that they would close. They're the only cancer care place in the Bronx, 1.3 million people. And they give great care. They're the only one. They would close. So the devastation of these cuts, the American people should realize is just enormous from one end of the country to the other, in middle class communities, in upper middle class communities like Long Island, middle class like Staten Island, poor communities like the Bronx.

10:43 AM - Tariffs

SENATOR SCHUMER: But on tariffs, let me ask a question. So here we are, right on the edge of April 2nd. Today is April Fool's Day, but the tariffs that the President is proposing unfortunately are not part of an April Fool's trick. They're real and they're devastating. And my question to my colleague, with these tariffs, which is estimated would cost the American family $6,000 more on average, would raise costs on everything across the board and would throw devastation into our economy. Look at the stock market. It goes down when Trump is serious about tariffs, then goes up when he says maybe he is not so serious. And with the chaos that it has caused so businesses which love certainty--small businesses, medium-sized businesses, large businesses need certainty.

So my questions are these, does the great Senator and great Giants fan from New Jersey agree that prices could go way up, all the way up to as much as $6,000?

And does he agree that the chaos from Trump's tariffs is discombobulating the economy in very serious ways? And again, does he agree that the reason that they seem to be doing this, they count the revenues. This guy Navarro seems to have no sense of reality and yet he seems to be in charge. And they count the revenues to help them get more tax cuts for the wealthy. Almost everything they do, including tariffs, it seems to me, is aimed at getting those tax cuts for the wealthy. Which, God bless the wealthy, as I've heard you say last night when we spoke, we're not against people who make a lot of money, God bless them, but they don't need a tax break.

SENATOR BOOKER: No, they don't.

SENATOR SCHUMER: They should realize the beauty of America helped them become or stay billionaires. The money we invested in education and roads and schools and helping kids get food makes a better workforce. So my question to my colleague on these tariffs, (A) does he agree that it could raise the price on an average family thousands of dollars? It's estimated $6,000. Does he agree that the chaos caused by Trump's on again, off again, this country, that country, this much, that much, this product, that product is hurting the economy and hurting business people do their jobs? And does he agree that it seems the motivation is tax breaks for the wealthiest people? Will you please answer my question?

SENATOR BOOKER: I will, Senator Schumer.

SENATOR SCHUMER: And I yield back to him.

SENATOR BOOKER: I will. So you and I both know that in 72 days now – it's the next day – the 72 days that Trump has been in office, he has caused havoc on the American economy, especially given the economy he inherited. Inflation is up, prices are up, consumer confidence is down, the stock market and people's 401(k)s and retirement plans are down. He continues to do things to rattle confidence, to raise prices and to hurt, not the billionaires, the people that can afford these things, to hurt average Americans who find housing prices too high and it difficult to make ends meet. Every time, and I've looked at the tariffs throughout history, in fact, one of my friends sent me this really funny clip, I hope somebody will put up for me, from I think it was Ferris Bueller's Day Off where he was talking about tariffs and was like, "Bueller, Bueller, the reality is..." Or maybe it was another movie, I'm mixing it up. It shows my pop. What's that?

SENATOR SCHUMER: You are entitled after 15 hours.

SENATOR BOOKER: Thank you right now. But the tariffs haven't worked out for Republican presidents who tried them during the depression. The evidence is here, learn from our history.

SENATOR SCHUMER: Does my colleague remember the names of Smoot and Hawley*?

SENATOR BOOKER: Smoot and Hawley? Yes, sir. I definitely remember those names from high school history. God bless you, Mr. Al Gore and Ms. Saru. So yes, what he's going to do tomorrow is going to rattle the markets. What he's going to do tomorrow is raise prices for Americans. What he's going to do tomorrow is lie to folks and say that this is something that China will pay or whomever will pay, when actually it's the American consumers that will pay with higher prices and more economic insecurity. I'll tell you this quote that Frederick Douglass once said — this I do remember. He said, "The limits of tyranny is prescribed by the endurance of those who are oppressed."

How much more will we take of this? How much more will we as America say, cut our Medicaid to give tax cuts to the billionaires, take the Affordable Care Act and take away tax credits, take away enrollment support? Hey, come after Social Security, cut thousands of people, make customer service get worse, as said The Wall Street Journal. How much more of these indignities will we take as he turns his back on our allies? How much more of a person that is doing tyrannical things as he takes our Constitution and continues to trash it as he's running into judge after judge, after judge that's trying to stop him.

But we've already seen that he wants to ignore judges or if he gets real rulings he doesn't like, he trashes the judges. And even the Chief Justice appointed by a Republican says to him, "No, this is not right. This is not who we are. This is not how we do things in America." How much more can we endure before we in a collective chorus of conviction in our country say, enough is enough? Enough is enough. You're not going to get away with this.

SENATOR SCHUMER: I thank the gentleman for his fortitude, his strength, and the crystalline brilliance by which he has shown the American people the huge dangers that face them with this Trump-DOGE-Musk administration. I yield the floor back to my colleague in New Jersey.

SENATOR BOOKER: Thank you.

* The Tariff Act of 1930, also known as the Smoot–Hawley Tariff Act

10:49 AM - Social Security and USAID

SENATOR ELIZABETH WARREN (MASSACHUSETTS): Mr. President.

PRESIDING OFFICER: I recognize the Senator from Massachusetts, but I think you have to ask him for a question.

SENATOR WARREN: Mr. President, will the Senator yield for a question?

SENATOR BOOKER: I yield for a question while retaining the floor.

SENATOR WARREN: Thank you. I am very grateful to the Senator from New Jersey for coming to the floor for such an extended period of time to give voice to all of those around this country whose voices evidently are not heard by the Republicans in the United States Congress. And I wanted to ask a question for the 73 million people who are beneficiaries of the Social Security system and for their families, for the people whose grandma is getting Social Security, for the people whose cousin, whose dad died, who is getting Social Security benefits, about what's happening right now between Donald Trump and Elon Musk, our current co-presidents, and what they're trying to do to the Social Security system.

So I start this question with just a basic observation. Social Security is not charity. It is not something we give away to those who are less fortunate and we do this out of the goodness of our hearts. Social Security is a contract that people who work in America pay into the system for all of their working lives. And when the time comes that they retire or something happens to them and they are not able to do that work, that they can count on the Social Security system and the payments that they are legally entitled to. I want to underscore here, legally. Now, if America wanted to change that contract, the place they have to go is right here to Congress. They have to come to the United States Senate or they have to go to the House of Representatives and they have to say, "We actually want to change benefits for Social Security recipients."

And by the way, that has happened dozens and dozens of times in our history, up through the late 1980s, where we made adjustments in the Social Security benefits. For example, for the fact that people lived longer, for the fact that people worked longer. And so we made minor adjustments in the system. We also made adjustments to make sure that there were cost-of-living changes in how much Social Security would pay out. So anyone who wants to change the benefits that people are legally entitled to has to come here to Congress and make that happen. But it appears that Elon Musk and Donald Trump have tried to figure out an end run. And the end run is to say, okay, we can't directly change benefits, but what we can do is we can effectively cut off benefits.

Now how can they do that? Well, one way is fire all the people who help people get their Social Security benefits. And think of it this way: someone who wants to collect Social Security – let's just say, at age 66 – they decide, okay, I'm ready. It's time for me to retire. I can't do this anymore. I want to collect my Social Security benefits. And they try to fill out the form, it turns out it gets rejected. There's a number off somewhere in the system. Somebody's got a confusion over what the name is or where somebody worked or an employer from decades back failed to fill out the right form. So now there's a problem in the system. So what does a person do? Well, first they might try calling. But if you fire the people who answered the phones, that's not going to work.

Okay, so what's the next thing you do? You go to your local Social Security office. Oh, but if they've closed the Social Security office near you, that's not going to work. So what do you do? You go to the Social Security office that you can find two hours away, three hours away, four hours away. Finally get to that Social Security office and when you get there, if they fired most of the people, you may encounter, what? Two people working the desk to help straighten out problems and a line that's 50 people long.

By the way, these come from real stories. People are telling what's happening out there. So by the time the day is over, our example here hasn't even made it to the front of the line. So doesn't get the question answered, doesn't get the problem resolved, has to go back home again, has to find somebody who can maybe take him to the Social Security office that's hours away and start this process over and over and over. If this person, let's just say for example, takes three months to get this problem ultimately resolved by the Social Security Administration, they don't get the money, that money is lost, it just simply is gone. They do not get the money they are legally entitled to and they have no right to go back and collect it — even pointing out that it was Social Security's error. So failure to correct these errors or to give people an opportunity to correct these errors is effectively the same as having cut their benefits.

And you do that for 1% of the people, drive up your error rate, you do that for 5% of the people, you do that for 10% of the folks who are getting Social Security. And man, those cuts really start to add up. They really start to add up for the people whose benefits are cut, they really start to add up for Donald Trump and for Elon Musk. But let's look at another possibility here, and that is just simply delay. Checks don't go out on time. When checks don't go out on time, then the promise that people relied on, that that check would come on the third of the month. That's what they count on for rent, that's what they count on to put groceries on the table, that's what they count on to support themselves. It's gone.

So maybe they'll get their check next month. Another billionaire Republican, Howard Lutnick, said, "Don't worry about it." His mother-in-law would simply count on the fact that they'd straighten the problem out and maybe next month she would get her payment. I suppose if your son-in-law is a billionaire, you can count on the fact that somebody will make sure your rent gets covered and groceries are on the table. But for the 70 million Americans relying on that check coming in every month, not so clear what you're going to do. So what do you do? Do you borrow money to make rent? Do you call on relatives if you've got them? Who do you go to be able to make it to the end of this month, and if the problem persists to the next month and the next month? Where do you go?

That is, in my view, as much a benefit cut as Congress having voted to say, we're just going to give a 10% across-the-board cut to everyone who receives Social Security benefits. There are a lot of ways to cut benefits and breaking your promise to seventy-three million Americans is a benefit cut. It is not a legal benefit cut, but it is an effective benefit cut. And I admire the Senator from New Jersey for being here today to speak out for those Americans who face these kinds of cuts and have no recourse. I admire him for standing up and saying to the Republicans who won't go do town halls, who won't go out and meet with these people and listen to them, listen to their concerns, listen to their fears, listen to their stories about what happens as thousands and thousands more Social Security employees are fired and correcting problems, straightening out your benefits, gets harder and more out of reach for more and more Americans.

That is what we face right now. So the question that I want to pose to the Senator from New Jersey is this: at a time when Donald Trump and Elon Musk are looking for an indirect way to cut Social Security benefits... And let's just pause here if I can to say why. Why go out of your way to cut Social Security benefits? Come on now. 73 million Americans rely on this. This has been the backbone of America's promise to its own people, that you did the work, you put in the money and now you are entitled to the benefit on the other side.

Why are they doing this? Because they want to reduce the amount of money that is available for Social Security and instead take that money over so that they can advance tax cuts for billionaires and billionaire corporations. They're just trying to grease the skids here for the billionaires to get even richer and ask the 73 million Americans who rely on Social Security to pay for it out of their own hides. So the question I have for the Senator from New Jersey is when Elon Musk and Donald Trump are determined to try to use a backdoor way to cut Social Security benefits, (A) are they acting legally? And (B) how do we put a stop to this?

SENATOR BOOKER: Amen. Reverend Warnock was here earlier and was preaching and quoting scripture, but you are preaching a gospel of the truth, my friend, from a civic gospel that speaks to the cares and the concerns of the American Hope and the American Dream and the American Constitution because you and I both know the answer to the question.

I have to say for folks who are watching, she's a great Senator from Massachusetts, but she used to be a professor in New Jersey. She was a Rutgers professor. I was listening to her way before I got to the Senate when she was fighting for the CFPB [Consumer Financial Protection Bureau], when she was fighting so people would not be taken advantage. It was establishing the first ever agency whose sole purpose is to stand up to big banks, to big corporate powers and defend people. An institution that got billions and billions of dollars back into the pockets of the American consumer.

And what did Donald Trump and DOGE do to an institution that we set up in Congress in a bipartisan way? They did something that is against the Constitution and went after to hack it to pieces so that it's no more. But add insult to injury, down here we just had a vote on overdraft fees. That was stunning to me because there was just no defense of it. It was a clear thing. Some of the big banks said, "You know what? We don't need those usury fees. It's actually wrong." Some of the big banks just stood up and they did the right thing, but a handful of others were still taking advantage of people and this Senate got to vote, which side are you on? And we failed.

So your question is right. You detail what is right, how people are getting hurt already, how the benefits of Social Security are already being affected, how rural Social Security offices are being closed already. And the question of why? Under the guise of efficiency, but you're hurting our elders who deserve dignity in their retirement. It's stunning to me, Senator Warren, stunning to me that we're actually even having this discussion and having this debate when there's been not one congressional hearing about what Elon Musk is doing. The letters I read earlier about Social Security were painful because people wanted to know what was being done with their most confidential and private information.

I want to continue because we were working through national security. And given the time, I want to rush to just read some stories of voices. I wanted to come to the floor and read people's voices, elevate voices. And so here's a voice, a statement from Julia Hurley from Bergen County, New Jersey. Thank you, Julia. I see you.

> My family's roots are deep in New Jersey all the way back to my great-grandparents, with my mom's side from Bogota, Fair Lawn, and Upper Saddle River. And my dad's side from Spring Lake and Wall Township. I have north and south roots. My grandfather started a manufacturing company that my cousin still runs and my other grandfather ran a trucking company based in New Jersey.
>
> I was born and raised in Park Ridge and learned from a very young age about the importance of serving and community. Both of my grandfathers served in World War II. {What a family.} My family was always involved in charity and our churches. And ever since I can remember, I wanted to help people, doing my first fundraiser for homeless people in Bergen County when I was maybe eight or nine. The passion for service took an international bend after I went abroad for the first time during an exchange trip to Germany with Park Ridge Junior Senior High School in 2001 and fell in love with travel. Shortly after that, September 11th happened. Seven people from my little town were killed in the Towers and we could see the smoke from ground zero from a hill in the next town over.

For those of you who don't know, Park Ridge is very close to where I grew up, and my childhood best friend died in the Towers.

" This was when I learned how my little suburban bubble could be impacted by things worlds away. I became obsessed with trying to help and wanting to drive a career that would be in service to my country and people elsewhere, so those people would be more inclined to work with us than against us. I went on to study diplomacy and international relations at Seton Hall University, graduating magna cum laude and determined to work for the State Department at some point.

My 15-year winding career path after that took me into the advocacy space and onto humanitarian and peace-building work in Gaza with the UN as well as in Tunisia and Egypt. In 2022, after a year as a policy advisor with the International Committee of the Red Cross, I was recruited to join USAID. And I couldn't have been more excited. This was a dream job. An opportunity to serve my country and impact policy in a real way, sharing what I had learned from working abroad and at home to shape US foreign policy and efforts to advance development and humanitarian assistance on the ground.

I was eventually promoted to a senior policy advisor role in USAID's Office of Policy where I was developing policy that was shaping the way USAID worked, trying to break down silos across the agency to be more effective and efficient in our response to some of the toughest crises in the world. I got the opportunity to not only prepare talking points for high-level events and for our leadership, but even brief the administrator a couple of times. That all came crashing down around January 28th as my colleagues began being terminated and furloughed. I went into the Trump administration like any other bureaucrat, ready to engage and help because I want every administration to succeed and lean on us as experts to help advance American policy.

I worked with our team and I briefed our political appointee director who started on inauguration day and hoped to see what I could do to continue building on the reform work I had been doing for a year at that point. Instead, everything quickly unraveled. Elon Musk called USAID, 'A criminal organization that should die,' he said. And the President of the United States deemed us radical left lunatics. I was terrified, afraid of what people might do when two of the most powerful men in the world were saying things like that. Our jobs were then in question and the USAID offices were quickly closed with our belongings still in them. We were left not knowing what our fate would be for weeks. As DOGE dismantled USAID, I watched in horror as the programs shut down, the people we served, suffered, and friends and colleagues from the agency and our partner organizations lost their livelihoods and their mission-driven careers. On March 14th, I was finally terminated.

I've been heartbroken since, shifting between deep depressions and rage. Because of the sledgehammer approach that DOGE took, the entire foreign assistant architecture was broken. Organizations I would have gone on to work for are going bankrupt, cutting staff and definitely not hiring. I spent 15 years building up this career that I loved beyond words. Every time I would leave my late father while he was dying in a hospital in 2012, he would tell me to, "Go save the world." This wasn't just a career, it

> was a calling to serve. I have no idea what I will do next. In some ways, I feel lucky because I got married last May {God bless you} and I am on my husband's health insurance. {Thank God.} But he also works for the government and he could be riffed with a moment's notice. I also have a supportive family who will help me if it really gets bad. But the uncertainty has probably been one of the most painful parts of all of this. Not knowing what will come next and just fearing it will be worse than the day before. All we wanted to do was serve.

I want to say thank you to Julia Hurley from Bergen County, my home county in New Jersey. Thank you for your voice. Thank you for laying your pain plain and your anger, making it real in my heart as I know it's in yours. I stand for you today.

Personal statement from Catherine Baker, from Neptune, New Jersey:

"   I have been furloughed from my job at my USAID implementing partner since February 14th, 2025. I have 13 years experience supporting USAID contractors in business development and recruitment efforts, mostly in conflict and post-conflict settings. The following is how I got here today. I was born in Neptune and raised there until I went to college. My father is a lifelong Neptune resident, whose Jersey roots date all the way back to the early 1700s {Wow!} when my Scottish ancestors came here in search of religious freedom and economic opportunity to help build much of what is Gloucester and Mercer Counties.

My mother is an immigrant, born in Coro, Venezuela, to refugees escaping fascism, bombs, and economic ruin in Spain and Sicily. Every summer, my mom and I traveled to Venezuela to see her mother, my aunts and uncles and countless cousins. Coro, the capital of Venezuela's state responsible for most of oil refining, sits on the Caribbean coast and is about 15 minutes plane ride from Aruba, surrounded by sand dunes. Our family friends lived in homes with dirt floors, corrugated aluminum roofs, and a hose out back you would use to shower while fending off the chickens that roamed freely.

Coro is a city in constant drought. We would get water every other day and you'd use a trash bin filled with water and a ladle to shower on your non-water days. Coro, as you can imagine, couldn't be more different from Neptune, New Jersey. I went to St. James Elementary and Red Bank Catholic High School in Red Bank from kindergarten through 12th grade. If 13 years of Catholic school teaches you anything, it's the importance of taking care of one another, especially those that are suffering from poverty, famine, and disease.

I remember being given small cartons when we were tasked with filling with spare change so that we could ship them off to some faraway place where we were told stories of children just like us who were facing unimaginable hardships. I was so moved by the notion that a child, not so different from myself, didn't have enough to eat or had lost their parents in a conflict I couldn't begin to understand. My senior year at RBC, I took a class called Globalization and Social Justice. The class was taught by a long time family friend, Mary Logan, herself a former nun. Ms. Logan taught us about the Rwandan genocide and had us watch Hotel Rwanda as a class. She made sure we knew the reasons why this happened, understood how dehumanization and hatred can lead to mass torture and executions, and critiqued the international response to the genocide that led to nearly ONE million deaths in 100 days.

That year, Ms. Logan took us to Kean University to see Nick Kristof speak about Darfur and made sure we knew the signs of genocide when we saw it. "How can we let this happen again?" We asked her. I wore my Save Darfur green rubber bracelet and t-shirt everywhere I went. What could I, a kid living at the Jersey Shore, do to help? During this period of enlightenment led by Ms. Logan, the Maryknoll Missionaries funded school in Kibera, Kenya, that we were supporting was threatened by electoral violence. In December of 2007, we received letters from nuns there who were

Ms. Logan's personal friends about how the fires nearly reached the school and the children who were already living in Africa's largest slum stood poised to lose the little they had, including their lives.

Upon returning from Christmas break, Maryknoll Affiliates Club sprang into action. We raised awareness and funds and proudly sent money from bake sales and door knocking to our friends in Kenya. We received media attention from WCBS in New York and our story got picked up by other channels and newspapers. I was amazed that my efforts in Monmouth County were having such meaningful and real impact on a crisis happening thousands of miles away. I was passionate about this work. I was seemingly good at it or as good as an 18-year- old could be. Could I actually turn this into a career? Could I help even more people across the world?

I'd like to think I did that. I'd like to think I did that. And I'm crying as I write this because I wonder if I ever will do it again. The past ten years, I've focused on conflict prevention, stabilization, preventing, countering violent extremism, and citizen security in conflict or post-conflict areas. Not only did I conduct desk research and analyze problem sets from behind a desk, but I got to travel to those countries and meet with local governments, civil society organizations and advocacy groups to hear from them about the issues and discuss solutions.

I spoke with survivors of the devastating 2004 tsunami in Sri Lanka, and Tamils whose fathers and brothers disappeared during the Civil War and are likely burned in unmarked graves somewhere on the island. I worked closely with a woman my age whose family fled Kosovo to the United States during the war when we were about nine years old and returned as soon as she could to her home country to promote continued peace between Albanians and Serbs. My recent trips to Kosovo were so illuminating, not because of the pain or struggle of these people, but because of the respect and admiration and gratitude they had towards the United States of America. Anyone who has been to Pristina knows of the Bill Clinton and Bob Dole statues {I didn't know about that} as well as the Hillary Boutique.

A few years ago when I was negotiating an employment offer with a Ghanaian candidate for a USAID funded Preventing Violent Extremism program, I couldn't meet his salary expectations. He said to me, "That's okay. I will take whatever you can give me. If the United States will make sacrifices for the people of Ghana in support of this program, I'm willing to make a sacrifice too with a pay cut." He proudly accepted the offer. The recognition of these funds could be spent elsewhere was not lost on him. Generosity and kindness are always more greatly appreciated by those who have less. All but one of my company's USAID contracts – which totaled nearly $400 million – were terminated almost overnight by DOGE. Over 80% of our Virginian based office was laid off or furloughed. I bought my first condo last year, a milestone we all strive for, but too few people my age are able to achieve.

I applied to 60 jobs in one month, all of which I'm qualified for. I have received two interview requests. This after being a sought-after professional in my industry with a

> strong network cultivated through years of hard work. This has ruined me. My mortgage payment isn't what makes me cry, though. It's our local staff and partners that come to mind every night as I say my prayers.
>
> My colleague, a Sudanese refugee living in Kampala, working on a terminated USAID peace-building program from Sudan, texts me every week to ask how I'm doing. He called me to make me smile because he knew I was crying. He now calls me Sad Eyes and has made it his mission to never see tears fall from these lashes again. I obviously lie to him and say, 'Mission accomplished', but it will never be true.
>
> Not only is the United States not stronger, not safer, not more prosperous, but the beacon of our democracy grows dim across the globe. Without leadership, other countries hostile to the United States will step in and innocent people will continue dying. When I close my eyes, the specter of very real people from my travels and projects appear, and I hear the echoes of suffering they shared with me. Suffering they were sure to note was alleviated, however, temporally by the United States of America, through USAID. And wherever they could, they would thank me. Whatever they could, they would thank me and America, they would thank me and America for it.

Thank you, Catherine Baker from Neptune, New Jersey, and Catherine. I see you. I see you. Catherine, I hear you. I stand for you, but I want to share something with you. One of the most extraordinary trips I've had as a United States Senator was to Chad, to go up to the border of Chad and Sudan, and see the horrors.

I've been to refugee camps all around the globe, but see the horrors of what was happening again in Sudan, you wore that 'Save Darfur' t-shirt in your earlier days, but the ethnic cleansing is going on right now. I've never seen so many malnourished babies, barely able to hold up their heads. People fleeing tyranny and they fled across the border to meet Americans, because we were there. With less than 1% of the American budget, we were there. Standing for our values, our highest ideals, our faith traditions, the understanding that when we are out there making the world safer, responding to crises, not only were people seeing the help they need, but they saw the light and the beacon of this democracy.

And it pains me that Chris Coons comes down here and shares the headlines from today's newspaper that in Myanmar, in this horrific earthquake, the agency that used to respond to that tragedy – that human tragedy – doesn't have the resources. America's not there. It's a void. And then, Chris Coons says in the article I'm surely to read today or tomorrow, whenever I can't stand anymore. He says, "Who fills that vacuum? Who showed up, but the PRC — China showed up." Less than 1% of our budget, *less than 1% of our budget*. And people like the folks I read, whose whole life, all they wanted to do was to be the light of the American torch of freedom and hope to the world. And they had the rug pulled out from under them. But here's what's worse, because we've had Chris Murphy, we've had meetings with some of the people behind the scenes that are savagely cutting and the stories are horrible. People in dangerous places that we sent there, having their emails cut, having their phones turned off, pregnant women who don't know how they're going to get out of those areas. And James Mattis, as we discussed, said, "If you cut these kind of programs, buy me more bullets, because there'll be more instability. There'll be more political democracies being overthrown. There'll be more terrorism, there'll be more violence."

And we are old enough as a nation in 250 years to know that if we don't meet these terrorists abroad, they will visit us at home. As Chuck Schumer said, "I was there watching the towers come down."

And in the Sahel – in the Sahel before, I do this in Africa – that's the threat in Togo and Ghana, in Benin, the northern parts of their country, they're fighting terrorism.

SENATOR MURPHY: Gentleman, yield for a question?

SENATOR BOOKER: Oh God, yes, I will. I yield for a question while retaining the floor. Chris Murphy.

SENATOR MURPHY: We have a few more colleagues who are going to join us before the top of the hour, but I just wanted you to round this out and ask you the question this way. Often when we talk about the withdrawal of USAID from the world, the withdrawal of the United States from international bodies like the WHO [World Health Organization], the beneficiary is China.

But I think you were hinting as you talked about the African continent, that the threat is much broader than that, because USAID is not just doing counter-China programming, it's also doing counter-extremism programming. In Lebanon, for instance, it's doing the primary work to push back against Hezbollah's political influence there. It's doing work to counter Russian influence around its periphery. And so, isn't it the case, Senator Booker, that as USAID is pulled off the playing field for reasons we still don't understand, that it is all of our adversaries, state adversaries and non-state adversaries, who are tragically celebrating at this opening that we have given them to gain additional influence?

SENATOR BOOKER: Senator Murphy, that is correct. You've been one of the most articulate voices for this decision. I shouldn't even call it decision. This reckless trashing of USAID, this vilification of the proud men and women that stand in Ebola outbreak, that stand against terrorism, that stand against hardships and ethnic cleansing, that stand against malnutrition. You're so good at pointing out that those are American interests and that not to do that makes this a more dangerous and unsafe world. A world where countries like ours want to lob missiles into Yemen post-facto of crises. So I hear you, Chris Murphy, and I answer your question with a simple understanding that what you're saying is right.

And I'm going to tell you that I've got so many other to read, but we are way behind the schedule of where we wanted to be at this point. We're way behind at about 16 hours and 24 minutes.

11:25 AM - Housing

And so, to obey my staff, as senators are told to do, I want to move quickly to just the housing issues. I'm sorry, unless of course. So I want to move quickly to housing and start really with the theme of affordable housing. Again, we keep returning to the economy and how the Trump administration is making things worse in every area, especially for people struggling. And so, let me be clear that for decades under Democrat and Republican presidents, it's become increasingly difficult for working-class Americans to afford a home. In recent years, this nationwide housing affordability crisis for so many Americans has nearly reached a breaking point. The crisis now impacts nearly all Americans shared across all demographics, regardless of partisan identification, race, age, gender, education, or whether you own or rent your home, we in America are in a housing crisis. According to the Center for American Progress, 80% of Americans living in rural communities believe housing affordability is getting worse.

While 72% of residents in urban areas feel the same way. In October 2024, the Center for American Progress found no matter your zip code, the goal of homeownership in America's drifting further out of reach all across the country. Over the past two decades, housing costs have dramatically outpaced income growth in the United States, increasing the rent burden, heightening barriers for homeownership. The housing price index, a gauge of house selling prices for single-family homes have changed over time was more than 50% higher in July 2024 than it was in July 2019.

According to the Brookings Institution, the US housing market was short 4.9 million housing units in 2023 relative to the mid-2000s. Decades of policy at the federal, state, and local level have all contributed to this reality. Let's not blame some rank partisanship. It's been decades in the making. There are few too homes in the United States and there are few too homes being built in the United States. The cost of housing keeps rising, rents continue to skyrocket. Median home prices are on the rise, which makes it harder and harder for families to make ends meet. The vast majority of young Americans are hard-pressed to save for the chance of one day having enough for a down payment to buy a home. Almost half of all renters in America struggle to pay their rent. Almost half of all renters are struggling to pay the rent, devoting more than one third of their income to housing costs.

Since the pandemic, rents have jumped more than 12% year over year, hidden rental fees and other expenses on already cost burdened tenants continue to mount, as landlords assume more and more power and leverage leaving tenants and prospective home buyers with nowhere to turn. Last year, NPR methodically walked through the supply shortage that's impacting our country. But before I read this article, I see that my colleague, my friend, extraordinary leader from Maryland is here and I think he has a question for me first.

11:29 AM - Empty Promises

SENATOR CHRIS VAN HOLLEN (MARYLAND): Will the Senator yield for a question?

SENATOR BOOKER: I will yield for a question while retaining the floor.

SENATOR VAN HOLLEN: Well, I want to thank my friend and I want to start by thanking the Senator from New Jersey, the senior Senator of New Jersey for shining a spotlight on what is happening in our country at this moment and specifically what is going to be happening here in the United States Senate later this week or next. And I have a question for the Senator, but I want to take some of the threads of what you've been saying as I put this to you because you are shining a light on the great betrayal, and that is candidate Trump went all over the country saying that he was going to be a president for the forgotten Americans, that he was going to be a president that looked out for working people. And he said he was going to focus on bringing costs down and prices down in the United States of America. And yet ever since he was sworn in, he has done just the opposite.

Prices are going up, including as the Senator was talking about, housing prices. Affordable housing is a crisis in this country, and yet we see Elon Musk and his DOGE cronies cutting deeply into affordable housing programs over at the Department of Housing and Urban Development. We see also, and tomorrow he calls it Liberation Day. It's actually going to be Sales Tax Increase Day. There was testimony that we got in the Banking and Housing Committee that when you increase these tariffs on Canada as he's proposed to do, not in a targeted way, but in across-the-board way, according to the National Association of Home Builders, that will increase housing prices for Americans up to 10% more, at a time we're already facing an affordable housing crisis. And of course, the folks who benefit the most are those billionaires who are part of his cabinet and others in the hedge fund industry, who are going out and buying up a lot of houses, not because they need the house for their family, but because they want to flip it at a big profit, making it even less affordable to the American people.

So the housing crisis is one part of what is getting even worse, because of the actions of Donald Trump and Elon Musk. And it's part of this greater theme of the great betrayal. And later this week, Republicans here in the Senate say they're planning to bring the floor, what we call a budget resolution, which is a framework that will be providing for very big tax cuts for the ultra-rich Americans, tax cuts for big corporations, some of which are offshoring all of their profits. Senator Wyden and I were on the floor just last week talking about how Pfizer has half of its sales revenues here in the United States, but books none of its profits here. And therefore by this scheme called round-tripping, where you sort of push your money around the world, they lower their taxes, which means the

American people get short-changed. So all of this is part of a scheme to provide tax cuts for the very wealthy at everybody else's expense.

And the Senator from New Jersey has been shining the light on what it means when we say this will come at the expense of other Americans, that this tax cut for the very rich and big corporations will come at the expense of the rest of America. So I want to amplify that as I do a wind-up to the Senator. Number one, it's Elon Musk and the DOGE operation. Let me be very clear that this is part of the most corrupt bargain we've seen in American history. Elon Musk spent $280 million to help elect Donald Trump president, and Donald Trump has turned the keys to the federal government over to Elon Musk. Not for efficiency, but to rig the government in favor of people like Elon Musk. That's why they want to get rid of the Consumer Financial Protection Bureau. This is a bureau that has returned billions of dollars to Americans who were cheated by scam artists and they are coming in to dismantle the CFPB, because they want to be on the side of the scam artists and deny American consumers the benefit of getting their dollars back when they've been cheated.

So this has nothing to do with government efficiency. It has to do both with rigging the government for people like Elon Musk and trying to lay the groundwork, claiming lots of cuts that they will then use to pay for, they say, tax cuts for the very rich. So who's being cut by Elon Musk? I don't know, Senator, just if you saw the other day in the sort of spin room at the White House, did you catch that, where Elon Musk and some of his folks were explaining the work they did? They said, "We're really doing this with a scalpel."

Well, the reason that's especially interesting is it was just weeks earlier that Elon Musk brandished a chainsaw at CPAC, which is actually they met over here in my state of Maryland. That's what they're doing. They're taking a chainsaw and they're taking a chainsaw to departments that help our veterans. These are people who care for our veterans and our veterans are being especially hard hit, including when they did these firings, arbitrary firings of probationary employees and veterans were saying, "Why are we being hit so hard?"

And the White House spokesperson said, and I'm quoting, "Perhaps they're not fit to have a job at the moment."

That was the response from one of the White House spokespersons, as if individuals who'd served our country in the military were not fit to serve our government as civilians. That's the kind of attitude we've got. We just learned today that the RIFs, the reductions in force letters, were received by folks in the Department of Health and Human Services. So these are people who help with the public health of all Americans and they do important work at the FDA, the Food and Drug Administration, right? They make sure that the foods that we eat and the medicines we take are safe and that they do what they say they're going to do in the case of medicines. They do work at NIH, the National Institutes of Health to develop cures and treatments for diseases that hit every American family. And they're cutting there. They're cutting in these places not for government efficiency, but to create what they believe is the space for tax cuts for the very rich. We talked about what they're doing over the Department of Health, Department of Housing, and Urban Development. At the Social Security Administration, which by the way has its headquarters in my state of Maryland, we have thousands of workers who are there to deliver hard-earned benefits to the American people.

And the reality is that the Social Security Administration operates incredibly efficiently. The former commissioner for Social Security, Martin O'Malley, reminds us that Allstate, insurance company, operates at an 11% overhead. Liberty Mutual operates at a 23% overhead, the Social Security Administration 0.5% overhead. The Social Security Administration workforce is now at a very low level in terms of personnel compared to what it was years ago. And yet they're serving a record number of Americans, 73 million Americans, and they've never missed a payment. Never missed a payment. So this talk about going after social Security and they're going to somehow make it more efficient. And of course, Elon Musk called it a Ponzi scheme, when the Senator and I know it's not a Ponzi scheme, it's a promise to the American people. So first they discontinued telephone service, as if all the seniors could somehow just connect by WiFi or whatever it may be.

A lot of people, of course, rely on telephones. So they cut that. They said, "Well, if you have trouble, go to one of the local regional social security offices."

Well, they're cutting regional social security offices, lots of them. And then, when you go there and you don't find many people there, well, whoops, we just cut 7,000 people from Social Security. So a benefit isn't meaningless if you can't actually access the benefit. And what they're doing is making it harder for Americans to get those benefits. So when we hear about the Musk DOGE operation, make no mistake. Not about efficiency. It's about trying to put together some kind of savings that they then want to use to at least partially pay for tax cuts for the very rich. Another way they're doing that, we've heard a lot about that, Senator has spoken about it, is cutting Medicaid and food nutrition programs.

In fact, I think we recall a number of weeks ago, we had a couple of amendments here on the floor of the Senate saying, "Okay, if you're going to do these tax cuts, at least don't cut Medicaid or Medicare, or food and nutrition programs."

Every Republican Senator voted against those amendments. In other words, not to protect those programs, meaning they're fair game for big cuts to pay for tax cuts for the very wealthy. So that's another area where they're very focused, which is cutting important programs that benefit millions and millions of Americans. There's another way they're doing it. And Senator from New Jersey, and again, thank you for shining a light on all this, has talked about it, which is these across-the-board tariffs.

So I think all of us know that strategically targeted tariffs, they can be useful, certain points in time, to protect strategic American industries. I'm for those. But across-the-board tariffs, and across-the-board tariffs on a friend and ally like Canada or Mexico? All that is, is a tax increase on the American people. Let's be clear. So these are the areas where Donald Trump having said that he was going to be there for working people, is doing the opposite, right? These across-the-board tariff cuts are going to increase costs and prices for the American people. Cutting Medicaid and food nutrition programs is going to hurt the very people that Donald Trump on the campaign trail said he was fighting for. And the DOGE Musk operation is taking a chainsaw to important services and important consumer protections that benefit all Americans in order to claim that they're providing some savings for tax cuts for the rich.

So it wasn't that long ago that just down the hall here, Donald Trump was sworn in as president and I remember what he said. He said, "This is going to be a golden age for America."

And who was sitting right behind him? Elon Musk, the richest person in the world, and other billionaires in the Trump cabinet, including one who just said not that long ago that Americans on Social Security wouldn't miss one of their social security checks. Only the fraudsters would notice that. Say that to the 73 million people who get social security. But that's the attitude of the billionaires in this Trump cabinet, the people he's really looking out for. And so, when he says a golden age for America, that's who he means. He means Elon Musk and the billionaires, Elon Musk who's rigging the government for the billionaires, and all the others in the cabinet who don't think Americans would miss a social security payment that they earned.

So my question to you, and I want to again thank the Senator from New Jersey. I know it's been a long day's journey into the night, but it's important that we address these issues in the courts and the courts are upholding the rule of law, that we address these issues and fight them in Congress, and that we do so in communities across the country and people need to understand what's happening. So the core issue here, is it not, my friend, that Donald Trump really is betraying the people he said he was going to fight for. And at the end of the day, and we're going to see that later this week in the Senate, the goal is to provide these big tax breaks to wealthy people at the expense of everybody else in America. That is the big betrayal. So if you could just zero in once again on the central narrative that we're seeing play out during the Trump administration.

SENATOR BOOKER: Well, you are putting it right. Donald Trump made commitments to America. We have quotes of him rally after rally. I'm going to bring your, he used to, "Oh, grocery, that's a really great word," I think he said. "I'm going to bring down grocery prices."

Well, grocery prices are up dramatically. The American dream, and many of us see that as owning a home. Well, you said it, home prices are already up, but with these tariffs, they could go upwards of 10% more. You can be sure that Canadian lumber coming down here is going to be expensive. You can see Donald Trump making it more difficult to access healthcare. And this massive Reconciliation is going to be a direct attack on working-class healthcare, on healthcare of expectant mothers, on healthcare of Americans with disabilities, on healthcare of the majority of seniors in nursing homes.

I'm about to go, my next chapter is all going to be about how Trump is rolling back commonsense protections for clean air and water. And Elizabeth Warren said it very powerfully. He's reducing services, which is a service cut to people with social security. In so many ways, Americans should see these crises looming, these attacks. But ask yourself one economic question. With the stock market who just had its worst quarter in years and people's retirement savings, if they have it in 401Ks is going down, ask yourself this question. I ask America to please ask yourself this financial question, am I better off than I was 71 days ago? Am I better off or worse off? And this is before he's even gotten going, because we see what's about to happen with this whole sham reconciliation process. They're already trying to change the rules to obscure what they're doing. This is what they're doing.

Three things you should take home. Are we going to let them again, like they did with the ACA, with the Affordable Care Act, come after healthcare for 70 plus millions Americans by doing their proposed $880 billion cuts? Or are we going to allow them to blow a hole so big in the trillions of dollars, they're going to push it out for over ten years? Are they going to create such a deficit in our country that our children's children, they're stealing from our children's children and putting on a deficit that they're going to have to pay for? And number three, are they going to let them do all of that to renew tax cuts that the Congressional Budget Office and every independent agency says very clearly would give trillions of dollars of tax cuts that go disproportionately to the wealthiest in our nation. That's the addition.

That's what we know. And it doesn't account for the things that he's doing to our allies. It doesn't account for how he's turning his back on NATO. It doesn't account for how he's praising Putin and calling Zelenskyy a dictator. It doesn't account for how he's giving advantage to China around the world from the region in Southeast Asia all the way to Africa. It doesn't account for how he's already made it harder to enroll for the Affordable Care Act. It doesn't account for all the other things he's doing that we wake up and hear every day. Not to mention trying to threaten Greenland, trying to threaten Panama, trying to change the name of the Gulf of Mexico. All these things he didn't tell us he was going to do, didn't promise. He promised to lower your grocery prices. They're higher.

He promised I'll be a better steward of the economy. It's worse than when inherited. Over and over, he's breaking promises and doing outrageous things, like disappearing people off of American streets, violating fundamental principles of this document, invoking the Alien Enemies Act from the 1700s that was last used to put Japanese Americans in internment camps. Do we see what's happening? How much is enough? That we have to stand and do something different, not just in this body. In America. Because you know this, how we stopped him in his last term was the American people rose up, spoke up, stood up, rose up, in the most extraordinary nonviolent demonstrations and demands. So thank you.

SENATOR VAN HOLLEN: Will the Senator yield for another question?

SENATOR BOOKER: Yes, I will yield for a question while retaining the floor.

SENATOR VAN HOLLEN: And I see that my friend and colleague, Senator Alsobrooks from the great state of Maryland is on the floor. So I'm going to be very brief with this question. And I want to thank you for reminding us of course, of the other great betrayal that's been going on over the last 70-plus days. There's the betrayal against the American people and working people here at home, but then there's the betrayal of our allies, like the Ukrainians who Donald Trump is throwing under the bus as we speak, and other close partners and allies around the world. And I have to depart here for a moment, because we have a hearing in the Senate Foreign Relations Committee, and I'm privileged to serve on that committee with the gentleman from New Jersey and one of the people before the committee is their nominee to be our ambassador to Turkey.

Now of course, Erdogan just locked up his major opponent, the popular mayor of Istanbul. We've not heard a peep from the Trump administration about the question of how this undermines democracy. But I want to close on the point that you just raised. It's kind of hard for Donald Trump to complain about Erdogan disappearing people, when right here in the United States of America, you had a Turkish student at Tufts disappeared by people who showed up without any identification, some with hoods on, and sent her apparently to Louisiana, because she spoke out on an important issue of national concern. And the First Amendment is pretty clear. You can engage in controversial speech that someone may like or dislike, but you're protected. And that includes everybody here in America, because that's an important value to us. Apparently it's not an important value to Donald Trump, who like Erdogan, essentially wants to whisk away anybody who disagrees with him. I thank again the Senator from New Jersey and just ask him to elaborate on that. But I also see my friend and colleague, the Senator from Maryland.

SENATOR BOOKER: Answer to your question, which is the irony, the irony that this president is remaining quiet about folks that are violating international law in many ways. So I think it's absurd, and you're right, it's another betrayal.

11:51 AM - Tax Cuts and Housing

SENATOR ANGELA ALSOBROOKS (MARYLAND): Will the Senator yield for a question?

SENATOR BOOKER: I yield for a question while retaining the floor.

SENATOR ALSOBROOKS: First, I'd like to commend my colleague. I want to thank you, first of all, for your spiritual obedience. Want to thank you so much as well for your commitment and your dedication, and want to thank you as well for your courageous leadership. I want to thank you also, Senator Booker, for your recognition of the times that we are living in. These are times that we will recount, our children will recount. And I think all of those of good conscience who watch during this time and say nothing will also be held to account. As the senator has eloquently remarked, these are not normal times. We're watching an administration that is drunk with vengeance, hatred, and surrounded by incompetent people who are taking callous actions, who are inhumane, and because of their incompetence are making costly mistakes that will harm the American people and denigrate the hardworking people of this country by proposing tax cuts.

And these tax cuts are not designed to help the average American person. They are designed to help billionaires, and they're doing so by firing thousands of middle-class workers and more. What we are seeing before our eyes is not only unconscionable, we know as well that it is deeply immoral, that it is inhumane, it is wicked. We are seeing with glee the actions of people who are so happy to tear down. But I am watching and waiting to see what it is they intend to build in this country. And in your remarks over these hours, you have made that plain for the American people to see. You've uplifted the stories of everyday people. And what we recognize is we hear about the firings and we hear about the devastation and chaos, is we're not talking about numbers, we're talking about humans, about people. These are our friends, these are our family members, these are our neighbors, these are our church friends, these are our colleagues who this administration has harmed. And so, my question today centers around the topic of housing.

We have a housing crisis in this country, that's no secret. And in fact, we recognize that through the actions of this administration, what is harmful will be exacerbated. Maryland is nearly 100 thousand housing units short, and, as you know, it is both about an affordability and a supply problem. We need to make home ownership, which is part of the American dream, and how the average American builds wealth in this country, accessible to more Americans.

I think about my parents, Mr. Senator, who married at 21 and 22 years old. And at the time that they married, although my father was a car salesman and selling newspapers, and my mother was a receptionist, five years into their marriage they could afford to buy a home. This is no longer the expectation of the average American family. My own 19-year-old daughter doesn't have the realistic hope that she can follow even her grandparents.

This problem affects red states and it affects blue states, which is the theme that you have hit on in all of these hours of speaking. When this president acts against the interest of the middle class, we recognize that he is not just harming Democrats, as he intends, but unfortunately his actions harm everyday Americans.

It affects those who voted for him, it affects those who didn't vote for him, and it affects those who did not vote at all. He's harming Republicans too. He's harming Americans. And so this administration is slashing funding and personnel at the very agencies that are tasked with addressing this crisis. He is illegally firing HUD employees. And this administration has stalled millions of dollars in previously allocated funding intended to help those who need affordable housing. And again, his actions are so indiscriminate, so immoral, so callous, so heartless, that he is impacting the very people who supported him, as well as those who didn't.

This administration has effectively ended enforcement of the Fair Housing Act, one of the most important American civil rights laws. This administration is considering privatizing the Federal Housing Finance Agency, which guarantees over half of the US mortgage market. And to make matters worse, this administration is proposing sweeping tariffs on our allies, driving up the cost of home construction. And let's be clear, absolutely none of this will help to build homes. None of this will make home ownership more accessible to Marylanders or Americans. And in fact, we understand that it is not the intention of this administration to do so, it's for the billionaires to be able to afford their tax cuts.

And so I've heard from people all across my state, blue areas, red areas, purple areas, every area, who are concerned about this. And so I have a question for you. And I want to thank you as I ask the question for sacrificing your own body today to bring attention to this. What are you seeing in the state of New Jersey about how this administration's unconscionable actions are making housing less affordable and home ownership less accessible?

SENATOR BOOKER: The senator, I want to thank her for the question. I want to thank her for being my colleague. But more important than even being my friend, she is a spiritual sister of mine. And was very kind to me when I was telling her that I was going to do this. And gave me so much encouragement and prayer. And I just love you and I'm grateful.

And you read the litany of things. I had a whole section, whole binder that my staff told me to skip and go to this one, about all the things. Going in deep, in depth to all the things the Trump administration is doing to make housing more unaffordable, more unaccessible, more expensive, more discrimination in housing, which we know is still a problem, more challenges, more pain heaped upon rural areas, and more complications and problems for building affordable housing in all areas.

It is so frustrating to me that this is a problem. We cannot lay the crisis of housing at one administration in the United States, we need to have bold visions and ideas to address this. I am so excited about this next generation of Americans that are rising up with bold visions. And I want to give a shout-out to Ezra Klein, his book is a must-read, Abundance. This is a vision of doing great things again, of building housing, of redeeming the American dream.

But to have a president that is dead set on for the next four years to do the kind of things that you made a litany of, and now tomorrow is going to bring tariffs that are going to raise the price even more of housing is outrageous. Where are his promises to make this country more affordable and more accessible?

You heard the data that I read, about we have so many millions of Americans, close to the majority of renters now spend more than a third of their income on rent. Which is the very definition our government has of housing insecurity. So it should anger people in this country. Even if you own your home, have paid off your mortgage, you should be angry about what they're doing to the American dream. And that there's no bold ideas coming from this administration to help. In fact, they're hurting. They're hurting.

11:59 AM - Energy and Environment

So thank you very much to my colleague [Senator Angela Alsobrooks]. Thank you for giving me strength, as you did in prayer. And I just thank you for the question that should anger people, that should inspire people, that should activate people, that should engage people, that should demand from us that we take our country away from those who want to do so much harm. I want to start by reading until someone... I know, the prayer, I'm going to keep going. I want to talk about environmental protections and how this country is becoming less safe for people with emphysema or with asthma, because Donald Trump is rolling back common-sense environmental protections, threatening our children's future and hurting our nation's economy.

Energy costs in America are continuing to rise, making it harder and harder for working families to pay their bills. And at a time that we should be investing in clean energy, this administration is canceling projects that would create more jobs for Americans and lower energy prices. He claims he supports an all of the above strategy, but that's clearly not what we're seeing.

And there's too much silence about it. All Americans, regardless of where you're born, we deserve safe drinking water, clean air, and an equal opportunity for a healthy and fulfilling life.

President Trump promised America the cleanest air and the cleanest water, but on entering office he immediately instructed the EPA, the Environmental Protection Agency, to cut a long list of common sense environmental protections. This administration is rolling back efforts to reduce emissions from power plants. He's letting polluters pollute our air more. That affects the health of Americans. It drives up, aggravating the rates of asthma and emphysema. Weakening rules that keep our rivers and our water systems clean as well.

12:01 PM - Prayer

SENATOR JOHN CURTIS (UTAH), PRESIDING OFFICER: Pursuant to the order of February 29th 1960, the hour of 12 noon having arrived, the Senate having been in continuous session since yesterday, the Senate will suspend for a prayer by the Senate Chaplain.

SENATE CHAPLAIN BARRY BLACK: Let us pray. Lord of hosts, you have done great things for us, filling our hearts with determination to do your will. You protect us from unseen dangers, supply us with wisdom and direct our steps. Today we are grateful for the efforts of the floor staff, the capitol police, the stenographers, the pages, and all those who have worked through the night. We pray you give them the strength they need for this day.

Today, give our Senators the assurance of your presence. Inspire them with a calm faith, a steady peace, and a firm resolve to do your will. Let no weapon formed against them prosper.

We pray in your omnipotent name. Amen.

SENATOR BOOKER: I'm going to continue.

SENATOR CURTIS: The senator from New Jersey is recognized.

SENATOR BOOKER: Thank you. I'm going to continue until one of my colleagues asks me a question.

12:03 PM - Agriculture and Frozen Obligations

SENATOR TAMMY DUCKWORTH (ILLINOIS): Senator, yield for a question?

SENATOR BOOKER: One of my heroes in the Senate — a living legend. My partner on some bills that I'm so passionate about, about expanding IVF. Someone that is just freaking awesome. I yield for a question while retaining the floor.

SENATOR DUCKWORTH: Thank you, Senator Booker, for taking this important stand and for doing so much to make it clear how much pain Donald Trump and Elon Musk are inflicting on the American people in every sector of our society.

I'm going to be asking you a question about what you've heard from agricultural businesses in your state, about the damage that this administration is doing, and the jobs that either have been or will be lost as a result. But I thought I would give you some background on what I'm hearing as well.

I want to focus this body's attention on our nation's farmers and ranchers, who seem to be getting punched day after day, week after week by the Trump-Musk oligarchy. Whether it's their harmful tariffs that hurt our soy and corn farmers, canceling and freezing more than one billion dollars in funding for schools and food banks who purchase food from local farmers, or halting reimbursement and contract payments that our farmers are already owed.

The Senator from New Jersey and I are both working together to undo some of the most harmful impacts of these disastrous decisions, including joining forces on to push his Honor Farmer Contracts Act forward.

We're also starting to hear reports from farmers about just how damaging the Musk-Trump dismantling of USAID is to jobs and businesses right here in America. For example, I don't know if this senator has heard, but in North Carolina, they had 2.2 billion in USAID awards, including for 27 large-scale farmers who were fulfilling orders for humanitarian food assistance, and four universities who were receiving agricultural research funding. More than 300 North Carolina workers have lost their jobs as a result of this freeze.

In Georgia, they had over $389 million in USAID awards, including nine large-scale farmers fulfilling orders for humanitarian food assistance, and six universities receiving agricultural research funding.

Arkansas had over $210 million in USAID awards, including purchases of rice, grain and beans from our farmers.

Florida has lost $91 million in USAID awards, including 38 million to the University of Florida to improve livestock productivity and food security in developing countries.

Texas lost over $48 million in USAID awards, including nine large-scale farmers, fulfilling orders for humanitarian food assistance, and eight universities receiving agricultural research funding. The list goes on and on.

My neighbors in Iowa over time now have lost over four million dollars in USDA food commodity sales. They had a total of over $149 million in purchases through USDA and other programs for USAID. Illinois has lost $245 million in farm income that would go towards USAID and food programs.

I think that our farmers have been hit with body blow after body blow from this administration, an administration that in their first term and even in the second term promised that they would look out for America. But I have to say to my friend from New Jersey, I don't think that this administration has lived up to their promises to farmers.

Remember that a nation that cannot feed itself, if we lose those family farms, if we lose our ag sector, we cannot lead the free world if we cannot feed ourselves. And frankly, farmers have been hit over and over again. These incoming tariffs are going to be disastrous for our farmers.

I was just in South Central and Southern Illinois, just across the Mississippi River from Missouri, talking to our farmers in St. Clair County, Illinois. And you know what they tell me? They tell me that the tariffs are going to affect their products being sold overseas — our top products in Illinois, corn, soybean, pork. We're also the largest grower of pumpkins, so if you get that Libby can of pumpkins at Halloween time and Christmastime and Thanksgiving, that's thanks to Illinois. (If you ever want to come, I'll just take you out to the pumpkin fields — the best pumpkins in the country.)

But frankly, they're being hurt over and over and over again. And so they're going to see the prices on their commodities affected. They can't sell their products overseas to the top countries that purchase their products.

At the same time, their inputs, the fertilizer, the equipment that they need will be more expensive. The tariffs against Canada in terms of steel and aluminum is affecting John Deere. John Deere, hundreds of years old, an American company founded in the heartland of this great nation, is laying off people.

And so we have to do better by our farmers. And our farmers have been betrayed time and time again by this Trump administration. They promise big things, but then they come in, and by cutting programs like USAID, they are hurting our farmers, their bottom line.

I sat down and I met with farmers who were seventh generation, eighth generation, watching the teenage son of the farmer. And they're afraid that they're not going to have a farm there anymore. Their products, their margins are so tiny that they don't think they're going to make it.

So my question to my colleague from New Jersey is what are you hearing from farmers? And why do you think this administration is taking so many actions that hurt them and hurt American jobs?

SENATOR BOOKER: I love my colleague. I love my colleague. I love how she's been standing up quite figuratively time and time again on issues. She's really inspired me. I've told folks that on social media I have been celebrating elevating, liking her content. She is truly fierce and is a voice that gives me strength.

And today she's asking me about one of my favorite subjects. A lot of people were surprised – my staff knows this story well – that I'm on the ag committee. And when one of my staffers, a guy sitting over here, Adam Zipkin, who's been with me since 1998, came to me and said, "You should go on the farm committee." This is going to get me in trouble. I laughed at him. Committees I loved. And what's that old saying? At first they laugh at you, then they fight you, and then they finally accept it. He told me all the issues I care about intersect with our farm and food system. That our farmers are such vital parts of America, they need more people standing up and fighting for them, because the American farmers are getting screwed. We're losing thousands of farms in this country. Family farmers are going belly up. The math doesn't work for them.

And this President, as you've pointed out, oh gosh, President Trump is causing an unprecedented amount of chaos, instability, and harm for farmers. Farmers already deal with so much uncertainty from prices, weather, pests and more, they should not have to deal with uncertainty that our government won't follow through, as you said, on contracts. On contracts.

I've had farmers from New Jersey to Texas coming to my office about this president freezing contracts that we approved in a bipartisan manner. Putting them in financial crisis. One of the first things that Trump and Musk did is freeze thousands of contracts and agreements that have been already made with our farmers. Farmers applied to grant programs and were selected on their merits. They made legally binding contracts. Yet, starting in late January, farmers found themselves not getting reimbursed, sometimes reading in the news that a particular grant was frozen, or sometimes no information at all other than that they were not getting their payments processed.

SENATOR DUCKWORTH: Would the Senator yield for a question?

SENATOR BOOKER: I yield for a question while retaining the floor.

SENATOR DUCKWORTH: Thank you. I think the issue of contracts is especially important, because so much of these cuts are claimed to cut waste in government spending. But we have a law in the books that says that if we don't make payments according to existing contracts, then we have to pay the interest on those payments that we are late in providing.

And so if we, for example, freeze funding payment on two billion dollars in contracts, as we did with USAID, that means that we're going to have to pay, say, 2% interest rates, $60 million in interest. I don't see where that is a savings for taxpayers. That is a waste of taxpayer dollars. I think that that is something that we should be talking about.

And I also think that, as you were mentioning, the issue with our farmers, they are important to our national security. The SNAP [Supplemental Nutrition Assistance Program] program is a good example of it. That program was instituted after World War II. We had the very famous example of Audie Murphy, who was the most highly decorated soldier coming out of World War II. He could not pass the initial test to enlist into the army during World War II because he didn't weigh enough, due to malnutrition post the Great Depression.

And so we created the SNAP program to make sure that America's young people were fed or no longer malnourished, so that they could get food in our schools while they were going to school. Because it was good for the United States military to have a workforce that could enlist in the military and meet the standards. That is the origin of the SNAP program, and that has been a program that has sustained our farmers over time. And I think that we are losing sight of that.

And so my question to the Senator from New Jersey is to hear a little bit more. Have you heard about the SNAP program? And also the work that the farmers in New Jersey have been doing in terms of organic and sustainable farming, which is really where the beginning of the organic and sustainable farming movement has begun in this country?

SENATOR BOOKER: Yeah, I'm aware of another one of my colleagues. I just want to say, yes, I'm aware of that. The way that Trump, I'm just going to summarize, contract freezes. This is one of the ways Trump and Musk are causing havoc, program cuts. They've eliminated programs, as you said, that support local food systems, including those that connect farmers with food banks and schools, and promote regenerative practices. It's stunning.

USDA destabilization: Trump and Musk have laid off USDA employees, closed USDA offices, hindering the agency's ability to provide essential services to farmers.

Tariff policies: Trump's tariff policies, implemented without consultation or support from farmers, will increase farmer costs and consumer food prices.

And finally, general chaos, which seems to be something, as you're pointing out, that they're very good at. Farmers already deal with so much uncertainty from prices, weather, pests and more. They should not have to deal with uncertainty from Donald Trump's administration that will undermine everything that they do.

SENATOR DUCKWORTH: I have a further question for the Senator from New Jersey.

SENATOR BOOKER: I will yield for a question while retaining the floor.

SENATOR DUCKWORTH: I would like to ask the Senator from New Jersey a question pertaining to the farm bill.

You speak to uncertainty. One of the things that I've heard from my agricultural sector and my farmers are farm rural in Illinois is the desperate need for this body to pass a farm bill, especially when it comes to crop insurance, the crop insurance program as well as, again, retaining SNAP benefits.

I do think that crop insurance is something that our farmers care deeply about. It is a tool that they use to make sure that they are able to survive when there are bad crop years, whether that is through disease, whether that is through drought or floods. Our farmers, certainly this is a program for them to sustain themselves and be able to look out for themselves. So it is a personal responsibility on the part of farmers.

It is especially important for young farmers who are just starting out. Those margins are so tiny. And when you take away the commodity program and the USAID, when you take away SNAP program, and then you don't provide them with crop insurance, you're going to lose those family farms.

And what is going to happen? Large agribusinesses are going to take over. And they don't have the wellbeing of the American people at their heart.

And so I would love to hear from the Senator from New Jersey, is would you agree that what we should be doing right now is not attacking farmers and cutting commodity programs, and cutting and freezing funding for USAID that it provides a market for farm products, but instead we should be working on passing a farm bill?

SENATOR BOOKER: Yeah. I love you, I love you, I love you, for bringing these things to point. And by the way, with Adam Zipkin, we did a farm tour. And we were in southern Illinois meeting with Republican farmers. This is now before the pandemic. And you see that we have so much common cause, as they're trying desperately to hold onto their farms.

And so the crop insurance program, we need to reimagine it so it's more accessible to independent family farmers, not just big agribusinesses. We need to be visionary about our farm building, to create a food system that the farmers want that help them to be better stewards of the land.

The oversubscribed programs for regenerative farming and cover crops and environmental practices, they want those things. To preserve their soil, reduce their dependence on chemicals, they want those things. They want a farm bill that works for them. And we should be delivering that in a bipartisan way.

So you are right on point. But do you hear that from the White House? Not at all. Not at all.

12:17 PM - Questions and Praise for a Colleague

SENATOR MAGGIE HASSAN (NEW HAMPSHIRE): Would the Senator yield for a question?

SENATOR BOOKER: I will yield for a question while retaining the floor.

SENATOR HASSAN: Well, Senator Booker, I have a question for you about Medicaid and Medicaid expansion. But I want to start with a little bit of background.

SENATOR BOOKER: Please.

SENATOR HASSAN: As you may recall, when I was Governor of New Hampshire, thanks to the Affordable Care Act, the program Medicaid expansion became an option for my state. And I worked with people of both political parties to make sure that the people of New Hampshire could actually get the benefit of Medicaid expansion.
  Expanded Medicaid meant that, for the first time, working adults who couldn't earn enough money to actually buy insurance themselves, but who were working and single could actually get healthcare coverage. Medicaid expansion meant that people with mental illness who wouldn't be covered by traditional Medicaid actually could get healthcare and could get coverage. People with substance use disorder, with addiction could finally get Medicaid coverage and get better.
  And we worked across party lines, took a few tries, but we got Medicaid expansion done in New Hampshire. And today Medicaid covers more than 180,000 people in my state, including more than 90,000 children, more than 15,000 people with disabilities and nearly 10,000 seniors.
  And here's another number that people don't always think about — it covers 10,000 people who are getting addiction treatment. My state, as you know, has been very, very hard hit by the fentanyl crisis. And just when the president gave his joint address in March, I brought a woman from New Hampshire with me who had been suffering from addiction.
  Medicaid expansion covered her treatment. She got into recovery. She's now working in the private sector, but also offering counseling and peer recovery services to people who are trying to get their addiction treated through Medicaid expansion. And she is now on private insurance.
  I remember talking to another Granite Stater while we were working to pass Medicaid expansion. She had been laid off from her job as part of the Great Recession. She had an ongoing chronic stomach condition. So as she got laid off, her health insurance went away too. And she couldn't afford the COBRA fee to keep her health insurance, so she couldn't get healthcare. So she got sicker and

sicker, so she couldn't go to work. But because she was a single adult, she couldn't get Medicaid coverage.

So here's somebody who has been working, wants to work, has a chronic illness, can't get to work. We passed Medicaid expansion, she got coverage, she got treatment and she got back to work. The other great benefit of Medicaid expansion covering people with addiction in New Hampshire has been that as people have gotten better, as more and more physicians have learned to integrate addiction care into primary care, we have a lot more people in recovery. And like many of our states, we also have a workforce shortage.

What's been happening now, New Hampshire is a leader in recovery-friendly workplaces. So that people who got this Medicaid expansion coverage, got their addiction treated, got better, can go to work in the private sector and get private insurance. That's some of the benefit of Medicaid expansion.

But of course what we are hearing about now from the House and Senate Republicans is their desire to make massive cuts to Medicaid, including Medicaid expansion. And they're doing it. They want to rip away healthcare from millions of Americans, so that they can pay for big tax breaks for billionaires and corporate special interests.

So the Republicans have proposed cutting up to a third of federal funding for Medicaid. If those cuts go into effect, that could mean 30,000 children in my state will lose their healthcare coverage. That means one in five seniors in New Hampshire could lose their nursing home care. And all told, that could mean 60,000 people cut off for Medicaid.

Including, for instance, a young man whose parents I just met at the airport actually who has autism. And Medicaid pays for his healthcare, but he could be cut off too.

So if Republicans continue with this plan, I am really, really concerned about what is going to happen to millions of Americans who currently get their healthcare through Medicaid.

So Senator Booker, can you address the ways in which Medicaid helps provide healthcare for Americans, and the disastrous impact it would have if Republicans proceed with their plan to take coverage away from up to 25 million Americans? Just so that they can pay for big tax breaks, by the way, for people who are already billionaires.

SENATOR BOOKER: So before I answer the Senator's question, I just want anybody who's watching to know that, I'll put it bluntly, this is one of the baddest-ass human beings serving here in the Senate. You have been a governor of a state with all the challenges. You are beloved. I've spent a lot of time in New Hampshire, folks. After New Jersey, it's one of my favorite new states. No disrespect to New Mexico over here on my right. But I love your state, I love the people of your state, and they love you.

You are an extraordinary governor. You are a trailblazer, a glass ceiling breaker, a name-taker. You are a badass. And to have served with you as my colleague, you have the kind of leadership in the Senate that is needed more of. Somebody that stands in the middle and draws people together to common sense and pragmatism.

I started on healthcare some 16 or so hours ago. And I read, you would be proud of me, because she's one of these voices that comes to me and says, "Hey Cory, let's bring people together." I know that the presiding officer, who's new here, but he has the same spirit of trying to bring people together. And this might be the third time I've seen him in the chair over the last hours. 17 hours. Thank you, sir.

But you whisper in my ear all the time, "we've got to find a way to do this together." We've got to find a way to put more 'indivisible' into this 'one nation under God'.

And so I hope that you would be proud, because I told my staff who prepared, days, days preparing all these sections from farming to environment, all the ways that Donald Trump is betraying his promises, betraying America, driving up costs, wrecking our economy, endangering us globally and here at home, and turning us back on a lot of our values, all while disrespecting this document more than any president that I've seen.

But I wanted to make sure, I told the instructions to my staff, "Pull from all the Republicans you can. We want to use the Wall Street Journal. We want to use the Cato Institute. We want to bring this together." Because what we're standing up here is not to talk about Left or Right, we're talking about what is right or wrong.

I do not want to talk about this being a Democratic moment, it is a moral moment. And you are the perfect Senator to be asking these questions about healthcare to me because of what you stand for. You, when you got elected as governor, twice I think, when you got elected to the Senate here, you had to get votes from Democrats, independents and Republicans or you can't win in New Hampshire. I've been in your state. I've met the people. And god, you have a very participatory democracy up there.

If people feel like if you're not going north to south house parties, you have to engage directly with the people. They don't care what party you ascribe to, they want to feel you, see you. They don't care how much you know, until they know how much you care. That's why I think you're such a badass leader.

And so you would've been proud of me when I did the healthcare section, because I read from Republican governors and Democratic governors. 40 states expanded Medicaid, and all of these governors, all of these voices said exactly what you're intimating here, is do not let Donald Trump cut $180 billion out of Medicaid. It will crush rural hospitals. It'll crush level one trauma care centers. It'll crush organizations that deal with beautiful disabled children. It'll crush people who are struggling for healthcare. It'll crush nursing homes. It'll hurt red counties and blue counties. It will hurt America. Republican voices were saying that.

And to have a bipartisan Senator who embodies the spirit this place should ascribe to more to say these things is affirming the truth. Why, why are they rushing to cut $180 billion which voice after voice that I read said it would do so much damage to people's lives, so much damage to healthcare providers, so much damage to hospitals?

Why? The only two things that will result from that is that they'll extend the Trump tax cuts, where the disproportionate benefits went to the wealthiest among us who are doing better than they've ever done in this country. They don't need it. Taking money from struggling folks and giving it to them is not the answer.

And then the other thing to a person who, like me, when we were executives, you were a governor, I was a mighty mayor, we had to balance our budgets. But they're not balancing the budget. They're not lowering the deficit, they're increasing it by trillions of dollars.

This makes no sense to a pragmatic person who has balanced budgets, who expanded healthcare access, who made her Senate state work, who has love and respect and votes, frankly, from Democrats and Republicans. You know this makes no sense.

And so if you're standing up and colleagues of mine further to the left of me, then why aren't other people? Why did only one Republican in the house vote against it? He told the truth. Massie. I see some of my Republican colleagues here. He's a fiscal hawk, he told the truth, "This budget is going to explode the American national debt stealing from future generations. I can't vote for this." He was not bullied, like other people in the house, into doing what *dear leader* Donald Trump says.

And so my colleague, you are on the money. I have internalized your voice. There's only a few people's voices I've internalized. One of them is my mother, but you're more my peer. You are one of those voices in America right now that we need that does not slip into a partisan argument, but makes the pragmatic argument that what Donald Trump is trying to do with the aiding and abetting of Congressional Republicans is wrong.

It is fiscally wrong. It is morally wrong. It will hurt Americans. It is not for the common welfare. It's not for the common defense. Read the start of the Constitution: Please, I beg of you, we all swore to uphold it. How do our founders begin? We the people of the United States, in order to form a more perfect union, establish justice, ensure domestic tranquility, provide for the common defense, promote the general welfare and secure the best blessings of liberty to ourselves and our prosperity.

Trillions of dollars of deficit doesn't secure the blessing of liberties. It endangers our country. The common welfare is this idea that everybody should have access to what makes us free. What makes us free is not having medical debt. What makes us free is not being chained to uncertainty and security that if someone in my family gets sick, I will not be [able to] afford it. Still the majority, or close to the majority, of bankruptcies in the United States of America are people who can't afford their healthcare bills. We need to find better ways to expand access and not cut more people off.

You know this, former governor. There are a number of states that have these things called triggers, automatic triggers that if the funding for Medicaid reduces to covering 90% of the costs, what happens in those states? Boom, Medicare expansion goes offline. So if you don't even cut it 880 billion, maybe you say, "We'll just do 250 billion of an ax," states are going to lose their expansion, people are going to suffer and get hurt. Why? You've said it, you've said it and you've said it.

You and I are the two people that want to see entrepreneurs make money. You and I want to see small business people thrive. We don't hate rich people. We think that's great. It's often (not always Donald Trump)... it's often a sign of people in America using the ingenuity, applying it and being successful. But you and I both know that the richest people in this country don't need more tax cuts. It is morally wrong. It is fiscally wrong. It is wrong in the name of God and America. How could we be doing this to ourselves?

SENATOR HASSAN: Will the Senator yield for another question?

SENATOR BOOKER: I can't call you one of the baddest-ass people I've ever worked with and not yield to your questions, but I have to read the words. I yield for a question while retaining the floor.

SENATOR HASSAN: Well, thank you for yielding for a question while retaining the floor, and thank you for the very nice compliments. I do have a question for you about Social Security and then I think another colleague of mine has additional questions. But look, as you know, you just talked about my wonderful state, New Hampshire. You also just talked about your mother and I should just also let you know that my mother always made me memorize the preamble to the United States Constitution. So as I listened to you read it-

SENATOR BOOKER: Shots fired on the Senate floor. Where's the parliamentarian?

SENATOR HASSAN: I hope my mom is watching right now.

SENATOR BOOKER: Rule 19 her*.

SENATOR HASSAN: But here's my question, and just by way of background, as you know, New Hampshire's a small state. It's a very rural state, and recently the Trump-Musk forces have announced that they want to close a Social Security office in Littleton, New Hampshire. Now Littleton, New Hampshire, that Social Security office, which takes applications and provides technical assistance for people who need Social Security or need Medicare or who have questions about their current coverage, it is the northernmost office in New Hampshire.

So they closed that office and now my folks in the north country, and there are about 334,000 people in New Hampshire with Social Security, right, my people in the north country will have to drive as far as one hundred miles to go to another New Hampshire Social Security office. And meanwhile, of course, they're laying off people from Social Security offices and they're making it harder to get assistance via the telephone, which as you know, many people who are on Social Security find the telephone the easiest way to make a connection, get technical assistance.

Elon Musk has called Social Security a Ponzi scheme. He says he wants to cut $700 billion from Social Security and Medicare. So my question to you as we're looking at an administration that says that it wants to make things more efficient but is actually laying people off, closing offices, making it harder for people to actually connect with the Social Security office, my concerns of course are that this is just going to delay claims, delay coverage, make it harder for people to get on Social Security because actually Trump and Musk want to cut Social Security. Trump said, of course, that he was going to protect it when he was running for office, but now he's letting Musk do his cuts.

So Senator Booker, can you speak to the ways in which seniors across the country count on Social Security benefits that they have paid into? This is not charity. People pay into the Social Security system. They earn the benefit. And can you talk about the disastrous impacts if this administration takes benefits, Social Security, Medicare, away from our seniors?

SENATOR BOOKER: Earlier or last night, I had a whole chapter on Social Security outlining not just what you said, my colleague, my friend, but stories from seniors and some of them really got to me. They were hard to read through. I have to say I had prepped this by reading a lot of them, but somehow on the floor when I read about the woman who had Parkinson's, when I read about the person taking care of their elderly parents, a spouse with dementia, children with special needs, and Social Security, it helps a lot of folks.

But here's the craziness, the craziness of the Trump attacks on the Social Security administration. First, he makes people insecure about it. My mom lives in this amazing senior home Las Ventanas in Las Vegas, Nevada. Most of the people there, first of all, I love them all for who they are, not their party affiliation, but it's more Republicans than Democrats. And the stories my mom tells me about just the worry that they or other people in their family have because of Elon Musk calling it a Ponzi scheme, of Donald Trump talking about utter lies from the highest post in the land during a joint address, savaging Social Security with lies that everybody from conservative papers to democratic papers to left-leaning papers have all called out, lie, lie, lie, lie, lie.

There are not millions of people receiving false payments. They've insinuated so much insecurity that people were writing me letters talking about they're losing sleep, they have so much anxiety because they only live on their Social Security check. And brother Howard Lutnick, who I know, and I don't know what he was thinking when he said it, a billionaire talking about his mother-in-law, I don't know what you were thinking, Howard. I just don't understand it how you're saying if she misses a payment, she's okay, but if people complain, they're probably fraudsters. Do you understand how many millions of Americans only have that as their only protection between poverty and destitution, that if they miss a payment, they can't make their rent, they can't buy food?

And so they've created so much insecurity, so much fear, and I compared it, Governor, I compared it to the difference between an FDR and a Donald Trump. FDR knew people were suffering. They knew people were afraid and he stood before the American public and didn't lie to them, didn't attack people, didn't demean people, didn't degrade people. He comforted people. He allayed their fears. He inspired them. "You have nothing to fear but fear itself." What an opposite in leadership.

And so yeah, there are a lot of people who right now don't know, but then my colleague from Massachusetts comes in and makes the very clear point, the professor we have in our caucus, she makes a very clear point. They've already done benefit cuts because when you close offices in rural areas that that person who is missing a check or has an issue, now they have to drive, how many miles?

SENATOR HASSAN: One hundred miles.

SENATOR BOOKER: One hundred miles. Now, what is that hardship to a senior? I heard from people in their 90s. They already are having benefit cuts. The Wall Street Journal – I told you, I was trying to make you proud, I wanted to get as many sources from anybody that was more centered or right – and I read from the Wall Street Journal and said the customer service in Social Security is going from bad to worse. That was the title of the article. So they're already doing cuts. They're already launching heaping insecurity on our seniors, heaping inconvenience on our seniors, heaping fear upon our seniors, heaping insecurity, making people lose sleep. This is wrong, wrong, wrong, wrong, wrong. This is not a model of leadership. It's a model of cruelty and mean-spiritedness and hurting people.

When is it enough, America? When is it enough that we say it may not be my grandmother that depends on that Social Security check, but I love America and you cannot love Americans, you cannot love America, you cannot call yourself a patriot... please listen to me... you cannot say you love this country and that you're a patriot because patriotism is love of country, but you can't love your country unless you love your country men and women. And love means that if somebody, some mother or grandmother is hurting, is afraid, that I'm going to stand up and do what I can to comfort them and fight for them, because today it might be your grandmother, it might be your family with a disabled child. This is not Right or Left, it is right or wrong. This is not a partisan moment, it is a moral moment. Where do you stand?

We started this by talking about John Lewis. It is time for good trouble, necessary trouble. Thank you. Thank you, my friend, even though you made fun of me for in my tired state not remembering the very important preamble to the Constitution.

SENATOR HASSAN: You're very welcome.

SENATOR BOOKER: Thank you very much. That actually means... I take your compliments because you don't give them abundantly or overly well, so thank you very much.

SENATOR BEN RAY LUJÁN (NEW MEXICO): Will the Senator yield for a question?

SENATOR BOOKER: Heck no. Not to you, not to you, not to you. Let me tell you, I have something to get off my chest about you. I woke up this morning, or this morning. I woke up yesterday morning and the first thing I did, now this shirt's all wrinkled and a little ripe, but the first thing I did is grab a gift from you. People don't get upset ethics-wise. We're allowed to give each other gifts. This was like, I don't know how much it costs, but you gave me... I was talking to you about traveling and how we have to pack bags and go all the time, and you told me, "I travel with a steamer," and I pulled out this little steamer for this shirt that I'm wearing right now.

You are one of the kindest, sweetest people I know. You're one of my closest friends here in the United States Senate, and I want to say something about you because in this moment if people are watching, I want people to go there. We had a conversation. You came to my office. It's always a sign of respect when you come to the Senator's office and you came to my office and we were talking about social media and I was encouraging you. You were a little resistant, if you don't mind me outing you, to open up and get more on the platform. We were talking about ideas and talking about Social Security, talking about Medicare, Medicaid.

You opened up to me, and I hope I'm not betraying confidences, and I asked you just like, "What do you do?" You are such an amazing human being. You're one of the kindest people I know. I asked you, "What do you do on your weekends? What do you do for fun? Let people see it." And then you kind of made me pause when you said, "Well, my mother's getting kind of old, is getting older. I love her so much," and you said that, "My brothers, my siblings and I, we alternate weekends just spending time with our mother." It was one of the sweetest things I heard.

And then I said to you, "What do you do with your mom?" And then you brightened up and you choked me up, you jerk, because you said, "What I love to do with my mom is to dance with her in the kitchen. When we're in the kitchen making food or something, I just love sometimes to put on a song and we dance." I don't know why it struck me as beautiful, and this is what I hope people will do right now. I said, "Well, why don't you record that?" And I didn't think you would do it, you would ask her if you could do it, but you then put up one of the most beautiful videos I've ever seen from one of my colleagues of you and your mom in the kitchen. I think it's on your Instagram page. And I have looked at that... I'm probably all the views right now of my colleague, this big United States Senator loving his mother so much.

And we are talking about that. I've talked about this on the floor. Great nations respect their elders. They take care of them. One of my colleagues, when they asked me a question about Social Security, they reminded me of what it was, the greatest anti-poverty program in the history of America, that Social Security rescued millions of Americans from being in poverty. It virtually ended poverty, although the checks now are becoming meager and meager as prices are going up more and getting lower and lower towards poverty, and people who live on those checks live very austerely.

But you're just this amazing guy that turns your own lived experience into greater and greater urgencies to fight for the people of New Mexico. So I did not want to yield for a question. So getting that off my chest, you are my friend, you are my colleague, you are my brother. And more than you know it, you're my inspiration. So yes, I yield for a question while retaining the floor now. I feel like I have so much power here to yield to my colleagues are often more eloquent. I'm afraid of Whitehouse because he's one of the brainiest people in the Senate, but I now have the control, but for you, now that I've gotten this off my chest and hopefully embarrassed you, but maybe added a few more views to my favorite video, I yield for a question while retaining the floor.

SENATOR LUJÁN: Well, Senator Booker, thank you. I won't be surprised if mom's watching right now, so you're probably going to get some messages from her. But I want to thank my friend and colleague from the great state of New Jersey. You've been holding this space for the American people now for well over 17 hours. While we represent different parts of the country, Senator Booker, we have the same values. I learned from you the importance of treating people with respect and dignity. That's what we should all be talking about here today, every day. I've also learned a lot about grace from you.

* Standing Rules of the United States Senate, Rule XIX, regarding accusations of incivility or disrespect (said in jest in this context)

12:44 PM - Food Concerns

SENATOR LUJÁN: Now, I come to the floor to ask you a question about farmers. You and I both appreciate the long hours that farmers put in to take care of that soil, their families, the planning that goes into this, sowing seeds. Sometimes you have to do a little weeding to make sure that we're going to all benefit from the fruits of their labor. Now, having fresh food in a grocery store is not something that can be taken for granted. And for a lot of our constituents, I've had these conversations with nominees that have come before us when they ask me, "Well, why is someone just eating potato chips or Doritos from that local store?" I'll educate them by saying, "That's the only store around."

SENATOR BOOKER: Yes.

SENATOR LUJÁN: There's food deserts everywhere, but we could do something about that. We have programs in place that recognize the importance of getting someone a meal that needs that meal, supporting our farmers out there to sow those seeds, to help them with their planting. But what I'm seeing right now, Senator Booker, is our farmers have been on the receiving end of these federal funds being taken away from the United States Department of Agriculture, these reckless tariffs that are hurting farmers and ranchers just as much as they're hurting anyone in America. Outbreaks — bird flu. People know what the cost of eggs are at the store now. And then they look into what's going on here. There's this bird flu that's going around and my constituents ask, "Why did the United States Department of Agriculture under Donald Trump fire the people, epidemiologists that are responsible for containing this thing?" It didn't make any sense to folks.

I was in the ag committee earlier today, Senator Booker, and I was asking some questions to USDA and I learned that on March 7th, 2025, under the Trump administration, the United States Department of Agriculture terminated the Local Food in Schools program and the Local Food Purchase Assistance Cooperative Agreement, and then they went further and they also notified grant applicants on March 24th that the fiscal year 2025 competition for the Patrick Leahy Farm to School grant program was canceled.

Why does this matter to farmers and ranchers and people back home? These programs allow food banks and schools and others to purchase food from our local farmers. Now, our local farmers aren't just making a decision on what seeds are going to be planted so they can sell the lettuce next week. They start this a year going back. So when the United States Department of Agriculture a year ago started talking to these farmers and ranchers about what programs were going to be in place, and then these farmers responsibly went and found customers to sell their food, food banks, different groups around the country, they planned the rest of the year to be able to get that nutritious food into the bellies of people that need it most. That sounds like respect and dignity. What's not respectful is when the Trump administration gives them a few days notice and pulls the rug from under them and cancels the program that's going to allow the food bank, their customer, to buy their food. What do the farmers have to do now across America?

Now, it gets worse and worse. I won't go into all of it, Senator Booker, but here's one of the dirty little secrets — all of these programs that are being taken away from the American people, it's to find an extra dollar for this tax policy under Donald Trump that my constituents started calling back in 2017 the Trump tax scam. Well, why are you calling it that? And they said, well, everyone promised me... I'm making less than the median income, making less than $80,000, which is a lot of money in New Mexico. Across America, the median income there is a little lower. I was told that we were going to get the brunt of this tax cut recognizing that we're hardworking and how hard it is to make ends meet. But that's not what happened. Most of this went to families and folks making over $2.8 million.

I don't have anything against those families. I wish them well. I want them to make more, ten million next year, but they don't need a tax cut. That should be going to those hardworking families that were told that they were being prioritized, but they're the ones that told us, told me anyway, that this was a Trump tax scam. That's the secret. That's where all this money's going.

So Senator Booker, whether I'm in a grocery store and I'm chatting with constituents, we're out there looking at egg prices or whatever it may be, they're concerned about what's going on here and all they're asking for me to share with my colleagues here is just tell them to tell us the truth.

SENATOR BOOKER: Yes.

SENATOR LUJÁN: If they're going to vote to take these programs away, they have the votes by Republican colleagues.

Just be honest. Treat my constituents with the respect and dignity so that they can plan, so that a single mom that has a child that whose Medicaid may get ripped away, but that child has cancer, how are they going to plan for care in six months, so that farmer who started planting seeds recently but was planning over a year on what to do so they could find another customer, so that they're not going to lose that farm as well.

Now, before I ask you this question, sir, I want to end with this. Senator Booker, you often share a story of Abraham Lincoln's inaugural address, his second, and the man whose review mattered most to the 16th President of the United States.

SENATOR BOOKER: One of my favorite stories.

SENATOR LUJÁN: When asked his opinion of Lincoln's performance, former slave and abolitionist, Frederick Douglass replied, "It was a sacred effort." Let me be the first to say this is a sacred effort, Senator Booker, and I'm proud to stand alongside you.

So, Senator Booker, the question that my constituents and I have for you is can the farmers and ranchers of America afford to pay for another Trump tax scam with all this nonsense that's going on? I mean, it's a question I get when I'm at church. I say not during church, but after church is okay, or at the grocery store. But when I'm visiting with folks back home, this is what they're asking me.

SENATOR BOOKER: And thank you for the question. You said the same words that literally... I didn't write these words. My staff wrote this little paragraph here. "Trump is pulling the rug out from under producers that need stability and reliable markets," because you and I sit right by each other in the ag committee and we see this connection that you so beautifully say, this idea that we are separate from each other, the invisible lines that divide us in this country are bunk compared to the strong ties that bind us. That farmer producer in a rural neighborhood is deeply connected to the person in my community, and I live in inner city Newark, New Jersey. There is a powerful spiritual connection.

And you talk to that farmer and they've got pride that they're feeding America and they have pride in the ground. You described it so beautifully. They have pride in their soil. They want to be stewards of the land and they want to create a vibrant American food system and they rely on people that empower them in that process and don't pull the rug out from under them, drag back contracts, cut programming, especially not those programs that help them get fresh fruits and vegetables, healthy foods to food banks.

You talk to the food banks, they'll attest that families how grateful they are for that fresh fruits and vegetables. You said it right. Parents want the best quality food for their kids, but this food system is killing them. And when I heard the new Secretary of HHS talk about, "Hey, we need to get greater access to fresh, healthy foods, food is medicine," things I've been saying for years, and what do they do when they get in there? They cut the very programs that help our farmers and get fresh fruits and vegetables to kids to deal with chronic disease. How could you say out of one side of your mouth, Trump, "Oh, I'm going to let the MAHA [Make America Healthy Again] people go their way," and then the first thing you do is cut the programs that help kids get healthy, nutritious foods? It makes no sense. It makes no economic sense. It hurts our farmers. It hurts our farm workers. It hurts our end users. It's not fair, and I appreciate your question, sir. Thank you.

12:44 PM - Looters and Polluters

SENATOR SHELDON WHITEHOUSE (RHODE ISLAND): Will the senator from New Jersey yield for a question?

SENATOR BOOKER: Let me think about this for a second.

SENATOR WHITEHOUSE: You take your time thinking about it, sir.

SENATOR BOOKER: I want to thank Senator Whitehouse. He's been a colleague and a friend for a long time and he stands right there at that desk for very long speeches. I think I'm trying to go a long time. You go a consistency of times and you've talked about the climate crisis. You've talked about the Supreme Court scams. You've not only educated members in this body on these issues, you've educated America. You are a YouTube star now, and I learn from you every time I hear you speak. So I'm a little worried right now, but I'm going to step out on faith and yield for a question while retaining the floor.

SENATOR WHITEHOUSE: So first question, it's been 17 hours. How are you doing?

SENATOR BOOKER: I shall not complain. I shall not complain. But thank you for checking in on me, my friend.

SENATOR WHITEHOUSE: Yeah, well thank you for what you're doing. Second question, if you would yield for a second question without yielding the floor.

SENATOR BOOKER: Yes, I yield for a question while retaining the floor.

SENATOR WHITEHOUSE: One of the ways in which I try to discuss what's going on in this country when people are horrified, anxious, astonished, whatever, is to describe it as the rule of the looters and the polluters. The looters are the creepy billionaires coming to government trying to figure out how to get even more for themselves. It used to be that people thought that there was a thing, too rich to steal. That doesn't seem to be a thing for these creepy billionaires. They're more than happy to wreck Social Security so that they can send in their tech bros and their private equity folks to put right what they have broken. And the looting goes on across the entire face of government, scarred and disfigured by Musk, and his little Musk rats, I like to call them.

And then of course you've got the polluters who are doing a similar thing, which is to steal from the public, only instead of stealing through government, they're stealing by dumping their pollution into our common air, into our common climate future, into our waters, into our lands, and defending through political influence and clout and power and dark money in this building their privilege to pollute for free. And the end point of both of those is regular Americans who are getting, to put it bluntly, pretty hosed so that people on the other side of that, the creepy billionaires who are behind the climate denial scheme, who are out to wreck the American government so that it can't regulate their conduct or make them behave like honest bankers and investors or insurers or whatever, react for a moment, if you would, to that framing of our beautiful country now being subject to the really malevolent whims of the big looters and the big polluters.

SENATOR BOOKER: Well, first of all, I will say to you that I meet wealthy people like a group called the Patriotic Millionaires who advocate for progressive tax policy and are the first to say and speak out against this tax scam. Again, to me, what does patriotism mean to you? Patriotism by definition means love of country. If you don't love your fellow country men and women, how do you love your country? So what would you do… I actually know what you would do, I don't even have to answer to this question… if somehow you would came into a billion or more dollars? You would not be asking for more. You would literally say, " Wait a minute, Republican Congress, wait a minute, Donald Trump, what you're trying to do is take away healthcare from expectant mothers, from disabled children, from seniors in order to give me more tax credit?" I would think that the patriotic thing to do that, the thing in love, in love, you would say, "Donald Trump, go screw yourself."

SENATOR WHITEHOUSE: If the Senator would yield for another question while retaining the floor.

SENATOR BOOKER: I yield for a question while retaining the floor.

SENATOR WHITEHOUSE: I would add to your comment and request your response to the observation that not only is this an appalling manifestation of greed by people who already have more money than they're able to spend in their entire lifetimes, but the manner in which they are accomplishing their purpose is pretty loathsome in and of itself because the manner in which they are accomplishing their selfish purposes is to corrupt and degrade this great American democracy that we are all here to defend.

SENATOR BOOKER: Yes.

SENATOR WHITEHOUSE: And they do it by taking their billions and running it through phony front groups so it pops up as dark money in elections, and of course the beneficiary of the dark money, the candidate figures out exactly who's behind the big dark money contribution that ends up in the super PAC that is supporting them, and of course the big donor knows that they gave the money, so the deal between the creepy billionaire and the in-hock-to-them political candidate is made. But because it's dark money, because it's secret, because it goes through front groups and into the super PAC and ultimately into the campaign, courts don't know, public doesn't know, voters don't know. Everybody else is left out of the joke.

SENATOR BOOKER: Yes.

SENATOR WHITEHOUSE: And so bad enough that they're here arguing for excess benefits for themselves compared to regular Americans. Worse, they're using dark money corruption to get there. So how is that patriotic?

SENATOR BOOKER: I want to answer this question so badly, but the crazy thing is the person best to answer this question is the person who asked it. You've sat here and given this detailed analysis to show how this group of very wealthy billionaires in this country are so perverting our system by creating these front groups that then interfere in our democracy in the most disgusting of ways.

Even if you are like me and you that can't stand the decision of Citizens United, even in Citizens United, the majority opinion really projected that we should do the Disclose Act, which we have tried to bring to this floor and get passed that says no more dark money. How do we have a political system that is so corrupted by billionaires who so with all of their money drown out the voices and politics of other Americans? A great example of that is they're getting so reckless that many billionaires aren't even hiding it anymore, i.e., Elon Musk.

SENATOR WHITEHOUSE: Elon Musk.

SENATOR BOOKER: He's saying, "Hey, I'm going to roll up into a Supreme Court case up in one of our best Great Lakes states, and I'm just going to dump a hundred million dollars there and then give away as if to insult our democracy, million dollar checks as part of my effort to influence an election with my overwhelming flood the zone amount of billions of dollars. And by the way, hey, it's a pretty good investment, right? Donald Trump's biggest campaign contributor, and as soon as he gets elected, a lot of my stock goes up," — although Tesla stock isn't doing so great right now.

The reality is we live in a country right now that we are giving more and more ability for billionaires to use their wealth to rig the system and then get more wealth as a result of that. It is so corrupt and so corrupting to this. [HOLDS UP POCKET CONSTITUTION] We have been talking about this, as you said, for 18 hours now, this big unchecked corporate contributions, billionaire dollars, dark money in front organizations that nobody in the Senate has outlined better than you is corrupting our Constitution. And even the bad case, Citizens United, even they said this shouldn't happen. You all should write laws in this place that force people to disclose where that money's coming from. But how many years has it been since Citizens United? Many. And how many times have we failed? Fifteen?

Guys, I don't know, and I'm so grateful for this man because all my colleagues who were assembled here know doggedly and determinedly, you have stood right there with charts and graphs.

You've outlined it ad nauseam. They've attacked you because your truth is so threatening to them that more people will know about how big money is corrupting democracy.

And so how many assaults are we going to have to watch in 71 days when we now have a president that can create a memecoin? Isn't there something here, my great constitutional scholar, a big word called emoluments? This president has basically created a memecoin where we now know, hard to trace this, that millions of dollars have been put into his pocket. I have my team reading about it right now — foreign countries, Russian oligarchs, incredible Arab wealth. You want to pay off the Donald Trump because his government is being run like this. It's not JFK, "Ask not what your country can do for you, but what you can do for your country."

You've seen how he's behaved? It's, "Ask not what your country can do for you; Ask what you can do for Donald Trump." That's how he does business. How do we know that? Look at the evidence of the last 71 days. If you are a law firm that comes to him and offers him $40 million of pro bono work... God, how many people I love in Newark who had that kind of legal representation, pro bono. He is beating you up, threatening to ruin your business until you come to him and tell him what you're going to do for him. We're seeing it. You want a merger? What do you do? Give a million dollars to his inaugural committee and then find ways to get money to him, through his memecoin, kowtow to him in any way possible.

Senator Whitehouse, nobody has outlined this more than you have. And I encourage people. I feel like now I'm advertising everybody's social media. Go to his YouTube. I call him a YouTube star. I'm not joking. You have on YouTube, I know, just great details and outline about how the corruption of money in politics is getting worse and worse and worse in this era of billionaires like Elon Musk who have no shame anymore. And I'm going to say it on the Senate floor. There are so many reports and stories of him threatening elected leaders — threatening to put a hundred million dollars in a primary challenge if they don't kowtow to what the Great Leader is telling them to do.

You use the word all the time, and I'm going to say it over and over. This is corrupting to our democracy and amounts to another assault on our Constitution. How much will we take America until we say enough, until we say no more, until we say pass the Disclose Act? Bring back the dark money, put light on it. Shine the light of truth on this web of dark money lies. How long will we endure this? I hope that you and I are in the Senate when you no longer have to give that speech because we took action on the Senate floor to end this nightmare of billionaires trying to outsize influence in our democracy.

1:06 PM - Impact on Veterans

SENATOR PATTY MURRAY (WASHINGTON): Will the Senator yield for a question?

SENATOR BOOKER: Not immediately. I just want to say to Patty Murray, thank you. You are a co-conspirator in my life of trying to cause good trouble. You are one of the most powerful people in the United States Senate, yet you have never lost your compassion and your care for people. You're like somebody else I talked about in the Senate, two of my favorite people who lives this ideal that I may be a United States Senator, I may be head of appropriations, I may be president pro tem of the Senate, but I will never lose my connection to the people I represent and to the convictions that brought me to this place. You are such an honorable soul. You're such a great American and you've been such a dear friend to me. This Congress, I savor the times where you let me come to your a lot more seniority than me. You've got a great hideaway with with a view, one day maybe.

But I just want to say thank you Patty Murray for being so kind to me and you're showing up right now gives me a lot of strength, puts more fuel in my tank. And so now, I feel all this power. Now, you outrank me in every imaginable way here and you're the head of our Democrat appropriation. So I am obligated by the state of New Jersey to be very obsequious to you.

I yield for a question while retaining the floor.

SENATOR MURRAY: Well, I thank the Senator from New Jersey. Thank you for your kind words. And I would just say the country is so grateful for what you are doing right now because so many people are so frightened, worried, scared and angry about what is happening to the basic values of this country that so many people have just thought would be there. That their kids would be able to go to school and get an education and not have to worry that the Department of Education was going to be gone and there wasn't a watchdog anymore or somebody to help them, or that the research at NIH was going to be dismantled. Perhaps they had a family member who was in the middle of some kind of scientific experiment that is now being dismantled, what happens to their hope?

I hear from people on so many topics, seniors who are waiting on hold for hours and then getting hung up on because there's nobody to answer the phone anymore. These are basic values that we have as a country, that we care for other human beings and we're there as a country for them. And you are showing that fight today and inspiring so many people. And I will ask you a question in a minute, but I wanted to personally thank you for what you are doing today. It is so important. You are the voice of so many people today and I so appreciate it.

Now, I want to change the dynamic a little bit. I wanted to come today, you have talked about the impact in so many areas in our country, but I wanted to come and ask you about something really personal to me and that is the impact on our veterans today. The Senator may not know this, but when I came to the Senate many years ago, I asked to be on the Veterans Affairs Committee. I was the first woman ever to ask to be on the Veterans Committee. And the reason for me was very personal. As you may know, my dad was a World War II veteran and my family relied on his VA care when he was diagnosed with multiple sclerosis.

But I also, when I was in college during the Vietnam War, many of my friends and colleagues were on the streets demonstrating and my heart was out to them. But I was thinking about those men and women my age who were going over to Vietnam and coming back and injured in many different ways. So I actually did my college internship. I asked to be at the Seattle VA. And I went to the Seattle VA during the Vietnam War and served on what was the psychiatric ward at the time. And I sat and worked with young men and women who were my age, in college age, who'd been sent there and came back with severe mental health impacts. Now, today we call that PTSD, but at the time we didn't know it.

And I was looking at these men and women who volunteered to go over or sometimes their number came up at the time and came home and were going to be impacted the rest of their lives. And I learned firsthand what it means when somebody says, "I will go for my country to fight for all of you so that you have that America that you've been talking about here for you when you get home." And our promise to each and every one of them was, if you serve your country in the military, we will take care of you when you get home. That is a promise I hold near and dear to my heart, which is why I asked to be on the Veterans Committee when I first came here, first woman ever.

And I will tell you, I've seen the impact time and time again. I go home and I hold town halls when I was newly here and there'd be a lot of veterans who'd come and talk to me and tell me what's going on, what needed to be fixed. But always at that time, I will share with my colleagues, women never said anything. There were a few always in the back of the room and it wasn't until the regular meeting was over and they'd come up quietly to me and say, "I need to tell you what's happening to women veterans. I need to share with you sexual assault. I need to share with you that there's not the facilities. I go to the VA and it's a men's only kind of place. There's no OBGYNs. There's nobody to do mammographies. And I often don't feel comfortable sitting in that waiting room with a whole lot of people after I have had the experiences that I've had. And there's no place for women to go."

So we've worked really hard to make sure the VA works for women. We've worked really hard to make sure the VA addresses the issues of today, the PACT Act that we worked so hard to make sure that men and women who were victims of toxic exposure overseas got the services they need. I could speak for two hours here about all the things we've done, but then I see what this administration is doing to those men and women who we asked as a country to serve overseas or to here at home in service of all of us and the promises we've made them. And I think what are they doing? They're undermining the very value that all of us have given to Americans who serve above and beyond.

So when I hear of 2,000 layoffs a few weeks ago, I go, "Wow. Where's that coming from?" Well, I know because I'm getting the phone calls like I'm sure you are from a VA researcher who has been taken off the job, fired, unexplained, told he wasn't doing a good enough job somehow. Doing research on basic things like prosthetics or doing basic research on PTSD, or doing basic research on the kinds of things that our men and women who serve overseas are subjected to and need to come home and have the specialized service and resources that they need. Or I hear from veterans who can't get the services that they've been asked for. So now when we are hearing this administration is about to cut 80,000, you didn't hear me wrong. 80,000 more people from the VA. A vast majority of themselves are veterans. I wanted to ask the Senator, how does that hit you? How do you feel about that?

SENATOR BOOKER: I'm so grateful you brought this up, and especially all the work we had to do when I got elected 12, 13 years ago, one of the earliest things I did is meet with women veterans in my state and heard these awful stories about how long it took to get gynecological care, the weights that they had to do, the indignities they had to endure. And I'm glad we've made so many strides in part thanks to your leadership in New Jersey with special dedicated facilities to our women veterans with shortening those wait times, with prioritizing them. But you're now right. Their proposal is to cut 83,000 positions from the VA. And you said it, this just years ago. This governing body passed the PACT Act with overwhelming bipartisan support. It was signed by President Biden in August of 2022, the largest healthcare and benefit expansion in VA history. You were one of the leaders increasing disability compensation and extending eligibility for VA care.

To meet this increased demand, the VA added 61,000 employees in 2023. These new hires included claim processors, physicians, nursing staffs, medical support assistance, food service workers and housekeeping staff. And now the progress this body made is in jeopardy by this president. We added 61,000 just to keep up with the demands and the needs, and now he's cutting 83,000. This is an article, if you don't want me to yield. DAV [Disabled American Veterans] urges Veteran Affairs to be more transparent about vet care amid layoffs and budget costs. Veteran Affairs Secretary Doug Collins says Veterans care won't be impacted. We saw the largest expansion of VA healthcare benefits in a generation under the PACT Act. Collins attended DAV's recent midwinter conference where he came from behind the podium, walked into the audience and told attendees that vet care and benefits would not be impacted by the Trump administration.

In recent appearances on CBS *Eye on Veterans* podcast, DAV Communications Chief and Air Force [Marine] Veteran Dan Clare said the VA has not demonstrated how it's going to keep its promise. They have not demonstrated it. DAV also does not have "a lot of information about what's planned", he said. Can you imagine that? Leaving all these veterans with insecurity and uncertainty.

> Now, we're hearing about the 83,000 people losing their jobs. 20,000 or so folks might be veterans themselves. We're concerned about how we're going to be able to cut that many people and maintain care and benefits.

The VA hired thousands of staffers since 2022 in response to the PACT Act, which brought 800,000 new enrollees into its systems. Columns has said cutting the VA workforce by 83,000 would bring it back down to its 2019 level. Before we did all those expansions to help women's vets, Clare said he has not heard about specific performance problems with those who've been laid off. Well, *you* haven't heard about it. Veterans' needs have not changed and they remain great.

> The people who are sick from the burn pits didn't necessarily get better overnight. And some of these folks are going to have a long row to hoe when it comes to their health. {DAV is getting calls frequently from veterans who are} scared, angry, and don't understand what's going on and how it's going to affect them.

Clare was one of the first whistleblowers on burn pits in Iraq, which eventually inspired the fight to pass the PACT Act to help veterans who became sick or even died from their toxic exposures.

> When we started talking about dioxin, Vietnam veterans heard that they immediately thought of Agent Orange. And that's probably what this is — our generation's Agent Orange. There's a lot of decisions being made behind closed doors {he continued}. We want to know what the plan is. {*We want to know what the plan is.*} We're not against efficiency of government. We're not against even removing VA employees who may not be fit performers. {A veteran has a unique understanding of another veteran's needs. Clare continued...} When you lose those folks out of the VA, the veterans, you lose an institutional capacity to understand veterans.

It is also unclear how these cuts will impact VA research, which Clare also stresses, has helped veterans deal with complex issues that are service-connected such as traumatic brain injuries and post-traumatic stress.

In addition to being concerned about how recent budget cuts and staff reductions will impact veterans' care and caregivers, Clare said DAV is also concerned about the impact on veteran-owned small businesses. DAV is asking veteran business owners whose contracts have been recently canceled, or who have been fired from their VA jobs to reach out here. DAV is actively keeping a list of veterans negatively affected by the Trump administration's cuts and plans on fighting for them in the weeks and months to come. And those lists that they're keeping are getting longer and longer and longer of people affected by this.

So to answer your question, it's absurd. It is offensive. It's ready, fire, aim. Tens of thousands of veterans laid off, veterans who do business and work in contracts, contracts ended. Why is this another group that the President of the United States is scaring frightened veterans, angry veterans? I'm hearing from them in my state. I know you're hearing them from yours. What's the plan? What's the plan? What's the plan? They have no answer for us. All they're doing is cutting social security staff, undermining the delivery of those services, the cutting the VA services. And why, by the way? Is it creating efficiency or effectiveness? No. Is it to create savings, because we got to create savings to give more of those tax cuts to billionaires like Elon Musk. It is not fair. It is not right. When we send people off into the most dangerous environments on the planet Earth and ask them to put their lives on the lines for us, the least we can do as a nation is not penny pinch on their backs of the service that they deserve.

SENATOR MURRAY: For one additional question.

SENATOR BOOKER: I yield for a question while retaining the floor.

SENATOR MURRAY: The Senator's right. So many veterans are afraid right now, and I had a veteran tell me that he was one of those people that got the letter, "You haven't performed well." He worked for the National Park Service actually. And he said, "I've been saving lives. I've been cleaning trails. I've been making sure that the national parks are safe for all of you." And then he said to me, "I'm a veteran. I served in the war and I served my country there because I wanted to serve my country and my fellow Americans. And I came home and worked for the National Park Service to do the same. And now as a veteran, my country's not there for me."

And I would just say to my colleague and to everyone who's listening, these men and women that we make a promise to that we say we will be there for you when you come home, that does not mean slamming a door in your face. It doesn't mean that you have to wait for hours to get the services that you earned. It doesn't mean that you'll be mistreated. It means that we will honor you. And I would thank the Senator for his response and just say to him again, do you think we're treating men and women in this country as great Americans by the actions that are being taken by this administration?

SENATOR BOOKER: Thank you for the question. No. And I'm just going to read another article that's going to make even clearer the point you just laid that's so strong and so important. This is from Axios — *How White House Firings are Hurting Veterans*:

> The Trump administration's big cuts to the federal government are hitting one group particularly hard — the country's veterans. Why it matters? Many of those who served in the military derive a sense of purpose and belonging from their government work, viewing it as a way to serve their country and help their peers outside of active duty, the big picture. It's not clear yet how many vets have been fired or will be. Last year veterans made up 28% of the federal workforce. 28% per federal data, a far bigger share than the 5% in the private sector.
>
> "About 36% of the vets working in civil service, more than 200,000 in total are disabled or have serious health conditions per federal data. 36% of the vets working in civil service are disabled vets. This is the largest attacks on veteran employment in our lifetime," says William Attig, executive director of the Union Veterans Council, a large group that represents many of these workers. Attig who was deployed in Iraq from 2003 to 2009, has been talking to newly unemployed members trying to get a tally of everyone whose job was lost.
>
> Zoom in now: Some veterans still holding on to their jobs for now are waiting for the hammer to drop. We're being smeared as leeches, but I just want to serve my country and provide for my family, an employee at the Department of Defense who's a disabled veteran and requested anonymity because he didn't want to put his job at risk. {Talk about free speech.} "We're being smeared as leeches," says a disabled veteran who stood for us. He was thrilled to land his job, he said a few months ago, but it is anxiously waiting to see if he'll be one of the more than 5,000 workers that the Pentagon said it would fire next week.
>
> Privately now, GOP lawmakers are growing uneasy with the cuts to veterans. {I know this because I know the heart of so many of my Republican colleagues.} Political reports adding that vets have been disproportionately affected by firings. And again, GOP lawmakers are growing uneasy about it. The White House did not say how many veterans have been fired. At least one department, the Department of Interior, has rapidly carved out an exception for them. "President Trump has consistently stood up for our brave men and women delivering crucial reforms that improve VA healthcare," said White House spokesperson Anna Kelly in an email...
>
> There are a few reasons government work attracts vets. The federal government has a veteran's preference put simply when deciding among a group of qualified candidates, they're first in line. {I think that's right.} "You'd have to jump through a lot of hoops to not hire a veterans" said a former official. With more veterans working in government more feel welcome to work among people who understand them. Others are drawn to their retirement veterans benefits — years of military service counts towards your federal pension. Plus, though many of these folks feel drawn to mission-driven employment. "Most veterans feel like they're putting on another uniform" {when they go work in other federal agencies}. "These jobs are a crucial piece of the puzzle in most military life," he says. Adding that is also a key part of suicide prevention for

this at-risk group. One of the most important things you can do for a veteran is help them with a job.

How can we expect to maintain what is in America an all-volunteer force if we fail to show those folks willing to serve, how we care for our service members when they come home? Slashing more than 83,000 jobs from the VA alone, it's clear that these cuts are going to have a disproportionate impact on veterans, veteran contractors and the services they receive. I'm angry about these cuts, but most of all, it should make all Americans feel a sense of sadness. We ask our veterans to sacrifice so much. And we all know who knows veterans. It's not just the veterans. It's also veteran families that make that sacrifice, that share in that service, that share in that commitment. And these veterans, some of the more talented, dedicated leaders I know, they're not doing it for the money. They're doing it because they're called to serve. You know how many people jumped into service after 9/11? Friends of mine rushed to join the military to serve in Iraq and Afghanistan and now they're home. Many of them with invisible wounds, many of them with visible wounds, and the services they rely on for their healthcare, the services they rely on as lifelines, the services that they rely on often that give them hope and opportunity, not compounding their trauma. This is now being attacked by a president who's not keeping his promises. He says he values veterans, but the facts are different.

She devoted her life to serving the US then DOGE targeted her. It has been six days since Joy Marver was locked out of her office at the US Department of Veteran Affairs, five days since she checked herself into hospital for emergency psychiatric care. And two days since she sent a letter to her supervisors, "Please, I'm confused. Can you help me understand?"

Now, she followed her wife into the storage room of their house outside of Minneapolis, searching for answers no one could give her. A half dozen bins held the remnants of 22 years spent in service to the US government. First as a Sergeant First class in Iraq, then as a disabled veteran, and finally as a VA support specialist in logistics. She devoted her career to a system that had always made sense to her, but now nobody seemed to know whether she had officially been laid off or for how long, or even why. "Are you sure you never got an email?" asked her wife, Mickey Joe Carlson, 49. "How would I know?" Asked Marver, 45. "They deleted my account. Maybe it's because you were still probationary. My boss said I was exempt," Marver said, "I was supposed to be essential."

In the last few months, more than 30,000 people across the country were fired by President Trump's new initiative called the Department of Government Efficiency. Historic reduction of the federal workforce that has been all the more disruptive because of its chaotic execution. Entire agency divisions have been cut without explanation or mistakenly fired and then rapidly rehired, resulting in several lawsuits and mass confusion among civil workers. After a court ruled last week that many of the firings were illegal, the government began reinstating workers, even as the Trump administration appealed the decision and promised more layoffs. The VA alone said it planned to cut about 80,000 more jobs this year, including tens of thousands of veterans.

And for Marver, the shock of losing her job was eclipsed by the disorientation of being repeatedly dismissed and belittled by the government she served. She had watched on TV as Trump's billionaire advisor, Elon Musk, took to the stage at a political conference wielding a chainsaw to the beat of rock music, slicing apart the air with what he called his 'chainsaw for bureaucracy'. She had listened to Trump's aids and allies deride federal employees for being lazy, parasitic, unaccountable, and essentially wasting taxpayer money in their "fake jobs."

In Marver's case, that job had meant helping to retrain soldiers for civilian work and coordinating veteran burials while earning a salary of $53,000 a year.

> "Here's the note I got a little while after I was hired," Marver told Carlson pulling a form letter from the government. "You represent the best of who we are as Americans," it read, "You could have chosen to do anything with your talents, but you chose public service. Kind of boilerplate, but it's nice," Carlson said.

1:30 PM - Child Tax Credits

SENATOR MICHAEL BENNET (COLORADO): Senator Booker-

SENATOR BOOKER: Madam Chair.

SENATOR BENNET: -Senator Booker, will you yield for a question?

SENATOR BOOKER: Before I yield, I just want to acknowledge my friend in the chair and she's tracking a tight whip. So I appreciate you following the rules here. I got to read this now and then I'm eager to get your question because you are one of the few people I knew before I got to the Senate.

SENATOR BENNET: That is what I wanted to talk about.

SENATOR BOOKER: Well, I'm sorry. I didn't yield for a question. I still can't say anything, sir, the parliamentarian will jump all over you. I have the floor. So much power. It's going to my head.

SENATOR BENNET: Sir, will you yield for a question?

SENATOR BOOKER: Man, known you for 25 years. I wanted to talk about you, but you're being so insistent. I reward your insistence and say, I yield for a question while retaining the floor.

SENATOR BENNET: And let me ask you, Senator Booker – can I ask you now, through the chair, [or] you directly – how long a question you would like, would you have... I'm happy to provide you with a five-minute question or a five-hour question. It depends entirely on how you feel.

SENATOR BOOKER: I actually believe that you would go a five-hour question to try to help me power through. Senator, we've been at this for-

SENATOR BENNET: My wife Susan, would-

SENATOR BOOKER: I love you and your wife Susan, but I love your children more. Your girls are-

SENATOR BENNET: Well, that's why I came down here. I remember-

SENATOR BOOKER: Is this a question? Because I yield for the question while retaining the floor.

SENATOR BENNET: This is a question, please.

SENATOR BOOKER: Okay. Let's make it a seven-minute question.

SENATOR BENNET: This is a question. And I would say to the senator from New Jersey and to the presiding officer, thank you very much for being here and for enduring this. When I started here, I was sitting in the chair all the way to the right of where you are today, Senator Booker. And I can remember the day you walked in to be sworn in. You came through those doors right there. And I had a huge smile on my face because I knew when you were walking through those doors, when you were walking into this chamber, you would bring with you the kids you used to work for in Newark, New Jersey.

And the reason I knew that was that when you were working for the kids in Newark, New Jersey – as the mayor of Newark, New Jersey – I was working for the kids in Denver as the superintendent of the Denver Public Schools. And at that time in our country's history, we were engaged in a pretty profound effort to try to make better the schools in our respective communities. Not that everything was perfect, but we were trying to drive achievement for the kids at Newark and the kids in Denver. And we talked about it over many years. And here you walked into this chamber, a place where it would be easy to imagine has long had the habit of treating America's kids like they're someone else's kids. Not like they're America's kids.

I know that because if the kids were in America, represented by the 100 desks that are in the Senate, roughly nine of them would be graduating with a college degree in our country — nine of these desks. If we thought about the rates of literacy, the failure in our country to be able to teach people how to read or do mathematics decade after decade after decade, the proficient students would consume just a few desks in this place and everybody else would not be able to do basic levels of reading and basic levels of math. But here you were somebody who understands that, and here you are, somebody who understands that.

And one of the very first projects you and I worked on, this is coming to my question, was the Child Tax Credits. This was an effort to turn back 30 or 40 years of trickle-down economics, that said that what we're going to do is cut taxes for the richest people in the country and just have it trickle-down to everybody else. Some people don't know what that means. And if I could, let me just say what that actually means.

For you to understand what that tax policy is, that tax policy that Donald Trump has pursued now twice – once when he was president before and now again – you have to imagine that there is a mayor in Newark or there is a mayor in Denver, or a mayor in San Diego or in Miami who is saying to the people that live in his community, "I have an idea. I'm going to go out and borrow more money than we have ever borrowed before as a community. I'm going to go out and borrow a ton of money", and your constituent, my constituents to say, "Wait a minute, mayor, wait a minute, that makes me nervous. What are you borrowing all that money for? Because I'm worried about the fiscal condition of my city and my town."

This conversation would happen in every city, in every town in Colorado or New Jersey, whether they're Democratic or Republican mayors, you'd have to answer the question, what are you spending the money on? What are you going to borrow all this money for? Is it for our parks? No. Is it for our schools? No. Is it to give mental health services to kids who desperately need it? No. Is it for our roads and bridges, our infrastructure? No. Are you going to do something important for our water systems? No. What is the answer? What are you going to do with that money that you are borrowing, that you are mortgaging our kids' future? What is this important thing that you're going to do with it? The answer is, we're going to give it to the two richest neighborhoods in New Jersey or Newark or Denver, and we're going to expect that it's going to trickle-down to everybody else.

That is the theory. That is what trickle-down economics is. That is what the Trump tax plan is. And there's a reason why no mayor in America has ever done it because you would be run out on a rail because you couldn't explain it. You're going to borrow money from the kids of our police officers, our firefighters, our teachers, in order to cut taxes for the richest people in the community, in the hope that they'll buy a little bit of an extra, I don't know, luxury, and that that's going to somehow generate economic activity for everybody else. It is demonstrably true that that has never worked. And by the way, these tax cuts, I say they're presiding officer and everybody else within the sound of my voice have literally never, ever come close to paying for themselves.

That is a complete lie. That's why the Congressional Budget Office says this is going to blow a $4.6 trillion hole in our deficit. And for what? To give tax cuts the richest people in America when they need them least, and when the income inequality is as great as it has been in our country since the 1920s.

Which brings me to my question, my cherished colleague from New Jersey, what was it we were trying to do with the Child Tax Credits? There were a lot of people who believed that we couldn't even get it passed, that we couldn't even get the IRS to administer it. And then we did get it passed during part of the Biden administration, and lo and behold, more than 90% of the families in New Jersey got a tax cut. Lo and behold, more than 90% of the families in Colorado got a tax cut. Not waiting for a trickle-down from the wealthiest people, but they got a tax cut directly that did what? Cut in half — *cut in half* the childhood poverty rate in America. In the richest country in the world, for one moment, we said, we don't have to accept this level of childhood poverty as a permanent feature of our democracy or a permanent feature of our economy. We can do something different than that.

And Senator Booker, that is what you said when you were mayor of Newark. We don't have to accept these generational outcomes of poverty or of poor schools or of lead in the water. We can do something different, and that's what you've brought to the United States Senate as well. The tragedy from my perspective is... There are many tragedies about the election of Donald Trump. And by the way, I'll say again on this floor, I don't blame him for getting elected president. He ran and he won. Those of us that were trying to offer a different vision have something to explain about why we were not successful.

The one thing I am certain of is that the kids in Newark and the kids in Denver are completely invisible to our current president — that he is not concerned with their welfare or even loses a minute's sleep over the next generation. So I wonder if you could talk a little bit about... This isn't a numbers and sense question because I know even though you don't look tired, I'm sure you must be tired after all these hours and hours and hours. But can you talk a little bit, Senator, about how a society should be judged with respect to how we treat the next generation of Americans, how a tax bill should be judged by how we treat the next generation of Americans, how almost nothing else matters except what we do with respect to the next generation of Americans?

I can tell you that my daughters, Caroline, Helena, and Anne understand better than most your commitment to them and your commitment to their generation because you've been such an inspiration to them. Not just today. Not just today – but thank you for what you're doing – but for basically their entire lifetimes.

SENATOR BOOKER: Well, thank you for the question. My long, long-time friend, one of the folks I've known the longest, who I get to serve with and what you did for me when I came here is you and Sherrod Brown who sat right there by the door. You let Bennett and Brown become Bennett Brown Booker, three B's and joined together with some of the most extraordinary House members and brother Warnock and fight for the Child Tax Credit. And it took years, but we found our opening when we called Ron Klain together before the election was even settled and said, "Please, this is the best thing our country can do, is to expand the Child Tax Credit, make it fully refundable." Because we knew, as you said, it would give the overwhelming majority, between 80 and 93% depending on what state you are, the people in those states, if we expanded the Earned Income Tax Credit, it would give them all a tax break.

It was unarguably one of the greatest tax cuts in the last 50 years and it cut child poverty in America nearly in half. And child poverty is a moral obscenity. Child poverty is violence against children. Violence. And here's the thing that you and I both know from the research. Every dollar you spend in raising a child above the poverty line, you return to society between five and $7 in economic growth and activity or in lesser costs. Because kids above the poverty line have, for example, less visits to the emergency room.

I just don't understand how we are a nation – again, the wealthiest nation – that has one of the highest child poverty rates. It makes no sense. Zero sense. When we proved once and for all with that one-year effort, because we couldn't make it permanent. We were short one vote in this body. We proved forever in America that child poverty is a policy choice, not an inevitable reality.

And so you asked the great question why in a nation that was founded on men that studied virtue, the ideals of virtue, they were imperfect geniuses. They were imperfect geniuses, but they really struggled with moral philosophy. We have the power, we've proven it, to cut child poverty in half.

What's the argument against it? Wasteful spending? Come on. Come on. Giving trillions of dollars of tax cuts to the wealthiest in America, I'm sorry, it's wasteful spending, especially if it ends up blowing a hole. Those tax cuts don't pay for themselves. Trump won, tax cuts didn't. Renewing them won't. Doing the same thing over and over again and thinking you're going to get different results is the very definition of insanity.

You are one of the most passionate... I remember a stem-winder of a speech you gave in this body. You were so angry. I love it when it's 'Bennet unchained'. You were so angry when you started talking about the horrible policies of this nation that has eaten away the inheritance of children to come. Why you went off on the trillions of dollars spent on stupid foreign wars where our brave men and women fought for this country, but this country made bad mistakes in these long wars. You talked about the money we spent there and you talked about the first time in American history, common sacrifice, every war before that. Not just the men and women who are brave enough to go out and fight. You said the first time in American history that we said the only people that are going to bear a burden are the people that are going to go. The rest of you get tax cuts.

George Bush, first time ever, we went to war and we gave tax cuts. From the Civil War to the Revolutionary War to World War I to World War II, it was a common collective effort. My grandmother talked with pride about victory gardens and pride about war bonds. Everybody pitched in. And so here we are at another crossroads and is America going to tolerate... Is America going to tolerate this idea that we're going to give extraordinary tax cuts to the overwhelmingly disproportionately will accrue to the wealthiest amongst us? For what? If I was a mayor, I'd have to answer it.

So I appreciate your question, but I also appreciate your moral indignation. I really do. I keep saying over and over again, elevating the voices of Americans on this floor, elevating the point. I hope that we can't keep doing things like this as business as usual. These are real issues, not of Right or Left, of right or wrong. This is a moral moment in America. And you point out a very clear choice we have when we talk about our tax policy. It should reflect our values. Thank you, sir.

1:46 PM - Health and Human Services

SENATOR JACK REED (RHODE ISLAND): Will the Senator yield for a question?

SENATOR BOOKER: For Jack Reed, I would do just about anything. So I yield for a question while retaining the floor.

SENATOR REED: First, thank you for continuing to highlight the harm that's being done by the Trump administration on average Americans, working Americans — flouting the law, withholding federal funds, illegally shutting federal agencies, ruining long-standing alliances, increasing prices, taxes on American consumers, it goes on and on and on.

Last week, the Department of Health and Human Services announced that it would fire 20,000 employees. Those cuts appear to be taking shape right now. Is the Senator aware that there are reports that thousands of HHS staff have been locked out of their offices this morning?

SENATOR BOOKER: To answer the Senator's question, I've been on the floor since last night. I haven't read any news reports. But when you say that am I aware of thousands and thousands of HHS employees who've been laid off of their jobs? I'm not aware of it. I'm not surprised. The question isn't is Donald Trump going to lay more people off? The question isn't is Donald Trump going to lay more disproportionately veterans off? The question is what are we going to do to stop it when it isn't thoughtful, reasonable cuts? When he talks about the people he's cutting as leeches, demeans and degrades their commitment to service and their noble obligations.

We were told that HHS would be about making America healthy again, and I haven't seen that. I've seen them cut services to give access to children to fresh and healthy foods. I've seen them cut regulations on polluters that make our air quality worse, which hurts people with emphysema, with asthma, with other respiratory diseases. In fact, a lot of the actuary will show more Americans die when polluters are allowed to go back to polluting more. I could go through the things they're doing that are not making our water healthier and safer, not making our air healthier and safer, not making more access to healthcare that stops and treats chronic disease, not giving access to healthy foods.

We're not making America healthy. And so these cuts, they don't surprise me, but they hurt me. They hurt me. These are Americans, these are disproportionately veterans and I thank you for speaking up for them today.

SENATOR REED: If the Senator would yield for another question...

SENATOR BOOKER: I yield for a question while retaining the floor.

SENATOR REED: President Trump and the Secretary of HHS, Secretary Kennedy, are, as I indicated and made you aware, they are firing a host of people today. But the critical staff functions will be undercut. For example, the Low Income Energy Assistance Program and the National Institute for Occupational Safety and Health, they focus on worker safety. LIHEAP, as you know, provides essential support to literally keep people warm in the winter and cool in the summer in our southern states. And with LIHEAP undercut like that, there will be effects. People will become unhealthy. In fact, possibly could even pass away and perish.

NIOSH, on the other hand, is an agency that looks after 164 million people in this country so they're safe. And we all know, we all remember back all those stories about the Gilded Age, which sometimes I think the administration wants to bring back, where children labored in shops, where garment workers were killed in fires because there was no way to get out. All the exits were sealed. National Institute for Occupational Safety and Health prevents that. And work-related injuries and illnesses cost our economy about $250 billion annually. So that will double, triple, quadruple.

And we're seeing all sorts of reports about the National Center for Injury Prevention and Control at CDC. They do critical work. They're under the gun. We're seeing reports that the director of the FDA Center for Tobacco Products has been fired. We can see that President Trump and Secretary Kennedy would rather stand up for big tobacco than for young kids who get hooked on it and it ruins their health.

These are just a few of the cuts and I know you're aware of these. I know you're focused on these. They're going to destroy years of progress and basically, it's being shouldered by working Americans. Nobody who lives in Mar-a-Lago needs LIHEAP heating. Nobody who dines at Mar-a-Lago needs occupational health support, but the waiters do and the grounds people do. So Senator, just your comments and thoughts on this.

SENATOR BOOKER: I so appreciate the question from my friend. I really think empathy is a superpower and you are Superman in that character because you're thinking about the people affected. We throw these acronyms down here and they sound like government programs, but you meet with the people.

I remember when I was starting out my political career in service in Newark and I had this dear friend named Kim, and she was one of these people that worked trying to sign people up for LIHEAP. And the stories that would affect her of people that that was a lifeline for them to have a little bit of resources. A little bit of resources to help them get their energy costs in a place where they could afford heat in the winter and some air in the summer. Stories of elders and vulnerable.

I don't understand how we can be a nation with so much wealth and abundance and we haven't figured out a way to design a system where when you invest in the well-being of people, people thrive. Kids growing up in quality housing, with great public schools, with clean air without lead in their water, above the poverty line. You know what I love about young people in this country is their resiliency.

I meet these beautiful children with light in their eyes, that all they need is a little fertile ground and they go beyond our imagination in what they can achieve. And so here we are taking our national treasure, the resources being paid into, our taxes are our national treasure. And what do we invest in? What do we do with it? Well, we're running up more debt. We're not going to pay for these tax cuts that are overwhelmingly going to go to the wealthiest. But we're taking all these things that people rely on from our veterans to our seniors, to our disabled, to expectant moms. We're just taking as much as we can to defer as much of this gross tax cuts that go disproportionately to the wealthy.

And so again, I return to where I've been for closing in on 19 hours. I go back to what are we going to do about it? It can't be business as usual. There are too many things we've already covered that show that this is a moral moment in America. Where do we stand? It's time as John Lewis, as I keep repeating. He says, "It's time to get into good trouble." Necessary trouble to redeem the soul of our nation. And what you're talking about goes directly to the soul. What do we stand for? Who do we stand for? We should stand for each other. Thank you, sir.

1:55 PM - Setting the Record Straight

SENATOR MARIA CANTWELL (WASHINGTON): Will the Senator from New Jersey yield for a question?

SENATOR BOOKER: To my dear friend, I yield for a question while retaining the floor and I thank you for being here. I thank you for your leadership. I thank you for what you stand for and I look forward to your question.

SENATOR CANTWELL: Well, I so appreciate the Senator from New Jersey trying to articulate the urgency of this moment. And I think that I know you've discussed many things in the last I don't know how many hours it is, but it's been many, many hours. And we just had a hearing this morning related to the markup of the Social Security nominee. And somebody we're just trying to find out because a whistleblower said that he was involved in helping DOGE. And we're here today trying to bring attention to the American public that people are trying to rearrange essential services, contractual obligations. Things like Social Security or Medicaid or even Medicare by basically saying well, we have this efficiency strategy. When in reality, they're over there with numbers just trying to carve something out of the budget. Billions of dollars out of Social Security efficiency or billions and billions and billions of dollars out of Medicaid, which would really come right out of our hospitals who are saying they don't even think they could stay open. But this notion of Social Security, I don't know if you've heard that not only are they closing offices and cutting jobs. They're asking people to re-register.

So my constituent, who they basically said was dead, was not dead. He wanted his Social Security. So not only did they not give him his check in January, they tried to claw back checks from the previous months out of his bank account. And even though this has got national press and attention, you would think that everybody on the other side would be like, no, that's not what we're trying to do. Even though the president in the State of the Union said all these people were getting Social Security checks when my constituent is standing in line with less and less staff trying to get his Social Security. And guess what? They're still at it. As of last Friday, they were still at not giving him his Social Security.

So what are we unleashing on America? What are we unleashing that even... And I don't know whether you addressed these Social Security issues in your statements. I so appreciate you emphasizing the urgency here because this is the dismantling of contractual agreements between the American people and the people's body that we're here to represent them and stand up for it. And people are acting like they don't care.

So you are here in an extraordinary athletic achievement. Thank you. Makes your Stanford days look like nothing, right? You've achieved this great long effort to bring illumination to the American people that they're getting screwed over the fact that these cuts are not some efficient way to deliver better service. But in Social Security, they're undermining Social Security.

So have you heard of these cases, the whistleblower issue and others? And do you believe that that's what we should be paying attention to? That before we get a vote on Mr. Bisignano, that we should be finding out what whistleblowers are saying and his involvement related to DOGE and making sure that Social Security checks are protected?

SENATOR BOOKER: I thank you for the question, my friend and my chairwoman. I did talk about this, but it is so worth repeating. At some point in the night, we covered Social Security and we read story after story after story of senior citizens that are frightened and afraid that the President of the United States would stand in a joint address and attack Social Security, make fun of it with lie after lie after lie, about millions and millions of people getting fraudulent checks. When the people who do the fact checking and even the Social Security folks themselves say that it's a minuscule amount of people getting checks and usually it's an overpayment.

But they didn't stop there. Elon Trump called it a Ponzi scheme. Elon Musk called it a Ponzi scheme. The richest man in the world and the most powerful man in the world, himself a billionaire, are attacking the program that millions and millions of our senior citizens rely on.

I read letters of people that say, "Don't forget about the people who are disabled who rely on SSI", begging us to remember and speak their names and tell their stories. A lot of fear, a lot of terror, a lot of insecurity. But we spoke about this on the floor that their benefits are already being cut. What do I mean by that? Well, if you are cutting Social Security offices, as one of our colleagues said from New Hampshire, in a rural area forcing people to have to drive 100 miles, if they have a problem, they can't talk on the phone with the waits on the phones. I read an article from the Wall Street Journal, no left-wing mag, from the Wall Street Journal talking about how the customer service is going downhill because of the cuts that they're making. And now you're forcing seniors...

We read letters from 85 year olds, 90 year olds, 93-year-old. They're going to drive 100 miles? I read letters from Social Security workers who now work in inadequate spaces with inadequate staff, unable to do their job that they love. They're not leeches. They're not people that should be demeaned or degraded by the most powerful people in our land. They are public servants who love their jobs and want to serve seniors, but now can't do it because they cut, cut, cut before they thought, thought, thought.

SENATOR CANTWELL: Will the Senator yield for a question because I-

SENATOR BOOKER: I will yield for a question while retaining the floor.

SENATOR CANTWELL: I thank the Senator from New Jersey. The issue that I think is not being illuminated enough for the sheer numbers here in my state of Washington, 1.4 million people on Social Security, 1.8 million people on Medicaid. So you're talking about a big federal relationship.

Now, I know that some people in... I actually worked in the private sector. I could tell you one thing about the private sector, the bigger it gets, usually the more inefficient it gets. It just happens. Big organizations can be inefficient. So just because the federal government is the government doesn't mean that Social Security and Medicaid are fraught with fraud. In this case, my constituent's not even getting his check and no one is responding. And you would think with all this commotion that Social Security would want to jump right on it and fix it. But they're not.

And the question I have for the Senator of New Jersey is in my state, I have, as I said, nearly 1.8 million people who are on Medicaid. And the same problem is now where our colleagues are trying to say they're going to get $880 billion out of the energy and commerce budget of the House of Representatives. When in reality, 90% of that money is Medicare or Medicaid. And if Medicare is supposedly off the table, then the majority of that is going to come from Medicaid.

So in my state, I'm hearing from hospitals that that means they could close. That means essential Medicaid services that are used even in our jails or for fentanyl treatment or Medicaid that is used as a Obamacare expansion for healthcare that so many literally red Republican states, Republican governors have said we want that. The Governor of Idaho, yes, we want that. That's an expansion of Medicaid and it's successfully working at providing healthcare to millions of Americans.

But now our colleagues are entertaining a notion that they could cut this system. They're not really making it clear. So again, the illumination of you showing the urgency is like a big flag that we're trying to show to the American people. This is not a drill. This is now. This is happening. The beginnings of it are happening, and now this debate that's going to ensue is going to be a massive cut into those programs unless the American people wake up.

Now are your states, and are you hearing this in New Jersey about the Medicaid cuts, the impacts on hospitals, on the delivery system, on essential services?

SENATOR BOOKER: I cannot emphasize to you strongly enough, we decided to start this whole thing at 7:00 PM last night with Medicaid. And we read story after story after story after story of people who are Medicaid beneficiaries, who are terrified, who are afraid. Who didn't say if they cut 880 billion. If they diminish the cuts in any way to their services, they're holding together their lives in this fragile financial equilibrium that one little tug of a transportation service, one little tug of a home healthcare giver, it all crumbles. They're terrified and afraid. Some of the Americans that are dealing with the greatest challenges. Not of their own making. Some of them working full-time jobs and getting an injury costs extraordinary amounts of chaos to their lives.

So yes, I read from the people who are recipients. I read from the people who run hospitals, from rural hospitals to urban hospitals to level one trauma centers who all said that if they cut hundreds of billions of dollars, that it'll affect them. I did something really important. I read from Republican governors and Democratic governors because I keep over and over America, this is not Right or Left. It's right or wrong. It's not a partisan moment. It's an American moment. It's a moral moment. I read voices from Republicans specifically, Republican governors in Medicaid expansion states. They have this trigger. You know this. Many states that the funding from the federal law of government ever dips below 90%, boom, Medicare expansion is over, millions of people in financial crisis and healthcare crisis.

What is it going to take for us to say no? With such a firm voice, such a chorus of conviction, thousands, hundreds of thousands of Americans – Red, White, and Blue – every state saying do not do this for no good reason but to give the majority of your tax cuts to billionaires like Elon Musk, it makes no sense.

Who are we as a country? This is not normal times. This is not usual. We should be standing up because I read the stories of Republicans who run hospitals, Republicans who are governors, who are all saying don't do this. Don't do this.

2:06 PM - Fear, Anger, and Courage

SENATOR ALEX PADILLA (CALIFORNIA): Will the Senator yield for a question?

SENATOR BOOKER: Senator Padilla. I was teasing. I'm not yielding yet, Senator Padilla. I was teasing that man over there named Bennet that he and I had known each other for years, but you and I have known each other longer. I knew the Senator from Washington before I got here. Mutual friends, so these are three people that were friends of mine before I met this institution. Had Coons here, I have all four. You though, I knew longer than Bennet and longer than the great Senator from Washington and the chairwoman. We met in 1998-99, around then? We were both city council people and the dear friend, a beautiful man who introduced us, told me before we walked into your office that you were a rising star. You were a man of deep decency. That you were going to do extraordinary things in your career, and he did not overstate the fact. You are one of my close friends and I definitely yield for a question while retaining the floor.

SENATOR PADILLA: Thank you. And let the record reflect that he said the exact same things, probably better things about you. And he was absolutely correct. But I couldn't help but interject right at the moment where I did because once again, your passion is coming through. Well, first of all, I tremendously admire what you've been doing here on the floor of this Senate today, starting with last night. And as I've been watching off and on, there's these moments where your empathy and your sympathy and your care and concern is coming through. You can't help it. It's who you are.

There's been other moments as you've been talking about some of the key issues and dynamics of this current political climate that we're in where your passion is coming through and at times, anger. I know it because I've seen it. I know it because we're getting calls in my office about this. I know it because if you monitor comments and commentary on social media about what my colleague is doing here on the Senate floor, some people have asked, "Why is he so angry?"

I'd like to say here right now that Senator Booker has every right to be angry because of what's going on. I know I'm angry with so much of what's going on, and the American people have every right to be angry with what's going on. Because none of what we're seeing come out of the Trump White House is normal. But every day, this approach of flooding the zone with more and more extreme actions runs the risk of making people grow numb to these attacks, and we certainly can't surrender to the feeling of just being overwhelmed by their tactics. And so I want to thank the senior Senator from New Jersey for doing what he's doing to shake and awaken the conscience of our country.

Now as I listen to my colleague talk about the real dangers of the Trump administration, what it poses for our nation, I also reflect on what it means for our environment. Because I know it hits home for many folks, but especially in my home state of California. California, many of you have come to visit time and again, is home to some of those beautiful parks and natural wonders in the nation. But if you grew up in Southern California like I did, you also know there's a flip side to this climate discussion.

SENATOR BOOKER: Definitely feeling it.

[Other inaudible discussion, seemingly with his staff, until he mutes his mic.]

SENATOR PADILLA: And we've seen, we lived through the real costs of climate inaction. Now growing up, I can tell you not just about the smell of diesel exhaust, which I'll never forget, sitting on a school bus, going to and from school. Or the regular days where school would be shut down early. We'd all be sent home because of the smog, toxic smog in the air in the greater Southern California area. These were concrete reminders of the real threats that emissions pose to our health. California also knows the dangers posed by extreme weather. We know the droughts, we know the floods and yes, all too often, we've come to know wildfires. Devastating wildfires like the ones we experienced in Los Angeles County at the beginning of this year.

Now, Senator Booker was kind enough to come visit a few weeks ago to tour Altadena, the epicenter, if you will, of the Eaton Fire that devastated so many. And I think we both agree and anybody who's visited the area to see for themselves would agree that you cannot see what happened in and around Altadena and come away unmoved. I go on and on with examples and reasons to say to you that this is exactly why California, for decades, has worked so hard against pollution and against the impacts of climate change. Everything from being aggressive on tailpipe emission standards to our ambitious conservation goals. The 30x30* goals set up by the Biden administration, were modeled after the 30x30 goal set out by the state of California. California is also home to the very first Earth Day, which is now celebrated nationally each and every year.

But today, much of our progress is now at risk because just in the first two months of the second Trump administration, we've seen nothing but attacks on this progress of environmental protection. The Trump administration has sought to reverse the endangerment finding, which is the most basic finding of climate science. That yes, greenhouse gases harm public health. They've taken the steps of illegally freezing funding that this Congress, this Congress, had previously appropriated. I'm talking about the types of investments that keep our kids in our communities healthy.

Now, earlier this month, the EPA, Trump's EPA announced that they would be rolling back more than 30 environmental rules. By doing so, they're not just going to make Americans less healthy, they're also going to hurt our economy, and it's going to clear the way for China to become the world leader in green technology. So much for America first if they continue down that road.

But even while the Trump administration has refused to fight climate change, it's one thing to not be helpful, they've actually taken a number of steps that are actually harmful and hurtful, making it harder, for example, for states to respond to natural disasters. They've toyed with tying wildfire disaster assistance to political demands. They've proposed eliminating FEMA. They've implemented federal freezes on things like hazardous fuel removal and the hiring of federal firefighters.

Things that we need to do in the winter months to prepare for the hot and dry summer months when the risk is greatest. They've even brazenly opened up dams and flooded portions of the Central Valley to pretend President Trump was helping with the Los Angeles wildfires when the fact is those fires were contained when they released this water, water that's no longer available in the hot, dry summer months.

So, they're not just refusing to act or to help. They're making matters worse for states like California and many others. So, that's what this fight is about. Our fight for the environment is about America's health and safety. It's about American jobs and it's about America's future. With all that being said, my question to Senator Booker is this, for the next generation of Americans, for the young people who are tuning in and wondering, "Well, what is it that I can do? Do I have a voice? Do I have any power?" What would you say to them? How can they take action?

SENATOR BOOKER: I love you for that question, my friend. And I just want to talk about anger because I've been all over the place. I read these letters and they make me sad. I read these letters, they make me angry. I read these letters, they make me embarrassed that we are a country where people have to rend their pride and beg for help because of the little teeny modicum of support they get from a service like Medicaid.

But I've been saying over and over again, as I've tried to learn from my elders, as I've tried to learn from the heroes I revere, that I learned from my parents that anger is not a bad emotion. It's what you do with that emotion that's important. Does it consume you? Does it drive you to hate other people? Or do you allow it to fuel you? Because it was ferocious love that had ancestors of all of ours in this country make it through the insults, "No Irish need apply." The injuries of Japanese internments. It's what do you do with those feelings? You're not defined by what happens to you. You're defined by how you choose to respond. So, I tell people, if you're not angry, if you're not angry, let that fuel you.

Well, what about the heartbreak that I feel? Well, I get emotional sometimes because I read a letter and something in it makes me remember somebody I know, or to feel the hurt of constituents begging for help. And it breaks my heart. But I tell you, if America hasn't broken your heart, you don't love her enough, because there's so much heartbreak and fear and pain in a nation where people are seeing their economic hopes and dreams of maybe buying a home or having the money to help their kids with school, or to meet their basic needs, where so many Americans are one flat tire, one $400 hit to their account and they're suddenly doing payday loans or having to struggle to find a way through. There's so much heartbreak in this country. Great love means you make yourself vulnerable to having that heartbreak. But the heart's this powerful tool that even when it's broken, it still beats.

And what about people that are afraid? I get afraid sometimes. I think about this legislation if it goes through what's going to happen in my state. I know the hospitals, I know the recipients. But you are telling me, look at our history. Is there anybody in American history that you revere that didn't face extraordinarily fear? Because you cannot have great courage without great fear. Fear is a necessary precondition to courage.

And so, you ask me, my friend, what can people do? I want to remind people, as I've said before on this floor, to remember the truth that I heard before I came here. That change does not come from Washington, it comes to Washington by the people who demand it. I said this earlier, do you think that we got suffrage in this country because a bunch of men on this Senate floor right here put their hands in and said, "Hey, fellas, on the count of three, women get the right to vote. Ready? One, two, three, go." No, that's not how it happened. It happened because of Alice Paul. She was a young, young person from New Jersey. She broke with the course of human events.

Alice Paul, one of my greatest heroes. You know what she did? She caused a heck of a lot of good trouble, necessary trouble. She's the first American ever, young American in her early 20s, the first American ever to protest in front of the White House. She broke with the older, more mature suffrage organizations and went to the White House and did what she called a silent protest. She held up signs quoting President Woodrow Wilson's own words about freedom and equality and say, "Aren't they true for me?" Like a great Black woman would later say, "Ain't I a woman? Don't I deserve rights?"

You don't think she was afraid? Let me tell you how afraid she was. Hundreds came out to jeer her, blocking the street, and then they arrested her for obstructing public passage. And then what do you do with a strong, powerful woman? You say that she's crazy and you throw her in the insane asylum before Gandhi. Sitting in jail, before Gandhi, Alice Paul, this young American from New Jersey goes on a hunger strike and they don't honor her hunger strike. They shove tubes down her throat, crack eggs into the tube, force-feeding her. And thank God for the First Amendment, which is under attack here in America, the freedom of the press under attack here in America. Look at them dragging the journalist Jeffrey Goldberg right now, for doing what? Getting the highest security officials in the land, just showing them the laws that they were breaking.

A journalist covered what Alice Paul did. She gets out of jail because of public outrage. She goes back to protesting in front of the White House and Woodrow Wilson, the president of the United States, finally comes out and joins her in supporting suffrage. You don't think she was afraid, angry, heartbroken? But she did something different. She chose a new and unusual pathway to show that, "This is not the America I believe in." The poetry of Langston Hughes, *"America never was America to me, but I swear this oath, America will be."* The poetry of Langston Hughes, *"There's a dream in this land with its back against the wall. To save a dream for one, we must save the dream for all."* It's what you do with those emotions that matters. Does it call you to greater service? Does it call you to greater sacrifice? Does it call you to greater love?

And let me say one more thing. As we were speaking, I just wanted to bring this up. You know I love history, and this is one of my favorite letters, Alex, my colleague, Senator Padilla. It's one of my favorite letters in all of American history because an obscure, unknown American, obscure and unknown, would never have been known, writes a letter to a powerful, powerful man. This obscure American woman that nobody know or would have heard of ever if somebody didn't hear about her story and write a book, she would be gone like most of the great heroes in American history that we don't know their names.

It reminded me of the last healthcare debate when Donald Trump tried to take away the ACA and how many amazing, heroic people – who I don't remember their names, but rose up – and say,

"No, no, no." They got three of my colleagues, McCain, Murkowski, and Collins, to change their vote on this floor and stop healthcare being stripped away from 20 million Americans.

Well, here is what I mean. It's not the powerful people with titles and celebrity and offices and billions of dollars that have ever shaped this country. What shapes this nation is hardworking, determined Americans who say, "I'm going to redeem the dream of America. I'm going to heal the soul of this country. I'm going to demand that we do better, that we rise higher, that we make change happen." What can you do, that you ask if you're a young person?

I love this letter. It's written by Frederick Douglass to an unknown person that would have never been heard of if it wasn't for this book. And he writes to his friend,

> I'm glad to know that the story of your eventful life has been written by a kind lady, and the same is soon to be published. You ask for what you do not need from me {...Frederick Douglass writes.} You call upon me for a word of commendation. I need such words from you far more than you could need them from me. {...He says to this unknown woman.} Especially where your superior labors and devotion to the cause of the lately enslaved of our land are known as I at least know them. The difference between us is very marked...

...says the great Frederick Douglass, one of the most known people. He was the most photographed man, period, in the 1800s.

> "The difference between us is very marked {...Frederick Douglass says} Most that I have done and suffered in the service of our cause has been in public and I have received much encouragement at every step of the way. You, on the other hand, {he says to this woman...} you on the other hand have labored in private. I have wrought in the day, you in the night. I have had the applause of the crowd and the satisfaction that comes of being approved by the multitude. While the most you have done has been witnessed by a few trembling, scared, and foot-sore bondsmen and women whom you have led out of the house of bondage and whose heartfelt, 'God bless you,' has been your only reward.
>
> The midnight sky and the silent stars have been the witnesses of your devotion to freedom and to heroism. Excepting of John Brown of much encouragement, excepting of John Brown of sacred memory, I know of no one who has willingly encountered more perils and hardships to serve our enslaved people that you have. Much of what you have done would seem improbable to those who do not know you as I know you. It is to me a great pleasure and a great privilege to bear testimony for your character and your works, and to say to those to whom may come that I regard you in every way truthful and trustworthy.

He gave his legitimacy to this book project, Frederick Douglass, to then an unknown woman who did the most heroic things. Her name was Harriet Tubman.

How did we get here, America, to this privileged place? Well, we got here because of that incredible infrastructure project that this place didn't fund called the Underground Railroad, where Black Americans and White Americans broke laws, did civil disobedience to stop slavery. How did we get here? We got here because young 20-somethings got up on a bridge named for a grand wizard of the KKK — named the Edmund Pettus Bridge. We got here because they marched. We got here because they were beaten. We got here because they bled. And I may know one or two of the people on that bridge. I may know one or two of their names, but I am in this body because of them.

How did we get here, America? We got here because of people whose names I don't know who fought at Seneca Falls. How did we get here? Because of people whose names I don't know who stood at Stonewall. We got here because of people's names I don't know who were there at Selma.

This is the answer to your question. This is an American moral moment. This is the question of where do we stand for healthcare? Where do we stand for Social Security? Where do we stand for VA benefits? Where do we stand for our American neighbor when the call and commandment of every faith in our land is to love your neighbor? What is the quality of our love, America?

Now is the time to get angry, but let that anger fuel you. Now is your time to get scared for what's happening to your neighbors and let that fear bring about your courage. Now is your time to stare at despair and say, "You will not have the last word because I'm going to stand up and at least I can give one person hope in this country. Can I give one person hope in this country?"

And so, what do I want from my fellow Americans? Do better than me, do better than we in this body. We are flawed and failed people. I see people showing up at our town halls yelling at us, Democrat and Republican, "Do more. How are you letting this happen?" Well, I hate to tell you we're doing all that I can think of. This is why I'm standing here to try to give voice to those people.

But what is more needed from now is less people sitting on the sidelines, less people being witnesses of American history, and more people determined to make it, to make history, to call to the conscience of this nation, to say, "I will not stand for another American to lose their healthcare for a billionaire. I will not stand for another veteran who's dedicated to stopping the suicide of other veterans to lose their job. I won't stand for the air quality in my community to be worse because we're letting polluters pollute more. I won't stand for the collective assaults on the Constitution by a man who even the highest judge in our land, a Republican appointed judge said, 'Stop threatening and bullying other branches of government.'"

When is it going to be enough? My voice is inadequate. My efforts today are inadequate to stop what they're trying to do. But We the People are powerful. We are strong. We have changed history. We have bent the arc of the moral universe. And now is that moral moment again — it's the moral moment again. God bless America. We need you now. God bless America. If you love her, if you love your neighbor, if you love this country, show your love. Stop them from doing what they're trying to doing.

For almost 20 hours we have laid out what they're trying to do. 20 hours. I want to stand more and I will, but I'm begging people, don't let this be another normal day in America. Please God, please God, don't let them take Medicaid away from 10, 20, 30, or 40 million Americans who desperately need it. Don't let them do it.

SENATOR ANGUS KING (MAINE): Will the Senator yield for a question?

SENATOR BOOKER: I will yield to my dear friend who I owe an apology, the last hours of your birthday, as I was preparing for this, I realized that we have a special bond. Before I yield, I want to tell this guy-

SENATOR KING: The Senator was discussing-

SENATOR BOOKER: Hold on. I yield, but I retain the right to the floor. So, I yield, but I retain the right to the floor.

SENATOR KING: I want to ask some questions about veterans in this country, but before I do so, you talked a lot about courage-

SENATOR BOOKER: Yes, sir.

SENATOR KING: -and how the world has been changed by people of courage. And I look down at my tie that I have on today, which has the signers of the Declaration of Independence. And we think of that as a sacred document, an important document in our history. But these people had the courage to put their lives on the line for a radical idea that people could govern themselves and that we could be independent of a monarch. And they were putting their lives on the line. That's courage.

And I'm afraid we have people around here, Senator, who won't put their jobs on the line for the idea of America, for our Constitution, for the guarantees that are provided in the Constitution, for the First Amendment, for the structure of the Constitution, for the independence and separation of powers, which is what provides the protection, the essential protection for our freedoms.

But let me ask a question about veterans. We had a hearing this morning in the Veterans Affairs Committee. We were hearing nominees. And I commented that here we are mostly voting on nominees in this extraordinary historic time as if everything is normal. What I said in the committee this morning was, "We're playing Nearer, My God, to Thee, on the deck of the Titanic. And we're talking about all these nominees and all these votes that we're having and not talking about what's happening to our country."

And in terms of veterans, here's what's happening. Number one, every time the guy with the chainsaw takes so much pleasure in firing people, if you hear about a thousand people fired in this government, chances are over 300 of them are veterans. 30% of the federal workforce are veterans. In the VA I suspect it's even a higher number. So, what's happening in the Veterans Administration? The first thing that happened was a hiring freeze. And the hiring freeze affected everybody in the Veterans Administration until somebody said, "Well, wait a minute, what about doctors and nurses?

What about direct care workers?" And they said, "Oh, oh, wait a minute. We didn't mean for that." And that's sort of symbolic of the way this thing is going, because they're not thinking. It's ready, fire, aim, time after time.

And so, you have a hiring freeze. Then they say, "Oh, well wait a minute. There's this group we want to do." But then they leave the hiring freeze in place for the people that are working behind the scenes. I think the Senator will agree that if nobody's there to answer the phone when a veteran calls to make a claim or make an appointment, that's a denial of benefits, just as if they've cut the benefits.

Okay. So, 2,400 people fired. And by the way, those people being fired are getting emails that say, "You're being fired for poor performance." There was no analysis of performance. There was no examination of how they were actually doing or what these people were contributing. It was random. It was people who were on probation. You know why? Because they're easier to fire under our laws. So, we've got people being fired ostensibly for poor performance. Think of that as somebody who's put their life on the line for their country because they're a veteran, and then they go to work in public service for the Veterans Administration and they're being told poor performance, when everybody knows that's a sham.

So, the next thing that happens is the Veterans Administration announces they're going to fire 83,000 people over the next six months. Now, they say, "We're going to return to the size of the Veterans Administration it was in 2019." Number one, that's an arbitrary number. Why not 2020 or 2016? It's an arbitrary number. It's not based on any analysis or deep thought.

Here's the problem, Senator, and I want you to be ready to respond to this. Here's the problem. There have been seven major pieces of legislation benefiting veterans since 2019. The biggest of which, of course, is the PACT Act, the largest expansion of veterans benefit program in probably the last 30 or 40 years. And you need people to administer that program. And instead, they're firing people. And the secretary of the Veterans Administration says, "Don't worry, it's not going to affect services at all." I don't think that statement passes the straight face test. And then we have a statement from the VA that says very proudly, "We've canceled 600 contracts." But they won't tell us what they are. I'm on the Veterans Affairs Committee. We don't know what they are. We don't know what the plan is for those 83,000 people that are going to be fired.

And I guess my question is, what do you think of an organization that says to a veteran, "Thank you for your service. You're fired"?

SENATOR BOOKER: Well, as we were talking earlier, the firings are adding up. It's going to be now about 80,000 people from the VA alone. A disproportionate number of them are veterans. And so, that is a rollback in service. We already know that veterans in all of the government agencies represent about 24% of the government workers we're talking about that are getting fired. And these are veterans, as I read their stories, that just want to keep serving their country from the national parks to serving their fellow veterans and helping them get healthcare. And we are seeing people that get exemplary reviews and then they're fired as probational workers under the only way they can, according to the law, is to say that they're a bad federal worker. And then they get insult on top of it when the highest or the most powerful man in the world and the richest man in the world, Trump and Musk, come together and call the guy making $45,000 serving other veterans, they call him a leech. They call him a parasite.

And so, I hear what you're saying. These are folks that I read their stories, they did things that few Americans would do. They went overseas and served in combat. We had one of our dear friends here who lost her legs in combat, but she stands taller than most all the people in this body. These are the people that are so ingrained in their bodies and minds and souls to serve America, to love America. This president calls somebody like John McCain a sucker. The guy who dodged the draft.

And so, I hear what you're saying and one of the things you're just saying is it makes no sense. Nobody came to the Veterans Committee in the Senate who actually approves the resources, establishes the agencies, and should have the say, according to this document, this vaunted, sacred, civically sacred text, our Constitution. And so, what are you going to say to them? If you don't even know what the plan is, you can't even explain to us what your plan to making the VA system more efficient.

Now here's the other thing. We passed in this body ... Some of my favorite Senators like John Tester, who I miss so much, maybe I even just miss bumping into the guy, because he was the only person in the Senate that let me run from one hallway all the way and hit him. I used to joke that it was this test to see what happens when the unstoppable force meets the immovable object. He is a void in this place. But he stood for that PACT Act. He gave some of the most fiery speeches and finally we got that bill passed. And we had to add tens of thousands of jobs because of the increased hundreds of thousands of people that were affected from these burn pits or from other challenges. And now we're cutting back 83,000 employees.

Patty Murray came down here and said something that affected me in my first weeks as a Senator when I in New Jersey, sat down with women veterans and they told me how long they had to wait for gynecological care. And so, what is this administration doing in its 83,000 cuts? They're going to improve services to our female veterans? I don't believe it. I don't believe it. Show me I'm wrong. Because we have an Article I duty, oversight, checks and balances. Are we doing that right now?

One of the worst things I've seen happen in national security ... And by the way, there are national security screw-ups on both parties. Nobody has a monopoly on this. Let's not be overly partisan here, but weeks ago, we who are supposed to be the pros and set the example, our national security leadership was using a commercial app to communicate classified documents and they had it on disappearing messages. So, they're violating a law of the land called the Preserving Public Records Act.

Now, I've heard from Republicans and Democrats, "This is outrageous. There should be an investigation. We should be asking common sense questions. Was this a pattern and practice of communication? How many other things that are classified have you been communicating about? There's a lot of really important questions that they should have to answer to." But where are the hearings, folks?

I just wonder why this body is shrinking from the articulated duties that we all raised our hands and said we would defend and preserve this Constitution and what it says we should do, what it says our jobs should do. But you, you're a Senator, I'm a Senator. I can't tell you what the cut VA plan is. I can't tell you it. They haven't come in here and told us. Are we doing our job? I can't tell you are we preserving and fighting for national security after one of the biggest national security scandals I've seen since I've been here. They don't have a providence in a partisan way, but they should answer for it. Are we doing our constitutional duty?

What about the administration that is ending the Consumer Finance Protection Bureau, ending that agency, ending the Department of Education? Do they have the right to do that according to this document? No. Are we saying, "Hey, we're going to stand up for the people and preserve this document?" No. Thank God for the Article III branch of government because they're being dragged into court and Republican appointed judges and Democratic appointed judges are saying, "You can't do it."

But you know what Trump is doing? He's ignoring the courts and then he's demonizing the judges. You know that threats on judges in America, the threats have gone up 400%. You know that I had a federal judge, God bless her, where somebody thought they were going to her house. They did, but she wasn't home, and they murdered her son and shot her husband. And Trump is out there threatening judges, dragging them on Twitter or X or whatever he's calling it now.

This is America. I know people on both sides of the aisle. We believe in common decency. We believe in respect. We believe that the highest office in the land should represent the best of our values, not the worst. Not a guy that we wouldn't even let babysit our kids. And so, I don't know what's going on with veterans, but I'm not going to sit by and do nothing. That's why I'm standing here. That's why I read the voices of so many veterans. Let's elevate the voices of the Americans who are being hurt and harmed. Let's talk for them if they can't talk for themselves. Let's tell them that, "We see you, we love you, and that all of us, we're going to fight for you."

SENATOR ADAM SCHIFF (CALIFORNIA): Will the gentleman yield for a question?

SENATOR BOOKER: From you, my friend, who doubled the number of vegans in the Senate? I yield for a question while retaining the floor, and I thank you for being here.

SENATOR SCHIFF: I thank you for being here. Senator Booker, I always knew you were a towering intellect and a phenomenal and passionate speaker and advocate, but I did not know your stamina until today. And I am delighted to join you on the floor and have this opportunity to engage in a dialogue with you.

SENATOR BOOKER: You can't engage in a dialogue. The parliamentarian is going to stare me down. You can ask me questions.

SENATOR SCHIFF: I stand corrected. I'm happy not to engage in a dialogue with you but to ask you a question.

SENATOR BOOKER: And I will yield for a question while retaining the floor.

SENATOR SCHIFF: And let me ask the question this way — I was in the airport yesterday when someone handed me a note that said, "Please save our country." *Please save our country*, and I think the genesis of the note was her profound concern over the direction of this country, over the increasingly authoritarian direction of this country and what is happening to the rule of law in America. We look at institution after institution and we see the guardrails of our democracy coming down, we see an assault on the rule of law unlike anything we have seen in modern history, maybe in the entire history of the United States of America, each and every institution. And why? Because they can. Because they feel they can.

So they're going after the colleges and universities. They're going after the institutions of higher learning. This was an attack that was presaged by JD Vance years ago in a speech where he talked about the professors are the enemy. They have to go after the seat of learning, so they're going after the universities and they're using an enormous cudgel. "We'll cut off your funds. We'll cut off hundreds of millions in your funds if you do things, if you say things that we in the administration don't like. If you irritate the personal predilection of the president, you'll have your funding cut." It is unlawful, it is illegal, and yet they're doing it because they can.

They're going after major American law firms because these law firms had the audacity, the unmitigated temerity to hire lawyers or have lawyers who would take on causes inimicable to the president's personal interests. So they're going after these firms and they're threatening the livelihood of these firms. "We'll close the courthouse doors. We'll cut your clients off from contracts unless you kiss the ring." And of course, it's not just the firms or what they represent. It's everyone who is in need of a lawyer who now needs to know that if they run afoul of the policy preferences of the administration, they may never get a lawyer. And why are they doing this to law firms? Because they can.

And they're going after judges. They're calling for the impeachment of judges. The latest is Judge Boasberg in a case involving the administration grabbing a bunch of people, designating them as part of a Venezuelan gang, and without any due process, without any process at all, taking them to some maximum security prison in El Salvador. And in fact, it would appear doing so even against the court order when the judge said, "Turn those planes around."

Now why are they, are they encouraging the impeachment of a judge? Well, I impeached a judge here. I was a lead manager before there was an impeachment of Donald Trump or two of them. I led an impeachment of a corrupt judge. It's the same standard of high crimes and misdemeanors. It is not a high crime or a misdemeanor to disagree in a case brought before a federal district court, to disagree with the flawed reasoning of the government. Why are they doing this to judges? Because they can. Because they can.

They're going after the press. They're going after the press and saying, "If you don't call the Gulf of Mexico the Gulf of America, we're going to prevent you from attending press events at the White House or on Air Force One." And why are they doing this to the press? This party that claims to be against censorship, why are they doing this to the press? Because they can, and they will continue to do so as long as they believe that they can, until we, and not just we in this body, but we in this country, stand up to them and tell them, "No, you can't. No, you can't."

If the slogan years ago was, "Yes, we can," today it has to be "No, you can't. No, you can't." No, you can't trample the rights of the American people. No, you can't censor our speech. No, you can't bring the weight of the Justice Department down on the American people. No, you can't, because we're going to stand together. We universities are not going to let you pick one of us off. We're going to band together. No, we're not going to let you go after the law firms. We're going to band together. No, we're not going to let you go after the press organizations. We're going to demand free speech. Until we come together, until we mobilize in a massive way together to say, "No, you can't. No, you can't," they'll continue to believe that yes, they can violate the law with impunity.

So my question, Senator Booker, is how do we tell them, "No, you can't. Not with our country. No. You can't violate the law, violate our values. Violate our interests. No, you can't." How do we tell the administration no?

SENATOR BOOKER: My friend and colleague, I'm hoping that we could figure out thousands of ignition points where Americans can stand up and do that, call to their fellow Americans to do more. I'm not upset at the folks that have been saying to Democratic Senators and House members and me and challenging me. I've talked to so many of my constituents who've said, "You've got to do more," and all of us have to interrogate ourselves.

Because like I said at the very beginning of this, at 7:00 PM on Monday night, I said we have to say to history where we stood — where we stood when they were coming after our constitutional principles, where we stood when they were threatening judges to impeach them for making just decisions, where we stood when they were taking law firms and threatening their business (unless they came and kowtow to the leader), where we stood when they were disappearing people from America with the due process that even Anton Scalia said they should have.

Where were you when they came after the healthcare of the disabled, the healthcare of the children, the healthcare of the expectant mothers, the healthcare of seniors? Where were you when they attacked veterans, laying them off for no justifiable reason and attacking the VA services that they rely on? Where were you when we turned our back on Ukraine? Where were you when we turned our back on our alliances? Where were you when they took the economy down with tariffs? When they took the economy down by threatening it so consumer confidence drops, where were you? How many things are going on?

Before we answer the question... As it says in Hebrew, "Hineni, hineni. Behold, Lord, here I am." [הנני]

And so I confess that I have been imperfect. I confess that I've been inadequate to the moment. I confess that the Democratic Party has made terrible mistakes that have given lane to this demagogue. I confess we all must look in the mirror and say, "We will do better." And it's not just defining ourselves what we're against. We, the next generation, as the Baby Boomers are leaving the stage – the last Baby Boomer president – we have to say that we are going to redeem the dream. We're going to dream America anew. We're going to start talking about bold things that don't divide people, that unite people. Bold things that excite the moral imagination of a country to do better, to go higher, to call us together. This is the time where new leaders in our country must emerge. I'm not talking about Senators, I'm talking about citizens.

This time of despair and darkness doesn't demand more darkness. We don't need to demean and degrade people who disagree with us. This is a time for us to do something bigger than that. Do you think Martin Luther King in Birmingham hated Bull Connor, or said, "I'm going to defeat this guy by bringing bigger dogs and bigger fire hoses"? No, but he did say we're going to be so creative, we're going to inspire the moral imagination of the nation. We're going to call to the conscience of the country. We're going to excite them about who we could be. When he went to the march on Washington, he didn't stand there and complain about the demagogues. Listen to his speech. He didn't stand there and demean and degrade the governor of Alabama. He didn't stand there and talk down to Bull Connor. No. He stood before the American people and said, "It's not what you're against. It's what you're for. I have a dream."

And now it's our generation. We have to redeem the dream. We have to excite people again. He in the highest office of our land wants to divide us against ourselves, wants to make us afraid, wants to make us fear so much that we're willing to violate people's fundamental rights. We're willing to go after the speech on college campuses. We're willing to go after law firms, go after the freedom of the press. Don't let them do that. Don't become like him. Be an American that says, "I look to the future and I'm excited." Yes, things are tough right now. They're hard, they're scary, they're hurting, but we can overcome this. Our American history, if it's nothing else, American history, if it's nothing else, it is a perpetual testimony to the achievement of impossible things against impossible odds.

We are a nation that is great not because of the people that are trying to whitewash our history, to remove great people, Native Americans, Black people and women from our military websites. I don't want a Disneyfication of our history. I don't want to whitewashed history. I don't want to homogenized history. Tell me the wretched truth about America because that speaks to our greatness. And so what do I want people to do? It starts with us, man, and you're doing it. I've seen courage of my colleagues. We're doing it, but we have to do more. And I'm sorry, I'm not going to be a politician that's going to say we are going to do more for you. I'm going to be a politician, I'm going to be a leader that demands more from America.

SENATOR SCHIFF: Will the Senator yield for one last question?

SENATOR BOOKER: I yield for a question while retaining the floor.

SENATOR SCHIFF: Well, this gets to exactly – Senator Booker – your point. I'm optimistic about this country. Notwithstanding this deep, difficult, dark period we are in, I'm optimistic about this country, and I'm optimistic because of something that Alexis de Tocqueville might have said. There is some dispute about whether he actually said this.

SENATOR BOOKER: The mere fact that you can quote Alexis de Tocqueville, you got me. You have me.

SENATOR SCHIFF: I would like to believe he said this. "America is a great country because America is a good country."

SENATOR BOOKER: Yes.

SENATOR SCHIFF: If he didn't say it, he should have said it, because it is true of this country. It is what makes me an optimist. There are wonderful, beautiful, patriotic people in every state of the Union, and they will see us through this, but it does, I think, require all of us to be reminded every now and then of the better angels of our nature. Now, I remember standing in that well during the first impeachment of Donald Trump.

SENATOR BOOKER: I remember sitting right here in this seat watching you.

SENATOR SCHIFF: And I'll tell you, I had approached that case as a prosecutor would approach a case, that I just needed to prove the president guilty of what he was charged with. But it became apparent very quickly that that was not enough, that notwithstanding the abundant evidence of his guilt. I needed to show something more. I needed to show that it was dangerous to keep him in office. Well, tragically events since have proven my point, but I made a different argument at that point of the trial which I think gets us to the present moment, which is that truth should matter to us. What's right should matter to us, and even if it doesn't matter to the President, it should matter to us that we are decent as Americans.

We are decent, we are good and decent people. As Americans, that's who we are. We don't believe that when someone is needing medical help, that they should be turned away. We don't believe that we should turn our back on our neighbor. We believe in extending our hand. We believe we should be able to disagree with each other without it becoming a personal hatred or antagonism. We're Americans, this is who we are. I do think sometimes we forget, and we have to remind ourselves that as Elijah Cummings used to say, we're better than this. We are better than this.

SENATOR BOOKER: Yes. I miss Elijah.

SENATOR SCHIFF: And you remind us of this all the time, Senator Booker, you really do. You also remind us that we're not defined by what we're against, we are defined by what we're for. And I am fully on the same page with you that we haven't lived up to our responsibility as a party and what we're for. I think our democracy is in trouble because our economy has been in trouble, and I think our economy has been in trouble because it's not like after the Depression or during the Depression or the Great Recession when people are out of work.

The problem today is not that people are out of work. The problem today is that people are working. They are working and they still can't get by. And you have too many millions of Americans who see their quality of life and they look at what their parents had and see it as better, and they look at the future for their kids and see it as worse. And amidst that economic difficulty, they're ready to embrace anyone who offers something different, any demagogue who comes along and promises they alone can fix it. And while this demagogue is not going to fix it, and indeed, he's made their lot much worse, it is not going to fix itself. It falls on us to come up with those big ideas.

Now, some of those big ideas are not new. Medicare for All, which I support, is a big idea that would expand healthcare access for millions of people, and make sure parents can go to work and understand that if they get sick or their kid gets sick, that they will have access to healthcare. We haven't kept pace with changes in the nature of work, changes that are going to accelerate with artificial intelligence. Changes which have meant that over the last several decades as the country's become more productive, that productivity and prosperity has simply not been shared with the people who made it possible. And I think this economic anxiety which is felt all over the world with these global changes in the marketplace have put great stress on the whole democratic experiment.

If democracy is not working for people, they will flirt with other models like authoritarianism. But we are here to tell folks that is not the direction we want to go in, but it's still incumbent on us to offer bold ideas for how we can make the economy work for people again. But I do think that what has led people into such bitter antagonisms with each other has been a lot of this uncertainty, the feeling that they are only a car payment or a health problem away from failure, and it's up to us to address that.

And so I join you, Senator Booker, in your optimism about the American people. I join you in the call on all of us really in both parties, but if they're not going to do it, it falls on us to put forward the big, bold economic plans that will ensure that we can answer the central question of our time, which is if you're working hard in America, can you still earn a good living?

SENATOR BOOKER: Yes.

SENATOR SCHIFF: We need to be able to answer that question, yes, you can. And right now, what we are seeing with this tax cut for billionaires and large corporations is just going to make the problem so much worse. But I want to thank you, Senator Booker, for your irrepressible optimism about the country, which I share. I want to thank you for seizing the helm today and every day to put forward that positive vision for our country. And my question is, where do you find the energy, my friend?

SENATOR BOOKER: I don't know. I'm finding it from my colleagues right now. I'm finding it from my friends. I'm finding it from their heart and their commitment, and I'm finding it from the people whose names and stories we're reading. And more than you know, I appreciate your friendship. I'm so happy you're my colleague now, and I believe that our future, our tomorrows, as bad as things seem, I still believe that our tomorrows are better than our yesterdays. Thank you, and I know you share that.

SENATOR SCHIFF: Amen.

SENATOR RICHARD BLUMENTHAL (CONNECTICUT): Will the Senator yield for a question?

SENATOR BOOKER: Before I yield to you, I just want you to know, I love you my friend, and thanks. We're doing some good things recently, you and I. We're trying to solve some big problems, and I appreciate that. So I yield for a question while retaining the floor.

SENATOR BLUMENTHAL: Thank you, Senator. Unlike Senator Schiff who said that he didn't know of your stamina before now, I knew well the stamina of Cory Booker, and I've always admired it. Not just physical stamina, but moral stamina, the courage of conviction, the stamina to stand up and speak truth to power, which has become now one of the most common phrases that is used in public life. But Cory Booker has epitomized it throughout his career, not only in this body, but as mayor of Newark, and as a leader in sports when he was an All-American athlete at Stanford. That physical stamina was matched by a moral stamina that is invaluable in life today, because Americans have come to prize above all, integrity, authenticity, genuineness, which Cory Booker epitomizes.

And so it's not just his eloquence today on the floor and the soaring rhetoric that we have heard from him. It's his understanding and his sense of real life impacts of what we do here on everyday Americans, and what everyday Americans are doing right now as we speak here on the floor. Everyday Americans are in the grocery stores where they're seeing higher and higher prices. Everyday Americans are at the VA hospital where their doctors and nurses and clinicians and schedulers and counselors may be out of a job because they may be among the tens of thousands targeted for dismissal. Everyday Americans are in schools, K through 12 and higher education, where the resources available for their teachers in the classrooms right now in real time are going to be cut. In fact, the workforce at the Department of Education will be cut by one half as we speak, and funds will be no longer available to teach everyday Americans.

And of course, everyday Americans right now are in hospitals and clinics. They're undergoing treatment for life-threatening diseases. Right now, they are lying on a hospital bed with needles in their arms, or receiving other kinds of treatment that have been made available, lifesaving treatments by the research at NIH that will be crippled because of the cuts that we're seeing.

And of course, everyday Americans are receiving social security checks, and social security will be cut by this administration. Medicaid that provides for those everyday Americans who are in doctors' offices right now in America. Even as we engage in this kind of soaring rhetoric, everyday Americans are contending with the real life problems of living in America.

We live in a country that has never been so unequal in terms of wealth and pay. And if we look back to our own history, we see that that inequality is a danger to all of us. The stock market crashed and depression occurred after the Gilded Age when inequality became so drastic that the middle class was in danger.

And of course, everyday Americans who are right now in the military are experiencing anger, disgust, fear, because the secrets about what they are doing, even as they engage in operations around the world. Like those pilots who are going to bomb the Houthis, engaged in that top secret mission, have learned that the details of that mission, the time of their launch, the targets, the timing of their strikes, the weather, the identity of their targets, all were being discussed over a non-secure channel by a careless, reckless Secretary of Defense.

And I don't need to go into the details of what was discussed except to say our allies are reacting with that same disgust, anger and fear, and they are having doubts about sharing intelligence with us. The Israelis are outraged by what they've seen. The intel communities of other countries are aghast and appalled, and we have yet to explore fully all of the potential ramifications, like what other conversations may have been on that unsecured kind of platform? Who else knew about them, what the motives were? There needs to be a criminal investigation. I've called for it, and everyday Americans have a right to be fearful and angry, just as those pilots should be, and our allies and intelligence communities all around the world.

So we need not only an investigation, we need action to hold accountable the individuals, beginning with the Secretary of Defense, who should resign, the National Security Advisor, who should resign, but a criminal investigation launched by the FBI National Security Division to hold accountable anyone responsible for this breakdown of security, to meet the standard of public service that Senator Booker has outlined as what we should demand of ourselves, and the responsibility that the American people have a right to deserve.

So my question really is about the standard of public service that we should expect of our leaders, and whether there is something we can do. I'm asked so often, Senator Booker, as I go back to Connecticut, and I'm sure you are in New Jersey, what can we do? What can we do? You are leading us on the floor of the Senate by showing what we should be doing. Fighting back, sounding the alarm for everyday Americans who are in the grocery store, in their schools, at the VA Clinics, Social Security offices. What can we do?

* 30 by 30 (or 30x30) is a worldwide initiative for governments to designate 30% of Earth's land and ocean area as protected areas by 2030. In the United States, it was called the "America the Beautiful" initiative.

3:11 PM - Personal Comments

SENATOR BOOKER: I'm going to answer your question.

I just first want to say thank you. There's been so many Congresspeople coming onto the floor from the House of Representatives. It reminds me of some other times where big things were happening and people would come to the floor, but this is a lot more, and I just want to express thank you for their kindness.

Also, I called the chairwoman of the CBC [Yvette Clarke, Congressional Black Caucus] last night and then texted her, and the force of the CBC, which has been giving me spirit and strength for a long time, is really one of the best parts of my time here as a United States Senator, and the fact that they have come through constantly means a lot to me.

I'm grateful that my cousin, Pam, has been here the entire time, just like Chris Murphy, the entire time in the gallery and I'm so grateful for her. I love her and she's sitting now next to my brother, and I'm just thankful for that.

I want to answer your question because I get it all the time, and I'm not sure how to answer it all the time. I read letters and it actually got me emotional in the middle of the night where somebody would detail all their challenges. They would render personal information to me in letters about their struggles with healthcare, about their conditions, about their pain, about their hurt, just sending it out to their government official that they've never probably met, hoping that they might just listen to you and be activated by your voice, but then many of them ended the letter with that question.

I am here to help you in any way. It really moves me because I believe in the deep decency of our country, and so I just want to try to answer that question more with me trying to think creatively about more that I can do as a leader. Because as I've said before, I think we as Democratic leaders have to start thinking more creatively, because obviously we don't control the Senate, we don't control the House, but we have positions that were given to us in trust by the people we represent. And moments like this require us to be more creative or more imaginative, or just more persistent and dogged and determined. And I say that in front of some of my colleagues on this floor who I know personally like you, but also some of my CBC colleagues who are sitting over here to my right who have been my rock for almost 13 years.

And I just know, before I turn to my left, to the woman who represents the most important person in my 55 years, my mom, I just want to say that the answer to that question has to be something, that I will do something more than I'm doing now. Because the cause is so great, the challenges are so real, that I will do something that I have not done before to try to help my neighbor in a time of moral crisis in our country. And that I may be afraid, my voice may shake, but I'm going to speak up more. I may be demoralized by what's happening, but I'm going to find a way to get out of bed and breathe and know that I can make myself feel a little bit better by helping another person.

I don't know what it is, but we've got to help each other now through this, and know I am a person of faith, and it was said to me by a colleague that know that we've been willing to work through the night, but joy will come.

I'm going to turn to my left because I always say that she's a Senator, but she's had one of the hardest jobs in all of America, which is to be the president of a shul [synagogue]. I met her and I realized she could probably do anything.

SENATOR SCHIFF: I know about that.

SENATOR BOOKER: Yes. I am not Jewish, but my name is Booker so I always say I'm Mish Booker. So there's a formal way I have to do this. So I see you, I love you, and I am wondering if you have something to ask me.

SENATOR JACKY ROSEN (NEVADA): Yeah. Will, the Senator yield for a question?

SENATOR BOOKER: I yield for a question while retaining the floor.

SENATOR ROSEN: Well, Booker, or a people of the book. People of the book.

SENATOR BOOKER: That is powerful. Yes.

SENATOR ROSEN: There you go. It's very powerful. The book you believe in, the books you believe in, but you read — we've heard everyone quote the Bible, philosophers, great thinkers and leaders, and you are one of them. And it has been my privilege to sit here next to you on this desk for the last six years I've been here, the best seat in the Senate.

SENATOR BOOKER: You and I, and I'm going to-

SENATOR ROSEN: And take care of your mother, who is my constituent. She is my constituent, so I have your precious mother in our hands.

SENATOR BOOKER: Who I suspect like my cousin and my brother in the gallery, that my mom is watching from Las Vegas.

SENATOR ROSEN: Yes. And we appreciate what a good mother she was and how she raised you to be strong and to be smart and to be kind. And boy, oh boy, did she give you some damn stamina. I'll just tell you that, sir. We are in awe. But my question is, thank you, Mr. Booker. Thank you for what you're doing. Thank you for using your voice to stand up against Trump's administration, reckless and extreme policies. And we've got a lot to talk about here, so I'm going to bring it back to Nevada.

SENATOR BOOKER: Yes.

SENATOR ROSEN: Because we've got a lot of families in my state, and just like you, those letters, they're overwhelming and they bring me to tears. The stops in the grocery store and the airport and the shopping mall and the gas station, over and over again. People are worried. People are worried and they want us to help, and they're wondering about this. People have talked to me about-

SENATOR BOOKER: Oh, Senator-

SENATOR ROSEN: [AIDE REPLACES MIC] -oops, thank you. People have talked to me about how high costs at the grocery store are squeezing their budgets. They're concerned that the Trump tariffs, well, what are they going to do? Prices ain't going down. They are going to make prices go up instead of going down. President Trump declared tomorrow is 'liberation day'. *Liberation day.* This is what he plans — to impose the latest round of across-the-board tariffs for goods on several nations, tariffs that amount to a national sales tax on every single person that goes to a grocery store in Nevada, in New Jersey – I see my esteemed colleague, Senator Duckworth – in Illinois, and every state in this nation. Tariffs that amount to a national sales tax.

Now, Nevada's economy relies heavily on tourism. I don't have to tell anyone that, and these tariffs don't target tourism specifically, but make no mistake, they will have a profound impact on a city like Las Vegas, the entertainment capital of the world. Because when prices go up across the board, what happens? Families' budgets at the kitchen table, those kitchen table budgets there are squeezed. It means the number of visitors coming to Las Vegas, the visitors that fuel our economy, go down. It means the price that every single person, every single hotel, every single service we have goes up because of those tariffs and so it's going to have a devastating impact on Nevada, on our local economy, on our small businesses. Ninety-nine percent of businesses in Nevada are small businesses. *Small businesses.* It's going to have a devastating impact on them and the good paying jobs it supports. We see the impact. International travel down in the United States. Down. Now, that's a whole 'nother discussion. Someone will be asking that question too. It's driving down our visitor numbers. It hurts our economy in Nevada, hurts our economy all across this great nation. In fact, booking for flights in Canada, they're already down by 70% compared to last year. Canada, our great neighbor, partner and ally to the north, down 70%. The most troubling part as a recent report estimates that up to 14,000 jobs, hospitality jobs, could be at risk due to decreased international travel as a result of these horrible, misguided tariffs.

I just want to tell you that I'm looking at all of my colleagues and I'm looking at you and you have given us the inspiration to stand here, to use our voice, to use our power, to show that we are not without a say in this country. We are not without a say and we cannot go quietly ever without that fight. Senator Booker, I want to ask you what you think these tariffs are going to do. Well, not to just the place where your mom lives in Las Vegas, but where families live all across this country and every price at the market, every price at the gas station, the mall, wherever you go, wherever you go and where people depend, like my Nevadans on their livelihood for tourism. I will repeat what Senator Blumenthal said. Senator Booker, what can we do? That's the question we're asked. What can we do?

SENATOR BOOKER: I want to answer your question, but first I want to just say what you already know. You represent my mom. You represent one of her best friends, Lou. You represent my Aunt Shirley. You represent my Uncle Butch. You represent my Aunt Marilyn. You represent so much of my family. This is the place where my father died, when Harry Reid came to his bedside when he was sick and I was still running for this office and showed me the extraordinary kindness of Senators from Nevada. That tradition has continued. I'm so grateful for you. My family's grateful for you. I'm grateful that we were founders of the Black Jewish Caucus and in fact I'm going to...

SENATOR ROSEN: Juneteenth Seder coming up.

SENATOR BOOKER: Juneteenth Seder coming up. I'm going to put this on as you have it on, as I think about Edan Alexander and all those who are suffering. I'm just so grateful for our friendship and what we've done against anti-Semitism, what we've done for the Abraham Accords.

You are somebody that you and I find a lot of ways to work with and one of the best things I saw in you was on January 6th sitting in this row, me, you Mark Kelly and I always say that often in the most difficult circumstances, you see the best of people and I don't know if you remember this, but staffers started coming, rushed in. Usually you have to have special identification and then some of them stood behind us and they were crying and they were upset and they were frightened and I just watched you go from Senator to mother and I watched you comforting people in their times of fear when they thought they were going to be killed – literally – and you were this voice of comfort, voice of calm. I saw you in one of our country's worst crises. I saw your light. I saw your love. I saw the Jewish mom and I benefited from that.

I just feel that Trump mocks us. What does his 'liberation day' mean to the people that are shackled to debt — from medical debt. They're shackled with student debt, they can't afford the rising cost of groceries. What does liberation mean to people who are chained by fear right now, waiting with bated breath to see if the Medicaid programs they rely on are going to be cut. What does his liberation mean? To people who are literally in jails right now because they were disappeared from our streets. What does his liberation mean to people who can't afford homes because of his tariffs? Who dreamed of a new car? That's going to go up as well. I don't know what he means by liberation. I honestly don't. I wish he'd explain it to the American people. Who's liberated? In this financial times, who's liberated? I don't think the law firms feel liberated — that were so threatened by you that they felt the only way they could get from out from under the threat of you is to come to you and beg them and offer them and say, we'll do this and say, we'll give you millions of dollars of pro-bono work. I don't think they feel liberated.

What about the people that are banned from the Press Corps because they won't call it the Gulf of America? The idea of the press, the freedom of the press. Do they feel his liberty? What does his liberty mean? What does Donald Trump's 'Liberty Day' tomorrow mean? In a nation where I read letter after letter of people that feel like their liberty is gone, that they're losing sleep at night worried about Social Security. What does liberty mean to the veteran that was laid off? That fought for my liberty? What does Donald Trump's liberty mean? What is he talking about? What does his liberty mean to Canada, who fought next to us? Who died next to Americans fighting for our causes. What does his liberty mean to them?

I don't understand Donald Trump. I really don't. There are going to be PhD students writing about him for generations. He'll love that. In heaven he'll look down and say, I'm so happy people talking about me, but I will tell you this.

I love great presidents. I love that Lincoln said, "With malice towards none, with charity towards all" — but I hear Donald Trump say with malice towards everybody that does not tell me how great I am and Charity? I don't know if he understands that, what it means to show sympathy and compassion and empathy and to help people whether they like you or not. I love great presidents. I love FDR. You have nothing to fear, but fear itself, but the letter, after letter, after letter, the word fear, the word terror, I was reading from voices from my state and across the country. It's as if Donald Trump is saying, "Be afraid. Be afraid of me, the big man with the power. Be afraid. Be afraid. Be afraid."

There was another president that said, "Mr. Gorbachev, tear down this wall" and yet Ukrainian Americans are watching their president go, not Mr. Gorbachev tear down the wall. They're saying, "hey, Mr. Putin, come in and take the Donbas. I'm going to start the negotiations, not with Zelenskyy at the table. I'm going to call him a dictator. I'm going to start the negotiations from a position to giving Putin what he wants – Ukrainian sovereign land – and that's where we'll start the negotiation".

I love John F. Kennedy quoting a poet saying, "Ask not what your country can do for you. Ask what you can do for your country." Donald Trump, it's ask not what your country can do for you. Ask, what can you do for Donald Trump because I will threaten you until you kowtow. I will threaten to run primaries against you. If you don't fall in line and vote for things you know are wrong. I will terrorize your law firm unless you come to me and kiss my ring. I will make political your applications for your merger. I will drop cases against you. I will pardon you if, as he said in a recent pardon, he was a pro-Trump guy.

I don't understand this. I really don't. I don't understand how he tries to divide Americans. I got on a plane once. I'm on a plane and I'm juggling to put my carry on up and I get lots of reactions in airports. I have to say on the whole part, good, but occasionally, I think my colleagues this May next month should send me a Mother's Day card because occasionally I get called 'you mother' with something following it.

Here I am putting up my overhead baggage and I sit down next to two people. The presiding officer before this, my friend from Alabama, two Alabamans. One 80 years old, one 60 years old, mother and daughter, and they see people paying attention to me and they said, "Who are you? Are you a professional athlete?" and as a middle-aged, overweight black guy, my ego wasn't insulted. I wanted to say, "Well, I could be, but I chose to serve the people", but no, I go, "No ma'am, I'm not." "Well, who are you then?" I go, "Well, I'm a Senator." And we are so conditioned in America, if we meet a congressperson out and about, the first thing we want to know is whose team are you on, my team or their team? 'Us' versus 'them'. Horrible dynamic of tribalism in our country and I took a deep breath and I looked at these two great American women and I said, "Ma'am, I'm a Democrat." The woman next to me looks at me suddenly soured and she said, "I should have brought my Trump hat," and she wheeled away from me. Immediately, I said [to myself], "You know what, I'm not going to play. I'm not going to dance to this tune. I'm going to scratch this record, scratch this record."

I looked at her and I go, "Oh my gosh. Donald Trump signed two of the biggest bills I wrote in Congress into law." The First Step Act, which we passed in this body, 87 votes. We would've got 88 if one of my dear friends and colleagues was not off trying to do whatever in the world and he wasn't here to vote on it and I talked about opportunities. I was working with Tim Scott to get billions of dollars invested into some of our country's poorest rural and urban areas. Now they were confused, but by the end of that flight, Donald Trump didn't divide us though. By the end of that flight, I was talking to them like fellow Americans and we found so many points of connection, so much common humanity and so much common cause.

These outrage machines, TV and these devices, [HOLDS UP CELLPHONE] I want to say to America, their financial interest is to keep your eyes on the screen as much as they possibly can. You know what sells? Division, divide, moral indignation.

I will tell you this. I have this great friend, part of the bald club, named Van Jones. He told me this story that he was on Crossfire on CNN and Van Jones got on with Newt Gingrich. Van Jones, a green activist – a guy I met in law school, extraordinary man, speaks like a poet to me – and he worked in the Obama White House and then Newt Gingrich, very known Republican. The two of them sit down, but Brene Brown writes something extraordinary. She writes, "It's hard to hate up close, so pull people in." They get on this show called Crossfire and they find out with all the differences they have, they also have commonalities, things they agree on and they actually kind of like each other. They go to the producers and they say, "Could you let us do the final segment called Ceasefire? Can you let us do the final segment called Ceasefire?" The producers say, "Yeah, go ahead. Go ahead." They do this last segment talking about the areas they agree, but the producers run in after a few shows and stop them. Can't do it. Why? Ratings are going down.

There are a lot of legitimate differences and places I'm going to stand my ground and fight for people's healthcare, for people's Social Security, I'm going to fight, but I'm never going to get into a position where anybody in this country can make me hate another American, because this is the age where we have to figure out how to live up to those words up there of *E Pluribus Unum*. That's the call of our ancestors, to put more indivisible into this one nation under God. That's the challenge and there's enough things that we agree on in America and especially when we stop and talk about things like the child tax credit. Most Americans are for that.

SENATOR DUCKWORTH: Will the Senator yield?

SENATOR BOOKER: Oh gosh. I've been waiting for you, for crying out loud. Why didn't you interrupt me earlier?

SENATOR DUCKWORTH: You were on a roll. You were on a roll.

SENATOR BOOKER: Come on, Senator.

3:32 PM - Betrayal of Veterans

SENATOR DUCKWORTH: Will you yield for a question?

SENATOR BOOKER: I yield for a question while retaining the floor.

SENATOR DUCKWORTH: I don't know what kind of food you eat on that vegan diet of yours, but I need to figure out more of that vegan diet.

One place where we can and do care that unites us as a nation is the role of our nation's veterans, the heroes who have sacrificed for us, although with this President, I guess he doesn't hold veterans in the same esteem. As someone who has bled for this nation, I guess I joined the ranks of the suckers and losers who have bled and died for this nation in the President's estimation, but I just wanted to start off by saying thank you again, Senator Booker, for all that you're doing as you hold the floor today, but also every other day. To underline the pain and damage Donald Trump and Elon Musk are doing, not just to our country, but to middle-class Americans throughout our country and tragically that harm even extends to our nation's veterans, who have sacrificed so much to protect this country and keep Americans safe, who should be shielded from this needless chaos and uncertainty.

Senator Booker, I know you are well aware that this administration is firing more veterans than any other administration in modern history. It's been reported that this administration, in these first few months in office, has fired approximately 6,000 veterans from federal service across this country. This list of firing, especially at the VA, has resulted in operations for our veterans being canceled. We've seen reports of the caregivers hotline, a hotline that was set up to support the caregivers who provide medical caregiving to their loved ones who served and sacrificed and are now disabled. There are delays in that hotline being answered because Donald Trump fired all of these veterans. There are people who support the crisis hotline were also fired. I know this because some of them aren't my constituents and asked for help. I had one individual who'd served in the military for over two decades, did such a good job on the crisis hotline as a frontline person answering the phone, trying to prevent their brothers and sisters from the idea of suicide. They did such a good job that they were promoted to be a trainer. They were promoted to be a supervisor, which then made them probationary and they were fired.

We were able to get some of these people their jobs back. Some of them are still out there without their jobs. This is what Donald Trump and Elon Musk has already done. This does not help our nation's veterans. This does not help our nation's heroes. If anything, it is a betrayal to them, is a betrayal, a cruel betrayal to the men and women who bravely answered the call to serve our country in uniform. A call that this President dodged five different times when he had the opportunity to serve. Our men and women in uniform came home from serving and many of them chose to continue their service to our country as federal employees. How are Elon and Trump thanking these brave, selfless Americans? They're doing it by showing them the door and leaving them wondering how they'll be able to afford next week's groceries or next month's rent, forcing them to look for a new job. The Senator from New Jersey and I are both working together to help our heroes get their jobs back, which is why I've introduced a Protect Veterans Jobs Act to reinstate all veterans who are wrongly fired from their federal jobs by Trump and Musk.

It is a critical bill to help those who've already been fired, but according to recent reports, Trump and Musk are just getting started. From everything that we've seen. They're planning on firing another 80,000 VA employees, almost a third of whom are veterans themselves. That's going to be another 25 veterans on a chopping block on top of the 6,000 who've already been fired. It is a complete betrayal from Trump and from Musk. Firing these VA employees will even harm veterans that Trump is not firing because it's going to force them to wait longer to see their healthcare providers. It's going to make them wait longer to have their disability claims adjudicated. It is going to make them wait longer to have someone pick up their calls at the veterans crisis line. It is going to make them wait even longer and their loved ones wait even longer to have their burial and funeral expense reimbursements request process and so much more, all while the VA's backlog of unprocessed claims continues growing.

I have another question for you, but first, for the Senator from New Jersey, I was wondering if you could tell us if you have heard from your veterans who have been fired — If you have heard from your veterans who've seen their services delayed in New Jersey and around the country?

SENATOR BOOKER: Yes, yes, yes, yes, yes, yes, yes. This is my veteran's book. This is what I was reading from earlier and everything you're saying is right and it's such an insult. I read stories from our veterans. It's such an insult to the highest calling of our country to stand and serve as you did, as you did. Injured veterans, disabled veterans. I read an article about thousands of disabled veterans that want to serve their country, love this nation so much that they want to serve in humble jobs, doing noble things and how do we treat them?

They say 83,000 people being laid off. A quarter of them are veterans from the VA itself, but this doesn't include VA – excuse me – veterans that do things for the park Service and our national parks. Veterans that do things for us in the Defense Department. Veterans that do things for us across this country. I found in my state some of the greatest leaders I have met, in my state are veterans who are still serving veterans, and then veteran entrepreneurs — you know the data. They're incredibly successful. They contribute to our economy. The VA is cutting not just veteran jobs, they're cutting contracts with veteran owned businesses. I don't understand how you can say out of one side of your mouth, you honor and respect our veterans, which is not what our President's always said. Dear God, what he said about John McCain.

I still remember John McCain is in a town hall with Barack Obama fighting fiercely to be the President of the United States and somebody gets up and says that Barack Obama, as if it's an insult – it's not – is a Muslim or something and he grabs the mic back and corrects her. One of his voters, he corrects her on national TV. This is wrong. He's a guy who loves his wife, Christian, loves his family. I mean, that is character and honor. Can you ever see that from our President now? This is how wrong I was and I want to admit I've made mistakes. I've been wrong. I remember where I was when he said in his campaign that he's no hero, that people who are captured are not heroes. I said to the people that were with me, up, there goes his 15 minutes of fame. I thought that was the end of Trump, but somehow you could become President of the United States when you insult the veterans who serve.

I want to read you and I know you have another question, but can I read you... I don't know. John Lewis and John McCain. The two Johns coming up a lot in so far in my 20 hours, but I want to read you this. I want to read this when you are here because I read this.

This is John McCain writing:

> Let me all tell you what I think about the Pledge of Allegiance, our flag, and our country. I want to tell you a story about when I was a prisoner of war. I spent five years in the Hanoi Hilton. In the early years of our imprisonment, the North Vietnamese kept us in solitary confinement or two or three to a cell.
>
> In 1971, the North Vietnamese moved us from these conditions of isolation into large rooms with as many as 30 to 40 men to a room. This was, as you can imagine, a wonderful change and was a direct result of the efforts of millions of Americans led by people like Nancy and Ronald Reagan, on behalf of a few hundred POWs, 10,000 miles from home. One of the men moved into my cell was Mike Christian. Mike came from a small town near Selma, Alabama. He didn't wear a pair of shoes until he was 13 years old. At 17, he enlisted in the US Navy. He later earned a commission. He became a naval flying officer and was shot down and captured in 1967. Mike had a keen and deep appreciation for the opportunities his country and our military provide for people who want to work and want to succeed.
>
> The uniforms we wore in prison consisted of a blue short sleeve shirt, trousers that looked like pajama trousers, and rubber sandals that were made out of automobile tires. I recommend them highly. My pair lasted my entire stay. As a part of the change in treatment, the Vietnamese allowed some prisoners to receive packages from home and some of these packages were handkerchiefs, scarves and other items of clothing. Mike got himself a piece of white cloth and a piece of red cloth and fashioned himself a bamboo needle. Over a period of a couple months, he sewed the American flag on the inside of his shirt. Every afternoon before we had a bowl of soup, we would hang Mike's shirt on the wall of our cell and say the Pledge of Allegiance. I know that saying the Pledge of Allegiance may not seem the most important and meaningful part of our day now, our day in the Senate, but I can assure you that for those men in that stark prison cell, it was indeed the most important and meaningful event of our day.

[*Senator Booker chokes back tears, struggling to continue*]

> One day, the Vietnamese searched our cell and discovered Mike's shirt with the flag sewn inside and removed it. That evening, they returned, opened the door of the cell, called for Mike Christian to come out, closed the door of the cell and for the benefit of us all, beat Mike Christian severely for the next couple of hours. Then they opened the door of the cell and threw him back inside. He was not in good shape. We tried to comfort and take care of him as well as we could. The cell in which we lived had a concrete slab in the middle of which we slept, four naked light bulbs in each corner of the room. After things quieted down, I went to lie down and go to sleep. As I did, I happened to look into the corner of the room. Sitting there beneath that dim light bulb with a piece of white cloth, a piece of red cloth, another shirt and his bamboo needle was my friend Mike Christian, sitting there with his eyes almost shut from his beating, making another American flag.
>
> He was not making the flag because it made Mike Christian feel better. He was making that flag because he knew how important it was for us to be able to pledge our allegiance to our flag and our country. Duty, honor, country.

We must never forget those thousands of Americans who with their courage, with their sacrifice, with their lives, made those words live for all of us. That is our veterans. That is you. That is you my friend, and Trump is coming after them. DOGE is coming after them. They're firing them right now and are we silent America? Are we silent? When the bravest amongst us, the most honorable amongst us, the most noble amongst us are losing their jobs. Did you speak up when they came for American veterans? When they fired them for no good reason? What did you do? What did you say? I say no.

SENATOR DUCKWORTH: Will the Senator yield for a question?

SENATOR BOOKER: I yield for a question while retaining the floor.

SENATOR DUCKWORTH: Thank you for what you have said. John McCain was a true hero. He said the same thing to me when I first met him. I do have a question for you, which will come later, but I thought I would tell you the story of how I met John McCain. I was recently wounded. Within weeks of being able to finally sit up for the first time, I was in physical therapy and Senator McCain came and visited us. The nurses and occupational therapists and physical therapists came running in and said, "Senator McCain, this is Captain Duckworth. She's a hero just like you" and said to me, "You're a hero like Senator McCain. You were both shot down." Senator McCain looked at me and said in that voice of his, "Didn't take no hero to fly into a missile. The good pilots don't get shot down."

I knew then and there that I really liked him because he was right. The real heroes were the buddies who carried me out of that field in Iraq. The real heroes are the sergeant in the rescue bird that carried me out and has to live with the post-traumatic stress. The real heroes are all the men and women who survived and came home and need the care, that they have rightfully earned. The care that we're providing with the PACT Act, a bill that you supported, a bill that you spoke up for.

Even while our colleagues across the aisle, many of them said it was too expensive and at a time when we should be expanding the PACT Act, when we should be recognizing more of the illnesses and injuries that came out of service around burn pits and toxic substances, you have a President who is cutting the VA, who wants to cut those jobs, who want to go after our veterans benefits, whom, just like Elon Musk has said, sees veterans as a people with their hands out. We don't have our hands out. We're simply asking for what this country promised us. Where were you, Mr. President?

Where were you, Elon, when this country asked for someone to serve? When this country asked, who amongst you will leave your family, leave your friends, leave your neighbors and put on her colors and defend her, not for your mom, not for your dad, not for your family members, but for strangers who will never know your name, will never know your sacrifice. Who among you will do that? Thank God that from Lexington and Concord, from Iwo Jima, from Ia Drang Valley, from Kandahar, from Fallujah. There were Americans who stood up and said, I will. I will defend this great nation. I will wear her colors with pride.

All we have to do as a nation is live up to one tiny little percentage of that sacrifice that they made. Let them have the benefits that they've earned and yet Donald Trump and Elon Musk are cutting those benefits.

The biggest predictor, the biggest predictor of veterans homelessness is not post-traumatic stress disorder. It is not a health condition. The biggest predictor of veterans homelessness is lack of employment. Not having a job. That begins the spiral downwards for veterans that ends up with them becoming homeless. I will tell everyone in these chambers and in this nation, we are all dishonored when a veteran must lay their head down on the very same streets that he or she defended to sleep that night. We are all dishonored.

The VA has done tremendous work, tremendous work to fight veterans homelessness and that has been a bipartisan effort. These cuts, these cuts that are costing veterans their jobs are going to start some of those veterans, unfortunately, on that path to homelessness. These cuts are going to mean those veterans homelessness programs that will prevent our veterans from becoming unhoused, those programs will not be able to take care of all the veterans of the demand. I'm already seeing it.

I spent this past weekend in Missouri at the Cochrane VA Medical Center, hearing about the challenges that they're facing. They need to expand. They don't need to shrink. They said there's going to be another 25,000 veterans moving into the area. They actually have to expand their services, and yet Elon Musk enabled by Donald Trump is cutting veterans jobs, veterans benefits because according to them, veterans aren't heroes. We are suckers and losers.

Well, I beg to differ. I beg to differ. I am sure that my colleague from New Jersey knows that firing 80,000 employees from the Department of Veterans Affairs wouldn't just cost longer delays for veterans, it will doom our VA's ability to process the influx of claims under the PACT Act, a law that is helping ensure veterans who were exposed to toxins while serving can get the care that they have earned, with more than one million claims already approved in a short time since it's become law. I can't think of a single good reason to hurt so many veterans and I'll just ask this Senator from New Jersey, can you think of any reasons?

SENATOR BOOKER: Oh God. I'm very moved by your comments. I want to say that from John McCormick, to Jack Reed, the Senate has a good number of people who serve this nation who answered the call. They should all get our honor and respect. Senator Blumenthal served, and he has a son — a Navy Seal. We should have a reverence for those people because a lot of them didn't make it back. A lot of people didn't make it back and a lot of people who came home came home with horrible wounds, visible and invisible. We should all be ashamed of the veterans that are committing suicide. We should all be ashamed of veteran homelessness. We have the capacity. We are a great enough nation to help them, but the ones that didn't come back, they watch over us. They look down upon this nation.

I want to read you one more thing. Because I was raised by parents, they really worried raising me in an affluent town, in a beautiful home, that I wouldn't recognize how extraordinarily privileged I was. My dad used to say to me, "Boy, don't walk around this house like you hit a triple. You were born on third base." My dad would say things to me like, "Boy, don't sit at this table and not realize that you drink deeply from wells of freedom and liberty that you did not dig. You eat from banquet tables of blessings prepared for you by your ancestors. You must metabolize those blessings, not so that you could pay your ancestors back, but that you could pay it forward."

My dad, when I got degrees from Stanford, Oxford, and Yale, said, "Boy, you got more degrees than the month of July, but you ain't hot." [LAUGHTER IN CHAMBER] Life ain't about the degrees you get. It's about the service you give.

McCormick and Reed and Tammy, I'm here because of people that died for this country, that stormed beaches in Normandy in this country. They were at Iwo Jima for this country. They liberated Nazi concentration camps for this country. They are buried. I've seen their burials. In Thailand, fields full of American soldiers who never made it home. Every time I see one of those, I get overcome with emotion. I can't think about it when I look at their ages — 18, 19, 20, 21... Let me read this and I'm going to compose myself because you got me all emotional, Tammy. (I thought you were my friend.)

This is a poem written by Billy Rose. You know it probably – it's called *The Unknown Soldier* – and just listen to the words and let them echo, and see if we are living up to them — if our President lives up to them, the most powerful person in the world, or the richest man in the world, are they respecting.

> There's a graveyard near the White House where the unknown soldier lies
> and the flowers there are splendid with the tears from a mother's eyes.
> I stood there not long ago with roses for the brave
> and I suddenly heard the voice speak out of the grave,
> "I am the unknown soldier," the spirit voice began,
> "and I think I have the right to ask some questions, man to man.
> Are my buddies taken care of? Was their victory so sweet?
> Is that big reward you offered selling pencils on the street?
> Did they really win the freedom they battled to achieve?
> Do you still respect that Croix de Guerre above that empty sleeve?
> Does a gold star in the window now mean anything at all?
> I wonder how my old girl feels when she hears the bugle call.
> And that baby who sang Hello Central, give me no man's land,
> can they replace her daddy with a military band?
> I wonder if the profiteers have satisfied their greed.
> I wonder if a soldier's mother ever is in need.
> I wonder if the kings who planned it all are really satisfied.
> They played their game of checkers and 11 million died.
> I am the unknown soldier and maybe I died in vain,
> but if I were alive and my country called, I'd do it all over again."

Thank you, Senator. Every time I see you, I have such reverence and gratitude that I get to serve alongside of you. I didn't serve in the military alongside of you like those courageous soldiers, like those people who carry you at risk to themselves. People who saved your life, the people that helped you in rehab, the people that empowered you to get back on your feet and run for one of the highest offices in the land. And then you serve here with distinction because you don't forget who helped you get here.

SENATOR DUCKWORTH: Just take care of my buddies.

SENATOR BOOKER: Exactly. And my dad who's in heaven with a lot of the other good folks from American history, I don't know what he'd think of his son, but I know he'd be proud of you. All right, let's talk about the economy.

SENATOR COONS: Will the Senator yield?

SENATOR BOOKER: Ah. Christopher Coons.

SENATOR COONS: Will the Senator yield for a question?

SENATOR BOOKER: I yield for a question while retaining the floor.

SENATOR COONS: Is the Senator familiar with Rory Badger of Delaware? Is the Senator familiar with my guest to the speech to a joint session of Congress delivered by President Trump just a few weeks ago?

SENATOR BOOKER: So every time I answer the question, we have to go through the same thing. I am slightly familiar, yes, because we talked about it, but I would be really happy if you asked me another question and filled in some gaps.

SENATOR COONS: If I might, I simply want to ask my colleague.

SENATOR BOOKER: Then I yield for a question. If you want to ask me a question, I yield for a question while retaining the floor with the recognition that I have to do it because I'm standing between two Delawareans and I'm a little nervous. [Laughter on the floor] Jersey never wants to be between two Delawareans.

SENATOR COONS: To my colleague and friend from the great state of New Jersey, I simply am asking the question — are you familiar with a Marine from Seaford, Delaware? His name is Rory Badger. He is not a man of politics. He is not a partisan and he only came to my attention when he called my office for assistance. Rory Badger volunteered to serve our nation, was deployed to Afghanistan, and is a decorated combat veteran of the United States Marine Corps. Working through the impact of his service, he's returned to the United States and was engaged by Fish and Wildlife in Delaware and doing great work to promote conservation with a young wife and a young son.

Marine Badger reached for what was his dream job to work for the U.S. Department of Agriculture Rural Conservation Service. All Rory wanted to do – he conveyed to me in a letter and then in person when he came to visit here – all he wanted to do was to help farmers on the Delmarva Peninsula conserve their land, create wildlife habitat, protect the environment, and be in places both beautiful and still. As you, my friend and colleague have documented in long discussion and debate in the last hour, he is one of thousands of veterans who woke to receive an unjust and unwarranted termination email that said it was for cause without citing any cause, and that threw him into the chaos and hurt of having been summarily fired by the American government. He's ultimately been rehired, thankfully, but that period of chaos and of loss made him question our nation and its commitment to our veterans.

I also, I will share with my colleague, had the opportunity to visit with our friend Senator McCain to the prison where he was imprisoned for five and a half years, tortured repeatedly, and lived through the experiences you've just shared of fellow veterans risking their lives to do the most simple thing that we take for granted at the beginning of every day here to pledge allegiance to our flag. I had a chance on visiting the Hanoi Hilton with our friend and former colleague, Senator McCain, to ask him a simple question, which was at the end of his describing the period when friends were beaten horribly, when some were killed, and when his Vietnamese captors told him, "We found out who your father is, a four-star admiral, and so we will release you any day." I simply asked him, "Knowing that you could at any moment on any day raise your hand and say, 'I will accept your offer and go home.' How did you endure another five years of torture and imprisonment?" His answer simply, "To do so would not have been honorable."

My question to you, my friend and colleague was the firing of Rory Badger honorable? Is the leadership of our current administration and its treatment of our veterans honorable? Is the value shown by the decisions being made by Elon Musk and his team at DOGE honorable? Are we putting at risk the very honor of our nation in the mistreatment of the veterans of this country? This question I put to my friend and colleague.

SENATOR BOOKER: I thank you Senator Coons, by your strength of voice, by your tone by the colleague and citizen that you invoke, you are saying the answer with strength, my friend. How do we judge our nation? What measure do we judge America? Is it by how tall our buildings are? Well, those are great marvels, but other countries have taller buildings. God, maybe Ezra Klein has got me so focused now on making our nation do bold and build great things, but does the speed of our rails as an Amtrak guy speak to the greatness of our nation? No. Other nations have faster rail. Does the wealth of our people, we have more billionaires than any other country, does that speak to the greatness of our nation? No. I think the things that speak to the greatness of a nation is how do we take care of each other?

How do we take care of our elders who deserve our respect and our reverence and gratitude for building America, for sustaining America, for doing the hard jobs to raise families, to set the next generation on their way? I think we should be judged by how we treat our children. They are the only true hope we have of seeing tomorrows that we will never live through. I think we should be judged by how we treat the sick, whether it's people with the disease of alcoholism or mental health or crippling cancers or chronic diseases. What do we do? I think we should be judged by how we nurture our families. God, we put American families under crazy stress, affordable child care, paid family leave. Other nations, our competitors have these things. I think we should judge the greatness of our nation by how we treat our veterans. These honorable men and women, some of them who gave their last measure, the last measure of their devotion on fields across the world, from Thailand to Gettysburg. They gave their lives and those who came home, those who came home, the America they experience will speak to the truth of who we are. And so I'm in this place like you're in this place.

3:56 PM - The Economy

SENATOR BOOKER: We've been friends for a long time. I'm blaming you a little bit because you're one of those people I called and said, "Hey, I'm thinking about running for Governor. I'm thinking about running for Senator." You told me to come here, man... I'm joking. I love you for it. I'm honored and blessed that New Jersey sent me here. I know that you and I are working, and let's talk like we talk when we're not on the floor of the Senate. We both are deeply devoted Christians.

You told me one of my favorite stories in the Senate, which I won't tell right now. I've been asking you to tell that story. I hope you'll tell it, but it's just about how your parents, James Baldwin said, "Children are never good at listening to their elders, but they never fail to imitate them." You are a great reflection of the stories of your parents you told me. And you and I grapple with this faith of ours which demands the most radical love. Radical love.

What does the Bible say about immigrants? I mean, come on. What does the Bible say about the poor? What does the Bible say about the hated, the prostitute, the leper, the people who are looked down upon? What's the story of the prodigal son? What's Matthew 25 say about how we should live? "Even as to the least of these you did unto me." How many times does the Bible mention poverty? How many?

SENATOR COONS: Two thousand.

SENATOR BOOKER: I am abiding by it. I will not yield to you, but I knew you would know it and I don't. Two thousand times it mentions poverty, and does it say we should scorn the poor? Does it say we should ignore the poor? No, it calls us to love our neighbor. No exceptions to that.

SENATOR COONS: Will the Senator yield for a question?

SENATOR BOOKER: Thank you, man. I've been waiting for that question. The prayers of the righteous availeth much. You are a righteous man. I have a lot of work to do so I yield for a question while retaining the floor. I tried to instigate you, Chris. I tried to throw out Jesus bait.

SENATOR COONS: You have, sir. Good.

SENATOR BOOKER: Thank God. I yield for a question about whatever you want to ask me for, but I'm retaining the floor.

SENATOR COONS: To my good friend and colleague, as we transition to comments about the economy, are you familiar with the very first time that Jesus stood in his home synagogue in Nazareth to preach? He read from the scroll a passage from ... I believe Isaiah 61, verse one to two. This is recorded in Luke, chapter four, and it is a well-known passage, and I rely upon it to understand what was the ministry of Jesus centrally about. He says this is fulfilled in your hearing today, *"The spirit of the Lord is upon me. He has anointed me to preach good news to the poor."* I don't think it is possible to read the Gospels and to read the Torah and to understand righteousness without hearing over and over and over in the course of the Old and New Testaments, a call to respect those at the margins of life. A call to be generous and open-hearted and kind to those who suffer and struggle, to be attentive to and present to those who are in prison, who are widows, who are orphans. To allow the gleaning of a field, which means to make sure that out of the abundance of our productivity on our farms, we make sure that we feed those who hunger here at home and abroad.

You cannot miss the central message, which is, as you have said, kindness to those on the margins, attentiveness to those in need. Good news to the poor. And so in this season of Lent, I ask my friend and colleague whether he's aware of our President's intention to impose significant tariffs sometime today or tomorrow that may raise the costs for working families in our nation, that may make harder the lives of those who struggle to pay for their children's food and medicines and schooling that instead of meeting his promise to make America affordable again, will almost certainly make America less affordable for those who are exactly those to whom we are called to give attention, kindness and service.

I ask my colleague and my friend, are you aware of President Trump's so-called 'liberation day' that will impose in fact thousands of dollars of additional costs on the working families of America who struggle so hard to make ends meet in a direct violation of a call to care for those in need?

SENATOR BOOKER: Yes, I'm aware. I said earlier that he calls it 'liberation day' and I'm not sure what he means by that because Americans will not, by this move, be liberated from high prices. They won't be liberated from watching their 401Ks dwindle in value as the stock market goes down. They won't be liberated from the high cost of groceries. They won't be liberated by the high cost and hard availability of housing. He calls it 'liberation day', but Americans won't be liberated from crushing debt, from medical debt, from student loan debt. Parents who are struggling to take care of their parents and their children who rely on Medicaid because a parent has Alzheimer's and a child has a disability and they're trying to make it all work, but yet they're shackled in fear because they see that recommended to a house committee on energy and commerce was to find $880 billion of cuts to the programs that they are relying on as a lifeline to keep their family together.

Who's liberated? Who's liberated by the tariffs that he's going to come and bring onto a country where half this nation is dealing with a tough, tough economic reality where half of the renters in this country, you and I, we're both local leaders. We know it is technically the definition of housing insecurity if you are paying more than a third of your income on rent.

Chris Coons, you love people, you know people you travel Delaware — it's a much smaller state. I do say that with some little bit of twisted non-Christian arrogance and from New Jersey looking down, but you know people in your state, I've been with you in your state. You're connected to your communities, so you know people that are struggling just to make ends meet. People that are one emergency away like a car accident or a sickness that forces them to miss a week of work and a paycheck that that will throw their lives in financial ruin. Is this President doing his promises to make their lives better?

President Trump is calling his tariffs 'liberation day'. You think Canada feels liberated from the bully neighbor that is Donald Trump? Do you think Greenland feels liberated from the bully nature? Do you think the Panama feels liberated? What about universities that are cutting NIH funding, that are cutting the scientific research that will cure the diseases in the future that will alleviate suffering that now aren't allowing post-docs to come to their school. They're not hiring, they're slashing the number of engineering students that they're allowing in because they're terrified because this president is menacing indirect costs. Is that liberation?

Seventy-one days in — now 72 days. I asked you, are you better off than you were 72 days ago economically? I asked that question. Ask it to your friends. Are they better off economically? Well, I don't see how they could be because prices are up. Stock market's down. The risk of recession is climbing. Consumer confidence is in the gutter. 401K plans are losing value. Are you better off than you were 72 days ago? Under this president's leadership on the verge of his so-called 'liberation day', that's going to drive prices up even more. And he's doubling down on tax cuts for the rich.

e wants an economy that works for him, his billionaire donors, his powerful special interests and it's coming at the expense of working people or struggling to get by and a lot of the programs that they rely on for their healthcare, like for their Social Security, he wants an economy where the richest people get the biggest tax cuts, where the largest corporations, heck, they may get to skip out on taxes altogether and where hardworking Americans are getting crushed by rising food prices and rising rents.

This idea that that might trickle down, but we know it doesn't work. He's continuing the same reckless economic approach he used in his first term. Massive tax cuts that are mostly to the wealthy, unchecked spending, rapacious spending, big, big, big holes in our national debt, trillions of dollars of more debt and no serious plan on how to pay for any of these things that he's doing. From Social Security to public health to the education to supports children with disabilities and scientific research, the safety nets that millions of people depend upon.

Here's the New York Times — *Trump's policies have shaken a once-solid economy economic outlook*. This is from March 7th:

> President Trump inherited an economy that was, by most conventional measures, firing on all cylinders. Wages, consumer spending and corporate profits were rising. Unemployment was low. The inflation rate, though higher than normal, was falling.
>
> Just weeks into Mr. Trump's term, the outlook is gloomier. Measures of business and consumer confidence have plunged. The stock market has been on a roller coaster ride. Layoffs are picking up and...

By the way, this was March 7th. We just finished March — the worst performing quarter in years in the stock market. Back to the article ...

> Layoffs are picking up according to some data and forecasters are cutting their estimates for economic growth this year with some even predicting that the US gross domestic product could shrink in the first quarter, and some commentators have gone further arguing that the economy could be headed for a recession, a sharp rebound in inflation or even the dreaded combination of the two, stagflation. Most economists consider that unlikely saying growth is more likely to slow than to give way to a decline.

Still the sudden deterioration in the outlook is striking, especially because it is almost entirely a result of Mr. Trump's policies and the resulting uncertainty. Tariffs and the inevitable retaliation from trading partners will increase prices and slow down growth. Federal jobs cut will push up unemployment and could lead government employees and contractors to pull back on spending while they wait to learn their fate. Deportations could drive up costs for industries like construction and hospitality and the agricultural sector that depend on immigrant labor.

{In quotes...} "If the economy was starting out in quite good shape, it probably is in less good shape after what we've seen the last few weeks," said Donald Rizmiller, chief economist at StratGas research firm. "The U.S. economy has repeatedly shown its resilience in recent years and there are parts of Mr. Trump's agenda that could foster growth. Business groups have responded enthusiastically to a Republican plans to cut taxes and reduce regulation. A streamlined government could in theory make the overall economy more productive. So far, however, the Trump administration's approach to economic policy has been characterized more by chaos – tariffs that are announced and then delayed, government workers who are fired and rehired – than careful planning."

Michael Strain, an economist at the conservative American Enterprise Institute {I know AEI well... } said Trump's policies on trade and immigration and his slash and burn approach to federal job cuts would have a damaging effect. {This is a conservative think tank.} "What President Trump has proposed will not cause a recession," he continued, "but it will slow economic growth. It will take money out of people's pockets. It will increase the unemployment rate. It will cost people jobs. It will make American businesses less competitive.'" {That's AEI folks.}

It is certainly possible for Mr. Trump's policies to come together in a way that causes a recession. His tariffs alone could shave a full percentage growth in the domestic products this year, according to some economic models, enough to cut in half the 2% growth rate that economists expected going into this year.

Many economists contend that deporting millions of immigrants – as Mr. Trump promised to do on the campaign trail last year – could be even more harmful than tariffs, given the US economy's need for workers, particularly in industries like construction and healthcare.

And the administration's push to shrink the federal government, an effort led by Elon Musk, could leave hundreds of thousands of federal workers and government contractors looking for jobs when hiring has slowed. That could set up a chain reaction. Workers who lose jobs or worry they might would pull back on spending, which would force businesses to cut costs leading to more layoffs and further reductions in spending.

Ordinarily, that would prompt the Federal Reserve to cut interest rates and shore up the economy, but that could be difficult if tariffs were also pushing up prices, making policymakers nervous that cutting interest rates could spur inflation.

"It's a death by a thousand paper cuts," said Jay Bryce and Chief Economist for Wells Fargo. {Certainly not a great liberal organization, Wells Fargo. He says ... } "All things individually aren't enough to cause a recession, but if you layer them on top of one another it might be."

Most economists think such an outcome is relatively unlikely, however, Mr. Trump has repeatedly delayed full enforcement of his promised tariffs. For example, on Thursday {...this article's from March 7th...} he suspended tariffs on most imports from Mexico and Canada until April. {What month are we in? April.} His deportation efforts have likewise gotten off to a slow start and some of the cuts to the federal workforce have been tied up in court. {As they should be.}

Such delays and reversals will help blunt the impact of Mr. Trump's policies and could make a recession less likely, at least in the short term, but the prolonged uncertainty could have its own costs leading businesses to delay investment and hiring decisions.

"If we don't get clarity by the back half of this year, economic uncertainty can be like a deer in the headlights," said Nancy Lazar, chief global economist at the investment bank Piper Sandler. "Things just stop. Business confidence is muted, employment is muted, and capital spending is put on hold."

Even if Mr. Trump's policies don't cause a recession, they could do long-term damage. Lower immigration will leave the country with a smaller labor force as a native-born population is aging. Trade barriers will be a relatively modest drag on growth, while in place a chronic condition rather than an acute one.

"It's less the economy is in a car wreck and it's more like the economy has decided to start smoking a pack a day," said an economist at the Roosevelt Institute.

In certain places and for certain groups the consequences could be harder to ignore. Veterans who make up a disproportionate share of federal workers could be particularly hard hit by government layoffs. So could parts of the countries that depend heavily on federal jobs. Apparently there are signs that home prices in the Washington metropolitan area are falling.

"It's going to be substantial for certain communities ... When you look at the aggregate, it's going to be challenging."

SENATOR TIM KAINE (VIRGINIA): Will the Senator yield for a question?

SENATOR BOOKER: I talked or texted with this person who's asking me to yield the floor. I've been letting this power go to my head. I've never in the Senate had the ability to hold the floor and leave a person in a little bit of a limbo. I just want to say that Tim Kaine is one of the friends and honestly, he's like a pastor to me. He's one of the more honorable men I've met in my life and struggles like me about faith and public service. I read your book, I really hope more people read your book*. I didn't think it was going to be as beautiful as it was. I laughed. I wept. When you were attacked by spiders and things like that. I'm sorry I was laughing at your misfortune, sir. It's a book about you going through your whole state by walking the Appalachian Trail, canoeing. Every story you told moved me. It's a great book. I've read a lot of my colleagues' books, but this one really touched me. You have this beautiful view of America and I want people to read your book. I really want people to read your book, so if I should yield, I'll yield only if you'll tell people the name of your book and maybe tell something about it. This is extortion on the Senate floor. I'm going to hold onto the floor unless you agree to that, you could shake your head up and down if you agree.

All right, then of course, to my dear friend and somebody that I probably wouldn't be standing here, we had some discussions about procedural opportunities and things like that. He had to make some concessions to me. I won't give details, but he's an honorable man and in the crux before I came here, he really helped to clear the pathway for me to stand here now. I owe you a lot of my 12 years. You are like a big brother to me and I yield for a question while retaining the floor.

SENATOR KAINE: Well, thank you to my friend Senator Booker and to all who are gathered to watch this very, very important vigil. And the question that I'm going to ask in slow motion to give you a chance to think of a response-

SENATOR BOOKER: God bless you.

SENATOR KAINE: -is a question that was inspired by your colloquy with Senator Coons where you guys were-

SENATOR BOOKER: Not a colloquy, that's not allowed. It was a question.

SENATOR KAINE: Discussion, where you were doing some Bible quoting back and forth. And as you know, I'm a big Bible reader and the thing I thought about, and actually I've thought about it during your talk since last night, is this part of the Gospel of Matthew where he's challenging people that he thinks are hypocrites. And he says to them, "*You can discern the faces of the sky, but you can't discern the signs of the times.*"

SENATOR BOOKER: Wow.

SENATOR KAINE: That's Matthew 16, two and three. "*You can discern the faces of the sky, but you cannot discern the signs of the times.*" The way I view this vigil that you have been powerfully engaged upon is you are attempting to discern and explain the signs of the times to your colleagues and to our country, and that's very important that we do. I'd like to ask you one question about the signs of the times economically to follow the discussion of what we're seeing. But then I want to ask you a question about the signs of the times more in the nature of our democracy.

So to begin on the economy, you walked through how strong the economy was on the day this president was inaugurated and two months later the challenges of a volatile stock market, the challenges of rising prices, the challenges of declining consumer confidence, the challenges of predictions that there might be slow growth or even a recession.

* *"Tim Kaine: Walk Ride Paddle", not talked about after all.*

4:25 PM - Canada

SENATOR KAINE: We will have a vote on the Senate floor tomorrow about Canadian tariffs. Based on a resolution that I've introduced that we will have a vote on. You talked at length about those tariffs and the effect that they have on Americans as Mr. President and others. As I've traveled around my Commonwealth, my farmers and my small businesses, they've seen it before. They saw it in Trump-term-one. They know how dangerous it will be. They don't want to pay more for groceries, they don't want to pay more for building supplies. Farmers don't want to pay more for fertilizer. My shipyards don't want to pay more for aluminum and steel. They were promised that they would pay less, not pay more.

They don't want to be part of a campaign to demonize a nation that has been a friend of the United States and stood side by side with us in every war since the War of 1812. They don't want to be part of a juvenile assertion by this President, that that sovereign nation is the 51st state. They don't want to be part of a name-calling effort to call the Prime Minister of a sovereign nation 'governor'. They're trying to read the signs of the times. Why is this administration that came in with such a strong economic hand doing so much so quickly to both hurt us economically, but also to tarnish a relationship that has stood the test of time with an ally?

The President often says that his goal is America first. We would all agree as members of this body in America first, but we would all passionately disagree with America alone. What is America alone going to get us? What will we turn to? Who will we turn to when the allies that we've spent decades building relationships with now feel pushed aside? Yesterday, China announced that they were going to be working with Japan and Korea on a free trade zone, possibly to respond to U.S. tariffs.

SENATOR BOOKER: Wow.

SENATOR KAINE: Other nations are having to engage in hedging behaviors because they thought we were friends and now they doubt that reality anymore. And so as you look at the signs of these economic times, and then I'll get to a second question about the signs of the times in our democracy. How are we to understand this and more importantly, how are we best to rectify it? How can we stand up for our families and reduce their burdens, not increase them? How can we stand shoulder to shoulder with linked arms with our allies to face off against adversaries, reflect on the signs of the times and point us in the right direction, please?

SENATOR BOOKER: I appreciate that. I'm going to try to keep it short, but I want to reminisce with you about something that... Do you remember in Trump's first term that he used a national security waiver to put tariffs on Canada then?

SENATOR KAINE: Yes, and my citizens really remember it because they suffered.

SENATOR BOOKER: Yes, but do you remember we had a Foreign Relations Committee meeting and a leader, I don't want to embarrass the leader, but a leader from Canada came, it was a woman, and she sat there. It was a bipartisan group together. You do remember this?

SENATOR KAINE: Yes, I do.

SENATOR BOOKER: So she sat there and then she started very slowly going back to the War of 1812 and marched through Canadian American history. I confess, I have a degree in history but I didn't know all this history, but these amazing stories of Canadian sacrifice to stand next to Americans, to die next to Americans, to fight for America, to join our artists, our cultural communities, our arts, our agricultural communities, all the things we've done hand-in-hand to make both of our nations stronger and more prosperous.

Then she looked at us and said, "And then your President, in a sense, calls us a national security threat and you all put tariffs on us." I remember the quiet, the silence around that committee table. I felt like, whoa, this is such an ally, such a friend, such a consistent ally of us throughout the hardest, difficult times of history, never left our side, that her litany was so admirable, and then she looks at us, "A national security waiver to put hardships on our economy, national security waiver to put tariffs on." They hurt Americans and they hurt – embarrassingly hurt – our northern neighbor.

But I thought that was bad enough, and now what kind of bully are you? What kind of mean spirit do you look at your northern neighbor and say, I'm going to call you governor, not with the title you earned by the people that put you in that office. It is the worst kind of behavior and nobody calls it out of our Republican colleagues. Not enough of them call it out, I should say.

So we are in, as I read in that article, in an economic crisis, and I question, how long will we wait until more of us join in a chorus and say, "Enough is enough"? I don't know the answers, I don't know how we can stop him, but I know we did in the first term. We pushed back on him successfully on his attempts to try to take healthcare away from tens of millions of Americans, and we can do it again, but more people have to do things differently.

They have to do like we've been talking all day, and I'll turn to my colleague again, as John Lewis called us, get in good trouble, necessary trouble, heal the soul of America. We have to do more and follow the examples of our forefathers and foremothers who never gave up. With conviction and determination, with an indefatigable spirit, unyielding grace, they continued time and time again pushing back, and bending the arc. It's our turn. What are we going to do? All of us have to answer that question, but I know part of the answer is we have to do more.

4:31 PM - Democracy and Tyranny

SENATOR KAINE: Will you yield? Will the Senator yield for another question?

SENATOR BOOKER: I yield for a question but I will retain... while retaining the floor.

SENATOR KAINE: This is a question about the signs of the times in our democracy. We will celebrate 250 years of American democracy in 2026, and I want it to be a celebration, not a coronation, not a requiem, not a wake, but a celebration. A week ago Sunday, 250 years ago, Patrick Henry stood on the floor of Henrico Parish, now known as St. John's Episcopal Church on Church Hill in Richmond, at a moment of decision where people were challenged to understand the signs of the times, at a moment of tyranny. He asked the immortal question, and I almost view your vigil as asking the same question about where we would stand in such a moment. There were different forks in the road, a phrase that has attained some meaning recently, and Patrick Henry said, "As for me, give me liberty or give me death."

You're giving a liberty speech, my colleague. You're giving a liberty speech as the nation begins to think about 250 years of democracy. The opposite of liberty, that which Henry was fighting against, was tyranny. It was tyranny. I am one that believes that we should mark anniversaries. We shouldn't just act steady state like this country was ordained and will just go on forever, regardless. We are coming up on 250 years of American democracy and there is a live question about its continued existence that this generation is grappling with. Henry gave that speech at St. John's Church and a few months later, July 4th, 1776, the US declared its independence from England and our history in this new chapter began. At various points along the way during the 1850s, say, or during the 1950s, generations just like ours have had to grapple with the question of whether the experiment will continue or not.

Some of our national symbols have some unusual aspects to them that point to this experiment. We have a National Anthem that ends with a question – not an assertion, not a declaration – but whether the flag will still stand over the home of the free and the land of the brave, question mark. The state flag that Virginia adopted on July 5th, 1776 is a most unusual flag. It has a woman representing Roman virtue standing astride a deposed tyrant whose crown is knocked off, who is holding a broken chain in his hand, and he's laying on the ground. It's one of only six state flags with a woman on it. It's the only state flag that features toplessness, which occasionally creates some raciness in schools as students ask about it, but it's also the flag with the most unique state motto of any state. All states have mottoes. Forty-nine states' mottoes are positive. *Hope, eureka, excelsior, onward and upward, ad astra per aspera.* Michigan's has the most unusual positive motto, in Latin, "*If you seek a pleasant peninsula, look around you."* Well, I wasn't looking for a peninsula, but I'd rather it be pleasant than not.

Virginia's is the only flag and the only state with a motto that's not positive. It's a rebuke. *Sic semper tyrannis*. Thus be it always, thus be it ever to tyrants. George Wythe, Thomas Jefferson's teacher, was in charge of designing the flag and chose that as the motto. Think about the verb tense, right? It's the only one that's a rebuke and it has stayed on our state seal and state flag since July 5, 1776. Many state flags have been changed in the last 20 years. Utah's changed, Minnesota's changed, Mississippi's changed, Georgia's changed. Virginia has essentially not changed since 1776. Neither the figure of virtue standing astride a deposed monarch or the motto *sic semper tyrannis*. Again, the verb tense, semper, always, ever. It's not in the current tense, no tyrants or down with tyrants. It's in the future tense, thus be it always to tyrants, thus be it ever to tyrants.

The Virginia flag that we pass by in Virginia every day without thinking about it, it's in every school we pass it by, it asks us two questions 250 years later. Do we retain the ability to recognize tyranny? Do we retain the virtue to defeat it? Can we recognize tyranny? Can we retain the virtue to defeat it? My friend, you are standing on the floor in the tradition of Patrick Henry, 250 years later. You are raising a question about liberty and our fidelity to it. So my question to you would be what gives you hope that the answer we will give to these questions as Americans, as those commemorating a quarter millennium of American democracy, what gives you confidence that we will answer these questions in a way that will honor those who came before us?

SENATOR BOOKER: I want to answer that question. I want to first say that Hakeem Jeffries is here, and now I'm worried because two Brooklynites are shaking hands. [LAUGHTER IN CHAMBER] I confess, when I had the floor and Schumer – for the only time in my life I could deny him the right to speak on the Senate floor – I confessed to my friend, who's part of the X Generation, Hip Hop generation, my brother who is part of this transition in American history from the Greatest Generation to the Baby Boomers, from the Baby Boomers now we're seeing leaders emerge that are X-Geners, Millennials, and he represents so much of the best of the future. I want to before I... This question's so good... Okay, because you didn't honor your commitment to me and talk about your book. [LAUGHTER IN CHAMBER] But I just want to say that I insulted Brooklyn for stealing my Nets. I told the leader, I abused my power to retain the floor and I told the leader that there's only one football team in New York, the Buffalo Bills. The other two are from New Jersey. [LAUGHTER IN CHAMBER] I should have reminded the leader that the chairman of the board, who sings New York, New York, is actually from New Jersey. I could go on with this litany, but I do want to get back to your very serious question about tyranny.

I think many of us have read books like "On Tyranny", and we're doing a lot, we're reading articles and people are talking about the fears that they have, fears that they have about this document. [HOLDS UP POCKET CONSTITUTION]

You and I have had serious conversations over the last 72 days of Donald Trump's presidency. How much of the encroachments – I would say encroachment is a gentle word – of the separation of powers is happening? We're watching justices or judges from Republican appointees to Democratic appointees trying to stop him from doing things, which one of our great Bill of Rights amendments from freedom of the press. He's doing things to the press that in my opinion are bullying them, breaking with traditions the Presidents have done in the past, trying to create press corps like Putin or Erdogan have, where they only let people in the room who will give obsequious supplications, often for the *dear leader*. What about the freedom of speech?

You and I both know that reprehensible speech is protected, disappearing people for what they said. Scalia talked very clearly about having rights even when you're in the country. One of the most conservative justices said, "You have rights." We're seeing him invoke emergencies. You've been the leader in our caucus talking about the absurdity of these emergencies he's doing and you've tried to rally this body to say, "Don't let this happen." You've talked to me about all of these things.

So what is the limit of tyranny? Well, you and I, and we talked about this with your book, I'm trying to get back there, I told you once when Skip Gates did my history that he traced my history back to Virginia. I tried to show you that I have more Virginia legitimacy because my roots go back to 1640 in your state. The Stampers came over, and following down, down, down. Then Henrietta Stamper, who my mom still talks about as a relative, John Stamper, and the chart that Skip Gates gave me, the only thing he could say about John Stamper. The mother of Henrietta Stamper was a slave woman. Born Henrietta Stamper, they called her on her documents mulatto, and Stamper fought for her ownership because it would later come out that that was his child.

These are the traditions in my family. It's really amazing what Skip Gates did and showed me that I'm the direct descendant of slaves and slave owners. I'm the direct descendant of a Confederate soldier that was captured in retreat. I'm a direct descendant of Native Americans and people that fought in the Creek Wars to kill Native Americans. And this traditions in our country, I draw upon all of them. I'm proud of all of them. They speak to us, they speak to the complicated history of America. But perhaps one of the best things I got about this complicated history was a visit to my office by... I don't know if I told the leader this... I'm sorry, I'm going to return to this question, but I think I know how busy the leader is, so if the leader asks me a question, if he asks if I'll yield for a question.

SENATOR SCHUMER: Yes, will the Senator yield for a question?

SENATOR BOOKER: I yield for a question while retaining the floor.

SENATOR SCHUMER: Now, before I ask my question... What a tour de force. You are amazing. It's not only the amount of time that you have spent here on the floor, what strength, but the brilliance of your indictment of this awful administration that is so destroying our democracy, that is taking so much away from working people in the middle class, and at the same time all for tax cuts for the billionaires. You're amazing. We salute you. America salutes you. All eyes are on you. You're incredible.

Now, here is my question that is related to what our Republican friends are trying to do to all the things that you were so opposed. So are you aware that while you were here on the floor today, Senate Republicans are declaring that using the current policy baseline is up to Lindsey Graham, not the parliamentarian? I believe that this is going nuclear and it shows how hell-bent they are on giving tax breaks to the rich even if it goes nuclear, even if it violates all the norms that they have had, even if it breaks all the promises they have made.

Do you agree with me that this is just a move that is so, so against what the traditions of the Senate have been about, but not just the traditions of the Senate, fairness, decency, ability to debate issues fairly? They're afraid to debate them. They're afraid to defend tax cuts for billionaires. They're afraid to admit they're taking away Medicaid from so many Americans. So they come up with this nuclear option showing that they don't care anymore about norms, about rules, and even about going nuclear, which the leader, the Republican leader and all of them said, "Oh no, they're not going to do that." Well, now they say they're going to do it. What does the Senator think? Does he agree with me that it's going nuclear? Does he agree with me that is a nasty, vicious, and self-seeking for the billionaires, which is what they're doing, way of proceeding?

SENATOR BOOKER: Chuck, I'm not 100% right now and you just hit me with stunning news that I can't even think about how to respond right now. I'm stunned by that and I wish, if you want to ask me a question – it has to be a question – I wish you would explain it a little bit more because what you're basically saying to me is that we're not going to go through the parliamentarian, that this is a gimmick that is going to be done to try to break really what the Byrd Rule requirements of reconciliation*. I'm using Senate speak and I don't think we should use that. So what they're going to try to say is obscure the impact of the reconciliation. They're going to obscure this, the incredible tax cuts, the cost of trillions of dollars to our economy, blowing up our debt. So-called fiscal hawks are going to blow it up. I'm stunned by this news.

SENATOR SCHUMER: So I'm asking the Senator, the great Senator Booker, a question.

SENATOR BOOKER: I yield for a question while retaining the floor.

SENATOR SCHUMER: Does he agree that this is just a blow to the people of America and it shows that the folks, the people on the other side are only interested not in playing decent, not in playing fair, not in being honest with the American people, but taking money out of the pockets of working people and the middle class and putting it in the hands of billionaires? Is that something that this country should just countenance because it does so much harm to the country, and does it not show what our colleagues are really like and what they're after?

SENATOR BOOKER: Yes. The answer to those questions is yes, but I just want to more say it's the further breaking of the Senate in a severe way. It's breaking the Senate. Every time you break the Senate like that to do another big nuclear option thing, the next time around, when the pendulum swings ... I've been here for 12 years, I've watched it swing back and forth, there's no going back now.

SENATOR SCHUMER: Would the Senator yield for another question?

SENATOR BOOKER: I yield for a question while retaining the floor.

SENATOR SCHUMER: Does the Senator remember that when this was done in the past, McConnell said, "They would regret it, and they'll regret it sooner than they think"? Does the Senator agree that that applies to the Republicans — they will regret it, and they will regret it sooner than they think?

SENATOR BOOKER: I hate to answer the question this way, but America will regret this day. American people will regret this day. All of us will regret this. All of us will.

SENATOR SCHUMER: I hate to bring the Senator bad news-

SENATOR BOOKER: You have to ask me-

SENATOR SCHUMER: -but I'm asking him a question.

SENATOR BOOKER: Yes, I yield for-

SENATOR SCHUMER: I needed his answer, given how eloquent he has been about what America should be and what America should not be, and so I yield the floor to the Senator.

SENATOR BOOKER: You cannot yield the floor because I have the floor, sir.

[LAUGHTER IN CHAMBER]

SENATOR SCHUMER: Yes.

SENATOR BOOKER: I retain the floor. This is one of the few times in my life that I'll ever get to tell Chuck Schumer what the rules are here. I just want to get back to you, and maybe there's a better way to get to you by sharing a story I don't think I've ever told you. It was a few years ago with one of Biden's last State of the Union speeches, and we all had to vote on the floor about an hour before the speech and then we would come back here and assemble to do this extraordinary walk — this extraordinary walk through history.

So days before that I was with the leader, Hakeem, and I was with some other people in the Oval Office with the President, and the President had put his arm around me as we finished the meeting and said, "Hey, Cory." I'm like, "Yes, Mr. President." "I got a big speech coming up." I said, "I know, Mr. President." He goes, "I'm going to go to Camp David and work on it." I said, " Okay, Mr. President." He goes, "Can I call you if I need some help?" I said, "Yeah, right, Mr. President. Sure." That was it. That weekend he didn't call me for help with his speech, and we came here and did that vote an hour before.

Then I like walking out that door, and many people know this, if I can, I go straight out the next doors onto the steps. I love those steps, maybe because I watched *Schoolhouse Rock* as a kid and that's

where Mr. Bill, "I'm just a bill."** So I pause sometimes there and just feel the sense of gratitude and the Supreme Court right in front of me, the Library of Congress, and stand in the right place you see the gold dome behind you.

As I'm standing there in that moment, an hour before we have to hustle back here, my phone rings. I answer my phone and it begins with what I think is one of the top stupidest questions in America. You've gotten this question, I think you would agree with me. You're not the kind of guy that uses words like, "Hey, this is stupid," but this is stupid. The thing I heard, the stupid question, "This is the White House operator. Will you hold for the President of the United States?" Who says no to that question, as one does when they get a call from the President of the United States? So I say, "Yeah, I will hold." No, wait. Wait a minute, I'm washing my hair. I say, "Yes, of course."

The next thing you know, it's Joe Biden. He goes, "Cory." I go, "Mr. President." He goes, "I'm struggling with my speech." At that point, I know you weren't this kind of student in college, but all of my guilt from my college days of waiting until the last minute to finish a paper were gone. If the President of the United States is waiting until the last minute to finish his speech, heck, I feel good. So he goes, "Cory, can I read you a section of the speech?" He read me a section of the speech where I have a lot of policy depth, and I couldn't believe it. The President of the United States, hour before his speech, rehearsing a part of the speech. Then he asks me that immortal question. You're a married man, you have to give me good advice on how to answer this question. When your spouse looks at you and says, "How do I look?" You're torn between two things, right? Maybe to tell the truth or tell your spouse what they want to hear. Tell me what you answer with. You can't do it now because I have the floor.

[LAUGHTER IN CHAMBER]

So I take a moment, am I going to tell the President what I really think of this section or am I going to just say, "Yes, Mr. Leader"? So I decide, he called me up, hour before speech, he must really want my advice, and I gave some hard input. Turn this dial down more, turned this one whatever. He said, "Okay, Cory." Abruptly, he's gone. I go home back to the office. I tell my chief of staff, "I just got a call from the President of the United States. He asked for help with a speech." What a crazy life moment while I stood on the steps like the bill, "I'm just a bill."

Anyway, we get back here and it's a wonderful moment in the Senate. I don't know if anybody has the privilege of seeing what we do. We all gaggle around those doors, we talk to each other. People think we always fight and yell, that's not the case. Democrat, Republican, merge into this ball of senatorial humanity and then those doors open. I love it because you walk out, you walk past a Thune's office, which used to be the Library of Congress. You walk past the old Senate chamber where some of the greatest debates in American history and violence on that Senate floor with the caning of Sumner. You walk through the dome, the statue by an 18-year-old woman named Reams [Vinnie Ream] of Lincoln, the suffrage leaders, Martin Luther King, Presidents, extraordinary Presidents.

Then you walk past where the old House used to meet – and you'd love this, I love this – those little gold plates on the floor where Presidents had their desks. Exactly where the Presidents had their desks. Most people go in right under Junipero Serra, California's statue, under that cross is Lincoln's gold plank, people that were in the House and served in the presence. That's not my favorite one though. It's John Quincy Adams. Why? You know this. The only person in American history ever – it'll probably never happen again – where somebody went from the Presidency and came back to the House. Ran for a House seat, worked at that spot where that desk was until he collapsed, was carried off the floor. He would soon later die. Amazing.

Maybe a future President will, maybe Obama's going to get, you know... I got to run for the House.

Then you get into that old chamber and we sit down, we find our seats, and that great moment, I don't care if you're a Republican or Democrat, when that person walks in and says, "The President of the United States of America," I still get that feeling. Joe Biden comes in, and I think he sets a record for the longest it would take to get from those doors all the way down. Everybody he's talking to. "Marjorie Taylor Greene, what's up?" He's just touching everybody. He gets up there, he gives a speech.

Now, you know that this is an aerobic event. You stand up, you sit down, you stand up, you sit down. You got to get your squats in when you're doing it, you get the exercise for a little while. Well, this part of the speech he called me on is, and I'm sitting down and I hear my input in the speech. I don't know if you all noticed it, my colleagues, but I was the first person to stand up for that section. I was looking at Schatz, "Get up, man. This is the best speech ever given." It was amazing.

I go home, I'm kind of buzzing about the whole experience. Then I'm lying in bed and I unfortunately have my phone on my nightstand, it goes off and I see a number I don't recognize. I open it up and it says, "Senator Booker, this is Jon Meacham" — the great historian. "Thank you for helping the President of the United States with his speech. You made more of a difference than you'll ever know." My first thought was, how do I print this out? How do you print out a text? So he gave me his cell phone number and now I'm going to troll him. I'm going to keep calling him until this historian comes to my office and finally he relents and he comes.

Now he steps into your domain, my brilliant friend of history. I express worry, fear, concern, demagoguery in our land, rising of tribalism. I dump on him. I'm normally a prisoner of hope, I'm normally a purveyor of finding your joy even in the toughest of times. He listens for a while and then he looks at me and says, "Cory, there's nothing about this time that is unprecedented. It's all precedented. You want to talk about demagoguery?" He goes through every generation of Americans having extraordinary demagogues. I read Margaret Chase-Smith's incredible speech on this floor against a demagogue and the demagoguery within her own party. He talks about the number one radio show in all of America — the majority of Americans listen to his anti-Semitic screeds-

SENATOR KAINE: Father Charles Coughlin.

SENATOR BOOKER: Father Coughlin. He went through them all and he said, "You want to think worry?" He said that there was an American general in the Depression – he said his name, I'm forgetting it now, I'm not at my best – and said that this guy was calling for a military takeover of our democracy***. You want to talk about authoritarianism? He talked about a Senator here on the Left, Huey Long, who was calling for the people to storm the Capitol. He went through this all and he said every single time. Nazis in Manhattan, at Madison Square Garden. I couldn't believe it, it was unbelievable.

I wish people were there listening to this guy as he went through all these times when America was at a crossroads, when we came upon a moral moment, and he said what happened how we chose the right paths, when people were trashing this document, or treading on it, or undermining it, when demagogues rose to the highest points of popularity in our land, how did we stop it? Well, he looked at me with some sympathy and said,

> Not you guys. Not a Senator. It was that the better majority of American people said, 'Enough.' They chose to define the soul of our country." He gave that phraseology to our President and he said, "The soul of America is not the people in office. It is the everyday citizens who choose the better angels of their nature, who choose right over wrong, who recognize a moral moment and know that they have to stand up and bend the arc of the moral universe, or more importantly, steer the ship of our state out of the troubled waters into the clear, open sea.

I rose here – and I've gotten into lots of questions with my colleagues – but I rose hoping to read more and more of the stories of as many Americans as I could. During the night my friend Chris Murphy and I read a lot of them. You know me well, my friend, you know the truth of all of us in this place. You know the truth of everybody. We're all mountain ranges, we all have peaks and we all have valleys. You, my friend, have seen my valleys, me at my worst. I've failed as a leader at times, or at least come up short from my own personal expectations. You've seen me at some of my better moments. I know we have obligations. I know people are right to be upset or demanding of us right now. Please help us. What are you doing in the face of people that might make it so that we might not have elections or might make it so that we do break things in this government that can never be fixed?

As one of the speakers that came into our caucus, the people that wrote the book "How Democracies Die" [Harvard professors Steven Levitsky and Daniel Ziblatt], great nations, great civilizations – forget democracies – don't necessarily die from external threats. They die from internal corruption. Think of the Roman Empire. Think of the Soviet Empire, it crumbled from its own corruption, failure to live up to its promises and ideals.

We are at this moment. I am here to tell you, America, to tell my friends and colleagues and anybody who cares to listen to a Senator from New Jersey, that we are at that moment. We're past that moment. Every day things are happening. The 72 days of this administration, God, if there's not enough to upset you, to ignite you, to realize that maybe you and your family are not getting hurt but other Americans are, our veterans are, our seniors are, we've told their stories here over these last 21 hours, 22 hours. We've told their stories.

People are getting hurt, people are afraid, people are worried, and people I don't even agree with are getting disappeared. Law firms that I've known for my entire career, for my entire career, are being forced to kowtow to this President. Universities that should be the bastions of free speech, free thought, free enterprise, intellectual research, academic research, scientific research are getting torn up by cutting indirect costs. I read stories of PhD programs that are virtually being canceled, from the best scientific minds not being able to build the state-of-the-art labs. The country that has led humanity in scientific invention is taking a blow. Fareed Zakaria, I read his article here, and he's saying that China is doubling down on investments on the universities as this President is cutting them, unless of course you come to the leader and make all these commitments, meet all of these demands. There should be enough already. It should be enough already.

So this is that moment John Meacham told me about. I want us to try in the Senate. I know my colleagues — I see Tammy Baldwin, I see Chris Murphy, I see Angela Alsobrooks. I love you guys. I've served side-by-side with you. I know your passion, I've heard your anger, I've heard your fear, I've heard how you want to fight for this country, but we are not enough. We can do demonstrations, we can do demands, we could try to do things differently. In fact, we must.

The "Byrd Rule" is the Senate is part of the budget reconciliation process.

*** "I'm Just a Bill" is a song written by Dave Frishberg. In 1976, a segment debuted with the same name as part of "America Rock," the third season of the Schoolhouse Rock! animated series.*

**** The Business Plot (1933), where Marine Corps Major General Smedley Butler alleged that wealthy businessmen plotted a military coup to install a fascist government. A special House of Representatives committee investigated and claimed details of the allegations could be corroborated.*

5:02 PM - Paying the Price

SENATOR TAMMY BALDWIN (WISCONSIN): Will the Senator yield-

SENATOR BOOKER: I will definitely yield to Tammy Baldwin, my friend and my colleague.

SENATOR BALDWIN: -to another question?

SENATOR BOOKER: Thank you very much. I don't have that much gas in the tank, but hold on, let me say it right. I yield for a question while retaining the floor.

SENATOR BALDWIN: So noted.

SENATOR BOOKER: Thank you.

SENATOR BALDWIN: Senator, since you have taken the floor, which I suppose is nearly a full day now, there have been new breaking news of mass firings. Perhaps others have come to the floor to talk about it. But you were just talking about how great democracies are shredded, sometimes from within. Look, one of the pieces of breaking news today was the mass firing of our nation's public health agency within it. Today it was reported that the Health and Human Services Department began firing up to 10,000 more people. It's more than the previous firings, including researchers, scientists, support staff, and senior leaders.

These are people who are doing work to keep our children safe from preventable illnesses and researchers who are searching for cures and treatments for diseases that plague our families, like cancer and diabetes and Alzheimer's. And look, we can all agree that government could be and should be more efficient, but here is where I disagree with the unelected Elon Musk and people like our president. People stopping the spread of measles, researchers finding cures for Alzheimer's disease are not waste, fraud, or abuse. The slash and burn that is being led by Elon Musk's DOGE will make Americans less healthy, less safe. And Elon Musk's DOGE and Donald Trump are callously ripping away treatments, cures, from millions of Americans suffering from Alzheimer's disease, cancer, ALS, and other devastating diseases.

Behind these cures are of course workers, and they are some of our nation's brightest and best and most devoted. They keep our nation healthy and our economies running. But this administration is not respecting their work, their mission. And I have to point out the why. What is the why to all of their actions today announced that they're starting that slashing of 10,000 workers within the

Department of Health and Human Services? By the way, with more in store, because last week they announced a reorganization that would result in 20,000 people losing their jobs.

But what is the why? Ripping the rug out from under cancer and Alzheimer's disease and ALS patients is all in service of finding the money that Elon Musk and Donald Trump need to cut taxes for themselves and billionaires like them. And yes, big corporate tax breaks. They are cutting cancer cures for corporate tax breaks.

Senator Booker, these cuts to health and human services are going to crush families in Wisconsin, whether it be people not having hope for a cure for a disease, or to the workers who are doing this groundbreaking research all across the United States who are going to be fired. In New Jersey, what will these firings mean for the people who you represent?

SENATOR BOOKER: I'm so grateful for the question because that's what we said we are here about. We're here to try to elevate the voices of people affected by what they're doing to our government. And frankly, as they cut the Department of Education completely or the Consumer Finance Protection Bureau. They're getting rid of agencies that were created by Congress. And many people are right to believe that it can't be eliminated without Congressional action. We were talking before with people here that the majority, the biggest plurality of people being laid off from all of these departments are our veterans.

And again, I'm going to be back in New Jersey this weekend. I'm going to try to be at a rally, a town hall. I know everywhere I go in my state, I'm going to hear from people who are rightfully angry, who are rightfully afraid, who are affected by this, who are fearful of what's to come. These are such important human emotions. But the question then is going to be for all of us, and I know people will be questioning me, "What are we going to do? What can I do? What are you going to do, Senator?"

And so I don't have a brilliant response. I don't have some prescient idea that we are going to be able to change the course of this, but I know we're going to fight. And I want to be honest with you, I wasn't sure we could stop Donald Trump when he tried to take down the ACA. I just wasn't sure. I really wasn't. I did not know how that would end. People gasped. Do you remember that in this room?

SENATOR BALDWIN: I remember that.

SENATOR BOOKER: People gasped. We did not know. This room usually has very predictable actions. That's why I'm still standing here, because I didn't want the predictable. I didn't want business as usual to happen. It's rare that we have unpredictability on this floor. It's usually finely orchestrated. You and I both know this. But that day, no one expected that, or at least wasn't sure. It was drama, it was a moment, and we won.

And I want to tell you this. I said this earlier. When I say we won, I don't think there's one Senator here and the 99 others that convinced John McCain of his vote. I know who did though, Arizonans, who stood up, who spoke up, and demanded more from their leadership not to hurt people, not to hurt folks who needed that healthcare, not to hurt folks with preexisting conditions, not to hurt children.

I am one of these people that wants to learn from our history. I want to stand here today and tell you I'm going to do everything I can. I'm willing to go to some lengths. But I am inadequate. You are inadequate. We're Senators with all of this power, but in this democracy, the power of the people is greater than the people in power. This is a moral moment that more Americans need to stand up and say, "Enough is enough." I'm sorry. The Civil Rights movement wasn't won because of just a few black folks who stood up and were really articulate. No, they called to the conscience of this country and the country responded. And it was a rainbow coalition that said, "This ain't who we are in America."

I know New Jerseyans are hurting. I know. I've been to your state. I love your state. I love sitting side by... We had some fun in your state together. We've some young artists, business people. You are this person that says this word over and over again more than any Republican or Democrat, "Buy American, buy American," and created so many jobs in your state. We were in some packed restaurant, people packed not to see me as a special guest, but to listen to your story. You are a trailblazer too in this Senate. You are doing things that our founders did not expect, and you know that. You want to stand up. I heard you in our caucus. I heard you in Schumer's leadership meeting standing up for people that are most marginalized, most looked down on, most talked about. I hear you, Tammy.

SENATOR BALDWIN: Will the Senator respond to another question?

SENATOR BOOKER: I won't respond to a question. I'm going to read this for the 75th time. I will yield for a question while retaining the floor.

SENATOR BALDWIN: Thank you, Senator Booker. You just talked about your visit to Wisconsin. You've had many. But there was one that you're talking about that I remember really well and really fondly — I had the privilege of hosting you and showing you what our state had to offer.

SENATOR BOOKER: Yes.

SENATOR BALDWIN: Something that I likely bragged about then, like I often do, is that the Badger State is known for making things. While I know you don't indulge in all of the things that we do make, because of course we have our iconic products like beer and brats and cheese, but we also build motorcycles and big industrial ships and engines that power our Navy and so much more.

SENATOR BOOKER: Some people will give a ship.

SENATOR BALDWIN: That's right. Make one too.

SENATOR BOOKER: Make them too. Yes.

SENATOR BALDWIN: Build them. And of course behind it all is our workers, as you were just talking about. And whether they are in a marsh harvesting cranberries, we're number one in cranberry production in the country.

SENATOR BOOKER: We're in the top five in New Jersey.

SENATOR BALDWIN: I know, but we're number one; not that I'm competitive here. Or whether we're on a foundry floor or whether that worker is on an assembly line, workers are what make our economy go round. And so naturally they are the ones we should be prioritizing in all of our policy, but that's not what this administration is doing. They are going to get a slap across the face when the administration slaps across the board tariffs and gets us into a trade war.

SENATOR BOOKER: Yes.

SENATOR BALDWIN: It's going to be these workers who pay the price. And Wisconsinites are really worried about what we're going to see this week. They worry about their businesses. You met so many of them when I hosted you. Their livelihoods, their communities; they're worried because we have all been here before.

Wisconsin was one of the hardest hit states by retaliatory tariffs last time Donald Trump started a trade war. During Donald Trump's last trade war, American farmers lost $27 billion in export sales. And according to further records, the state's economy lost more than $3 billion worth of product sales, product exports. And our manufacturing economy in Wisconsin, well, we lost about $26 billion in exports. And you know what? The exports that Wisconsin manufacturers make is supported by more than 460,000 jobs. And our agricultural economy is supported by 350,000 jobs. And so a trade war would be devastating to the workers of Wisconsin.

And then the prices. People have been struggling with the high price of things in grocery stores, at gas stations. A number of our business leaders have spoken out about the impending tariffs. Ariens Company in Brillion, Wisconsin, which makes outdoor power equipment like snowblowers, told Reuters news that policy whiplash in this arena is making it difficult to plan, especially as price hikes are likely in the works. And Roden Echo Valley in West Bend told one of our media outlets, WTMJ4, and I quote, "I don't like this tariff business. It's going to be on the backs of farmers because we have to depend on the world to export our commodities." He highlighted the dependency of the dairy industry on global trade, noting that 15-20% of dairy products are exported. "And if we lose," I quote again, "15% of our markets for dairy — it's going to be absolutely devastating." We've seen this before, again, in service to a big tax break for billionaires and corporations.

But to my esteemed colleague from New Jersey, thank you for visiting the state of Wisconsin. I want to ask what the impact would be in New Jersey. What would President Trump's tariffs mean for the workers of the Garden State?

SENATOR BOOKER: I love that you focus it there, because that's who President Trump made promises to in my state, that things are bad with this economy because it's not serving people who are working every day. He promised that he would make things better. "I'll make grocery prices go down." He said that. And so people were expecting that's where he'd focus. They didn't think that he'd focus on Greenland. Didn't think that he'd focus on the Gulf of Mexico. Didn't think he'd focus on bullying Canada. Didn't think he'd focus on turning his back on Ukraine. Didn't think that he'd focus on gutting the Department of Education and ending it. This is not the reason why people voted for them. They did something that Reverend Warnock calls, is a vote is a sort of prayer. He says it's like a civic prayer that I'm putting a prayer out there that you will be who I hope you can be — you'll be a blessing to my life and not a burden.

But you're talking about the burdens that he's bringing. This economy under 72 days has not gotten better for working Americans, and they don't even see the president trying to make it better. They see what he's doing to make it worse. And one of the things that's going to be these tariffs which are going to raise costs on working Americans. Then what Chuck Schumer said to me, it's sounding like it's going to just sail through a plan that's going to blow trillions of dollars of holes into our budget, give trillions of dollars of tax cuts to the wealthiest, and gut your Medicaid and gut your services for your grandparents in nursing homes.

People believed. People put their trust. I don't blame them. They're my fellow Americans. They wanted for them, families, they wanted America that was more affordable. They wanted America to be first, prioritized. They wanted a safer America, strong America, more prosperous America. I heard that. And so I know when I'm back home this weekend, I know that I'm going to encounter a lot of folks who are workers in my state who are getting hurt. They want better. They want better from their government.

And so the burden upon us and each other is what are we going to do? Are we going to do the same old thing over and over again? Or are we going to try to do things different? Are we going to be willing to, again, get in good trouble, necessary trouble to try to save the soul of this nation?

5:19 PM - Our Children

SENATOR BOOKER: I think my colleague, my dear sister, my prayer partner, my soul lifter, I thought I heard you say something?

SENATOR ANGELA ALSOBROOKS (MARYLAND): Yes. Will the Senator yield for a question?

SENATOR BOOKER: Ah yes. I yield for a question while retaining the floor.

SENATOR ALSOBROOKS: Well, I first of all want to thank you so much again, Senator Booker, for your spiritual obedience. I think it's necessary for me to say as well today to you on behalf of so many of us who are watching right now how extraordinarily proud we are of you. I would dare say that you are in so many ways our ancestors' dream, and how powerful it is for all of us who are watching to recognize that in this very chamber you are standing today 67 years after this podium was used for the 24 hours that you have used the podium that was used to block the passage of the Civil Rights Act of 1957. And today you have taken over the podium, sacrificed your own comforts. You have suffered over 22 hours to stand here today to talk instead about the greatness of America and to speak about it in such a way that reveals the love you feel for our country. We thank you for that.

This country needs right now bravery. It needs leaders who are unafraid to stand up and speak truth to power, to not hold back when calling out these callous and inhumane acts that are perpetrated by this president against the American people. And when I talk about the American people, we know who we're talking about — against our veterans, against our seniors, against our children, from every corner of our country.

I want to talk specifically today about our children. Mahatma Gandhi noted that the true measure of any society can be found in how it treats its most vulnerable members. This president is failing America's children, and he's doing so by harming our education system. We remember as well very fondly when Nelson Mandela said, "Education is the most powerful weapon which you can use to change the world." And I think many of us recognize that that is exactly why we are seeing all of the attacks that we've seen on this system because we recognize that education allows us to change the world.

Last Friday, Secretary McMahon shut yet another critical lifeline off to our states and our schools, canceling extensions that the department had previously granted to states to draw down their COVID relief money. States like Maryland originally got extensions to finish spending the remainder of these critical dollars on long-term projects like teacher recruitment, tutoring, and other services for students. We know in particular Anne Arundel Public Schools brought Chromebooks for students with their funds, but Maryland still has a remaining ESSER [Elementary and Secondary School Emergency Relief] balance of nearly $150 million. $150 Million — that's on top of the millions that have already been clawed back, frozen, or withheld from the state by this administration. These are funds that districts like ours from all across the country were using for school construction projects and mental health supports for students. This administration is refusing to acknowledge the lasting effects of the pandemic on our nation's students, cruelly stripping educational opportunities from our students, and leaving our states and our districts on the hook.

So let me be clear that these are dollars that Congress authorized, dollars that have already been allocated, dollars that have already been earmarked by Maryland and our local districts for projects that will help all of our students. Our schools planned and committed these funds in good faith, in good faith. Our states have acted in good faith, and this administration is acting in bad faith, pulling the rug out from underneath them, blowing a hole in their education budgets. Our governor had this to say, and I quote, "The clawback of these previously committed funds would place an undue burden on our school systems and undermine our collective efforts to strengthen education across the state."

And this is only the latest attack on public education by this administration, the latest attack on our schools and our students, the latest attack on our teachers. We saw this administration attack HBCUs by freezing funds for the 1890 School Scholars Program, which provides tuition for students at our land grant institutions. We saw this administration and Secretary McMahon slash teacher training grants which helped prepare our educators to serve our communities. We saw this administration proposing to move the student loan program to the small business administration, threatening students' access to aid in the promise of higher education. We saw this secretary and this administration lay off half of the staff at the Department of Education several weeks ago, firing over 1,300 staffers.

I want to talk for a minute about who the department fired. And by the way, these are people who are not incompetent. These are people who are not DEI. These are professionals, well-educated. The administration fired civil servants at the department's Office of Civil Rights, and shuttered Office of Civil Rights regional offices, including the regional office that handles discrimination cases.

I want to make really clear, and I want the American people to hear this, that what decimating the Department of Education and the Office for Civil Rights means, it means that attorneys who intervene when schools ignore complaints from students who are repeatedly called racial slurs or who are subjected to hateful speech or imagery like swastikas on campus, it provides the technical assistance that schools need to train staff on anti-harassment practices, combat harmful behaviors, and build welcoming environments. It holds K through 12 schools and colleges that failed to keep students safe accountable. It ensures that families have recourse if their child with a disability is not being served appropriately by their district, that if a child is not getting the speech therapy or other services outlined in their individualized education program, that they will have an advocate to help them.

At the time that this administration took over, there were over 270 open Office for Civil Rights cases impacting 1.3 million students in my state alone. Without enough OCR staff to do the job, investigators' caseloads will grow to an untenable level. So we spoke to some of the lawyers that work in the division that serves Maryland schools, and all of these patriotic civil servants, all they want to do is to do their jobs. They want to combat discrimination in our schools. They want to ensure that every child has the opportunity to learn in a safe environment. These civil servants don't know that that mission is possible as they and so many of their colleagues are ruthlessly fired by this administration. These cuts are catastrophic. I dare say that they, like so many other decisions by this administration, are wicked.

Senator Booker, here is my question. What are you hearing from families in the state of New Jersey as this administration dismantles the Department of Education and slashes opportunities for students and families?

SENATOR BOOKER: I'm so grateful for the question from my friend, and that's the centering that we've been trying to do, which is what are families in New Jersey and around America thinking? As you said, the Department of Education – and we read that earlier today – doesn't dictate or educational policy to states, but it does do a lot to do funding for special needs kids in the states. And so I'm already hearing from parents of kids with special needs and what the impact it will have if those resources are cut. Everything from the programs that help children afford, young people afford college, to programs that I've worked with people that help schools afford advanced scientific equipment, so the bright minds, the geniuses of our state and the country can have the equipment they need.

This administration is cutting things that are hurting families, and we are hearing from them. We're hearing from veterans. We're hearing from the elderly. We're hearing from people that are taking care of the elderly. We're hearing from people who run our hospitals. We're hearing from people that run our universities and who talk about the science funding and the cutting of PhDs. We're hearing from people who rely on Medicare and Medicaid, who rely on social security. We're hearing from people that are appalled that their nation bullies smaller nations like Canada or Greenland. We're hearing from people that are shocked at what they're doing to the most vulnerable people who come to our nation, who have American children, who have an American spouse, are being disappeared off of our streets that have no criminal record. We're hearing from people that don't think it's right, that a president should have a memecoin that allows him to enrich himself to hock his power and position for even greater wealth.

And so I've done everything I can, and I'm going to do more. I've still got a little gas in the tank to elevate those voices, to elevate those voices.

5:24 PM - Tax Policy Failures

SENATOR ALSOBROOKS: I want to talk for a minute about who the department fired. And by the way, these are people who are not incompetent. These are people who are not DEI. These are professionals, well-educated. The administration fired civil servants at the department's Office of Civil Rights and shuttered Office of Civil Rights regional offices, including the regional office that handles discrimination cases.

I want to make really clear, and I want the American people to hear this, that what decimating the Department of Education and the Office for Civil Rights means, it means that attorneys who intervene when schools ignore complaints from students who are repeatedly called racial slurs or who are subjected to hateful speech or imagery like swastikas on campus, it provides the technical assistance that schools need to train staff on anti-harassment practices, combat harmful behaviors, and build welcoming environments. It holds K-through-12 schools and colleges that failed to keep students safe accountable. It ensures that families have recourse if their child with a disability is not being served appropriately by their district; that if a child is not getting the speech therapy or other services outlined in their individualized education program, that they will have an advocate to help them.

At the time that this administration took over, there were over 270 open Office for Civil Rights cases impacting 1.3 million students in my state alone. Without enough OCR staff to do the job, investigators' caseloads will grow to an untenable level. So we spoke to some of the lawyers that work in the division that serves Maryland schools, and all of these patriotic civil servants, all they want to do is to do their jobs. They want to combat discrimination in our schools. They want to ensure that every child has the opportunity to learn in a safe environment. These civil servants don't know that that mission is possible as they and so many of their colleagues are ruthlessly fired by this administration. These cuts are catastrophic. I dare say that they, like so many other decisions by this administration, are wicked.

Senator Booker, here is my question. What are you hearing from families in the state of New Jersey as this administration dismantles the Department of Education and slashes opportunities for students and families?

SENATOR BOOKER: I'm so grateful for the question from my friend, and that's the centering that we've been trying to do, which is what are families in New Jersey and around America thinking? As you said, the Department of Education, and we read that earlier today, doesn't dictate educational policy to states, but it does do a lot to do funding for special needs kids in the states. And so I'm already hearing from parents of kids with special needs and what the impact it will have if those resources are cut. Everything from the programs that help children afford, young people afford college, to programs that I've worked with people that help schools afford advanced scientific equipment, so the bright minds, the geniuses of our state and the country can have the equipment they need.

This administration is cutting things that are hurting families, and we are hearing from them. We're hearing from veterans. We're hearing from the elderly. We're hearing from people that are taking care of the elderly. We're hearing from people who run our hospitals. We're hearing from people that run our universities and who talk about the science funding and the cutting of PhDs. We're hearing from people who rely on Medicare and Medicaid, who rely on social security. We're hearing from people that are appalled that their nation bullies smaller nations like Canada or Greenland. We're hearing from people that are shocked at what they're doing to the most vulnerable people who come to our nation, who have American children, who have [an] American spouse, are being disappeared off of our streets that have no criminal record. We're hearing from people that don't think it's right that a president should have a memecoin that allows him to enrich himself to hock his power and position for even greater wealth.

And so I've done everything I can, and I'm going to do more. I've still got a little gas in the tank to elevate those voices, to elevate those voices.

SENATOR MARK KELLY (ARIZONA): Will the senator yield for a question?

SENATOR BOOKER: Before I yield, because I just keep wanting to exercise this power that I might have for a little while longer, and exercise it over a man that I have a real chip on my shoulder. He's a senator from Arizona. Yeah, he's been a military fighter pilot. He's been an astronaut, has been out of this world.

But what ticks me off, sir, I've said nice things about everybody else, but I'm not saying them about you, sir. Because when I go home to New Jersey and I walk through my airport, I was the Newark mayor. My airport... I see your big bald head up in, a big big picture of you saying "New Jersey Hall of Fame Mark Kelly". Why the heck am I?

[LAUGHTER IN THE CHAMBER]

You're the senator from Arizona, but yeah, yeah, you're right, okay, you're this great celebrated military veteran and astronaut, who grew up in New Jersey. Who went to high school in West Orange, whose parents were cops. And so you have the accolades in my state. And I am proud of that. I'm proud I get to serve with you. I still have the floor, stop trying to speak. [LAUGHTER] There's rules in this place, don't make me sick the parliamentarian or the presiding officer. (Thank you sir, thank you sir.)

SENATOR KELLY: Senator, my apologies.

SENATOR BOOKER: Well, with that sort of deference I will now yield for a question while retaining the floor.

SENATOR KELLY: My apologies for my giant mug at your airport-

SENATOR BOOKER: Where you overshadow me, literally. [LAUGHS]

SENATOR KELLY: [LAUGHS] As Senator Booker knows, I did grow up in the state of New Jersey. And, growing up in New Jersey I came from a very working class family. My family didn't have a lot of money. My dad was a cop. He was a union member. From my earliest days of remembering my mom going to work she started out as a waitress. I remember those days after working these night shifts at these banquets, how tired she was. She would work some long hours. Then she became a secretary but she would also work as a waitress at the same time and this was just to make ends meet.

Eventually, my mother decided that she wanted to become a police officer like my dad, but this was New Jersey in the 1970s, and for a woman to become a cop, it was really really hard. It was practically unprecedented. My mom had to take a written test and then a physical fitness test, and the physical fitness test — it was designed for men. Part of this test required that my mom climb over this seven-foot-two-inch wall. Now my mother was all of about four-feet-13-inches tall. To help my mom out in passing this test my dad built a replica of this wall, made out of a door between two pine trees in our back yard. He didn't tell her he made it an inch higher at seven-foot-three. And I'd watch my mom go out there after dinner every night and try to get over this thing. Initially, she couldn't reach the the top, and when she finally could, she would usually just fall off into the dirt.

But my mom, she wasn't one to give up. Eventually, she was able to get over this thing, but it took her a long time. She practiced for months. And when she finally took this test, instead of getting over in the required nine seconds, she got over in four and a half, much faster than almost all the men. My mom became one of the first female police officers in Northern New Jersey.

She kept that job for a long time until eventually she was injured. And by the way, it was the union that protected her rights after being injured on the job. But I remember how this job changed our lives economically. Both of my parents having good-paying union jobs, it meant more money coming in the door, more money for our family, more money to play sports.

It was part of what allowed my brother and me to chase our American dream, to serve in the U.S. Navy and, eventually, both of us as astronauts in NASA. We were able to do that because our parents worked hard, and they sacrificed for us. Because of the support we had, including some really good

public schools — that is harder today for a lot of families, including the school part, by the way.

I hear from so many folks in Arizona who feel like they are working harder and harder, and they just are not getting ahead. The cost of groceries and gas and housing – especially housing – makes these folks feel like they are just running in place. It shouldn't be that way.

Elon Musk and Donald Trump, they are making it worse. Trump's tariffs are going to jack up prices on nearly everything that families rely on — groceries, rent, cars, housing. They are even trying to do away with the Department of Education. Now, how is that going to help kids get a good education?

If they are successful, their plan to gut Medicaid in order to pay for a giant tax cut for rich people, it is going to be even tougher for hardworking Americans, hard-working New Jerseyans and Arizonans to get ahead and achieve their American dream.

So as a fellow kid from New Jersey, and I never expected – never expected – that tax cuts for rich people would potentially kill the American dream of kids all over this country, but it could. And as a kid – you, Senator Booker, growing up in New Jersey – I am interested to hear what was your American dream and why, *why*, would these giant tax cuts make that kind of dream harder?

SENATOR BOOKER: I appreciate a New Jersey Hall of Fame member, the only one in the US Senate; I appreciate his question. I appreciate the service of his parents, out there every day putting their heart and soul into serving the community in a dangerous job where you often see people at their worst.

I said this earlier, James Baldwin said, "Children are never good at listening to their elders, but they never fail to imitate them." You are living up to the example your parents set in so many ways. Then you go and pull something off that really makes me jealous is you are one of the guys in the Senate that probably most married up. We are both are Jersey boys. We both grew up there in grade schools and high schools. We both know those teachers that did so much for us — they coached sports, they taught us.

I am going back for a funeral for a great man in New Jersey, named Ed Koehler, this weekend, who was one of the greater influences in my life in high school. And you know how much people invested themselves. I remember learning Little League from a guy that would come back from working at a gas station, a parent of another kid. I still remember his big thick hands teaching us how to hold the bat. This guy is working a job at a gas station and rushes home to teach his kid Little League and treated me – the only Black kid – like one of his own kids.

Special communities, special heritage, special culture that we share — this is the Jersey culture. We got a chip on our shoulders. We are tough. We are strong. We are proud.

And a lot of New Jersey is watching. Thousands of letters and emails and phone calls from all over New Jersey. Andy Kim and I are hearing from so many people, and they are afraid. They are angry. They are worried. They don't understand why they are going after our Social Security programs, cutting benefits by cutting so many employees and cutting the service people get. They don't understand why they are seeing veterans being laid off from their government jobs. They don't understand why Social Security is being called a Ponzi scheme. The President of the United States is making up lies. They don't understand why veterans and Medicaid and Medicare — there are so many things that are making people worry. I am hearing their letters, and they are praying we stop some of these things like $880 billion dollars' worth of it. And the question is, why? Why are we doing this?

We are doing this. And they are saying it is to extend or make permanent the Trump tax cuts, the overwhelming disproportionate benefit that went to the wealthiest amongst us, the wealthy corporations.

So Trump's economy in the first 72 days is pretty bad because of his reckless chaotic behavior. Prices are up. Inflation is up. The stock market had its worst quarter in two, three years. Consumer confidence is down. And now we are going to see his tariffs tomorrow, which are going to further drive up prices, create more chaos. Trump squandered the progress we were making on the economy. He tanked the market, jacked the prices.

Is it any surprise that Americans are feeling more pessimistic, as I said, with consumer confidence going down. And what's his first major legislative push? This is what we're talking about, my colleague, my friend, my fellow New Jerseyans. His first big legislative push in this body is not to help families. No plan to lower costs — that's what he said he would do. Is his first legislation coming here about lowering costs? No. Is it any relief for seniors? Is it some big idea like we did to lower prescription drug costs? No, that's not what he's doing. Is his first priority helping our veterans? No.

What is his first priority? As I said, it's extending the 2017 Trump tax cuts, a multi-trillion-dollar giveaway that slashed corporate taxes and overwhelmingly benefited the wealthy and left the middle class with crumbs, relative crumbs. He and his allies promised that the benefits would trickle down to workers. That's what we heard. "It would pay for itself," was said. But in 2022, the Fed and the Joint Committee on Taxation confirmed the truth. Ninety percent of workers, 90% of folk in our states saw no benefit.

Now Trump and his GOP allies want to double down with even bigger tax cuts that have increased the deficit by over $4.5 trillion, the majority of which would go to the wealthiest people. Let me read what the Center on Budget and Policy Priorities and how they describe the plan. Here's a quote of their writings:

> Following a presidential campaign in which Donald Trump promised to improve the economic circumstances of working families, House Republicans are instead pushing to extend all expiring provisions of the costly 2017 tax law, which are heavily skewed to people with the highest incomes and add new tax cuts on top of that. The Republican controlled House passed a budget resolution on February 25th, authorizing the $4.5 trillion in tax cuts through 2034 and called on committees to partially offset the cost with $2 trillion in cuts...

Are they cuts to the wealthiest? No. These cuts will inevitably hit programs such as Medicaid and SNAP, which help millions of families afford essential needs.

> Extending the inspiring tax cuts for individuals and large estates would double down on the flaws in the 2017 law by, one, giving benefits, the biggest benefits to the wealthy. Households with income and the top 5% who have incomes over $320,000 would receive roughly half of the benefits.

So millionaires above that, billionaires, altogether they would receive roughly half of the benefits.

" Ballooning the deficit: along with the 2001 and 2003 tax cuts enacted under President Bush, the 2017 law has severely eroded our nation's revenue base. The House budget would compound the damage, adding hundreds of billions of dollars to the deficit each and every year. Extending the 2017 tax cuts would cost $3.6 trillion through 2034.

Failing to significantly boost economic growth, workers' earnings and other benefits will not be seen. The trickle-down benefits that proponents claimed in the 2017 law that they said it would produce never materialized. And the law hasn't come close to paying for itself {as I heard on the Senate floor from my colleagues. They said, "Oh, this is going to pay for itself. All this is going to pay for itself."} Yet the House budget claims that extending the tax cuts would generate trillions in revenue, far more than any independent estimate.

As of 2017, an alternative path is available. Congress should work towards creating a fairer federal tax system that raises more revenue from wealthy people and corporations and supports high value investments, high value investments that expand opportunity and promote more shared prosperity...

During the 2017 debate, Trump administration officials and prominent proponents claimed the tax law would yield broadly shared benefits by boosting economic growth. President Trump's Council of Economic Advisers claimed the centerpiece corporate tax rate cut would very conservatively lead to a $4,000 boost in household income. {What a lie.} But the research to date has failed to find evidence that the gains from the corporate rate trickled down to most workers. {Surprise, surprise, surprise.} A study by economists from the Joint Committee on Taxation and the Federal Reserve Board found that workers below the 90th percentile of the firm's income scale, a group whose incomes were below roughly $114,000 in 2016, saw no change in earnings from the tax cut.

Proponents claim that the tax cuts would pay for themselves hasn't panned out either. In fact, a study by economists from Harvard, Princeton, the University of Chicago, and the Treasury Department estimate that the law's total corporate tax cuts, the rate cut as well as full expensing for capital investments and international tax charges, reduced revenue by roughly 98 cents for every dollar of tax cuts, reduced revenue in our country by roughly 98 cents for every dollar of tax cuts, even after accounting for increases in economic activity due to those cuts.

Similarly, proponents argued the law's 20% deduction for pass through businesses, partnerships, S corps and sole proprietorships would boost investment and create jobs. Then Treasury Secretary Steven Mnuchin, for example, argued that the deduction would be good for the economy and good for growth. But researchers have found no evidence that provided any significant boost in economic activity and little evidence that increased investment or broadly benefited workers, other than the owners themselves.

> Despite the underwhelming performance, the House Republican budget resolution assumes that in enacting a $4.5 trillion in new or extended tax cuts will produce enough additional economic growth to generate an extra $2.6 trillion in revenue through 2035. They think it's going to offset the tax cuts. The Committee for a Responsible Federal Budget has derided this claim as fantasy math, noting that it is many times greater than even the most optimistic independent estimate.

They lied to us, or at least just put out really expansive hope in the past. And none of it came true. Fool me once, shame on you. Fool the American people twice, well, we should not let it happen. This idea in this country that if you make the wealthiest more wealthy by giving them more tax cuts and deny services to our veterans, deny health care to our seniors, cut social security benefits, cut scientific research, cut programs that protect people's safety and security, that that is going to somehow help our nation to prosper as a whole, you're kidding yourselves. We have the evidence. We have the analysis.

And this is the crazy thing. As I heard from Chuck Schumer, that Republicans are now trying to hide the true cost of their billionaire tax cuts with accounting gimmicks. The New York Times interviewed budget experts from across the political spectrum to shed light on the Republican's trickery. And this is the article I want to read. I know some people have questions. I want to read this article because Schumer shook me, shook me. So here's the New York Times. The title of the article is *The Budget Trick the GOP Might Use to Make $4 Trillion Tax Cuts Look Like They're Free*.

> How much does a tax cut cost? It depends on what you compare it to. Republicans in Congress trying to advance a giant bill that includes $4 trillion in tax cut extensions are considering a novel strategy that would make the extension appear to be free money. The trick, budgeting with the assumption that current policies extended indefinitely to the future, even those with an expiration date like the 2017 tax cuts set to end next year. It's the difference between making the extension appear to cost $4 trillion, which is the true cost, or hiding it and say it costs nothing. Using this 'Current policy baseline' wouldn't change the bill's real effect on our deficits or debt, but it would make it easier to actually make the tax cuts lasting by sidestepping a rule governing budget reconciliation, the process Republicans are using to pass the bill. Yes, this sounds technical. That's why we've enlisted some of our Washington's top budget veterans to explain this maneuver using a metaphor.
>
> Across the ideological spectrum, nearly all of the more than 20 experts we heard from disliked changing the baseline {that Chuck Schumer just came in here and said, "The Republicans have already decided that they're going to do it." This is outrageous. But here, The New York Times interviewed across the ideological spectrum, whole bunch of experts from the center, from the Right, from the Left, and let's hear what they're saying about this gimmick.} "If budget reconciliation is like taking the express lanes on a highway — there's extra rules and tolls, limited stops, but it gets you where you want to go faster, using a 'current policy baseline' for taxes is like slapping a fake license plate on your car," says Zach Moeller, director of the economic program at Third Way, which describes itself as a center-left research group.

And they don't like this gimmick. They think it's fakery. Here's another person using an analogy. "It's like taking an expensive week-long vacation and then assuming you can spend an extra $1000 per day forever since you are no longer staying at The Plaza." That's Goldwyn, Senior Vice President and Senior Policy Director for the Committee For a Responsible Federal Budget, a nonpartisan group that tends to be hawkish on deficits.

Here's another person, Jessica Riedl, Senior Fellow at the Manhattan Institute. I've worked with them in the past, a conservative research group and the Chief Economist for the former Republican Senator Ron Portman of Ohio:

> Last year, despite being deeply in debt, I bought a $100,000 sports car. So next year, buying another $100,000 sports car is not irresponsible because I'm merely spending the same amount of money as the year before. And if I purchase only a $70,000 car, then I should be congratulated for reducing my annual spending by $30,000.

A conservative think tank is basically calling this a hoax and a lie. Lying to yourself, that if I keep spending, spending, spending the same amount I've kept spending, spending, spending to drive up the costs, then I'm just doing the same thing I've done before. So it's not adding.

Well, it is adding. There's no way to not call what the Republicans are trying to do a gimmick that's trying to hide the truth that they're going to add trillions of dollars to the deficits that we, that our children, that our children's children are going to have to pay for. The debt payments alone to service the debt are going to be bigger than any of the programs we think we should be investing in, like science research or education or affordable childcare or lowering prescription drug costs or expanding the child tax credit. Things that we know if we invest in, we'll get some returns.

But no, what they're investing in is bigger tax cuts for the wealthiest. Conservatives, independents, left left-leaning folks all come to the same conclusion. Pretending $4 trillion in tax cuts will cost nothing may not be easy math. Many Republican lawmakers who are concerned about the deficit are well aware that the bill will increase the deficit by a lot.

Here's the integrity call. One Republican in the House showed his integrity. One budget hawk named [Thomas] Massey said, "I can't vote for this stuff. I'm a budget hawk. I do not want to see increased deficits." He called it what it was. I saw him in an interview say, "Hey, hey, wait a minute. By your own numbers, Republican colleagues, you're driving up the deficit by trillions of dollars, and you're making the rich richer and you're leaving future generations more bankrupt."

So this article assumes that this was all going to be decided by the Senate parliamentarian who advises legislators on chamber rules. This parliamentarian I thought could rule that the current policy baseline isn't allowed, forcing the Republicans have to make a choice, overruling or replacing my friend, parliamentarian, somebody that on both sides of the aisle we respect. It's very rarely done. I've been here for 13 years, we've had the same parliamentarian. But that doesn't mean the Republicans won't try, this article assumes, and I guess they did try. They found a way around the parliamentarian. They found a way around the rules of the Senate. They found a way around the ideals of reconciliation and the Byrd Rule. They are deciding that the way we're going to do this is break the Senate and make up our own rules.

This is how they're going to get a bill through that gives trillion dollars of tax cuts to the wealthiest in our country who are doing very well. Let's not hate on other Americans. I celebrate success. God bless you, but you don't need tax cuts, especially not that are going to be given to you on the backs of the poor, on the backs of our elders, on the backs of our children, on the backs of expectant mothers, on the backs of my mom's, your mom's social security. What does it say about our values and our priorities to allow that to happen? Who are we, America, if you don't think this is a moral moment where the character of our country is being tested?

I tell you, the Senate has stopped crazy gimmicks like this before, but the persuasive power of Democratic Senators probably won't be enough. We as a country, like these economists, that are Republicans, that are Democrats, that are nonpartisan, who called out this budget gimmickry for what it is, when is it enough? When they came after journalists, when they came after colleges and universities, research and science, when they came after law firms who had the audacity to defend clients or to represent clients that were suing the president who, God bless America, lost in civil courts, lost in criminal courts.

When do you cross your line? We can't let this happen. It's not a Right or Left moment. It's a right or wrong moment. It's a moral moment in America. I've read Republican after Republican, from Republican governors to Republican mayor groups, from the Cato Institute to the Manhattan Institute, to AEI calling out this budget gimmickry for what it is and the result will be the same. Blowing up our federal deficit to stratospheric, almost unimaginable levels. This is wrong every way you look at it.

And if your values are fiscal conservatism, then vote with your integrity and vote against that. If your values are a fiscal hawk and you hate deficits, well vote against this bill because it violates you. Don't make up some fantasy that this is going to pay for itself. The 2017 tax cuts didn't. And you're going to extend them and say, "Well, it's going to happen this time. Oh, don't worry about it. It's going to happen this time." No, it's not.

Here's an article:

> Donald Trump built a national debt so big that it'll weigh down the economy for years. One of President Trump's lesser-known but profoundly damaging legacies will be the explosive rise in the national debt that occurred on his watch. The financial burden that he's inflicted on our government will wreak havoc for decades, saddling our kids and grandkids with debt. The national debt has risen by almost $7.8 trillion during Trump's term in office. That's nearly twice as much as what Americans owe in student loans, car loans, credit cards, and every other type of debt other than mortgages combined, according to the Federal Reserve Bank. It amounts to about $23,500 in new federal debt for every person in the country. {Every person — $23,500.}
>
> The growth in the annual deficit under Trump ranks as the third biggest increase relative to the size of the economy of any US presidential administration," according to the calculation by a leading Washington budget maven, Eugene Steuerle, I'm pronouncing the name wrong, co-founder of the Urban Brookings Tax policy. And unlike George W. Bush and Abraham Lincoln who oversaw the larger relative increases in deficits, Trump did not launch two foreign conflicts or have to pay for a civil war.

In peace times, he's number three — not the reason you want to be like Lincoln...

> Economists agree that we needed massive deficit spending during COVID-19 crisis to ward off an economic cataclysm, but federal finances under Trump had become dire even before the pandemic. That happened even though the economy was booming and unemployment was at historically low levels. By the Trump administration's own description, the pre-pandemic national debt level was already a crisis and, "A grave threat to our nation." The combination of Trump's 2017 tax cut and the lack of any serious spending restraint helped both the deficit and the debt soar.
>
> So when the once-in-a-lifetime viral disaster slammed our country and we threw more than a trillion dollars into COVID-19 related stimulus, there was no longer any margin for error. Our national debt has reached immense levels relative to our economy nearly as high as it was during the end of World War II. But unlike 75 years ago, the massive financial overhang for Medicare and Social Security will make it dramatically more difficult to dig ourselves out. Falling deeper into debt is the opposite of what the Trump... Falling deeper into the red is the opposite of what Trump, the self-styled king of debt, said would happen if he became president. In a March 31st, 2016, interview with Bob Woodward and Robert Costa of the Washington Post, Trump said he could pay down the national debt, then about $19 trillion.

This is President Trump's promise back then, over a period of eight years by renegotiating trade deals and spurring economic growth. God, this man breaks his promises over and over.

> After he took office, Trump predicted that economic growth created by his 2017 tax cut combined with the proceeds from the tariffs he imposed in 2017 on a wide range of goods from numerous countries would help eliminate the budget deficit and let the United States begin to pay down its debt. On July 17th, 2018, he told Sean Hannity of Fox News, "We have $21 trillion in debt. When this, the 2017 tax cut really kicks in, we'll start paying off the debt like it's water." {That's Trump on Fox News — lying.} Nine days later he tweeted, "Because of tariffs, we will be able to start paying down large amounts of the $21 trillion in debt that has been accumulated, much by the Obama administration."

The guy can't help blaming Obama. That's not how it played out. Nothing he said came true.

> When Trump took office in January of 2017, the nonpartisan congressional budget office was projecting that the federal deficit would be 2% to 3% of our gross domestic product during Trump's term. Instead, the deficit reached nearly 4% of gross domestic product in 2018 and 4.6 in 2019. There were multiple culprits. Trump's tax cuts, especially the sharp reduction in the corporate tax rate to 21% from 35%.

Again, I was here, a lot of my colleagues were here. The big business groups were coming in asking for 25%, from 35%, and Trump said, "Nah. You're asking me for 25, I'm going to give you 21% — cut your taxes even more."

> It took a big bite out of federal revenue. The CBO estimated in 2018 that the tax cut would increase deficits by about $1.9 trillion over 11 years. Meanwhile, Trump's claim, {I wish the author wrote Trump's lie, but he says...} Trump's claim that increased revenue from the tariffs would help eliminate or at least reduce our national debt hasn't panned out. {Surprise, surprise.}
>
> In 2018, Trump's administration began hiking tariffs on aluminum, steel, and many other products, launching what became a global trade war with China, the European Union, and other countries. The tariffs did bring in additional revenue. In the fiscal year 2019, they netted about 71 billion. Up about 36 billion from President Barack Obama's last year in office. But although 36 billion is a lot of money, it's less than one-750th of the national debt. That 36 billion could have covered a bit more than three weeks, just three weeks of the interest on the national debt. That is, had the Trump administration not unilaterally decided to send a chunk of the tariff revenue to farmers affected by his horrible trade wars. Businesses that struggled as a result of the tariffs also paid fewer taxes offsetting some of their increased tariff revenue.
>
> By early 2019, national debt had climbed to $22 trillion. Trump's budget proposal for 2020 called it a grave threat to our economic and societal prosperity... {He called his own damage that...} and asserted that the US was experiencing a national debt crisis. However, the same budget proposal included substantial growth in the national debt. By the end of 2019, the debt had risen in our country to 23.2 trillion and more federal officials were sounding the alarm. "Not since World War II have we seen deficits during times of low unemployment that are as large as those that we project, nor in the past century has it experienced large deficits for as long as we project," said the CBO.
>
> Weeks later, COVID-19 erupted and made the financial situation far worse. As of December 31st, 2020, about a month left or three weeks left in his term, the national debt had jumped to 27.75 trillion, up 39% from the 19.95 trillion when Trump was sworn in. He increased our deficit by 39%. The government ended its 2020 fiscal year with a portion of the national debt owed to investors. The metric favored by the CBO at around 100% of GDP. The CBO had predicted less than a year earlier that it would take until 2030 to reach that approximate level of a debt, but not under Donald Trump, including the trillions owed to various governmental trust funds. Under his leadership, the total debt grew and grew and grew. It's now at about 130% of GDP. {Where are the fiscal hawks?}
>
> Normally, this is where you give Trump's versions of events, but we couldn't get anyone to give us Trump's side. Judd Deer, a White House spokesman, referred us to the Office of Management and Budget, which is a branch of the White House. OMB didn't respond to our requests. The Treasury directed us to comments made by the OMB director Russell Vought in October in which he predicted that, "As the pandemic eases the economic growth rebounds, the fiscal picture will improve," he said. The

> OMB blamed legislators for deficits when Trump submitted his proposed 2021 budget.
> Unfortunately, the Congress continues to reject any efforts to restrain spending. {"It ain't me," he's saying. It's them.} Instead, they have greatly contributed to the continued ballooning of the federal deficits and debt, putting the nation's fiscal future at risk. Still, the deficit growth under Trump has been historic. The Tax Policy Center has said that a comparison of every American president using a metric called the primary deficit, they are saying Trump had the third biggest primary deficit growth, 5.2% of GDP.

He's our biggest debt man. Deficits have ballooned under this president because of his tax scam, of his lies about his tax bill in 2017, none of which came true. It didn't pay for itself. It didn't close deficits. It blew up our deficits. The benefits didn't go to working people. The benefits, as it says, over 90% would go to wealthier Americans and corporations.

> Even some Republicans have been calling out the hypocrisy. One of our colleagues, Rand Paul, in 2018, " I can't, in all honesty," Rand Paul says, "In all good faith, just look the other way because my party is now complicit in these deficits." The other thing is, there's a huge hypocrisy factor. Republicans lambasted President Obama to no end for trillion-dollar deficits and now they have to put forward a multi-trillion-dollar deficit.
> Mick Mulvaney, Trump's former Chief of Staff, said in 2020, "My party is very interested in deficits when there is a Democrat in the White House. The worst thing in the whole world is deficits when Barack Obama was president, then Donald Trump became president and we're a lot less interested in deficits as a party. We don't care at this point."

And here's a guy I've mentioned numerous times, Thomas Massie, a Republican member of the House, said earlier this year about Republicans, "We have no plan whatsoever to balance the budget other than growth, but what they're proposing is going to make deficits worse."

This is what our president is trying to do with the complicity of a lot of people who call themselves deficit hawks, who call themselves fiscal conservatives. They're going to try to blow it through here, gaming the system, creating some kind of scam to obscure the real cost of this when we all know them on the Republican side, us on the Democratic side, we all know the truth about these tax increases and what they're going to do, how much they're going to cost, but we're going to play a game it looks like here unless more Americans speak up, Republican and Democrat, people who know numbers who know what we're doing to future generations in this country.

This is wrong. And I say again, this is not Right or Left, it is right or wrong. This is a moral moment in America. What are we going to do?

6:00 PM - Chaos and Abuse of Power

SENATOR BOOKER: I'm so glad my friend, the Senator from Hawaii, is here. I try to keep M&Ms in my desk occasionally if she wants to partake of New Jersey's state product. The M&M was invented in Newark. It's the truth. [LAUGHTER IN THE CHAMBER] Get great trivia here.

I'm waiting for the Senator from Hawaii, my dear friend, to ask me a question because I have the floor.

SENATOR MAZIE HIRONO (HAWAII): Will the Senator yield to a question?

SENATOR BOOKER: I will yield for a question while retaining the floor.

SENATOR HIRONO: Okay. I'm glad you mentioned M&Ms. Both of us are lawyers and I remember I got through the studying for the bar exam by eating mounds and mounds of M&Ms. So I thank you, the senator from New Jersey, for continuing to provide me with M&Ms.

I want to thank you, Senator Booker, for standing here for hours on end to push back, to fight against this administration's lawlessness. And in fact, a reporter asked me today, "Do you think this is a good use by Senator Booker of his time to be on the floor to do this?" And I said, "Anytime any of us gets up and use our voices to counter, to fight against the lawlessness of this administration, it is a good use of our time."

So thank you, Senator Booker, for yielding to me and for standing up [for] the American people. And is it making a difference? Millions of people are watching you, Senator Booker. Millions have watched and are watching you. It's making a difference. So I want to ask you a question about the lawlessness of this administration. As you yourself said last night, "These are not normal times in our nation." In fact, these are the very words that I often use when I meet with anybody who comes to see me from Hawaii. Individuals, organizations. I say, "These are not normal times." So Donald Trump has made no secret of the fact that he fancies himself a king with total disregard for the rule of law. And from day one, he and his administration have taken one illegal action after another. On his first day in office, Donald Trump issued an executive order reporting to end birthright citizenship, a right protected in our Constitution for more than a century — birthright citizenship.

He tried to unilaterally freeze federal funding, funding for everything from cancer research to disaster aid. Funding that had already been appropriated by Congress and that the executive branch is required by law to spend it. It is not as though it's up to the President to decide what programs he's going to release money for. Congress already made that determination. By law, he is supposed to expend these funds. But again, he thinks he's the king. He can do whatever he wants. So he's put a freeze on these funds.

He's enabled Elon Musk, an unelected billionaire, the richest person in the world, whose only qualification is the more than 200 million he spent to get Trump elected to run roughshod through our government. Together, they've attempted to shutter USAID and the Consumer Financial Protection Bureau, just for two examples. This Consumer Protection Bureau, which has returned more than $21 billion to consumers through its enforcement actions. $21 billion going to our consumers. And apparently, King Trump can't stand that and neither can Elon Musk. These are agencies that do critical work at home and abroad and represent just a minuscule part of the federal budget. But this doesn't stop either Trump or Musk from going after these programs.

And Musk's so-called DOGE team has gained access to sensitive databases and payment systems across our government containing the personal information of millions of Americans. So he has access to the Treasury Department database, all our social security numbers, our tax payments, all of that. He is running roughshod, until stopped by a court, on these databases. And they've done all this without any transparency or accountability whatsoever, meaning we still don't know the full extent of where DOGE has been or what they've done.

Trump has launched an all-out assault on our federal workforce. He attempted to fire tens of thousands. He actually fired them, who are on probationary status overnight, and only for courts to order them, these thousands and thousands of federal employees in probationary status, to be reinstated weeks later. Talk about chaos, talk about sowing fear. So now he's attempting to reclassify whole swaths of federal employees to strip them of civil service protections, and in some cases, eliminate their ability to bargain collectively.

SENATOR HIRONO: He fired Department of Justice and FBI officers for seemingly no other reason than their involvement in January 6th cases. Cases they were assigned to as rank and file officials, not as though these people at DOJ and FBI had a choice in the kind of cases they were going to be assigned. They were assigned January 6th cases. And the names of these people – there's some 6,000 FBI and DOJ employees who worked on January 6th cases – and there's a fear that those names would be disclosed.

He's going after schools, from kindergartners to universities as part of his war on diversity, equity, and inclusion. There are many examples of the kind of government outreach, overreach, that they are exercising through their effort to ferret out what they call diversity, equity, and inclusion, which actually, that is a positive. Don't we want to be inclusive?

So I want to give you just one example. There was a teacher in Idaho who had a poster in her classroom that said, "Everyone is welcome here." And there were handprints – different colors – white, black, yellow handprints. And she was told she had to take this poster down and that if the handprints were all White handprints, she could have kept the poster up, but she was told she had to take this poster in her classroom that says, "Everyone is welcome here." She took it down at first, but she felt so bad about it that she put it back up. And then she was told by the powers that be at her school that she had a certain amount of time to take this poster down, otherwise there will be disciplinary action.

That is the kind of government overreach that is a hallmark of this administration. To date, the Trump administration has withheld millions of dollars from handpicked colleges and universities, conditioning the funding on unreasonable demands meant to bring these colleges to their knees. So he is starting with Harvard, Columbia. There's probably a whole long list of colleges that he's threatened to withdraw hundreds of millions of dollars from. They've slashed funding or staffing at the Department of Education.

In fact, they would like to dismantle the Department of Education, which is responsible for administering billions in funding for low-income students, students with disabilities, and something as critical as school lunch for kids. Every single state in our country relies on the funding they receive from the US Department of Education. In Hawaii, we're talking about some $300 million in funding for our schools to help our kids with disabilities, to provide school lunches through the US Department of Agriculture, the things that I mention.

And as Senator Booker knows well, the list goes on and on. This administration continues to abuse its power, acting with total disregard for the rule of law. And we have turned to the courts to stop these illegal acts. And now Republicans are calling to impeach these judges who are applying the law, who are doing what they're supposed to be doing and not just giving Trump whatever results he wants, but these judges are now deemed open to impeachment. It's clear Trump and his cronies will keep on doing whatever they want regardless of the Constitution or the law.

They are crippling government and sowing total chaos across our country while doing nothing to address the actual issues people care about. I know my colleague from New Jersey is just as concerned about lawlessness as I am. We both sit on the Judiciary committee. We know how important adherence to the rule of law is. And in fact, I have said many times it is the rule of law that separates a democracy from all other forms of government. And we now have a president who does not think that the rule of law applies to him. 'WTF' comes to mind. So Senator Booker, my question to you is, what are the consequences of this total lawlessness on our government, our country, and the American people?

SENATOR BOOKER: Thank you, Senator Hirono. I think I needed somebody to say what- 'WTF'. And to come from you is particularly precious and I'm grateful. And this rule of law is really important. It's part of this whole moment in American history that I keep calling a moral moment, something beyond the normal, where we shouldn't respond in a normal fashion. This is a moment where judges rule in his favor and he praises them. Judges that don't rule for him, he drags them and threatens them. So much so that Chief Justice of the Supreme Court has to tell them back to back up.

When officials, elected officials speak up, many of them fear what the consequences would be for them or their re-election if they speak against him. Lawyers decline possibly to represent people because they're worried that this President has already showed that if you represent the wrong people or represent, God forbid, people against him, he's going to try to shut down your law firm in ways that are against the rules of law that this country believes in. Journalists and media organizations, they don't report in a way that he likes or confirm his arbitrary name changes of the Gulf of Mexico, there's a punishment that he dishes out to try to make them succumb to submission.

State and local governments literally could get extorted for their funding if they don't carry out his demands. Schools and universities who are starving for dollars, trying to invest them in research and science that will propel humanity to new heights, well, they could get targeted by this President if you don't do what he says.

It feels like his ultimate goal is to create a country where you cannot trust the outcome of elections that he loses because he's going to tell you if he lost that election, it's the big lie. "It's wrong. I won. I won. I won. I won. I don't care what judge after judge, court after court says. I won. And if you don't believe me, if you don't say that the election I won, well, there'll be consequences for that too." This is a President who even as we've read people on both sides of the aisle isn't respecting the Constitution, the separation of powers, isn't respecting the rights that we hold precious, isn't honoring what you call the rule of law.

I want to go a little bit into this for a second. Let's talk about the separation of powers. There's many, many different cases right now. But we know that James Madison, the founding father who devised the basic framework of our Constitution, devoted some of The Federalist Papers to the ways the Constitution addresses the danger of concentrating too much power in one person or one branch of government. Written in 1788, Madison's words still have resonance today. This is what he wrote in Federalist No.47:

> The accumulation of all powers, legislative, executive, and judiciary, in the same hands, whether of one, a few, or many, and whether hereditary, self-appointed, or elective, may justly be pronounced the very definition of tyranny.

So what is this President trying to do? He's trying to jam any court decision that's not in his favor. And either the judge is corrupt and should be impeached, or he's just going to deny the ruling or not follow it. Madison explained that the Constitution set up the executive legislative and judiciary branches to be separate and distinct and equal and bound together by checks and balances.

> It is agreed on all sides that the powers properly belonging to one of the branches ought not to be directly and completely administrated by either of the other branches. It is equally evident that none of them ought to possess directly or indirectly an over ruling influence over the others in the administration of their executive respective powers.

That's Federalist No.48.

I'm nerdy enough to have a favorite Federalist Paper. I'm going to read from my favorite one, Federalist No.51.

> In order to lay a due foundation for the separate and distinct exercise of the different powers of government essential to the preservation of liberty, it is evident that each department should have a will of its own. So constituted that each should have as little agency as possible in the appointment of the members of the others. But the great security against a gradual concentration of the several powers in the same department consists in giving to those who administer each department the necessary constitutional means to resist the encroachments of the others.

To resist the encroachments of the others. We're not doing that in the Senate or in the House.

> It may... {Federalist No.51 continues...} It may be a reflection on human nature that such devices should be necessary to control the abuses of government. {And here's the quote folks. Here's the quote from our Founders:} If men were angels, no government would be necessary. If angels were to govern men, neither external nor internal controls on government would be necessary. {But our President is no angel.} In framing a government... {This is Federalist No. 51 continuing...} In framing a government which is to be administered by men over men, the great difficulty lies in this. You must first enable the government to control the government. And in the next place, oblige it to control itself.

They are talking about at great length, our Founders, in the separation of powers, in the checks and balances of these institutions. And yet for 72 days of this administration, has the Congress, the Article I, the people's House, the Senate, the deliberative body, have we once held this President to account?!

The most powerful man in the world and the richest man in the world have taken a battle axe to the Veterans Association. A battle axe to the Department of Education. A battle axe to the only agency solely focused on protecting consumers against big banks and other factors that might abuse them, bringing it down. Congress established the Department of Education. Congress established the Consumer Finance Bureau. Congress. But the President doesn't care, he's going to push as hard as he can against the principles of our Founders. And what will we do in this body? What will we do in the House of Representatives? Right now, the answer is nothing.

Has Elon Musk, the unelected, un-Senate-confirmed billionaire, number one campaign contributor of Donald Trump who has admitted he's made mistakes, heck, his website, he keeps taking down the mistakes, keeps getting called out from him, fires people from the FAA, then begs him to come back, fires the people that protect us from nuclear accidents.

[To aid] Oh, wait, come back.

Have we ever in the Senate or the House called him in for one oversight hearing to account for what he's doing to address the fears of a nation? No. Separation of powers.

Hey, we have hearings here all the time, but not Elon Musk. You know why? You know why I think why? Tell me I'm a conspiracy theorist, because what Elon Musk is doing to some of my colleagues on the other side of the aisle is threatening them, threatening to run primaries with what to me would be a quarter, but to him is a hundred million dollars. I'm going to drop a hundred million dollars against you in a primary if you step out of line. Or if you dare to say Hegseth is not qualified to be the Secretary of Defense, we're going to drag you through X, we're going to awaken a mob to threaten you.

Our Founders spoke so eloquently to protect against that kind of corruption, to protect that kind of egregious tyrannical power that says, "Only I can save this country. Give me all power. Let me be the strong man." And we know who he respects on the global stage. I was stunned. I thought it was a joke during the election when he said his favorite leader is Viktor Orbán, who has rolled back democratic principles, who has concentrated power. I see, who does he choose to call a dictator? The man who is trying desperately to lead his country in defense against the authoritarian dictator and preserve his democracy, or does he call the dictator a dictator? No. Simple test. Most high school students would simply pass it, but no, he calls a hero a dictator. We have any conversations about that in a formal capacity to talk about the Ukrainian war? Which I know people on both sides of the aisle. Maisie Rono brings up the separation of powers.

Why is history's lesson so relevant today? Why do we study history? Why did I learn that in high school that you study history so you don't repeat the mistakes of the past. You study history to gain inspiration and insight and courage against tough times. You study history to be inspired by heroes who stood up against despots. Who sacrificed themselves. What is the lesson in history? How is it relevant to us today? Because the separation of powers between the branches of government has allowed our democracy to thrive for nearly 250 years. And now we have a person in power that's barely being checked. And if the courts check him, what he does to the courts...

President has in my lifetime ever has had 140 federal lawsuits in about nine weeks. It's a staggering figure. We should consider it a staggering figure. He must be the most sued President in US history. Somebody should fact-check that*. But at least in my lifetime, I don't remember Reagan, don't remember Bush, don't remember Obama or Clinton or Biden being dragged into court in the first nine weeks so many times and losing case after case.

He may have a record for the most lawsuits filed by a President himself, because he's a guy that says he loves to sue folks. In support of the big lie, he did so many lawsuits and lost them all. The lawsuits against Trump and his administration are not frivolous. Federal judges appointed by Republican Presidents and Democratic Presidents alike have found Trump's executive actions illegal, temporarily pausing many of them too. Trump's executive actions and the outcomes of these lawsuits have a direct effect on Americans. These lawsuits challenge Trump.

Here are some of the examples folks. And I'm wondering where the American people stand on these lawsuits, not the people who are blindly loyal to him because they believe the lies that he so artfully creatively and convincingly tells, but just tell me where do you stand on these issues. Attacks on veterans who have served our country in the military and civil services.

Well, there's lawsuits challenging his right to attack our veterans. There's lawsuits challenging Trump on his attacks on government agencies that protect your grandmother from online scams. I don't know where you stand. With the grandmas getting scammed, to defend them or the President? Lawsuits against Trump because of his attacks on lawful American citizens born in this country and guaranteed their citizenship under the US Constitution. There are lawsuits against the President for withholding National Institute of Health funds to support studies of horrific diseases like Alzheimer's, and disrupting life-saving medical research and ongoing clinical trials. Now, if you're a student of history, this is the problem often with lawsuits. Brown V. Board of Education, we celebrate it as this wonderful case. It was. But was it obeyed? No, it wasn't. I have a picture of Ruby Bridges in my office because it wasn't obeyed, the court didn't declare this and suddenly everybody said, "Hey, let Black folks go to school with White folks."

No, the President had to call in the National Guard to escort a little girl into a class. That's the problem with lawsuits, is you have a defiant executive leadership, they'll defy them. These, where you stand, do you stand with veterans? Do you stand on with your grandmothers against online scams? Do you stand with American citizens born in this country? Do you stand withholding National Institute of Health funding? It was clearly that. We know the majority of Americans are with that. But people are having to bring him to court to fight on these issues. So many cases being done, so many cases I have here before me, so many cases. I can read them all, but you all know many of them. They're stunned in the press as he pushes, as Elon Musk push. They push the bounds of the authorities of the Constitution of the United States, and people are bringing lawsuits, but that is not enough.

Martin Luther King didn't step down because of Thurgood Marshall's law, legal work. John Lewis didn't step down. Ella Baker didn't stop. Abraham Joshua Heschel didn't stop. The great rabbi Yohan Prince didn't stop. The people of the United States of America, more powerful than courts. The people of the United States of America, more powerful than the Constitution. I just said something controversial, so let me defend myself.

I believe in the people. I believe in the words of the great Learned Hand. He said the like of what I just said. So let me read somebody far greater, far more vaunted than this Senator from New Jersey. Learned Hand, serves as a federal judge from 1909 to 1951. He was nicknamed the 10th Justice of the Supreme Court for his many influential decisions. And he wrote this speech about our Constitution, about our liberties, about the tyrants in every generation who have tried to subvert our democracy, some of them from this body, like the Red Scare that had so many Americans being unjustly fired, unjustly deported, unjustly jailed, that infringed on freedom of speech, freedom of expression. I'm sorry, every generation of Americans have seen demagogues rise to try to undermine what American stands for. And Learned Hand knew that. He had so much wisdom about our Constitution.

> We are gathered here to affirm a faith, a faith in a common purpose, a common conviction, a common devotion. Some of us have chosen America as the land of our adoption. The rest have come from those who did the same. For this reason, we have some right to consider ourselves a picked group, a group of those who had the courage to break from the past and brave the dangers and the loneliness of a strange land. What was the object that so nerved us, or those who went before us to this choice? We sought liberty, freedom from oppression, freedom from want, freedom to be ourselves. This is what we sought. This we now believe that we are by way of winning. What do we mean when we say that first of all, we seek liberty? I often wonder whether we do not rest our hopes too much upon constitutions, upon laws and upon our courts. These are false hopes. Believe me, these are false hopes. Liberty lies in the heart, in the hearts of men and women. When it dies there, no constitution, no law, no court can save it. No constitution, no law, no court can even do much to help it. While it lies in our hearts there, it needs no constitution, no law, no court. And what is this liberty, which must lie in the hearts of men and women? {Please, please, please listen to what he writes next.} What is this liberty, which must lie in the hearts of us Americans? {This is what he says next.} It is not the ruthless, the unbridled will. It is not freedom to do as one likes. That is the denial of liberty and leads straight to its overthrow. A society in which men recognize no check upon their freedom soon becomes a society where freedom is a possession of only a savage few as we have learned in this country to our sorrow.
>
> What then is the spirit of liberty? I cannot define it. I can only tell you my own faith. The spirit of liberty is the spirit which is not too sure that it is right. It's the spirit of liberty, is the spirit which seeks to understand, to understand the minds of other men and women. The spirit of liberty is a spirit which weighs their interest alongside its own without bias. The spirit of liberty remembers that not even a sparrow falls to earth unheeded. The spirit of liberty is a spirit of him who near 2000 years ago taught mankind that lesson it has never learned, but has never quite yet forgotten, that there may be a kingdom where the last shall be heard and considered side by side with the greatest. And now in the spirit of that great America for which our young men are at this moment fighting and dying, in that spirit of liberty and America, I ask you to rise and say with me the pledge of our faith in the glorious destiny of our beloved country. I now ask you to raise your hands and repeat after me this pledge. {And he says The Pedge of Allegiance.}

He believed that the Constitution dies if the spirit of it dies in the hearts of men and women. I will tell you. This Constitution has saved my life. It made my life. Because people marched to make real on the promise of our democracy. People bled to make real on this democracy. When some people told us that this Constitution didn't apply for us, this body, this body, Republicans in America stood up and said, "No. President Johnson, we're going to do amendments." We saw the 13th

Amendment, the 14th Amendment. The 15th Amendment would guarantee my ancestors finally full citizenship in the United States of America and the protections of the Constitution. I am here in this body because of past generations that fought to uphold the Constitution, not because the Constitution was real to them, but because they brought reality and hope and love and promise to the Constitution. They were Americans that said like Langston Hughes, "America never was America to me, but I swear this oath America will be."

They loved this country so much even when it didn't love them back. I am here because of that. I'm the fourth Black person popularly elected to this body because of generations that believed so much in this document. That they were going to make it real. It lived in them. I quoted earlier today, and it's worth quoting her again, the great Margaret Chase Smith. A US Senator from Maine, a Republican in her famous Declaration of Conscience speech, delivered on June 1st, 1950 [see back of book]. Thank you. Thank you. My good senator friend Whitehouse, because Lord knows I would have slipped and fallen on my tuchus, and have ended this long filibuster because I fell to the floor. That's what you mean when the brother has your back.

What did this Republican say in a time of tyranny in her times, in a time where the Constitution stopped living in people's hearts, where people believed that whipped up fears of others by demagogues, where people believed the fear that they heard again and again on the radio that we should fear other Americans when people believed their fear justified them inhibiting the greatness of the Constitution? What's that old saying from one of our great leaders of the past? "If you're willing to give up your liberty in order to ensure your security, you will lose them both."

And so here was this courageous Republican who in a time that demagogues were whipping up fear, where First Amendment rights were being trampled, where people were being intimidated into silence, where people were afraid to go up against the big and the powerful and the rich, where people were being deported from our country, where Jews were being deported and accused of being communists as justification to take them out of the country because they didn't have permanent legal status — yeah, that's our history.

What did she stand up and say in the Senate? This Republican putting her own career at risk to call out Senator McCarthy. She said, "I don't believe the Republican Party is in any sense a party of fear. I do believe that the Republican Party has made an alliance though with the four horsemen of fear, the fear of communists, the fear of labor unions, the fear of the future, and the fear of progress." There are people fear mongering now. There are people trying to tell Americans to hate Americans — either with the great *Dear Leader*, or you're a danger and enemy. And it's not just Democrats that are being drug, there are being other Republicans, I saw it happen. I saw it happen to one of our vice president's daughters, a congresswoman. I saw it happen to colleagues of mine like Jeff Flake, like John McCain, like Corker, who stood up in this body and told the truth about *Dear Leader* and they saw the consequences politically.

You want to talk about where the Constitution lives? And defending the Constitution, first make it real in your heart like those women did before the amendment that granted them the right to vote, who loved this country so much. You want to know where the Constitution lives in your heart? I just met with extraordinary men and women who are Native Americans to this country, who were here before any of us. They love this country so much even with the sins against them.

You want to know where the Constitution lives? Let it live in the hearts of all Americans now and ask yourself, is the leader of our country, is he living the Constitution in his heart? Because as Learned Hand says, "It's not braggadocious, it's not mean." It is loving. It is kind. It is expansive. We are Americans. Our creed above the presiding elder says it all. E pluribus unum. Trying to remind our country that despite racial differences, gender, besides Republican or Democrat, ethnics, all the lines that divide us are not nearly as strong as the ties that bind us. That's what *e pluribus unum* means.

What about the pledge that Learned Hand read? Listen to the words. It says things. It says things in that pledge. It says that we are one nation under God, that we are indivisible and we pledge ourselves to liberty and justice, not just to the people who agree with the President, but for all. God bless my courageous colleagues who have spoken out in the past and suffered the consequences. The liberty and the Constitution lives in their hearts. They put patriotism over politics. We are in this moral moment now. We are in this moral moment now. This is not Right or Left. Don't let them say this is a partisanship. It is not Left or Right, it is right or wrong. America, this is a moral moment. Does the Constitution live in your heart?

* *Yep, by a landslide.*

6:38 PM - Historical Moment

SENATOR MURPHY: Senator, a question.

SENATOR BOOKER: Before I yield, I love this power trip. [LAUGHTER] It's the only time in 13 years I've really felt this power. I don't have to let my colleagues speak. And I, first amongst us all, really love to speak. [LAUGHTER] I just want to say thank you to Chris Murphy. I repeated this 10, 15 hours ago, but I just want to tell the story and then I'll let you go.

Chris, nine years ago on this floor after the Pulse shooting, we called Chuck Schumer, Chris and I. I saw a moment, he saw a moment that we couldn't do business as usual. We just said, "How can you have this mass shooting, yet another mass shooting, and this body just go on as business as usual?" It's why I'm standing here right now. And we agreed with Chuck Schumer's help that we would get control of the Senate. And Chris Murphy went down to that desk and I promised him, "I'll be with you. I'll stand with you. I won't sit down. We'll go as long as we possibly can."

And he began a filibuster nine years ago, and it lasted 15 hours, and he still had fuel in the tank. I know he did. I was a hurting guy. I told you my back was hurting, my feet were hurting. But we had a direct end when Mitch McConnell agreed to give us votes on common sense gun safety, which I think every American, most gun owners agree on, just universal background checks. And it failed to get 60 votes in the Senate. But you stood, and I stood with you, and he said to me days ago, "If you're going to do this brother, I will be your aide-de-camp this time." And you've been with me... You have been with me far past 15 hours. You've been with me for 23 hours and 49 minutes.

[APPLAUSE IN THE CHAMBER]

My cousin Pam in the gallery, she's been the same amount of time.

[LAUGHTER FROM SENATOR MURPHY]

All right. So I'm going to yield my power. It's not going to go to my head. This is why we need separation of powers, checks on men, because men are not angels.

I yield for a question while retaining the floor.

SENATOR MURPHY: Senator Booker, it has been a wonder to be with you on the floor these last 24 hours. You indeed did something extraordinary and performed a sympathy filibuster with me nine years ago where as I stood at that desk for 15 hours, you stood on the Senate floor. You didn't need to, but you did in solidarity. I have been with you for the last 24 hours, but I've sat for most of it. You've done the hard work. You are an extraordinary Senator. You are an extraordinary American. And I think I can say on behalf of everyone in this chamber and many people in the gallery, you are an extraordinary friend.

And so I think all of us feel privileged to be here with you at this moment, this moment of peril, this moment of danger, this moment of opportunity for the nation, but also this moment of history. On August 28, 1957, at about 8:45 P.M., Strom Thurmond took this floor. And he took the floor with the intent of trying to block the 1957 Civil Rights Bill. This was the most significant, really the only civil rights bill that had been before the United States Senate in 90 years. Most famously, about ten years before when he was running for President as a Dixiecrat, he had said, "There's not enough troops in the army to force the southern people to break down segregation and admit the Negro race into our theaters, into our swimming pools, into our homes, and into our churches." And he sat on this floor for just over 24 hours, and he made the case for why this nation should continue to segregate Black and White. He started in fact by reading every single state's voting rights laws. Every single state's laws, he read into the record, apparently as proof that every state adequately protected all of its voters and that no additional laws were necessary. He had friends in his cause to preserve segregation that came down to the floor and asked him long questions to give him breathers. At the end of that 24 hours at around 9:00 P.M. the following night, he could go no longer. His final words in his 24-hour record-breaking filibuster were, "I expect to vote against the bill."

But within hours, the bill passed. It became law. It established the Office of Civil Rights at the Department of Justice. It was not nearly enough, but it broke 90 years of inaction. What you have done here today Senator Booker, couldn't be more different than what occurred on this floor in 1957. Strom Thurmond was standing in the way of inevitable progress towards equal political and economic rights for Black Americans. It was inevitable only because the people of this nation were standing up at that moment, the beginning of the civil rights movement, to make clear that progress was inevitable.

And I say that that moment is so different from this moment, because today you are standing in the way not of progress, but of retreat. You are standing in the way of retreat from the rule of law, retreat from our commitment to provide care to the most vulnerable, retreat from our common cause, at least we used to be in common cause that we would have zero tolerance from corruption at the highest levels of government.

And you have recognized rightly that this multifaceted retreat from everything that makes this country so special and the speed of that retreat over the last 71 days, it is an exceptional moment. You've said that word over and over again. It is not normal what this administration has been doing to rob from us the values that used to unite left and right in this nation. And so you made this bold decision to engage in an exceptional tactic, to declare 24 hours ago that you are going to stand on this floor for as long as you could to try to raise the specter of failure in our fight against this retreat for our colleagues and for the American public.

The exceptional nature we have heard so eloquently from you over the course of the last 24 hours, the massive transfer of wealth in this reconciliation bill from the poor and the middle class to the wealthy, the industrial scale harassment of journalists, of universities, of law firms, the destruction of the independence of the Department of Justice, the destruction of the American knowledge economy and the research economy, the use of the White House in violation of the Constitution, to make those in power richer. You have laid out the case. And it's funny, I remember this from nine years ago. When you're sitting in your spot, you haven't moved in 24 hours, you have no idea what's happening outside of this building. You don't actually know how many people in this country have engaged in the conversation that you started 24 hours ago. On one social media platform alone, there have been 150 million clicks on your live stream. This is a country of 300 million Americans.

You have been able to pique a conversation here amongst our colleagues, who we need to stand with us eventually against this retreat and across this country. And I think we are here as we reach a pivotal hour to just say thank you for having the courage, the audacity, to bring us on this journey. And so my question is pretty simple. I think you'll find when you finally leave this chamber that you have done something extraordinary, that you didn't solve the problem, that we are still a long ways from being able to successfully beat back this retreat, but that you have accomplished something extraordinary.

And so I guess that's just my question. When you set out with this idea, when this was starting to germinate in your mind, my question for you, Senator Booker, is, what did you hope to accomplish?

SENATOR BOOKER: I thank my colleague and my friend again. He and I talked about this, that I was challenged by my own constituents to do something different, challenged by my own constituents to do something, challenged by my own constituents to take risks. My staff here who should get a lot of credit for making it thus far, I'm not sitting down, but I'm mindful of what you said about Strom Thurmond. I'm mindful of that right now, as I watch that clock tick for another 20 minutes.

SEVERAL VOICES IN CHAMBER: You got it. You're good.

SENATOR BOOKER: I'm grateful for my staff. I'm grateful for the parliamentarians, the clerks. I'm grateful for the Republican presiding officers.

I don't know if I want to out Curtis on the note that he... I'm sorry, the good Senator or the Presiding Officer, forgive me on the note he sent me.* But this is the kind of specialness in this place that I love.

I want to tell a few connecting stories. I think some of my colleagues know a few of these, but I want to explain why I started this whole 24 hours talking about John Lewis and good trouble. Sixty years ago when he was on the Edmund Pettus Bridge he shook New Jersey as he shook the nation. When Bloody Sunday happened, there was a White guy on a couch in New Jersey who was watching TV and was so shaken. This lawyer said, "I got to go to Alabama." He realized he couldn't afford a plane ticket, so this man slumped back down on his couch and then he said, at a moral moment in America, "I'm not going to let my inability to do everything, undermine my determination to do something, to do something different."

And he got up and said, "Okay." It was a meager calculation, but it was different. "I can afford one hour, one hour a month of pro bono work." And he called around and he found this woman named Lee Porter who was heading up an organization called the Fair Housing Council and said, "Can you use a lawyer?" And she's like, "Hallelujah. Thank you, Jesus. Yeah, we need some help." And they worked together and they designed a sting operation where they would send black families in areas of New Jersey that would not sell homes to Black people where usually the best public schools were. And if they were told the house was sold, they'd send a White couple behind them to expose that the house was still for sale and expose all of this. Well, they had a lot of success getting things written about the severe housing discrimination in my state.

And he said that after about five years – four years – I got this case file of a Black family trying to move to New Jersey and they were frustrated because every time they'd look at homes and the places with the best public schools, which happened to be White communities, they said they couldn't find a home. So they did the sting operation, they sent a Black couple in. They were told this incredible house was not for sale. They loved the house. So then when the White couple went, they just threw in a bid to see if it would be accepted. The bid was accepted, papers were drawn up on the day of the closing the White couple did not show up. The Black man did. Lawyer Marty Friedman marched in, confronted the real estate agent. You would think 1969, a year after the Fair Housing Act, that he would capitulate, but he didn't.

This real estate agent gets up so angry, he punches the lawyer in the face and sends a Doberman Pinscher on the Black guy. They get out of there, shaken up and they start writing letters back and forth. The good owners of the home found out what was going on. They were so aghast. They said, "Let us sell the house directly to the Black family." The Black family moved in and 43 years later, the baby from that family became the fourth popularly-elected Black Senator in our country — *me*.

Now, I tell that story because I started with John Lewis 24 hours ago and it was John Lewis and a bunch of marchers on a bridge that influenced the destiny of my life and my family's life. We're all interconnected. As King says, "We're all caught in an inescapable network of mutuality tied in that common garment of destiny."

But I want to tell you the second time John Lewis shook up my life, I was mayor of the city of Newark and I got called to be on a TV show. I got called by a guy named Skip Gates who I love, admire, and he calls me and he jazzes me up. He fills my ego. He just flatters me, "Hey, I got this show called Finding Your Roots, Cory Booker, and you're a rising star. You're this hot shot. We should feature you in this." And I'm like, "Oh, great. Oh, don't say that Skip, but okay, yeah, of course." [LAUGHTER] And then I said, "Okay, well who are you going to pair me with?" And I thought it was going to be another young hotshot up-and-coming politician in America. No. He goes, "I'm going to pair you with John Lewis."

And my heart sank a little bit. Actually, maybe it was my ego that sank. My heart got excited because I know how these shows start. They start with biographies. And so imagine the show starting [using a deep announcer voice:] *John Lewis, hero of the Civil Rights Movement, literally bled the southern soil red for freedom and justice.* And then it goes to my biography, *Cory Booker riding his big wheel in suburban New Jersey.* [LAUGHTER] The show was unbelievable – mountain and boy – but I got to meet John Lewis. I got to tell him that story that he changed my life and I didn't even know it, on a bridge in Alabama, changed the course of events in New Jersey that led to me.

Third take on John Lewis. My colleagues know I got here in a special election in 2013. What all my colleagues might not know is I came here with a broken heart. My mom and I came here with a broken heart. Because I was elected in October, sworn in October, but also in October my dad died of Parkinson's. That's why I got choked up reading these letters from people with Parkinson's. And so we came down here, we were grieving. My dad was not with us. My mom lost her husband of nearly 50 years and I'm going to get sworn in. It's a big event. But my parents and my campaign decided, "You know what we should do right before you get sworn in, or are brought over here to be escorted to the Vice President, that you should go and sit with John Lewis." And so we went to John Lewis's office and a lot of my colleagues from the CBC, a lot of my colleagues from the House, a lot of my colleagues that are here who came over to the House know his office.

You walk into his office and it looks like a civil rights museum except he's in all the pictures, [LAUGHTER IN THE CHAMBER] and this is John Lewis. We who knew him, this was him, mountain of a man. He had already prepared eggs and grits, a good southern breakfast, and wouldn't let my mom and I get up, and he serves us all and he humbly is saying, "This is why I marched. This is why I sacrificed for history-making days like this." He told us how special this was for him. He told me that he would be right here where my friends are sitting watching me get sworn in and how proud he was going to be, in a sense he stood in for my dad on this floor and then BOOM — I'm a Senator. I find colleagues and friends here and I find a lot of colleagues and friends in the CBC.

At that point, I was the only African-American in our caucus and found so many friends, so many heroes that have gone on from the Senate now who looked at me, adopted me, helped me. Dick Durbin, you were amazing in those early months, and this is the next time I meet John Lewis for a moment that changed my life. Chris Murphy, Brian Schatz – remember this moment – it was during the 2017 healthcare debate when I didn't know how we were going to stop that bill from passing and taking away healthcare from 20 million Americans, but John Lewis, "Hey Cory, let's do something different. What you got in mind?" And I said, "Well, John Lewis, I got this phone. It's very powerful. Let's do a Facebook Live."

[LAUGHTER]

And so I opened it up, Facebook Live, we meet in between in the capitol and then he says, "Hey, where can we go to sit down for a wild place?" And I got my favorite place to sit. I watched Schoolhouse Rock so much. It's right on the steps of the Capitol. Let's just sit there and talk. Chris Murphy, Brian Schatz first people out to sit with us and the time-lapse. The time-lapse is amazing. First two, three people, then ten people, then 50 people, then hundreds of people. I have it all coming because of the moral magnetism of this man, John Lewis. And he talked to people that night who were looking for what can I do? I'm just one person and this guy who in his 20s, who is just one person and caused a heck of a lot of good trouble, he told them,

> Don't lose faith, don't lose hope. Get angry, but let it fuel you. Be afraid. But know that's a necessary precondition to courage.

He was amazing that night and I know my colleagues remember that. And then there was the next time... Oh, Brother Warnock, you're going to love this one. The next time I was with John Lewis, Jimmy Carter had gotten a little sick, but then he got better and went back to teaching Sunday school and I thought, this man is in his 90s. I need to go to Sunday school. And so who do I know? Because there's a waiting line. It's like people sleep out all night. I might've been a little selfish. How do I know I can get in? Call John Lewis. I say, "Hey, I got this great idea. Why don't we go to Jimmy Carter to watch him teach Sunday school?"

So I have the singular greatest road trip. I fly into Atlanta, we get into a car and we drive all those hours to Plains, Georgia. Indeed, people were waiting outside, but it's John Lewis. Come on in. We sit in the front row. I must be in the front row and we sit down and then this marvelous, incredible moment comes. Somebody comes and says, "Congressman Lewis, Senator Booker, the President, first lady would love to see you beforehand." It's my first time meeting President Jimmy Carter. But I walk in, I'm sort of on the sidelines. These two men are hugging each other. He and the first lady and the two of them whisper for a second and Jimmy Carter walks over into me and says, "I hear you're thinking about running for President of the United States" and he does something incredible. He says, "I think you should run, but only if you run." And he pokes my heart. "Only if you run from here." [The Senator is clearly moved]

The last time of the powerful moments I've had in my life with that man, that so many of us have had these powerful moments. The last time happened because of a man named Michael Collins. I know there are people in this room that got the same phone call I got that it won't be long now that John Lewis is going to pass very soon. He can't speak, but I know he would want you to have your moment to say goodbye to him.

And what do I do? What do I do to say goodbye to a man that's a legend in my life, a legend in our nation? What do you do to say goodbye to him? I wasn't prepared. I can't say I said anything eloquent. Michael Collins, God bless you man. You put the phone by his ear and you just gave me my time to have a conversation with the man that would soon die. The man that changed my life, that helped my family get into a neighborhood that loved me and cherished me. God love Harrington Park, the man who stood in for my father when heaven brought him home, the man that showed me on the steps of this capitol, how powerful the people are wasn't about him. It was about them. The man that brought me to see a President who flattered every Senator's ego, tell them what they want to hear, "Run for President." And so I said everything I could, but the last thing I said, I remember very well. I said, "I love you." I said, "I love you." And I said, "John, I know you're going to be in heaven looking down on us, and I promise you, I promise you John Lewis, that I'll do everything possible, that we'll do everything possible, to make you proud."

The civil rights generation is starting to be called home. Leaders are leaving us. We in the CBC have lost a lot of greats and I can't remember – forget – the promise I made to John Lewis with all that he gave me with all that he gave his country that I said we would make him proud. And so this is one of those moments that John Lewis, he would not be sitting still. He would be calling me up and say, "You still got that Facebook thing?" I go, "No, I don't really use Facebook anymore." [LAUGHING, LAUGHTER] But there's a thing called TikTok or...

I don't know what John Lewis would say right now. I know what he said in 2017, but I'll be honest with you, I don't know what he would say, but John Lewis would say something. He would do something. He wouldn't treat this moral moment like it was normal. John Lewis knew what King said. That what we have to repent, for all of us here will have to repent for, is not just the vitriolic words and violent actions of so-called bad people. What we will have to repent for in our day and age is the appalling silence and the inaction of good people. This is our moral moment. This is when the most precious ideas of our country are being tested where the Constitution and the question is being called, where does the Constitution live? On paper or in our hearts? This is the moment. Generations get them. We're on a crossroads here, folks. Healthcare is on the balance. Veterans are in the balance. Priorities are in the balance. Where's our priorities, America? More tax cuts disproportionately going to the wealthy, greater budget deficits in the trillions and trillions of dollars.

Or are we going to do something different like John Lewis would call us to do? He would call us to get into good trouble, necessary trouble. Save the soul of America. But you all know John, don't hate each other. Don't let anybody pull you so low as to hate them. I said this about the presiding elder, different parties, but he showed me an act of kindness during this speech. He and I have talked about energy policy. He has amazing ideas. I want to partner with him. Don't hate anybody. Did the folks in Birmingham and Martin Luther King, Fred Shuttlesworth, Dorothea Cotton, James Bevel, did they bring bigger dogs and bigger fire hoses to match the Sheriff's — Bull Connor... Thank you. I've been standing here a long time.

They didn't do that. They were creative artists of activism. They called to the conscience of a country. They challenged our moral imagination not to focus on hate, but focus on what is possible in America. If we redeem the dream, if we dream America anew that generation in their 20s and 30s, that's what they demanded. Martin Luther King didn't go to the march on Washington with a list of grievances against the racists in our country. He went there and called to the conscience of a country. He said he had a dream.

That's what we need in our generation vision now. That's what we need in our generation. A vision to redeem the dream, to call our country together. Yes, there is a man in the White House who's the most powerful man in the land, and his partner is the richest man in the world. But as long as this is a democracy that we can still protect, the power of the people is greater than the people in power — if they use their powers.

A great African-American woman author once said, "The most common way people give up their power is not realizing they have it in the first place." I've been calling out names, folks, to tell them they have power. I read the stories of Diana, of Wendy and Cassie, of Tanya, of Cameron, of Jean, of Susan, of Edna, of Randy, of Dylan, of Teresa, of Pamela, of Sally, of Mike, of Carol, of Rosemary, of Danielle, of Judith, of Elizabeth, of Sandra, Alicia, Maggie, Nibel, Laura, Michael, Robin, Mary, Allison, Ash, Roseanne, Carrie, Samantha P, Raphael, Will, Anthony, Sean, and so many more. I read their stories here because while we were elected, they are the power of our country.

I've made mistakes. We all have. Both parties have a lot of mistakes to account for the ballast of this country. What will anchor us to our ideals? What will call us to new heights? Lift our heads, lift our hopes. What will call us to rise is each other. We need each other. We need a greater love in this country. We need a greater fight in this country. We need a greater determination. We can't act as if this is normal times. These people's stories that I [read] were calling out for help. Senator help me. Someone help me. I'm in danger of losing my healthcare. Someone help me. I'm a veteran. Look what happened to me. It's not fair. I fought for this country. Help me, help me. I'm worried about my Social Security and the rural office I go to is being closed, help people calling out for help, and what [did] Americans do and people are calling out for help?

They built an infrastructure. The greatest project ever, called the Underground Railroad, where Quakers, White folks joined with Black folks to shuttle people to freedom. What did they do when people were worried and fearful? They called people together from across our country. Let's have a conference. Let's go to Seneca Falls. What did they do when they faced violence? Well, look at the people at Stonewall who stood up, who pushed back, who organized, who won. What do they do when the dogs are unleashed on us, the fire hose are unleashed on us? Look at what they did in Selma.

I'm getting close to a record folks, but... [APPLAUSE] There's a room here in the Senate named after Strom Thurmond. To hate him is wrong. And maybe my ego got too caught up that if I stood here maybe, maybe just maybe I could break this record of the man who tried to stop the rights upon which I stand.

I'm not here, though, because of his speech. I'm here despite his speech.

I'm here because as powerful as he was, the people were more powerful. [APPLAUSE] But I remind you, all those people who believe like me, that we've got to redeem the dream. Turn again to John Lewis because you all know the story my colleagues of when the man that beat him savagely, drew blood, cracked bones. Decades later, he was a Congressman. That man brought his grandson with him to ask for forgiveness from John Lewis. I heard about this story when I was in the car in Georgia with him. "What did you do, John? This man that so viciously beat you, wounded you, bruised you, battered you. What did you do when he came to ask you for forgiveness? What did you do?" And a good Christian man, man of faith simply said, "Every one of us needs mercy. Every one of us needs redemption. I forgave him. I hugged him, we wept. And I looked at the boy, 'This nation needs you too.'" John.

SENATOR SCHUMER: Would the Senator yield for a question?

SENATOR BOOKER: Chuck Schumer, it's the only time in my life I can tell you no. [APPLAUSE]

SENATOR SCHUMER: I just want to tell you a question. Do you know you have just broken the record? Do you know how proud this caucus is of you? Do you know how proud America is of you?

[STANDING OVATION]

SENATOR JOHN CURTIS (UTAH, PRESIDING): Ladies and gentlemen, ladies and gentlemen, [GAVEL] ladies and gentlemen, ladies and gentlemen, [GAVEL] order, order. The Chair does not wish to take away from this moment, but I think the best way to honor this great accomplishment to our guests in the gallery, to make a rare exception and let you stand to show your appreciation. I will not constrain my fellow Senators.

SENATOR BOOKER: [TO SENATOR CURTIS] Thank you.

Chuck Schumer, I have yielded for a question and you asked me did I know. I know now. I want to not quite wrap this up yet.
[LAUGHTER IN THE CHAMBER]

VOICE IN CHAMBER: Twenty-four more!

SENATOR BOOKER: I don't want to wrap this up yet. Senator, my mom's been watching. I know Catherine Cortez Masto has a podium in front of her. She can give me a rest. I'd like to go a little further if we can. Just a little further. I love, and again, I know people are trying to train each other and all of our media operations, they give the worst images of the people of the other party. But I want to tell you one of the funny tweets my staff gave me is something Ted Cruz said is he's around 19, 20 hours. He said, "Maybe I should pull a fire alarm. He's going to break my record."
[LAUGHTER]

I'm going to pause in a moment if she has a question for me to Catherine Cortez Masto, because she's my mother. But I do want to just say again, two points to make if I can. One is how grateful I am to my staff. When we decided to do this many days ago-
[APPLAUSE]

-When we decided to do this days ago, they were like, "We have to do this." And we started preparing and working on this. And they did an extraordinary job. They were with me late nights, writing, writing, writing. I just feel guilty. Because they wrote about ten books, and we didn't use all of them. They were really substantive stuff pulling from Republicans and Democrats in critique of this moment, pulling from Democrats and Republicans, Republican governors that are saying, "Do not cut Medicaid." States that know, as my colleagues do, that have a trigger that if the Medicaid funding goes below 90%, they stop the Medicaid expansion.

My staff really worked hard to not make this just democratic voices to make it people in our country that Republicans and Democrats, you heard mentioned in the speech, the Cato Institute, the Manhattan Institute, all people who are honest arbiters and are saying that what Trump is doing is wrong. That a budget like this that blows massive holes in our deficit, it will be something our children are trying to pay for.

And what are they ultimately paying for that's caused this big deficit? It's trillions of dollars of tax cuts that people like DOGE, multi-millionaire, multi-billionaire Musk will benefit from, but children won't. They did such a good job bringing together authorities on both sides of the aisle. I just want to thank them. I want to thank my cousin Pam and my family, cousin Pam, like Chris Murphy was here for the whole time. I want to thank Chris Murphy again who never stopped telling me we could do this, we can do this, we can do this. And said, "I will stay with you." He's been with me on the floor. I hope you don't look as tired as I look because you look beat man. Do I look that bad?

SENATOR MURPHY: You look great, man. You look great.

Sen. John Curtis of Utah was presiding when the record was broken, and had previously sent Sen. Booker a yet mysterious note of encouragement. Senator Curtis also allowed and exception to the rules for the Senators in the chamber to give a standing ovation when the record was broken. (Senate decorum rules prohibit Senators from applauding or "commit(ing) any other type of demonstration either by a sound or sign".)

7:15 PM - Final Words

SENATOR BOOKER: All right, I want to go a little bit past this and then I'm going to deal with some of the biological urgencies I'm feeling. [LAUGHTER] But I'm going to wait here, 'cause I have the power. I have the floor. Somebody has to ask me perhaps from my mom's state the way that it's supposed to work.

SENATOR CATHERINE CORTEZ MASTO (NEVADA) : So will the good Senator from New Jersey yield for a question?

SENATOR BOOKER: My mom would be so upset with me. My Aunt Marilyn, my Uncle Butch, my Aunt Shirley, all the people that are your constituents, not mine. They would be upset with me if I didn't yield to you for a question while retaining the floor.

SENATOR MASTO: Well, first of all, Senator Booker, I have to say we in Nevada are so proud of you. We are proud to be 'Nevada strong'. You are one of us. You are definitely New Jersey, 'Nevada strong'. I'm so proud of what you have accomplished so far, and willing to stay here as long as it takes to help you get your message across. And I think that's the important moment. We are all here right now. So I want to pose a question to you actually a couple of questions. But I want to start off and set the stage here because you have been here now what for over 24 hours. You are missing some of the national news things that are happening out there. But one of the things I want to point to that is happening that you may not be aware of, and you've touched on it a little earlier today, is this notion that we have now a President who is actually focused on billionaires and tax cuts for billionaires at the expense of the American public.

And one of the things we have watched him do is cut funding for medical research. Now what you may not know is just today, just today I found out that HHS laid off the entire healthy aging branch of the CDC just today. This office administers Alzheimer's disease programs and it oversees the funding from the bold infrastructure for Alzheimer's Act. And it is a piece of legislation that I was so proud to partner with Susan Collins on. And she has fought for and we have fought for funding for it to support caregivers and their families. And Congress just reauthorized this funding. And now we have a President that has stopped the critical work that scientists are doing to try and cure Alzheimer's. And I bring this to your attention, Senator, because like you and I think like all of us, there are personal moments in the work that we do.

My personal moment is my grandmother, who I'm named after, died from Alzheimer's, and she died at a time in Las Vegas when there was not enough research, when there was not enough healthcare, when there really not enough providers to understand what was going on. And so for many of us, this fight, not only is it personal, but we recognize the impact that it has outside the Beltway in so many families and lives across the country. And that's what this is about. In Nevada as of 2023, there are 49,000 people 65 and older are living with Alzheimer's. And that's projected to reach 65,000 this year.

Not only did we hear that HHS laid off the entire healthy aging branch of the CDC, but Donald Trump also recently terminated a $14,000 NIH research grant that had been supporting Alzheimer's research at the University of Nevada, Las Vegas. And he's continued, continued to cut the grant for essential research for so many reasons. We've seen these funding cuts, we've seen mass layoffs and the impoundment of grants that have already been approved by Congress. This is a violation of the rule of law. And you have been talking about that for the last couple of hours. President Trump is forgetting that this is personal — it is happening to so many families. So my question, Senator Booker, to you is what do you think families and caregivers of those impacted by Alzheimer's. How they are feeling about what is happening right now?

SENATOR BOOKER: So this bothers me for two reasons and the first you've already mentioned is this is the point of bipartisan work that we do. I talked about Chris Murphy and the bipartisan gun bill that lots of people here worked on with Senator Cornyn and others. And how upset my state is that some of that community violence intervention money that I worked so hard to get in that bill is being clawed back by a President. There are people in this room. I know so many of you and I know on the other side that have done such great work to work with our colleagues to find common ground and get really important programs passed that bring resources to families. And it's being clawed back by a President, not with consultation, not with a hearing, not with a discussion of even why you would target Alzheimer's research.

That is a violation of the separation of powers. And I wish my Republican colleagues would hold more hearings about that. These are programs that they like. I saw that with USAID. I worked with Marco Rubio on some of that, programs and those investments that are now been cut and clawed back. So it's a separation-of-powers issue. It's an offense to the common goals that we share in this community of leaders. For the second reason it bothers me is that an article I read hours ago by Fareed Zakaria and he talked about what's happening to a nation that cuts so dramatically, what is one of the best taxpayer investment dollars in biomedical sciences. If you are an investor and I told you there's an investment that every dollar you invest, you would get five dollars back for your economy, folks would be invested in that vehicle.

Well, that's NIH funding. Every dollar you invest, who would cut a profit center? And it's not just a profit center though. The outcomes, the discoveries could change the lives of people who are suffering in your nation and around the world. But he's attacking them. I read all these universities from around the country. This shows you how magnanimous I'm trying to be. I even read stories from USC-

[LAUGHTER]

VOICE FROM CHAMBER: *Whoa.*

-I'm sorry, I'm sorry, rival, that all of these universities are cutting their postdocs, cutting their PhDs, cutting them because they don't know as Donald Trump threatens the direct costs, they're stopping. And Fareed Zakaria said so painfully to all Americans with American's pride as we are doing that China who, when they had that culture revolution, they first went after their universities. Now modern China, their government is doing the opposite. They're trying to out America us, they're massively increasing their investments in scientific research because they know if they get ahead of us on quantum computing, all of our subs can be located and God knows what could happen. Any kind of cryptology, they could break. They know they get ahead of us on scientific research, the power and advantage that will give them. So they're doubling down.

But what are we doing in America? We're tolerating a president that is cutting the funding that will predict who defines the future and what values will define those futures. Will they be democratic values or will be the values of the country that's competing with us to beat us? And right now we're giving them a head start. And then the final reason that question bothers me is because my father died of Parkinson's, and he had Parkinson's-related dementia, and I know what that's like. I know the pain families are enduring. I remember the time that my dad and my mom, we were in the movie theater and my mother just shook my world, she was in Georgia. And so many people here in this room have had the same experience. We're in a movie theater and my mom leans over to me and said, "You need to take your dad to the bathroom." I never imagined the years of my dad as a two year old and three year old, taking me to the bathroom, that one day I'd have to take him.

And so in this Atlanta movie theater in the middle of a movie, which I was like, "Okay, it's time for me to do this ritual" that so many families know. I pick my dad up, who's shuffling with his Parkinson's. I'm not seeing any light in his eyes that he's there, I'm just letting him hold me and he's shuffling into the bathroom. And then we get to a public bathroom, his hands are shaking, he's standing in front of the urinal. And then I realize I got to unbuckle this man's pants. So many families know this. And my ego, I'm sorry, I was leaning over and I'm saying, "Wait a minute. I'm in a public bathroom leaning over, unbuckling another man's pants. Please, please, God, don't let somebody come in." And as if God heard my call, someone walked in. [LAUGHTER] And I hear the person walk in and I'm like, "Just please keep walking. Go into a stall, please keep walking."

And then suddenly I hear the feet walk past me and stop. And then the man turns around and says, "Oh my God, Cory Booker." [LAUGHTER] And then I look up at my dad and I see the clarity in his eyes. He is 100% there and he's grinning and loving my mortified embarrassment. [LAUGHTER]

Alzheimer's is devastating so many American families who are watching the loved one of their lives diminish and we're cutting funding, Donald Trump is cutting funding democratically, bipartisanly approved. So forget the separation of powers. It's important, it's so important. If that doesn't get you, then maybe think about the competition with China. If that doesn't get you, if those two don't get you, America, then think about the millions of Americans struggling with Alzheimer's, the struggles it does to those families.

This is a moral moment, America. This is going to define the character of our country for years and years to come. Has the Senate called a hearing on your bipartisan funding, Senator? No. Have we done our oversight responsibility? Have we checked, as I read from the Federalist Papers, as our founders wanted us to do, is to check the executive? Be the check of the executive that balances our governmental powers. No, we're not checking that executive.

With Signalgate, I have heard from Republicans that serve in Congress of the 535 with us, I know other colleagues here have heard, they're mortified. You talked about that, mortified about that. And again, this is not partisan. The Biden administration made foreign policy mistakes, Obama made foreign policy mistakes, Reagan, when I was growing up, I was hearing about the Iran-Contra scandal.

So I'm not going to be one of those people that says we are the pristine, perfect Democrats. We've made mistakes, we've made failings, we've let the public down. We have some reckoning in our own party that we're working on right now, but that doesn't say that you should just be one of these people that says, "Well, Biden did it." No, you should be a leader of character that says, "There's something wrong here." And in fact, it could point to real problems in the national security of our country and the laws that we established. One of those laws is very simple, you're supposed to preserve records. How can a Signal chain that disappears not be a violation of the law of this land? Is there a hearing on that, head of the Intel Commission? Not a hearing at all.

Where are the checks and balances spelled out in the Constitution? We are derelicting our duties here in the Senate, we really are. And the consequences of that is the very national security of our country. How many times, do you think this was the first time they created a Signal chat, or is this a pattern of practice? You're a really rational man. I keep looking at you, Mark. You're my leader on these issues or Jack Reed. No, this indicates a real problem. And the Senate, the United States Senate should get to the bottom of it. [LAUGHTER]

This is a moral moment. I keep saying it, it's a moral moment. Who are we going to be, what's going to define us? And it's time not for the typical tribalism, it's time for leaders to start standing up and saying, "You know what? We can go a different way. We can imagine a different country." That's why I pointed out the new leader of the Democratic Party on the house side, we're a different generation. There's a rising generation of people. I've talked about my friend who wrote this great book, Abundance. There's a whole bunch of new ideas out there that are about the future, about the possibilities, about the hope, about the greatness of America, not the greatness that is braggadocios, not the greatness that says, "I'm better than you," not the greatness that says, "Only I can fix things." That's not the America we want. We want America that says, "We the people." An America that says, "*E pluribus unum*," an America that says that our history shows that rugged individualism and self-reliance are important values, but rugged individualism didn't beat the Nazis, it didn't take us to the moon. We did that together, America.

We need bigger visions that can unite us beyond our narrow partisan desires to get a real mandate. And you know what a real mandate should be? It should be government efficiency, it really should be. God, I have heard from so many of my colleagues on this side of the aisle that have said if they formed a commission of former executives in this body, I see you, Maggie Hassan, it was hard, but I had to cut 24% of my... One out of four employees, it was really hard. It caused a lot of pain but we had to reduce my government. There are a lot of people here that are executives on both sides of the aisle that would have said, "Pick me, pick me. Let's form the most exciting team possible."

Because Jack Reed knows that the military of the United States of America could do things more efficiently, a little bit of waste over there because they haven't passed an audit.

Where's Mary Cantwell? The Commerce Committee, so many ideas about how to create profit centers in the American government. You have talked to me about them, you're brilliant on some of these ideas.

I look around here, but I can look to the other side of the aisle — the man, the farmer sitting over there. The guy who's been so good to me, Chuck Grassley. [LAUGHTER] I forced that man to hug me when we passed. I forced you to hug me, sir. I have pictures, can't deny it. I don't know how you're going to get reelected now, sir, you hug this Black dude from New Jersey. You're so sweet to me still. We passed a big bipartisan bill because people like him, like the presiding officer, I've met with you, you still have big ideas. You still have big ideas that aren't partisan.

If President Trump, from his inaugural address to his first speech before a joint session of Congress said, "Enough, there are big ideas in this country. I want the best, I want people to come together. I'm tired of us talking down at each other. It's time for us to come together and imagine ways to create real abundance in America for all Americans. I trust the genius of America, the kindness and the decency." But this President doesn't do that. He violates all of our common senses of decency. And don't say it doesn't happen, folks, don't say that. I listen to him, I listen to how he talks about people. We have a government now, as I said earlier, that isn't, "Ask not what your country can do for you, but what you can do for your country." We have a country now where a President says, "Ask not what your country can do for you, ask what you can do for Donald Trump."

And you're seeing who gets the special treatment. Some law firms are really threatened right now with being bankrupted by Donald Trump targeting them. Others have decided a different path. I'm not hating on them, but they said, "We're going to go to Trump and we're going to offer him what he wants. We're going to give him tens of millions of dollars of free pro bono work." I wish they would bring some of that free bono work to Newark, New Jersey, a lot of people need lawyers, folks in my city. What are the standards here of our government? You want a merger? Well, maybe you should put a lot of money in Donald Trump's memecoin.

I read the document. There's something, a word called emoluments, and we sit by and act like, "Oh, no big deal. He's made millions and millions of dollars." From who, we don't know. We haven't held one hearing of oversight to know who is giving a millions of dollars to that memecoin. Is it the Turks, is it the Saudis, is it the Chinese? Is it the Russian oligarchs? Do we know? Should we know? Yes, America, stop falling into tribal lanes and closing your eyes to things that should not be normalized. Why are we normalizing these things? They're wrong. They're patently, on the face of it is wrong. If you use Signal to discuss a military attack, the time of the attack, the weapons that are going to be used and you do it on a commercial app and decide to include a reporter, there should be accountability. Am I crazy?

[APPLAUSE]

SENATOR CURTIS (PRESIDING): Order, order. Ladies and gentlemen, let me just remind you, expressions of approval and disapproval are not permitted by the gallery, thank you.

SENATOR BOOKER: He was forced to say that. Look at you, defiant man [pointing at someone who didn't stop clapping].

The Senate and the House should be checks and balances on the President of the United States. The Senate and the House should not allow business as usual in this moment when the President is insisting that no one has the power to check and balance him. When a judge does it, when a judge decides on the soundness of his legal observations to have a ruling, and then the President of the United States doesn't appeal the ruling like most people kind of do, but starts to drag and insult and threaten that judge with impeachment, and some people, astonishing to me in our government said, "Oh, that's right. We should impeach this guy." That's not a question of Left or Right, that's a question of right or wrong. We're normalizing this behavior. We're letting him do things that Republicans and Democrats should say together are wrong.

And so I want to say, I'm going to stop soon.

SENATOR JEANNE SHAHEEN (NEW HAMPSHIRE): Will the Senator yield for a question?

SENATOR BOOKER: Oh yes – God bless you – for a question while retaining the floor.

SENATOR SHAHEEN: Thank you. I want to start before I get to my question, with just saying how proud I am, how proud we all are of you. And I think I'm old enough to remember Strom Thurmond's filibuster. I can remember being in high school and seeing the news every night and the reporters coming from the steps of the Capitol because they were filibustering the Civil Rights bill. And what I'm proud of is that your focus on democracy and the opportunities that democracy opens up for all of our rights, in my mind cancels out what Strom Thurmond did to prevent African-Americans and others from getting the rights they deserve in this country, so I'm proud of that. [APPLAUSE] But I really want to... You talked earlier this afternoon about the rule of law and the overreach of this administration.

As part of that, you went through a litany of agencies that Congress had established that this President is trying to take away. And I just wanted to point out that, and you mentioned this earlier, one of those agencies that Congress established is the US Agency for International Development. And earlier today, we had a Shadow Hearing Roundtable, the Democrats on the Foreign Relations Committee. It was on the dangerous consequences of funding cuts to US global health programs. And I know that as a ranking member on the subcommittee on African Global Health Policy, you would have really been interested in this. I'm glad you were here on the floor, but I wish you could have heard what we heard from the people who testified.

We heard from Atul Gawande, who used to be the administrator of USAID, their global health program. We heard from Dan Schwartz, who was the Vice President of Management Sciences for Health. That's a contractor that works on global health programs. And we heard from Nick Enrich, who's the former assistant administrator for Global Health at USAID. And they started out by talking about what global health has accomplished through USAID. PEPFAR has saved more than 26 million lives. It's reversed the spread of HIV/AIDS. They've done malaria prevention and control for over half a billion people. They've eradicated smallpox and eliminated most of polio. They've reduced infant mortality by more than 59% since 1990. They've supported cholera, measles and Ebola outbreak response.

And one of the things Dr. Gawande pointed out is that they took the response to Ebola outbreak from two weeks, many of us remember that during the Obama administration, when Ebola was coming to the United States. They took that response from two weeks down to 24 to 48 hours, to be in there to be responding to the Ebola epidemic. And what has this President done? What has Elon Musk and DOGE done? They've gone in to USAID, they've cut the global health workforce from over 800 to about 60. They've taken the system that was designed to make programs more efficient and they dismantled it. And when the Inspector General Paul Martin reported on food rotting in ports, he was fired. USAID has been the largest civilian ground force to address global goals. As Dr. Gawande said, "What we learned from USAID is that prevention is a whole lot more efficient and a lot cheaper than emergency treatment."

He said that what we spend on global health through USAID has been nine dollars a household in America in a year. *Nine dollars*. Think about what we've done with that nine dollars. And as they were going through the litany of programs that have been cut, the one that caught my eye was 75% of the pandemic threat comes from diseases jumping from animals to humans. That program has been terminated — 75% of the threat of future pandemics. So as we think about rule of law and the overreach of this President, would you agree with me that there has been no consultation with Congress about any effort to move USAID into the Department of State, and that because Congress created this agency, Congress has got to be involved in reauthorizing whatever comes next, that this President and his DOGE boys need to understand that before they take any more steps at USAID?

SENATOR BOOKER: Yes, yes, yes. You and I both know that in a bipartisan way, we created some of these programs principally to keep America safe. Many of us remember that dramatic hearing where Trump's Secretary of Defense, James Mattis, sat before the American people when they were discussing the budgets for USAID and the State Department. And John Mattis knew the power of those programs to keep us safe. You mentioned infectious diseases, well we live in a world where an infectious disease anywhere is a threat to public health everywhere. So pulling our scientists out of the fight against Ebola, pulling our scientists out of drug-resistant tuberculosis fights, it makes no sense.

And then in terms of our safety, he just simply said, "If you cut these programs, buy me more bullets," because our fight's to spread democracy. There are nations in Africa, for example, where the Chinese are trying to influence a different way of life. That's why so many African countries now won't criticize China for things that the rest of the world say are bad, because they owe them so much debt, they're so engaged, they're so overplaying the fact. Kris Coons said something – I think it was Kris Coons – said something painful earlier about Myanmar. This horrific thing, America, the most generous country on the planet, when there's a crisis, we lead the rest. I've sat in meetings in a bipartisan way with ambassadors from other countries where we had the moral authority to tell them, "You're not doing enough." And in the Myanmar crisis right now, as Kris Coons said, who's standing there? Not Americans – we don't have the capacity anymore to help a horrific crisis like that – but the Chinese government's there.

Again, it's what defines us. I keep saying this is not a Left-Right moment, this is a moral moment. And we tell our truth with what we do with our resources. And here's the thing, when you poll people and ask them how much money you spend on USAID, they say, "Oh, it must be 10% of the American budget, it must be 5% of the American budget." It's around 1% or less. A penny of what tax dollars you send down to Washington goes to help us make sure that around the globe, we're countering the hard power of some countries with the power of our light and our soft power.

We have been the envy of the world where people see and know how special America is because we live the value of every major religion, that we're going to love our neighbors, we're going to be there for you in your times of need. And we all know with a terrorist group from far away to the most horrific attack, that in a lot of these countries, terrorist groups are trying to counter the democratic governments there.

Look in the Sahel region, look what's happening. When I was in Nigeria, I was shocked to say what they're talking about, instabilities in the North, the threats of terrorism in the North. I'm going to go for seven more minutes and stop, but I want to use these last seven minutes to return one more time to the people of my state and actually other states who demanded we do things different, who asked for help.

Before I do, I just want to thank Mike Lee today. He's my partner in antitrust, a specialty of my friend, Amy Klobuchar. I don't know if you got my text, but you got it, where I said to you, "I'm kind of going to the floor to hold it for as long as I can," and I may not make our first subcommittee together on antitrust where we have a lot of common ground. So I'm sorry I missed it today. I know you'll fill me in, but I know my friend filled in. Thank you.

I want to close back where we started, about us, about why I'm here. I believe that there is an urgent crisis in our country that we are not talking about. It's not a Left-Right crisis, it's a right-wrong crisis. It's a moral moment, and again, in America that's going to define our character, about who we are and what we stand for. There's a threat to the bedrock commitments we've made to each other as a country.

People are threatening that bedrock commitment of Social Security. They're calling it a Ponzi scheme. They're making up absolute lies about it. When I read American after American who said that that is their lifeline. They told stories that if they don't get their Social Security payment or they get caught up because nobody's answering their calls, if the rural Social Security office... I read states, Red and Blue, where they're closing Social Security offices. If I now have to drive not 100 miles, but 150 miles at 93 years old, it doesn't make sense. One of my colleagues stood up here and said, "That's already cutting benefits if you can't access the folks." I stood here because there's a threat to these bedrock commitments, the bedrock commitment we've made in healthcare in this country.

We won the defense of the Affordable Care Act, but my colleagues know when you start talking about Medicaid, that's not 20 plus million Americans, it's 70, 80, 90 million Americans. It's our elders in nursing homes, it's our children with disabilities. It's our moms giving birth, that are still giving birth in the country with about the highest maternal mortality rates in the industrial world. It's a moral moment. Who do we stand for?

Schumer shocked me when he said they're going to use some kind of budget gimmick to push this through. You shocked me, Chuck. I thought this was going to come down to the parliamentarian, but it doesn't sound like it now. It's just going to get done with the math, and I read from Manhattan Institute, criticized it on the Right, AEI criticized it on the Right. They said, "What are you doing? What are you doing, America?" You're going to rack up trillions and trillions of dollars in debt that our children and our children's children are going to have to pay for, passing the bucks that will grow. Are you doing that to help people get more access to healthcare, more access to retirement security, more access to the things we believe in? Big ideas like universal childcare, paid family leave? No, we're doing that in order to renew the tax cuts that I read.

Conservative budget folks, moderate budget folks all across the spectrum who said, "It will blow up our deficit." And the benefits of those tax cuts, not all, let's not use hyperbole, but most will go, most will go to the richest people in our country, who I promise you, I celebrate people who've brought their ingenuity and their expertise and their grit and their tireless work, who've built wealth in this country. But it should not be us versus them; but I'm telling you that those folks do not need another tax cut.

And the corporations who came here, you all remember, said, "We would like a 25% rate." The people I read said that when we kicked it to 21% – not even what they were asking for from 35% – it exploded. One of the main reasons it exploded our debt. And we read from conservative groups who just said all these promises, that we would grow our way out of our deficit, they didn't materialize, all the promises that were made. Trump, for those who don't remember or weren't here when I read it, was going around, telling folks that, "Oh, my tariffs." This is 2017. "My tariffs, the money that I get, that will be what we could pay down the debt." The math that they did, that would account for about one-750th of the debt at that time.

But he used that money to try to compensate the farmers that he was hurting with his tariffs. This is a moral moment and people are getting hurt and people are afraid because of the threats to Medicaid cuts. There were people writing in and said, "$880 billion would devastate me, but even small cuts to services, my whole family, fragile architecture of our finances, if you just pull out the transportation money that my disabled child uses, that will crumble my financial world." And so when you talk about the bigger cuts, we know the math. Many states who expanded Medicare have a trigger that if it goes below 90%, all the Medicare expansion goes off in that state and millions of Americans will be hurt. That's not right, guys. That's not right. And so this is the choices we have before us, our veterans and the VA.

You, I'm mad at you now — you made me get very emotional with your story. We've read John McCain's story. We read the stories of the poems of the unknown soldier, looking over us and saying, "What are you doing to the gold star families? What are you doing to the veterans? Are you living up to your promises that you made?" Well, right now with the cuts of tens of thousands, over 80,000 veterans who work for the VA, but even more because about 20% or so of all federal workers are veterans. And we read stories from veterans in America, who are shaken by what's happening, who are losing their jobs. But yet, all they want to do is serve. They're not what they're being called. They're not leeches, they're not criminals. They shouldn't be degraded for wanting to continue to serve their nation.

This is what we're talking about, our veterans, our seniors, our healthcare, our financial security going forward. I asked the question to all those people who voted for Donald Trump, who believed in him, that he would lower your grocery prices. I asked you, "Look at your financial self, are you better off than you were 72 years [days] ago financially?" Well, the answer for most people who believed in him is no, because he didn't set out to do anything to lower prices. He set out to rename the Gulf of Mexico, to threaten Canada, to say, "I'm going to take over Greenland." He's done a lot of things — 140 executive orders. Many of them actually drive up your costs, make it more expensive to enroll in the ACA, reduce a lot of the tax credits there. He's increased your costs, he's taxed your bedrock services, stock market tumbles, your 401k accounts are less.

Inflation is up, consumer confidence is down. This is what the voices we've brought into this chamber, the voices of our constituents, red states, blue states, the voices of Democrats and Republicans, Republican governors, Democratic governors. We brought all the people that are saying, "No, this is a moral moment. Not Left or Right, right or wrong."

And so I've tried over the last 25 hours and one minute, to center the conversation back on what will we do of good conscience? People who are saying, "I served this country, I risked my life. Shouldn't I be able to keep my job?" People are saying, "This country once made itself the envy of the world because we invested in high quality education for every child. I don't like what's going on with the end of the Department of Education." People are saying, "I worked harder than I ever have, but the prices on everything in my life are getting higher." People who are saying that, "The America I learned about in school, the one where people's rights are protected," the people are saying that, "Why are we yet again going through another healthcare battle that threatens millions of people?" The people are saying that, "I'm worried about the financial security and the future of my country," the voices of folks.

And so I end by saying simply this. Where I started was John Lewis. I don't know how to solve this, I don't know how to stop us from going down this road. Chuck Schumer has now told me that they're greasing the skids to do these things. I'm sorry, but I know who does have the power. The people of the United States of America.

The power of the people is greater than the people in power. It is time to heed the words of the man. I began this whole thing with John Lewis. I beg folks to take his example of his early days where he made himself determined to show his love for his country at a time the country didn't love him, to love this country so much, to be such a patriot that he endured beatings savagely on the Edmund Pettus Bridge, at lunch counters, on freedom rides. He said he had to do something. He would not normalize a moment like this. He would not just go along with business as usual. He wouldn't know how to solve it, but there's one thing that he would do that I hope you all can do that I think I did a little bit of tonight. He said for us to go out and cause some good trouble, necessary trouble to redeem the soul of our nation.

I want you to redeem the dream. Let's be bold in America, not demean and degrade Americans, not divide us against each other. Let's be bolder in America with a vision that inspires with hope that starts with the people of the United States of America.

That's how this country started, we the people. Let's get back to the ideals that others are threatening. Let's get back to our founding documents, that those imperfect geniuses had some very special words at the end of the Declaration of Independence – was one of the greatest in all of humanity – declarations of interdependence, when our Founders said, "We must mutually pledge, pledge to each other, our lives, our fortunes and our sacred honor." We need that now from all Americans.

This is a moral moment. It's not Left or Right, it's right or wrong. Let's get in good trouble.

My friend, Madam President, I yield the floor.

[OVATION]

Madam President! Madam President! Thank you to the Pages, thank you to the parliamentarian staff, thank you to the clerks, thank you to the doorkeepers. There are so many people that make this place special. I kept you up all night — kept you up 24 hours. I just want to say thank you. Thank you, everybody.

Senator Cory Booker

{Official Biography, September 2025}

Cory Booker believes that the American dream isn't real for anyone unless it's within reach of everyone. Booker has dedicated his life to fighting for those who have been left out, left behind, or left without a voice.

Booker grew up in northern New Jersey and received his undergraduate degree from Stanford University. At Stanford, Booker played varsity football, volunteered for the campus peer counseling center, and wrote for the student newspaper. He was awarded a Rhodes Scholarship and went on to study at the University of Oxford, and then Yale Law School, where he graduated in 1997.

After graduating law school, Booker moved to Newark and started a nonprofit organization to provide legal services for low-income families, helping tenants take on slumlords. In 1998, Booker moved into the Brick Towers housing project in Newark, where he lived until its demolition in 2006. Booker still lives in Newark's Central Ward today, where the median household income is less than $15,000.

At 29, Booker was elected to the Newark City Council, where he challenged the city's entrenched political machine and fought to improve living conditions for city residents, increase public safety, and reduce crime.

Starting in 2006, Booker served as Newark's mayor for more than seven years. During his tenure, the city entered its largest period of economic growth since the 1960s. In addition, overall crime declined and the quality of life for residents improved due to initiatives such as more affordable housing, new green spaces and parks, increased educational opportunities, and more efficient city services.

In October 2013, Booker won a special election to represent New Jersey in the United States Senate. In November 2014, Senator Booker was re-elected to a full six-year term. As New Jersey's senior Senator, Cory Booker has brought an innovative and consensus-building approach to tackling some of the most difficult problems facing New Jersey and our country. He has emerged as a national leader in the effort to fix our broken criminal justice system and end mass incarceration, helping craft the most sweeping set of criminal justice reforms in a generation, the First Step Act, which became law in December 2018. Booker has also worked to reform America's broken food system, address our nation's nutrition crisis, and end food insecurity.

Booker sits on the Judiciary Committee, the Foreign Relations Committee, the Committee on Agriculture, Nutrition, and Forestry, and the Committee on Small Business and Entrepreneurship.

Other Senators

{Senators listed here are in the order they first requested a yield for a question.}

Charles Ellis "Chuck" Schumer

Born 23 November 1950
Member of the New York State Assembly from the 45th District (1975-1980)
Member of the US House of Representatives from New York (1981-1999)
Senate Minority Leader; assumed office of United States Senator from New York in 1999

On 12 March 2025, he announced his opposition to the House-passed continuing resolution (CR) to fund the 2025 United States federal budget until 30 September 2025. He reversed his position the next day, saying on the Senate floor, "A shutdown would give Mr. Trump and Mr. Musk permission to destroy vital government services at a significantly faster rate". This drew the ire of many House Democrats, and caused his book tour to be postponed for security reasons. After the vote, Schumer faced pressure to step down as Senate leader, but he said he has no intention to do so.

Senator Lisa Blunt Rochester

Born 10 February 1962
US Representative for Delaware's at-large congressional district 2017-2025
Assumed office of U. S. Senator from Delaware Jan.3, 2025.

Member of the Senate Committee on Banking, Housing,and Urban Affairs and the Senate Committee on Health, Education, Labor, and Pensions (HELP).

On 2 April 2025, her office published a press release announcing a letter she led with 22 colleagues to the Secretary of Education, Linda McMahon. It addressed things spoken about in Sen. Booker's speech, and was co-signed by many of the Senators who participated in the Booker speech.

Senator Chris Murphy

Born 3 August 1973
Representative, CT 5th District 2007-2013
US Senator from Connecticut since 2013

Member of the Senate Foreign Relations Committee and ranking Democratic member of the subcommittee on the Middle East and Counter-terrorism.

His most famous speech was 15-hour filibuster on gun control in 2016 after the mass shooting at the Pulse nightclub in Orlando, Florida.

Book: "The Violence Inside Us: A Brief History of an Ongoing American Tragedy" (2020)

Senator Andy Kim

Born 12 July 1982

Civilian advisor at the US Department of State in Afghanistan during the Obama administration.

US Representative from New Jersey's 2nd congressional district 2019-2024

Junior Senator from New Jersey since 2024

Member of Committee on Armed Services, subcommittee on Cyber, Information Technologies, and Innovation, subcommittee on Military Personnel; Member of Committee on Foreign Affairs, subcommittee on Indo-Pacific, subcommittee on Oversight and Accountability; Member of Select Committee on Strategic Competition between the United States and the Chinese Communist Party

In February 2019, Kim introduced his first bill, the Strengthening Health Care and Lowering Prescription Drug Costs Act (SAVE Act).

Senator Peter Welch

Born 2 May 1947

US Representative for Vermont's at-large congressional district 2007-2023

Junior Senator from Vermont since 2023

Member of Committee on Agriculture, Nutrition, and Forestry. Subcommittee ranking member on Rural Development and Energy. Member of Committee on

Finance. Member of Committee on the Judiciary, subcommittee ranking member on the Constitution. Member of Committee on Rules & Administration.

Senator Welch has taken several legislative actions in his term and since the speech. There is a comprehensive list of these actions on his website on a page titled "Combating President Trump's Illegal Agenda"

Senator Dick Durbin

Born 21 November 1944

US Representative for Illinois' 20th congressional district 1982-1996

US Senator from Illinois 1996-present

Senate Democratic Whip since 2005. Durbin is the longest-serving Senate party whip in US history (the position was created in 1913)

Member of the Committee on Agriculture, Nutrition and Forestry. Member of Committee on Appropriations, Ranking member of the Committee on the Judiciary.

Senator Kirsten Gillibrand

Born 9 December 1966

US Representative from New York's 20th Congressional district 2007-2009

When Hillary Clinton was appointed Secretary of State In 2009, Governor David Paterson selected Gillibrand to fill the vacated Senate seat. She won the special election to retain the seat in 2010, and has continued to win re-election, most recently in 2024.

Member of the Senate Appropriations Committee. Member of the Armed Services Committee. Member of the Select Committee on Intelligence. She is the ranking member on the Special Committee on Aging.

When Sen. Gillibrand took congressional office in 2007, she began publishing her official schedule, earmark requests she received, and her personal financial statements. Her office calls it the "Sunlight Report", and this practice of transparency continues to this day. The reports are available on her website.

Senator Tina Smith

Born 4 March 1958

Lieutenant Governor of Minnesota 2015-2018

Appointed to US Senate seat vacated by Al Franken in 2018. (Won 2018 special election to the seat, and was elected to a full term in 2020. She has announced she will not run for re-election in 2026)

Member of US Senate Committee on Agriculture, Nutrition and Forestry. Member of the Committee on Banking, Housing and Urban Affairs. Member of Committee on Finance. Member of Committee on Indian Affairs. Subcommittee Ranking Member on Housing, Transportation, and Community Development. Subcommittee Ranking Member on Fiscal Responsibility and Economic Growth. Subcommittee Member on Digital Assets. Subcommittee member on Rural Development, Energy, and Credit. Member of the Subcommittee on Food and Nutrition, Specialty Crops, Organics, and Research. Member of the Subcommittee on Livestock, Dairy, Poultry, and Food Safety.

After the January 6, 2021 insurrection, Senator Smith called for Trump's immediate removal from office through invoking the 25th Amendment to The Constitution and by impeachment.

Senator Rev. Raphael Warnock

Born 23 July 1969

Has served as Senior Pastor at Ebenezer Baptist Church, the former pulpit of Rev. Dr. Martin Luther King Jr., in Atlanta since 2005.

Rev. Warnock was elected to the Senate in a special election in 2020. He was reelected to a full term in 2022.

Rev. Warnock rose to prominence in politics in Georgia while campaigning to expand Medicaid in the state, including leading a sit-in at the Georgia State Capitol to press for the Medicaid expansion offered by the Patient Protection and Affordable Care Act. He was arrested during the protest (as he and Senator Booker joked about during the speech documented in this book)

Member of the Agriculture, Nutrition and Forestry Committee. Member of Banking, Housing and Urban Affairs Committee. Member of the Finance Committee, and the Special Committee on Aging.

Senator Amy Klobuchar

Born 2 May 1960

Hennepin County Attorney 1998-2006

US Senator from Minnesota 2006- present

Member of the Committee on Agriculture, Nutrition, and Forestry. Member of Senate Judiciary Committee. Chairwoman of the Senate Democratic Steering and Policy Committee. Member of Commerce, Science, and Transportation Committee. Member of Joint Economic Committee. Member of Rules and Administration Committee.

Senator Ron Wyden

Born 3 May 1949

First elected office was in 2000, as president of the New Castle Couty Council He was then elected county executive in 2004. He served in that office for 6 years.

Representative of Oregon 3rd Congressional District 1981-1996

US Senator from Oregon 1996- present

Ranking member of Finance Committee. Member of the Committee on Energy and Natural Resources. Member of Budget Committee. Member of Select Committee on Intelligence. Leading Senate Democrat on Joint Committee on Taxation.

Has headers on his website that are links to "Submit A Whistleblower Complaint" and "Resources for Terminated Federal Employees"

Book: "It Takes Chutzpah: How to Fight Fearlessly for Progressive Change"

Senator Chris Coons

Born 9 September 1963

Elected in 2010 Senate special election for Delaware. Elected to a full term in 2014, and is currently serving.

Member of Appropriations Committee, Foreign Relations Committee, Judiciary Committee, Small Business & Entrepreneurship Committee, and is Chair of the Select

Committee on Ethics.

Coons co-chaired the 2017 and 2019 National Prayer breakfasts, and co-chairs the weekly Senate Prayer Breakfast.

Senator Ed Markey

Born 11 July 1946

Massachusetts House of Representatives from 16th Middlsex 1973-1975

Massachusetts House of Representatives from 26th Middlesex 1975-1976

US House of Representatives from Massachusetts 1976-2012, from 7th and 5th District

US Senator from Massachusetts 2013- present.

Ranking Member of Committee on Small Business and Entrepreneurship. Member of Committee on Commerce, Science, and Transportation. Subcommittee on Telecommunications and Media. Subcommittee on Consumer Protection, Technology, and Data Privacy. Subcommittee on Surface Transportation, Freight, Pipelines, and Safety. Member of Committee on Environment and Public Works. Subcommittee on Clean Air, Climate and Nuclear Safety. Subcommittee on Chemical Safety, Waste Management, Environmental Justice,and Regulatory Oversight. Subcommittee on Transportation and Infrastructure. Member of Committee on Health, Education, Labor, and Pensions. Subcommittee on Primary Health & Retirement Security (Ranking member). Subcommittee on Employment and Workplace Safety.

Senator Mark Warner

Born 15 December 1954

Governor of Virginia 2002-2006

Senator from Virginia 2009-present

Member of Select Committee on Intelligence (Vice Chairman). Member of Committee on Finance.Subcommittee on Energy, Natural Resources and Infrastructure. Subcommittee on International Trade, Customs, and Global Competitiveness. Member of Committee on Banking, Housing & Urban Affairs. Subcommittee on Financial Institutions and Consumer Protection. Subcommittee on National Security and International Trade and Finance. Subcommittee on Securities, Insurance,and Investment. Member of Committee on the Budget. Member of Committee on Rules & Administration.

Senator Elizabeth Warren

Born 22 June 1949

US Senator from Massachusetts 2013- Present

Member of Committee on Banking, Housing, & Urban Affairs. Subcommittee Chair on Economic Policy. Subcommittee on Financial Institutions and Consumer Protection. Subcommittee on Securities, Insurance, and Investment. Member of Committee on Finance. Subcommittee on Health Care. Subcommittee on Social Security, Pensions, and Family Policy. Subcommittee on Taxation and IRS Oversight. Member of the Special Committee on Aging. Committee on Armed Services. Subcommittee Chair on Personnel. Subcommittee on Emerging Threats and Capabilities. Subcommittee on Strategic Forces.

Senator Chris Van Hollen

Born 10 January 1959
Maryland House of Delegates Member from the 18th District 1991-1995
Member of Maryland Senate from the 18th District 1995-2003
Member of US House of Representatives from Maryland's 8th District 2003-2017
Chair of the Democratic Congressional Campaign Committee 2007-2011
House Democratic Assistant to the Leader 2009-2011
Chair of the Democratic Senatorial Campaign Committee 2017-2019
US Senator from Maryland 2017- Present
Member of the Appropriations Committee. Ranking member of the Subcommittee on Commerce, Justice, Science, and Related Agencies. Subcommittee on Financial Services and General Government. Subcommittee on Homeland Security. Subcommittee on Interior, Environment, and Related Agencies. Subcommittee on Transportation, Housing and Urban Development, and Related Agencies.

Senator Tammy Duckworth

Born 12 March 1968
Director of the Illinois Department of Veterans Affairs 2006-2009
Assistant Secretary of Veterans Affairs 2009-2011
Member of US House of Representatives from Illinois's 8th District 2013-2017
Vice Chair of the Democratic National Committee 2021-2025
Senator from Illinois 2017- Present
Member of Senate Democrats' Special Committee on the Climate Crisis. US Senate Armed Services Committee. Subcommittees on Airland, Personnel, and Readiness and Management Support. Member Committee on Commerce, Science & Transportation. Ranking member of the Subcommittee on Aviation, Space and Innovation.Subcommittee on Telecommunications and Media. Subcommittee on Surface Transportation, Freight, Pipelines and Safety. Member of the Committee on Veterans Affairs. Member of Committee on Foreign Relations. Subcommittee on Multilateral International Development. Ranking member of the Subcommittee on Multilateral Institutions and International Economic, Energy and Environmental Policy. Subcommittee on Europe and Regional Security Cooperation. Subcommittee of State Department and USAID Management, International Operations and Bilateral International Development.

Senator Maggie Hassan

Born 27 February 1958
Member of the New Hampshire Senate from the 23rd District 2004-2010
Majority Leader of the New Hampshire Senate 2008-2010
81st Governor of New Hampshire 2013-2017
US Senator from New Hampshire 2017- Present

Committee on Homeland Security and Governmental Affairs. Subcommittee on Border Management, Federal Workforce, and Regulatory Affairs. Permanent Subcommittee on Investigations. Member of Committee on Health, Education, Labor, and Pensions. Subcommittee on Employment and Workplace Safety. Subcommittee on Primary Health and Retirement Security. Member of Senate Finance Committee. Ranking member of the Subcommittee on Health Care. Member of Committee on Veterans Affairs. Member of Joint Economic Committee.

Senator Ben Ray Luján

Born 7 June 1972
Member of the New Mexico Public Regulation Commission from the 3rd District 2003-2009
Member of the US House of Representatives from New Mexico's 3rd District 2009-2021
Chair of the Democratic Congressional Campaign Committee 2015-2019
Assistant Speaker of the US House of Representatives 2019-2021
US Senator from New Mexico 2021- Present
Member of the Committee on Energy and Commerce. Subcommittee on Communications and Technology. Subcommittee on Health. Subcommittee on Digital Commerce and Consumer Protection. Member of Select Committee on the Climate Crisis.

Senator Sheldon Whitehouse

Born 20 October 1955
US Attorney General for the District of Rhode Island 1993-1998
71st Attorney General of Rhode Island 1999-2003
US Senator from Rhode Island 2007- Present
Member of the Committee on Budget. Ranking Member of Committee on Environment and Public Works. Subcommittee on Oversight, Subcommittee on Superfund, Toxics and Environmental Health. Subcommittee on Water and Wildlife. Member of Committee on Finance. Committee on the Judiciary. Member of Commission on Security and Cooperation in Europe.

Senator Patty Murray

Born 11 October 1950
Member of the Washington State Senate from the 1st District 1989-1993
US Senator from Washington 1993- Present
Vice Chair of the Senate Appropriations Committee. Ranking member of the Subcommittee on Energy and Water Development. Subcommittee on Defense. Subcommittee on Homeland Security. Subcommittee on Labor, Health, and Human Services. Subcommittee on Military Construction and Veterans Affairs. Subcommittee on Transportation, Housing, and Urban Development. Member of the Committee on Health, Education, Labor,and Pensions. Committee on the Budget. Committee on Veterans Affairs.

Senator Michael Bennet

Born 28 November 1964

Superintendent of Denver Public Schools 2005-2009

Chair of the Democratic Senatorial Campaign Committee 2013-2015

US Senator from Colorado 2009- Present

Member of Committee on Agriculture, Nutrition and Forestry. Chair of the Subcommittee on Conservation, Forestry and Natural Resources. Subcommittee on Rural Development and Energy. Member of Committee on Finance. Subcommittee on Energy, Natural Resources,and Infrastructure. Subcommittee on International Trade, Customs, and Global Competitiveness. Subcommittee on Taxation and IRS Oversight. Member of Committee on Rules and Administration. Member of Select Committee on Intelligence.

Senator Jack Reed

Born 12 November 1949

Member of the Rhode Island Senate from the 12th District 1985-1991

Member of the US House of Representatives from Rhode Island's 2nd District 1991-1997

US Senator from Rhode Island 1997- Present

Member of Appropriations Committee. Subcommittee on Commerce, Justice, Science, and Related Agencies. Subcommittee on Defense. Ranking member of the Subcommittee on Financial Series and General Government. Subcommittee on Labor, Health and Human Services, Education, and Related Agencies Subcommittee on Military Construction, Veterans Affairs,and Related Agencies. Subcommittee on Transportation. Housing, and Urban Development. Ranking Member of the Armed Services Committee. Serves in an Ex Officio capacity on the Subcommittees for Airland, Cybersecurity, Emerging Threats and Capabilities, Personnel, Readiness and Management Support, Seapower, and Strategic Forces. Member of Banking, Housing and Urban Affairs Committee. Subcommittee on Economic Policy. Subcommittee on Housing, Transportation, and Community Development. Subcommittee on Securities, Insurance, and Investment. Ex Officio Member of the Select Committee on Intelligence.

Senator Maria Cantwell

Born 13 October 1958

Member of the Washington House of Representatives from the 44th District 1987-1993

Member of the US House of Representatives from Washington's 1st District 1993-1995

US Senator from Washington 2001- Present

Chair of the Senate Committee on Commerce, Science and Transportation. Ex Officio member of Subcommittees on Aviation Safety, Operations and Innovation; Communications, Media,and Broadband; Consumer Protection, Product Safety, and Data Security; Oceans, Fisheries, Climate Change, and Manufacturing; Space and Science; Surface Transportation, Maritime Freight, and Ports; Tourism, Trade, and Export Promotion. Member of the Committee on Energy and Natural

Resources. Committee on Finance. Committee on Indian Affairs. Committee on Small Business and Entrepreneurship.

Senator Alex Padilla

   Born 22 March 1973
   Member of the Los Angeles City Council from the 7th District 1999-2006
   President of the Los Angeles City Council 2001-2006
   Member of the California State Senate from the 20th District 2006-2014
   30th Secretary of State of California 2015-2021
   US Senator from California 2021- Present
Ranking Member of the Committee on Rules & Administration. Member of the Committee on the Judiciary. Subcommittee on Immigration, Citizenship, and Border Safety. Member of Committee on the Budget. Committee on Environment and Public Works. Committee on Energy and Natural Resources.

Senator Angus King

   Born 31 March 1944
   72nd Governor of Maine 1995-2003
   US Senator from Maine 2013- Present
   Ranking Member of the Committee on Rules & Administration. Member of the Committee on the Judiciary. Subcommittee on Immigration, Citizenship, and Border Safety. Member of Committee on the Budget. Committee on Environment and Public Works. Committee on Energy and Natural Resources.
Member of the Committee on Veterans' Affairs. Select Committee on Intelligence. Committee on Armed Services. Chair of the Subcommittee on Strategic Force. Subcommittee for Airland. Subcommittee on Seapower.

Senator Adam Schiff

   Born 22 June 1960
   Member of the California Senate from the 21st District 1996-2000
   Member of the US House of Representatives from California 2001-2004
   Ranking Member of the House Intelligence Committee 2015-2019
   Chair of the House Intelligence Committee 2019-2023
   US Senator from California 2024- Present
   Member of the Senate Committee on The Judiciary. Ranking Member of Subcommittee on Intellectual Property. Member of the Subcommittee on The Constitution. Subcommittee on Privacy, Technology, and the Law. Subcommittee on Antitrust, Competition Policy, and Consumer Rights. Member of Committee on Environment & Public Works. Ranking Member of the Subcommit-

tee on Fisheries, Water, and Wildlife. Subcommittee on Transportation and Infrastructure. Member of Committee on Agriculture, Nutrition & Forestry. Subcommittee on Conservation, Forestry, Natural Resources,and Biotechnology. Subcommittee on Commodities, Derivatives, Risk Management, and Trade. Committee on Small Business and Entrepreneurship.

Senator Richard Blumenthal

Born 12 February 1946
US Attorney for the District of Connecticut 1977-1981
Member of the Connecticut House of Representatives from the 145th District 1984-1987
Member of the Connecticut Senate of the 27th District 1987-1991
23rd Attorney General of Connecticut 1991-2011
US Senator from Connecticut 2011- Present
Member of the Committee on the Judiciary. Member of the Senate Committee on Homeland Security & Governmental Affairs. Ranking Member of the Permanent Subcommittee on Investigations. Member of the Committee on Armed Services. Committee on Veterans' Affairs.

Senator Time Kaine

Born 26 February 1958
Member of the Richmond City Council from the 2nd District 1994-2001
76th Mayor of Richmond 1998-2001
38th Lieutenant Governor of Virginia 2002-2006
70th Governor of Virginia 2006-2010
Chair of the Democratic National Committee 2009-2011
US Senator from Virginia 2013- Present
Member of the Armed Services Committee. Member of Budget Committee. Member of Foreign Relations Committee. Ranking Member of the Subcommittee on Western Hemisphere, Transnational Crime, Civil Security, Democracy, Human Rights, and Global Women's Issues. Member of Health, Education, Labor and Pensions Committee.

Senator Tammy Baldwin

Born 11 February 1962
Member of the Dany County Board of Supervisors from the 8th District 1986-1993
Member of the Wisconsin State Assembly from the 78th District 1993-1999
Member of the US House of Representatives from Wisconsin's 2nd District 1999-2013
US Senator from Wisconsin 2017- Present
Member of Committee on Appropriations. Subcommittee on Agriculture, Rural Development, Food and Drug Administration, and Related Agencies. Subcommittee on Defense. Subcommittee on Energy and Water Development. Ranking Member on the Subcommittee on Labor, Health and

Human Services, Education, and Related Agencies. Subcommittee on Military Construction, Veterans Affairs, and Related Agencies. Member of Committee on Commerce, Science, and Transportation. Subcommittee on Consumer Protection, Technology, and Data Privacy. Subcommittee on Coast Guard, Maritime, and Fisheries. Ranking Member of the Subcommittee on Science, Manufacturing, and Competitiveness. Member of Committee on Health, Education, Labor, and Pensions. Subcommittee on Employment and Workplace Safety. Subcommittee on Primary Health and Retirement Security.

Senator Angela Alsobrooks

Born 23 February 1971
State's Attorney of Prince George's County 2011-2018
8th Executive of Prince George's County 2018-2024
US Senator from Maryland 2025- Present
Member of the Committee on Banking, Housing, and Urban Affairs. Subcommittee on Financial Institutions and Consumer Protection. Subcommittee on Housing, Transportation, and Community Development. Subcommittee on National Security and International Trade and Finance. Subcommittee on Securities, Insurance, and Investment. Member of the Committee on Environment and Public Works. Ranking Member on the Subcommittee on Transportation and Infrastructure. Subcommittee on Fisheries, Water, and Wildlife. Member of the Committee on Health, Education, Labor and Pensions. Subcommittee on Education and the American Family. Subcommittee on Employment and Workplace Safety. Member of the Special Committee on Aging.

Senator Mark Kelly

Born 21 February 1964
Time in Space: 54d 2h 4m
US Senator from Arizona 2020- Present
Member of the Committee on Armed Services. Committee on Environment & Public Works. Member of the Special Committee on Aging. Member of Joint Economic Committee. Member of Select Committee on Intelligence.

Senator Mazie Hirono

Born 3 November 1947
Member of the Hawaii House of Representatives 1981-1994
10th Lieutenant Governor of Hawaii 1994-2002
Member of US House of Representatives from Hawaii's 2nd District 2007-2013
US Senator from Hawaii 2013- Present

Ranking Member of Senate Committee on Armed Services. Subcommittee on Readiness and Management Support. Member of Committee on the Judiciary. Committee on Energy & Natural Resources. Committee on Small Business & Entrepreneurship. Committee on Veterans' Affairs.

Senator John Curtis

Born 10 May, 1960
44th Mayor of Provo 2010-2017
Member of the US House of Representatives from Utah's 3rd District 2017-2025
US Senator from Utah 202- Present
Member of Committee on Commerce, Science, and Transportation. Committee on Environment and Public Works. Subcommittee on Chemical Safety, Waste Management, Environmental Justice, and Regulatory Oversight. Committee on Foreign Relations. Chairman of the Subcommittee on Western Hemisphere, Transnational Crime, Civilian Security, Democracy, Human Rights, and Global Women's Issues. Member of the Committee on Small Business and Entrepreneurship.

Senator Catherine Cortez Masto

Born 29 March, 1964
32nd Attorney General of Nevada 2007-2015
Chair of the Democratic Senatorial Campaign Committee 2019-2021
US Senator from Nevada 2017- Present
Member of Senate Finance Committee. Member of Committee on Banking, Housing & Urban Affairs. Member of Committee on Energy & Natural Resources. Member of Committee on Indian Affairs

Senator Jeanne Shaheen

Born 28 January, 1947
Member of the New Hampshire Senate from the 21st District 1990-1996
78th Governor of New Hampshire 1997-2003
US Senator from New Hampshire 2009- Present
Ranking Member of the Senate Committee on Foreign Relations. Member of the Appropriations Committee. Ranking Member of the Appropriations Subcommittee on Agriculture, Rural Development, Food and Drug Administration and Related Agencies. Senior Member of the Armed Services Committee. Member of Committee on Small Business.

{As per the National Archives, the following text is a transcription of the Constitution as it was inscribed by Jacob Shallus on parchment. The spelling and punctuation reflect the original.}

We the People of the United States, in Order to form a more perfect Union, establish Justice, insure domestic Tranquility, provide for the common defence, promote the general Welfare, and secure the Blessings of Liberty to ourselves and our Posterity, do ordain and establish this Constitution for the United States of America.

Article I

Section 1. All legislative Powers herein granted shall be vested in a Congress of the United States, which shall consist of a Senate and House of Representatives.

Section 2. The House of Representatives shall be composed of Members chosen every second Year by the People of the several States, and the Electors in each State shall have the Qualifications requisite for Electors of the most numerous Branch of the State Legislature.

No Person shall be a Representative who shall not have attained to the Age of twenty five Years, and been seven Years a Citizen of the United States, and who shall not, when elected, be an Inhabitant of that State in which he shall be chosen.

Representatives and direct Taxes shall be apportioned among the several States which may be included within this Union, according to their respective Numbers, which shall be determined by adding to the whole Number of free Persons, including those bound to Service for a Term of Years, and excluding Indians not taxed, three fifths of all other Persons. The actual Enumeration shall be made within three Years after the first Meeting of the Congress of the United States, and within every subsequent Term of ten Years, in such Manner as they shall by Law direct. The Number of Representatives shall not exceed one for every thirty Thousand, but each State shall have at Least one Representative; and until such enumeration shall be made, the State of New Hampshire shall be entitled to chuse three, Massachusetts eight, Rhode-Island and Providence Plantations one, Connecticut five, New-York six, New Jersey four, Pennsylvania eight, Delaware one, Maryland six, Virginia ten, North Carolina five, South Carolina five, and Georgia three.

When vacancies happen in the Representation from any State, the Executive Authority thereof shall issue Writs of Election to fill such Vacancies.

The House of Representatives shall chuse their Speaker and other Officers; and shall have the sole Power of Impeachment.

Section 3. The Senate of the United States shall be composed of two Senators from each State, chosen by the Legislature thereof, for six Years; and each Senator shall have one Vote.

Immediately after they shall be assembled in Consequence of the first Election, they shall be divided as equally as may be into three Classes. The Seats of the Senators of the first Class shall be vacated at the Expiration of the second Year, of the second Class at the Expiration of the fourth Year, and of the third Class at the Expiration of the sixth Year, so that one third may be chosen every second Year; and if Vacancies happen by Resignation, or otherwise, during the Recess of the Legislature of any State, the Executive thereof may make temporary Appointments until the next Meeting of the Legislature, which shall then fill such Vacancies.

No Person shall be a Senator who shall not have attained to the Age of thirty Years, and been nine Years a Citizen of the United States, and who shall not, when elected, be an Inhabitant of that State for which he shall be chosen.

The Vice President of the United States shall be President of the Senate, but shall have no Vote, unless they be equally divided.

The Senate shall chuse their other Officers, and also a President pro tempore, in the Absence of the Vice President, or when he shall exercise the Office of President of the United States.

The Senate shall have the sole Power to try all Impeachments. When sitting for that Purpose, they shall be on Oath or Affirmation. When the President of the United States is tried, the Chief Justice shall preside: And no Person shall be convicted without the Concurrence of two thirds of the Members present.

Judgment in Cases of Impeachment shall not extend further than to removal from Office, and disqualification to hold and enjoy any Office of honor, Trust or Profit under the United States: but the Party convicted shall nevertheless be liable and subject to Indictment, Trial, Judgment and Punishment, according to Law.

Section 4. The Times, Places and Manner of holding Elections for Senators and Representatives, shall be prescribed in each State by the Legislature thereof; but the Congress may at any time by Law make or alter such Regulations, except as to the Places of chusing Senators.

The Congress shall assemble at least once in every Year, and such Meeting shall be on the first Monday in December, unless they shall by Law appoint a different Day.

Section 5. Each House shall be the Judge of the Elections, Returns and Qualifications of its own Members, and a Majority of each shall constitute a Quorum to do Business; but a smaller Number may adjourn from day to day, and may be authorized to compel the Attendance of absent Members, in such Manner, and under such Penalties as each House may provide.

Each House may determine the Rules of its Proceedings, punish its Members for disorderly Behaviour, and, with the Concurrence of two thirds, expel a Member.

Each House shall keep a Journal of its Proceedings, and from time to time publish the same, excepting such Parts as may in their Judgment require Secrecy; and the Yeas and Nays of the Members of either House on any question shall, at the Desire of one fifth of those Present, be entered on the Journal.

Neither House, during the Session of Congress, shall, without the Consent of the other, adjourn for more than three days, nor to any other Place than that in which the two Houses shall be sitting.

Section 6. The Senators and Representatives shall receive a Compensation for their Services, to be ascertained by Law, and paid out of the Treasury of the United States. They shall in all Cases, except Treason, Felony and Breach of the Peace, be privileged from Arrest during their Attendance at the Session of their respective Houses, and in going to and returning from the same; and for any Speech or Debate in either House, they shall not be questioned in any other Place.

No Senator or Representative shall, during the Time for which he was elected, be appointed to any civil Office under the Authority of the United States, which shall have been created, or the Emoluments whereof shall have been encreased during such time; and no Person holding any Office under the United States, shall be a Member of either House during his Continuance in Office.

Section 7. All Bills for raising Revenue shall originate in the House of Representatives; but the Senate may propose or concur with Amendments as on other Bills.

Every Bill which shall have passed the House of Representatives and the Senate, shall, before it become a Law, be presented to the President of the United States; If he approve he shall sign it, but if not he shall return it, with his Objections to that House in which it shall have originated, who shall enter the Objections at large on their Journal, and proceed to reconsider it. If after such Reconsideration two thirds of that House shall agree to pass the Bill, it shall be sent, together with the Objections, to the other House, by which it shall likewise be reconsidered, and if approved by two thirds of that House, it shall become a Law. But in all such Cases the Votes of both Houses shall be determined by yeas and Nays, and the Names of the Persons voting for and against the Bill shall be entered on the Journal of each House respectively. If any Bill shall not be returned by the President within ten Days (Sundays excepted) after it shall have been presented to him, the Same shall be a Law, in like Manner as if he had signed it, unless the Congress by their Adjournment prevent its Return, in which Case it shall not be a Law.

Every Order, Resolution, or Vote to which the Concurrence of the Senate and House of Representatives may be necessary (except on a question of Adjournment) shall be presented to the President of the United States; and before the Same shall take Effect, shall be approved by him, or being disapproved by him, shall be repassed by two thirds of the Senate and House of Representatives, according to the Rules and Limitations prescribed in the Case of a Bill.

Section 8 The Congress shall have Power To lay and collect Taxes, Duties, Imposts and Excises, to pay the Debts and provide for the common Defence and general Welfare of the United States; but all Duties, Imposts and Excises shall be uniform throughout the United States;

To borrow Money on the credit of the United States;

To regulate Commerce with foreign Nations, and among the several States, and with the Indian Tribes;

To establish an uniform Rule of Naturalization, and uniform Laws on the subject of Bankruptcies throughout the United States;

To coin Money, regulate the Value thereof, and of foreign Coin, and fix the Standard of Weights and Measures;

To provide for the Punishment of counterfeiting the Securities and current Coin of the United States;

To establish Post Offices and post Roads;

To promote the Progress of Science and useful Arts, by securing for limited Times to Authors and Inventors the exclusive Right to their respective Writings and Discoveries;

To constitute Tribunals inferior to the supreme Court;

To define and punish Piracies and Felonies committed on the high Seas, and Offences against the Law of Nations;

To declare War, grant Letters of Marque and Reprisal, and make Rules concerning Captures on Land and Water;

To raise and support Armies, but no Appropriation of Money to that Use shall be for a longer Term than two Years;

To provide and maintain a Navy;

To make Rules for the Government and Regulation of the land and naval Forces;

To provide for calling forth the Militia to execute the Laws of the Union, suppress Insurrections and repel Invasions;

To provide for organizing, arming, and disciplining, the Militia, and for governing such Part of them as may be employed in the Service of the United States, reserving to the States respectively, the Appointment of the Officers, and the Authority of training the Militia according to the discipline prescribed by Congress;

To exercise exclusive Legislation in all Cases whatsoever, over such District (not exceeding ten Miles square) as may, by Cession of particular States, and the Acceptance of Congress, become the Seat of the Government of the United States, and to exercise like Authority over all Places purchased by the Consent of the Legislature of the State in which the Same shall be, for the Erection of Forts, Magazines, Arsenals, dock-Yards, and other needful Buildings;—And

To make all Laws which shall be necessary and proper for carrying into Execution the foregoing Powers, and all other Powers vested by this Constitution in the Government of the United States, or in any Department or Officer thereof.

Section 9 The Migration or Importation of such Persons as any of the States now existing shall think proper to admit, shall not be prohibited by the Congress prior to the Year one thousand eight hundred and eight, but a Tax or duty may be imposed on such Importation, not exceeding ten dollars for each Person.

The Privilege of the Writ of Habeas Corpus shall not be suspended, unless when in Cases of Rebellion or Invasion the public Safety may require it.

No Bill of Attainder or ex post facto Law shall be passed.

No Capitation, or other direct, Tax shall be laid, unless in Proportion to the Census or enumeration herein before directed to be taken.

No Tax or Duty shall be laid on Articles exported from any State.

No Preference shall be given by any Regulation of Commerce or Revenue to the Ports of one State over those of another: nor shall Vessels bound to, or from, one State, be obliged to enter, clear, or pay Duties in another.

No Money shall be drawn from the Treasury, but in Consequence of Appropriations made by Law; and a regular Statement and Account of the Receipts and Expenditures of all public Money shall be published from time to time.

No Title of Nobility shall be granted by the United States: And no Person holding any Office of Profit or Trust under them, shall, without the Consent of the Congress, accept of any present, Emolument, Office, or Title, of any kind whatever, from any King, Prince, or foreign State.

Section 10 No State shall enter into any Treaty, Alliance, or Confederation; grant Letters of Marque and Reprisal; coin Money; emit Bills of Credit; make any Thing but gold and silver Coin a Tender in Payment of Debts; pass any Bill of Attainder, ex post facto Law, or Law impairing the Obligation of Contracts, or grant any Title of Nobility.

No State shall, without the Consent of the Congress, lay any Imposts or Duties on Imports or Exports, except what may be absolutely necessary for executing it's inspection Laws: and the net Produce of all Duties and Imposts, laid by any State on Imports or Exports, shall be for the Use of the Treasury of the United States; and all such Laws shall be subject to the Revision and Controul of the Congress.

No State shall, without the Consent of Congress, lay any Duty of Tonnage, keep Troops, or Ships of War in time of Peace, enter into any Agreement or Compact with another State, or with a foreign Power, or engage in War, unless actually invaded, or in such imminent Danger as will not admit of delay.

Article. II.

Section 1. The executive Power shall be vested in a President of the United States of America. He shall hold his Office during the Term of four Years, and, together with the Vice President, chosen for the same Term, be elected, as follows

Each State shall appoint, in such Manner as the Legislature thereof may direct, a Number of Electors, equal to the whole Number of Senators and Representatives to which the State may be entitled in the Congress: but no Senator or Representative, or Person holding an Office of Trust or Profit under the United States, shall be appointed an Elector.

The Electors shall meet in their respective States, and vote by Ballot for two Persons, of whom one at least shall not be an Inhabitant of the same State with themselves. And they shall make a List of all the Persons voted for, and of the Number of Votes for each; which List they shall sign and certify, and transmit sealed to the Seat of the Government of the United States, directed to the President of the Senate. The President of the Senate shall, in the Presence of the Senate and House of Representatives, open all the Certificates, and the Votes shall then be counted. The Person having the greatest Number of Votes shall be the President, if such Number be a Majority of the whole Number of Electors appointed; and if there be more than one who have such Majority, and have an equal Number of Votes, then the House of Representatives shall immediately chuse by Ballot one of them for President; and if no Person have a Majority, then from the five highest on the List the said House shall in like Manner chuse the President. But in chusing the President, the Votes shall be taken by States, the Representation from each State having one Vote; A quorum for this Purpose shall consist of a Member or Members from two thirds of the States, and a Majority of all the States shall be necessary to a Choice. In every Case, after the Choice of the President, the Person having the greatest Number of Votes of the Electors shall be the Vice President. But if there should remain two or more who have equal Votes, the Senate shall chuse from them by Ballot the Vice President.

The Congress may determine the Time of chusing the Electors, and the Day on which they shall give their Votes; which Day shall be the same throughout the United States.

No Person except a natural born Citizen, or a Citizen of the United States, at the time of the Adoption of this Constitution, shall be eligible to the Office of President; neither shall any Person be eligible to that Office who shall not have attained to the Age of thirty five Years, and been fourteen Years a Resident within the United States.

In Case of the Removal of the President from Office, or of his Death, Resignation, or Inability to discharge the Powers and Duties of the said Office, the Same shall devolve on the Vice President, and the Congress may by Law provide for the Case of Removal, Death, Resignation or Inability, both of the President and Vice President, declaring what Officer shall then act as President, and such Officer shall act accordingly, until the Disability be removed, or a President shall be elected.

The President shall, at stated Times, receive for his Services, a Compensation, which shall neither be encreased nor diminished during the Period for which he shall have been elected, and he shall not receive within that Period any other Emolument from the United States, or any of them.

Before he enter on the Execution of his Office, he shall take the following Oath or Affirmation:—"I do solemnly swear (or affirm) that I will faithfully execute the Office of President of the United States, and will to the best of my Ability, preserve, protect and defend the Constitution of the United States."

Section 2. The President shall be Commander in Chief of the Army and Navy of the United States, and of the Militia of the several States, when called into the actual Service of the United States; he may require the Opinion, in writing, of the principal Officer in each of the executive Departments, upon any Subject relating to the Duties of their respective Offices, and he shall have Power to grant Reprieves and Pardons for Offences against the United States, except in Cases of Impeachment.

He shall have Power, by and with the Advice and Consent of the Senate, to make Treaties, provided two thirds of the Senators present concur; and he shall nominate, and by and with the Advice and Consent of the Senate, shall appoint Ambassadors, other public Ministers and Consuls, Judges of the supreme Court, and all other Officers of the United States, whose Appointments are not herein otherwise provided for, and which shall be established by Law: but the Congress may by Law vest the Appointment of such inferior Officers, as they think proper, in the President alone, in the Courts of Law, or in the Heads of Departments.

The President shall have Power to fill up all Vacancies that may happen during the Recess of the Senate, by granting Commissions which shall expire at the End of their next Session.

Section 3. He shall from time to time give to the Congress Information of the State of the Union, and recommend to their Consideration such Measures as he shall judge necessary and expedient; he may, on extraordinary Occasions, convene both Houses, or either of them, and in Case of Disagreement between them, with Respect to the Time of Adjournment, he may adjourn them to such Time as he shall think proper; he shall receive Ambassadors and other public Ministers; he shall take Care that the Laws be faithfully executed, and shall Commission all the Officers of the United States.

Section 4 The President, Vice President and all civil Officers of the United States, shall be removed from Office on Impeachment for, and Conviction of, Treason, Bribery, or other high Crimes and Misdemeanors.

Article. III.

Section 1 The judicial Power of the United States, shall be vested in one supreme Court, and in such inferior Courts as the Congress may from time to time ordain and establish. The Judges, both of the supreme and inferior Courts, shall hold their Offices during good Behaviour, and shall, at stated Times, receive for their Services, a Compensation, which shall not be diminished during their Continuance in Office.

Section 2 The judicial Power shall extend to all Cases, in Law and Equity, arising under this Constitution, the Laws of the United States, and Treaties made, or which shall be made, under their Authority;—to all Cases affecting Ambassadors, other public Ministers and Consuls;—to all Cases of admiralty and maritime Jurisdiction;—to Controversies to which the United States shall be a Party;—to Controversies between two or more States;— between a State and Citizens of another State,—between Citizens of different States,—between Citizens of the same State claiming Lands under Grants of different States, and between a State, or the Citizens thereof, and foreign States, Citizens or Subjects.

In all Cases affecting Ambassadors, other public Ministers and Consuls, and those in which a State shall be Party, the supreme Court shall have original Jurisdiction. In all the other Cases before mentioned, the supreme Court shall have appellate Jurisdiction, both as to Law and Fact, with such Exceptions, and under such Regulations as the Congress shall make.

The Trial of all Crimes, except in Cases of Impeachment, shall be by Jury; and such Trial shall be held in the State where the said Crimes shall have been committed; but when not committed within any State, the Trial shall be at such Place or Places as the Congress may by Law have directed.

Section 3. Treason against the United States, shall consist only in levying War against them, or in adhering to their Enemies, giving them Aid and Comfort. No Person shall be convicted of Treason unless on the Testimony of two Witnesses to the same overt Act, or on Confession in open Court.

The Congress shall have Power to declare the Punishment of Treason, but no Attainder of Treason shall work Corruption of Blood, or Forfeiture except during the Life of the Person attainted.

Article. IV.

Section 1. Full Faith and Credit shall be given in each State to the public Acts, Records, and judicial Proceedings of every other State. And the Congress may by general Laws prescribe the Manner in which such Acts, Records and Proceedings shall be proved, and the Effect thereof.

Section 2. The Citizens of each State shall be entitled to all Privileges and Immunities of Citizens in the several States.

A Person charged in any State with Treason, Felony, or other Crime, who shall flee from Justice, and be found in another State, shall on Demand of the executive Authority of the State from which he fled, be delivered up, to be removed to the State having Jurisdiction of the Crime.

No Person held to Service or Labour in one State, under the Laws thereof, escaping into another, shall, in Consequence of any Law or Regulation therein, be discharged from such Service or Labour, but shall be delivered up on Claim of the Party to whom such Service or Labour may be due.

Section 3. New States may be admitted by the Congress into this Union; but no new State shall be formed or erected within the Jurisdiction of any other State; nor any State be formed by the Junction of two or more States, or Parts of States, without the Consent of the Legislatures of the States concerned as well as of the Congress.

The Congress shall have Power to dispose of and make all needful Rules and Regulations respecting the Territory or other Property belonging to the United States; and nothing in this Constitution shall be so construed as to Prejudice any Claims of the United States, or of any particular State.

Section 4. The United States shall guarantee to every State in this Union a Republican Form of Government, and shall protect each of them against Invasion; and on Application of the Legislature, or of the Executive (when the Legislature cannot be convened) against domestic Violence.

Article V

The Congress, whenever two thirds of both Houses shall deem it necessary, shall propose Amendments to this Constitution, or, on the Application of the Legislatures of two thirds of the several States, shall call a Convention for proposing Amendments, which, in either Case, shall be valid to all Intents and Purposes, as Part of this Constitution, when ratified by the Legislatures of three fourths of the several States, or by Conventions in three fourths thereof, as the one or the other Mode of Ratification may be proposed by the Congress; Provided that no Amendment which may be made prior to the Year One thousand eight hundred and eight shall in any Manner affect the first and fourth Clauses in the Ninth Section of the first Article; and that no State, without its Consent, shall be deprived of its equal Suffrage in the Senate.

Article VI

All Debts contracted and Engagements entered into, before the Adoption of this Constitution, shall be as valid against the United States under this Constitution, as under the Confederation.

This Constitution, and the Laws of the United States which shall be made in Pursuance thereof; and all Treaties made, or which shall be made, under the Authority of the United States, shall be the supreme Law of the Land; and the Judges in every State shall be bound thereby, any Thing in the Constitution or Laws of any State to the Contrary notwithstanding.

The Senators and Representatives before mentioned, and the Members of the several State Legislatures, and all executive and judicial Officers, both of the United States and of the several States, shall be bound by Oath or Affirmation, to support this Constitution; but no religious Test shall ever be required as a Qualification to any Office or public Trust under the United States.

Article VII

The Ratification of the Conventions of nine States, shall be sufficient for the Establishment of this Constitution between the States so ratifying the Same.

The Word, "the," being interlined between the seventh and eighth Lines of the first Page, The Word "Thirty" being partly written on an Erazure in the fifteenth Line of the first Page, The Words "is tried" being interlined between the thirty second and thirty third Lines of the first Page and the Word "the" being interlined between the forty third and forty fourth Lines of the second Page.

Attest *William Jackson*
Secretary

done in Convention by the Unanimous Consent of the States present the Seventeenth Day of September in the Year of our Lord one thousand seven hundred and Eighty seven and of the Independance of the United States of America the Twelfth In witness whereof We have hereunto subscribed our Names,

G°. Washington
Presidt and deputy from Virginia

{As per the National Archives, the following text is a transcription of the enrolled original of the Joint Resolution of Congress proposing the Bill of Rights, ratified 15 December 1791. The spelling and punctuation reflect the original.}

Amendment I

Congress shall make no law respecting an establishment of religion, or prohibiting the free exercise thereof; or abridging the freedom of speech, or of the press; or the right of the people peaceably to assemble, and to petition the Government for a redress of grievances.

Amendment II

A well regulated Militia, being necessary to the security of a free State, the right of the people to keep and bear Arms, shall not be infringed.

Amendment III

No Soldier shall, in time of peace be quartered in any house, without the consent of the Owner, nor in time of war, but in a manner to be prescribed by law.

Amendment IV

The right of the people to be secure in their persons, houses, papers, and effects, against unreasonable searches and seizures, shall not be violated, and no Warrants shall issue, but upon probable cause, supported by Oath or affirmation, and particularly describing the place to be searched, and the persons or things to be seized.

Amendment V

No person shall be held to answer for a capital, or otherwise infamous crime, unless on a presentment or indictment of a Grand Jury, except in cases arising in the land or naval forces, or in the Militia, when in actual service in time of War or public danger; nor shall any person be subject for the same offence to be twice put in jeopardy of life or limb; nor shall be compelled in any criminal case to be a witness against himself, nor be deprived of life, liberty, or property, without due process of law; nor shall private property be taken for public use, without just compensation.

Amendment VI

In all criminal prosecutions, the accused shall enjoy the right to a speedy and public trial, by an impartial jury of the State and district wherein the crime shall have been committed, which district shall have been previously ascertained by law, and to be informed of the nature and cause of the accusation; to be confronted with the witnesses against him; to have compulsory process for obtaining witnesses in his favor, and to have the Assistance of Counsel for his defence.

Amendment VII

In Suits at common law, where the value in controversy shall exceed twenty dollars, the right of trial by jury shall be preserved, and no fact tried by a jury, shall be otherwise re-examined in any Court of the United States, than according to the rules of the common law.

Amendment VIII

Excessive bail shall not be required, nor excessive fines imposed, nor cruel and unusual punishments inflicted.

Amendment IX

The enumeration in the Constitution, of certain rights, shall not be construed to deny or disparage others retained by the people.

Amendment X

The powers not delegated to the United States by the Constitution, nor prohibited by it to the States, are reserved to the States respectively, or to the people.

The Structure of the Government Must Furnish the Proper Checks and Balances Between the Different Departments

{From the New York Packet. Friday, 8 February 1788}

To the People of the State of New York:

TO WHAT expedient, then, shall we finally resort, for maintaining in practice the necessary partition of power among the several departments, as laid down in the Constitution? The only answer that can be given is, that as all these exterior provisions are found to be inadequate, the defect must be supplied, by so contriving the interior structure of the government as that its several constituent parts may, by their mutual relations, be the means of keeping each other in their proper places. Without presuming to undertake a full development of this important idea, I will hazard a few general observations, which may perhaps place it in a clearer light, and enable us to form a more correct judgment of the principles and structure of the government planned by the convention.

In order to lay a due foundation for that separate and distinct exercise of the different powers of government, which to a certain extent is admitted on all hands to be essential to the preservation of liberty, it is evident that each department should have a will of its own; and consequently should be so constituted that the members of each should have as little agency as possible in the appointment of the members of the others. Were this principle rigorously adhered to, it would require that all the appointments for the supreme executive, legislative, and judiciary magistracies should be drawn from the same fountain of authority, the people, through channels having no communication whatever with one another. Perhaps such a plan of constructing the several departments would be less difficult in practice than it may in contemplation appear. Some difficulties, however, and some additional expense would attend the execution of it. Some deviations, therefore, from the principle must be admitted. In the constitution of the judiciary department in particular, it might be inexpedient to insist rigorously on the principle: first, because peculiar qualifications being essential in the members, the primary consideration ought to be to select that mode of choice which best secures these qualifications; secondly, because the permanent tenure by which the appointments are held in that department, must soon destroy all sense of dependence on the authority conferring them.

It is equally evident, that the members of each department should be as little dependent as possible on those of the others, for the emoluments annexed to their offices. Were the executive magistrate, or the judges, not independent of the legislature in this particular, their independence in every other would be merely nominal. But the great security against a gradual concentration of the several powers in the same department, consists in giving to those who administer each department the necessary constitutional means and personal motives to resist encroachments of the others. The provision for defense must in this, as in all other cases, be made commensurate to the danger of attack. Ambition must be made to counteract ambition. The interest of the man must be connected with the constitutional rights of the place. It may be a reflection on human nature, that such devices should be necessary to control the abuses of government. But what is government itself, but the greatest of all reflections on human nature? If men were angels, no government would be necessary. If angels were to govern men, neither external nor internal controls on government would be necessary. In framing a government which is to be administered by men over men, the great difficulty lies in this: you must first enable the government to control the governed; and in the next place oblige it to control itself.

A dependence on the people is, no doubt, the primary control on the government; but experience has taught mankind the necessity of auxiliary precautions. This policy of supplying, by opposite and rival interests, the defect of better motives, might be traced through the whole system of human affairs, private as well as public. We see it particularly displayed in all the subordinate distributions of power, where the constant aim is to divide and arrange the several offices in such a manner as that each may be a check on the other that the private interest of every individual may be a sentinel over the public rights. These inventions of prudence cannot be less requisite in the distribution of the supreme powers of the State. But it is not possible to give to each department an equal power of self-defense. In republican government, the legislative authority necessarily predominates. The remedy for this inconveniency is to divide the legislature into different branches; and to render them, by different modes of election and different principles of action, as little connected with each other as the nature of their common functions and their common dependence on the society will admit. It may even be necessary to guard against dangerous encroachments by still further precautions. As the weight of the legislative authority requires that it should be thus divided, the weakness of the executive may require, on the other hand, that it should be fortified.

An absolute negative on the legislature appears, at first view, to be the natural defense with which the executive magistrate should be armed. But perhaps it would be neither altogether safe nor alone sufficient. On ordinary occasions it might not be exerted with the requisite firmness, and on extraordinary occasions it might be perfidiously abused. May not this defect of an absolute negative be supplied by some qualified connection between this weaker department and the weaker branch of the stronger department, by which the latter may be led to support the constitutional rights of the former, without being too much detached from the rights of its own department? If the principles on which these observations are founded be just, as I persuade myself they are, and they be applied as a criterion to the several State constitutions, and to the federal Constitution it will be found that if the latter does not perfectly correspond with them, the former are infinitely less able to bear such a test.

There are, moreover, two considerations particularly applicable to the federal system of America, which place that system in a very interesting point of view. First. In a single republic, all the power surrendered by the people is submitted to the administration of a single government; and the usurpations are guarded against by a division of the government into distinct and separate departments. In the compound republic of America, the power surrendered by the people is first divided between two distinct governments, and then the portion allotted to each subdivided among distinct and separate departments. Hence a double security arises to the rights of the people. The different governments will control each other, at the same time that each will be controlled by itself. Second. It is of great importance in a republic not only to guard the society against the oppression of its rulers, but to guard one part of the society against the injustice of the other part. Different interests necessarily exist in different classes of citizens. If a majority be united by a common interest, the rights of the minority will be insecure.

There are but two methods of providing against this evil: the one by creating a will in the community independent of the majority that is, of the society itself; the other, by comprehending in the society so many separate descriptions of citizens as will render an unjust combination of a majority of the whole very improbable, if not impracticable. The first method prevails in all governments possessing an hereditary or self-appointed authority. This, at best, is but a precarious security; because a power independent of the society may as well espouse the unjust views of the major, as the rightful interests of the minor party, and may possibly be turned against both parties. The second method will be exemplified in the federal republic of the United States. Whilst all authority in it will be derived from and dependent on the society, the society itself will be broken into so many parts, interests, and classes of citizens, that the rights of individuals, or of the minority, will be in little danger from interested combinations of the majority.

In a free government the security for civil rights must be the same as that for religious rights. It consists in the one case in the multiplicity of interests, and in the other in the multiplicity of sects. The degree of security in both cases will depend on the number of interests and sects; and this may be presumed to depend on the extent of country and number of people comprehended under the same government. This view of the subject must particularly recommend a proper federal system to all the sincere and considerate friends of republican government, since it shows that in exact proportion as the territory of the Union may be formed into more circumscribed Confederacies, or States oppressive combinations of a majority will be facilitated: the best security, under the republican forms, for the rights of every class of citizens, will be diminished: and consequently the stability and independence of some member of the government, the only other security, must be proportionately increased. Justice is the end of government. It is the end of civil society. It ever has been and ever will be pursued until it be obtained, or until liberty be lost in the pursuit. In a society under the forms of which the stronger faction can readily unite and oppress the weaker, anarchy may as truly be said to reign as in a state of nature, where the weaker individual is not secured against the violence of the stronger; and as, in the latter state, even the stronger individuals are prompted, by the uncertainty of their condition, to submit to a government which may protect the weak as well as themselves; so, in the former state, will the more powerful factions or parties be gradnally induced, by a like motive, to wish for a government which will protect all parties, the weaker as well as the more powerful.

It can be little doubted that if the State of Rhode Island was separated from the Confederacy and left to itself, the insecurity of rights under the popular form of government within such narrow limits would be displayed by such reiterated oppressions of factious majorities that some power altogether independent of the people would soon be called for by the voice of the very factions whose misrule had proved the necessity of it. In the extended republic of the United States, and among the great variety of interests, parties, and sects which it embraces, a coalition of a majority of the whole society could seldom take place on any other principles than those of justice and the general good; whilst there being thus less danger to a minor from the will of a major party, there must be less pretext, also, to provide for the security of the former, by introducing into the government a will not dependent on the latter, or, in other words, a will independent of the society itself. It is no less certain than it is important, notwithstanding the contrary opinions which have been entertained, that the larger the society, provided it lie within a practical sphere, the more duly capable it will be of self-government. And happily for the REPUBLICAN CAUSE, the practicable sphere may be carried to a very great extent, by a judicious modification and mixture of the FEDERAL PRINCIPLE.

PUBLIUS.
[HAMILTON OR MADISON]

Senator Margaret Smith (1897-1995) was the US Representative from 1940-1949 and US Senator from 1949-1973, representing Maine. She was the first woman to serve in both houses, and as a Republican, was the first woman nominated by their party for the presidency. Her candidacy was announced 27 January 1964.

This statement and declaration was given less than four months after Senator Joseph McCarthy's "Wheeling Speech" and was a response to the House Un-American Activities Committee's words and actions against a perceived "Red Scare". Her speech was endorsed by six other Republicans considered Liberal to Moderate. They are listed with permission in the preamble to her declaration.

Statement of Senator Margaret Chase Smith
1 June 1950

Mr. President:

I would like to speak briefly and simply about a serious national condition. It is a national feeling of fear and frustration that could result in national suicide and the end of everything that we Americans hold dear. It is a condition that comes from the lack of effective leadership in either the Legislative Branch or the Executive Branch of our Government.

That leadership is so lacking that serious and responsible proposals are being made that national advisory commissions be appointed to provide such critically needed leadership.

I speak as briefly as possible because too much harm has already been done with irresponsible words of bitterness and selfish political opportunism. I speak as simply as possible because the issue is too great to be obscured by eloquence. I speak simply and briefly in the hope that my words will be taken to heart.

I speak as a Republican, I speak as a woman. I speak as a United States Senator. I speak as an American.

The United States Senate has long enjoyed worldwide respect as the greatest deliberative body in the world. But recently that deliberative character has too often been debased to the level of a forum of hate and character assassination sheltered by the shield of congressional immunity.

It is ironical that we Senators can in debate in the Senate directly or indirectly, by any form of words impute to any American, who is not a Senator, any conduct or motive unworthy or unbecoming an American -- and without that non-Senator American having any legal redress against us -- yet if we say the same thing in the Senate about our colleagues we can be stopped on the grounds of being out of order.

It is strange that we can verbally attack anyone else without restraint and with full protection and yet we hold ourselves above the same type of criticism here on the Senate Floor. Surely the United States Senate is big enough to take self-criticism and self-appraisal. Surely we should be able to take the same kind of character attacks that we dish out to outsiders.

I think that it is high time for the United States Senate and its members to do some soul searching -- for us to weigh our consciences -- on the manner in which we are performing our duty to the people of America -- on the manner in which we are using or abusing our individual powers and privileges.

I think that it is high time that we remembered that we have sworn to uphold and defend the Constitution. I think that it is high time that we remembered; that the Constitution, as amended, speaks not only of the freedom of speech but also of trial by jury instead of trial by accusation.

Whether it be a criminal prosecution in court or a character prosecution in the Senate, there is little practical distinction when the life of a person has been ruined.

Those of us who shout the loudest about Americanism in making character assassinations are all too frequently those who, by our own words and acts, ignore some of the basic principles of Americanism –

The right to criticize;
The right to hold unpopular beliefs;
The right to protest;
The right of independent thought.

The exercise of these rights should not cost one single American citizen his reputation or his right to a livelihood nor should he be in danger of losing his reputation or livelihood merely because he happens to know someone who holds unpopular beliefs. Who of us doesn't? Otherwise none of us could call our souls our own. Otherwise thought control would have set in.

The American people are sick and tired of being afraid to speak their minds lest they be politically smeared as "Communists" or "Fascists" by their opponents. Freedom of speech is not what it used to be in America. It has been so abused by some that it is not exercised by others.

The American people are sick and tired of seeing innocent people smeared and guilty people whitewashed. But there have been enough proved cases to cause nationwide distrust and strong suspicion that there may be something to the unproved, sensational accusations.

As a Republican, I say to my colleagues on this side of the aisle that the Republican Party faces a challenge today that is not unlike the challenge that it faced back in Lincoln's day. The Republican Party so successfully met that challenge that it emerged from the Civil War as the champion of a united nation -- in addition to being a Party that unrelentingly fought loose spending and loose programs.

Today our country is being psychologically divided by the confusion and the suspicions that are bred in the United States Senate to spread like cancerous tentacles of "know nothing, suspect everything" attitudes. Today we have a Democratic Administration that has developed a mania for loose spending and loose programs. History is repeating itself -- and the Republican Party again has the opportunity to emerge as the champion of unity and prudence.

The record of the present Democratic Administration has provided us with sufficient campaign issues without the necessity of resorting to political smears. America is rapidly losing its position as leader of the world simply because the Democratic Administration has pitifully failed to provide effective leadership.

The Democratic Administration has completely confused the American people by its daily contradictory grave warnings and optimistic assurances -- that show the people that our Democratic Administration has no idea of where it is going.

The Democratic Administration has greatly lost the confidence of the American people by its complacency to the threat of communism here at home and the leak of vital secrets to Russia through key officials of the Democratic Administration. There are enough proved cases to make this point without diluting our criticism with unproved charges.

Surely these are sufficient reasons to make it clear to the American people that it is time for a change and that a Republican victory is necessary to the security of this country. Surely it is clear that this nation will continue to suffer as long as it is governed by the present ineffective Democratic Administration.

Yet to displace it with a Republican regime embracing a philosophy that lacks political integrity or intellectual honesty would prove equally disastrous to this nation. The nation sorely needs a Republican victory. But I don't want to see the Republican Party ride to political victory on the Four Horsemen of Calumny -- Fear, Ignorance, Bigotry and Smear.

I doubt if the Republican Party could -- simply because I don't believe the American people will uphold any political party that puts political exploitation above national interest. Surely we Republicans aren't that desperate for victory.

I don't want to see the Republican Party win that way. While it might be a fleeting victory for the Republican Party, it would be a more lasting defeat for the American people. Surely it would ultimately be suicide for the Republican Party and the two-party system that has protected our American liberties from the dictatorship of a one party system.

As members of the Minority Party, we do not have the primary authority to formulate the policy of our Government. But we do have the responsibility of rendering constructive criticism, of clarifying issues, of allaying fears by acting as responsible citizens.

As a woman, I wonder how the mothers, wives, sisters and daughters feel about the way in which members of their families have been politically mangled in Senate debate -- and I use the word 'debate' advisedly.

As a United States Senator, I am not proud of the way in which the Senate has been made a publicity platform for irresponsible sensationalism. I am not proud of the reckless abandon in which unproved charges have been hurled from this side of the aisle. I am not proud of the obviously staged, undignified countercharges that have been attempted in retaliation from the other side of the aisle.

I don't like the way the Senate has been made a rendezvous for vilification, for selfish political gain at the sacrifice of individual reputations and national unity. I am not proud of the way we smear outsiders from the Floor of the Senate and hide behind the cloak of congressional immunity and still place ourselves beyond criticism on the Floor of the Senate.

As an American, I am shocked at the way Republicans and Democrats alike are playing directly into the Communist design of "confuse, divide and conquer." As an American, I don't want a Democratic Administration "white wash" or "cover up" any more than I want a Republican smear or witch hunt.

As an American, I condemn a Republican "Fascist" just as much as I condemn a Democrat "Communist." I condemn a Democrat "Fascist" just as much as I condemn a Republican "Communist." They are equally dangerous to you and me and to our country.

As an American, I want to see our nation recapture the strength and unity it once had when we fought the enemy instead of ourselves.

It is with these thoughts I have drafted what I call a "Declaration of Conscience." I am gratified that Senator Tobey, Senator Aiken, Senator Morse, Senator Ives, Senator Thye and Senator Hendrickson, have concurred in that declaration and have authorized me to announce their concurrence.

The Declaration

1. We are Republicans. But we are Americans first. It is as Americans that we express our concern with the growing confusion that threatens the security and stability of our country. Democrats and Republicans alike have contributed to that confusion.

2. The Democratic administration has initially created the confusion by its lack of effective leadership, by its contradictory grave warnings and optimistic assurances, by its complacency to the threat of communism here at home, by its oversensitiveness to rightful criticism, by its petty bitterness against its critics.

3. Certain elements of the Republican Party have materially added to this confusion in the hopes of riding the Republican party to victory through the selfish political exploitation of fear, bigotry, ignorance, and intolerance. There are enough mistakes of the Democrats for Republicans to criticize constructively without resorting to political smears.

4. To this extent, Democrats and Republicans alike have unwittingly, but undeniably, played directly into the Communist design of "confuse, divide and conquer."

5. It is high time that we stopped thinking politically as Republicans and Democrats about elections and started thinking patriotically as Americans about national security based on individual freedom. It is high time that we all stopped being tools and victims of totalitarian techniques -- techniques that, if continued here unchecked, will surely end what we have come to cherish as the American way of life.

LIFT EVERY VOICE AND SING

"Lift Every Voice and Sing" came out in 1900 as a ballad of the struggles of African Americans during the Reconstruction and Jim Crow Eras. The lyrics were written by James Weldon Johnson (1871–1938) and was set to music by his brother, J. Rosamond Johnson (1873–1954). The NAACP, established in 1907 out of the Niagara Movement, advocated it as a "Negro national anthem".

The song came to new popularity with the Black Lives Matter movement in 2020 and is known today as the "Black National Anthem". Mike Phillips and West Byrd quoted "Lift Every Voice and Sing" as part of their rendition of "The Star-Spangled Banner" at NASCAR's 2020 Pocono 350. As of February 2025, the song has been performed at five consecutive Super Bowl pregame ceremonies.

It is sung frequently at Juneteenth celebrations today.

> Lift every voice and sing,
> Till earth and heaven ring,
> Ring with the harmonies of Liberty;
> Let our rejoicing rise
> High as the list'ning skies,
> Let it resound loud as the rolling sea.
> Sing a song full of the faith that the dark past has taught us,
> Sing a song full of the hope that the present has brought us;
> Facing the rising sun of our new day begun,
> Let us march on till victory is won.
>
> Stony the road we trod,
> Bitter the chast'ning rod,
> Felt in the days when hope unborn had died;
> Yet with a steady beat,
> Have not our weary feet
> Come to the place for which our fathers sighed?
> We have come over a way that with tears has been watered.
> We have come, treading our path through the blood of the slaughtered,
> Out from the gloomy past,
> Till now we stand at last
> Where the white gleam of our bright star is cast.

God of our weary years,
God of our silent tears,
Thou who hast brought us thus far on the way;
Thou who hast by Thy might,
Led us into the light,
Keep us forever in the path, we pray.
Lest our feet stray from the places, our God, where we met Thee,
Lest our hearts, drunk with the wine of the world, we forget Thee;
Shadowed beneath Thy hand,
May we forever stand,
True to our God,
True to our native land.

ABBREVIATION GUIDE

401K : an employer-sponsored, defined-contribution, personal pension (savings) account, as defined in subsection 401(k) of the U.S. Internal Revenue Code

AARP : American Association of Retired Persons

ACA : Affordable Care Act, formally known as the Patient Protection and Affordable Care Act (PPACA) and informally as Obamacare, a federal statute enacted in 2010

AI : Artificial Intelligence

ATF : Bureau of Alcohol, Tobacco, Firearms and Explosives

CBC : Congressional Black Caucus

CBO : Congressional Budget Office

CDC : Centers for Disease Control and Prevention

CFPB : Consumer Financial Protection Bureau

CHIP : Children's Health Insurance Program, formerly known as the State Children's Health Insurance Program (SCHIP). Not to be confused with the CHIPS and Science bill

CIA : Central Intelligence Agency

COVID : Coronavirus disease 2019, a contagious disease caused by SARS-CoV-2 that spread worldwide in 2020 as the COVID-19 pandemic

C-SPAN (Cable-Satellite Public Affairs Network) : A private, nonprofit television network created in 1979 for televising proceedings of the United States federal government and other public affairs programming.

DAV : Disabled American Veterans

DEA : Drug Enforcement Administration

DEI (Diversity, Equity, Inclusion) : organizational frameworks that seek to promote the fair treatment and full participation of all people, including marginalized groups and those with disabilities

DHS : Department of Homeland Security

ABBREVIATION GUIDE

DOGE (Department of Government Efficiency) : Formerly designated as the U.S. Digital Service, it comprises the United States DOGE Service Temporary Organization started by President Trump in 2025 and is scheduled to end on 4 July 2026.

DOJ : Department of Justice

EU : European Union

EPA : Environmental Protection Agency

FAA : Federal Aviation Administration

FBI : Federal Bureau of Investigation

FDA : Food and Drug Administration, a federal agency of the Department of Health and Human Services

FDR : Franklin Delano Roosevelt, 32nd president of the United States

FICA : Payroll taxes as per the Federal Insurance Contributions Act

FMAP (Federal Medical Assistance Percentage) : the percent of Medicaid program costs covered by the federal government

GAO : U.S. Government Accountability Office

GDP : Gross domestic product, a measure of the total market value of all goods and services produced

GOP (Grand Old Party) : The Republican Party, currently "right-wing" in the American political spectrum

HHS : United States Department of Health and Human Services

HIV : The human immunodeficiency viruses that infect humans thatcan cause acquired immunodeficiency syndrome (AIDS)

HUD : U.S. Department of Housing and Urban Development

ICE : U.S. Immigration and Customs Enforcement

IDEA : Individuals with Disabilities Education Act, a law that makes available a free appropriate public education option to children with disabilities

KKK : The Ku Klux Klan, or "The Klan", an American Protestant-led Christian extremist, white supremacist, far-right hate group

LGBTQ (Lesbian, Gay, Bisexual, Transgender, Queer) : A term inclusive to all identities and individuals who are part of a sexual or gender minority

M&Ms : brand name of a color-varied sugar-coated, chocolate confectionery made by Mars Inc. {endorsed by publisher without compensation}

MAHA (Make America Healthy Again) : American populist slogan and political movement led by Robert F. Kennedy Jr., serving as Secretary of Health and Human Services in the second Trump administration

MS13 : A Salvadorian gang that Trump declared a foreign terrorist organization

NASA : National Aeronautics and Space Administration

NATO : The North Atlantic Treaty Organization, also called the North Atlantic Alliance

NIH : National Institute of Health

NIOSH : National Institute for Occupational Safety and Health

OCR : Office for Civil Rights

OMB : Office of Management and Budget

LIHEAP : Low Income Home Energy Assistance Program

PACT Act : a law expanding healthcare and benefits for veterans exposed to toxic substances

PBS (Public Broadcasting System) : An American publicly-funded nonprofit, free-to-air television network. It is the most prominent provider of educational programs to public television stations in the United States.

PRC : The People's Republic of China, governed by the Chinese Communist Party (CCP)

SBA : Small Business Administration

SNAP : Supplemental Nutrition Assistance Program, formerly and colloquially known as the Food Stamp Program

SSA : Social Security Administration

STEM : Science, technology, engineering, and mathematics, in an educational or vocational context

USCIS : U.S. Citizenship and Immigration Services

USDA : U.S. Department of Agriculture

USAID : United States Agency for International Development

USPS : United States Postal Service

VA : U.S. Department of Veterans Affairs

WHO : World Health Organization

ACKNOWLEDGEMENTS

I would like to express my deepest gratitude for all of your support, mentorship, encouragement, and inspiration through my political "career": my partner and spouse, Rob McCrady; my children and grandchildren, who are my motivation to change the world, and those in my family that have supported my endeavors; my co-author, Ken Stuczynski, for this awesome opportunity. For organizations, I wish to include The Iredell County Board of Elections, The Iredell County Democratic Party, The Catawba County Democratic Party, The Board and Alumni of Women's Campaign School at Yale Class of 2011, The Young Democrats of North Carolina, and The North Carolina LGBTQ+ Caucus.

Posthumously, I express these sentiments toward Mary Lynch Sullivan, Victor Crosby, Henry Gordon, Woody Woodard and Rev. Joseph Lowery.

Special appreciation goes out to David and Sally Parker, Betty Dobson, Billy Kennedy, Robert Stidd, Neal and Louise Grose, Xavier Zsarmani, my "Gay Husband" Scott Testerman, my "SEC husband" Chris Telesca, Ron Danley, Erin Rochelle, Vinod Thomas, Graig Meyer, Beth McMahon, Kay and Richard Holshauer, Andy Ball, John Sylvester, Michael Quadrozzi, Cliff Moone, Tony McEwen, Sam Spencer, George Battle, Lainey Edmisten, Eli Glynn, Deb Kozikowski, David Byrne (yes, that David Byrne), Aisha Dew, Kim and Faith Naff, Andrew Schwaba, Jesse Presnell, Wanda Kelley, Tricia Stevens, Gene and Fay Mahaffey, Beth Kendall, Diane Hamby, everyone who voted for me when I ran for office, and especially all of my amazing volunteers through the years!

September McCrady, co-Editor

PUBLISHER'S NOTE

The content of this book was originally to be part of a sequel to "40 Days In... The Beginning of the Second Trump Presidency". The intention was to provide a snapshot of current events, so that future historians and others could deep dive into this contentious time. I obviously wished to include Senator Booker's historic speech, but quickly realized it would take up the lion's share of its pages. I was still ambivalent about making it a stand-alone volume, thinking it could be one tome in a larger series. In short, I had to ask myself, did it deserve its own volume?

To be honest, I didn't have high expectations before I read it. Like many people, I considered the response to quickly-rising authoritarianism to be lackluster in the DNC. Was this speech going to merely performative, pressing the usual partisan talking points to moving the ball down the field of business-as-usual politics? To further betray my ignornace, I asked myself, who was this Senator, anyway? What was he trying to achieve?

Hold that thought for a moment.

When I wrote "Some White Guy's Book" about race, ethnicity, and allyship in America back in 2020, I came out a changed person on the other side. Research and contact with such material is an experience that only an editor-author can appreciate. It had laid bare how much I still had to learn, but also challenged assumptions I had not considered, and forced my positions to shift, or at least fruitfully evolve.

Working on this project feels almost like another chapter in that narrative. Over these crammed weeks (months) of producing this book, I got a glimpse of Cory — his story, his values, and an estimation of his character.

His respect for colleagues and willingness to openly work with those across the aisle is the admirable opposite of the poisonous, divisive rhetoric that now plagues the United States. I saw no disingenuous propaganda or duplicity, but an aim for objectivity and sanity. This wasn't the grandstanding I expected. This doesn't feel like a futile symbolic act, at least to anyone who can brave listening to the hours he stood.

Unlike the previous record-holder, he wasn't trying to kill a bill, but delay the machinations of government in the same way a pilgrim might engage in a fast — to get the attention of Providence, both human and divine.

In short, yes, it deserved its own book.

There is no illusion here. The written word is not equivalent to watching the video, which captures gestures and inflections. And if you desire only words and facts and figures, those are available elsewhere online. Anyone can look up the Constitution, for example, and yet citizens across the nation have pocket copies, some even on their person as a matter of habit. Why? Because *it means something*.

That's why I think this book is special. "Cory Booker: Proof Through the Night" is something you can hold in your hand and browse on your lap. His speech as a book is a statement in itself. It's something that can sit on your coffee table or bookshelf, in some way reminding yourself and others what you value, and that the goodness of America is worth fighting for.

What is happening today, in the Senator's words oft repeated, "It's not who we are." In times that seem to demand a merger of realism and pessimism, I cannot help but think of the Rev. Dr. King's words, "We must accept finite disappointment, but never lose infinite hope." The revelation that hope does not depend on optimism is a saving grace — one that seems to pour from a certain Senator from New Jersey.

That is why this work – what seemed at first to be not much more than an ISBN entry in my publishing company – turned out to be dear to me. I am proud to have some meager connection to this great historical speech.

My involvement is only a small thing. Most of my time was spent comparing an AI transcript to the Congressional Record and teasing out the punctuation to best fit nuance. Neither transcript nor official record were perfect, with contradictory lines here and there. It was my partner on the project, September McCrady, who went through the resulting hybrid version while watching the video. For the record, we made only the most modest nominal grammatical adjustments for readability and accuracy of meaning. A few verbal fillers were omitted if excessive, but most were kept in to capture the tenor of the statements made. September made valuable suggestions regarding the overall editing process, including the addition of footnotes.

The fact is, I set about his work by myself, with a ridiculous timetable. When I asked if she would be interested in editing the work, there was no hesitation. In theory, this work could have been done by me or someone else, but the result would have been lacking. Her attention to detail (while in the middle of a family crisis, nonetheless) and passion for the subject matter are what make this book what it is.

On a personal note, I've known September since frequenting The Topic Cafe in the Allentown neighborhood of Buffalo, NY, back in the 90s. Later, we argued many a time over fiscal policies on Facebook, me being on the conservative side of the battlefield. I could never share her long-term dedication to a particular party, but highly respect her efforts to be part of the solution. It is people like her, and even friends who are (still) Republicans, that have given me hope that working within the system is still meaningful. Whatever this book means to me, it means even more to her, and the opportunity to have her share the role of editor is a welcome, mutual blessing.

We are also pleased to provide (in the back matter) a few documents — ones that were quoted extensively and are worthy of reading in their full form. All are believed to be in the public domain, and although available elsewhere, we hope the reader appreciates this convenience.

Though most readers will not notice or be concerned, timestamps didn't line up perfectly between video and transcript, but were close enough to not merit correction. We also were unable to provide a comprehensive list of Senators acting as Presiding Officers, but in so as far as we could find, they include: John Husted (Ohio); Todd Young (Indiana); Bill Cassidy (Louisiana); John Curtis (Utah), and Bernie Moreno (Ohio).

By the time of this first printing, we hope to have a promotional page here for Cory Booker's upcoming book. It will be done by a different publisher, but there are more important considerations than market competition. I wish his book the best, and hopefully, some will find our own book a supplement or a compliment to that work.

Lastly, to Senator Booker — my hat is off to you, sir.

Ken JP Stuczynski
Co-Editor, Publisher
Amorphous Publishing Guild
Buffalo, NY

21 September 2025

ABOUT AMORPHOUS PUBLISHING GUILD

Amorphous Press is a small, private publishing company specializing in new independent writers. We provide on-demand printing of hardcover, softcover, and eBooks with distribution availability to over 38,000 outlets, including Amazon, Barnes & Noble, independent booksellers, universities, and libraries.

Other Titles in Political Science and Current Events Commentary

Some White Guys Book (Ken Stuczynski, 2020)

An admitted "White Guy" tackles the complicated subject of race and ethnicity in America. With unique life experiences and unconventional ways of thinking, the author covers the disparate ways we view history, society, and ourselves. From White guilt to cancel culture, Southern pride to religious intolerance, no subject is off-limits. Challenging political correctness and canned arguments, Some White Guy's Book candidly explores different sides of issues, why we believe what we do, and what roles White people and People of Color can play in building a common future. This work digs deep into how prejudices of color intersect poverty, crime, the justice system, religion, and patriotism. It includes first-hand experience and research of the George Floyd protests, contrasted with the Civil Rights Movement of the 1960s.

40 Days In ... The Beginning of the Second Trump Presidency (Ken Stuczynski, 2025)

A compilation of voices from America's first forty days of the second Trump presidency, including historical documents, letters, speeches, editorials, and social media posts. Topics include the inauguration, executive orders, DOGE, social media platform policies, White House achievement declarations, CPAC, Ukraine, commentary, and the State of the Union.

Learn more at

www.Amorphous.Press

Stand, by Cory Booker
Available February 2026
St. Martin's Press

In trying times, our nation demands more of us. It is time for good trouble.

Senator Cory Booker captivated Americans across the political spectrum in early 2025 with his remarkable 25-hour speech on the Senate floor, when he spoke out eloquently and forcefully against the Trump administration's relentless challenges to civil liberties, government institutions, the rule of law, and our nation's international standing. In the process, Booker outlasted the record for longest continuous Senate floor speech set by segregationist Strom Thurmond during a filibuster of the Civil Rights Act of 1957, which was delivered at another time of great uncertainty for our country when it felt like the odds were hopelessly stacked against justice and unity.

Stand expands on that message and offers a compelling vision for the future to readers who are eager to make a difference. It focuses on the virtues that are vital to our success as a nation and the lessons we can draw from past generations of Americans who fought for them. Now is not the time to surrender to cynicism or abandon our most noble ideals. Now is the time to defiantly declare, like our ancestors before us: "I, too, stand for America."

Stand is a celebration of the Americans who chose to get up in the face of injustice, who championed the uniquely American values central to making our nation a more perfect union, despite seemingly insurmountable obstacles. It is also a guide for today: leadership is not derived from position or title, it comes from action and example.